INTRODUCTION TO

Mass Communications

INTRODUCTION TO

Mass

Communications

Ninth Edition

Warren K. Agee
University of Georgia

Phillip H. Ault
South Bend Tribune

Edwin Emery
University of Minnesota

HARPER & ROW, PUBLISHERS, New York
Cambridge, Philadelphia, San Francisco, Washington,
London, Mexico City, São Paulo, Singapore, Sydney

Sponsoring Editor: Barbara Cinquegrani
Project Editor: Jo-Ann Goldfarb
Text Design: Laura Ferguson
Cover Design: Katharine Urban
Text Art: Vantage Art, Inc.
Photo Research: Mira Schachne
Production Manager: Jeanie Berke
Production Assistant: Paula Roppolo
Compositor: ComCom Division of Haddon Craftsmen, Inc.
Printer and Binder: R. R. Donnelley & Sons Company
Cover Printer: Lehigh Press

Composite Cover Photo: NASA, An Onboard Scene; Johnson Space Center, Houston
Texas; Max Headroom/Coke visual, Courtesy of Coca-Cola USA, Division of The
Coca-Cola Company; VideoMovie, Model GR-C7U courtesy JVC Company of America,
Divison of US JVC Corp.; Walkman, Courtesy SONY Corporation of America; Courtesy
International Business Machines Corporation; NASA, Earth View; *Rolling Stone*
Magazine (The "Magazine"), issue #506, August 13, 1987, Straight Arrow Publishers,
Inc.; NASA, TDRSS Ground Station.

Introduction to Mass Communications, Ninth Edition

Library of Congress Cataloging-in-Publication Data

Agee, Warren Kendall.
    Introduction to mass communications.

    Bibliography: p.
    Includes index.
    1. Mass media.   I. Ault, Phillip H.
II. Emery, Edwin.   III. Title.
P90.A35 1988   001.51   87-25203
ISBN 0-06-040181-8

55,576

87 88 89 90 9 8 7 6 5 4 3 2 1

Contents

Preface

Since the first edition of this text helped shape the introductory mass communications course in scores of colleges and universities more than 25 years ago, the book has chronicled the evolving media scene. Because of the far-reaching and sometimes disturbing changes in mass communications during recent years, the description and analysis of the media both for future practitioners and the consumers of their products are reaching a new and telling importance in our society.

Public interest in the ethical and social responsibilities of the media has deepened, accented by the report of the Commission on Pornography and the toughening of ratings for movies that depict illegal drug use and excessive violence. Video has emerged as an entirely new medium. An explosion in computerized graphics and photography has strongly affected the print media, television, and the movies. So-called "desktop publishing" is a new phenomenon. The emergence of worldwide mega-agencies has shaken advertising. American interest in global news events has reached new heights. Transmissions by communications satellites have re-sorted audiences and reached new ones, especially in Europe, where commercial television and other new telecommunications forms are emerging.

A tumultuous churning in the ownership of the media has shaken American communications industries and professions. Spinoffs, buyouts, and trades of media units, financed by enormous borrowing, have created conglomerates of almost baffling complexity. Critics fear that the mountainous debts incurred, and the pressures by stockholders and bankers to make the risks pay off, have enshrined money earning as the dominant factor in management decisions, resulting in severe cost cutting in operational budgets at the expense of socially valuable products.

These changes are reflected in the significant revision and updating of this edition, including a new chapter on *video;* a major section dealing with *graphics;* new information on *media ethics;* and the introduction of vignettes designed to spark reader interest.

In addition, a new Chapter 2 explores the role of the media in society with emphasis upon ethical standards and the media's influence upon political, economic, and social spheres of activity. Because of the affinity of their subject matter, the former Chapters 2 and 3, dealing with the process and effects of mass communication, have been combined into a new Chapter 3, with additional models provided. The historical sections dealing with magazines and news services have been moved from former Chapter 5 to their respective industry chapters. Chapter 5 now examines solely the growth of newspapers.

A logical organization thus is followed: (1) summary of recent changes in technology and methods produced mainly by the computer and the satellite; (2) delineation of the principal roles of the media in society; (3) exploration of the process and effects of mass communication, upon which the entire field is based; (4) explication of historic press freedoms and the development of newspapers; (5) examination of the operation and principles of newspapers, news services and syndicates, magazines, and book publishing; (6) review of the growth of telecommunications and film and of the individual industries—radio, recording, television, film, video, and photographic and graphics communication; (7) insight into the supporting fields of advertising and public relations; (8) overview of mass communications research and of education for mass communications; and (9) in-depth exploration of criticisms and challenges to the media in the areas of ownership, credibility, law, social and ethical responsibilities, and international mass communications.

New information has been added to update all the chapters of this edition; for example, there are discussions of the isolation and privacy needs of the individual, communication process and effects, landmark court decisions, new production processes, desktop publishing, audio versions of books, the laser disc, cable television, 3-D and other special effects, controversial changes in accrediting schools of journalism and mass communications, and increased coverage of international developments, among many others.

The selected, annotated bibliography has been updated and a glossary containing almost 250 items is included.

The revised *Instructor's Manual* for the first time is accompanied by *Harpertest,* a computerized version of the test bank. This program enables instructors to readily replace questions or intersperse their own to design their own exams. In addition, the manual contains study questions and projects, lesson plans, and an audiovisual list. A number of successful approaches to the study of mass communications have been provided in the manual by instructors who have taught with this text during the past almost three decades and whose adoption of the book has made it the most widely used text in the field.

For supplementary use in this course, and others, the authors have produced a reader, *Maincurrents in Mass Communications.* It contains articles, surveys, speeches, and commentaries by prominent people designed to clarify further much of what is happening in mass communications. Essays by the editors introduce the six parts: "The Media's Role in Society," "Ethical and Legal Challenges," "The Technology Revolution," "The Communicators," "Media Trends and Techniques," and "Living in the Information Society."

ACKNOWLEDGMENTS

This ninth edition of *Introduction to Mass Communications* represents a pooling of the professional media experience and scholarly interest of its authors, who wish to thank the more than 100 professors whose suggestions and criticisms, elicited by questionnaire and expressed personally to the authors, have helped shape these nine editions.

Among professionals in the mass media with whom the authors have consulted (including their titles at the time) were James A. Byron, general manager and news director, WBAP and KXAS-TV, Fort Worth; Jack Douglas, general manager of WSBT and WSBT-TV, South Bend, Indiana; Andrew Stewart, president, Denhard & Stewart, Inc., advertising agency, New York; David F. Barbour, copy chief, Batten, Barton, Durstine & Osborn, Inc., Pittsburgh office; Chandler Grannis, editor-at-large, *Publishers' Weekly;* Earl J. Johnson, vice-president, United Press International; William C. Payette, president, United Feature Syndicate, Inc., New York; J. Carroll Bateman, Insurance Information Institute, New York; K. P. Wood, vice-president, American Telephone & Telegraph Company; William Oman, vice-president, and Edward F. Webster, editor, Dodd, Mead & Company, Inc.; and Barbara Cinquegrani, editor, Harper & Row, Publishers, Inc.

Professors of journalism and mass communications who have made valuable contributions to the book during the past 28 years include Leslie G. Moeller, University of Iowa; Jack Haskins, University of Tennessee; R. Smith Schuneman, Roy E. Carter, Jr., Nancy L. Roberts, Harold Wilson, and James W. Brown, University of Minnesota; Everette E. Dennis, Max Wales, and Warren C. Price, University of Oregon; Joseph A. Del Porto, Bowling Green State University; John T. McNelly, University of Wisconsin; Hugh E. Curtis, Drake University; Milton Gross, University of Missouri; R. C. Norris, Texas Christian University; I. W. Cole and Baskett Mosse, Northwestern University; William A. Mindak, Tulane University; Sam Kuczun, University of Colorado; Henry Ladd Smith, University of Washington; John R. Wilhelm, Ohio University; Michael C. Emery, California State University, Northridge; Félix Gutiérrez, University of Southern California; Emma Auer, Florida State University; Emery L. Sasser, University of South Florida; Frank Pierce, University of Florida; William Robert Summers, Jr., and James R. Young, West Virginia University; Mel Adams and Lee F. Young, University of Kansas; James E. Dykes, Troy State University; John Merrill, Louisiana State University; Leo Jeffres, Cleveland State University; and James L. Aldridge, William S. Baxter, Beverly Bethune, Scott M. Cutlip, A. Edward Foote, Al Hester, Worth McDougald, Barbara McKenzie, Ronald Lane, Frazier Moore, Charles Martin, J. Thomas Russell, and Leila Wenthe, University of Georgia.

Many other professors contributed examination questions, suggested projects, and other materials for the *Instructor's Manual* accompanying each of these nine editions.

The authors express a special note of thanks to their wives, Edda Agee, Linken Ault, and Mary Emery, who have considerably shared much of their husbands' time with this enterprise for almost three decades.

The authors wish to thank all these persons, as well as others who have expressed their interest in the book. Thanks also are extended to the United States Information Agency, which has placed successive editions of the book in its reading libraries throughout the world and for which translations have been published in Malaysian, Arbabic, Korean, French, Spanish, and Portuguese, joining the editions published in India, the Republic of China on Taiwan, and the Philippines. We hope that the many changes incorporated in this edition will meet with the approval of all who read it.

Warren K. Agee
Phillip H. Ault
Edwin Emery

INTRODUCTION TO

Mass Communications

PART ONE

The Role of Mass Communications

The Communication

Explosion

Millions of Messages

Precisely what is the communication explosion? These are some of the things it does:

Scene 1: Twelve thousand telephone calls between two cities are going on at the same moment. Business deals, gossip, sales pitches, lovers' quarrels, data transmissions: they run the gamut of human affairs.

All 12,000 are transmitted simultaneously through a pair of glass strands thin as human hairs. And they don't get mixed up!

At work is fiber optics, using laser light.

Scene 2: A terrorist bomb in Europe destroys a night club; the severe casualties include numerous Americans. Television crews hurry to the scene. Within minutes their pictures and reports are beamed upward from mobile transmitters to satellites, bounced back to earth in New York, and shown nationwide in the United States on network TV news shows.

Computers made this possible. So did scientists who figured out that a satellite orbiting 22,300 miles in space stays constantly over the same point on earth.

Scene 3: Villagers in a remote region of Pakistan gather in a tea shop. One inserts a tape in a videocassette recorder and they watch Eddie Murphy cavort in *Beverly Hills Cop.*

Note: In the time you took to read this vignette, it could have been transmitted around the world by satellite.

*A*n explosion of information and entertainment, spread around the world by electronic methods, recently has intensified humanity's ability to communicate by an incalculable degree.

A space camera sends photographs of the planet Uranus 1.8 billion miles back to earth. These pictures in turn are bounced off orbiting satellites and distributed to television audiences worldwide. Only a relatively few years ago such actions were inconceivable.

The purpose of this opening chapter is to explain what is happening in the methods of mass communication and how the changes affect individuals and society. We look first at how computers and satellites have revolutionized communication. Examples show what can be achieved using these remarkable tools.

After that we explain how new methods have altered the operation of newspapers, television, radio, recordings, and motion pictures. The rapid growth of cable television and the emergence of the video industry receive attention. So does the concept of information on demand.

Finally, we discuss the negative side of this profusion of new communication techniques, pointing out the areas of danger it has created. ◆

THE ELECTRONICS REVOLUTION

The ancient barriers of time and space have fallen. Swept away by the tremendous strides in electronic communication, these obstacles no longer impede the mass dissemination of news and entertainment even to remote corners of the world.

Within seconds a news bulletin or television picture can flash around the globe. Much of humanity's accumulated knowledge and contemporary information is recorded in computer storage, waiting to be called up by those who desire it. A computer in New York calls a computer in San Francisco and disgorges into it masses of information at the rate of 10,000 words a minute. A person sitting in the family living room presses buttons on a keyboard and, without leaving the chair, reads on a screen the latest sports scores, makes a bank deposit, and casts a vote in a straw poll being taken on a local cable television channel.

Today's news stories, instead of being transmitted along the earth's surface by wire, are beamed to a satellite 22,300 miles above the earth. There they bounce off a transponder pad back to the ground and are delivered into homes on the television screen or by radio. Neither barriers of nature, such as mountains, nor artificial barriers, such as national frontiers, can block their passage.

Yet, many people remember when the fastest form of communication was represented by a telegrapher in a green eyeshade tapping out the dots and dashes of Morse code at 30 words a minute.

Propelled by these new electronic methods, the tools of mass communication have penetrated virtually everywhere in the developed countries of the world. Increasingly, they are reaching into the more primitive areas as well.

A study showed that when President John F. Kennedy was assassinated, 90 percent of the American people knew about the shooting within an hour. That was in 1963. Today, a quarter century later, catastrophic news flashes worldwide at even greater speeds and with more intense penetration.

The immediacy and abundance of worldwide communication created by these technical marvels influences all levels of society. The concept of the global village, in which all inhabitants of planet Earth are drawn together in shared knowledge and needs, has been brought closer to reality. Life moves faster. Political and social ideas spread more rapidly. More information is available for making decisions, personal as well as governmental. Comprehension of the lives, desires, and rights of other individuals and other countries has been intensified.

Nevertheless, the stifling hand of political censorship still restricts the full use of these communication capabilities, as the world witnessed during the Soviet nuclear plant disaster at Chernobyl in 1986. The explosion created a radiation danger for people within the Soviet Union and in neighboring countries, yet the Soviet Union suppressed the news for three days. Not until Scandinavian countries reported exceptionally high radiation in their atmosphere did the Kremlin make its first brief announcement.

It is evident that the availability of communication tools is greater than humanity's demonstrated ability to use them wisely.

At great speed, transmission by satellite delivers to the world pictures of important news events, such as this news conference in which President Reagan and the Tower Commission discuss its report on the secret sale of U.S. arms to Iran. Rising as the president enters the room are commission members Edmund Muskie, Chairman John Tower, and Brent Scowcroft. (AP/Wide World)

In the United States, to cite one example of this availability, 98 percent of the homes have at least one television set. Approximately 46 percent of television homes are wired to receive cable television, with its profusion of offerings. Radio sets number nearly 500 million. After a period of decline, daily newspaper circulation has risen to about 63 million copies a day. Motion pictures are reaching additional millions of viewers through cable TV. Development of videotape has enormously enlarged the flexibility of sound motion picture presentation, at home and commercially. By use of videocassettes and videocassette recorders, individuals can watch movies and television programs whenever they wish. The number of computers is said to exceed the world's population.

Given such enormous advances in the means of communication within a short time, it is not surprising that society does not yet fully comprehend the significance of the tools at its command.

THE MEDIA AND THEIR PURPOSE

The mass media fall into two categories with certain attributes in common but with unlike physical characteristics. These groups are:

PRINT. Newspapers, magazines, and books. Their words create images in the mind as well as transmit information.

ELECTRONIC AND FILM. Radio, recordings, television, motion pictures, and video. These media deliver their messages through visual and audio impact on the senses, sometimes with great emotional intensity.

This book will discuss the ways that society uses its mass communication tools. We will examine the relationship of the mass media to the social structure and the social responsibilities faced by men and women who, through their jobs in the media, hold enormous power. Because contemporary thinking and methods cannot be understood fully without knowing the background from which they have sprung, we shall trace the history of the various media.

Ingenious tools in the hands of clumsy workers are almost useless, indeed dangerous. A builder who has the equipment and material but can't read a blueprint will erect a rickety structure that may collapse on its occupants. Similarly, media people who use the spectacular machinery of communication described in this chapter carelessly or without constructive purpose can create dangers to society. At the very least, they are guilty of failing to take proper advantage of tools whose existence could not even have been imagined by their grandparents.

The media deliver information in the form of news, commentary, and advertising, and also in the guise of entertainment. A popular television program such as "The Cosby Show" creates laughter while exploring family problems and social issues. A well-crafted spy novel, designed to entertain readers, also delivers facts about how the shadowy world of espionage functions. The usually wacky comic strip, "Funky Winkerbean," deals sympathetically and constructively with the problems of a pregnant high school girl, perhaps reaching persons who need the information but find the reading of factual books difficult and attending group sessions embarrassing.

In order to understand how the media deal with issues and situations, we must understand how they are organized and how they operate. The first step is to learn how the machinery of mass communication functions.

Marvelous as the electronic revolution is, it carries perils as well as immense possibilities for good. The danger that persons of evil intent will pervert truth by electronic trickery needs close scrutiny. Invasion of privacy and destruction of security become more critical dangers as the means for accomplishing them multiply. Thoughtful consideration must also be given to the ethical dilemmas that challenge those who work in the mass communications field.

Above all, it is vital to remember that the techniques of mass communication, fascinating as they are, exist only as tools. The ability to deliver words and pictures to the remotest villages of the world swiftly and abundantly has opened doors, yet it is the content of the messages transmitted that can open minds. As Henry David Thoreau wrote in 1849, "We are in a great haste to construct a magnetic telegraph from Maine to Texas, but Maine and Texas, it may be, have nothing important to communicate."

Once people hungered for information. Today, the problem has become *information overload.* We are so inundated with information and entertainment that individuals face a perplexing problem of selectivity and evaluation.

SATELLITES AND COMPUTERS

Two major electronic creations of the past four decades form the core of the revolution in communications. The first is the *computer.* The second is the *satellite.*

Basically, a computer is a machine capable of accepting and processing information and supplying the results in a desired form. The digital computer, the primary element in so much communication, performs operations with quantities represented electronically as digits to solve arithmetical problems at high speed.

Computers are almost everywhere. They guide space vehicles and operate automatic bank teller machines, microwave ovens, and automobile engines. Our concern with the computer focuses on its role in processing news, other information, and entertainment for mass audiences. Material fed into computers can be stored, analyzed, codified, prepared for publication, and transmitted from place to place at speeds far beyond the capacity of the human mind and hand. One result has been an enormous increase in the amount of news published. Small personal computers have many uses in media work.

The interconnection of both portable personal and fixed-position computers over telephone circuits has created a new and expanding way to communicate called *electronic mail.* This exchange of business and personal messages, which eliminates postal delivery time, forms a loosely knit network for almost instantaneous dissemination of information separate from the standard forms of mass communication and not subject to the editorial control most such forms receive. Electronic bulletin boards are an increasingly popular way to circulate messages and information. Misuse of bulletin boards to distribute racist literature and stolen credit card numbers has created debate over possible controls on such computerized communication.

Marvelous as today's computers are, a spectacular leap forward appears probable in the near future with a revolutionary change from computers that simply calculate to computers that reason. These "thinking" computers, equipped with artificial intelligence, have potential uses so numerous that they cannot yet be fully comprehended. Talking computers and those that operate robots have opened still other possibilities.

Most human endeavor involves reasoning and problem solving rather than calculation and data processing. If computers can be harnessed to diagnose and solve problems, their aid to humanity will be enormous. Japan obtained a head start in research on the "thinking" computer by making a very heavy investment, but the United States is trying strenuously to catch up.

When early communication satellites were launched into space, their role as distributors of news and entertainment was limited. The Telstar satellite sent aloft in 1962 received, amplified, and returned signals to earth but could relay messages only when its orbit placed it between the sender and the intended receiver.

This problem was solved by firing a satellite to the precise altitude of 22,300 miles above the equator, where a satellite has an orbital period of 24 hours. It thus remains stationary above a fixed point on the earth's surface, always available for relaying back to receiving dishes on earth the news and entertainment transmissions beamed up to it from originating points on the ground.

Demand for satellite transmission facilities grows constantly, and an ever-increasing number of satellites are parked far above the equator in what scientists call the geostationary belt. Not only is satellite transmission much cheaper and more reliable than along-the-ground transmission, but it is far faster. One computer can "talk" to another computer thousands of miles away about 160 times faster via satellite than can be done over landlines. As *National Geographic* magazine points out, such computer-to-computer communication via satellite is fast enough to transmit Tolstoy's massive novel *War and Peace* from one point to another within a few seconds.

The recent launching of RCA's more powerful K-2 satellite permits a broadcaster to reach every television station in the United States with one satellite, a technical advance with great commercial potential. One company has formed its own client grouping to receive exclusive broadcasts of major programs, independent of the networks.

In specific terms, what do the computer and satellite mean to the process of communication? Here are a few samples:

- The Live Aid concert to raise funds for Ethiopian famine relief at JFK Stadium in Philadelphia and Wembley Stadium in London, described as the largest single musical event in history, was broadcast around the world by satellite in 1985 to an estimated 1.5 billion viewers. Seen simultaneously in 105 countries, the telecast was relayed by 22 transponders on 13 satellites. Approximately $82 million was raised.

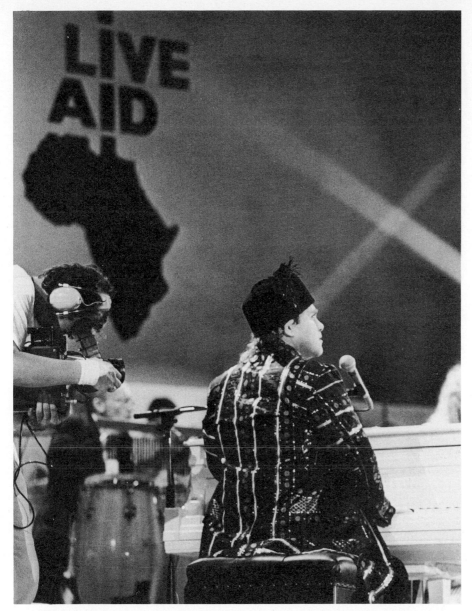

Cameraman shoots closeup of a performer during the Live Aid concert telecast worldwide by satellite to raise relief funds for Ethiopian famine victims. (Sygma)

• Pictures of rescuers digging through the ruins of the U.S. Marine Corps barracks in Beirut, Lebanon, where 241 Marines and Navy men died in a terrorist bombing, were transmitted almost instantly by satellite onto millions of television screens throughout the world. The emotional impact, particularly in the United States, was intense. When the shuttle Challenger disintegrated in midair, the dramatic satellite-transmitted film became the first foreign news event ever to open the nightly television news program in Beijing, China.

- *The Wall Street Journal* publishes a daily Asian edition in Singapore, consisting primarily of pages created by computerized phototypesetting in New York and transmitted by satellite to a printing press in Singapore.
- The president of one of the world's largest banks carries a personal video display terminal whenever he travels. He can plug it in and "talk" at any time with a dozen of his top executives, who have similar equipment. He also can plug it into his office computer file, which holds up-to-date information on 8000 business acquaintances, including their golf handicaps and spouses' nicknames. Thus, he can always refresh his memory before he meets some of them.
- Soviet scientists, speaking from Moscow by satellite, discussed with a group of American scientists in Washington the suicidal peril of nuclear war. They called the arms stockpile "a cancerous growth," expressing views similar to those of their American counterparts contained in a report under discussion.
- Over its international data communications network, the First Bank of Boston transmits a document from London to New York in a minute. Formerly, several days were required for a loan application made in London to be mailed to Boston, processed, and mailed back to England.

This is merely a tiny sampling of what the new electronic methods do.

Even the language has been altered, for better or worse, by the upsurge of high technology. Computer users identify a *bit* as the smallest unit of computer data: a 1 or 0 at a particular point within a computer memory. "Bit" stands for binary digit. Users know that eight bits make a *byte,* enough to identify one character. They are aware, too, that a diskette (or *floppy disc,* as it is also called) is a thin, magnetic, circular plate that stores data or programs, and that *software* is a set of instructions written in computer language that makes a computer do as it is told. In still another usage new to the language, they define a *chip* as electronic circuits etched onto a tiny disc, generally of silicon. On these chips information in the form of words, numbers, sounds, or pictures is stored and processed as electrical impulses—sometimes more than a half million components on a chip smaller than a cornflake.

Computer jargon has also made verbs out of several nouns, a process that makes language purists wince. Users *access* a computer—gain admission to its system by pressing certain keys—and *input* news stories into a computer through video display terminals (VDTs). *Interface* is used to mean *connect,* as in "My computer interfaces with yours." Satellite transmission has produced the words *uplink* and *downlink,* meaning the ground stations from which signals are beamed to a satellite and the round white receiving dishes that capture them on earth again.

TECHNOLOGY'S IMPACT ON THE MEDIA

As we examine the media in subsequent chapters, we shall discuss how each uses the new technologies. Here, to provide an overview of their cumulative impact, is a brief summary of how electronics has altered our major means of communication.

The electronic chip, on which thousands of circuits are etched, is an essential part of a computer. (AT&T Bell Laboratories)

Newspapers

In earlier days newspaper stories were typed or handwritten on copypaper, then set into lines of hot metal type on a Linotype machine, eight lines per minute. After manual correction by a proofreader, the lines were assembled in a metal page form. A soft cardboardlike sheet, rolled under heavy pressure, drew off an image of the page. This sheet was placed in a machine into which hot lead was poured, and the type image was thus transferred to a half-circular lead form called a stereotype plate. This heavy plate was locked onto the press for printing. The system was slow, cumbersome, and errorprone.

Compare that with today's electronic newsroom: A reporter types a story on a video display terminal keyboard, corrects it on the terminal screen, and dispatches it into a central computer. Editors call it up onto their screens for editing and headline writing, then with a push of a button release it into a phototypesetting machine, from which it emerges at speeds up to 4000 lines a minute as type on paper strips. These strips are pasted onto a sheet the size of a newspaper page, and this in turn is run through a plate-making machine that produces a printing plate weighing only ounces.

An even faster form of newspaper production, *pagination,* is just coming into extensive use. Under this system an entire newspaper page is made up electronically on a videoscreen, then by a push of a button is transmitted directly onto a printing plate. This process virtually eliminates the composing room of a newspaper. Control over the type and news pictures on each page lies entirely in the hands of newsroom personnel.

By use of digital processing, newsphoto services have begun to deliver better photographs to newspapers in less time. When an ordinary photograph is fed into this new machinery, its content is transformed into digital signals. An editor can call up the picture on a screen, enhance areas of it to improve its appearance, crop (cut) it to desired dimensions, then order it transmitted in digital form to subscribing clients.

Down in the pressroom, where the newspaper is printed, intriguing changes are taking place, too. One of these is development of magnetically charged ink that "leaps" onto the newsprint without actual pressure.

Some newspapers add to their regular publications with presentation of the news on cable television in text form. This leads to the concept of the "electronic newspaper"—delivery of the daily newspaper on the home screen rather than to the front doorstep in newsprint form. Tests to date indicate, however, that the public prefers electronic news as a supplement to print newspapers rather than as a replacement for them.

Dispatches from the news services formerly arrived in newsrooms on rolls of paper emerging from a clattering teletype machine. Now they are transmitted from a news service's computer by satellite into the newspaper's computer, ready for editing. Typewriters and paper have virtually disappeared from newsrooms.

Radio

Radio disc jockeys of an earlier era broadcast music entirely by playing phonograph records made of vinyl, either short ones at 45 rpm or long-playing ones at 33 rpm. In fact, pioneer disk jockeys played some 78 rpm records, now almost forgotten except by record collectors. Today much of the music is contained on tape cassettes, as are commercials. Laser digital recordings called compact discs, a third form of recorded music, have exceptional fidelity. A laser is an intense beam of light energy created when solid, liquid, gas, or plasma molecules are excited by electricity, heat, or other means. Sales of the CDs are multiplying swiftly, and radio stations have begun to use them in broadcasts.

For decades radio network programs were delivered to affiliated stations from their point of origin by telephone circuit over a microwave relay system that replaced the still-older overhead wires. Today network "feeds" are delivered to the stations by satellite.

Television

Since the creation of satellite transmission, cable television has immensely enlarged the scope of programs available to viewers in homes wired to receive it. The cable systems receive a number of programs by satellite and deliver them by cable to subscribers' sets. Using computerized text and graphics, many systems distribute national and local news summaries, along with weather information and the time, to home screens.

In another form of transmission called *direct broadcast satellite* (DBS), television programs bounced off a satellite are picked up directly by home reception dishes, bypassing the cable system entirely. Some organizations that distribute programs by satellite have begun to scramble the transmissions to prevent owners of home dishes from watching them without paying. Decoding attachments purchased from the organizations are needed to unscramble the transmissions, and monthly fees are charged for viewing privileges.

Equally dramatic, and just coming into use, are news and information services that allow viewers to call up onto their screens the information they wish. This is *information on demand.* The simpler form, called *teletext,* is a one-way system that displays indexes, or menus, of the material stored in the computer from which viewers, by pushing the proper buttons, can bring onto the screen the things they wish to see. These include such information as news bulletins, stock market reports, entertainment guides, games, community service listings, and airline schedules.

The more complex form of on-demand service is called *videotex.* It is a *two-way* system. On videotex, viewers call up what they wish to watch and, by using telephone circuits, are able to respond to what they have seen. For example, they may order goods they have seen on the screen, conduct banking operations, answer questions posed to them on the screen—plus, of course, watching whatever type of news they wish. On some systems they can send electronic mail, computer to computer.

In fact, the marriage of the computer and the telephone is at the heart of much new communication technology. Use of an instrument called a *modem* enables computer signals to travel by telephone.

Anxious to participate in electronic news delivery, numerous newspapers have leased cable channels and begun delivery of textual news summaries and video newscasts to homes. Their actions blur the traditional dividing line between print and broadcast journalism. This has created legal problems. Under the First Amendment, newspapers are free to publish anything they wish within such legal boundaries as libel and privacy. But the broadcasting industry does not have First

Amendment protection, although efforts to obtain it are being made. Is a story published in a newspaper under First Amendment protection when transmitted on the newspaper's cable news channel? Or is it subject to possible government broadcast rules? This is only one of numerous still-unanswered questions raised by the arrival of teletext and videotex.

Much of television's progress as a dispenser of news and entertainment was made possible by the creation of videotape, on which sights and sounds are recorded magnetically. Earlier, a television camera crew in the field made a film of the news event, then had it developed in a laboratory in a time-consuming operation before it was aired. With videotape, which can be erased and is then reusable, a TV news photographer sends the sound and pictures back to the studio by microwave, satellite, or vehicle. There it can be put on the air almost immediately because no developing process is involved.

From this original use of videotape, hundreds of other applications emerged. When the videocassette recorder (VCR) for home taping and viewing came onto the market, the booming video industry was born.

Still other television innovations are emerging from the laboratories and being offered to consumers. Television programs in stereo are broadcast in growing numbers on some commercial stations. Sets using flat picture tubes are less than two inches thick, small enough to fit into a pocket or purse. *High-definition television* will bring viewers clearer, sharper pictures. A system recently developed in Japan scans 1125 lines a minute, compared to the American standard 525 lines, greatly increasing picture detail. A bit further into the future will come *digital television.* By replacing receiver components with computer circuits, this system will reduce color TV production costs and cut down on ghostlike screen images.

Hundreds of low-power television stations have been approved by the Federal Communications Commission and more than 400 were in operation by 1987. Without disrupting the signals of present stations, they serve small areas where reception is inadequate, appeal to groups of special interest listeners, and offer pay television programs sent over the air instead of by cable.

In fact, the home video center is increasingly becoming a focal point of family life. Already the television set is not only a source of pictures and words but a place to play movies on videotape and receive prerecorded instruction. As the latest technologies come into general use, it will also be a place to transact business and do various kinds of work.

Technological and economic factors will determine how soon some of these innovations become everyday realities. Although in certain cases they may change shape from present expectations, the cumulative effect of the new forms will be intense.

Motion Pictures and Video

Thanks to new technologies, producers of Hollywood entertainment films have found additional home audiences to watch their pictures, first over cable television and more recently on videocassette recorders attached to television sets.

Until fairly recently, motion pictures were made for showing only in movie houses and drive-ins. Some of the more popular films are now played on network television, and old movies taken from the studio vaults have a seemingly endless replay life on independent television stations. The producers also shipped films to the lucrative foreign theater market.

Then came cable television. Its channels show movies, uncut and uncensored, many hours a day. Cable programs are distributed to home TV sets by wire, both above and under ground, from the headquarters of a local cable system; most of them are transmitted by satellite to the local systems from networks such as Home Box Office and Showtime. The home set owner pays a monthly fee to the local system to receive the material.

The enormous popularity of videocassette recorders has multiplied home viewing of movies, brought additional millions of dollars to filmmakers, and reduced attendance at theaters. Home viewers either rent videocassette movies from video shops or purchase them for their permanent libraries.

Foreign markets for videocassettes are thriving. In Saudi Arabia, for example, the homes of wealthy oil businessmen may contain seven or eight cassette recorders, one in every bedroom. Even in the midst of intense fighting in Lebanon, the sale and rental of videocassettes was a thriving business. In the evening, people there go to video clubs, where they drink coffee, select videocassettes of recent American movies, and sit in darkened viewing rooms. One dealer carries a stock of 16,000 videocassettes.

Videodiscs, which resemble phonograph records, failed to win public acceptance as competitors of videocassettes. Discs are valuable for storing information, however, and specialized uses for them have been developed. A new type of disc, the laser video disc, popularly known as laser vision or LV, appeared on the market recently. Critics praised the quality of its picture and sound.

This summary gives only a brief outline of how the electronic explosion has increased the global flow of communication. Ideas, information, and entertainment flashing around the world even penetrate regions where dictatorships try to control the lives of their citizens by restricting what they can see, hear, and read.

Electronic News Reporting

Gathering the news has been speeded up through electronic methods.

Vehicles carrying transmission equipment that beams signals to a satellite can speed to the scenes of timely news events such as disasters. From them reporters can send their televised dispatches directly to a network or individual station for immediate broadcast.

Newsgathering from space by cameras on commercial satellites has begun in a limited way. The first news pictures of the 1986 nuclear plant disaster at Chernobyl in the Soviet Union reached the world from the American Landsat and French SPOT satellites. Eventually, analysts predict, a group of American news organizations will launch their own satellite. Existence of newsgathering cameras in space able to report military movements could lead to a confrontation between

Transmission by cellular telephone helps pilots navigate rivercraft safely on busy waterways, just as it enables reporters to send in stories from moving automobiles. (Courtesy, GTE)

U.S. national security interests and the freedom of the press guaranteed by the First Amendment to the Constitution.

Newspaper reporters also have fast electronic tools for use in the field. They can type their stories on lap-size personal computers in their automobiles, connect the computers to *cellular telephones* in the cars, and transmit the stories directly into their newspapers' central computers. A cellular telephone system consists of numerous interlocking low-power transmitters, each covering a small geographic zone. As a vehicle equipped with a cellular telephone moves from one zone into another, its phone transmission is switched automatically by computer into the next zone's transmitter.

On the Horizon

Other dramatic forms of transmission are emerging to supplement or perhaps succeed some of those we have mentioned. Perhaps the most intriguing is *fiber optics.* Instead of transmitting signals by wire, this system uses highly transparent strands of glass thinner than a human hair. Replacing electronic signals, pulses of light flash along these glass strands at the rate of 90 million per second. A single fiber optics cable can carry 240,000 telephone calls at once. Use of fiber optics is expanding swiftly because of its efficiency and economy.

A Hungarian physicist, Dennis Gabor, developed the theory of *holography*—the projection of a three-dimensional image of an object—in the late 1940s. The theory could not be demonstrated, however, until a reliable source of coherent light, the

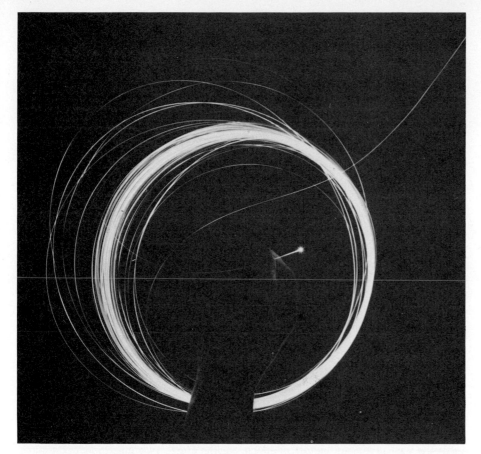

Fiber optics, consisting of glass strands finer than a human hair, makes possible transmission of a multitude of messages simultaneously at almost unbelievable speed. (AT&T Bell Laboratories)

laser, was later developed. During the last decade or so, holographic pictures have been created and used commercially on a limited basis. Observers can view all sides of the object seemingly projected toward them. The use of holography in motion pictures has been demonstrated to be possible, but numerous technical problems must be overcome before holographic films become a commercial reality.

An economic change that may have a profound impact on communications, especially within the United States, is the breakup of the giant American Telephone and Telegraph Company. Under a consent agreement with a federal court to settle an antitrust suit, AT&T in 1983 gave up ownership of its Bell telephone operating subsidiaries. It kept control of its long-distance services, manufacturing facilities, and laboratories from which so many communication advances have come. After a waiting period of at least seven years, AT&T, in 1990 or later, may be permitted to market its own data services over its own facilities. Historically AT&T has been only a common carrier transmitting other people's information for a fee. If it also becomes an electronic publisher—a creator and seller of information in sophisticated forms—AT&T will undoubtedly become a major competitive force in the marketplace of high-technology communication.

AREAS OF DANGER

The electronic developments we have described inevitably are having an intense impact on society. The behavior, thinking, and expectations of humans everywhere have been altered and will be molded even more extensively as the full influence of the information flood is felt. This proliferation of information and the swiftness of its distribution improve the human condition. Along with the positive values it provides, however, the communication explosion has created areas of danger that must be recognized and controlled.

Among them are these five major concerns:

1. Perversion of the truth by electronic trickery.
2. Invasion of privacy.
3. Violation of security, both governmental and institutional.
4. Impact on the democratic process.
5. Isolation of people.

Five Major Concerns

MANIPULATION. Clever users of electronic devices can alter the meaning of recorded visual and audio material, making it appear to be what it really isn't.

A high school teacher in North Carolina showing the family film *Annie* to a class was startled to find nude scenes appearing on the screen in the midst of the movie. With a home recorder four students had taped scenes from the Playboy channel on cable TV and secretly spliced them into the *Annie* videocassette the teacher had rented. In the motion picture *Zelig* trick photography and clever editing made the character played by Woody Allen mingle on screen with famous personages from the past, a glaring historical anachronism. These two innocuous examples, one a prank and the other a commercial entertainment device, suggest how political demagogues and unscrupulous entrepreneurs might electronically create a facade of truth for antisocial purposes.

PRIVACY. As two-way electronic communication increases, persons who use it for a variety of transactions will be placing more and more information about their private affairs into the memory banks and storage files of computers. In these records could be such information as the names of products a person had purchased by videotex, the content of electronic mail, lists of X-rated films the person might have ordered, and details of banking transactions.

Marketing firms, criminals, even just plain neighborhood snoops might like to obtain this information. Some system operators might be tempted to sell it for supplemental revenue, just as mailing lists are sold.

In an effort to prevent improper disclosure, a few states have adopted laws to prevent cable operators from supplying unrelated third parties with data about cable users without the users' consent. Important legal questions remain unresolved. For example, would a newspaper that operates a videotex service have the right to search its computerized records for evidence of illegal behavior by a suspected criminal who happens to subscribe to the service? Could police inspect the files merely by obtaining a search warrant?

Existence of control laws does not in itself provide automatic protection for such private material because electronic snoopers have shown remarkable skill at breaking into computer systems and obtaining information they should not have.

SECURITY. Protection of secret government information, private financial transactions, and institutional records in computer systems has caused much concern. Disclosure of instances in which computer "hackers" have ingeniously penetrated storage and transmission systems has increased public awareness of the danger.

Although banks are reluctant to admit they have been victimized, security specialists estimate that hundreds of millions of dollars have been stolen by computer criminals from the $600 billion a day that financial institutions transmit by computer. Using a home computer, one electronic "whiz kid" broke into and tampered with radiation-therapy records of cancer patients at Memorial Sloan-Kettering Cancer Center in New York. In California a 19-year-old student was arrested and charged with illegal entry into a Department of Defense computer system and 13 other systems, including confidential university research files. Protection against break-ins is costly and not always foolproof.

DEMOCRATIC PROCESS. It is axiomatic that democracy functions best when voters are widely informed on all problems and issues.

Given power to select the information they desire with the new technologies, will citizens expose themselves to a sufficiently broad range of knowledge? By choosing to see and hear only what interests them most—for example, sports, stock market quotations, and entertainment—will they be able to vote intelligently? Might this power of selectivity actually serve under some circumstances as a limiting factor in the education of the citizenry rather than a broadening one?

Because of the power of television and its ability to project personality, the danger grows that the nation may make decisions about leaders and policies based on image rather than substance. Already, the election campaigns of some candidates consist primarily of cleverly crafted 30-second TV commercials. Poorly financed candidates, no matter how well qualified they may be, often are overwhelmed by the TV barrages of less deserving opponents.

ISOLATION. While the communications revolution has the power to draw the global community closer together and frequently does so, it simultaneously isolates individuals and small groups.

Instead of mingling with crowds at movie theaters, couples and families stay home to watch videotapes on their TV screens. Both adults and children sit at computers for hours, aware only of what appears on the small screen, Often they seem visually drugged, almost bewitched. A growing number of workers do their jobs at home, linked to their offices by personal computer. This isolation from human contact and camaraderie, this loss of the group dynamic, has forced some intense users of computers to seek psychological help. The negative influences of such aloneness on society as a whole, if there are any, are not yet discernible.

Obviously, society has far to go in comprehending and controlling the communication explosion. More than a little awed by these feats of electronic wizardry and new marvels just coming into use, we are still struggling to harness their capacity in ways that will improve the human condition everywhere. More than ever before, responsible citizens need to learn how the mass communication system works and how to deal intelligently with the deluge of information it delivers.

The Media and Society

2

"Just Say 'No' "

The mass media can't solve a social problem, but, by focusing attention on it, they can arouse the public to act against the danger. The campaign against drug addiction shows what the media can do.

First, the media broadcast and published news reports on the spread of drug abuse. Through them the people learned of the dangers and extent of drug abuse.

Then the counterattack began. The media continue to publicize the anti-drug campaign in dozens of ways. Professional football players make pleas on television, "Don't use drugs." So do certain groups of rock musicians.

Newspapers publish medical reports on what drugs do and advice columns on where to seek help. Television, newspapers, and magazines show pictures of captured drug caches and stacks of money taken from arrested drug dealers. Videotapes depicting drug abuse and urging children, "Just say 'no,' " are shown in schools.

From the White House, Nancy Reagan has used the national media to publicize the slogan. Hospitals specializing in treatment of drug addiction run TV commercials telling the stories of persons they have helped.

Sports associations publicize their testing programs. The National Collegiate Athletic Association announced a ban against some college players playing in bowl games because they flunked drug tests.

Through the media, society has defined the problem and begun an educational campaign that is achieving results.

*A*s one of many elements making up the contemporary social fabric, the mass media draw more than their share of attention and controversy because of their high visibility. This chapter examines the place of the media in society and the nature of their influence.

We provide examples of how the media touch our lives at diverse levels, often without our realizing their impact. We examine how the media function in relation to other social forces. Are the media merely the messengers of society, or do they intentionally attempt to shape society to their interests, as some critics charge?

Since the media are so important, those who work in them have a responsibility to exercise ethical and moral leadership. The chapter discusses basic elements of that leadership.

After that, we look specifically at the role of the media in politics; in the economy, especially through the advertising they carry; and in social change. Numerous examples drawn from current situations are used to illustrate these issues, including ways in which the media both affect and are affected by the problems. ◆

EXAMPLES OF MEDIA IMPACT

The ways, large and small, in which the mass media touch our lives each day are beyond counting. Often we do not realize that we are being affected by what we see, hear, and read because we take the media's presence for granted. Their impact can be subtle as well as compelling. Here is a sample of diverse ways in which they influence individuals and events.

- President Reagan complains that his secret arms sales to Iran would have been accomplished unnoticed if "that rag" of a Lebanese publication had not broken the story.
- For nine days people of many nations follow news reports with growing enthusiasm as a man and a woman cramped into the flimsy aircraft Voyager fly nonstop around the world without refueling. Television cameras show crowds cheering as the bone-weary crew crawl from the Voyager after its successful landing. For a moment millions of people are uplifted by a shared sense of triumph.
- Parental organizations charge that the lyrics of rock-and-roll recordings seduce their children into drug abuse and sexual activity. They demand that warning labels be placed on offensive albums.
- *Seventeen* magazine publishes an article and pictures about a new hair style, and within weeks the style appears frequently on high school campuses.

- The happy escapism of the fantasy film *Star Trek IV* sends audiences out of theaters feeling contented. Meanwhile, another space film *Star Wars* took on an additional grim meaning as the label for a grandiose plan of nuclear defense in real life.

THE MEDIA AS MESSENGERS

Obviously the role of the media as the messengers of contemporary society is a great one. Aided by the methods of electronic communication described in the previous chapter, the media deliver words and images almost everywhere. Far swifter and more extensive systems of delivery are in operation today than ever before. As pointed out in Chapter 1, approximately 98 percent of American homes have at least one television set; half a billion radio sets exist in the United States alone; and American newspapers sell about 63 million copies a day. In addition, best-seller books such as Bill Cosby's *Fatherhood* and Lee Iacocca's autobiography sell more than 2 million hardback copies, often with several readers to a copy.

As they deliver messages, the mass media illuminate the social fabric of the nation. They report political, economic, and religious developments. Through the media we know that Pope John Paul II is the most traveled pontiff in history. On television we watch him perform his ritual of kissing the ground as he alights from his airplane in each country and see him ride through the streets in his "popemobile." In another manifestation of media-oriented religion, a television evangelist, Pat Robertson, announces his intention to seek the Republican nomination for president if his followers provide enough support.

When performing merely as messengers, the mass media generate relatively little of the controversy that has come to surround them. Much of their work is of this nature, such as reporting routine police news and civic meetings in newspapers and TV news programs. The controversy arises when the media—television in particular because of its potential for emotional intensity—become, or are perceived as, interpreters of society. In the minds of many, interpreting becomes "slanting" if the interpretations conflict with the recipients' opinions.

Yet flat presentation of cold fact alone is inadequate to inform the people sufficiently. The media must analyze, interpret, and compare the facts in order to give them meaning.

Many persons dislike the facts the messengers bring on certain types of stories because those facts disturb their prejudices or reveal unpleasant realities they would prefer not to know about. When the media add interpretation and analysis, as they must to do their job fully, animosity against the messengers may become intense. In the minds of hypersensitive recipients, the messengers turn into antagonists.

HOW MUCH MEDIA POWER?

Do the media shape society by forming its attitudes, habits, and manners of thinking, as critics often charge?

The phrasing of the question is flawed, because it implies that the media stand

This news photographer taking pictures in a guerrilla warfare zone delivers vivid visual messages that help readers to understand what such combat is like.
(Kong/Sygma)

aside from society as a separate entity. In reality, the media form a part of society just as churches, schools, and minority groups do. While the media unquestionably do influence societal thinking and behavior, their own conduct in turn is shaped by the standards and strictures of other social elements. The media do not stand alone, although their high visibility focuses attention on them. Later in this chapter we shall examine a situation in which the media are caught between conflicting social attitudes.

The concept that the media exercise extreme power over society is fostered, curiously, by two contradictory elements: (1) enthusiasts within the media who see their impact, especially that of television, without giving sufficient heed to their limitations; and (2) those who in their irrational hatred and fear see the conduct of the media in terms of dark, byzantine motives.

In his book *Media The Second God,* Tony Schwartz, a television advertising specialist, typifies the enthusiasts when he states, "Godlike, the media can change the course of a war, bring down a president or a king, elevate the lowly and humiliate the proud, by directing the attention of millions on the same event and in the same manner."

This advertisement soliciting contributions to the Guide Dog Foundation shows how advertising is used for social and charitable causes, as well as for commercial purposes. (Courtesy, Guide Dog Foundation for the Blind, Inc.)

The Conspiracy Theory

Among certain segments of American society, especially the political far right, belief persists that the media participate in a conspiracy to distort the news. Their goal is seen to be imposition of liberal attitudes on the audience, thus bending the people to their will. The primary targets of this belief are the major television networks, the New York *Times,* the Washington *Post,* and the weekly news magazines, all of which command large national audiences.

Always latent, the conspiracy theory surfaces most vehemently when a Republican president gets into political difficulty. Because their coverage reports and explores the president's problems, the media are accused by these critics of trying to undercut the chief executive and control the course of government. This happened during the Watergate crisis when President Nixon was forced to resign, and it happened again after disclosure of President Reagan's secret arms sales to Iran and the diversion of money from those sales to the rebel *contra* forces in Nicaragua. The sight of reporters and photographers swarming around newsmakers in disorderly displays of "pack journalism" heightens the disdain of these critics.

Typifying this animosity, especially toward the television networks, is a letter to the editor published in *The Sunday Oklahoman,* of Oklahoma City. Similar to letters published in other newspapers, it condemns the three major networks for what the writer sees as an attempt to destroy Reagan.

"A lot of people don't realize that these networks consider themselves the fourth branch of government," the female writer stated. "They don't want to just report the news, they want to mold minds and shape policy.

"They are the most dangerous element in this country today. The communists don't need a television station in this country—they have CBS, ABC, and NBC."

When their news coverage engenders such vitriolic reaction, the mass media have passed beyond the stage of being simple messengers. They have become socio-political forces, whether or not they desire to do so. They must assume the responsibility the role involves.

ETHICAL AND MORAL LEADERSHIP

The mass media do not exist to serve as moral preceptors or ethical taskmasters, although some of the material they deliver serves these purposes. Their principal task is to distribute information and entertainment. Nonetheless, those who write, speak, and edit the media have a heavy obligation to conform to acceptable standards. These standards are described below.

Acceptable Standards

HONESTY. News coverage must not consciously include falsehoods. Critics such as the letter writer cited above always hurl the "lie" accusation at stories that disturb their personal views. That cannot be avoided. But those who prepare and deliver stories must satisfy their own consciences that they are being honest.

FAIRNESS. The facts in a news story, magazine article, book, or broadcast may be true, and yet the publication may be unfair. Selective use of facts to create a headline, while consciously omitting qualifying or contradictory information, is an unfair practice. Unfortunately, just enough examples of this method exist for critics to raise the "slanting the news" cry and unjustly condemn the bulk of honest, balanced coverage being delivered by the media.

GOOD TASTE. Deciding the boundaries of good taste in broadcast, filmed, and printed material is highly subjective. Contemporary standards have been liberalized to the point that all social problems, even the most personal, are dealt with in the media. Topics that were forbidden or quietly ignored a generation ago are explored in dramatic films and TV shows, in radio advice programs, and in print. The problem centers on the manner in which the topics are handled.

Newspaper and television news editors had to make a delicate decision on good taste when Pennsylvania state treasurer R. Budd Dwyer unexpectedly committed suicide before the cameras during a news conference. Although some editors used a picture of him pulling the trigger with the gun in his mouth, most chose this less graphic one taken a few seconds earlier. (AP/Wide World)

Boundaries vary from medium to medium, depending upon the audience each reaches. Obscene and profane words used freely in many motion pictures, certain magazines, cable television, and videos are deleted from newspaper stories and network TV programs. The rationale for this difference is that the permissive media reach selective audiences that find the material inoffensive, or only mildly so, while newspapers and the networks reach a general family audience. The fact that approximately half of American homes now have videocassette recorders, making very easy the entry into the home of films containing strong language, nudity, and sexual situations blurs the lines of this argument.

Much of the controversy about good taste involves excessive use of violence, especially in motion pictures and television. With extensive research to support them, critics argue that these two media contribute strongly to make the United States a violent nation. Film and TV leaders deny this, contending that they give the public only what it desires and that violence is inherent in American character and history. This is an area in which society as a whole can exercise control over the media.

A detailed discussion of ethical and social responsibility in the media appears in Chapter 24.

THE MEDIA AND POLITICS

The influence of the mass media on the political process is strong and easily discernible. Politicians maneuver to obtain 30-second interview "bites" on the evening TV news shows. Election campaigns are fought with 30-second TV commercials designed to project a calculated image of the candidate rather than the discussion of an issue. And two decades after the Vietnam War, motion pictures such as the uncompromising *Platoon* remind us of war's horrors and the American political failures of that struggle.

Democracy flourishes only when a free flow of information about the operation of government reaches the people. That is accomplished primarily through the media. Daily news stories report spot developments while magazine articles, books, and discussion groups in the electronic media examine trends and background influences at greater depth.

Recent emergence of the TV commercial as a principal campaign tool disturbs many students of politics. The method is so enormously expensive that some candidates appear to spend more time raising money to buy television time than they do in meeting voters. What TV watchers see is not the candidate in person but a shrewd advertising specialist's image of the candidate. It is ironic that at a time when the tools of communication far exceed those of the past, live interplay of personality and ideas between candidates and voters has shriveled.

This observation is not intended to condemn use of TV commercials, for they are a proven method for reaching large audiences. Nor is it to condone those citizens who say they seldom vote because, as a letter writer in a California newspaper put it, "the issues presented each year are delivered to us by the commercial media in a form so vague as to leave many individuals wondering what the hell the measure or proposition is about." (Notice the implication that the fault lies with the media, not with the politicians who place the advertisements.) Rather, it is a plea by worried political observers for better balance so that the political process does not become distorted.

In the democratic process, the media perform a two-way function. Political leaders use media channels to explain their actions and promote their causes. Simultaneously, they study the media to determine what voters think, what they desire, and how a mesh of political goals and voter attitudes can be achieved.

A comprehensive examination of these issues appears in Chapter 22.

THE MEDIA AND THE ECONOMY

Advertising makes a free economy function by telling potential purchasers what is available and explaining the advantages of buying. As the machinery through which advertising messages are delivered, the media play a crucial role. Without the media to present these messages, business would stagnate.

The principal media for advertising are television, radio, newspapers, and magazines. Neither books nor entertainment motion pictures carry advertising, except for occasional items of a self-promotional nature. Neither do recordings.

Advertising on television and in magazines usually introduces and describes

products, while the majority of newspaper and radio advertising is designed to make the cash register ring by listing prices and detailed information about purchasing.

Some advertising is hard-fisted and harsh, but messages of deft subtlety also are employed. Jordache, a manufacturer of jeans, recently ran a television campaign for its Jordache Basics in which the product was neither mentioned nor described. These advertisements played on the alienation of young women. One featured a sulky teenage girl who resented but admired her mother; another focused on an angry high school girl running away from home despite the protests of her friends. The situations struck familiar chords with potential customers for Jordache products and lingered in their minds. Such conceptual advertising is challenging work because stories must be told and points made or implied within the space of 15 or 30 seconds.

Advertising is discussed more fully in Chapter 17.

The media also deliver news about the economy, to enlarge people's general knowledge and to guide them in their personal finances. Newspapers publish stock market price lists and other statistical tables. The newspaper with the largest daily circulation in the United States is the *Wall Street Journal.* Financial magazines such as *Barron's, Forbes,* and *Fortune* probe business trends, as do programs such as Louis Rukeyser's "Wall Street Week" on television.

In the business community a popularly held misconception is that the news media are out to "get" corporations. Many corporate executives regard reporters as antagonistic and ill-informed individuals who try to tear down the business structure.

Those who hold this view overlook a crucial fact: the media themselves are big business and have no desire to destroy others. Huge multimedia corporations such as the Gannett Company, Time Inc. and the Times Mirror Company own arrays of newspapers, magazines, book publishing firms, radio and television stations, and film subsidiaries. Critical stories about the performances of corporations and individuals in the financial community are based on legitimate news values, just as are similar stories about other fields of endeavor. Better training of business reporters in recent years has improved the business–media relationship.

Media ownership is examined in Chapter 21.

THE MEDIA AND SOCIAL CHANGE

During the immense changes in the social structure of the past quarter century, the media have been the instruments through which the promoters of change have advocated their causes. At times the media themselves have been advocates, as in the campaign against drug abuse, but on occasion they have been slow to recognize change in progress.

When the flaming racial riots of the 1960s exploded in Los Angeles, Detroit, and other metropolises, leaders of the media were startled. Their publications, films, and broadcasts had done virtually nothing to alert the public to the potentially explosive situation. An extremely important story existed under the noses of editors, and they had not covered it. Indeed, the mass media as a whole soon realized that they possessed few contacts within the angry racial minorities.

That shock did the media a world of good. Their leaders realized belatedly that they had a responsibility to search for broad social trends beyond routine daily news coverage.

In general, the media since then have done an adequate and occasionally excellent job in identifying and reporting social trends. Changing relationships between men and women, both in the workplace and in personal life, the problems of racial inequality, alienation of young people and their rejection of traditional living patterns, the increase in violence and growth of the drug culture—all of these have been examined in broadcasts, books, magazine articles, news stories, and films. Some of these examinations have been sensational and irresponsible, but the crucial point is that examinations have occurred. The media are unlikely to be caught dozing, as they were by the notorious Watts riot in Los Angeles.

So we return to the question, do the media create and foster social trends, or do they merely reflect what is happening? The question can be argued in both directions, with evidence to support yes *and* no answers. Media coverage of informal live-in arrangements between unmarried men and women, for example, has conditioned the public to accept this unconventional life style. Yet it cannot be said that the media have intentionally promoted it. Similarly, emergence of the gay rights movement and open homosexuality has been reported extensively, but mainstream broadcasters and writers do not attempt to foster the trend.

As emphasized earlier, the media are an integral part of society, not an unrelated force, and their treatment of social change is influenced and constricted by other portions of the social fabric.

For example, the three major broadcasting networks recently were caught in

Punk hair styles are a device some young people use to symbolize their revolt against tradition. Coverage of social trends is an important function of the media. (Weisbrot, Stock, Boston)

a dispute about airing commercials for birth control devices, specifically condoms. Society is plagued by a distressing increase in teenage pregnancies and by the swift spread of the fatal acquired immune deficiency syndrome, or AIDS, which primarily is sexually transmitted. The surgeon general of the United States, C. Everett Koop, urges use of condoms as "the best protection against infection right now, barring abstinence."

Some television stations have run discreetly worded commercials for the birth control devices, but the networks have refused to do so on the grounds that such commercials would offend large segments of their audiences. The Catholic Church and some other religious groups oppose their use. Planned Parenthood has placed full-page advertisements in several newspapers, condemning the networks' decision.

These advertisements charge the networks with sending a "dangerous double message to American teens" by carrying programs and commercials promoting sexuality while turning down birth control advertising. One of the advertisements was headlined: "They did it 9000 times on television last year. How come nobody got pregnant?"

Thus powerful social forces oppose each other on the issue, and the networks are caught between them. The individual stations that have run such commercials, including some stations owned and operated by the networks, have family audiences but have reported no surge of protest.

Social change often does not come easily, and, as the messengers of society, the media must suffer the bruises of conflict.

SUMMARY

Because they form the primary channel through which the elements of society communicate, the mass media illuminate and interpret the constantly changing societal relationships. Some critics contend that the media, or at least certain of the national electronic and print media, try to mold society to their own desires by influencing its attitudes, habits, and political beliefs. Other observers see the media role as more passive, reflecting rather than promoting change.

On balance, it seems fair to conclude that the bulk of the print, electronic, and film media do not consciously try to shape society, although a small minority of them vigorously and openly plead their special causes.

The media as a whole are concerned in a news sense with reporting and interpreting society's conduct, in an entertainment sense with presenting material that will earn a profit because it pleases audiences, and in a commercial sense with marketing goods and services through advertising, at a profit for themselves.

Mass Communication:

Process and Effects

3

Oh, Is That a Fact?

Nearly everyone has played the parlor game called "pass the word along" or "telephone." Designed as a genteel means of breaking the ice at a social gathering, it also serves to illustrate the perils of interpersonal communication.

Someone, perhaps the hostess, whispers a message into the ear of a male guest seated alongside. To do this the pair must huddle their heads closely, probably holding hands to ears. The man then whispers the message into the ear of the woman next to him, and so on around the circle until the message is returned to the hostess.

If the message is as garbled as the hostess hopes, there may be a moment of mirth. An opening statement that Betty had dinner in a lively night spot with bachelor friend George while husband Jack was out of town will almost certainly be magnified into an eyebrow-raising incident, complete with drinks, dancing and a lingering question mark.

Delivering a message involving facts—"the new tax rate is up 7 percent for singles, down 9 percent for couples"—will also demonstrate the inability of people to remember details long enough to pass them along. Zip codes or phone numbers are even harder to remember. That is why media people write down and recheck their facts.

*B*ecause the new technological systems have brought even greater speed, complexity, and power to affect human life than in the past, it is more imperative than ever for mass communicators to understand the nature of the art and the scientific applications in which they are engaged. The study of mass communications begins with a knowledge of the basic theory and process of communication itself.

Communication in its simplest form consists of the transmission of information, ideas, and attitudes from one person to another. A communicator sends a message through a channel to an audience, seeking some effect.

Mastering interpersonal communication requires consummate skill, but communicating to a mass audience is even more difficult. Not only must the mass communicator know what to communicate but also how to deliver the message, through complex systems, to make the greatest possible impact on an audience of diverse character from whom reactions cannot be immediately obtained.

In this chapter we explore the basic communication process and the various problems encountered by both the individual and the mass communicator. We then turn to the questions of how much effect the mass media have in shaping people's thoughts, changing their attitudes, or actually moving them to action. Various theories and research findings are examined. ◆

WHAT COMMUNICATION MEANS

The need to communicate with our fellow human beings is as fundamental as the physical requirements of food and shelter. This urge for communication is a primal one and, in our contemporary civilization, a necessity for survival.

Simply defined, *communication* is the act of transmitting information, ideas, and attitudes from one person to another.

Upon this foundation society has built intricate, many-faceted machinery for delivering its messages, the latest developments of which were described in Chapter 1. Yet these costly structures lose meaning unless their users have something significant to say. The study of communication thus involves two aspects—a broad comprehension of the mechanical means and the underlying theories of communication and, more importantly, an understanding of how we use these tools in our daily round of informing, influencing, inspiring, convincing, frightening, and entertaining one another.

Each of us communicates with another person by directing a message to one or more of the person's senses—sight, sound, touch, taste, or smell. This is known as *interpersonal communication,* in contrast with *intrapersonal communication* in which one "talks to oneself." Both forms are subjects of much research study. When we smile, we communicate a desire for friendliness; the tone in which we say "good morning" can indicate feelings all the way from surliness to warm pleasure; and the words we choose in speaking or writing convey a message we want to "put across" to the other person. The more effectively we select and deliver these words, the better our communication.

Contemporary society is far too complex to function only through direct communication between one individual and another. Our important messages, to be effective, must reach many people at one time. A consumer who is angry at high meat prices may talk to a half-dozen neighbors interpersonally about a boycott; if he or she then gathers some of them together for a coffee cup discussion, *group communication* is taking place. Some of the elements of physical or emotional proximity that characterize one-on-one interpersonal communication remain, but the level of involvement for individuals varies. One step further: If the editor of the local newspaper publishes a letter from the consumer advocating the boycott, the idea is communicated to hundreds of others in a fraction of the time it would take to visit them individually. This is *mass communication*—the process of delivering information, ideas, and attitudes to a sizable and diversified audience through use of media developed for that purpose.

Figure 3.1 shows the degrees to which the *frames of reference,* or mind sets, of the sender (A) and the receiver (B) overlap in various forms of communication. The more they overlap, the more likely will there be understanding and possible acceptance of the message. One-on-one communication has heavy overlap when people are close friends or agree wholeheartedly on the subject of interpersonal discussion. As the size of the group increases, those attributes decline and so does the degree of interpersonal communication success.

The art of mass communication, then, is much more difficult than that of face-to-face discussion. The communicator who is addressing thousands of different personalities at the same time cannot adjust an appeal to meet their individual reactions. An approach that convinces one part of the audience may alienate another part. The successful mass communicator is one who finds the right method of expression to establish empathy with the largest possible number of individuals in the audience. In some instances, such as network television shows, the audience for a message numbers in the millions. In the case of weekly newspapers, it may be only a few thousand. The need to catch and hold the individual's attention remains the same.

The politician reaches many more individuals with a single television speech

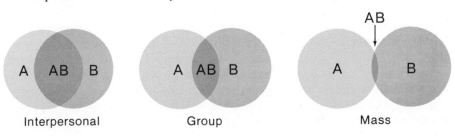

AB

Interpersonal	Group	Mass

FIGURE 3.1
Three visualizations of the sender-message-receiver relationship. (Source: From *Men, Messages, and Media* by Wilbur Schramm, p. 43. Copyright © 1973 by Wilbur Schramm. Reprinted by permission of Harper & Row, Publishers, Inc.)

than through handshaking tours, but that person's use of mass communication may be a failure if the same feeling of sincerity and ability that is conveyed through a handshake and smile cannot be projected on a radio broadcast.

Thus, the mass communicator's task breaks down into two parts: knowing *what* to communicate and *how* to deliver the message to make the greatest possible impact on an audience. A message of poor content, poorly told to millions of people, may have less total effective impact than a well-presented message placed before a small audience.

Every day each of us receives thousands of impressions. Many of these pass unnoticed or are quickly forgotten. The effectiveness of the impression is influenced in part by our individual circumstances. A news story from Washington about plans by Congress to increase unemployment benefits raises hopes in the mind of the person who fears being laid off a job; the same dispatch may disturb the struggling entrepreneur who sees in it the possibility of higher taxes. The communicator's message has differing effects upon these two members of the audience; it may have none at all upon another consumer who is somehow distracted while scanning the newspaper or listening to a newscast.

Obviously, the mass communicator cannot know the mental outlook and physical circumstances of everyone to whom the message goes. There are many principles and techniques that can be used, however, to ensure that the message has an effective impact on the greatest possible number of individuals in the largest possible audience. Some of these are learned by mastering the basic techniques of journalistic communication (writing, editing, newscasting, graphic presentation); others are learned by studying the mass communication process and by examining the character of the mass media.

THE COMMUNICATION PROCESS

Researchers call our attention to four aspects of the communication process: the *communicator,* the *message,* the *channel,* and the *audience.* (In research language, the communicator is also known as the *encoder;* the message—whether words, pictures, or signs—becomes *codes* or *symbols;* the channel, in the case of mass communication, is one of the mass *media;* the person in the audience is known as the *decoder.*) A properly trained communicator understands the social importance of his or her role and also knows what to transmit as the message. The communicator understands the characteristics of the channels (media) to be used and studies the varying interest and understanding levels of groups of people who make up the total audience. The message is molded to the requirements of each channel used and to the capabilities and interests of the audiences being sought.

Figure 3.2 presents the widely used HUB model of mass communication, visualizing the process as a circular, dynamic, ongoing progression. Its set of concentric circles forms a pool into which the familiar pebble (communication content) is dropped, sending ripples outward as the message progresses toward the audience.

In the center are the communicators, who in mass communication are a group of individuals forming the newspaper staff, the television news team, the advertising agency members. Their messages (called *codes*) involve language or symbol

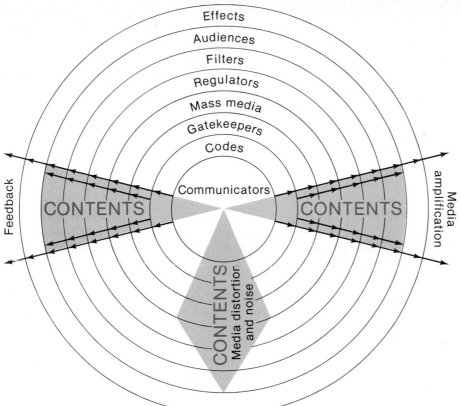

FIGURE 3.2
The HUB model of mass communication. (Source: From *Mass Media IV* by Ray Eldon Hiebert, Donald F. Ungurait and Thomas W. Bohn, p. 25. © 1985 by Longman, Inc.)

systems, such as the visual symbol systems that replace dialogue in motion pictures. Before a message reaches a mass medium, it must pass through the organization's *gatekeepers* who make decisions about what will be communicated as they shape the content of their broadcast show, magazine or news service. Another set of gatekeepers working for newspapers makes decisions as to which specific news stories will be used on a given day. They are the news editors and copy editors. On the other side of the mass media ring are the *regulators*—public pressure groups, government agencies, advertisers, consumers, courts, and legislatures—that exert influence on the media, affecting content and performance. Beyond are the *filters,* or frames of reference, through which audiences receive messages and which may enhance or cripple the *effects.* These terms will be discussed in greater detail later in this chapter; for the moment we shall focus on filters, media distortion and noise, feedback effects, and media amplification.

The receiver filters the message in terms of a frame of reference, as we have said. Each person has a *stored experience,* consisting in part of individual, ego-related beliefs and values and in part of the beliefs and values of the groups to which he or she belongs (family, job, social, and other groups). A message that challenges these beliefs and values may be rejected, distorted, or misinterpreted. Conversely, one whose beliefs on a given subject are under pressure may go out of the way to seek messages bolstering his or her viewpoint. In cases where beliefs are firmly fixed, the communicator finds it is often more effective to try to redirect existing attitudes slightly than to meet them head on. Another audience problem is called *dissonance.* This occurs when an action is taken that is inconsistent with what a person knows or has previously believed, or the action is taken after two or more attractive alternatives are considered. The person is uncomfortable until some dissonance reduction is achieved by seeking out messages that help adjust beliefs to action (a familiar example is the person who, having bought one make of car from among several attractive ones, continues to read advertisements for the car purchased; if makes have been switched, even more reassurance is required).

The communicator also knows about the limitations and problems communications researchers have studied. One of these is *channel noise,* a term used to describe anything that interferes with the fidelity of the physical transmission of the message (such as static on radio or type too small to be read easily); but broadly speaking, channel noise may be thought of as including all distractions between source and audience (Figure 3.3). The professional communicator helps overcome its effects by attention-getting devices and by careful use of the principle of *redundancy* (repetition of the main idea of the message to ensure that it gets through, even if part of the message is lost).

A second kind of interference, called *semantic noise,* occurs when a message is misunderstood even though it is received exactly as it was transmitted (Figure 3.4). The communicator, for example, might use words or names that are unfamiliar to an audience member (material outside that person's *frame of reference*). Or the words used may have one meaning for the communicator and another for the listener or reader (the common or dictionary meaning is called *denotative,* the emotional or evaluative meaning is called *connotative*—a word like *socialist* has widely differing connotations). Semantic noise can be reduced if the communicator will take pains to define terms and adjust vocabulary to the interests and needs of the audience. Sometimes, difficult or strange words are understood because the reader grasps the *context* in which they appear, but it is also possible for a poorly defined word to be misunderstood this way. And if the material presented is too complex, the reader either will be forced to *regress* and restudy the message or, more likely, will turn to some other more rewarding and pleasant material.

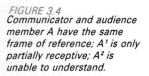

FIGURE 3.3
The communication process: Communicator (C) places a message in selected channel to reach audience (A) but is subject to "noise" interferences.

FIGURE 3.4
Communicator and audience member A have the same frame of reference; A¹ is only partially receptive; A² is unable to understand.

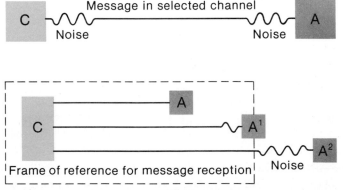

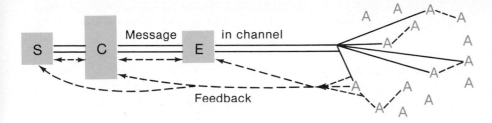

FIGURE 3.5
Mass communication for a given message at one moment in time is illustrated here: Source (S) has the message reported by communicator (C) in channel controlled by editor (E); some audience members (A) receive the message directly, others indirectly, but some are inattentive; feedback interactions may occur along the communication route.

The communicator is aided by what are called *feedback effects* (Figure 3.5). These are reactions that take place along the communication process and that are transmitted backward: by the communicator (reporter) to the original news source; by another media worker (editor) to the reporter; by members of the audience to the editor, the reporter, or the news source; and by different persons in the audience to each other. Obviously, there is much more discernible feedback in person-to-person communication than in mass media communication, and thus a better opportunity to deliver a convincing message face to face. But the communicator who has knowledge of feedback reactions in mass communication and who solicits them may enhance acceptance of the messages.

Nonverbal communication is an important aspect of the communication process. Popularly known as "silent language" or, in some of its aspects, "body language," nonverbal communication may include such attributes as facial expression, eye movement, posture, dress, cosmetics, voice qualities, laughing, and yawning. For example, a TV newscaster may, consciously or unconsciously, alter the meaning of the spoken message through a lifted eyebrow or a shrug of the shoulders. A weak voice may convey uncertainty or an arms-folded stance defiance. A politician's rolled-up sleeves and tieless shirt may produce votes from laborers.

Media amplification is familiar to all of us—appearance in the media amplifies the importance of a Johnny Carson, a Geraldine Ferraro, a Jack Nicklaus, even a president. We shall find in Chapter 19 research evidence about the media's role of *agenda-setting.* While the media may not determine what we think, very often they determine what we think about.

All this is summed up in Professor Harold D. Lasswell's question: "Who, says what, in which channel, to whom, with what effect?" The different types of studies carried on by the mass media and by individual scholars to aid in more effective communication will be examined later in this chapter and in Chapter 19. Essential steps for a would-be communicator, however, are to gain an understanding of the role of the communicator in our contemporary society and to examine the mass media through which audiences are reached. To take the communicator through these steps is the purpose of this book.

COMMUNICATION: HOW MUCH EFFECT?

How effective are the mass media in shaping thought (the cognitive aspect of mass communication)? In changing attitudes (the affective aspect of mass communication)? Or in moving people to action (the behavioral aspect of mass communication)? Scholars have been asking these questions for decades. Historians and journalists have found many convincing examples of media effects involving the cognitive aspects of mass communication: attention, awareness, information. These indicate that people do learn from mass communication, and sometimes then change their attitudes and opinions.

Social scientists, however, in their research of the 1940s and 1950s, chose to emphasize the affective and behavioral aspects of mass communication. Focusing their attention on voting behavior and using precise measurement and analysis techniques, they found only minimal direct effects of mass communication on attitudes and behavior. When they later concentrated on cognitive aspects, they found new paths. In the 1980s communication researchers generally agreed that the mass media have effects and are used by many people in ways that are important to them.

In the remainder of this chapter, we examine the topic of communication effects, and the evolving theories developed by communication researchers since Walter Lippmann advanced his "the pictures in our heads" theory in his 1921 book, *Public Opinion.* Harold D. Lasswell a decade later put forth the "hypodermic model" theory based on the argument that communication is something one does to someone else with powerful effect.

The next generation of media research leaders, using scientific studies developed in carefully designed experiments in laboratory atmospheres, rejected the theory of the "hypodermic model" and advanced the theory of minimal effects. By the 1970s still another school of thought swung the pendulum back by distinguishing between the media's affective and behavioral aspects. In the 1980s the focus of research about communication effects was on agenda-setting: the ability of the media to select and call to the public's attention both ideas and events.

THE CONVENTIONAL WISDOM

Every writer on the topic of communication effects elects to recall the panic that seized part of the eastern seaboard on October 30, 1938. That night, Orson Welles and the CBS radio theater group broadcast a terrifying and realistic report of an invasion from Mars taking place near Princeton, New Jersey. Conventional radio news bulletin devices convinced thousands of citizens that giant mechanical monsters were roaming the countryside, and people fled without waiting to hear that the report was only an adaptation of H. G. Wells' novel, *War of the Worlds.*

Wilbur Schramm, a distinguished communication research scholar, cites the Orson Welles hoax as an obvious communication effect, saying that many people were emotionally aroused, and that some of them abruptly changed their behavior in a way that could never have been predicted before the broadcast. Indeed, the incident ranks high among classic examples of a mass medium's effects on its audience.

Other examples of the conventional wisdom are:

- Both participants in the 1960 debate between presidential candidates John F. Kennedy and Richard M. Nixon agreed with the experts that the positive image of Kennedy, perceived by a majority of the great television audience,

"War" Victim

Caroline Cantlon, WPA actress, listening to this radio in West 49th St., heard announcement of "smoke in Times Square." Running to street, she fell, broke her arm.

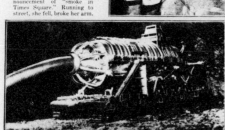

Story on Page 2

"I Didn't Know". Orson Welles, after broadcast expresses amazement at public reaction. He adapted H. G. Wells' "War of the Worlds" for radio and played principal role. Left: a machine conceived for another H. G. Wells story. Dramatic description of landing of weird "machine from Mars" started last night's panic.

—*Story on page 2.*

Front page of the New York Daily News reports the fear created nationwide in 1938 when Orson Welles presented a dramatized adaption of the H.G. Wells novel, War of the Worlds, in a network radio broadcast. (New York Daily News photo)

gave him the necessary edge for election. Jimmy Carter enjoyed a positive reaction during his 1976 debate with Gerald Ford, which buttressed his campaign. But in 1980 Carter was perceived negatively in contrast to Ronald Reagan, and pollsters said his popularity slumped immediately after the debate. Walter Mondale suffered similarly in 1984. These events illustrate the effect of mass media upon voting behavior.

- Historians of the American Revolution, reviewing their literature during the bicentennial year, generally agreed that the colonial weekly newspapers and pamphlets such as Tom Paine's *Common Sense* played a crucial role in first informing colonists about events and ideas and then persuading them to support the Declaration of Independence. This is an example of political communication, since the radicals espousing independence had a carefully planned propaganda effort.
- Press historians point out that public consciousness of Lincoln's "Gettysburg Address" or William Jennings Bryan's "Cross of Gold" oration could have been developed only by the print media during the nineteenth century. Many Americans learned Lincoln's lines by heart. Bryan was nominated for the presidency three times.
- One can argue that the mass media are capable of creating a presidential candidate if the public fails to find other candidates attractive. In 1940 Americans learned about Wendell Willkie, a relatively unknown businessman, through the print media and radio. A "We Want Willkie" chant swept other hopefuls aside in the Republican nominating convention. In 1976 "Jimmy Who?" caught the public fancy and catapulted Carter to the lead in the Democratic party primaries, with voters in some states becoming aware of him solely through television and radio newscasts, newspapers, and news magazines.

  Lt. Col. Oliver North became an instant folk hero when he dominated the Iran-Contra congressional hearings during the six days on television in 1987. The beribboned former White House aide called himself "Ollie" and so did much of the American public, which believed he was being framed. "Ollie for President" clubs were organized, and the public rushed to buy "instant" videos and books extolling his beliefs and exploits.
- A classic story of mass media effects is, of course, that of Watergate. In this instance the effects of mass media brought about the forced resignation of a president in the face of changing opinions of him among members of the Congress and the general public. The media effort in the Watergate story was primarily an informational one. When convincing evidence accumulated, it had a persuasive effect that brought about changed attitudes and behavior. That, in brief, is what journalism has been all about over the centuries.

EARLY THEORIES OF POWERFUL EFFECTS

Walter Lippmann spent his life as an editor of magazines and newspapers, an author, and a highly influential political columnist. He also was a member of the academic and intellectual communities centered at Harvard University and in the liberal political and media clusters of New York and Washington. With this background he wrote a brief book in 1921, *Public Opinion,* which served as a challenge to the development of scholarly research and writing in the fields of public opinion and mass communications.

The first chapter of *Public Opinion,* "The World Outside and the Pictures in

Our Heads," was rich in provocative thought. "The world we have to deal with politically," he said, "is out of reach, out of sight, out of mind. It has to be explored, reported, and imagined." Each person gradually makes for "himself a trustworthy picture inside his head of the world beyond his reach." The pictures in the minds of citizens collectively constitute public opinion, Lippmann continued. Fragmented, distorted, and subject to preconceptions and prejudices, the pictures inside people's minds often mislead them in their dealings with the outside world. Part of Lippmann's analysis is how the pictures in our heads affect the "trickle of messages from the outside," which includes mass communications.

Harold D. Lasswell, a professor of law at Yale University, contributed much to the study of propaganda during World War II. From his writings came the concepts popularly called the "silver bullet" and hypodermic model theories of mass communications effects. These assume that communication is something someone does to someone else; the communicator, not the consumer or receiver, is the causative person. This was a natural avenue for Lasswell to take, steeped as the academic world was in wartime studies of the influence of propaganda and its use in political and social spheres. His famous query, "Who, says what, in which channel, to whom, with what effect?" structured the thinking and research of communication scholars and students for two decades. The fields of research became, in the order of the phrases in the question, communicator or systems analysis, content analysis, media analysis, audience analysis, and effect analysis. Though Lasswell was a valuable guide in many of these fields, he misdirected effect research by focusing so heavily on the affective role of mass communications.

Lasswell also described the function of communication as "(1) the surveillance of the environment; (2) the correlation of the parts of society in responding to the environment; (3) the transmission of the social heritage from one generation to the next." In simpler terms these are (1) collecting and distributing information and news; (2) interpreting that information and writing editorials suggesting reaction to it; and (3) educational activity. Entertainment and marketplace roles are also added to the functions of mass communications.

SCIENTIFIC STUDIES: MINIMAL EFFECTS

With the image of powerful mass media created by the hypodermic model it was natural for large-scale research projects to be launched. One was the Yale Communication Research Program, directed by psychologist Carl I. Hovland for the U.S. Army in wartime and later for Yale University. Another was an intensive field study of voting behavior in Erie County, Ohio, conducted by sociologist Paul Lazarsfeld and his colleagues at Columbia University.

The Yale University studies were at first designed to analyze differences in communication techniques and the effectiveness of various types of messages and communicators. Using carefully designed experiments in laboratories, schools, and military units, the researchers examined one variable after another in different combinations and situations, with attitude change as the dependent variable. Out of these years of experiment came what Wilbur Schramm calls a wealth of information about variables in communication and descriptions of then-new research designs. Hovland obtained greater effects in his laboratory studies than Lazarsfeld and others found in field studies, a result that Hovland defended as scientifically valid. Even so, there was little resemblance between the results of Hovland's experiments and the concept of the hypodermic model.

Lazarsfeld, Bernard Berelson, and others in the Columbia University voting study found no evidence of the "hypodermic needle" in their 1940 study of Erie County voting behavior. Lazarsfeld reported in *The People's Choice* that the media have relatively few direct effects on voting during an election campaign. Rather, the Columbia researchers said, the media serve to reinforce preconceived beliefs. Whatever influence the media do have on voting change they attributed to the "two-step flow." Opinion leaders obtain information and opinions from the media and pass along their ideas to other members of their voting groups. Magazines could thus become important sources of voter information through the two-step flow concept. Later research determined that this model was too simplified. Many researchers concluded that the more personal a medium is, the more likely it is to be persuasive. Face-to-face communication is most effective, followed by television, film, radio, and print.

Lazarsfeld and Robert K. Merton published a paper in 1948, as part of the book, *The Communication of Ideas,* which argued that the primary social effect of the mass media is to maintain the status quo, exercising a status-conferral power. They have a "narcotizing dysfunction" of absorbing their audiences' time without energizing them. According to Lazarsfeld and Merton, the media have the ability to "canalize" behavior, directing persons who already accept one idea or product to accept a similar one.

In 1960, Joseph T. Klapper, a disciple of Lazarsfeld and a professor at Columbia University, summed up the "minimal effects" research in his book, *The Effects of Mass Communication.* "Mass communication *ordinarily* does not serve as a necessary and sufficient cause of audience effects," he wrote, "but rather functions among and through a nexus of mediating factors and influences." He qualified that statement, however, with the following remarks: "It must be remembered that though mass communication seems usually to be a *contributory* cause of effects, it is often a major or necessary cause and in some instances a sufficient cause. The fact that its effect is often mediated, or that it often works among other influences, must not blind us to the fact that mass communication possesses qualities which distinguish it from other influences, and that by virtue of these qualities, it is likely to have characteristic effects."

To many observers, the impact, influence, and effect of the mass media on audiences seemed obvious. Granting that the effects of mass communications may have been judged to be too powerful, particularly in the ability to persuade, observers insisted that the generalizations of some social scientists, who said that the media had "nil effects," were equally misleading. Those who believed the mass media could affect audiences noted the conflict in findings by researchers using laboratory methods and those working in the field. They noted that generalizations were being based on a limited number of controlled experiments and studies. The time was ripe for what historians call a revisionist school of thought, to bring the balance of judgment back toward the middle.

CONSISTENCY THEORIES: SELECTIVE PERCEPTION

A series of consistency theories, developed during the 1950s, hypothesized that people want their beliefs and judgments about things to be consistent with one another. Professor Leon Festinger's cognitive dissonance theory is the most well-known of these theories. In order to reduce dissonance created by inconsistencies in belief, judgments, and action, people expose themselves to information that is consistent with their ideas and actions, and they shut out other communication.

As Professors Maxwell E. McCombs and Lee B. Becker stated in *Using Mass Communication Theory,* "a key part of each individual's experience that influences his or her perceptions is the set of previously acquired attitudes and opinions. Stereotypes straddle the boundary between cognitions, our mental pictures of the world about us, and affective attitudes, our feelings and evaluations of persons, issues, and situations in the world around us."

In *selective perception,* items in the news that are regarded favorably are more likely to be recalled by a viewer than items that are regarded unfavorably. Further, the viewer will, if possible, shape his or her interpretation of a news event to be congruent with the viewer's existing attitude. In a study of reactions to the surgeon general's warning about the hazards of smoking, Festinger found that the more cigarettes an audience member smoked each day, the less convinced the smoker was that an actual link had been established between smoking and lung cancer.

Two areas similar to selective perception are *selective exposure* and *selective retention.* Some persons habitually listen to news on Channel 4 rather than on Channel 5, or read *Time* rather than *Newsweek.* Some persons consistently avoid materials they know to be distasteful, or that would create dissonance. Researchers find that selective retention plays a role in the effectiveness of efforts to change attitudes through informational campaigns. People remember what they want to remember.

Professor L. John Martin points out that the consistency theories switched the Lasswellian paradigm around. Rather than "Who says what to whom?" the question for researchers now seemed to be, "Who needs to receive the message from whom?" "The emphasis was on the seeking and avoiding of information rather than on the transmission of instruction or urging of opinion change," Martin says. "Furthermore, a distinction began to be made between informational communication and persuasive communication" in discussions of the effects of mass communications.

MEDIA SYSTEMS AND AGENDA-SETTING

Lasswell's concept of a surveillance function of the media, and early studies of what became known as gatekeeping by editors who were charged with selecting or rejecting items to fit a daily newspaper's available space, pointed to new avenues of research. As sociologists Melvin L. DeFleur and Sandra Ball-Rokeach have written, "The ultimate basis of media influence lies in the nature of the three-way relationship between the larger social system, the media's role in that system, and audience relationships to the media." One avenue was *systems analysis,* the other the *agenda-setting* function of the press.

Some researchers have examined mass media as a part of the larger social system. Sociology professors George Donohue, Phillip Tichenor, and Clarice Olien have done extensive research and writing to demonstrate that "mass media represent subsystems which cut across other subsystems and transmit information among and between them." This means that the mass media have the ability to penetrate other aspects of society with their messages. It also means that control of the media subsystems, and of gatekeeping activities within them, is crucial.

Information control has been practiced for centuries with the realization that knowledge is vital to social power. Those who control the flow of communication have the ability to exercise power over other people. Gatekeeping, the three sociologists point out, should be viewed as more than the simple exercise of choice among available news stories. The editor accepting or rejecting a story is part of a subsystem that has input into many decisions regarding information control.

Television network news editors prepare a broadcast. Selection of stories to be used in a newscast or publication is known as "gatekeeping."
(Taylor/Sygma)

These include message selection, shaping, display, timing, withholding, and/or repetition. Thus the study of mass media as social subsystems plays a part in the overall study of mass communications effects, including agenda-setting.

Professor David Manning White's classic 1949 study of the news selection behavior of one wire news editor portrayed the subjective selections and rejections of stories by the gatekeeper, dubbed "Mr. Gates." Later researchers who reviewed White's study and other gatekeeping research data found that the larger the number of news items offered the local newspaper news editor about a given category of news (national, political, crime, and so forth), the larger will be the proportion of his or her selections for that category. Professors Charles Whitney and Lee Becker summed up their own and others' studies in 1983 as suggesting quite strongly that the local media, at least, are influenced greatly by the decisions of a relatively few gatekeeper editors operating in the regional, national, and international press association bureau offices. Agenda-setting thus is a complex procedure.

Agenda-setting became a leading area of mass communications research in the 1970s. The basic idea of agenda-setting—the ability of the media to influence the salience of events in the public mind—was a part of Walter Lippmann's description of "the pictures in our heads." In 1963 political scientist Bernard C. Cohen declared in his book, *The Press and Foreign Policy,* that "the press may not be successful much of the time in telling people what to think, but it is stunningly successful in telling its readers what to think *about."* Theodore White wrote in 1972: "The power of the press is a primordial one. It sets the agenda of public discussion. . . . No major act of the American Congress, no foreign adventure, no act of diplomacy, no great social reform can succeed in the United States unless the press prepares the public mind. And when the press seizes a great issue to thrust onto the agenda of talk, it moves action on its own."

Two professors of mass communication, Maxwell E. McCombs and Donald L. Shaw, offered in 1972 their scientific concept of the agenda-setting function, that media emphasis on an event influences the audience to also view the event as important. This impact of the mass media—the ability to effect cognitive change among individuals, to structure their thinking—is characterized by McCombs and Shaw as perhaps the most important effect of mass communication, "its ability to mentally order and organize our world for us."

McCombs and Shaw made the first empirical attempt at verification of the agenda-setting function of the mass media in a study of voters in the 1968 election. Among undecided voters, there were substantial correlations between the issues emphasized in the news media and what those voters regarded as the key issues of the election. The voter agenda was ascertained independently of what the media were reporting, the results indicating that indeed the press had set the agenda for its audience. Since the mass media provide many of the facts that make up the cognitive world of each individual, it could be possible that the press merely relays information, as a transmission belt. But agenda-setting studies have developed evidence that the press selects certain issues to play up at times when they are not significant in the public mind; they then become part of the accepted agenda.

Support for the McCombs–Shaw thesis was given by publication in 1981 of a book by Professor David Weaver and associates analyzing media agenda-setting in the 1976 presidential campaign. The study found the newspaper agenda was highly stable over time, more so than the television or voter agendas. Television agendas became increasingly similar to newspaper agendas, and, by summer, the voter agendas tended to become increasingly similar to both in content. The authors concluded that the media not only may determine who will be nominated, but by projecting images for candidates and linking them to issues, may also decide who will be elected. Political campaigns are altered to meet the media's needs and preferences; adroit candidates have, of course, shaped the dialogue and events to influence media agendas. Professor Thomas Patterson reviewed the same election in a book-length study.

In Sweden political scientist Kent Asp studied that country's 1979 national election campaign and found that the degree of agreement between the priorities which the media assigned to issues and those which voters assigned to them was very great. As a consequence the agendas of the political parties lagged in influencing how voters appraised the issues. Asp characterized this as another dimension of journalists' "power." The concept of agenda-setting was well established, although its status as a detailed theory remained to be determined.

McLUHAN'S "HOT" AND "COOL" MEDIA

A theory that the medium is the key element in the mass communications process evoked widespread attention and controversy during the 1960s. This was mostly due to the colorful writing and lecturing of its originator, Marshall McLuhan, a professor of English and director of the Center for Culture and Technology at the University of Toronto. His books, *The Gutenberg Galaxy* (1962), *Understanding Media* (1964), and *The Medium Is the Massage* (1967), coupled with extensive lecture and television appearances, projected McLuhan as the prophet of a new age of electronics in which the medium, in his opinion, is more important than the message and conventional values less relevant than "depth involvement."

In his work, McLuhan carried forward explorations of various earlier observers. Among them was the late Harold Innis, whose *Empire and Communications* (1950) and *The Bias of Communication* (1951) analyzed the relationship of media to power structures, beginning with those of ancient times.

McLuhan declared that each new medium alters our psychic environment, imposing on us a particular pattern of perceiving and thinking that controls us to an extent we scarcely suspect. For example, the written language, mass produced by print, was the main cultural transmission belt for many generations. Knowledge and ideas were necessarily processed into the linear, one-step-at-a-time form required by the medium. People were thus pushed into sequential habits of thinking that are quite unlike the complexity and richness and all-at-onceness of face-to-face communication, and without the resonance of the human voice.

Today, however, the electronic media have restored the resonance (radio) and reintroduced the complexity and all-at-onceness (film, television), and have done it on a scale that gives the world potentially a tribal unity. McLuhan viewed modern men and women as in a state of shock, unable to adjust to the rapidly changing state of communication and clinging to linear habits in an all-at-once world. Given to puns and a measure of flippancy, McLuhan insisted not only that "the medium is the *message*" (that is, more important in itself than what is transmitted) but also that "the medium is the *massage*" (that is, it "roughs up and massages" our senses, altering the environment of the preelectronic world).

Two key terms in McLuhanese are "hot" and "cool." The cooler the medium, the more information must be supplied by the audience, and that is why wide-screen movies are "hot" and a fuzzy television picture is "cool." The more information the audience supplies, the more involved it becomes, and television has given its audience a sense of "depth involvement" more far-reaching than any previous medium, McLuhan believed. "When you go to the movies," he states, "you are the camera, but when you watch TV, you are the screen. The image is not projected from you, but charges at you. The movies were an extrovert orgy, but television is a depth experience."

Critics charge that his theories are confusing, illogical, mystical, and lacking in documentation. They deplore his "pop-art intellectualism," his puns, and his seeming call for a return to the jungle, for the abandonment of print-based civilization as we have known it. McLuhan retorted that he was merely an investigator and explorer of ideas, trying to persuade us to think about the changes in our environment caused by successive mass media, and that he saw no need to offer logical explanations.

By the 1980s, excitement generated by McLuhan's far-reaching theories had died down, but his ideas were still being reviewed in classrooms and in scholarly circles in many countries. McLuhan died in 1980.

USES AND GRATIFICATIONS RESEARCH

Psychologist Elihu Katz of Israel has led the argument that there should be less attention paid to what the media do to people and more attention on what people do with the media. The *uses and gratifications* concept is associated with Katz's writing and research. But Katz points out that studies of the gratifications that the media provide their audiences were well represented in the Lazarsfeld-Stanton collections of the 1940s and other early research.

Katz summarizes recent direct empirical investigations of audience uses and gratifications as "being concerned with the social and psychological origins of needs, which generate expectations of the mass media or other sources, which lead to differential patterns of media exposure, resulting in need gratifications and other consequences, perhaps mostly unintended ones."

Uses and gratifications research might have important, practical policy effects in daily mass media operations, Professor Everette Dennis points out in his book, *The Media Society.* Audience gratifications research could be used to change those media policies that do not help to satisfy media-related needs, wants, and expectations of the audience. Dennis points out that research in the area is somewhat fragmentary, and that it "flies in the face of the more humanistic popular culture critics of the media."

Study of communication as a consequence is more rewarding than study of communication as a cause, says Professor Alex S. Edelstein, an international communications scholar. Researchers should study the process of change in time and space, the consequences of that change in uses of communicated messages, and the effects of the change on the personal life of the subject. In research based upon the uses and gratifications concept, Edelstein studied audiences in both the United States and Yugoslavia and concluded that they evaluated sources of information not in terms of the sources' credibility but in terms of content, breadth of perception, and availability. Newspapers ranked ahead in content, television in breadth of perception, and radio in availability. The consumer determines which medium to use, the decision depending on which medium gratifies his or her needs.

THE POWERFUL MEDIA REVISITED

In a research paper published in 1973, German communication researcher Elisabeth Noelle-Neumann reviewed the state of mass communication effects research, found the "minimal effects" literature badly wanting, and called for a "return to the concept of a powerful media." Noelle-Neumann, insisting that "the decisive factors of mass media are not brought to bear in the traditional laboratory experiment designs," was joined in this attack on the minimal effects concept by sociologists DeFleur and Ball-Rokeach. By 1980, support was growing rapidly.

One assault was upon the selective perception theory, which limits the possibility of media effects. Noelle-Neumann said that "real life" is different from laboratory-controlled studies; the media are so ubiquitous that it is difficult for a person to escape a message; repetitive messages have reinforced impact; and, news stories are so much the same that there are few options for selective perception. Noelle-Neumann's long-term studies demonstrated that the effects of mass media increase in proportion to the degree to which selective perception is made difficult. The larger the marketplace for ideas is, the more attitudes can be influenced or molded by the mass media.

Noelle-Neumann's position as a world leader in communication research was solidified by her development during the 1970s of a theory of "The Spiral of Silence" and the 1983 publication of her book by that title. The theory of the spiral of silence states that one's perception of the distribution of public opinion motivates one's willingness to express political opinions. When people look to the media to determine the majority position on an issue, those who think they are in the majority are more willing to speak out, while those who perceive themselves to be in the minority have an extra incentive to stay silent. Groups of individuals, who perhaps may constitute a majority, lose confidence and withdraw from the public debate, thus speeding the demise of their position through the self-fulfilling prophecy of the spiral of silence. The media have played a role in determining the issue.

In another revisit of the powerful media concept, mass communication researcher John P. Robinson, in a study conducted under the auspices of the University of Michigan Survey Research Center, found that the media can affect voting

Voters mark their ballots in the privacy of individual cubicles. Researchers debate how much influence the media have in the decisions voters make. (Price, The Picture Cube)

behavior after all. Data from studies of the presidential elections of 1968 and 1972 showed that "a newspaper's perceived support of one candidate rather than another was associated with about a 6 percent edge in the vote for the endorsed candidate over his opponent." The study in 1972 revealed that independent voters who had been exposed to a newspaper endorsing Democratic candidate George McGovern were twice as likely to vote for McGovern as independent voters exposed to a newspaper supporting President Richard Nixon for reelection. Robinson pointed out that the numbers of voters affected were small, and the effects of newspaper endorsements peripheral. But in a closely contested election, a change in attitude and behavior by a small group of voters could be decisive.

The research studies made by Weaver, Asp, Becker, McCombs, and Jack McLeod all pointed toward the concept of a powerful media. Professors Becker and Sharon Dunwoody, in a 1982 study involving a local election, linked media use to knowledge and knowledge, in turn, to voter behavior. Professor James Lemert's 1981 book, *Does Mass Communication Affect Public Opinion After All?*, answered the query strongly in the affirmative. But social science researchers still looked for conclusive evidence.

As Everette Dennis summarizes, "One thing seems certain: the press is neither the all-powerful giant imagined by the propaganda researchers nor the peripheral influence seen by the political researchers." Instead, mass communications effects research has found exciting areas to explore and new assessments to make.

THE MEDIA'S IMPACT ON A REVOLUTION

Probably the most dramatic example of the power of the media to affect public opinion and produce an historic turn of events was the Philippines revolution of 1986.

President Ferdinand Marcos seemed firmly in power in Manila, supported by his good friend in the White House, even after reporters for the San Jose *Mercury News* of the Knight-Ridder group broke a documented story in July 1985 of the looting of billions of the Philippines' wealth by Marcos and his shoe-loving wife. But as agitation arose Marcos called an early election—and drew Corazon Aquino, widow of the martyred political leader, as his opponent.

This was high drama. The world's media, print and visual, reported the election, the theft of the ballots by the Marcos regime, and the dilemma of Cory Aquino as crowds shouted "Cory!" in the streets. Then two leading Marcos generals rebelled and set up a makeshift command camp.

Raw drama unfolded before the television cameras. "People power" opposed the Army. Hundreds of thousands of Filipinos formed human barriers about the rebel camp; nuns fingered their beads as they confronted tanks; thousands of families, children and all, joined in the face-down. Marcos faltered.

A wave of support for Cory Aquino swept across the United States as the drama flooded television screens. The wave swept through the Congress and into the White House. A reluctant Ronald Reagan bowed to public opinion, passed the word to Ferdinand Marcos to "cut and run," and recognized the new government of President Corazon Aquino.

Professors Peter Clarke and F. Gerald Kline, moving away from the narrow focus of the attitude-change literature, suggest that "what people learn from communication activity is a more rewarding topic for media effects research than attitude formation or change." Those carrying forward research in agenda-setting, uses and gratifications, media systems, and information-seeking join in this spreading of media research interests, which will provide a better picture of the place and influence of the mass media in the lives of all citizens.

PART TWO

The Print Media

Historic Press Freedoms

Press Freedom Must Be for All

The plaintiff was described by Fred Friendly in the book *Minnesota Rag* as an unprincipled bigot, extortionist, and rumor-monger whose sleazy newspaper shocked even the crime-ridden city of Minneapolis, also known in the 1920s as the "anti-Semitic capital of the world."

But the case, *Near* v. *Minnesota,* became bedrock doctrine for constitutional defenses involving prior restraint. Chief Justice Charles Evans Hughes, reading a five-to-four decision June 1, 1931, to a packed Supreme Court chamber, declared, "It is no longer open to doubt that the liberty of the press and of speech is within the liberty safeguarded by the due process clause of the 14th Amendment from invasion by state action."

Near v. *Minnesota* made press freedom history. Those involved in the story did not. In 1925 the Minnesota legislature passed a public nuisance bill aimed at the publisher of the free-swinging Duluth *Rip-saw,* John L. Morrison, who had attacked a Duluth legislator. The law allowed a newspaper to be put out of business if a single judge declared it to be "malicious, scandalous or defamatory." But Morrison died before the axe could fall on his scandal sheet.

Jay M. Near and Howard Guilford were running the *Saturday Press* in Minneapolis in unprincipled fashion, but they were also crusading against a corrupt mayor and police chief, thereby spoiling the game of bribery played by many citizens. Why not apply the new "gag law" to the *Saturday Press?*

Ironically, the complaint against Near was brought by county attorney Floyd Olson, soon to become Minnesota's most liberal governor. When a judge permanently banned the sheet from publication, nearly everyone applauded, including the city's leading newspapers. They and Olson failed to realize that the gag law could also be used to silence any publication. Chicago *Tribune* publisher Robert R. McCormick saw the danger and took Near's case to the U.S. Supreme Court. The rest is history.

*T*he basic freedoms of a democratic society are freedom of speech, freedom of the press, freedom of assembly, and freedom of petition. Upon these freedoms rest freedom of religious expression, of political choice, of intellectual growth, and of communication of information and ideas.

In this chapter, we trace the historical evolution of press freedom under the older authoritarian theory and our current libertarian theory. Three basic rights the communicator needs in order to assure the public its right to know are examined: the right to print, the right to criticize, and the right to report. These concepts remain constantly under attack in the United States and are denied in many parts of the world.

The controlled society of the Renaissance era functioned from the top down, on the assumption that a small and wise ruling class should determine what others should read, hear, and know. Thus the printing press operated under license in an authoritarian atmosphere. The Reformation brought about a democratic modern era and, by the nineteenth century, the dominance in the Western world of the libertarian theory. The press, freed of constraints of licensing and seditious libel, was not an instrument to speak for the governors, but rather a free marketplace of ideas and information to be utilized by the governed. ◆

SOCIETY'S CRUCIAL FREEDOMS

The history of journalism and of the development of the mass media begins with the story of the long struggle of people for personal liberty and political freedom, upon which the freedom to write and speak depends. Without that freedom, the magic of print and electronic technologies is of no value to free minds. One basic tenet of Anglo-American society has been freedom to print without prior restraint. How fragile such concepts are became apparent during the 1970s when, for the first time in the history of the American republic, the government succeeded in imposing a temporary prior restraint upon publication of a news story—once in the influential New York *Times* and again in the obscure *Progressive* magazine. Both stories were eventually published, but the future of press freedom was left undetermined, as it has always been in the historic duel between the people's press and the people's governors.

Five centuries ago, the printing press began to revolutionize people's ability to communicate information and ideas. But almost from the moment Johann Gutenberg introduced movable type to the Western world around 1440 in Germany, barriers were erected against its use to influence public opinion through the free flow of news and opinion. In the English-speaking world printers and writers struggled until 1700 to win the mere right to print. They fought for another century to protect that liberty and to win a second basic right: the right to criticize. Addition of a third right—the right to report—came equally slowly and with less success. Today's journalist knows that there remains a constant challenge to the freedoms to print, to criticize, and to report and that therefore the people's right to know is in constant danger. This is true in the democratic Western world, where freedom of the press is a recognized tenet, as well as in the larger portion of the world where it is denied. And it is true of the twentieth-century additions to the printing press: film, radio, television, cable and video.

Freedom of the press is intertwined with other basic freedoms. These are freedom of speech, freedom of assembly, and freedom of petition. Upon these freedoms rest freedom of religious expression, freedom of political thought and action, and freedom of intellectual growth and communication of information and ideas. A society possessing and using these freedoms will advance and change as it exercises democratic processes. Very naturally, then, these freedoms will come under attack from those opposed to any change that might diminish their own power or position in society—today as in past eras. The press, occupying a key role in the battle for these basic freedoms, is a particular target. To the closed mind, the press has been a dangerous weapon to be kept as far as possible under the control of adherents of the status quo; to the inquiring mind, it has been a means of arousing interest and emotion among the public in order to effect change.

Two Press Theories. The social and political environments of the past five centuries have produced two basic theories of the press. The older we call the *authoritarian theory*. The controlled society of the Renaissance era, into which the printing press was introduced, functioned from the top down; a small and presumably wise ruling class decided what all of society should know and believe. This authoritarian concept of the relationship between citizens and the state could brook no challenge from those who thought the rulers were reflecting error, not truth. Publishing therefore existed under a license from those in power given only to selected printers who supported the rulers and the existing social and political structure. The authoritarian press theory still exists today in those large parts of the world where similar controlled societies are dominated by small ruling classes. A variant of this theory, called the *Soviet Communist theory* of the press by the authors of *Four Theories of the Press* (Fred S. Siebert, Theodore Peterson, and Wilbur Schramm), arose with the twentieth-century dictatorship. Whether fascist or communist, its government-owned and party-directed press is dedicated to furthering the dictatorship and its social system.

As the Western world advanced through the Renaissance and Reformation into the democratic modern era, the second basic theory of the press developed. This we call the *libertarian theory*. Its roots extend back into the seventeenth century, but it did not become dominant in the English-speaking world until the nineteenth century. In libertarian theory the press is not an instrument of government, nor does it speak for an elite ruling class. The mass of people are presumed able to discern between truth and falsehood themselves and, having been exposed to a press operating as a free marketplace of ideas and information, will themselves help determine public policy. It is essential that minorities as well as majorities, the politically weak as well as the politically strong, have free access to public expression in the press of a libertarian society.

In the battle against authoritarianism, the printer gradually became an ally of thinkers and writers who struggled for religious, political, and intellectual freedom and of the rising commercially based middle class that demanded economic freedom and political power in its contest with feudalism. Slowly the journalist developed dual functions: the opinion function and the news function. The journalist's media were the printed broadside and the pamphlet before the development of regularly issued newspapers in an established format. Such newspapers appeared on the European continent after 1609, in England after 1622, and in the American colonies after 1704. In the eighteenth century they were joined by the early magazines. By our standards early newspapers were poorly printed, haphazard in content, and limited in circulation. But their influence can be measured by the amount of effort expended by those in authority to erect barriers against them and the stimuli to thought and action they contained. The traditions of freedom their printers and editors won by breaking down the barriers in the seventeenth and eighteenth centuries are the heritage of the modern newspapers and magazines developed in the nineteenth and twentieth centuries and of the film and electronic media of our times.

It was John Milton in his *Areopagitica* of 1644 who argued against repression of freedom of expression by advocating reliance upon truth: "Let her and Falsehood grapple: who ever knew Truth put to the worse in a free and open encounter?" Those who are afraid of truth will of course seek to prevent its entrance into a free marketplace of thought, but those who believe in the public liberty should realize that its existence depends upon liberty of the press. Thomas Jefferson put it well in a letter to his friend, Carrington, in 1787:

> I am persuaded that the good sense of the people will always be found to be the best army. They may be led astray for a moment, but will soon correct themselves. The people are the only censors of their governors; and even their errors will tend to keep these to the true principles of their institution. To punish these errors too severely would be to suppress the only safeguard of the public liberty. The way to prevent these irregular interpositions of the people, is to give them full information of their affairs through the channel of the public papers, and to contrive that those papers should penetrate the whole mass of the people. The basis of our government being the opinion of the people, the very first object should be to keep that right; and were it left to me to decide whether we should have a government without newspapers, or newspapers without a government, I should not hesitate a moment to prefer the latter.

Jefferson qualified his final statement, however, by adding: "But I should mean that every man should receive those papers, and be capable of reading them." Jefferson used the word "reading" because the problem of literacy still was a major one in his day; he also meant "understanding" in the sense of intellectual literacy. In these words of Milton and Jefferson are found the libertarian arguments for freedom of printing and other forms of communication, for freedom to criticize, and for freedom to report. They also argue for public support of the kind of mass media that carry out their responsibilities to provide the free flow of news and opinion and to speak for the people as "censors of their governors." The ability of journalists to discharge their responsibilities to society is conditioned, as Jefferson warned, by the level of public education and understanding; there is a public responsibility implied in this philosophic statement of the role of press liberty in supporting all of society's crucial freedoms.

There is also a public responsibility, and a journalistic one, to maintain the libertarian theory that everyone can be freely heard in the press, through a variant concept called the *social responsibility theory* of the press. Today it is no longer economically feasible for one to start printing or airing one's views. Concentration of much of the mass media in the hands of a relatively few owners imposes an obligation on them to be socially responsible, to see that all sides of social and political issues are fairly and fully presented so that the public may decide. The social responsibility theory contends that should the mass media fail in this respect, it may be necessary for some other agency of the public to enforce the marketplace of ideas concept.

THE RIGHT TO PRINT

PRIOR RESTRAINT IN ENGLAND. William Caxton set up the first press in England in 1476. It was more than two centuries later, in 1694, before the freedom to print without *prior restraint* became a recognized liberty of the English people and their printer-journalists.

Prior restraint means licensing or censorship before a printer has a chance to roll the press. Unauthorized printing in itself becomes a crime. Under our modern concept anyone is free to have his or her say, although subject to punishment if what is printed offends society (obscenity, sedition) or harms another individual (libel). Authoritarian government does not care to grant this much freedom; it wishes to control communication from the start and to select the communicators.

Caxton printed the first books in the English language and otherwise aided in

The shop of William Caxton, who set up the first printing press in England in 1476. Caxton learned printing on the Continent, where it had been a craft since the middle of the fifteenth century. The press was established "at the Sign of the Red Pale" in the abbey at Westminster. Nearly two centuries elapsed, however, before England had a genuine newspaper. (Culver Pictures)

bringing the culture of the Continent to England. He enjoyed royal support and needed subsidizing by the ruling class since his market was limited by illiteracy. He and his successors improved the quality and volume of printing during the next half-century, which saw the rise of the Tudor dynasty. Henry VIII, in his efforts to grasp absolute power, issued a proclamation in 1534 requiring printers to have royal permission before setting up their shops. This was a licensing measure, imposing prior restraint. Except for short periods, the theory of prior restraint remained in effect in England until 1694.

Henry VIII took other measures to control the press, including banning foreign books, issuing lists of forbidden books, and punishing ballad printers who offended Henry and his powerful Privy Council. But neither he nor Queen Elizabeth I was able to frighten all the printers and writers into compliance. After 1557 the Stationers Company, an organization of the licensed publishers and dealers, was given power to regulate printing and to search out bootleg jobs that had not been registered with it. Severe penalties for unauthorized printing were imposed in 1566 and 1586, in the latter year by the authority of the infamous Court of the Star Chamber. But despite arrests and smashing of presses of unlucky printers, some defiance always remained.

The struggle between the rising commercial class and the crown, which broke into revolution in 1640 and brought the establishment of the Commonwealth in 1649 by Oliver Cromwell, gave printers some temporary freedom. James I and succeeding Stuart kings found that Puritan opposition was increasingly difficult to contain, and the journalists were more alert to their opportunities. Public interest in the Thirty Years' War in Europe and in other political and economic affairs inevitably brought increased publication. Nathaniel Butter, Thomas Archer, and Nicholas Bourne produced the first regularly issued news book in 1621, on a weekly basis. Containing translated news from European news sheets, it was called a coranto. Diurnals, or reports of domestic events, appeared first as handwritten newsletters and later, after the Long Parliament raised the crown's ban on printing in 1641, in print.

But freedom was short-lived. By 1644 Milton was protesting against new licensing laws. After the execution of Charles I in 1649, Cromwell and his Puritan regime permitted only a few administration publications, censored by none other than Milton. The return of the Stuarts under Charles II in 1660 merely brought a switch in the licenser and censor to the royal party and more strict repression of unauthorized printing. Noteworthy, however, was the founding of the court newspaper, the London *Gazette,* in 1665. It remains today the oldest English newspaper.

The decline of the Stuarts, preceding the Revolution of 1688 that brought William and Mary to the throne, restored freedom to printers. Parliament allowed the licensing act to lapse in 1679. It was revived temporarily but finally died in 1694. Though severe seditious libel laws remained, and taxes on print paper and advertising were to be instituted beginning in 1712, the theory of prior restraint was dead. Newspapers by the score appeared in London, among them the first daily, the *Daily Courant,* in 1702. The early eighteenth century saw a flowering of newspapers and popular "essay" papers, edited by such literary figures as Daniel Defoe, Richard Steele and Joseph Addison, and Samuel Johnson.

Licensing and the theory of prior restraint did not die immediately in the American colonies. The Puritans imported the first press to New England in 1638 to print materials for their schools and Harvard College. Commercial presses followed, and some news broadsides and pamphlets appeared. In 1690 a refugee editor from London, Benjamin Harris, issued the first number of a Boston newspaper, *Publick Occurrences,* but his frank reporting nettled the colonial governor and council, which promptly ruled him out for not having a license. When the postmaster, John Campbell, brought out the first regular weekly paper, the Boston *News-Letter,* in 1704, he voluntarily trotted to the authorities for advance censorship and put "Published by Authority" at the top of his columns. It was not until 1721, when James Franklin began publishing his famed *New-England Courant,* that a colonial editor printed in defiance of authority.

RESTRAINTS IN THE UNITED STATES. Freedom to print became an accepted principle in America; nine colonies had already provided such constitutional protection by 1787, when the Constitutional Convention met in Philadelphia. Many felt it was solely a state matter, but when the Bill of Rights was added to the Constitution, the First Amendment included freedom of the press among the basic liberties that Congress could not violate. Under British common law and American judicial interpretation, prior restraint violates press freedom. Suppression of publications in anticipation of wrongful printing, or licensing measures to control those who would publish, cannot be authorized by Congress. In two landmark cases, *Gitlow* v. *People of the State of New York* (1925) and *Near* v. *Minnesota* (1931), the Supreme Court applied the press guarantees of the First Amendment to the states, through the due process clause of the Fourteenth Amendment. The written decision in *Near* v. *Minnesota* became bedrock doctrine for all future cases involving prior restraint. In Chapter 23, this discussion and others involving media law will be continued.

The Post Office, with its power to exclude publications from the mails under certain conditions, has given publishers many censorship troubles. Matters came to a head in 1946 after it sought to withdraw use of the second-class mailing rate from *Esquire* magazine on the grounds that the rate was a privilege intended only for those making a "special contribution to the public welfare." *Esquire,* faced with an additional half-million dollars a year in postal bills, appealed to the Supreme Court, which ruled in its favor. The court commented: "But to withdraw the second-class rate from this publication today because its content seemed to one official not good for the public would sanction withdrawal of the second-class rate tomorrow from another periodical whose social or economic views seemed harmful to another official." The decision put the Post Office back to judging specific issues on the basis of obscenity or illegal news of lotteries.

The motion picture industry instituted its own regulatory code in 1922, as a form of self-censorship, through the Motion Picture Association of America. Even before that date, state and city censorship boards were exercising precensorship functions by viewing and ordering the clipping of films in advance of movie showings, or banning them, a practice that still continues despite court challenges. Extralegal pressures have been brought by such unofficial groups as the former

James Franklin's weekly defied authority but it also entertained in the style of England's essay papers. Here half-brother Benjamin offers readers his famed essay on drunkenness, using the pseudonym "Silence Dogood."

THE
New-England Courant.

[Nº 58]

From MONDAY September 3. to MONDAY September 10. 1722.

Quod est in corde sobrii, est in ore ebrii.

To the Author of the New-England Courant.

SIR,   [No XII.

IT is no unprofitable tho' unpleasant Pursuit, diligently to inspect and consider the Manners & Conversation of Men, who, insensible of the greatest Enjoyments of humane Life, abandon themselves to Vice from a false Notion of *Pleasure* and *good Fellowship.* A true and natural Representation of any Enormity, is often the best Argument against it and Means of removing it, when the most severe Reprehensions alone, are found ineffectual.

I WOULD in this Letter improve the little Observation I have made on the Vice of *Drunkeness*, the better to reclaim the *good Fellows* who usually pay the Devotions of the Evening to *Bacchus.*

I DOUBT not but *moderate Drinking* has been improv'd for the Diffusion of Knowledge among the ingenious Part of Mankind, who want the Talent of a ready Utterance, in order to discover the Conceptions of their Minds in an entertaining and intelligible Manner. 'Tis true, drinking does not *improve* our Faculties, but it enables us to *use* them ; and therefore I conclude, that much Study and Experience, and a little Liquor, are of absolute Necessity for some Tempers, in order to make them accomplish'd Orators. *Dic. Ponder* discovers an excellent Judgment when he is inspir'd with a Glass or two of *Claret*, but he passes for a Fool among those of small Observation, who never saw him the better for Drink. And here it will not be improper to observe, That the moderate Use of Liquor, and a well plac'd and well regulated Anger, often produce this same Effect ; and some who cannot ordinarily talk but in broken Sentences and false Grammar, do in the Heat of Passion express themselves with as much Eloquence as Warmth. Hence it is that my own Sex are generally the most eloquent, because the most passionate. " It has been said in the Praise of some Men,
" (says an ingenious Author,) that they could talk
" whole Hours together upon any thing ; but it
" must be owned to the Honour of the other Sex,
" that there are many among them who can talk
" whole Hours together upon Nothing. I have
" known a Woman branch out into a long extempo-
" re Dissertation on the Edging of a Petticoat, and
" chide her Servant for breaking a China Cup, in all
" the Figures of Rhetorick."

BUT after all it must be consider'd, that no Pleasure can give Satisfaction or prove advantageous to a reasonable Mind, which is not attended with the *Restraints of Reason.* Enjoyment is not to be found by Excess in any sensual Gratification ; but on the contrary, the immoderate Cravings of the Voluptuary, are always succeeded with Loathing and a pal-led Appetite. What Pleasure can the Drunkard have in the Reflection, that, while in his Cups, he retain'd only the Shape of a Man, and acted the Part of a Beast ; or that from reasonable Discourse a few Minutes before, he descended to Impertinence and Nonsense ?

I CANNOT pretend to account for the different Effects of Liquor on Persons of different Dispositions, who are guilty of Excess in the Use of it. 'Tis strange to see Men of a regular Conversation become rakish and profane when intoxicated with Drink, and yet more surprizing to observe, that some who appear to be the most profligate Wretches when sober, become mighty religious in their Cups, and will then, and at no other Time addres their Maker, but when they are destitute of Reason, and actually affronting him. Some shrink in the Wetting, and others swell to such an unusual Bulk in their Imaginations, that they can in an Instant understand all Arts and Sciences, by the liberal Education of a little vivifying *Punch*, or a sufficient Quantity of other exhilerating Liquor.

AND as the Effects of Liquor are various, so are the Characters given to its Devourers. It argues some Shame in the Drunkards themselves, in that they have invented numberless Words and Phrases to cover their Folly, whose proper Sgnifications are harmless, or have no Signification at all. They are seldom known to be *drunk*, tho they are very often *boozey, cogey, tipsey, fox'd, merry, mellow, fuddl'd, groatable,* Confoundedly *cut, See two Moons,* are *Among the Philistines, In a very good Humour, See the Sun,* or, *The Sun has shone upon them* ; they *Clip the King's English,* are *Almost froze, Feavourish, In their Altitudes, Pretty well enter'd,* &c. In short, every Day produces some new Word or Phrase which might be added to the Vocabulary of the *Tiplers* : But I have chose to mention these few, because if at any Time a Man of Sobriety and Temperance happens to *cut himself confoundedly*, or is *almost froze*, or *feavourish*, or accidentally *sees the Sun*, &c. he may escape the Imputation of being *drunk*, when his Misfortune comes to be related.

I am SIR,
Your Humble Servant,

SILENCE DOGOOD.

FOREIGN AFFAIRS.

Berlin, May 8. Twelve Prussian Batallions are sent to Mecklenburg, but for what Reason is not known. 'Tis said, the Emperor, suspecting the Designs of the Czar, will secure all the Domains of the Duke of Mecklenburg. His Prussian Majesty, to promote the intended Union of the Reformed and Lutherans in his Dominions, has charged the Ministers of those two Communions, not to make the least mention in the Pulpits of the religious Differences about some abstruser Points, particularly the Doctrine of Predestination, and to forbear all contumelious Expressions against one another.

Hamburg, May 8. The Imperial Court has order'd the Circles of Lower Saxony, to keep in Rea-

Legion of Decency. The same informal pressures have affected book publication and book purchases by public libraries and school systems. In addition, book publishers run the risk of having specific volumes barred from the mails as obscene.

Radio and television, like the printed media, are not subject to precensorship. But charges of censorship are often raised against media self-censorship or control of content in anticipation of adverse reaction. The broadcast media are more sensitive on this score because their managers realize that violations of what is considered to be "good taste" might cause difficulties for an individual station with the Federal Communications Commission under broadcasting licensing provisions.

If history has proved licensing to be a dangerous practice inimical to press freedom, why did the American public agree to licensing of radio and television stations? The answer is that by common consent we have recognized that broadcast channels are in the public domain. Congress in 1912 first legislated that the Department of Commerce should issue licenses to private broadcasters and assign them wavelengths so that they would not interfere with government wavelengths. During World War I, all wireless operations were put under government control, but by 1919 private broadcasters were again experimenting. The numbers of stations increased rapidly and chaos developed on the airwaves. The radio industry, the National Association of Broadcasters, the American Newspaper Publishers Association, and other groups petitioned the government for relief.

This came from Congress through the Radio Act of 1927, which established a five-member commission to regulate all forms of radio communication. The government retained control of all channels, granting three-year licenses to broadcasters "in the public interest, convenience, or necessity" to provide "fair, efficient, and equitable service" throughout the country. Federal authority was broadened in 1934 with the establishment of the seven-member Federal Communications Commission to exercise jurisdiction over all telecommunications. The responsibility of the license holder to operate a station in the public interest was more clearly spelled out. The commission was given the power to refuse renewal of a license in cases of flagrant disregard of broadcasting responsibility, but the FCC rarely used this power. The law forbade any attempt at censorship by the commission; no station could be directed to put a particular program on or off the air. But the FCC undeniably was able to exercise indirect pressure upon license holders, understandably wary of its ultimate powers. FCC insistence upon stations' building some record for broadcasting in the public interest led to attention to news and public affairs programs; on the other hand, the licensing problem led to broadcasters' dragging their feet in airing controversial issues.

American radio and television are as free as American newspapers and magazines to provide whatever news their news editors see fit. Radio and television have also widely broadcast the opinion programs of individual commentators. But they were long reluctant to broadcast opinion as that of the station itself. The FCC in 1941 issued a ruling that "the broadcaster cannot be advocate"; then in 1949 the commission decided that stations could "editorialize with fairness" and urged them to do so. Many broadcasters felt they did not have the trained staffs to do effective editorializing or did not wish to identify the station management as an advocate in controversial situations, but three decades later more than half the stations were broadcasting editorial opinions.

THE RIGHT TO CRITICIZE

SEDITIOUS LIBEL. Winning the liberty to print without prior restraint did not free the press from the heavy hand of government. In eighteenth-century England, and in the American colonies, the laws of seditious libel ran counter to the philosophical theory that the press should act as "censor of the government." To the authoritarian mind, the mere act of criticism of officials was in itself a crime, and "the greater the truth, the greater the libel" was an established tenet. This meant that publishing a story about a corrupt official was all the more seditious if the official indeed was corrupt.

The journalist's problem was to win acceptance of truth as a defense against charges of sedition or criminal libel. Mere fact of publication, then, would not be sufficient to determine guilt, and the accused printer or editor would be able to present the case in open court, preferably before a jury. Once the principle of truth as a defense could be won, governments would be less likely to press sedition charges, and laws defining what constitutes sedition could be revised.

THE ZENGER CASE. The landmark case in what is now the United States was that of John Peter Zenger, who was tried in New York colony in 1735 for seditious libel. Zenger was an immigrant printer who lent the columns of his weekly paper, the *Journal,* to the cause of a political faction opposed to the royal governor. Some of the leading citizens of the colony were aligned with Zenger in the struggle against the governor, whom they accused of various arbitrary actions in the *Journal's* columns. Zenger was jailed and brought to trial in a hostile court. At this juncture a remarkable 80-year-old lawyer from Philadelphia, Andrew Hamilton, entered the case as Zenger's attorney.

The crown prosecutor reviewed the laws of seditious libel and argued that since Zenger had admitted publishing the newspaper issues in question, the trial was as good as over. His aged opponent skillfully jousted with the presiding justice and the prosecutor and insisted that truth should be permitted to be offered as a defense, with the jury to decide upon the truth of Zenger's publications. These arguments were denied by the court, but Hamilton ignored the ruling and delivered a stirring oration to the jury. He ended with a plea for the jury to take matters into its own hands: "The question before the court . . . is not just the cause of the poor printer. . . . No! It may in its consequence affect every freeman . . . on the main of America. It is the best cause; it is the cause of Liberty . . . the liberty both of exposing and opposing arbitrary power . . . by speaking and writing Truth."

Zenger was acquitted, and the court did not challenge the jury's verdict, even though it ignored existing law. A similar court victory on the issue of admission of truth as evidence was not won in England itself until the 1770s. The threat of trials for seditious libel remained until the end of the century, although in the colonies no further court trials of editors were held. Some editors were harassed by governors and their privy councils, but in general the colonial press was free to criticize the English authorities and to promote the cause of American independence (the reverse was not true, however, and Tory editors were suppressed by colonial radicals). In the early 1770s such papers as the Boston *Gazette* were openly seditious in their attacks upon constituted authority, but they continued to appear and to fan the fires of revolution.

JEFFERSON AND HAMILTON. Once the revolution was won, there was sharp cleavage along political and economic lines in the new nation. The newspapers continued to take pronounced partisan stands. The two political factions, the Federalists headed by Alexander Hamilton and the Republicans headed by Thomas Jefferson, split on many domestic issues and particularly over the country's emotional reaction to the violence of the French Revolution. Most of the weeklies and the few dailies that had started after 1783 were published in seaboard towns for the commercial classes and tended to be Federalist in sympathy. Hamilton sponsored some party organs in addition: John Fenno's *Gazette of the United States,* Noah Webster's *American Minerva,* and William Coleman's New York *Evening Post.* Topping the Federalist editors in partisan criticism was William Cobbett with his *Porcupine's Gazette.*

Jefferson countered with Philip Freneau's *National Gazette* and also had other Republican supporters, including William Duane and Benjamin Franklin Bache at the *Aurora.* The impulsive Bache, grandson of Benjamin Franklin, more than matched Cobbett in vituperative criticism. When it appeared that war with France was imminent in 1798, the Federalists decided to crack down on their tormentors.

The Alien and Sedition Acts they passed in 1798 were aimed at deportation of undesirable aliens and at curbing criticism of the government. Undesirable aliens in Federalist eyes were those who supported Vice-President Jefferson; some were deported and others were harassed. The Sedition Act by its terms restricted prosecutions to those who "write, utter, or publish . . . false, scandalous and malicious writing" against the federal government, its officials and legislators, or its laws (including the Sedition Act itself). It provided for admission of truth as a defense. In theory, only false criticism was to be punished; but in practice, Federalist politicians and judges set out to punish anti-Federalist editors. One, for example, was jailed and fined for printing a letter to the editor that accused President John Adams of "ridiculous pomp, foolish adulation, and selfish avarice."

Vice-President Jefferson, fearful for his own safety, retired to Monticello, where he and his supporters drafted the Virginia and Kentucky Resolutions, advocating the theory of nullification by the states of unconstitutional acts of the Congress. But the issue did not need to be joined; federal excesses in administering the Alien and Sedition Acts contributed to a popular revulsion and to Jefferson's election as president in 1800. The dangerous Alien and Sedition Acts expired the same year. Jefferson insisted that his administration permit partisan journalism "to demonstrate the falsehood of the pretext that freedom of the press is incompatible with orderly government." He urged that individuals protect themselves against journalistic excesses by filing civil suits for libel. The calm course Jefferson took was vindicated when his party retained control of the government for a generation. Party newspapers, with one-sided news and fiercely partisan opinion, continued to flourish, but after the great crisis of 1798 no federal administration attempted to repress criticism. Soon after 1800 the libertarian theory of the press had eclipsed the authoritarian theory by common consent.

WARTIME RESTRICTIONS. During wartime, national safety requirements and emotional feelings bring some restriction of criticism. The Civil War saw suppression of a few newspapers in the North, but considering the violence of many editors' criticisms, retaliation by Lincoln and his generals was almost negligible. During World War I, the Espionage Act of 1917 widened the authority of the Post Office to bar periodicals from the mails, and the Sedition Act of 1918 made it a crime to write or publish "any disloyal, profane, scurrilous or abusive language" about the federal government. The axe fell heavily upon German-language newspapers, in many cases unfairly. It also fell upon socialist magazines and newspapers, because they opposed the war, and upon pacifist publications. Max Eastman's brilliant magazine, *The Masses,* was barred from the mails, as were two leading socialist dailies, the New York *Call* and the Milwaukee *Leader.* Socialist party leader Eugene Debs went to prison for criticizing America's allies as "out for plunder." Clearly the theory of liberty to criticize was disregarded in these violations of minority opinion rights. During World War II, only a few pro-Nazi and Fascist publications were banned—and they had few friends to plead their cause. But the black press was harassed by J. Edgar Hoover's FBI for complaining about racial discrimination in the armed forces.

Out of prosecutions for political expression arose what became known as the "clear-and-present-danger" theory to determine protection of freedom of speech and press. It was advanced by Justices Oliver Wendell Holmes and Louis Brandeis in four landmark case decisions rendered between 1919 and 1927. In *Schenck* v. *U.S.,* the court upheld the conviction of Socialist party members who distributed antiwar leaflets urging repeal of the draft law. Holmes wrote: "The question in every case is whether the words used, are used in such circumstances and are of such a nature as to create a clear and present danger that they will bring about the substantive evils that Congress has a right to prevent. It is a question of proximity and degree."

In *Abrams* v. *U.S.,* the court's conservative majority applied this clear-and-present-danger rule to uphold the conviction of five New York radicals whose pamphlets condemned American troop intervention in Russia's revolution and urged a general strike. Holmes and Brandeis dissented, Holmes using the phrase "immediately dangerous" in an effort to prevent such use of his theory as a two-edged sword. In the cases of Benjamin Gitlow, convicted of criminal anarchy under New York law for issuing socialist manifestos, and of Anita Whitney, convicted under a California law outlawing the Communist party, the two liberal justices forcefully restated the clear-and-present-danger theory. Its negative use to curtail free speech and expression prevailed again during the anticommunist tensions of the McCarthy era in the 1951 case of Eugene Dennis, convicted under the Smith Act banning the Communist party. But in many other cases, it fended off conspiracy and criminal sedition charges involving free speech and press for minority political beliefs.

POLITICAL AND LEGAL RESTRICTIONS. The right to criticize needs constant protection, as was demonstrated when Louisiana political boss Huey Long attempted to punish newspaper opponents through taxation. Long and his political machine imposed a special tax on the advertising income of larger Louisiana dailies, virtually all of which were opposed to him. The Supreme Court held the punitive tax unconstitutional in 1936. In the early 1950s courageous newspapers and magazines that spoke out against Senator Joseph McCarthy of Wisconsin and the movement known as McCarthyism were harassed and denounced. But neither McCarthy nor his followers could bring about actual legislation restricting criticism, much as they might have liked to do so.

Contempt-of-court citations bring about another kind of clash over the right to criticize. A series of Supreme Court decisions in the 1940s widened the freedom of newspapers to comment upon pending court cases and actions of judges. This was done by applying the clear-and-present-danger theory to a judge's contention that administration of justice was being impeded by newspaper comment. But judges have great power in contempt-of-court matters, and editors remain wary of criticizing their acts without urgent need to do so.

THE RIGHT TO REPORT

DEVELOPING A PHILOSOPHICAL CONCEPT. The right to report is not nearly as much a right safeguarded by law and legal precedent as the right to print and the right to criticize. Rather, it is based on a philosophical argument. What would be gained through the right to print and to criticize if no news were forthcoming? What good would a free press be for the reader if editors and reporters had no way to find out what government was doing? Denial of the right of access to news is a denial of the people's right to know, the journalist maintains.

Yet, no person can be compelled to talk to a reporter; no government official need grant an interview or hold a press conference; courts and legislatures admit the press through historical tradition and have the power to eject the press (unless specific statutes have been passed requiring open legislative sessions). There is another side to the coin: No newspaper can be compelled to print any material it does not wish to use, including paid advertising.

When the laws of seditious libel were in vogue, no right to report was recognized. The mere reporting of a government official's action, or of a debate in Parliament, was likely to be construed as seditious (unfavorable) by some person in authority. William Bradford in Pennsylvania, James Franklin in Massachusetts, and other colonial editors were hauled before authorities for reporting a disputed action of government. In England reporting of the proceedings of Parliament was banned until 1771, when the satirical writings of Dr. Samuel Johnson and the open defiance of newspaper publisher John Wilkes crumpled the opposition.

The House of Representatives of the American Congress opened its doors to reporters in 1789, two days after it was organized as a legislative body. The Senate, however, excluded reporters until 1795. Congress came to depend upon journalists, particularly the editors of the Jeffersonian party organ, the *National Intelligencer,* to publish a record of debates and proceedings. Not until 1834 did the government publish its own records.

TODAY'S RESTRICTIONS. Today there is little likelihood that Washington correspondents will be denied access to the congressional press galleries, except when the legislators are meeting in emergency executive session (a rare event). But reporters are admitted to sessions of legislative committees only with the consent of the committee chairperson and members. Some 40 percent of congressional committee sessions are closed to the press. The situation in state capitals is similar. Television and radio reporters and photographers have won access to legislative sessions only by persistent effort, and their ability to use all their equipment is often circumscribed.

Reporters similarly are admitted to court sessions only by the agreement of the presiding judge. They may be excluded, with other members of the public, if the court deems it necessary. Juvenile courts, for example, operate without reportorial coverage in most cases. Ordinarily reporters are free to attend court sessions, since public trials are the rule, but they have no automatic right of attendance. Photographers and television-radio reporters have had only limited success in covering trials with cameras or microphones, due to restrictions applied to them by Section 35 of the Canons of Judicial Ethics of the American Bar Association (ABA). A long campaign by the National Press Photographers Association, the Radio Television News Directors Association, and the American Society of Newspaper Editors to persuade the bar association to revise its Canon 35 failed when that group reaffirmed its stand in 1963. In 1972 the association replaced Canon

35 with Canon 3A7, equally as restrictive, and the impasse continued until 1982, when the ABA relented (see Chapter 23).

An important doctrine that has emerged is that of qualified privilege. This doctrine protects a news medium from the threat of libel suits when reporting the actions of a legislative body or a court, provided its report is accurate and fair. This doctrine carries with it the implication that the media have an obligation to report legislative and judicial sessions so that the public may know what government and courts are doing. Defamatory statements affecting the reputations of individuals made in legislative sessions and courts may therefore be reported without fear of damage suits.

The right to report is denied more often at the grass roots level of government than at the national level, insofar as legislative bodies are concerned. Boards of education, water commissions, city councils, county boards, and other similar groups often seek to meet in private and conduct the public's business in virtual secrecy. Newspeople wage an unending battle against this practice, without much avail, unless the public demands to know. Some editors and publishers accept the practice and forfeit their right to report the news firsthand, thereby forfeiting their most important right as journalists. Passage of "open meetings" laws in an increasing number of states during the 1950s, at the insistence of various news groups, somewhat improved the access to news at the local level. These laws provide that actions taken in closed sessions are invalid; but they do not force a reluctant legislative group to open the doors wide. By 1975 virtually all states had some form of open meeting law as well as laws guaranteeing the opening of public records to reporters needing access to them.

Perhaps the most publicized denial of access to news has been in the national executive departments. This increasing trend—stemming from the necessity for secrecy in limited areas of the national defense establishment and atomic energy research—has alarmed responsible journalists. The American Society of Newspaper Editors and the Society of Professional Journalists, Sigma Delta Chi, have well-organized campaigns demanding free access to news so that people may know the facts necessary to make intelligent decisions.

Appointment in 1955 of a House subcommittee headed by Representative John Moss of California to study the information policies of the government brought some relief. The Moss committee acted as the champion of the people's right to know and the reporter's right of access to news. By publicizing executive department refusals to make information available on public matters, the Moss committee forced some reforms, including passage of the Freedom of Information Act of 1966, giving the citizen legal recourse against arbitrary withholding of information by a federal agency. The law was strengthened in 1974 (see Chapter 23), but some presidents and government agencies still used every tactic to prevent disclosure of information they thought the public should not know. Even so, reporters determined to find out the facts can usually obtain them despite the opposition of such reluctant public officials.

Growth of Newspapers

Birth of a Great Newspaper

James Gordon Bennett was 40 years old, disillusioned, and deeply in debt when he founded the New York *Herald* in May 1835. His capital was only $500; he also had some credit from his printers. His office was in the cellar of a building at 20 Wall Street. His desk was a plank spanning two drygoods boxes, augmented by a second-hand chair and a file box.

This was quite likely his final bid for fame and fortune. Born in Scotland, he had studied economics at Aberdeen. He emigrated to Nova Scotia in 1819, taught school there and in Maine before drifting on down the coast doing proofreading and editing in Boston, New York, and Charleston. Finding the going difficult, he reverted to teaching and lecturing on economics—also hard going.

But by now Bennett had the newspaper bug. In 1825 he started the *Sunday New York Courier,* in imitation of Sunday-only English papers, but the keeping of the Sabbath was still a puritanical must. Hired as a Washington correspondent in 1827 by New York publisher James Watson Webb, he became an associate editor in 1829 and engineered the merger of the *Courier* and the *Enquirer* into a leading daily. But it was not his paper, and when it opposed President Andrew Jackson, he quit.

In 1832 Bennett supported Jackson for reelection, founding the New York *Globe* and declaring, "I am now in the field, sword in hand, with unfurled banner, resolved to aid the great cause of Jackson and Democracy." New York yawned, and the *Globe* folded within a month. Bennett founded the Philadelphia *Courier;* it too failed. In 1834 he looked up a printer–editor named Horace Greeley and tried to form a partnership with him. Greeley said no.

Suddenly Bennett won. With his *Herald,* he was the first to emphasize the principles of news enterprise—complete, accurate, skillful, and rapid reporting of important events—to create a great newspaper.

$\mathcal{F}$ewer than 300 years have gone by since the first weekly newspaper appeared in colonial Boston. The struggling weeklies of those colonial outposts of Europe that became the United States were instrumental in reporting news of commerce and politics, in developing a sense of community, and in fanning the fires of patriotism and revolution.

James and Benjamin Franklin led in making the colonial newspaper a readable product. Promoting the Revolution were propagandist Sam Adams and patriot editor Isaiah Thomas. With independence won, a political party press appeared, representing the divergent views of Alexander Hamilton and Thomas Jefferson.

The 1830s and 1840s saw the rise of the "penny press," low priced, popular in content, and tuned to ordinary readers. James Gordon Bennett and his New York *Herald* developed news enterprise; Horace Greeley and his New York *Tribune* first-rate opinion.

Joseph Pulitzer became the symbol of what was called the "new journalism" beginning in the 1880s and 1890s. His New York *World* gave aggressive editorial support to workers and immigrants with news coverage and crusades; it was also low priced, easily read, and popularized in content and appearance. With William Randolph Hearst, Edward Wyllis Scripps, and Adolph Ochs, he led the way into twentieth-century journalism. ◆

THE BASIC EDITORIAL FUNCTIONS

Newspapers, despite their impact on society, have a relatively brief historical tradition. Two hundred eighty-five years ago, there was but one struggling weekly in the colonial outpost of Europe that was to become the United States. It was only 150 years ago, in the 1830s and 1840s, that the "penny press" dailies ushered in America's first era of popular journalism, made famous by James Gordon Bennett and his New York *Herald,* Horace Greeley and his New York *Tribune,* and Henry J. Raymond and his New York *Times.* Bennett taught others how to search out and report the news; Greeley fashioned an editorial page; Raymond put his emphasis on news interpretation. With their contemporaries and successors, they laid the foundations for present-day American journalism.

The basic journalistic principles thus espoused were further advanced before the nineteenth century had ended by such noted publishers as Joseph Pulitzer, Edward Wyllis Scripps, and Adolph S. Ochs. These publishers had two goals. The primary goal was an ever-increasing concentration of effort on impartial gathering and reporting of the news and its comprehensive display. The other was demonstration of responsible opinion leadership, provided both through an intelligently written editorial page and integrity and zealousness in telling the news.

As even the colonial editor knew, however, there is a third editorial function of the press—to entertain the reader, as well as to provide information and instruction. What is called "human interest" news—stories with appeal based on writing skill rather than necessarily upon news value—has always been in great reader demand. Sensational news—stories involving the human passions, crime and violence, and spicy accounts of the doings of the famous—is likewise age-old in its appeal. The newspaper has also always contained a budget of nonnews material: short stories and other literary content (more prevalent a century ago than today), comics and Sunday feature sections (favorites since the 1890s), advice to the lovelorn (highly popular for early eighteenth-century readers), and a host of varying entertainment items.

The responsibility of the mass media has been to strike a balance among the functions of informing, instructing, and entertaining. The newspaper, as it reached out for mass circulation, sought to fulfill the first two functions in more popularized ways: a more readable writing style, skillful use of human interest elements in news, better makeup and headline display, effective pictures, and use of color. Such popularizing, in the interests of appealing to the entertainment desire, need not detract from the newspapers' social usefulness. There is no reason why the "hard news" of political and economic importance should not be presented as interestingly as possible and in company with other less important, but more attractive, ingredients. But there is a line to be drawn. Overemphasis on sensationalism at the expense of news and a lavish dressing up of purely entertainment features are merely cheapening, not popularizing.

How well American newspapers have responded to these basic principles over the decades is a matter of judgment. One thing is certain: They responded differently, for there is no such thing as a typical newspaper to analyze any more than there is a typical magazine, television or radio station, or book publishing house. What can be measured is the response made by the leaders in different historical periods, as they reshaped their journalistic products to fit the demands of their times and the desires of their audiences. As the sociologist Robert E. Park put it:

> The newspaper has a history; but it has, likewise, a natural history. The press, as it exists, is not, as our moralists sometimes seem to assume, the willful product of any little group of living men. On the contrary, it is the outcome of a historic process in which many individuals participated without foreseeing what the ultimate product of their labors was to be. The newspaper, like the modern city, is not wholly a rational product. . . . it has continued to grow and change in its own incalculable ways.

THE COLONIAL PRESS

Early Concepts of News

Reporting, as defined today, means gathering information of interest to other people and presenting it to them accurately in a way that makes them understand and remember it. This definition is broad enough to fit all media of information, and comprehensive enough to provide a measuring stick for present and past performance.

The first newspaper publishers were primarily printers, not editors. The majority had a sense of what interested people, but only a few had real reportorial instincts. Only a few, too, were good enough writers to tell their stories in an interesting way. Since their access to news was severely limited, and inadequate transportation and communication facilities made the collecting of news a very haphazard business, they scarcely could be expected to be either complete or accurate in their reports. But even so, very few made any move to go out and find the news; they ran what came over their doorsteps or what could be gleaned from other newspapers and periodicals, particularly those coming from London. None had local news reporters as we know them today. Nevertheless, what meager news and entertainment they offered were eagerly devoured by their readers, who had little other choice.

Benjamin Harris, with his ill-fated *Publick Occurrences* of 1690 in Boston, was banned because he reported too well, a fate avoided by John Campbell with his dull Boston *News-Letter.* James and Benjamin Franklin were early publisher-printers who were also journalists. James, in his *New-England Courant,* gave Boston readers of the 1720s the first readable and exciting American newspaper. He printed news, despite the opposition of Puritan political and religious authorities, and covered local issues in a dramatic and crusading fashion. He and his contributors, including his younger brother Ben, wrote well; and the paper, modeled on the successful "essay" papers of Joseph Addison and Richard Steele in England, had high literary qualities. Personality sketches, feature stories, and human interest material lightened the pages. Benjamin Franklin carried on the traditions in his *Pennsylvania Gazette,* editing his meager scraps of news more cleverly than his rivals and offering more substance.

During the Revolutionary War period, publishers such as Benjamin Franklin and Isaiah Thomas of the *Massachusetts Spy* were alert to forward the patriot cause, but even a well-to-do publisher such as Thomas did not attempt to have his own correspondent with Washington's army. The paper nearest to the scene of an event covered it; other papers copied the report or relied upon official announcements, messages sent to their local authorities from military and governmental headquarters, and reports of travelers.

The Political Pamphleteers

Throughout the eighteenth century, the political pamphleteer was more important than the editor-printer. Three examples from the years preceding the American Revolution are John Dickinson, Samuel Adams, and Thomas Paine—all well known in the pages of American history, and all of whom used the newspaper of their day as a vehicle to reach the public.

John Dickinson of Pennsylvania, an articulate spokesman of the colonial Whigs, wrote his "Letters from a Farmer in Pennsylvania" for the *Pennsylvania Chronicle* of 1767–1768. Dickinson was opposed to revolution and was actually a spokesman for the business class and its Whig philosophy rather than for the agrarian class. But he and the colonial Whigs could not afford to let the British Whigs impose commercial restrictions that were harmful to American interests. The mercantile system, which prevented development of colonial industry and trade, and taxation measures imposed by a Parliament in which the colonial Whigs were not directly represented, were threats Dickinson could not ignore. His forceful arguments for home rule helped swing Americans of his economic group to the revolutionary cause after it became apparent that compromise was no longer possible.

Samuel Adams, the great propagandist of the revolution, belonged to the Radical party. Only briefly an editor himself, he worked with the group of Boston patriots assembled in the office of the Boston *Gazette* that included the publishers, Benjamin Edes and John Gill, and the engraver, Paul Revere. Sam Adams was called the "master of the puppets" and the "assassin of reputations" by his enemies, and undoubtedly he was both. He wrote tirelessly for the columns of the *Gazette,* twisting every possible incident or administrative action of the British into an argument for revolution. When the news was dull and the fires of dissatisfaction needed fanning, he turned minor scrapes into events of seemingly major import. When a crisis arose, such as the passage of the Stamp Act or the imposition of the tax on tea, Adams worked with others to fire up resistance throughout the colonies. His Committees of Correspondence, organized in 1772, kept the word moving among patriot editors. When British rifles fired in Boston to restrain a street crowd, the *Gazette* called the affair the Boston Massacre. But a year later the *Gazette* was reporting on a memorial service held for the massacre victims, consisting of a propagandistic display in the windows of Paul Revere's house. Such touches as this were the work of Sam Adams, who knew how to stir the popular emotions.

Tom Paine, the political philosopher, arrived in the colonies from England in time to make two great pamphleteering contributions to the patriot cause. His *Common Sense,* which sold 120,000 copies in three months in the spring of 1776, was a hard-headed, down-to-earth argument for independence that the common citizen could understand. That December, when Washington's discouraged army was camped on the Delaware River across from Trenton, Paine was drafted to write the first of his *Crisis* papers for a Philadelphia weekly:

> These are the times that try men's souls. The summer soldier and the sunshine patriot will, in this crisis, shrink from the service of their country; but he that stands it NOW, deserves the love and thanks of man and woman. Tyranny, like hell, is not easily conquered; yet we have this consolation with us, that the harder the conflict the more glorious the triumph. What we obtain too cheap, we esteem too lightly; it is dearness only that gives every thing its value. Heaven knows how to put a proper price upon its goods; and it would be strange indeed if so celestial an article as FREEDOM should not be highly rated.

Paine's words lived to be broadcast to occupied Europe during World War II; at the time, they helped to spur the first American victory of the war.

PRESS OF THE NEW REPUBLIC

In the early years of the new nation, two types of newspapers were developing. One was the *mercantile* paper, published in the seaboard towns primarily for the trading and shipping classes interested in commercial and political news. Its well-filled advertising columns reflected the essentially business interest of its limited clientele of subscribers—2000 was a good number. The other type was the *political* paper, partisan in its appeal and relying for reader support on acceptance of its views, rather than upon the quality and completeness of its news. Most editors of the period put views first and news second; the political paper deliberately shaped the news to fits its views. In the struggle over the adoption of the Constitution and the establishment of the new federal government, these party papers played a key role.

The *Federalist Papers,* written for the newspapers of New York state and reprinted throughout the country, were largely the work of Alexander Hamilton, brilliant leader of the pro-Constitution party that took its name from the series of 85 articles. Written for mass consumption, they still rank as one of the best expositions of political doctrine ever conceived. When Hamilton's party assumed control of the new federal government, Hamilton directed the editorial opinion of the Federalist party papers he helped to establish. He dictated his ideas to his editors, who, with their Jeffersonian opponents, developed a briefer, one-argument form of editorial writing.

Ranged on the anti-Federalist side with Thomas Jefferson were his personally sponsored poet-editor, Philip Freneau of the *National Gazette,* and other masters of partisanship like Benjamin Franklin Bache of the *Aurora.* Editors on both sides attacked each other with biting sarcasm and bitter invective. Their political sponsors were also viciously treated; the climax came when Bache accused Washington of being a "front man" for the Federalists and said, "If ever a nation was debauched by a man, the American nation has been debauched by Washington." William Cobbett, the most fiery of the Federalist editors, retaliated in his *Porcupine's Gazette* with a classic character sketch of Bache in which the kindest word was "liar."

The American press survived the excesses of the 1790s and the dangerous effort at repression of press freedom through the Alien and Sedition Acts. But the traditions of partisan journalism lived on in the political party press of the nineteenth century. This was particularly true of the frontier papers that supported Andrew Jackson and the Democratic party. The *Argus of Western America* of Frankfort, Kentucky, was one of these grubby but virile sheets that helped to spark the Jacksonian revolution. Amos Kendall and Francis P. Blair, two of its editors, graduated to Jackson's "kitchen cabinet," where Kendall served as postmaster general and journalistic adviser to the president, and Blair as editor of the hard-hitting administration paper, the Washington *Globe.* The tradition of an administration organ in Washington had begun with the *National Intelligencer* of Jefferson's day, but none was edited with more single-minded driving purpose than Blair's *Globe.* "Give it to Bla-ar," Jackson would say, and Blair would pass the word along to the party faithful. The Whigs had their strong editors too, such as Thurlow Weed of the Albany *Evening Journal.* The attitude of the political paper was well expressed by the pro-Jackson New York *Evening Post,* which advised its readers to buy a Whig paper if they wanted the other side of the argument of the moment.

The political papers were much more important in the story of the development of the opinion function. The mercantile papers, however, played a role in the development of the news function concept. Even though their primary interest was in shipping news and digests of foreign news taken from European newspapers arriving in American ports, the leading mercantile papers took pride in excelling in their specialties. And as the struggle between the Federalists and the Republicans for control of the national government intensified, news of Hamilton's fiscal policies and Jefferson's moves became important to the business community. Competition was tough, too; in 1800 there were six dailies in Philadelphia (but only two in 1988) and five in New York. The weekly publishers had been forced into the daily field to meet the demands of patrons of the coffee houses, where the London papers were filed as soon as ships arrived with the latest issues and where news was freely exchanged.

So the individual papers began to go out after the news. Correspondents covered sessions of Congress in Washington as early as 1808 and were well established by the late 1820s. Seaport dailies hired boats to meet the incoming ships out in the harbor so their editors would have a head start on digesting the foreign news. The leading New York mercantile papers, the *Courier and Enquirer* and the *Journal of Commerce,* set up rival pony express services between Washington and New York to get presidential messages and congressional news faster.

What the mercantile papers did not do, however, was widen the appeal of their news columns to satisfy the demands of a new reading audience that was emerging from what is now called the Jacksonian revolution. More widespread education and extension of the right to vote increased interest in politics by a growing working class, and other socioeconomic factors were operating to pave the way for a more popular and responsive journalism that was destined to overwhelm the older types of newspapers.

THE PENNY PRESS

Between 1833 and 1837, the publishers of a new "penny press" proved that a low-priced paper, edited to interest ordinary people, could win what amounted to a mass circulation for the times and thereby attract an advertising volume that would make it independent. These were papers for the common citizen and were not tied to the interests of the business community, like the mercantile press, or dependent for financial support upon political party allegiance. It did not necessarily follow that all the penny papers would be superior in their handling of the news and opinion functions. But the door was open for some to make important journalistic advances.

The first offerings of a penny paper tended to be highly sensational; human interest stories overshadowed important news, and crime and sex stories were written in full detail. But as the penny paper attracted readers from various social and economic brackets, its sensationalism was modified. The ordinary reader came to want a better product, too. A popularized style of writing and presentation of news remained, but the penny paper became a respectable publication that offered significant information and editorial leadership. Once the first of the successful penny papers had shown the way, later ventures could enter the competition at the higher level of journalistic responsibility the pioneering papers had reached.

This was the pattern of American newspapers in the years following the founding of the New York *Sun* in 1833. The *Sun,* published by Benjamin Day, entered the lists against 11 other dailies. It was tiny in comparison; but it was bright and readable, and it preferred human interest features to important but dull political speech reports. It had a police reporter writing squibs of crime news in the style already proved successful by London papers. And, most important, it sold for a penny, whereas its competitors sold for six cents. By 1837 the *Sun* was printing 30,000 copies a day, which was more than the total of all 11 New York daily newspapers combined when the *Sun* first appeared. In those same four years James Gordon Bennett brought out his New York *Herald* (1835), and a trio of New York printers who were imitating Day's success founded the Philadelphia *Public Ledger* (1836) and the Baltimore *Sun* (1837). The four penny sheets all became famed newspapers.

Bennett and News Enterprise

James Gordon Bennett serves as the symbol of the penny press news enterprises. He had been a Washington correspondent, reporter, and editor for other dailies before he launched the *Herald* in 1835. Disillusioned by a previous venture with a political paper, he kept the *Herald* relatively free of political ties. He more than matched the *Sun* with sensational coverage of crime and court news, on the one hand, and challenged the more sober journals with detailed coverage of Wall Street affairs, political campaigns, and foreign news, on the other. As profits from his wide circulation and extensive advertising piled up, he spent money on news coverage. He matched his rivals in establishing pony express services to carry the news from Washington and other points. One *Herald* courier service reached all the way from Newfoundland, carrying European news by pony rider, boat, and train to the first telegraph point. Bennett was among the first to use each of the new means of communication as they burst upon the scene in the 1830s and 1840s, hiring locomotives to race presidential messages from Washington and utilizing the telegraph as soon as Samuel F. B. Morse's invention proved itself in 1844 and wires were strung from city to city. He personally toured the country with presidential candidates and sailed to London on the newest steamship to arrange for better coverage of foreign news. By the 1850s he had made the *Herald* the leading newsgathering paper and the richest in advertising.

Bennett's competitors were not left in the dust. The New York *Sun,* Philadelphia *Public Ledger,* and Baltimore *Sun* were all in the race for news. So were such older New York papers as the *Courier and Enquirer, Journal of Commerce,* and *Evening Post.* So were two new competitors, Horace Greeley's New York *Tribune,* founded in 1841, and Henry J. Raymond's New York *Times,* founded in 1851. Greeley shunned the sensationalism that had helped the *Sun* and *Herald* to their initial circulation successes and concentrated instead on building up an editorial page and offering news interpretation, but he also covered the running news. His managing editor, Charles A. Dana, directed a reportorial staff of high quality, although perhaps not as slam-bang as the *Herald's* group. By the

time Raymond entered the New York field with the *Times,* the lines of staff
organization were fairly well defined. The owner might still be editor-in-chief, but
he had a news executive and a business manager operating the day-to-day business. Raymond concentrated on foreign coverage and editorial policy, seeking to
give his reports more depth and meaning in the pattern of the *Times* of London.

The Civil War called for great efforts in news enterprise. The *Herald* sent its
own small army of correspondents into the field; other leading papers followed
suit. Printing advances of the previous two decades—the flat-bed cylinder press,
the type-revolving press, and stereotyping—were needed to handle increased
circulations. Sunday editions of daily papers came into being. The illustrated
periodicals, *Harper's Weekly* and *Frank Leslie's Illustrated Newspaper,* led the way
in using woodcut illustrations and maps, and newspapers followed suit as best they
could. Mathew Brady made his magnificent photographs of warriors and war, not
yet reproducible in newspapers. By the time the guns ceased firing, the traditions
of news enterprise and emphasis upon the news function had been well established.

Greeley and the Editorial Page

Horace Greeley is recognized as one of the most influential editors in the history
of American journalism. His New York *Tribune,* which he founded in 1841, was
the first American newspaper to develop an editorial page that was the product
of the thinking of a group of individuals. Not that it was the well-tailored, coher-
ently organized page many newspapers publish today. Orderly departmentaliza-
tion had not yet come to newspapers in Greeley's day, and, in any event, methodi-

calness and consistency were not part of the Greeley temperament. But what the *Tribune* printed represented a dramatic change from the tradition of the pamphleteer.

Greeley was deeply conscious of his responsibility to the reader. He knew the *Tribune* had to be enterprising in reporting the news if it was to compete successfully for readers. But he felt it his responsibility to be just as enterprising in seeking to influence public opinion by devoting much space to serious discussion, editorial argument, and interpretation of events. The *Tribune* examined issues and debated ideas; it did not follow a set party line or insist that there was only one solution to a problem. True, it advocated some of its opinions as vehemently as did the pamphleteer, but in total it illuminated the social and economic issues of the day, from differing viewpoints, far more than any other paper had.

Unlike Bennett's *Herald,* which minimized the opinion function while concentrating on news enterprise, Greeley's *Tribune* made the opinion function the key to its popular acceptance. And popular it was. His weekly edition, in which the best of the daily news and opinion was reprinted for mail circulation (a practice of some bigger papers of the period), had the largest circulation of any contemporary publication. It was called the "Bible of the Middle West," where many of the 200,000 copies went. "Uncle Horace," as Greeley was called, was as well known as any American of his time—only Lincoln, of the men of the period, has had more books written about him. Greeley lived through a period of momentous events and of great social change and, like Lincoln, was able to give expression to the aspirations and hopes of less articulate citizens.

To many, the activities of Greeley and the *Tribune* must have appeared strangely inconsistent. The editor was greatly concerned with the impact of the industrial revolution on society and the social ills unrestricted capitalism produced. He was willing to examine and debate any seemingly reasonable experiment in social reform or economic theory in the hope that it would give workers and farmers a more equitable share in the accumulating wealth. So the *Tribune,* ostensibly a Whig newspaper, advocated a form of collective living called "associationism" and ran many columns of material written by the socialist Albert Brisbane and the communist Karl Marx. Few of Greeley's readers were won over to socialism, but they enjoyed the debate. Greeley's fight for free land in the West, to which people in the slums could emigrate, was more popular—but that stand was inconsistent with Whig political principles. Eventually his stand on the slavery issue led him into the Republican party, and he ended his career by running unsuccessfully for the presidency in 1872 as the candidate of the Liberal Republicans and the Democrats, against General Ulysses S. Grant, candidate of the Whig-minded Republicans.

THE PERSONAL EDITORS

Greeley belonged to the group of editors of the middle nineteenth century called the "personal editors," men who were as well known to their readers as were their newspapers, in contrast to the much more anonymous editors of modern corporate journalism. Some of Greeley's farmer readers were surprised to keep getting the *Tribune* after his death; they assumed the paper would quit publishing, so much did he seem to be the newspaper itself.

William Cullen Bryant, who joined the New York *Evening Post* staff in 1825 and remained to edit it for a half-century, also fell into this category of the personal editor. His journalism was much more reserved than Greeley's and his thinking more logical, but through Bryant's personal editorial opinion, the *Post* exercised considerable influence. He supported Jacksonian democracy and, like Greeley, he showed sympathy for the worker. During the Civil War, he was one of the most effective interpreters of Lincoln's policies. Henry J. Raymond, founder of the New York *Times,* played a personal role outside the newspaper office as a leader in the Republican party, although he tried to make the *Times'* editorial columns calmly interpretive in character.

There were editors outside New York City who made their influence felt during the Civil War period. One was Samuel Bowles III, publisher of the Springfield *Republican* in Massachusetts, a daily of just 6000 circulation. Bowles' editorial ability was so great that his weekly edition of 12,000 copies rivaled Greeley's 200,000 circulation in reputation and did much to unify the North and Middle West in the pre-Civil War years. Another was Joseph Medill, builder of the Chicago *Tribune,* who was one of Lincoln's firmest supporters. The abolitionist editors, William Lloyd Garrison of the *Liberator* and the martyred Elijah Lovejoy, should be noted too, although they were agitator-pamphleteers.

In the post-Civil War years, the name of Edwin Lawrence Godkin stands out. Godkin founded the *Nation* magazine in 1865 and succeeded Bryant as the driving force of the New York *Evening Post* in 1881. Born in Britain, Godkin decided the United States needed a high-grade weekly journal of opinion and literary criticism similar to those in England. His distinctive style of writing and skill in ironic analysis made the *Nation* a favorite of other intellectuals. William James, the philosopher, said of him: "To my generation his was certainly the towering influence in all thought concerning public affairs, and indirectly his influence has assuredly been more pervasive than that of any other writer of the generation, for he influenced other writers who never quoted him, and determined the whole current of discussion." This was high accomplishment and praise for the editor of a weekly magazine with a circulation of no more than 10,000.

THE NEW JOURNALISM

Between 1865 and 1900, the dynamic capitalism of an expanding America, utilizing vast natural resources and the new machines of the industrial revolution, transformed the national economy. Industrialization, mechanization, and urbanization brought extensive social, cultural, and political changes: the rise of the city, improved transportation and communication, educational advances, political unrest, and the rise of an extensive labor movement. The mass media could not fail to go through great changes along with the society they served. In the world of newspapers, the era is known as that of the "new journalism," a designation used by people who lived through that time to describe the activities of the master editor of the period, Joseph Pulitzer.

The Linotype machine, on which an operator set lines of type in hot metal by fingering a keyboard, appeared in the 1880s and largely replaced hand-setting of type. The machine greatly increased the speed of preparing news for publication. The double row of Linotypes is producing type in the Los Angeles Times *composing room.* (Los Angeles Times photo)

In the 35 years between the end of the Civil War and the turn of the century, the population of the country doubled, the national wealth quadrupled, and manufacturing production increased sevenfold. It was the period of the coming of the age of steel, the harnessing of electricity for light and power, and the mechanizing of production processes. National growth and increased wealth meant cultural progress in literature, science, and the social sciences; a great stirring in scholarship and a rapid increase in the number and size of universities; and sharp increases in public school attendance and adult interest in popularized knowledge. Growing social and economic interdependence could be measured by two statistics for the year 1900: a third of the population was urban and 62 percent of the labor force was engaged in nonagricultural work.

Communication facilities expanded in this period of the nationalization of the United States. Telegraph lines and railroad tracks reached near-saturation points; the telephone, coming into use in the 1870s, provided direct communication through intercity lines that covered the country by 1900. The federal postal service greatly extended free carrier service in the cities and instituted free rural delivery in 1897. The low postal rate for newspapers and magazines in 1885 opened the way for cheap delivery of publications. By 1900 there were 3500 magazines with a combined circulation of 65 million an issue. Weekly newspapers tripled in number between 1870 and 1900, reaching a total of more than 12,000. During the same 30 years, the number of daily newspapers quadrupled and their total circulation increased almost sixfold; the figures for 1900 were 1967 general circulation dailies selling nearly 15 million copies each day. It was this tremendous increase in the circulation of the printed mass media that was the impetus for inventions such as the rotary press, the typesetting machine, photoengraving, and color printing, which transformed the newspaper into its modern form.

Obviously a new journalism would emerge for this new society. Again, as in the penny press period, there was a new audience: more people were interested in reading; the labor class increased rapidly; and there was a heavy concentration of immigrants in the rapidly growing eastern cities (New York City residents, who increased 50 percent between 1880 and 1890, were 80 percent foreign born or of foreign parentage). Such readers, stirred by political and social unrest in a period when reform movements sought to readjust the economic balance to bring relief to the worker and farmer, looked for aggressive editorial leadership and opinion-forming crusading in their newspapers and magazines. But they also wanted impartial and thorough coverage of the news. The newspaper that appealed to them was also low priced, easily read, popularized in content, and bright in appearance. Particularly in the big cities, the entertainment ingredient had to be high, and for the really new readers a new cycle of sensationalism was the major attraction.

Pulitzer and the News

Joseph Pulitzer serves as the symbol of the new journalism era. An immigrant himself, he served his apprenticeship as a reporter before founding the St. Louis *Post-Dispatch* in 1878. In the next five years Pulitzer built it into the city's leading paper by giving his readers what they wanted. He developed a liberal, aggressive editorial page and gave both the editorial and news columns a fierce crusading spirit. He insisted on accuracy, digging for facts, thoroughness of local news coverage, and good writing. One of his famous commands to his staff was: "Accuracy! Accuracy!! Accuracy!!!" Another was: "Terseness! Intelligent, not stupid, condensation." Still another showed his concern for the lighter side of the news: He reminded reporters to look for both the significant news and the "original, distinctive, dramatic, romantic, thrilling, unique, curious, quaint, humorous, odd, apt to be talked about" news.

In 1883 Pulitzer left the *Post-Dispatch* as his monument in St. Louis and invaded New York City by buying the run-down *World*. Within four years the paper had reached a record-breaking 250,000 circulation, had eclipsed the *Herald* as the leader in advertising volume, and had become the country's most talked-about newspaper.

Pulitzer's success lay in the fact that he had not forgotten the basic news function while he was wooing new readers with entertaining and sensational material. He gave his audience its money's worth in the quality and extent of significant news coverage and presented it in an enlivened style. He poured money into the building of a competent staff of reporters and editors and he kept pace with mechanical innovations that permitted them to fashion a better product. He combined a popular editorial aggressiveness and crusading spirit with great promotional skill to make the mass of readers feel the *World* was their friend. To attract them to its solid news stories and editorial column, the *World* offered big headlines, human interest stories, illustrations, and other sensationalized approaches. With the advent of color printing in the early 1890s, the *World* added popular Sunday supplements and the comic strip.

Some of Pulitzer's competitors did not sense the total character of his journalistic product and mistakenly assumed that sensationalism alone had made the *World* successful. One of these was William Randolph Hearst, who took over the San Francisco *Examiner* in 1887 and then invaded New York in 1895 by buying the *Journal.* The circulation war between Pulitzer's *World* and Hearst's *Journal* brought the cycle of sensationalism to a new height. Critics who eyed one of the comic strip characters of the times, the "Yellow Kid," dubbed the papers "yellow journals." The yellow journal prided itself on being the crusading friend of the "common man," but it underestimated the public's interest in significant news and overestimated its capacity for absorbing gaudy, oversensationalized news. The result was a degrading of the news function that reached its climax during the period of the Spanish-American War. After a few years the *World* and other serious-minded papers withdrew from the competition, leaving the techniques of yellow journalism to Hearst and his imitators. Although the yellow journals cannot be held solely responsible for causing the war, their news policies certainly contributed to the war fever of 1898.

There were other notable leaders in the new journalism era. The master teacher of the art of human interest writing was Charles A. Dana's New York *Sun,* which developed many a great reporter and editor. Dana, however, resisted change, and the *Sun* set its face against the general trend of the times. Edward Wyllis Scripps began developing his group of papers, headed by the Cleveland *Press.* They were low priced, small in size, well written and tightly edited, and hard-hitting in both news and editorial columns. Melville Stone's Chicago *Daily News* and William Rockhill Nelson's Kansas City *Star* were two more distinctive new papers fashioned in the new journalism pattern. In the South, Henry W. Grady became known as a master news executive because of his work with the Atlanta *Constitution* and his own reporting skill.

THE PEOPLE'S CHAMPIONS: PULITZER, HEARST, SCRIPPS

JOSEPH PULITZER. The rise of the architects of the new journalism in the 1870s and 1880s brought a heightening of attention to the exercise of the opinion function. Joseph Pulitzer, the leading exponent of the new journalism, has been named by his colleagues of this century as the leading American editor of modern times. A memo written by Pulitzer to an editor of his St. Louis *Post-Dispatch* summarizes his idealistic goal for the editorial page:

. . . every issue of the paper presents an opportunity and a duty to say something courageous and true; to rise above the mediocre and conventional; to say something that will command the respect of the intelligent, the educated, the independent part of the community; to rise above fear of partisanship and fear of popular prejudice.

No finer statement of the responsibility imposed upon those who exercise the newspaper's opinion function has ever been written. Those who can even occasionally meet such a challenge win the respect of both colleagues and readers.

Pulitzer and his contemporaries developed a growing independence of editorial opinion from partisan pressures. They did not hesitate to support political candidates, but they did not do this automatically as part of a political machine, as did the political press. Most of the leaders were champions of the "common man"—people's champions, doing battle against the trusts and monopolies that characterized big business, the crooked politicians who were "the shame of the cities," the moneylenders and the speculators, and the opponents of reform. The majority supported the political leaders of the Democratic party—Grover Cleveland, William Jennings Bryan, Woodrow Wilson—but they also gave aid to such progressive Republicans as Theodore Roosevelt and Robert M. La Follette. Pulitzer himself believed that the Democratic party best carried out the principles he espoused, but he bolted from the radical Bryan candidacy and gave aid and comfort to such New York Republicans as Charles Evans Hughes in the battles with Tammany Hall. His great editor, Frank I. Cobb, who carried on the traditions of the New York *World* after Pulitzer's death in 1911, was a close adviser to Woodrow Wilson and his solid champion. Cobb, however, insisted that it was part of his job to criticize the administration as well as to defend it. This is part of what is meant by "independence of editorial opinion from partisan pressures."

A distinctive feature of the new journalism paper was its eagerness to crusade in behalf of community welfare. Pulitzer developed the coordinated crusade, using both the news and editorial columns at the *Post-Dispatch,* and that paper remained famous for its tenacious attacks on wrongdoers in public or business life. These words written by Pulitzer in 1907, which became the *Post-Dispatch* editorial platform, sum up the crusading spirit:

I know that my retirement will make no difference in its cardinal principles; that it will always fight for progress and reform, never tolerate injustice or corruption, always fight demagogues of all parties, never belong to any party, always oppose privileged classes and public plunderers, never lack sympathy with the poor, always remain devoted to the public welfare, never be satisfied with merely printing news, always be drastically independent, never be afraid to attack wrong, whether by predatory plutocracy or predatory poverty.

WILLIAM RANDOLPH HEARST. William Randolph Hearst, in his New York *Journal* and the other newspapers, likewise was a crusading champion of the people. His editorial platform at the turn of the century called for nationalization of the coal mines, railroads, and telegraph lines; public ownership of public franchises; the "destruction of the criminal trust"; a graduated income tax; election of United States senators by popular vote rather than by state legislatures that could be

Three leaders of the "new journalism" who crusaded for reforms on behalf of all people. Top left: Edward W. Scripps, on his yacht. Top right: Joseph Pulitzer, as depicted by John Singer Sargent, American portrait and mural painter. Bottom: William Randolph Hearst, at the height of his career.

influenced by big business; and extensive new financial support for the public schools. To this he added an active support of labor unions that made them regard his papers as their champions.

One would suppose the liberals of the time would have clasped Hearst to their bosoms. But they did not. They distrusted Hearst's own political ambitions, which extended to the White House; they disliked the bitterness of his editorial attacks upon his opponents. Repelled by the sensationalism and near-cynicism of his news policies, they rejected his editorial page as shallow and insincere. But undoubtedly Hearst had great influence on the ordinary reader of the pre-World War I generation. By the 1920s, however, the Hearst papers were much less progressive in outlook, and by the 1930s their position was almost reversed from the one they had held in 1900. Always strongly nationalistic, in contrast to Pulitzer's support of international cooperation, the Hearst papers became bitterly isolationist by the time of World War I, and remained so until their founder's death in 1951.

EDWARD W. SCRIPPS. Edward Wyllis Scripps was the third of the great people's champions of the new journalism era. Scripps set his circulation sights on the working people of the smaller but growing industrial cities of the country as he developed his chain of newspapers from his headquarters at the Cleveland *Press.* His social goal was to improve the position of the mass of people through better education, labor union organization and collective bargaining, and a resulting reasonable redistribution of wealth. In this way, he reasoned, a peaceful and productive society could emerge in an industrialized America.

Scripps viewed himself as the only real friend of the "poor and ill-informed." He said his newspapers were the only schoolroom the working person had; the public school system did not serve him or her adequately, and other newspapers were either capitalistic in outlook or too intellectual in their appeal. He pictured himself as a "damned old crank" who was instinctively rebellious against the status quo in any field of human activity. He made a point of running small, tightly edited papers that could assert their independence of the business community and resist any attempted influence by advertisers. But he was businessman enough to make a profit on his journalistic ventures, and his employees found him to be cautious in wage policies. Politically, the Scripps papers were strongly liberal; they supported the third-party candidacies of Theodore Roosevelt in 1912 and Robert M. La Follette in 1924, Woodrow Wilson's New Freedom, the right of workers to organize, and public ownership. This liberal pattern continued after Scripps' death in 1926 and until the late 1930s when, under the influence of the late Roy W. Howard, the Scripps-Howard papers became substantially more conservative.

TWENTIETH-CENTURY NEWS TRENDS

Impartial gathering and reporting of the news were generally recognized to be the basic obligation of newspapers by the early 1900s. Some did the job in a much more comprehensive and intelligent fashion than others. But the editor who put views ahead of news, and who tied his newspaper to a political machine, had pretty well gone out of style. Slanting of news to fit the prejudices or political preferences of a publisher was also recognized as a detriment, although some newspapers continued the practice. The Canons of Journalism adopted by the American Society of Newspaper Editors in 1923 contain the following two paragraphs, which summarize the aspirations of modern journalistic leaders:

> The right of a newspaper to attract and hold readers is restricted by nothing but considerations of public welfare. The use a newspaper makes of the share of public attention it gains serves to determine its sense of responsibility, which it shares with every member of its staff. A journalist who uses his power for any selfish or otherwise unworthy purpose is faithless to a high trust.
>
> Partisanship, in editorial comment which knowingly departs from the truth, does violence to the best spirit of American journalism; in the news columns it is subversive of a fundamental principle of the profession.

No matter how impartial and well intentioned a newspaper's editors might be, they had to expend an increasing effort on comprehensive coverage and display of the news, and its intelligent interpretation, if they were to meet their full responsibilities. Great events of this century made the business of reporting the news far more complex, decade by decade. In the first decade, the story was one of economic and political reform in the United States. In the second decade it was World War I. In the third decade it was the world's effort at postwar readjustment. The fourth decade brought the Great Depression and a collapse of world order. The fifth brought World War II, the atomic era, and the cold war; the sixth and seventh the climactic crises of Korea and Vietnam. The eighth decade brought Watergate and international crises which have continued into the ninth.

The mass media made a reasonable effort to fulfill their increased responsibilities for interpreting the news of events that all but overwhelmed the world. Professional standards had to be raised to meet the challenge. Better-trained and more knowledgeable men and women came to occupy key reportorial assignments and news desk posts. The range of subject matter with which a Washington correspondent had to be familiar in the 1920s was narrow indeed compared to the complexities of Washington news in the 1980s. And since all news tended to become local in its impact with the narrowing of geographic barriers in the atomic age, every general assignment reporter had to know far more about such areas as international affairs, science, and economic trends than did his or her predecessors. The modern press associations, particularly, were put under heavy pressures. Newspapers were stimulated by the appearance of new competitors: radio, television, and the news magazine. Radio and television challenged the newspaper both in providing spot news coverage and in news analysis. The news magazines competed with the newspapers by giving the reader background information and point-of-view interpretation. Together, the print and electronic media offered a persistent reader-listener-viewer a sizable amount of information about the swirl of events that virtually engulfed even the most conscientious citizen.

The New York Times

The editors of the New York *Times* built what is generally conceded to be the greatest single news machine of this century, publishing what was called by its admiring competitors a "newspaper of record." The story of the growth of the *Times* since Adolph S. Ochs rescued it from bankruptcy in 1896 illustrates the trend in acceptance of the news function responsibility, even though it is the story of an atypical journalistic leader. For what the *Times* did in its methodical completeness was done at least in part, and in some respects as successfully, by other responsible newspapers.

Ochs told his readers in 1896: "It will be my aim . . . to give the news impartially, without fear or favor." He also promised them all the news, in concise and attractive form, and a paper that would be "a forum for the consideration of all questions of public importance, and to that end . . . invite intelligent discussion from all shades of opinion." He made no attempt to match the sensationalism of the yellow journals of the time, and he shunned many of the popularized entertainment features of most newspapers, including the comic strip. His Sunday magazine featured articles of current news significance and became, with its 1.5 million circulation of today, an important fixture in the magazine world. His book review section became the best known in the country. His coverage of financial and business news soon matched that of any older competitor. His editorial page, if quieter and more cautious than that of Pulitzer, was intelligently directed.

What made the *Times* great, however, was not so much these accomplishments as its persistence in gathering and printing the news in all its varied aspects. One of the great managing editors, Carr V. Van Anda, was given control of the *Times* newsroom in 1904 with the understanding that he should do whatever it took to do a comprehensive job with the news. Ochs was willing to spend money to get the news; Van Anda was willing to do the spending, and he knew how to get the news. World War I gave Van Anda an opportunity to show his ability. Using the cables and wireless almost with abandon, the *Times* added the reports of its own correspondents to those of the press associations and syndicates. It reported in detail not only on military operations but also on political and economic developments in the European capitals. War pictures were carried in a rotogravure section added in 1914. Most importantly, the paper began to publish the texts of documents and speeches. The Treaty of Versailles filled eight pages—more than any other American paper was willing to give that important document. This policy, combined with the publication of the annual *New York Times Index,* made the *Times* the leading newspaper for librarians, scholars, government officials, and other newspaper editors. Its major failure was biased, inaccurate coverage of Russian events during 1917 to 1920, stemming from Ochs's fear of radicalism either at home or abroad.

If there was any other complaint to be registered against the *Times* of the Van Anda period, it was that the paper presented a voluminous amount of news without sufficient interpretation or screening for the average reader. The objective fashion of reporting was considered the best, if impartiality was to be achieved, as late as the 1920s. But Van Anda did a goodly share of interpreting the news, and the editors who followed him did more. The Washington and foreign staffs built by the paper ranked with the best, and during the following decades they came to offer interpretive analysis along with factual reporting.

Copyreaders of the New York Times *telegraph desk in about 1940 edit stories received from other U.S. cities. Use of video display terminals has virtually eliminated such piles of paper from contemporary newsrooms. One editor wore his hat because of a draft.* (Library of Congress)

"Jazz Journalism"

One more wave of sensationalism, however, was to precede the "era of interpretation." The 1920s were known as the Jazz Age, and the papers that catered to a new group of readers won the dubious honor of being identified as "jazz journalism." Their sensationalism was accompanied by the two identifying techniques of the period: the tabloid format and great emphasis on photography.

Leading the sensationalist tabloids was the New York *Illustrated Daily News,* founded in 1919 by Joseph Medill Patterson, cousin of Robert R. McCormick and partner with him in the publishing of the Chicago *Tribune.* Patterson, unlike his ultraconservative Chicago cousin, was unconventional in his socioeconomic beliefs —socialistic, his wealthy friends said. He wanted to reach and influence the lowest literate class of Americans and was attracted to the tabloid format by the success Lord Northcliffe was enjoying with it in England. The *Daily News* appeared with a photograph spread across its front half-page and was well stuffed with pictures, human interest stories, and entertaining features. By 1924 it had the largest circulation of any newspaper in the country, a position it continued to hold until surpassed by the *Wall Street Journal* in 1980.

Close behind in reflecting the Jazz Age were Bernarr Macfadden's New York *Graphic* and Hearst's *Daily Mirror.* For all three papers, the most important news involved gangsters, murders, illicit love nests, bootleggers, and flappers.

The tabloid format, it should be noted, did not have to be equated with sensationalism. It was used by other papers that were similar to the dailies of conventional size in all respects but that of the half-fold style.

Interpretive Reporting

This type of more skillful, yet impartial, handling of the news was not unknown before the 1930s. But by then the socioeconomic revolution known politically as the New Deal, coupled with the impact of international crises, forced editors to emphasize "why" along with "who did what." Old-style objectivity, which called for the reporter to stick to a factual account of what had been said or done, did not give the reader the full meaning of the news. The new concept of objectivity was based on the premise that the reader needed to have a given event placed in its proper perspective if truth was to be served. Also discarded were older assumptions that subjects such as science and economics could not be made interesting to a mass readership. Reporter-specialists who could talk both to their subjects and to a popular reading audience emerged to cover politics, foreign affairs, business, science, labor, agriculture, and urban affairs.

E. W. Scripps' Science Service began blazing one trail in 1921, along with such reporters as William L. Laurence of the New York *Times* and Howard W. Blakeslee of the Associated Press. In labor news two pioneers were Louis Stark of the *Times* and Edwin A. Lahey of the Chicago *Daily News.* The 1960s saw the rise of urban and architectural specialists such as Ada Louise Huxtable of the New York *Times* and Wolf Von Eckardt of the Washington *Post.* Examples of successful interpretive writers in Washington are Jack Nelson, Los Angeles *Times* bureau chief; David Broder, Washington *Post* political columnist; Elizabeth Drew, the *New Yorker's* political correspondent; and syndicated columnist Mary McGrory.

ANOTHER NEW JOURNALISM

In the late 1960s, the literature of the mass media began to herald a "new journalism" that borrowed the title of the innovations of the 1880s. Its reportorial and writing techniques were variously described as tell-it-as-you-see-it, impressionistic, saturation, humanistic, investigative—and even interpretive. Its second and more controversial characteristic was described as advocacy, activist, or participatory. The latter trend merely reflected the widespread frustration of the era and the demand that the conservative establishment give heed and power to others—youth, minorities, women. The mass media should be used, the argument ran, to further such reforms.

Perhaps the leading spirit of this new journalism was Tom Wolfe, although he viewed his efforts as a revolt against old-fashioned book writing rather than news writing. Other major figures were Truman Capote, Norman Mailer, Gay Talese, and Jimmy Breslin. Their work appeared in *Esquire,* the *New Yorker, Harper's,* and the fast-rising *New York.* Those magazines, the old New York *Herald Tribune,* and such underground papers as the *Village Voice* served as vehicles for the new style of reporting, perhaps best described as "saturation." Capote's *In Cold Blood,* although a novel, demonstrated intense journalistic research; Mailer's description of the antiwar demonstrators' march on the Pentagon was powerfully impressionistic; Talese utilized incredible detail in his account of life at the New York *Times* in *The Kingdom and the Power;* Breslin made his readers feel the crunch of police clubs on their skulls as he wrote of the 1968 Democratic convention riots in Chicago for the New York *Daily News.*

Out of that 1968 crisis came the best-known example of advocacy journalism. The *Chicago Journalism Review* was founded in October 1968 in the wake of disillusionment among young Chicago newspeople over management and public reaction to the role of the press in the riots. Edited by Ron Dorfman, the monthly aggressively criticized the city's press and offered a forum for general media criticism and self-improvement until its demise in 1975. Across the country similar publications appeared, among them the late New York review [*MORE*]. In many city rooms "reporter power" movements developed among young staff members who sought to make their professional contributions more meaningful and also challenged the established system of command. Among the advocacy journalists were Gloria Steinem, Jack Anderson, Seymour Hersh, and Sander Vanocur.

First of the underground papers spawned by the sexual revolution and the credibility gap was the *Village Voice,* founded in 1955 and boasting such contributors as Norman Mailer, Jules Feiffer, and Jack Newfield. Art Kunkin's *Los Angeles Free Press* proved more radical and antiestablishment. Best known of the campus-based papers was the *Berkeley Barb,* founded by Max Scherr as spokesman for the free speech movement and a passionate opponent of the older educational order. San Francisco's *Rolling Stone* became highly successful in the mid-1970s. Among other underground papers that enjoyed at least brief fame were Chicago's *Seed,* Boston's *Avatar,* and New York's *East Village Other.*

Combining radical dissent and alternative press qualities were such pungent journals as *I. F. Stone's Weekly* (1953–1971), Dorothy Day's *Catholic Worker,* Deidre English's *Mother Jones,* the *Guardian* of New York, the *Texas Observer,* and Bruce Brugmann's *San Francisco Bay Guardian.*

THE BLACK PRESS

Only recently have the American mass media exhibited an understanding interest in the black 10 percent of citizens; even so, the capacity to be sensitive to blacks as readers or viewers has been severely limited. There has always been a clear need for a black press.

More than 3000 such newspapers—owned and edited by blacks for black readers—have appeared since the first, *Freedom's Journal,* in 1827. But the black community has had few socioeconomic resources to support a press. Historically, the average life span of a black newspaper has been nine years. Henry G. La Brie III, a research specialist on the black press, found that 213 black newspapers were being published in 1974, of which only 11 had founding dates before 1900, as compared to 90 founded since 1960. Total circulation was 4.3 million; only five were dailies; and only 38 had their own printing equipment. In 1979 he found only 165 black papers surviving, with a total circulation of 2.9 million. But by 1984 there had been a rebound to 185 papers with 3.6 million circulation (one-third free-controlled), including three dailies. Collectively this struggling press had made its impact on the country.

"We wish to plead our own cause. Too long have others spoken for us," said the editors of *Freedom's Journal,* John B. Russwurm and Samuel Cornish, in 1827. The first black journalist to do that effectively was Frederick Douglass, the re-markable ex-slave who founded *The North Star* in 1847 and became the symbol of hope for blacks of his generation and of today. Douglass helped rally public opinion against slavery and through his writing and speaking helped white men and women to see the degradation of slavery through black eyes. Published in Roches-ter, New York, *The North Star* reached a circulation of 3000 in the United States and Europe, particularly among influential readers. Renamed *Frederick Douglass' Paper* in 1851, it survived until the Civil War. Douglass then edited magazines for 15 years. He wrote three autobiographies, tracing the career of an ex-slave who became a skillful editor, polished orator, and inspiring leader.

Ranking in fame with Douglass is W. E. B. Du Bois, who founded *The Crisis* in 1910 as the militant-protest voice of the National Association for the Advance-ment of Colored People. "Mentally the Negro is inferior to the white," said the 1911 *Britannica;* to Du Bois, this belief was the crisis that had to be eliminated before discrimination in education, housing, and social status could be overcome.

Just as the standard daily press grew in numbers, circulation, and stature during the new journalism era between 1880 and World War I, so did the black press. Important papers today founded in that period include the New York *Amsterdam News* (1909); the leading papers in the two most important publishing groups, Baltimore's *Afro-American* (1892) and the Chicago *Defender* (1905); and the Pittsburgh *Courier* (1910), Philadelphia *Tribune* (1884), and Norfolk's *Journal and Guide* (1909). Among the major figures in black publishing up until 1910 were Robert S. Abbott of the Chicago *Defender,* John H. Murphy, Sr., of the *Afro-American,* Robert L. Vann of the Pittsburgh *Courier,* T. Thomas Fortune of the New York *Age,* and William Monroe Trotter of the Boston *Guardian.*

In 1970 Abbott's nephew, John H. Sengstacke, was elected to the board of the American Society of Newspaper Editors, the first black to be thus honored. Sengstacke was head of the Chicago *Defender* group, which included the Pitts-burgh *Courier* and the *Michigan Chronicle* of Detroit. John H. Murphy III headed the *Afro-American* papers.

Out of 45 efforts to publish dailies in the United States for blacks, as recorded by Professor Armistead Scott Pride of Lincoln University, only the Chicago *De-fender* and the Atlanta *Daily World* have published for long periods, the latter since 1932. Its founder, William A. Scott, was murdered in 1934; his successor, Corne-lius A. Scott, produced an essentially conservative newspaper. Most of the leading

TODAY'S WEATHER
Partly sunny; 30's

Chicago Defender

SENGSTACKE
Newspaper

Vol. LXXXI - No. 186   Wednesday January 28, 1987   30¢ Outside Chicago and suburbs   25¢

Watchers cry registration 'conspiracy'

by Chinta Strausberg

The last day of voter registration was riddled with scores of complaints from Black election judges and attorneys who accused the Chicago Board of Election Commissioners of "conspiring" to keep Blacks off the rolls.

Mayoral allies warned all voters to make sure their names are on the mailboxes "lest they be stricken from the rolls."

The *Chicago Defender* received numerous complaints that the precinct verification books containing computer printouts of current voters were not delivered to the precincts until as late as 2 p.m.

"What this means," said attorney Lawrence Kennon, "is that many Blacks who wanted to verify their registration couldn't (do so). This happened on the whole South and West Sides and some parts of the North Side."

He said the judges' manuals were reportedly not delivered either. "The judges need this because it contains their instructions. This is the biggest fraud and conspiracy ever perpetrated by the Board to avoid proper registration."

But Tom Leach, a spokesman for the Board, denied the conspiracy charges, saying the verification books aren't supposed to be at the polls Tuesday. They are to be delivered today. But because of the numerous complaints, Leach said, they were sent out many times in cabs to the precinct polls anyway.

Kennon said the lack of proper material "created so much confusion that some people went home without registering." Ald. Ed H. Smith (28) said two white officers allegedly were caught Monday canvassing voters. He has requested a probe by Police Supt. Fred Rice.

Peggy Smith Martin, an Operation PUSH spokesperson, said she was inundated with similar complaints. She said in the 76th precinct of the 6th Ward "there was no material at all" until later in the day.

McClinton lost in TV ratings battle

by Pat Jamison and Earl Calloway

Following two days of controversy over the dismissal of Marlene McClinton by WMAQ-TV, an executive at the station told the *Chicago Defender* Tuesday that both she and her co-anchor, Roy Weissinger, failed to maintain ratings.

McClinton, anchor-woman-reporter at the NBC affiliate since March, 1985, and Weissinger, who joined the NBC (Channel 5) news team in May, 1984, both were under three-year contracts, with yearly reviewing options.

Weissinger exited his position at WMAQ-TV two months ago, and decided against challenging the station's decision not to renew his contract. However, McClinton felt it was in her best interest to go public with the issue.

"Perhaps, by my not just walking away without saying a word, I can pave a smoother road for some future Black anchorwoman," McClinton said. "I am sure there will be repercussions, but I just couldn't keep quiet about this. I am not just looking out for myself, but for the future."

WMAQ's vice president and general manager, Richard Lobo, told the *Defender* that the duet was dismissed because of "all-important ratings." WMAQ is number two in local news ratings, behind WLS-TV, and ahead of WBBM-TV.

Lobo stated that the dismissals were not racially motivated, but instead, strictly business, adding, "Ratings are the name of the game."

"I am extremely sensitive when it comes to race issues, and I make every effort to see that the station's decision policy is based on professionalism and capability," Lobo said in an interview.

"Our job is to build audiences," Lobo continued. "And, if anyone on our team does not contribute to that progress, they will go.

"News is our most important area and we are working toward keeping our station number one. The electronic media is very competitive and every individual must be sharp," he said.

Super Dumpsters

Streets and Sanitation Comm. John J. Halpin, accompanied by Mayor Harold Washington and a crowd of area residents, yesterday unveiled the "Super Dumpsters" that will be used to collect refuse at ABLA CHA homes at 14th and Loomis and at Madden Park Homes on the South Side. *(Defender photo by Kenneth Wright)*

Collins cracks down on drugs in transportation

Congresswoman Cardiss Collins (D.-Ill.) announced today she has introduced a bill designed to "crack down" on pilots and engineers who may be working under the influence of alcohol or drugs.

"Pilots flying high, engineers 'highballing' down the track. How often does the public's safety have to be jeopardized before the government acts?" Collins asked.

"Americans have long taken comfort and pride in the fact they could get on a plane or train and arrive at their destination safely," she said. "But the Amtrak crash and recent media reports on our air transportation system raise serious doubts whether the safety of our rail and air systems is being compromised by the behavior of certain engineers and pilots."

Collins, chairwoman of a House Government Operations Task Force investigating the Amtrak collision, said, "current rules allow drug tests if there is a 'reasonable suspicion' a worker is drug im-

(continued on page 18)

Front page of the Chicago Defender. (Chicago Defender/Sengstacke Enterprises, Inc.)

black papers have been moderate in tone, heavily local in news coverage, strong in sports and social news, and occasionally crusading. The third black daily in 1986 was the New York *Daily Challenge,* founded in 1972.

Largest in audited circulation among all weeklies were Brooklyn's *Big Red News,* 57,400; the Cleveland *Call and Post,* 42,100; and the Los Angeles *Sentinel,* 34,900, edited by Ruth Washington as a mildly sensationalist and liberal paper. By far the largest in unaudited circulation was the *Bilalian News* (formerly *Muhammad Speaks*), voice of the Nation of Islam, reportedly rolling 625,000 copies weekly out of its ultramodern Chicago plant. The *Central News-Wave* group of free circulation weeklies in Los Angeles totaled 257,000 for seven editions. A 1982 entry, the tabloid *National Leader,* circulated 100,000 copies in 28 cities. The *Black Panther,* voice of the radical left, also once claimed 100,000 copies. The *Defender* group had circulation claims exceeding 100,000; the *Afro-American* group, some 50,000. Historically, black newspaper circulations peaked during the World War II period, when the Pittsburgh *Courier* achieved a national circulation of 286,000. As the regular press covered stories involving racial issues better, black newspaper readership declined, and community-based weeklies replaced the nationally circulating papers.

If there was a single major voice in black journalism, it was *Ebony,* the monthly picture magazine founded by John H. Johnson in 1945 in full imitation of *Life.* By 1986 it had a circulation of 1.7 million copies. Johnson also published *Jet, Tan,* and *Black World,* the latter an outlet for black authors. *Essence,* a New York-based women's magazine founded in 1970, had zoomed past 650,000 circulation. *Encore,* a biweekly news magazine, had a circulation of 150,000.

LATINO AND NATIVE AMERICAN MEDIA

By the late 1980s, Latinos were the fastest growing minority group in the United States, with an estimated population of 25 to 27 million, including the Chicano or Mexican-American population of the Southwest and the Puerto Rican and Cuban concentrations on the Eastern seaboard. While nearly 80 percent were bilingual, there was a cultural need for a Latino press and for a Spanish International Network (SIN) reaching 12 million radio listeners in 62 cities and 3.5 million households through 21 television broadcast affiliates and 256 cable outlets in the United States.

More than 50 major Spanish-language papers were listed in 1986, led by several important dailies: *El Miami Herald,* published by the Knight-Ridder group since 1976, with 73,000 circulation; *El Diario-La Prensa* of New York, purchased by Gannett in 1981, 69,000; *Diario de las Americas* of Miami, 63,000; *La Opinion* of Los Angeles, 63,000; *El Noticias del Mundo* of New York, 56,000; *El Mañana Daily News* of Chicago, 55,000; and the Laredo *Times* of Texas, 20,000. There were also bilingual papers, including bilingual sections of major Anglo dailies. English or bilingual magazines for Latinos included *Nuestra, Latin NY, Agenda,* and *Lowrider.*

The first Spanish-language paper in the United States was *El Misisipí,* printed during 1808–1810 in New Orleans. The first such paper in what is now Texas,

La Gaceta, appeared in 1813. More than 100 Spanish-language publications came and went before 1900, as New Mexico, Arizona, and California cities developed. In 1920 there were nearly 100, mostly tiny, voices of Latino pride and of protest against racial and economic discrimination. Fanning the activist movements of the 1960s were *El Malcriado,* voice of Cesar Chavez's union movement; *La Raza,* voice of Los Angeles Chicanos; *El Rebozo,* published by Chicano women in San Antonio; and such regional papers as *El Gallo* in Denver, *La Guardia* in Milwaukee, *Adelante* in Kansas City, and *Lado* in Chicago.

The Native American press of the 1980s was almost entirely printed in English. There were 325 newspapers listed by the American Indian Press Association in 34 states, more than 50 student publications, and four magazines. Two papers claiming 80,000 national circulation were *Wassaja* and *Akwesasne News.* The Cherokee tribe in Georgia produced the first papers in the 1830s.

SOME CURRENT NEWSPAPER LEADERS

Opinions differ about the quality of individual newspapers; any "list of ten" compiled by one authority would differ to some degree from the listing made by a second competent observer. But newspeople generally agree that a top-flight newspaper must offer both impartial and comprehensive coverage of the news as a first prerequisite for national recognition. The second prerequisite for recognition by the craft is a superior demonstration of responsibility in providing community opinion leadership and of integrity and zealousness in protecting basic human liberties. The second prerequisite is much harder to judge than the first.

The United States, unlike many other countries, has no truly national newspapers. It has three dailies without "home communities," however, that circulate nationally with their regionally printed editions. These are the *Christian Science Monitor* and the *Wall Street Journal* (neither of which carries a nameplate that seems to indicate the general interest character of the paper) and *USA Today.* The *Monitor,* founded in 1908 by the Church of Christ, Scientist, built a high reputation for its Washington and foreign correspondence and its interpretive articles. Edited by Erwin D. Canham from 1945 to 1970, it serves 150,000 readers from its offices in Boston. The *Wall Street Journal's* staff, led by Bernard Kilgore from 1941 to his death in 1967, has seen its readership rise from 30,000 to nearly 2 million to make the paper the nation's largest. It is produced in 17 regional plants, using satellite or microwave transmissions of ready-to-print pages from its New York office. It won its position on the basis of its excellent writing, coverage of important news, and specialized business reporting. *USA Today,* founded in 1982 by Allen H. Neuharth for the Gannett Company, reached 1.1 million circulation its first year. Printed in dozens of regional plants on presses of other Gannett dailies from plates sent by satellite from near Washington, D.C., the colorful five-day paper was sold in bright blue boxes blanketing larger cities. It was best known for its graphics, and revolutionized the appearances of many dailies, large and small (see Chapter 6).

The New York *Times,* generally recognized as the country's leading daily and newspaper of record, also has a sizable national circulation, particularly for its

Sunday edition. It clearly has been the leader over a period of time in developing its own Washington and foreign staffs, whose stories are also sold to other papers. Publisher-owner Arthur Hays Sulzberger ably carried on the duties of his father-in-law, Adolph S. Ochs, after Ochs' death in 1935 and maintained a remarkable news institution to which many staff members—editors and reporters—contributed leadership. His son, Arthur Ochs Sulzberger, succeeded to power in the late 1960s and favored the judgments of reporter-columnist James Reston and news executive A. M. Rosenthal, who directed the paper's Pentagon Papers publication. In the late 1970s the *Times* added popularized sections—Weekend, Living, Sports Monday, Business Day—to its solid fare in order to maintain its readership appeal.

Across the continent, the Los Angeles *Times* surged forward, beginning in the 1960s to reach the top levels of American newspaper journalism. Young publisher Otis Chandler and a competent staff turned the paper to a more progressive editorial outlook than it had exhibited in earlier years, plunged vigorously into civic affairs, and vastly improved the news content. Chandler joined with the Washington *Post's* owners in establishing a spectacularly successful news syndicate covering the nation's capital and worldwide news centers. The *Times'* editorial page showed intellectual depth and enjoyed the cartooning skill of Paul Conrad. By 1980 the paper had passed 1 million in circulation and reflected reportorial skill and influence in national and state affairs.

Rising to prominence since the 1930s has been the Washington *Post.* Financier Eugene Meyer and his son-in-law, Philip L. Graham, the paper's publishers, had as their aim the molding of a vigorous, intelligent, and informative editorial page for capital readers. This they accomplished, with help of an able staff who could tap Washington news sources for background and interpretation, and the provocative cartoons of Herbert L. Block. Meyer's daughter, Katharine Graham, maintained the *Post's* quality after the deaths of her father and husband in the 1960s, and with her son Donald pushed the *Post* to levels of news excellence that ranked it with the New York *Times* and the Los Angeles *Times.* The *Post's* role in Washington reporting (see Chapter 22) won it wide public attention and the admiration of others in the media.

A change of style and outlook from the ultraconservative stance given it by owner Robert R. McCormick brought the Chicago *Tribune* an enhanced national reputation by the 1980s and improved circulation in Chicago. Editor Clayton Kirkpatrick played a guiding role during the 1970s in reducing controversial activities and in encouraging revitalized reporting that won three Pulitzer prizes for local investigative work and one in international reporting. James D. Squires took control in the 1980s.

Moving up in rankings by media peers were the Miami *Herald* and the Boston *Globe.* The *Herald,* emerging as the most dynamic paper in the South, was started on its way by Lee Hills, later executive editor of all Knight newspaper group dailies, who built its Latin American area coverage. Boston's century-old *Globe,* guided by sons of earlier executives, publisher William Taylor and editor Thomas Winship, won attention for investigative reporting, political writing, and community leadership in a long school desegregation controversy.

The St. Louis *Post-Dispatch,* owned by a third generation of the Pulitzer family, continued to offer American journalism an excellent example of the exercise of the opinion function—excelling the standard set by Joseph Pulitzer's New York *World,* which ceased publishing in 1931. A talented *Post-Dispatch* editorial page staff, wrote superbly and with a depth of understanding on a wide variety of subjects.

Known as "Milwaukee's Dutch Uncle," the staff-owned Milwaukee *Journal* has demonstrated editorial page excellence since the days of founder Lucius W. Nieman. The *Journal* has paid close attention to city and state affairs and has cultivated good writing. The same characteristics have been exhibited by the Louisville *Courier-Journal,* long owned and edited by Barry Bingham, Sr., until sold to the Gannett Company in 1986. Both these papers enjoy local and regional news reporting of excellent depth.

Among other papers of high quality, those respected for news skills include Long Island's *Newsday* and the Philadelphia *Inquirer,* Baltimore *Sun,* and Toledo *Blade* in the East; the Chicago *Sun-Times,* Minneapolis *Star and Tribune,* and Kansas City *Times* in the Midwest; the Atlanta *Constitution,* St. Petersburg *Times,* Charlotte *Observer,* and Memphis *Commercial Appeal* in the South; and the Denver *Post,* Seattle *Times,* Dallas *Morning News,* San Jose *Mercury News,* and San Francisco *Chronicle* in the West. Another dozen could be named with almost equal justice to such a list of current leaders in exercising the news function.

Although all these newspapers have capable editorial pages, some have won particular attention. When one turns to newspapers that have won top recognition for their editorial leadership and for their aggressiveness in defense of basic principles of a progressive democracy, the names of four are readily apparent: the Washington *Post,* the St. Louis *Post-Dispatch,* the Milwaukee *Journal,* and the Louisville *Courier-Journal.* Examples of effective conservative opinion are found in the editorial columns of the Los Angeles *Times,* the *Christian Science Monitor,* the Chicago *Tribune,* and the *Wall Street Journal.*

As Gerald Johnson once said, "The greatest newspaper is as difficult to identify as the greatest man—it all depends upon what you require." Certainly an intelligent, honest, and public-spirited editorial page is as much an essential of an effective newspaper as is comprehensive and honest reporting and display of the news.

Newspapers Today

Murder, She Writes

Police reporters on newspapers cover the gritty underside of life. Those with intense curiosity and persistence find fascinating stories in the daily grist. Edna Buchanan writes murder stories—true ones. Her work as police reporter for the Miami *Herald* is so distinctive that *New Yorker* magazine published a profile of her, and she won a Pulitzer Prize.

Buchanan asks questions. Then she asks more questions, probing for the specific detail that lifts the story above the routine. What song was the murder victim playing on the juke box when he was shot? What was the family eating when the out-of-control car smashed into their dining room?

The concise, wry leads that Buchanan puts on her stories grab the reader's interest. They reach beyond humdrum recitals of facts to narrate the human dramas. Like this one:

> The man she loved slapped her face. Furious, she says she told him never, ever to do that again. "What are you going to do, kill me?" he asked, and handed her a gun. "Here, kill me," he challenged. She did.

Edna Buchanan says of the police beat: "It is people, what makes them tick —what brings out the best in them or drives them berserk." Reporting on what makes the world tick, from police stations to the White House, is what draws men and women into newspapering.

*A*s the written record of civilization, on a day-to-day basis, newspapers are a fundamental distributor of information. They continue to fill a basic role despite the proliferation of electronic news media.

Daily newspapers deliver news of the nation and the world, along with interpretation, advertising, and a leavening of entertainment. Weekly newspapers record local community news—the births and deaths, PTA meetings, bowling scores, traffic accidents, and Elks Club dinners that make up the grist of everyday life.

In this chapter we examine how newspapers operate, the positions men and women fill on their staffs, and the pressures and problems they face. We discuss the changes being brought about by new technology. Also, we look at the differences that exist among very small dailies, medium-sized ones, and the million-circulation metropolitan giants.

Creation of the first American general interest national daily newspaper, *USA Today,* is discussed. So are changes in reading habits that are stimulating a shift of many daily newspapers from evening to morning publication hours. The economics of newspaper publishing is explained.

Students also will learn what kinds of jobs, opportunities, and pay men and women can expect to find in the newspaper business. ◆

THE CHANGING NEWSPAPER

Today's newspapers are far different from those our grandparents read. Brighter graphically with splashes of color and open typography, they are more attractive and easier on the eye. Their writing is more informal. Most important of all, they cover a much wider range of subject matter.

During the past two decades in particular, newspapers have moved beyond their traditional news coverage formula emphasizing politics, crime, and tragedy. They examine social issues and devote space to articles concerning the personal lives, health, and needs of their readers. The better ones dig more deeply into the causes of events than many newspapers of earlier generations did.

Yet, with all these improvements, newspapers no longer stand alone as the dominant source for news. The rise of television news, in which the personality of the newscasters adds an attraction newspapers cannot match, has changed that.

Many Americans—the majority of them, according to some surveys—say they get most of their news from television. Nevertheless, newspapers probably still are the basic news medium because of the far greater depth and breadth of their coverage. With its speed and visual punch, television provides an eye-catching headline service, easily digested. That is all the news that some individuals desire. Only on occasional major stories, however, does television devote the time necessary to present the background and detail that newspapers provide. Also, newspapers cover far more stories, especially in local news.

Newspapers have benefited from borrowing some of television's techniques and, as in all competitive situations, the consumers gain from the rivalry.

Basic Purpose Remains the Same

The fundamental role of newspapers remains unaltered despite the challenge of television and the arrival of high-speed electronic newsgathering methods. They continue to be the written record of contemporary civilization, reporting in detail events great and small, from a presidential campaign to the automobile collision down the street. Despite the handicap of short-range perspective forced on them by the demands of deadlines, they seek increasingly to evaluate the news as well as report it.

The word *perspective* is heard and pondered more among today's editors than it was among those of the past. Achieving balance and significance tests the technical skill and intellectual capacity of editors and writers because they operate under severe time pressures in a society whose standards are in flux. Few absolutes guide the decisions of editors in the news media. They work not in the luxury of contemplation but under the tyranny of the clock.

Since television and radio newscasts have largely taken over the role of being first to report big news, and competition between rival newspapers within cities has almost vanished, today's newspaper staffs are less obsessed with the need to "get it into print right now!" The day when newsboys hawked extra editions containing huge headlines on late-breaking bulletins is gone. Some of the gung-ho excitement of old-time newspapering has vanished as a result, but newspapers are better-rounded products.

(See Chapter 21 for a discussion of the decrease in newspaper competition.)

New Trends in Advertising

Delivering advertisements to readers, as well as news, long has been an essential job of newspapers. Roughly 50 to 60 percent of a daily newspaper consists of display and classified advertising. Like the news content, newspaper advertising has undergone striking changes as the result of competition and new printing techniques. The growth of national and regional chain store merchandising is a significant factor in this change.

Old-time newspapers prepared all the advertising for local stores in their own composing rooms, requiring large staffs of compositors. Today chain stores often have their advertisements printed in multiple-page colored sections by an independent specialty shop, then shipped to newspapers in a number of cities for insertion into their editions. Thus readers in several states may receive identical advertisements on the same day, and one issue of a newspaper may contain inserts from several stores. In fact, on some small daily newspapers during the Christmas shopping rush, the basic newspaper looks like a newsprint shell around the slick-paper preprint sections.

The availability of preprint advertising has stimulated growth of free-distribution publications in competition to standard paid-circulation newspapers. Some of these are community newspapers with substantial news content and local editorial influence, circulated in easily identifiable neighborhoods of metropolitan areas or in small communities. Others fall into the "shopper" category, containing little or no news. Free-distribution newspapers operate on the economic principle that the cost of producing and giving away their copies can be more than offset, and a profit earned, by income from advertising placed by merchants who desire the nearly 100 percent saturation delivery to homes they provide. Standard newspapers cannot provide such blanket coverage with their paid subscriptions. To meet the competition, many publish supplemental shoppers of their own, which they deliver to nonsubscriber homes. This combination of paid and free distribution is called *total market coverage.*

BROAD RANGE OF PUBLICATIONS

Approximately 63 million copies of daily newspapers are distributed each day. The term *newspaper* covers a surprisingly broad range of publications. It includes publications ranging from the small weekly in which every task is done by a handful of people to the huge metropolitan daily with a staff of thousands and a daily circulation of more than 1 million copies.

No matter what their circumstances, all newspapers are alike in the sense that they are made of type, ink, and newsprint. They exist to inform and influence the communities in which they are published, and the men and women who produce them share a common urge to get the news and advertising into print. Into the pages of every newspaper goes an essential but intangible extra ingredient, the minds and spirits of those who make it.

Newspaper work is based upon a firmly disciplined routine, because "getting the paper out" on time is paramount, and this can be done only if a definite work pattern exists in all departments. Working on a newspaper is an open invitation to create ideas. The newspaper people who succeed best are those who handle the necessary routine meticulously and bring to their jobs an extra spark of creative thinking. Those for whom the atmosphere and work lose their excitement frequently move on to other media or occupations.

As one of the mass communications media, the contemporary newspaper has three fundamental functions and several secondary ones. The fundamental ones are (1) to inform readers objectively about what is happening in the community, country, and world; (2) to comment on the news in order to bring these developments into focus; and (3) to provide the means whereby persons with goods and services to sell can advertise their wares. The newspaper's secondary roles are (1) to campaign for desirable civic projects and to help eliminate undesirable conditions; (2) to give readers a portion of entertainment through such devices as comic strips, cartoons, and special features; and (3) to serve readers as a friendly counselor, information bureau, and champion of their rights.

When a newspaper performs all or most of these tasks well, it becomes an integral part of community life. Television "sells" its news by developing on-the-air personalities whose mannerisms and aura at times have more impact on the viewer than the content of the news they are delivering. Newspapers lack that personality advantage; a familiar by-line on a story carries the impress of authoritative knowledge to the steady reader but cannot match the congenial smile or the cynically lifted eyebrow of the TV news commentator. Therefore the newspaper must build a personality of a different sort based upon its complete contents and tailored to its audience. It may be brisk, breezy, and compact like the New York *Daily News,* whose readers often digest its contents while standing in a subway train; gray and consciously stodgy in appearance and full of long foreign and national stories like the New York *Times,* which aims to create an image of significance and permanence; or, in the case of a newspaper in a smaller city, where many residents know each other, filled with local stories on minor police actions, meetings of organizations, Eagle Scout awards, and local civic disputes, along with an adequate number of major national and foreign stories. The job of the editor is to give a particular audience what it wants and needs.

The printed word has a lasting power and precision beyond that of the spoken word or the visual image, although it has less ability to startle and shock. Readers can refer to it again and again. Stories may be clipped and saved by readers for many years and be readily examined in the newspaper's files decades later. This fact increases the reporter's feeling of writing history. It contributes to the newspaper's position as a stabilizing, continuing force in the community.

In the self-examination by the newspaper industry brought about by the challenge of television, editors as a group came to realize that too often the history they were recording was only the surface manifestation of the day's events—there was too much emphasis on who said this or did that, and not enough attention to why this had happened. This has led to an upsurge in *investigative reporting,* frequently by teams of reporters, in which the newspapers try to report frankly how our complex society is actually working. Reporters are given time to probe into such situations as conditions inside mental hospitals and nursing homes, the devious and sometimes illegal deals between political leaders and contractors, and the manner in which charitable institutions actually spend the money they receive from kindhearted donors. The possibilities are almost endless, if an editor is sufficiently curious and has a staff large and aggressive enough to carry out instructions for this type of story.

How far should reporters go in practicing deception to obtain stories? That question is sharply debated among editors. Some contend that having a reporter pose as a nurse or mechanic to gain access to a story is unethical. They point out that editors are angry when policemen pose as reporters. How then, they ask, can reporters pose as ambulance drivers to expose collusion between the police and private ambulance firms? Other editors dismiss this concern as unnecessarily self-righteous, arguing that when the public good is served by such reportorial deception, that takes precedence. More intense examination of reportorial ethics goes on today than ever before. (See Chapter 24 for a discussion of media ethics.)

Newspapers have changed dramatically in appearance during the past quarter century. Today only a few retain the format of eight narrow columns to a page, which creates a vertical stripe effect. Instead, most use six wider columns arranged in modular style on the page or spread horizontally under headlines running several columns wide. Graphics experts are experimenting with other combinations of type, pictures, and color, seeking ways to make pages more eye-catching without complicating production methods so much that deadlines cannot be met (see Chapter 16).

GENERAL ORGANIZATION OF NEWSPAPERS

No matter what their size, from small weeklies to metropolitan dailies, newspapers have a common organization. Each has five major departments: *editorial,* which gathers and prepares the news, entertainment, and opinion materials, both written and illustrated; *advertising,* which solicits and prepares the commercial messages addressed to readers; *production,* which turns the editorial material and advertisements into type and prints the newspapers; *circulation,* which sells and delivers the newspapers to the readers; and *management,* which oversees the entire operation.

The goal of a newspaper story is to present a report of an action in easily understood language that can be comprehended by a mass audience of different educational levels. Simplicity of writing is emphasized. If newspapers are to fill their role of communicating to the mass of the population, they cannot indulge in writing styles and terminology so involved that many readers cannot comprehend them. The best newspaper reporters are those who can accurately present complex situations in terms that are easily understood by the majority of their readers. Newspapers today put more emphasis on depth and less on excitement than in the past, a change that has opened new fields for the thoughtful, competent writer.

Newspaper advertising is divided into two types, *display* and *classified.* The former ranges from inconspicuous one-inch notices to multiple-page advertisements in which merchants and manufacturers proclaim their goods and services. Classified advertisements are the small-print, generally brief announcements packed closely together near the back of the paper; they deal with such diverse topics as help wanted, apartments for rent, used furniture and automobiles for sale, and personal notices. On almost all newspapers except the very smallest, display and classified advertising are handled by different staffs. Most newspapers receive about three-fourths of their income from advertising and one-fourth from circulation.

The staff setup of all newspapers is also basically the same, although naturally the larger the newspaper, the more complex its staff alignments. The top person is the publisher, who also may be the principal owner of the newspaper. On some papers the publisher's decisions on all matters are absolute; on others the publisher must follow policies set by group management or by the board of directors. The publisher's task is to set the newspaper's basic editorial and commercial policies and to see that they are carried out efficiently by the various department heads. On quite a few newspapers, especially smaller ones, the publisher is also the editor.

Usually a business manager or general manager under the publisher administers the company's business operations, which range all the way from obtaining newsprint to the purchasing of tickets as the newspaper's contribution to a community concert series. The heads of the advertising, circulation, and production departments answer to the publisher through the business manager, if there is one. But the editorial department, traditionally jealous of its independence to print the news without in theory being subject to commercial pressures, demands and generally gets a line of command direct to the publisher. The titles of executive editor and managing editor are most commonly used to designate heads of the news operations. The associate editor usually directs the newspaper's editorial, or opinion-making, function.

THE EVOLVING NEWSPAPER PATTERN

Switch to Morning Publication

The American newspaper industry consists of approximately 1660 daily newspapers and 7600 weekly newspapers, a total that fluctuates slightly from year to year. Despite concern about slow circulation growth, the newspaper industry is in a healthy and expanding condition. A slightly smaller number of daily newspapers are being published than at the end of World War II. Canada has 110 daily newspapers, including 10 in French, and about 850 weekly newspapers, of which about 150 in Quebec are in French.

Fewer than a third of the daily newspapers in the United States have a circulation above 20,000. About 115 of these exceed the 100,000 mark. Thus, while the greatest public attention is focused on huge metropolitan newspapers such as the New York *Times* and Chicago *Tribune,* their place in the total industry is relatively small.

If there is an average American daily (and the individualistic patterns of publishing make the description of a typical newspaper almost impossible), it has a

TEN LARGEST U.S. DAILY NEWSPAPERS

Newspaper	Circulation
Wall Street Journal (morning)	2,026,276
USA Today (morning)	1,311,792
New York *Daily News* (morning)	1,278,118
Los Angeles *Times* (morning)	1,117,952
New York *Times* (morning)	1,056,924
Washington *Post* (morning)	796,659
Chicago *Tribune* (morning)	758,464
New York *Post* (all day)	740,123
Detroit *News* (all day)	678,399
Detroit *Free Press* (morning)	639,720

SOURCE: Audit Bureau of Circulations report, March 31, 1987

circulation of about 20,000 copies and serves a city of about 30,000 in population and its surrounding trade area. A typical weekly has a circulation of about 4000 to 5000 copies in a small town and its surrounding countryside. Neither has direct newspaper competition in its own community.

Traditionally, evening newspapers have dominated the field. They still do numerically, more than 2 to 1 over morning newspapers, but a substantial and accelerating switch of papers into the morning field has occurred during the 1980s. Although outnumbered, morning papers have substantially more total circulation than evening papers. In cities where one ownership published both morning and evening papers, often the two have been combined into the morning paper. Also, in numerous instances a six-day evening paper has converted its weak Saturday afternoon edition into a Saturday morning enlarged weekend edition.

Changing American life habits are the principal reason for this trend. With so many women in the work force and away from home during the day, then busy with dinnertime work and television after they return home, their time available for reading has diminished. Television dominates the evening hours for many men, too. Surveys show that readers like to see the headlines and most urgent stories at breakfast time, perhaps saving more leisurely inside-page reading for later in the day. Since the P.M. papers often have been forced into earlier deadlines by problems of street traffic and production, some readers tend to regard them as "old news," repeating stories reported on television news programs the previous evening.

The shift to morning publication probably will continue. Eight of the ten largest-circulation American dailies are morning publications, and two are 24-hour papers. Evening papers retain a strong numerical superiority because most small-city papers cling to the traditional afternoon printing time.

The most striking manifestation of the changing American newspaper pattern has been in the great cities of the northeastern section of the country. One famous newspaper after another has been forced to quit publication, leading poorly informed observers to the false conclusion that the American newspaper industry was declining. What actually has happened is that newspapers have been heavily affected by altered patterns of American life. Earlier in the century metropolitan populations lived close to the center of the city, so the newspaper's newsgathering, circulation, and advertising efforts were concentrated near that center. As population spread to the suburbs, the problems of distribution grew, especially for evening papers, because of heavy traffic. Suburbanites developed loyalties to their outlying communities, which had their own governments, places of employment, and branches of downtown stores. Many people no longer commuted downtown. Higher purchasing power was concentrated around the fringes of the city, not in the core area.

Quickly, suburban daily newspapers in the largest metropolitan areas were created to serve this new audience. Some were longtime weeklies that went daily. Others were entirely new. Their growth has been one of the major publishing success stories of the last quarter-century. Between 1950 and 1968, the number of metropolitan newspapers in New York was reduced from eight to three; in Los Angeles, from five to two; and in Boston, from seven to four. The local newspaper's greatest advantage over larger "invaders" from out of town, and over local television and radio news broadcasts, is its more detailed presentation of hometown news. Many readers regard this as the most important ingredient in their newspaper.

A National Newspaper: USA Today

Until the arrival of satellite transmission, publication of a general interest national daily newspaper—one that is delivered simultaneously in all portions of the United States—was physically and financially impractical.

Then, in 1982, the Gannett Company launched precisely that kind of newspaper, *USA Today.* Assembled at a plant near Washington, D.C., Monday through Friday, the contents of *USA Today* are sent by satellite to plants around the country and abroad for printing and distribution. By the end of its third year, *USA Today* reported net paid circulation of about 1.1 million and availability in more than 2000 towns and cities nationwide. The newspaper lost heavily during its early phases, perhaps as much as $70 million in its first year, and drained talent away from other Gannett newspaper staffs. However, Allen H. Neuharth, chairman and president of the company, said that *USA Today* might be profitable in 1988.

Whether or not *USA Today* succeeds financially, its impact on American newspaper publishing has been intense. Abundant use of color and graphics, emphasis on brevity with short main stories and numerous capsulized summaries, unusually detailed and up-to-the-minute sports pages, a distinctive editorial opinion policy, and a full-color weather page are among its most conspicuous features. Photographers are part of the graphics art team that makes the paper stimulating in appearance. The paper is edited for an audience accustomed to the headline techniques, color, and brevity of television news stories. Almost immediately, editors of other newspapers began to imitate its color charts, weather layout, and other features.

Some critics called *USA Today* shallow and flimsy, with more flash than substance, and doubted that it would find a sufficiently large permanent audience. Its publishers and admirers asserted that it would change the nature of American newspapers because it was in tune with the times and would prove to be a major success, reaching a mobile audience with bulk distribution in hotels and on airlines.

Using satellite techniques, a few other American newspapers are distributed nationally on day of publication, but they are designed for more specialized audiences. The *Wall Street Journal,* with circulation of 2,026,276, is printed at 17 plants nationwide. The New York *Times* national edition is produced similarly in eight plants, appealing to those who desire detailed national and world news. The quiet, influential *Christian Science Monitor* also has nationwide distribution. The Washington *Post* distributes a weekly edition nationwide.

What Do Readers Want?

Industry leaders awakened during the 1970s to the disturbing fact that fewer Americans were purchasing newspapers than in the past. Between 1969 and 1975,

USA Today, *the first national general interest newspaper, is aimed at readers who are accustomed to television news. It emphasizes brevity in news stories, color, and graphics. (© 1986, USA TODAY; used with permission)*

total daily newspaper circulation declined from 62,059,589 to 60,655,431. Population rose during those years; obviously newspapers were not keeping pace with national growth. Why? The problem was intense for newspapers in large cities, with mobile population.

Editors and publishers subjected their newspapers to searching examination. They sought through polls, seminars, in-depth interviewing, and other forms of public contact to discover what contemporary Americans wanted in their newspapers and how to satisfy those desires. Editors were shocked to learn that large segments of the American population, especially young adults and low-income minority groups, felt little or no need for newspapers in their daily lives. Many claimed they received all the news they wanted from television. The "turned off" readers called newspapers dull. The age group from 21 to 35 was especially weak in newspaper readership and became a target for reawakened editors.

Equally disturbing to industry leaders was evidence that many Americans distrusted newspapers. Surveys disclosed a lack of credibility in what newspapers published and a dislike, sometimes vehement, of the ways they gathered and printed the news. Critics accused newspapers of being arrogant, inaccurate, unfair, slanted, and heartless in invading the privacy of individuals.

In a multitude of studies, speeches, and discussions, newspaper executives sought to determine how valid these criticisms were and what their publications could do to improve the situation.

Two companion studies in 1985, one by the American Society of Newspaper Editors and the other by the Associated Press Managing Editors Association, disclosed these composite findings:

- The public has a lower regard for the credibility of newspapers than the journalists who produce them do.
- While 66 percent of journalists perceived their newspapers as being accurate, only 49 percent of the public did so.
- Eighty-five percent of journalists perceived their newspapers as being objective, while only 63 percent of the public believed this.
- Sixty-three percent of the public—nearly two thirds—believed that newspapers took advantage of ordinary people, and 54 percent of journalists shared this view.

Although some newspaper officials contended that the credibility issue was exaggerated, it was clear that newspapers had much work to do in order to improve the public's opinion of their methods (see Chapter 22).

In order to reach new readers, the newspapers made changes in their format and content: magazinelike graphics to brighten pages and tell stories in visual form; more stories about daily living problems and styles; greater emphasis on personalities in the news; adoption of concise news summaries, often on the front page, to meet the challenge of television's brief news coverage, for persons who thought they didn't have time to read; more investigative reporting and analysis. In sum, they created briefer, brighter, and more searching newspapers.

Newspapers Redesigned

Convinced by research that a newspaper's readership consists of an accumulation of small audiences with special interests, rather than a homogeneous mass population, some publishers redesigned their papers to attract these groups. Their idea was that while all readers share an interest in general news developments, each audience segment desires something more from the newspaper. Demographic information gathered through market research identified groups by income, age, residential area, and type of background. To please them, these newspapers now produce enlarged special sections, usually weekly, focused on a field of interest such as entertainment, sports, contemporary living styles, and finance. Sections covering specific topics—sports cars or camping, for example—are included at intervals. Some papers produce sections of localized news for specific neighborhoods. Using computerized circulation lists, newspapers have experimented with delivering special sections only to those readers who desire them. Intensive research on methods of improving content and circulation was conducted by the National Readership Council, supported by leading industry associations.

Critics have argued that at times newspapers have gone too far in this change of direction, becoming soft in content and neglecting the hard news that traditionally is the primary function of a daily newspaper. They have urged, instead, greater attention to accuracy and thoroughness of basic news coverage. By the late 1980s, American newspapers as a whole had become more attractive and more relevant to changing social patterns. Their circulation was rebounding, too; not yet up to the pace of population growth, but advancing. Editors were doing a better job of producing newspapers with appeal to all ages and interest groups, but still had much to learn about what the American public wants.

Electronic News Delivery

Newspapers may face further changes in content as their proprietors learn more about electronic news delivery techniques.

Predictions heard a few years ago that the electronic newspaper—that is, news delivered into the home on the family television screen—would replace the traditional newsprint form have largely been withdrawn. The public apparently prefers to hold a newspaper in its hands.

Some newspapers have leased cable TV channels and presented news programs, as well as classified advertising. These programs, however, supplement the daily newspaper rather than replace it. The content of certain major newspapers is available to operators of computers through numerous commercial databases. By using a telephone hookup, the operator can summon news reports onto the computer screen, along with a vast amount of specialized information not usually included in newspapers. The popularity of personal computers has stimulated use of databases.

OPPORTUNITIES IN NEWSPAPER WORK

Not so many years ago, the newsroom was a white, male haven. The occasional woman who crashed the reporting staff was assigned to emotional feature stories and was dubbed a "sob sister." The only other women on the editorial department payroll worked in the women's department, generally known as "society" or more casually as "sock," where they wrote wedding stories and club reports. The chances of a black or other minority member getting a job on the news staff of a newspaper were minimal.

Newsrooms were not much different in this respect from many other business operations during the pre–World War II era. A change in attitude became apparent after the war, influenced by the social upheaval accompanying that conflict. A few black reporters began to appear on metropolitan news staffs. Young women hired as city room office "boys" during the wartime manpower shortage in some cases were able, through aggressiveness and demonstrated ability, to take over reporter jobs.

Change came slowly, nevertheless. Only in the late 1960s and early 1970s did women begin to get equal treatment in hiring. Now, in most newspaper organizations they are given equal consideration to male candidates as job openings arise. Long-overdue changes in social attitudes plus the competent performance of those hired have brought this about, and newspapers are much better for it.

The complaint remains, as discussed in Chapter 24, that few women hold high editorial posts on newspapers, that they still are regarded as second-line staff members. Although women are still largely not found in decision-making editorial positions, the situation is changing rapidly. Time will bring about the cure. In most cases they have been held back not by prejudice, but by seniority and the well-earned claim of longer-experienced male staff members to climb up the ladder as openings occur. Today women hold city editorships and managing editorships in growing numbers. Some are publishers. The American Newspaper Publishers Association reported in 1986 that the total of 185,000 women working for newspapers constituted more than 40 percent of the work force. Their numbers will increase; two-thirds of journalism school graduates in 1986 were women.

Progress of blacks and other minorities in newsrooms, unfortunately, has been much slower, in part because relatively few of them have graduated from journalism schools or come out of college with other suitable degrees and shown an interest in newspaper work. Despite extensive efforts by newspaper trade organizations to recruit and train them, a survey by the American Society of Newspaper Editors in 1987 showed only 3600 minority journalists in newsrooms, out of 54,700 newsroom personnel. Minorities form 6.56 percent of all newspaper journalists. Because of the demand, able young black and other minority journalists tend to gravitate to higher-paying metropolitan newspapers faster than their white counterparts (see Chapter 24).

Many news jobs open up on American newspapers each year. With about 9400 dailies and weeklies in operation, the turnover in personnel is extensive. After a surge of interest in newspaper journalism among young people during the preceding decade, college enrollments in the field declined in the 1980s. As a result, small and medium-sized dailies and weeklies in many parts of the country have been competing vigorously to fill vacancies. Major dailies generally draw their recruits from smaller papers. A college journalism degree is a prerequisite for most jobs. Employers especially seek young people with a liberal stock of knowledge, a variety of interests, and the ability to spell and write grammatical English (see Chapter 20).

A growing number of daily newspapers have intern programs for college undergraduates with journalistic ambitions, mostly during summer vacation periods but also at other times of the year. In obtaining jobs upon graduation, students who have served internships have a definite advantage over those who have not. Initial contacts should be made months before the internships will be open.

News and Editorial

There are two main divisions of newsroom work—*reporting,* which includes gathering and writing news and feature stories and the taking of news and feature photographs, and *desk work,* which is the selection and preparation for printing of the written material and photographs submitted by reporters, photographers, news services, and syndicates. Those who do the desk work are the editors.

This distinction between the newsgatherers and the news processors is quite sharp on large daily newspapers. Some editors will go a year or more without writing a single news story, and metropolitan reporters have nothing to do with the selection of a headline or page placement of the stories they write. On smaller papers an editorial staff member may spend part of the day as a reporter, photographer, and writer and the other part in selecting and processing the news for publication.

Some men and women find their greatest satisfaction in being reporters all their lives—probing for information, being close to events as they happen, and mingling with the people who make the news. Theirs is the most exciting part of newspaper work when big stories are breaking, and they are the people the public knows. Few outsiders have any knowledge of the inside office workers who really put the paper together.

The fact remains, however, that a reporter is rarely promoted directly to a high editorial place on a large or medium-sized daily. The top jobs go to those who have had desk experience. They are the organizers, the planners, and they also have demonstrated a keen sense of news value and judgment. By the same token, few

The busy newsroom of a daily newspaper. The man at right front is writing a story on a video display terminal. (Reprinted by permission from Presstime, *the journal of the American Newspaper Publishers Association)*

desk workers are truly successful unless they have had a thorough grounding in reporting.

A beginner may be a city hall beat reporter for a small daily or the telegraph editor, handling the wire and writing headlines. Sticking to the first choice could lead eventually to a metropolitan reporting staff; to the latter, to a large paper's copy desk. Or, in either capacity, the newcomer may remain with the small daily and soon rise to editorial management status.

On most daily newspapers there are specialized editing-reporting jobs in which the editorial worker gathers news and also helps to prepare it for print. The sports, business, entertainment, and lifestyle pages fall into this category. Varied opportunities for specialization may arise in one of the broader general news areas: politics, science, labor, religion, education, urban and racial problems, space and aviation, social work, and public health.

A very important area of work is the editorial page. Editorial page staffs run to eight or ten members on metropolitan papers that pride themselves on the quality of their opinion offerings. The editorial page director coordinates their work and consults with the publisher on major policy decisions. At the smaller daily level there may be only one editorial writer. Most weekly newspaper editors write editorial columns or more informal "personal columns."

Opportunities to advance on an editorial staff come in many forms. As a rule, when an important vacancy occurs, management chooses for promotion to a top position a man or woman with all-around experience and a record of dependability, good judgment under pressure, and creative thinking.

Photography

The newspaper photographer fills a large and growing role on the staff of every daily newspaper, large or small, as the field of photojournalism expands. On a newspaper the photographer's primary task is to record in a single picture or a sequence, rapidly and accurately, the news and feature developments of the day that lend themselves to pictorial treatment. The photographer may take pictures for the news, sports, life style and entertainment pages, as well as for the promotion and advertising departments, so versatility is important. On large staffs employing 20 or more photographers and technicians, individuals may develop specialties and work primarily in these fields. Reporters on small newspapers frequently take the pictures themselves.

Planning photographic coverage on good newspaper staffs is as meticulous as the arrangement of coverage by reporters. Large newspapers have photo editors who specialize in this work. Memorable newsphotos usually are the result of having a photographer assigned to the right place at the proper time, plus the photographer's instinct for the climactic moment in a news situation and technical ability to take an effective picture when that moment comes.

Newspaper photography has advanced far from the days when an aggressive copyboy of limited education could be taught the rudiments of a camera and turned loose as an ambulance-chasing photographer. Today many news photographers have college educations or have attended professional photography schools.

Newspaper photographers receive the same salaries as reporters under Newspaper Guild pay scales. They frequently supplement their salary with overtime assignments and with after-hour jobs such as photographing weddings. Freelance photographers, not on the newspaper payroll, are paid for newsworthy pictures that they submit for publication (see Chapter 16).

THE BUSINESS SIDE OF NEWSPAPERS

Although the news department is the most publicized part of a newspaper, it is only one portion of a publication's complex organization. Sale and preparation of advertising, efficient mechanical production, and the sale and reliable delivery of the newspaper copies are essential for success. Revenue from advertising and circulation sales must surpass the cost of production if a newspaper is to survive.

The task of overseeing the departments, coordinating their work, stimulating the generation of revenue, and setting goals falls upon management. In earlier times when competition from other media was less intense and operating costs lower, newspapers often succeeded despite inefficient management because readers liked their editorial and advertising content. That has changed. Many of the newspapers that failed in recent years, suffering from poor management, couldn't survive when the pinch came.

Management is recognized today as a critically important field, requiring across-the-board knowledge of all departments as well as, in many cases, specialized training in one. The corporate groups that now own a large majority of newspapers have created a professional class of media managers who frequently are moved from one member newspaper to another to solve problems. Below are some of the areas they examine.

Advertising

The advertising department is one of the most attractive for sales-minded persons. A good newspaper space salesperson must be much more than a glib talker. The advertising representative must be able to supply the potential advertiser with abundant and accurate figures about the paper's circulation pattern and totals, the advertising rates, and the kind of merchandising support the advertiser will receive. Knowledge of at least the rudiments of layout and artwork is important. In addition, the representative should be enthusiastic and able to give the merchant ideas about how best to use an advertising budget. Selling newspaper advertising requires the art of persuasion, a briefcase well loaded with facts and ideas (about competing media as well), and a strong personal belief that newspaper space will move merchandise off the merchant's shelves.

Advertising work for weeklies and small dailies is an excellent training ground. Some recent college graduates become advertising managers of weeklies, handling all types of business for their papers from classified ads to major local accounts. The same sort of opportunities for diversified experience come on small dailies, although as they increase in circulation the dailies tend to specialize their advertising staff functions. On smaller papers the advertising representative is likely to be copywriter as well; on larger dailies there are positions for copywriting specialists and artists.

Many advertising careers begin in the classified department of larger newspapers, where the newcomer deals with many small accounts in a variety of fields. A certain amount of classified advertising comes in voluntarily, but most of it must be solicited. Classified is sold on a day-to-day basis with deadlines only a few hours before publication. As on a reporter's beat, sales representatives have territories and detailed lists of accounts to cover.

Classified advertising is closer to the people than any other type. A well-written three-line ad offering a desirable item for sale at a reduced price may cause the private advertiser's phone to ring dozens of times within a few hours after the paper appears. A good classified copywriter seeks to learn the tricks of concise, alluring wording. Readership tests show that classified sections are among the best-read in a newspaper.

The young sales representative may advance into the local display department, and later perhaps into the smaller and more select national (or general) department. National advertising department members work with manufacturers and distributors of brand-name products, often weeks in advance of publication. Schedules are sold in multiple insertions, sometimes in color. A newspaper's national sales staff works in conjunction with its national newspaper representative organization, which solicits advertising for it in other cities.

Circulation

The circulation department offers some opportunities for college-trained individuals with organizing ability, promotional ideas, and a liking for detail. A supervisor who has a knack for working with carriers, much like a high school coach, is in demand. Although the top circulation jobs on large newspapers carry high salaries, the number of jobs available in this department for college-trained persons is somewhat less than in editorial and advertising.

Production

In the production department, which puts the words into type and prints the newspaper, the work is mechanical in nature, requiring technical skill. Most employees in the department work their way up through apprenticeship programs to journeyman status, and perhaps into supervisory positions. Graduate engineers and those with advanced training in electronics are becoming more frequent in production work (see Chapter 1).

Cost control is extremely important in newspaper production, just as in any manufacturing process. Elaborate accounting sheets are kept showing the cost of setting a column of type, making up a page, printing 1000 papers, increasing the size of an edition by two pages, working a press crew overtime because of a missed deadline, and other expenses. All these costs are weighed carefully in setting the newspaper's advertising rates. The publisher who pegs space rates too low will attract additional advertising but will lose money by doing so.

On larger newspapers several supplementary departments support the work of those directly involved in producing the paper. Chief among them are promotion and public relations, personnel, research, and data processing. Some newspapers put out their own institutional publications for employees.

Many editorial people on large newspaper staffs, it might be added, know little and care less about such production and cost problems. They regard the business aspects of publishing as something remote and of scant concern to them. This is unfortunate, especially if they have thoughts of striking off on their own some day on the small weekly they dream about.

SALARIES

Newspaper salaries, although not at the top of the list, compare favorably on large papers with those in other businesses and professions that require a good education and creative thinking. Except on many smaller papers, they have improved sharply during the past 30 years. The activities of the Newspaper Guild have been an important factor in this improvement. Organized in 1933 during the Depression when editorial salaries in particular were low, the guild has campaigned as an organized labor union for higher wages and more favorable working conditions. It has called strikes against newspapers to enforce its demands. A rise in daily newspaper salaries was inevitable, even without the existence of the guild, or the industry could not have held its workers as economic conditions improved. But the activities of the guild speeded the process.

Today the guild has 20,000 members, mainly on larger papers. Its contracts with management cover salaries, vacations, severance pay, and working conditions. The salary levels are minimums, covering all people in the categories specified. Some guild contracts cover just editorial departments; others, all nonprinting employees. The basic contract provides a graduated pay scale, with annual steps from the starting minimum through five or seven years to a top minimum. Salary advancement faster than, and beyond the top of, guild scales is by individual negotiation with management. Salaries on newspapers without guild contracts usually are in line with guild papers of similar circulation.

Although starting salaries at newspapers are less attractive than those in some other fields, the pay increases quite rapidly with experience. The larger the newspaper, the greater the salary. A survey by the American Society of Newspaper Editors in 1986 showed annual salaries for beginning reporters ranging from $10,816 at very small dailies to $22,894 at papers over 250,000 circulation. Average annual salary for top editors ranged from $22,366 at papers with less than 5,000 circulation to $165,539 for papers above 250,000 circulation. Higher starting salaries are urged by some newspaper industry leaders in order to attract the best beginners possible.

Veteran reporters on major newspapers receive more than $30,000 a year, and in New York the top minimum salary for the most highly experienced reporters under the Newspaper Guild contract reached $48,316 in 1986.

Newspaper salaries in general are comparable to those paid in broadcasting, (except for those of star television performers), but lower than those on large magazines and in public relations. This fact often attracts the young graduate directly into the public relations field. Many newspaper editors contend, however, that a few years of the discipline and challenging experiences of news reporting will generally make the person more effective in other fields later.

The guild salaries are for 37- to 40-hour weeks, for average people. Superior people get above-minimum salaries. But as in all professions, they must expect to work more than a mere 40-hour week to get extra pay. Any newspaper person can add income by becoming a specialist, or doing outside writing and speaking so long as this work does not conflict with the person's basic employment. Another route to the top pay levels is through skilled desk work, where a pronounced shortage of qualified personnel has existed in recent years, particularly since the introduction of video display terminals.

Although many men and women spend their entire careers in the newspaper business, others move on into related fields. Newspapers are a training ground for workers in all mass communications media. (A discussion of employment in the media for minorities and women appears in Chapter 24.)

THE PRODUCTION PROCESS

As described in Chapter 1, development of electronic typesetting has greatly simplified and accelerated the process of getting a writer's words onto newsprint. Electronic typesetting enables a news story typed into a video display terminal by a reporter to move all the way to the printing press without being retyped at any point while being edited and corrected, as was necessary under the old pencil-and-

Reporter receiving a story by telephone types it directly into a video display terminal, from which it may be sent into the electronic typesetting system or placed in computer storage for later call-up. (Reprinted by permission from *Presstime,* the journal of the American Newspaper Publishers Association)

paper method. The story goes into a central computer, from which the city desk and the copy desk editors call it up on their screens for review.

When a newspaper computer sends local stories to a news service computer for possible regional or national distribution, or to another computer elsewhere, these transmissions are called *electronic carbons*.

The phototypesetting machine contains a whirling disk of type letters in different faces or a cathode ray tube device. The flowing electronic commands of the computer cause the phototypesetter to record the indicated letters in sequence on fast film; this film produces a positive print of the words on a sheet of coated paper that emerges from the darkroom through a slot, ready to be pasted up in page form. This is called *cold type.* The type preparation process will be speeded up even more when pagination, described in Chapter 1, comes into general use. Some newspapers have pagination systems in operation, but further refinement of the electronic machinery must occur before their use becomes general.

Another electronic typesetting machine, sometimes used in conjunction with the VDT, is the *optical character recognition* device, or OCR. The reporter types a story on an electric typewriter using hard white paper. The writer and the editor

A system called pagination, just coming into general use, enables an editor to lay out a news page electronically, speeding up production and reducing the role of the composing room. Robin Fulton-Manly of the Pasadena, California, Star-News, seated at a makeup station, designs a news page with graphics. (Reprinted by permission from Presstime, the journal of the American Newspaper Publishers Association)

mark corrections on the story pages with a light blue felt-tipped pen to which the electronic eye is "blind" and strike out unwanted words with a heavy black pen. An operator types in the corrected words in certain positions under the original typed line. The copy sheet is placed face down into the OCR, or scanner, which resembles an office copying machine. A small electronic "reader" inside scans the copy line for line, inserting the corrections as marked, at tremendous speed. The output can be fed directly into a phototypesetting machine or into the computer storage bank for later callup, or produced as punched tape that can be placed physically into the phototypesetter at a desired time.

An important result of the typesetting revolution has been to break down the ancient barriers between the composing and news rooms. Control of typesetting has been largely moved "up front" into the hands of the editors, away from the composing room. The further the revolution proceeds, the smaller the role of the composing room becomes. The traditional proofreader may disappear, except for small special tasks. Weakened by these changes, the 40,000-member, 134-year-old International Typographical Union merged in 1986 with the Communication Workers of America, now known as the Printing, Publishing and Media Workers division of the organization.

In the pressroom, traditional printing methods have been almost entirely replaced by offset printing. By the mid-1980s, 1400 of the approximately 1675 daily newspapers had adopted offset in place of the old system, in which type contained on a semicircular revolving plate is inked and makes direct contact with the newsprint.

Offset printing is based on lithography, an older process in which printing was done from a smooth flat surface of stone. In surface printing the image is placed on the stone by a greasy substance that has an affinity for ink. The nonprinting surface is covered with a thin film of water that repels the ink. Thus only the image is printed on paper when pressure is applied. The image is transferred from the printing plate cylinder to a rubber blanket attached to a second cylinder. It is then transferred to the paper, which is carried by a third impression cylinder (Figure 6.1). Development of offset presses capable of printing on a continuous web of paper was a major step in adapting this process to newspaper printing. Newspapers printed by offset are noted for their excellent photographic reproduction and strong, solid black tones.

Competing with offset printing is another method recently adapted for newspa-

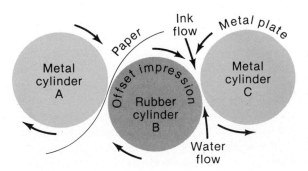

FIGURE 6.1
How offset printing works. The impression on the plate affixed to cylinder C is "offset" onto rubber cylinder B, then printed on paper passing between cylinder B and cylinder A. Because of the lack of wear on a metal plate, thousands of additional pages may be printed, and more clearly, with this method.

per work called *flexography,* long used in certain kinds of commercial printing. Flexography uses water-based ink rather than the traditional oil-based variety. Since this dries quickly, the vexing problem of ink ruboff onto readers' hands is virtually eliminated.

After several years of experimental work, most of the technical problems involved in adapting flexography to newspapers have been solved and its use by newspapers is growing. Flexography is economical because it reduces paper waste and power consumption, as well as print shop noise levels.

THE WEEKLY NEWSPAPER

A Midwestern weekly newspaper editor recently told a story about the pharmacist in his small county seat city who gave the wrong dosage for a prescription. The boy to whom the medicine was given died, and charges of negligence were brought against the druggist. His attorney obtained a change of venue to have the case tried in another county, so the trial publicity would not be seen in detail locally and damage the druggist's reputation. This offended the editor's principles of reporting the news, so although the extra expense strained his limited budget, he sent a reporter to the other county and covered the trial in detail. The druggist lived across the street from the editor. They saw each other every day. The druggist escaped without imprisonment, but because of the editor's action he still refused to speak to him more than two years after the trial.

This incident illustrates an essential point about weekly journalism—its intimacy. The people about whom the editor writes are neighbors, social acquaintances, and fellow members of churches and clubs. They pressure the publisher and editor of the weekly newspaper to conform, to shush up unpleasant news. Although less subject to time pressures than editors on daily newspapers, weekly editors have special problems. A large daily would not publish reviews of high school plays; the weekly is expected to do so, and if the review speaks ill of the performance, the editor can expect phone calls and visits from the actors' parents, accusing the newspaper of painting a false picture of the town's teenagers.

In thousands of American towns, the weekly newspaper is at the core of community life. It is the chief source of information about the activities of individuals and organizations, and the merchants look to its advertising columns as a weekly tool for selling goods. In the files of a small-town weekly are recorded the vital statistics of the town's life—the births and deaths, marriages, social events, and tragedies, and the ludicrous moments that give life zest. Even when it is overshadowed by a big-city daily a few miles away, the weekly newspaper often has a secure place in the heart of its community and can continue to thrive. The chief stock in trade it has to offer is names—subscribers reading about their neighbors and about themselves. The larger the newspaper, the less impact the names in news stories have on readers because they do not know all the people mentioned. This personal link is an advantage the community weekly newspaper has over its larger, more sophisticated city cousin.

The weekly newspaper illustrates editing and publishing in its simplest form, although anyone who believes that putting out a weekly is easy has been badly misled. All the jobs involved in any newspaper must be done: getting news and editing it, selling advertising, handling circulation, and seeing to it that the paper is printed on time. On a weekly everything is done by a handful of workers. The 40-hour week is only a dream to the editors and publishers of weekly newspapers. After the day's work at the office is finished, the weekly editor covers civic meetings, attends social functions in the hope of getting news, and listens to the complaints of fellow townspeople. Weekly newspaper publishing is a risky enterprise for a person who thinks only in editorial terms; unless the publisher quickly learns the business tricks of obtaining revenue from advertising and circulation, the paper won't live long.

The development of offset printing has changed life on weekly newspapers. In earlier days most were printed in the newspapers' own small hot metal shops, on aged equipment and a flat-bed press of nineteenth-century vintage. The resulting newspaper was poorly printed, often with miserable reproduction of photographs. Today, most weeklies are produced by offset, either in their own plants if the paper is large enough to justify the investment, or in a central plant along with several other weeklies.

Most weekly newspapers carry a Thursday publication date, for a sound commercial reason. It is the day on which local merchants want to reach readers with news of their weekend sales. The grocery stores in particular key their merchandise pattern to their Thursday newspaper advertisements, offering special items on sale through Saturday or Sunday. Some weeklies appear on Wednesday if many of their merchants desire a longer sales span.

A look at the operation of a typical up-to-date weekly newspaper in a small city gives us a picture of what this kind of newspaper life is like. The paper has been in continuous publication, with some changes of name, since 1879. It is published in a city of slightly less than 5000 population whose economy is based on farming and small manufacturing. The newspaper's circulation is 2700, most of it within the radius of a few miles of its downtown office. Usually its edition is 16 pages, dropping occasionally to 12 or rising to 22. Six persons compose its staff: a general manager who handles business affairs, sells and lays out advertisements, and takes news pictures and prints them in the darkroom; an advertising manager; a general worker and runner who makes the trips to the printing plant; a bookkeeper; an all-around staff member who handles subscriptions, helps out at the front counter, writes the society news and a chitchat column, and lays out advertisements; and the editor. The manager specialized in graphics at a two-year college. The editor is a recent journalism school graduate.

.The range of editorial excellence among weekly newspapers is wide. Splendidly edited weeklies are to be found throughout the United States, along with others that barely qualify for the label "newspaper." Weeklies are rarely of the crusading type, again with outstanding exceptions. Most weekly editors see their role as that of printing constructive, orthodox news without dealing in what is often called sensationalism. In some cases the newspaper's profit margin is so thin that the publisher cannot risk irritating an important advertiser by printing something the person dislikes. Frequently a weekly newspaper, such as the one we have examined, has no editorial page at all. Without resorting to big-city street sensationalism, many weekly editors could serve their communities better if they dealt more bluntly with local problems, despite the pressures not to do so. The American weekly press as a whole is conformist and conservative.

THE DAILY NEWSPAPER

The great difference in operation between weekly and daily newspapers is the addition of the element of timeliness. The principle of "today's news today" dominates minds of all daily newspaper staff members. Because the process of assembling and printing the newspaper is done six or seven times a week, thinking must be accelerated.

Working on a daily does not necessarily make a reporter or an advertising solicitor a better worker, but the worker must be fast. Deadlines take on a fresh, compelling meaning. On a daily, if the copy deadline is 12:40 P.M., any stories sent to the composing room after that minute may cause a late press start. That in turn can mean missed bus connections and lost street sales for the circulation department.

Weekly cities sometimes are larger than small daily cities, and some weeklies have more circulation and advertising than small dailies. What, then, causes some towns to have daily newspapers and other larger ones to have weeklies? Essentially it is a matter of geography, supplemented at times by the commercial audacity of the publisher. When a good-sized town is close to a large city, competition from the big neighboring paper may make successful operation of a small daily financially impossible. Yet there is room for a weekly newspaper to present community news and advertising. A small daily in a relatively isolated region may operate at a profit, whereas the same paper would fail if published in the shadow of a large city.

The primary problem a daily newspaper publisher faces is that the cost of producing the paper is the same every day, regardless of how much or how little advertising each issue carries. A bulky paper produced one or two days a week cannot carry all the burden if the other issues have little advertising content. Most newspapers try to average better than a 50:50 ratio between the amount of editorial and advertising content, with the greater weight going to advertising— up to 65 percent or more on some days.

Small-City Dailies

A small daily is excellent training ground for all journalists; many who later attain fame have started on such publications. On the smallest dailies, those in the 5000 circulation range, staff members "double in brass" by doing a little bit of everything. The key newsroom figure on the very small daily is the managing editor, who typically has a college education and perhaps five years of newspaper experience. The work of managing editor, city editor, and copy desk person is now performed by a single person responsible for producing a newspaper that fluctuates in size from 8 to 16, or occasionally 20, pages a day. Typically, the staff under the managing editor includes one or two persons with some college education and some local workers who have been hired at some time to help out, shown sufficient talent to fill lesser jobs, and become permanent fixtures.

The advertising staff of a very small daily often consists of a business–advertising manager who handles most of the big accounts, another display advertising salesperson, a clerk–secretary, and a classified advertising manager.

With mechanical facilities limited, the flow of copy must be closely scheduled, giving the beginner a sense of urgency. The editorial newcomer learns to make do with the available time and equipment, to cover local stories, to observe the workings of a news service wire, to write headlines. Mistakes in stories are quickly brought home to the writer because of close business and social ties with the news sources. Also, the person breaking into the business has an opportunity to practice photography and to get a taste of photojournalism under realistic operating conditions. If a beginner has that extra spark of creative writing and imagination so sought after by newspapers of all sizes, it will shine forth more quickly on a small daily than almost anywhere else in journalism.

Filling the Paper

Perhaps you wonder how a five-person editorial staff can produce enough copy day after day to fill the newspaper. Where does this small staff in a little city find sufficient news and get it all written fast enough to make the daily deadline? The answer is, help from other sources of copy. Part of the allotted editorial space is filled with feature material purchased from newspaper syndicates, and part is filled with stories selected from the global news reports delivered by the AP or UPI. Photographs help, too, and also add to reader interest.

Using a 500-word story from the news service is quicker than writing a local story of the same length. Even the smallest daily needs to give its readers highlights of major world developments, but overdependence on news service copy diminishes the local newspaper's value to its readers. They would prefer to read well-developed local enterprise stories and interviews than second-rate news service stories.

As the circulation of a newspaper increases, so does the staff. With somewhat larger staffs, the tasks performed by the managing editor of the small daily are divided among several persons, and the functional organization that reaches its peak on the staff of a metropolitan newspaper begins to emerge.

The managing editor's primary role is to oversee all the operations. Under that person is a city editor, who directs the work of the local reporters and photographers, and a national editor, who selects and edits stories from the news services. As the staff grows, a copy desk is set up to handle the editing of copy and the writing of headlines. With specialists at work, the result is a better-edited newspaper.

Medium-Sized Dailies

The medium-sized daily—say one approaching the 50,000 circulation point that is sometimes used arbitrarily to mark the start of the big-city group—often reaches far beyond the city limits because its copies are distributed by truck, bus, mail, and even airplane to surrounding rural areas. A motorist driving along a country road can often judge the impact of the newspaper published in a nearby city by the number of brightly painted tubes nailed on posts outside farmhouses to receive delivery of the daily editions.

Papers of this size are financially strong enough to have editorial staffs of considerable scope, usually with persons of outstanding ability (Figure 6.2). Some may eventually move on to metropolitan papers; others prefer to spend their working lives in the congenial atmosphere of a medium-sized paper.

At first glance the medium-sized daily operating under the shadow of a metropolitan giant would appear at a severe disadvantage. Usually it cannot offer the bulk that American readers too often associate with a desirable product. In fact, frequently the result is just the opposite. The medium-sized daily prospers because it provides the reader with as much, or nearly as much, news service and feature material as desired, and in addition provides detailed news of the local community. Density of population in these fringe areas is sufficient to provide a strong circulation potential. The presence of branch outlets of major downtown stores offers large advertising sources. Metropolitan newspapers in some cities, notably Chicago, have sought to counteract this trend by operating community dailies of their own that concentrate on local news as supplements to their downtown general publications.

The standards of medium-sized dailies in content, policies, and personnel are frequently high. For a young reporter whose ultimate goal is metropolitan journalism, a period of work on a well-regarded medium-sized daily is an excellent recommendation.

Selling the Papers

When it comes to selling the product it has produced, the daily newspaper is unique. It may have millions of dollars of equipment and a staff of experienced professional men and women to create it—yet leave the delivery of its newspapers and much of the selling effort to boys and girls, many of them not yet in their teens.

Management experts consider this a crazy system, yet it works. Under this carrier system, a large majority of the daily papers sold in the United States reach their purchasers. Circulation managers have put computers to work in their offices to handle billing, maintain circulation lists, and speed up truck loading, but so far they have not found an electronic replacement for the carrier who brings the newspaper to the subscriber's door. Use of older people, often retirees, as carriers instead of boys and girls is a recent trend in numerous cities.

Only in very large cities with heavy commuter traffic on public transportation do street sales of papers have the importance they once did. The home delivery carrier collects weekly or monthly for the daily service. Copies of an edition sold on the street, including through vending machines, are called single-copy sales.

Most methods of selling a newspaper are based upon the principle of having the publishing company sell copies to a distributor or delivery agent at a wholesale price several cents below the announced price per copy. The agent, including the

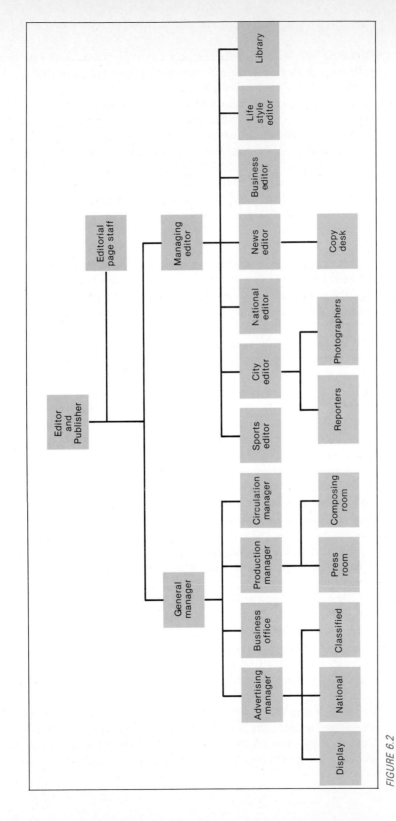

FIGURE 6.2

Typical organization of a medium-sized daily newspaper.

home delivery carrier, sells the papers to the public at the published price; the difference between wholesale and retail prices provides the agent's profits.

Single-copy street sales are affected by the weather, traffic, shopping conditions, holidays, and the nature of the main headline. These factors do not influence home delivery sale. Thus home delivery gives a newspaper assured income and a firm circulation figure to quote to advertisers.

Decades ago, in the fight to win circulation and outdo their rivals, some newspapers resorted to making exaggerated claims about their sales. Since advertising rates are based on circulation figures and on the cost of reaching each thousand readers, this led to many discrepancies and a chaotic situation in which honest publishers were placed at an unfair disadvantage by the unscrupulous operators. To correct this situation, the Audit Bureau of Circulations (ABC) was formed in 1914.

Newspapers that belong to the ABC, as most dailies do, submit detailed reports of their circulation every six months and open their books to a detailed examination by ABC auditors every year. Rigid rules are enforced. The organization puts limits on methods of solicitation, the number of low-cost subscriptions, bulk sales, and other devices used by publishers to inflate circulation figures. Types of circulation that fail to meet ABC standards are disallowed, and others of a somewhat transitory nature are appropriately indicated on the statements published by the ABC about each paper.

One widely used method of handling home delivery is known as the little merchant system. A carrier boy or girl has a route of several city blocks and is responsible for delivery of papers over that route, as well as for collecting the subscribers' fees. The more new subscribers or "starts" the carrier obtains, the more the carrier's monthly income will be. In effect, the carrier is an independent small merchant. Many newspapers encourage their subscribers to prepay for the service direct to the newspaper, which credits the payments to the carriers.

A swiftly growing phenomenon is the use of preprints. These are advertising sections printed in advance, separately from the basic newspaper, often by a commercial printer outside the newspaper plant. Properly labeled and dated, these are inserted into the newspaper. "On-line" stuffing machines insert the preprint sections into the regular papers as fast as they roll off the press. At some newspapers, insertion of the preprint sections is done by the carrier, who usually receives extra payment for the task. Seeking to increase its revenue, the U.S. Postal Service competes with newspapers as a distributor of preprints. When several advertising circulars are combined into a package distributed by third-class mail, the technique is called *marriage mail.*

Given proper adult supervision, the carrier system works for newspapers because the product is partly presold. An appetite for news exists, and in most communities the newspaper is a household word. The youthful appeal of the carrier is often the decisive sales factor. Some critics, however, contend that overheavy reliance on juvenile sales representatives has held newspapers back from reaching their full sales potential. Recognizing this, the American Newspaper Publishers Association engaged Massachusetts Institute of Technology management experts to study the newspaper distribution system in search of new ways to do the job. Among the facts uncovered was that it costs more than ten cents to get a copy of a daily newspaper into a reader's hand from the time it rolls off the press. The subscription price of a home-delivered copy is often little more than ten cents. This means that all other costs of writing and printing the paper, plus any profit, must come primarily from advertising sales.

THE METROPOLITAN PRESS

The newspaper as a mass communications medium reaches its highest development in our metropolitan centers. Here the publishers and editors think of readers in terms of millions. If we calculate three readers to each copy of a paper printed, which is a common rule of thumb, a big-city newspaper with a Sunday circulation of 1 million copies is read by 3 million persons. The impact of a single news story published in such an edition is easy to perceive.

Many newspaper workers look upon a metropolitan newspaper job as the goal of their careers, the sign of professional success. Ironically, quite a few big-city newspaper people in quiet talk sessions between editions speak longingly of escaping the scramble of metropolitan journalism for what they conceive of as a calmer, more orderly and satisfying life on smaller papers. Given an opportunity to break away from metropolitan work, however, many of this wistful brigade either refuse to do so or drift back to the so-called big time. The tempo, adventure, and prestige are alluring.

As stated earlier, metropolitan newspapers are the one group of the American press that has suffered severe attrition in the last quarter-century. Many of those whose names had been household words for decades have ceased publication. No matter how understandable the underlying social and economic reasons for these deaths, the passing of individual newspapers grieves both readers and staff members. A newspaper is such an ingrained part of public life that its sudden disappearance leaves a painful sense of loss.

Undoubtedly, the best-known newspaper in the country is the morning and Sunday New York *Times*. The *Times,* edited as the country's newspaper of record, publishes lengthy texts of official documents and exhaustive reports on national and international developments. Its circulation—1 million daily and 1.6 million Sunday—is nationwide. It appeals to readers who want an abundance of government and cultural news. The *Times* is not written for a general mass audience, however, and many Americans find it less interesting than their own more personalized local newspapers. Like all newspapers, the *Times* commits its share of errors and shadings of news coverage. Such missteps are not surprising in a publication of its size, but they underline the point that no newspaper is totally accurate, no matter how great its reputation. Primarily because of its work on the Watergate story, the Washington *Post* has also become a household word nationally.

Few if any stories in a metropolitan paper are read by all who purchase the paper. Every reader chooses selectively, picking a limited number of items from the huge tray of reading delicacies on the basis of personal needs, interests, and whims. Even so, every story in a metropolitan paper, no matter how insignificantly displayed, is seen by thousands of readers.

Thus the reporter's writing on a large newspaper is absorbed by a large number of persons. Yet the very size of the metropolitan region makes it impossible for the reporter to have direct contact with the audience. Except for personal acquaintances and the handful of readers who are either irate or thoughtful enough to report their reactions to an individual story, the metropolitan reporter has little opportunity to determine how stories are received. This is one of the most striking differences between big-city and small-town newspaper work.

The young person looking toward metropolitan papers as a place to work discovers two major differences from smaller cities: greater speed and greater specialization.

Most small dailies have one basic edition a day. Some may supplement this with a street-sale edition in which the front page is remade with larger, flashier headlines and late news bulletins for sale to casual purchasers. Or they may have an early, less complete edition for distribution in rural areas. In contrast, some metropolitan newspapers publish at least five editions within a period of eight hours. The edition schedule is an almost sacred document, whose stated deadlines govern the work of several hundred employees. If the press run of a big newspaper starts 15 minutes late, a bluntly spoken postmortem often results in the publisher's office.

A typical metropolitan deadline sheet has minute-by-minute rules stating when the final story must cross the city and copy desks and move to the production department; when the last photograph must leave the editorial art department; when the final page must move out of the composing room; and what minute the press must start. A smooth flow of pages through the assembly line is essential. In a huge newspaper plant, the production of a daily newspaper is a coordinated effort rarely exceeded in manufacturing.

The new reporter who obtains a metropolitan job right out of school usually considers himself or herself extremely lucky, as having gotten a big jump on classmates who go to work on weeklies or small dailies. Unfortunately, this is not necessarily the case. The big-city novice finds stimulation in associating with skilled veterans and watching exciting stories move through the production line. But too often the novice is shunted into a minor reporting job, like covering the overnight police beat, and is unable to get the all-around experience classmates are absorbing on smaller papers. Years may pass before the newcomer gets an opportunity to work on the copy desk. Seniority plays an important part in assignments on metropolitan staffs, and unless the young reporter is fortunate or shows exceptional talent for writing, advancement is slow.

Many editors and personnel managers of metropolitan papers advise beginners to work on small papers from three to five years before trying the metropolitan field. Often a young person coming to a metropolitan staff with a few years of small-city work will advance faster than one of similar age who has spent those same years on the big-city paper. The all-around experience of a smaller paper prepares the young reporter to fill many different jobs as they become available.

How a Metropolitan News Staff Functions

The key figure in the local newsgathering activities is the city editor, who has one or more assistants. Possibly 100 reporters, even more in a few cases, are deployed at the most productive news sources, held in reserve as general assignment reporters, or organized into investigative teams. The reporters placed on specific beats, such as the police department or city hall, are responsible for gathering all news that occurs in their territory and submitting it to the city desk. When time permits, they write the stories themselves. But the urgency of deadlines often makes this impossible, so they telephone their facts to a rewrite specialist. These writers are old hands, hardened under pressure, swift in their writing and quick at organizing a mass of facts into a story that reads smoothly and concisely.

When the story has been written, it is submitted to the city desk. There the city editor or an assistant reads it to catch errors, makes sure that it is easily understood, and finds "angles" that need further development. Writers and editors concentrate on finding a good "lead" for the story, an opening paragraph that summarizes the situation or entices the reader further into the article.

Much reporting is done by telephone. The reporter assigned to a story calls as many sources as possible to cross-check the facts for accuracy and to obtain the best-rounded story possible. Some metropolitan beat reporters, especially those covering the police department, may not write a story a week, even though they have worked on dozens by telephone.

While the city staff is gathering the local news, other groups are putting together other parts of the paper. News from the rest of the country and abroad arrives from the news services and special correspondents. This is edited and coordinated on the national desk.

City news and telegraph stories pass across the news desk, where they are weighed for importance and general interest. The news editor assigns them appropriate headline sizes and marks them into position on designated pages. The stories then pass to the copy desk for final editing. The language experts, supervised by the copy desk chief, give the stories a final polishing and write the headlines. From the copy desk the stories are released to the production department.

The sports department, the life style department, the financial editors, and other special groups are at work filling the pages allotted to them in a similar manner. Overseeing the entire operation is the managing editor; whose job on a metropolitan newspaper is one of the most demanding and responsible in all journalism.

SUNDAY PAPERS—WORLD'S LARGEST

By far the bulkiest newspapers published anywhere are the Sunday editions of American metropolitan newspapers. These mammoth publications wrapped in sections of color comics often contain more than 300 pages, nearly four pounds of reading matter covering everything from the current world crisis to interior decorating advice, theatrical notices, baseball scores, and weekly television logs.

In the United States there are about 20 such Sunday newspapers with 500,000 or more circulation, and several with more than 1 million. Even these mammoth figures are greatly exceeded by the circulation of several Sunday papers printed in London and distributed throughout the British Isles. They do not, however, have the advertising bulk of their American counterparts.

The Sunday paper is designed for family reading and is distinguished from the daily editions by two elements: a large feature package and bulk retail advertising. As a medium for late spot news, the Sunday paper is less important than the daily editions because less news occurs on Saturday (which it is covering) than on weekdays. Most newspapers print part of their Sunday editions well in advance because of the difficulty of printing such huge issues on the available press equipment on the publication date.

The Sunday editions of most newspapers have substantially higher circulation than the daily editions and sell at a price often more than double that of the daily paper. Publishing a Sunday paper is an expensive operation because of the heavy costs involved in buying the color comics and nationally syndicated magazine inserts and in preparing the abundance of locally created feature material. While the number of American daily newspapers has been shrinking slightly, the Sunday field has grown with a net increase of 223 Sunday papers from 1970 to 1986, for a total of 809.

News Services

and Syndicates

The World Gets the News

Howard Benedict of the Associated Press watched at the Cape Canaveral launch site, telephone in hand. He had an open line to the AP general desk in New York. As the space shuttle Challenger roared up from the earth, Benedict's bulletin reporting the takeoff was released onto AP circuits.

The time was 11:38 A.M.

Seconds later Benedict exclaimed, "Something is wrong. Something is terribly wrong!"

Challenger blew up as he spoke, killing the seven persons aboard. Benedict was stunned. Hardly pausing for breath he told New York:

> Space shuttle Challenger exploded today as it carried school teacher Christa McAuliffe and six crew members into space today.

The bulletin was timed off on AP circuits at 11:41 A.M. Two minutes later another bulletin cleared, reporting that the crew apparently had perished.

The news sped across the United States and to scores of foreign countries by satellite, arriving almost instantaneously.

Mobilizing its forces to cover many angles, by next morning the AP had delivered to newspapers 56 stories and full texts of statements about the disaster. Reporters for AP Network News dispatched on-the-scene reports to nearly 1000 stations.

That is what a global news service provides—swift, accurate reporting under pressure.

*M*uch of the material published in newspapers and included in radio and television newscasts does not originate from local staffs, but is created hundreds or thousands of miles away by global news services, supplementary news services, and syndicates that sell their material to clients. This chapter discusses how the news services operate and why they are so important to the flow of information.

The chapter describes how satellite dishes and computers are displacing the traditional teletype machine. By use of satellites, the news services can transmit a news bulletin from Rome to Tokyo via the United States in less than a minute. When a story is big enough, listeners to radio and television in countries around

Howard Benedict, Associated Press correspondent at the Kennedy Space Center, writes story about the explosion of the space shuttle Challenger. *He stares intently at the television monitor above his video display terminal, preparing to send another bulletin. Benedict's story was flashed around the world by satellite. At left is Dick Uliano, AP Radio; at right, Harry F. Rosenthal, Washington newsman. (AP/Wide World)*

the world can hear the bulletin almost immediately, and newspaper readers can have detailed accounts in their hands soon thereafter.

This swift dissemination of news is possible only because of the intricate organizations of the Associated Press and United Press International, the two rival American services, and their domestic and foreign competitors. The news services are an essential channel for international exchange of social and cultural knowledge.

From the syndicates, readers get comic strips, political commentaries, and other nonurgent material. This chapter discusses trends in comic strips and explains how the syndicates are organized. ◆

THE ROLE OF GLOBAL NEWS SERVICES

LONDON . . . SAN FRANCISCO . . . BEIRUT . . . WASHINGTON . . . PUNX-SUTAWNEY, PA. Every daily newspaper carries news stories from these and a thousand other datelines from far outside its city limits—stories it is able to publish only because it obtains the reports of one or more news services.

These international newsgathering agencies are a local newspaper's eyes and ears to the world. They take over where the local and area news coverage of the city desk ends. Only a handful of metropolitan newspapers can afford to have staffs of correspondents stationed outside their circulation areas, and even these newspapers depend upon the news services for many of the stories they publish.

Like other methods of mass communication, the news services are swept up in the new electronic techniques. They flash big news breaks around the world at remarkable speed, by bouncing signals off satellites, and can deliver voluminous information to subscribing newspapers and broadcasting stations almost everywhere. Indeed, they are the most extensive and fastest channel of global information exchange. News bulletins can be transmitted within a minute along a Rome–London–New York–San Francisco–Tokyo network.

For decades, the chatter of teletypes symbolized news excitement. Hour after hour, with automatic keys striking continuous rolls of paper, the machines typed out dispatches. Today, the teletype has nearly disappeared, just as did the Morse telegraph key it replaced. Most newspapers no longer have teleprinters in their newsrooms because dispatches are transmitted directly from a news service office computer into their computers, for editing on a video display terminal. The amount of material transmitted has increased enormously.

Supplying most news dispatches are the Associated Press and United Press International, the fiercely competitive American entries among the five major international newsgathering agencies. Intense hour-to-hour rivalry between AP and UPI exists in their effort to deliver simply written dispatches that are comprehensive, accurate, objective, and perceptive—and to get them there first. When they are reporting United States news to media abroad, or engaging in international newsgathering, they run into equally intense competition from Reuters, the British news agency, Agence France-Presse, and, to a lesser degree, TASS of the Soviet Union.

This competitive urge is one of the attractions of news service work, especially for younger reporters and editors; it adds a zest to newsgathering that has disappeared to some degree from the local news staffs in many cities where only one newspaper now exists. Commercially, to be faster and better than one's rival has great importance because the AP and UPI are in constant battle to take away customers from each other. (The AP calls them *members;* the UPI refers to them as *clients.*)

HISTORICAL DEVELOPMENT

Birth of the Associated Press

The invention of the telegraph in 1844 speeded the gathering of news, but it also increased the cost. In 1849 six New York morning newspapers formed the Associated Press of New York, forerunner of the modern news service of the same name. They did so to share the costs of telegraphing digests of foreign news from Boston and of routine news from Washington. Soon other papers asked to share in this common news report, and the New York papers began selling it. Papers in the interior of the country could now, with the telegraph, get the news as rapidly as their eastern metropolitan competitors. The excitement of the Mexican War and of the political crises leading to the Civil War spurred attention to the need for better mass communications.

THE RISE OF OBJECTIVITY. As has been previously noted, political biases colored much of the news reporting during the early decades of the Republic. Dispassionately presented mercantile news reporting characterized many of the large commercial newspapers during the first half of the nineteenth century in particular. Obvious biases toward narrow economic and political interests were avoided by the "penny press," which concentrated on local news and human interest stories. Counterforces, however, were working to produce a standard of objective news reporting. One was the Associated Press, serving newspapers of all sizes and political outlooks across the country. The AP developed a factual, condensed style of presenting news that eschewed partisanship and viewpoints. Reporters used only facts stemming from eyewitness reporting of events or those attributed to sources. The objective style fitted the needs of papers appealing to a wide cross-section of readers.

THE FIVE WS AND NEWS PYRAMID STYLE. The telegraph was used extensively to convey news from Civil War battlefronts, supplementing the old-style pony express. Because the wires frequently were cut or downed during storms, and because every word cost money, reporters (most of them serving Associated Press member newspapers) developed the so-called *inverted pyramid* style of transmitting the news. As many as possible of the five Ws—who, what, where, when, and why (and sometimes the how)—were placed in the first and immediately succeeding paragraphs, with the remaining paragraphs successively less important. This method helped assure the transmission of the most important news. Although news writing styles are not so strict today, this form of writing news still predominates.

STRUGGLE FOR CONTROL. The opening of the Atlantic cable in 1866 gave the AP better access to European news, which it obtained under exchange agreements with Reuters, Havas, and other news services. Regional AP groups formed, the most powerful of which was the Western Associated Press. The dailies outside New York City resented the tight-fisted control of the AP by the New York morning dailies that had founded it. The new evening dailies of the Midwest felt they were being ignored in the supplying of news on the two differing time cycles (morning and evening).

A bitter battle broke out among the newspapers in the 1880s. Control of the AP fell to the Western members, headed by Melville E. Stone, founder of the Chicago *Daily News.* Stone drafted exclusive news exchange contracts with European agencies, cutting off New York papers from the traditional supply of foreign news (see Chapter 25). Stone's rivals were broken by 1897. An adverse court ruling in Illinois threatened the membership status of the AP at this same moment, so its headquarters were returned to New York in 1900.

AP's NEWS MONOPOLY BROKEN. The basis of the AP was its cooperative exchange of news. The members found it necessary to finance a larger and larger staff, however, and that staff took over direction of the flow of news and eventually much of the newsgathering. Its organizational structure was not entirely democratic; the older and larger newspapers kept control of the board of directors by giving themselves extra voting rights during the 1900 reorganization. Until an adverse Supreme Court decision in 1945, an AP member could prevent the entry of a direct competitor into the group by exercising a protest right. This "blackballing" of a potential rival under the country-club style of bylaws could be overridden only by a four-fifths vote of the entire membership.

Newspapers that could not gain entry to the AP, or that disliked its control by the older morning papers of the East, needed news service from another source. Edward Wyllis Scripps, possessing both a string of evening dailies and an individualistic temperament that made him dislike monopoly, founded the United Press Associations in 1907 from earlier regional agencies. William Randolph Hearst, whose newly founded papers were denied AP membership, started the International News Service in 1909. Other agencies came and went, but the AP, UP, and INS survived until 1958, when the Hearst interests liquidated a losing business by merging the INS into the UP to form United Press International.

The strong men in the AP over the years were Stone, the first general manager, and Kent Cooper, general manager from 1925 to 1948. Builders of the UP were Roy W. Howard, who later became a partner in the Scripps-Howard newspaper group, and presidents Karl A. Bickel and Hugh Baillie. More recently, Wes Gallagher became president and general manager of AP, followed by Keith Fuller and Louis Boccardi.

Unlike the AP plan of organization, the UP and INS had a service to sell to clients. Howard set out to do this job for the young and struggling UP by building up a foreign service, first in Latin America and then in Europe. He embarrassed his agency by sending a premature flash announcing the end of World War I, but both Howard and the UP survived the incident. The enthusiasm and aggressiveness of the "shoestring" UP operation brought it into competitive position with the AP by the 1930s. In 1934 Kent Cooper brought an end to the restrictive news exchange agreements between the AP and foreign news agencies, and the AP joined in the foreign service race more determinedly. The AP also capitulated in supplying news to radio stations five years after UP and INS entered that field in 1935, and made the radio and television stations associate members, without voting rights. The INS, smallest of the three agencies, did not attempt to supply news at the state level except in a few states; it concentrated instead on outreporting and outwriting the other two on major news breaks and features. The UP–INS merger put United Press International in a position of competitive equality with its older rival in gathering and distributing the news until 1980, when substantial financial losses impaired its effort to ensure that there would be an intense rivalry between two well-managed global news services.

CURRENT AMERICAN NEWS SERVICES

In addition to the AP and UPI news reports, American newspapers publish dispatches supplied by supplementary news services. These services mostly are owned and operated by large newspaper groups, and the dispatches they supply primarily are created by staffs of the owned newspapers, in which they first appear. The best known of the operations are the New York *Times* News Service and the Los Angeles *Times*–Washington *Post* News Service. Others include the KNT Wire (sponsored by the Knight-Ridder newspapers and the Chicago *Tribune*), and the Gannett, AP–Dow Jones, Scripps Howard, and Copley news services.

These organizations distribute detailed dispatches covering top news events of the day, financial articles, background reports, and feature stories. While the global news services concentrate on speed and broad scope of coverage, the supplementary services emphasize depth and thoroughness on a narrower range of stories.

Many middle-sized and large daily newspapers that once took both the AP and UPI news reports now instead receive one news service report plus those of one or more of the supplementary services. Their editors believe that this combination gives readers better depth of coverage and more extensive reporting of cultural, health, and other significant nonspot news.

As the weaker organization, UPI has suffered more than AP from competition by the supplementary news services. For example, a Midwestern newspaper with more than 100,000 circulation that had received both AP and UPI services for 40 years dropped UPI and purchased the New York *Times* News Service. Although as an afternoon newspaper it does not use much of the New York *Times* spot news coverage, it publishes the service's news analyses on domestic politics and foreign affairs, health background articles, occasional political columns on its editorial pages, family living features, sports columns, and stories about motion pictures and television for its entertainment section. Its editors are careful not to overload any edition with material from the news service, however, lest their paper look like an imitation of the *Times.*

Although the services they deliver to newspapers, television, and radio stations here and abroad are similar, the two United States global agencies are organized quite differently. Each American newspaper that purchases the AP services becomes a member of the cooperative and has a voice in setting the association's newsgathering and financial policies; also, it is obligated to turn over its local news coverage to the cooperative. Television and radio stations taking AP service become associate members without voting rights; the total now exceeds that of newspaper members (Figure 7.1).

United Press International is a privately owned company, dealing on a contract basis with newspapers, television and radio stations, and other organizations that have need for a news report. Its individual clients influence the shape of the UPI news report through their suggestions and criticism, solicited by UPI management, or through their ultimate power to cancel the service. UPI has advisory boards of newspaper and broadcast clients to help management set goals and policies.

As previously stated, the new UPI was able to compete fully with the AP in gathering news and pictures worldwide, but it had only the smaller share of financial support from United States daily newspapers. Deficits incurred in that

FIGURE 7.1
The communications network of the Associated Press in the United States. "Hubs" are regional bureau offices. The AP also has an extensive worldwide communications network. (Courtesy of the Associated Press)

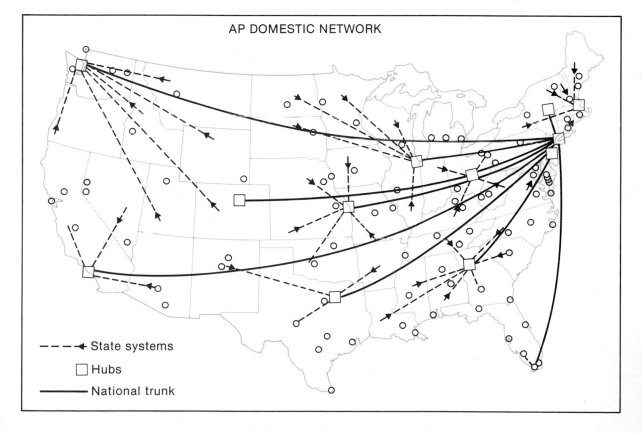

AP DOMESTIC NETWORK

- - - ◄ State systems
☐ Hubs
—— National trunk

area wiped out profits from service to broadcast, picture, and overseas clients, creating such severe losses that the Scripps Company sold UPI in 1982. The purchasers, four young men, obtained ownership for a symbolic $1 plus assuming the service's debts.

A complex and at times bizarre series of personality clashes among UPI's new owners and managers followed, along with odd financial maneuvers, until the service filed for bankruptcy on April 8, 1985, claiming $45 million in liabilities. A federal bankruptcy court in June 1986 awarded ownership of UPI to two men— Mario Vásquez Raña, a wealthy Mexican newspaper proprietor who took 90 percent ownership, and Joe E. Russo, a Texas real estate developer who took the other 10 percent. The men put up $41 million, of which $25 million went to pay creditors. It is remarkable that throughout this turbulence the UPI staff was able to maintain production of a competitive global news report.

The media world watched intently the steps the new owners took as they sought to strengthen UPI's prestige and enlarge its list of clients.

Already substantially ahead in income and number of members, the Associated Press grew even stronger during the turmoil within UPI. It collects and distributes news in 108 countries to more than 6000 newspapers and broadcast stations, including about 1365 newspapers and 3950 broadcast stations in the United States. More than 1500 news staff members serve AP around the world in 222 news bureaus. Daily the AP receives 150,000 words from abroad, of which 50,000 go onto its news circuits in the United States.

United Press International operates in more than 100 countries, serving 5000 publications and stations, including 700 newspapers and 3330 stations in the United States. More than 1200 staff members work in 260 news bureaus.

Regardless of whether a daily newspaper is called a member or a client, the net result is much the same. It receives the UPI or AP news report for a specified number of hours each day. For this service it pays a fee based on circulation. Most small dailies, and even some very large ones, operate successfully with only one of the two major wire services. Of the approximately 1660 American daily newspapers, fewer than 20 percent now subscribe to both services. When both provide stories on the same news events, as they do scores of times daily, the editor of the two-service newspaper selects the dispatch that arrives first, if an urgent news break is involved, or the one that seems more complete, concise, and interesting. Sometimes the two dispatches are combined to provide a more well-rounded and complete story.

The rival agencies keep close watch on selected lists of these two-service papers to determine the play their respective stories receive. Bad play on a big story—or worse, being badly beaten by the rival agency on a news break—brings sharp backstage criticism from the agency's home office to the head of the offending bureau.

OTHER GLOBAL AGENCIES

Reuters, the third international news service founded in 1851, is owned primarily by British newspapers and its policies are controlled by them, although some Class B stock with limited voting power is owned by outsiders. Ownership of 9.2 percent of Reuters stock is held by a large Arab investment organization, but the Reuters management insists that the Arabs' holding of Class B stock gives them no voice in policy-making.

In addition to delivering a general news report to media in 158 countries, the British agency provides an elaborate financial report to 35,000 subscribers in 112 countries. It operates 103 news bureaus in 74 countries, including 11 in the United States. Although the Reuters general news report is used by only a few U.S. subscribers, the agency hopes to expand in the American market. Worldwide, Reuters has a staff of 5400 persons, of whom 892 are journalists.

During the UPI crisis, Reuters purchased the American firm's photo operations outside the United States; thus foreign photographs distributed to American media by UPI are supplied by Reuters.

Agence France-Presse, although little known in the United States, is a major force in international newsgathering, having 12,000 subscribers in 160 countries. AFP distributes news in six languages, operates an international picture service, and employs 2000 full- and part-time persons in newsgathering. An English-language AFP news report is distributed in the United States through the Los Angeles *Times*–Washington *Post* News Service, and the company operates news bureaus in Washington and New York. Known as Agence Havas before World War II, Agence France-Presse is an independent company run by a board of publishers of French newspapers.

TASS has operated since 1918 as a Soviet Union government agency; it claims 5500 subscribers and has correspondents in all major countries and an extensive internal news network.

NEWS IN SATELLITE DISHES

Soaring costs of leasing 400,000 miles of telephone wires for their domestic services led AP and UPI to cooperate with a committee from the American Newspaper Publishers Association (ANPA) to work out a plan to transmit news and pictures to newspaper and broadcast station users via satellite. In April 1980 the first earth satellite station in an Associated Press nationwide network was dedicated at the Seattle *Times*. A retired AP Morse telegraph operator attached a gold-painted bolt to the receiving antenna, a 10-foot-wide "dish" on the roof. UPI opened a similar system in 1981. The signals were beamed to a satellite in view from any city in the United States, making possible line-of-sight microwave transmission to the dishes of the news service members and clients at a rate of 1200 words per minute. Both AP and UPI serve virtually all their United States users by satellite.

The services' satellite dishes can also be used to distribute syndicated material and to receive photos in a matter of seconds. ANPA began investigating transmission of advertising by satellite. *Time* magazine, using the Westar III satellite to transmit four-color pages and black-and-white photos and text to its regional printing plants in the United States, broke new ground in 1980 by using Intelsat IV to beam the same material to its Hong Kong printing plant, saving 24 hours for Asian subscribers. Its Netherlands printing plant did the same for Europe and Africa.

With use of this 10-foot-wide "dish" adjoining its plant, the Orlando (Florida) Sentinel *receives instant transmissions of Associated Press copy from the Westar III satellite. (Photo by David Cotton; courtesy of the Orlando* Sentinel)

HOW NEWS SERVICES FUNCTION

Each news service divides its flow of news into P.M. and A.M. reports, or cycles, the former for afternoon newspapers and the latter for morning papers. These reports always begin with a *budget,* or checklist, of the most important stories that are to be transmitted. The budget is a summary of the basic stories then available, or known to be forthcoming during the next few hours, plus sports and feature highlights. Usually it contains 10 or 12 items. The news editor is thus able to plan makeup to ensure space for stories that the paper most likely will want to run. Since the large majority of American newspapers are published in the afternoon, and most news occurs during daytime hours, the P.M. reports are generally handled with a greater sense of urgency.

Basic stories on major news situations are transmitted early in each cycle. If later developments occur on a story, a new lead is transmitted. This reports the latest news on the situation and ends with a transitional paragraph that blends into the earlier dispatch at a specified place. On big, fast-breaking stories a news agency, in some cases, may carry half a dozen leads in a cycle; these are edited so compactly that the dispatch that ultimately appears in a client newspaper reads with smooth continuity, even though it may contain segments of several leads.

Such methods are necessary because news service clients are constantly going to press and must print what is available on a given situation at press time. To use a phrase popular with United Press International, somewhere there is a

President Reagan talks with small group of reporters. Helen Thomas, UPI White House correspondent, is seated on couch facing him. Full-size presidential news conferences are held in a much larger room. (UPI/Bettmann Newsphotos)

deadline every minute. This is a major difference between news service and ordinary newspaper writing: the news service correspondent must keep feeding the latest developments in a spot story onto the news circuits immediately, even when their meaning and ramifications are not fully disclosed; the newspaper staff correspondent (called a *special* by the services) usually has more time before deadline to digest and consolidate the information. News service writers and editors usually work under time pressure. When we consider this, the amount of background and interpretation an experienced news service writer can weave into a fast-breaking story is remarkable.

News services have main trunk distribution circuits running across the country, serving the major metropolitan newspapers. Regional and state circuits from regional centers serve the smaller papers in different areas of the country. The editors who control the flow of news onto these secondary circuits must see that the newspapers on each receive a balanced menu of regional news along with the most important national and foreign dispatches. Thus an Associated Press member in Arizona will receive some stories of interest only to readers in the Southwest that will not be delivered to another member in Florida. These members, however, will receive identical dispatches on the day's major news from Washington and London. Proper channeling of the daily news report, so that each newspaper gets the largest possible number of stories pertinent to its needs, is a basic problem for the agencies.

The news services use video display terminals, on which reporters write their dispatches. Their stories go into computer storage from which they are called by editors on control desks. Once edited, the stories are ready for transmission as electronic signals directly into the newspaper's computer. Although newspapers with the direct computer intake system no longer require teletype machines, they have a special supplementary high-speed printer that provides a copy for reference when desired.

When the teletype circuit operated at 60 words a minute, news services faced the problem of having large stacks of copy on hand awaiting transmission. Newspapers received stories under this traditional method in the sequence determined by the editors who were newswire gatekeepers. Satellite transmission changed this. So did computer-to-computer transmission. In that system a brief abstract of each story is sent to the newspapers. With all the accumulated day's news stored in the newspaper computer within a short time, instead of having to await its arrival piece by piece, the newspaper's national editor can select and edit the stories desired for publication, then release them from the newspaper's computer to be put into type. Spot-breaking stories are transmitted on a priority basis from computer to computer as they develop.

SPECIAL WRITING TECHNIQUES

It is evident that a news story that goes through all these stages of editing from reporter to client editor's desk requires special writing techniques. It may be published 500 words long in one newspaper and only 100 words in another. Thus the writer must keep the fundamental information near the top of the story so the dispatch can be trimmed easily without having key facts omitted.

A news service reporter must write concisely, in simple sentences. Because the dispatches will be printed in newspapers of differing political persuasions, the writer must be carefully objective, especially in handling complicated, controversial stories. The primary goal is clear and swift communication of events and ideas. The staff writer's basic stock in trade is straight news, well written. More distinctive forms of self-expression increasingly find their way into the news reports; usually, however, those who wish to concentrate on this type of writing choose other, less restrictive outlets.

Broadcasting's instant news coverage of events in progress has had a heavy impact on the news service. Like newspapers, broadcast news staffs have changed their operating methods, increasing the stress on interpretive and analytical material. Until approximately the mid-1950s, news service reports primarily were happening-oriented, concentrating on reporting events as they took place. Today, they are more situation-oriented. Recognizing that the newspapers they serve no longer can be first with big news stories, the agencies supplement spot news with background and interpretive dispatches that help the reader understand the why of the situation.

Although the news services permit their established writers more freedom in interpreting news situations than in the past, they are on guard against political or social slanting of dispatches. The more complicated the world becomes, the more difficult it is for global news services to find a proper balance between quick-breaking facts and interpretation that gives them perspective without distortion. This calls for highly skilled reporting and editing.

OTHER NEWS SERVICE ACTIVITIES

Both United Press International and the Associated Press were founded to provide news for American newspapers. That remains their basic function, but they have branched out to additional services. Each supplies specially written news reports to thousands of radio and television stations in the United States, and news to newspapers and broadcasting stations in many foreign countries. A constant flow of news originating in the United States is being sent abroad while foreign news is arriving by a complex network of circuits. In Europe, the American agencies distribute their dispatches for translation into the local language in each country. Translation into Spanish for Latin American countries is largely done in the New York office of AP, and the Washington world headquarters office of UPI. Pictures are transmitted throughout the world by satellites.

The foreign bureaus of the American organizations usually are headed by an American, but they employ local nationals in substantial numbers as reporters, editors, and translators. The number of foreign correspondent jobs available to Americans in the agencies is thus smaller than many people may believe. It is apparent that the commonly held desire of young writers to become foreign correspondents is not easily fulfilled (see Chapter 25).

The American services have become important transmission belts for presenting a picture of life in America to foreigners. The hunger in many countries for news about the United States reflects this country's major role in world affairs. The Associated Press and United Press International carry a heavy responsibility in their selection and writing of news for the overseas audience, so that a well-balanced picture is presented. This does not imply censorship, the hiding of unpleasant news, or peddling of propaganda, but a judicious budget of stories to provide a multifaceted view of American life.

Special news service for television and radio stations is a major part of AP and UPI operations. This is transmitted on different circuits from the newspaper service and is rewritten from the stories in the basic report to please the ear rather than the eye. The style is more conversational, with simpler sentence structure and less detail. Distribution of a specially processed radio report was inaugurated by the United Press in 1935. The Associated Press followed reluctantly five years later.

Another important service provided to newspapers is news picture coverage. Both AP and UPI operate coast-to-coast circuits for transmission of news photographs and graphics, a growing number of them in color. Newspapers connected to these circuits receive photographs instantaneously as they are transmitted. The news agencies supply pictures to foreign clients by satellite, radio photo, leased circuits, and mail.

Some newspapers purchasing the nationwide direct service receive the newsphotos in their offices over facsimile machines, which translate the electrical impulses of the transmission circuit into black-and-white photographs by means of a scanning device; these pictures are ready for immediate printing in the newspapers. During the 1970s, the Associated Press introduced a new system of photo transmission by wire called Laserphoto, which uses a laser beam to provide improved clarity in the dry glossy prints it delivers to the member papers. Application of computerized digital technology to the transmission of pictures, enhancing their clarity and detail, is a recent development aiding the efforts of newspaper editors to make the graphic aspect of their publications more appealing (see Chapter 16).

Both AP and UPI have staffs of photographers who are assigned to stories much as are reporters. In addition, the Associated Press distributes many pictures taken by photographers on the staffs of member papers. UPI also supplements its staff picture coverage with photos from newspaper sources.

Both organizations deliver an audio news service for radio station voice pickups on news events. UPI operates a daily motion picture newsfilm service to TV stations and an audiovisual cable TV news service. AP offerings include a color slide service for television stations; a mailed tape service, TV Direct, a newsfilm service to television stations; in a joint venture with Conus Communications; and a book division that produces a news annual and other special volumes.

On still another front, the Associated Press provides a host of syndicated material for newspaper publication. United Features Syndicate, which was related financially to United Press International until the Scripps Company sold UPI, is one of the largest feature syndicates. The AP–Dow Jones service sells business news to clients outside the United States and Canada.

Thus the two organizations have journeyed far afield from their original purpose of providing dispatches for newspapers. The daily newspaper report, however, continues to be the core of each agency's operations, although they serve far more broadcasting stations than they do newspapers in the United States. The UPI and AP now serve not one but three mass communications media—newspapers, television, and radio—plus special services to magazines.

CRITICAL VIEWS OF AGENCIES

Students of the American press are sometimes critical of the heavy dependence of newspapers and broadcasting stations on the news services; this criticism is aimed more at the role of the services than at their daily performance. There is an undercurrent of uneasiness among these critics because nearly 1700 daily newspapers and 9000 broadcast stations look to these two organizations for the great bulk of their nonlocal news. Anyone who listens to a succession of radio newscasts and hears the identical words spoken repeatedly on different wavelengths realizes the dependence of radio stations in particular on the news services. In fact, an overwhelming percentage of the American people are largely dependent on the two organizations, through their various newspaper and TV-radio ramifications, as well as their use by the weekly news magazines, for knowledge of what is happening in the world. In the eyes of the critics this constitutes a danger involving conformity of reporting and thought, and some question the qualifications of editors to select the news that is transmitted.

The argument is more philosophic than practical. The economics of newspaper publishing makes it impossible for even the largest, wealthiest newspapers to have staff reporters stationed around the world in sufficient numbers to give them exclusive reports. The same is true of broadcasters. Therefore some form of cooperative newsgathering is necessary.

The editors of client and member newspapers, and news service executives themselves, subject the news report to constant scrutiny for accuracy and completeness. When instances of insufficient or inaccurate coverage come to light, steps are taken quickly to remedy the weakness. The competitive factor is a very wholesome one. The Associated Press Managing Editors Association has committees making continuous studies of AP operations. The UPI Advisory Council also makes studies.

The agencies are scolded at times by critics because in some parts of the world they use the reporting services of part-time local "string" correspondents. These are reporters who are paid according to the amount of their copy accepted for publication. When a major story breaks in a remote area, the big organizations must use the sometimes inadequate services of these part-timers until an American-trained correspondent can reach the scene. Governments of developing countries complain that the Western news services give a distorted colonialist view of their countries. At New Delhi in 1976 some of them formed a Pool of News Agencies of Non-Aligned Countries in competition. While admitting basis for their complaint, the Western press saw this as an attempt to distribute government-manipulated and censored news (see Chapter 25).

Another criticism of the news services is shared by the newspapers and broadcasters themselves: an alleged preoccupation with crisis reporting, or trying to find conflict and excitement in every situation, to the point of distorting the news. In particular, this charge has been made against the methods of handling political and legislative news. It is stated that too much emphasis is placed on the routine partisan postures of the two major political parties in the United States. This allegation results from the striving of each association to find sharp "angles" that induce editors to print its stories instead of its competitor's. In the last decade or so, however, both services have broadened their coverage by offering more thoughtful, interpretive articles in such fields as religion, race, health, education, labor, and social problems. They are much less open to charges of crisis overemphasis than they were two decades ago. The news services are also criticized for not carrying enough foreign news, to which they reply that their newspapers will print only a limited amount of such news, and there is no use in taking transmission time to give them what they will not use.

Actually, the conformity in presentation of national and foreign news by newspapers is less than might be expected. Checks of representative groups of newspapers receiving the same news service show a surprisingly wide variation in the stories chosen from the news report by editors for publication in their newspapers. Stories selected for prominent front-page play by some editors may be dismissed by others with brief mention on inside pages, or omitted entirely. This is not surprising when we realize that the news services deliver far more dispatches than most newspapers can use, and the pressures of local news vary from city to city. So do the news judgments of the individual editors. Because so many TV stations carry the network news programs, news conformity is greater in television than in newspapers.

JOB OPPORTUNITIES

The news services are among the finest training grounds in the entire field of mass communications for young people interested in a career of working with news. The work is challenging. It puts a premium on speed, conciseness, and judgment. These organizations have a tradition of hiring young writers of limited professional experience and training them. Since the turnover in personnel is relatively high, there are quite a few job openings each year. A large increase in the number of women on news service staffs has occurred in recent years. The same is true of members of racial minorities.

A beginner is usually given routine stories to rewrite from the local newspapers, items to check by phone, and similar simple duties. The writer must learn to look outward from the local community, to weigh each story for its interest to readers in other cities. Quite soon, the relative newcomer may be named night manager of a small bureau, an opportunity to exercise a limited amount of administrative responsibility. Because of the nature of the work, staff members do more editing and less original reporting than newspaper staffs do.

Those who stay with the news services for a number of years, as many do, usually become managers of small or medium-sized bureaus or are transferred into such large offices as those in Chicago and Washington. Members of the organizations' foreign staffs normally are given experience in New York or Washington before being sent abroad.

Salaries for news service work are approximately in line with those on large daily newspapers. For example, in 1987 AP news staff members with at least five years of experience received a base salary of $733 a week in New York and Washington, D.C., and between $668 and $683 per week in other U.S. cities, based on local living costs. Although quite a few newspeople spend virtually their entire careers in the news services, there is a fairly heavy turnover in personnel. Some staff members grow tired of the time pressures and the writing restrictions. They believe that although advancement is relatively fast when they are starting, it slows down as they mature.

They may find better salary opportunities in special reporting jobs and editorships on newspapers or in public relations, radio, television, and related fields of mass communications. Many of the country's best-known reporters, writers, television commentators, and editors worked for the news services in their younger years; almost unanimously they are grateful for the experience, especially for the writing discipline it taught them.

NEWSPAPER FEATURE SYNDICATES

The other major source of editorial material used by daily newspapers, and one that tends to bring uniformity to the American press, is the feature syndicate. Syndicates sell to the newspapers a multitude of material for the entertainment and education of their readers, edited and ready for publication upon delivery. Comic strips and other features are provided in proof form for newspaper reproduction; text features are available in proof or duplicated form, or by transmission directly into the purchaser's computer system.

An editor may load the newspaper with as much syndicated material as conscience and budget will allow. The larger the feature "package" in a paper, the less space is available to be filled with locally created news and news service dispatches. A publication too full of such "canned" features gets a reputation of being more an entertainment medium than a newspaper and of being deficient in editorial enterprise. Readership polls show, however, that a very strong desire exists among readers for certain syndicated features.

The newspaper editor tries to strike a suitable balance. There is no firm rule of thumb about this; one good newspaper of substantial circulation and a reasonably large editorial "hole" (the space left in a newspaper after the advertisements have been inserted) will publish 16 comic strips daily while a comparable one runs only 10 or 12. The same is true of political columns and other material offered by the syndicates.

Examination of a typical well-edited newspaper with 50,000 daily circulation shows the following material purchased ready-made from national feature syndicates: 12 comic strips, 12 cartoon panels, 5 political columns, medical column, personal advice column, crossword puzzle, astrological forecast, political cartoon, 2 entertainment columns, and juvenile information feature.

Certain features, especially comics, have run in newspapers so many years that they are household words. Some comic strips such as "Blondie" and the newer "For Better or Worse" reflect everyday life, often in exaggerated form. The purpose of most strips and panels is entertainment, not social or political commentary. In numerous strips fantasy plays an important part. This is evident especially in the trend to endow animals with the ability to think and talk. Some English teachers used to call the act of giving animals human abilities "the pathetic fallacy." Pathetic or not, the technique has been highly successful with the dog Snoopy in "Peanuts" and Garfield, the cat, among four-footed characters.

By far the most significant in terms of political and social relevance is "Doonesbury," whose creator Garry Trudeau resumed the strip in 1984 after a year's furlough. Because "Doonesbury" contains often biting political satire, some newspapers publish it on their editorial pages. Among other strips that employ subtlety and sophistication, in contrast to the simplistic jokes of the long-enduring "Nancy," are "Peanuts," "The Wizard of Id," and "Bloom County." The popular "Cathy" is drawn from the female point of view.

"Peanuts," drawn by Charles M. Schulz, became the first comic strip to appear in more than 2000 newspapers; it is published in 23 languages and is a repeat winner in *Editor & Publisher* magazine's annual poll of most popular comics.

Off-beat panels employing zany, often obscure, humor constitute the latest trend in comics. Gary Larson's "The Far Side" started the boom and was followed by such others as "Bizarro" and "Off the Leash." These panels, vastly more complex than the simplistic old favorite strip "Nancy," challenge the reader's perceptive powers.

The creators of some popular strips earn large additional income through merchandising tie-ins featuring their cartoon characters.

Among text features, the personal advice columns by Ann Landers and "Dear Abby" (Abigail Van Buren), who are sisters, have had extremely strong readership. Political columnists run the full spectrum of opinion, with writers such as Carl

Rowan, Tom Wicker, and Jack Anderson on the liberal side and James J. Kilpatrick, William Safire, and George Will expressing the conservative point of view. To provide balance, the majority of newspaper editors publish both liberal and conservative columnists on their editorial and commentary pages.

Approximately one dozen major syndicates provide the bulk of the features appearing in American newspapers, although there are more than 100 smaller companies, some of which operate in specialized fields such as boating and book serializations. The major syndicates have from 25 to more than 100 features on the lists they offer for sale to editors. An editor who has trouble saying no to the sales talk of the syndicate representative soon finds the paper overloaded with material for which the total weekly fee can run uncomfortably high. But an editor who can't say no is a contradiction in terms. On comics especially, many editors make a habit of dropping one feature whenever they buy a new one. Papers take occasional readership surveys to determine which comics and daily features are most popular. So attached do readers become to individual comic strips that the dropping of one sometimes provokes a torrent of complaints; consequently, fewer changes are made than many editors desire.

Features are sold to newspapers for prices scaled to the paper's circulation. Although some are sold for specific contract periods, many are on a "till forbid" (t.f.) basis, meaning that the feature runs until the editor sends in a cancellation, usually on 30- to 90-day notice.

Competition among the syndicates is intense. There are more than 250 daily comic strips on the market, many of which are also issued in color for Sunday comic sections, and about 40 health columns, 75 religious features, and a dozen competing columns on stamp collecting. Although many well-established features go on year after year, a new group of comic strips, panels, and text columns is brought onto the market annually. Features that lose popular appeal are dropped by the syndicates.

The feature syndicates do not offer very great potential for the young person seeking a job. Their editorial and sales staffs are small and mostly drawn from professional journalists with several years of editorial or business experience. Most of the artists and writers whose material is distributed by these organizations do their work outside the syndicate offices and send or bring it in for editing and approval. They work on a percentage arrangement with the syndicate, most commonly a 50–50 percentage split of the fees paid by the newspapers. Syndicate editing requires knowledge of the public taste, as well as the space problems, buying habits, and idiosyncracies of the various newspaper editors who are the customers for the syndicate products. Similarly, the odds against selling a comic strip, column, or other material to a syndicate for distribution are extremely poor. United Media receives between 5000 and 10,000 submissions a year, from which it introduces six or eight new features. King Features Syndicate annually releases about 10 new features, from between 3000 and 3500 submissions.

Magazines

8

Magazines Solve a Marketing Problem

Apple Computer faced a formidable marketing decision . . . how to launch its Macintosh personal computer in a highly competitive environment.

The company's Cecil B. deMille-type television commercial drew on Orwell's book *1984* to create awareness. But Apple, according to an analyst, "needed more than name recognition. It wanted to establish computers as a consumer product and needed a sophisticated way to inform people who were wary of computers, yet not alienate the more savvy customer who wanted the inside technical story.

"Apple needed to grab attention and *hold* it long enough to explain complex material in a way the average person could understand and to demonstrate how easily the Macintosh could be used.

"Apple also wanted something consumers could take to sales centers and consult when making purchase decisions. It needed to reach the *right* people with its message—upscale, educated people who were likely to act upon it."

Capitalizing on the numerous advertising options that magazines afford, advertising experts designed a 20-page insert, complete with fold-out sections. Pictures and text detailed the computer's operation. The insert was placed in split-run issues, conveying the insert to specific groups of readers deemed most likely to buy once they learned how easily the Macintosh could be used.

Within the first 100 days nearly 100,000 Macintoshes were sold. Word of the computer's desktop publishing capabilities quickly spread. Apple's experience demonstrated the values that magazine advertising offered over other media to solve its particular marketing problem.

*M*ore than 11,000 magazines provide information and entertainment for Americans, serving virtually every age, occupation, and lifestyle.

Largely because advertisers found a cheaper way to reach a mass, national audience, most of the general magazines that flourished earlier in the twentieth century vanished with the advent of television. Those that remained shifted largely to nonfiction content.

Commanding steadily increasing attention are thousands of specialized magazines serving almost every interest and need of their readers.

While the adult population grew 61 percent between 1954 and 1984, the average number of adults who read each magazine issue (4.36, according to studies) increased 91 percent. Several hundred new publications are established each year; nine out of ten, however, are destined to perish through failure to obtain sufficient reader and advertising support.

In addition to the general and specialized magazines, almost 10,000 industrial publications serve the interests of companies and organizations and the employees, customers, stockholders, and dealers to whom they are sent.

A new phenomenon, desktop publishing, swept the small magazine and newsletter industry in the mid-1980s. Under this system a single operator can write and edit copy and prepare an entire page for reproduction by use of a personal computer and a laser writer.

The expenses of production and delivery of most magazines, including printing, payrolls, and postal charges, have increased sharply in recent years, along with advertising, subscription, and newsstand purchase rates.

In this chapter we discuss these developments, describe the innumerable categories of magazines, explain how the industry functions, and identify opportunities and the level of salaries awaiting newcomers to the field. ◆

THE ROLE OF MAGAZINES

Much of the communication of ideas, information, and attitudes among American people is carried on through magazines. Thousands of periodicals fall within this field. They range from the slick paper, four-color monthly with circulation in the millions down to the small, special interest quarterly that, though virtually unknown to the general public, may have very strong influence within its field.

Like most other media, magazines seek to inform, persuade, and entertain their audiences and put before them advertising messages of national, regional, state, and city scope. Magazines never appear more frequently than once a week; thus their writers and editors, although generally part of small staffs that must meet deadlines the same as other media personnel, often have more time to dig into issues and situations than do those on daily newspapers. Consequently they have a better opportunity to bring events into focus and interpret their meaning. Says Katharine Graham, chairman of the board of the Washington Post Company, which publishes *Newsweek* magazine:

> Magazines are in many ways the ideal medium for serious treatment of the major issues of our day. However much the industry feels squeezed by soaring costs, the magazine still has certain luxuries. More lead time and perspective than the daily press, more permanence than broadcasting, more immediacy and wider readership than most books. It is no accident that long takeouts on major subjects in the daily press are called magazine pieces. It is no accident that some broadcasters describe some public affairs programs as magazines of the air. Nor is it happenstance that people are more and more depending on news magazines to give shape and substance to a week's worth of headlines.

Magazines are a channel of communication halfway between newspapers and books. Unlike newspapers or books, however, many of the most influential magazines are difficult or impossible to purchase at newsstands. With their color printing and slick paper (in most cases), magazines have become a showplace for exciting graphics. Until the 1940s most consumer (general) magazines offered a diverse menu of both fiction and nonfiction articles and miscellany such as poetry and short humor selections. With television providing a heavy quotient of entertainment for the American home, many magazines discovered a strong demand for nonfiction articles, their almost exclusive content today.

There is another basic difference between newspapers and magazines. Except for the *Wall Street Journal* and the zoned editions of some metropolitan newspapers that reach specific neighborhoods, a newspaper must appeal to an entire community and have a little of everything for almost everybody. Yet hundreds of successful magazines are designed for reading by such interest groups as computer operators, dentists, poultry farmers, and model railroad fans. Therein lies the richness of diversity that makes the magazine field so attractive to many editorial workers and to advertisers. The possibilities of advancement for a writer or editor who acquires specialized knowledge are greater than on most newspapers, although the number of editorial jobs on magazines is fewer.

Studies made for the Magazine Publishers Association reveal that from 1954 to 1984 magazine per-issue circulation grew 91 percent, while the U.S. adult population increased only 61 percent. *Per-issue circulation* refers to the finding that, on average, 4.36 adults each spend 37 minutes reading an issue, allowing that issue to garner 4.2 hours of total adult reading time. Ninety-four percent of all adults read an average of 9.9 different issues each month (see Tables 8.1 and 8.2).

Although average newsstand prices of magazines increased in the 1980s to more than $2 per issue and annual subscriptions to well over $22, total circulation climbed beyond 315 million copies and annual advertising reached $2 billion. The figures reflect the unprecedented role that magazines are playing in American life.

THE GROWTH OF MAGAZINES

Magazines have played an increasingly important role in American life since Benjamin Franklin published one of the first two short-lived colonial ventures in 1741. Fellow colonials preferred London magazines to his *American Magazine.*

U.S. MAGAZINE CIRCULATION LEADERS

Largest Circulation		Largest Newsstand Circulation	
1. *TV Guide*	16,800,441	1. *TV Guide*	8,482,246
2. *Reader's Digest*	16,609,847	2. *Family Circle*	5,688,100
3. *Modern Maturity*	13,597,330	3. *Woman's Day*	5,672,578
4. *National Geographic*	10,764,998	4. *National Enquirer*	3,944,496
5. *Better Homes and Gardens*	8,091,751	5. *Star*	3,399,127
6. *Family Circle*	6,261,519	6. *Cosmopolitan*	2,514,444
7. *Woman's Day*	5,743,842	7. *Penthouse*	2,140,098
8. *Good Housekeeping*	5,221,575	8. *Good Housekeeping*	1,755,528
9. *McCall's*	5,186,393	9. *People*	1,740,557
10. *Ladies' Home Journal*	5,020,551	10. *Glamour*	1,679,194

SOURCE: Audit Bureau of Circulations' FAS-FAX report of average circulation for the six months ending December 31, 1986. Does not include groups or comics.

But before the revolutionary war, Tom Paine was selling articles to the *Pennsylvania Magazine* and publishing genius Isaiah Thomas was printing his *Farmer's Weekly Museum* in New Hampshire. Mathew Carey's *American Museum* of 1787 was the best of the new country's efforts.

Forerunner of the news magazine was *Niles' Weekly Register,* a remarkable compendium of American events (1811–1849). Intellectual fare was offered by Harvard writers in the *North American Review* (1815–1914). But the splashiest and best selling was *Godey's Lady's Book,* which won 150,000 circulation with hand-colored engravings of fashionable clothing, fiction and poetry. Sarah J. Hale, its editor from 1836 to 1877, wrote 50 books and promoted women's rights, but won her greatest fame for a poem, "Mary Had a Little Lamb."

The Harper book publishing house founded *Harper's Monthly* in 1850, introduced extensive woodcut illustrations, published the writings of English and American authors, and ran up a world-record circulation of 200,000 before the Civil War. *Harper's Weekly* (1857) and *Frank Leslie's Illustrated Newspaper* (1855) used

TABLE 8.1   Magazine Reading by Demographics

	Average Month	
Adults	Read 1+ magazines	Average # of issues
18–44 years	96.2%	11.1
Attended/graduated college	97.5	12.1
$30,000 & over household income	96.6	11.0
Professional/managerial	97.4	11.9

SOURCE: Magazine Research Institute, Spring 1985. Special tabulation covering a four-week period. Courtesy of Magazine Publishers Association.

artists' drawings for woodcuts and maps to bring the war to 150,000 readers each. The *Atlantic Monthly* began its career in 1857, joined by *Century* and *Scribner's* in the 1880s as literary journals. Three new magazines of the same period that depended upon humor, cartoon, and satire were *Puck, Judge,* and *Life* (the original *Life* featuring the famed Gibson girl drawings). For the children, the legendary *St. Nicholas* challenged *Youth's Companion.*

Most influential in shaping American political and social life were the opinion magazines. An Englishman, Edwin Lawrence Godkin, began publishing the *Nation* in 1865 as a journal of opinion and literary criticism. It won influence among opinion leaders far beyond its 10,000 circulation. The *Independent, Forum, Outlook,* and *Review of Reviews* all discussed the rapidly changing political and social environment of the 1890s. The *Literary Digest* began summarizing contemporary editorial opinion in 1890.

Helped by cheap postal rates and expanding delivery service, magazine publishers struck out to win mass readership. Cyrus H.K. Curtis founded the *Ladies' Home Journal* in 1883 and soon won a half-million circulation with Edward W. Bok as his editor. In the low-cost weekly field, *Collier's* appeared in 1888 and Curtis put George Horace Lorimer in charge of the *Saturday Evening Post* in 1897. Both rode to success with current affairs and fiction. Three low-priced popular monthlies were *Munsey's,* begun in 1889 by Frank Munsey; *McClure's,* started in 1893 by S. S. McClure; and the *Cosmopolitan,* founded in 1886 and soon a Hearst property.

Nearly all these magazines took part in the "muckraking" era of exposure and reform during the Theodore Roosevelt administration. *McClure's* led the way in 1902 with Ida Tarbell's "History of the Standard Oil Company" and Lincoln Steffens' "Shame of the Cities." In 1906 Tarbell and Steffens joined Ray Stannard Baker, Finley Peter Dunne ("Mr. Dooley"), and William Allen White at the *American Magazine* to continue the muckraking movement. Coming on the scene in 1914 was the *New Republic,* featuring the political philosophy of Herbert Croly and Walter Lippmann. For those less concerned with idealism there were George Jean Nathan's *Smart Set* and H.L. Mencken's *American Mercury,* favorites of collegians of the 1920s.

Of all the magazines mentioned in this account, only a handful remained by the

TABLE 8.2 Average Reader of Average Magazine Copy

- 37.2 years old (U.S.=40.5)
- At least graduated high school
- Married
- Three-or-more-person household
- Employed full time
- $30,978 household income (13% above U.S. average of $27,330)
- Owns home

SOURCE: Magazine Research Institute, Spring 1985. Special tabulation covering a four-week period. Courtesy of Magazine Publishers Association.

1980s. The *Nation* and *New Republic* survived as magazines of opinion; *Harper's* and *Atlantic* continued as literary and public affairs magazines; and the *Ladies' Home Journal* and *Cosmopolitan* still appealed to women. But the 3500 magazines of 1900 had become the more than 11,000 of 1987.

TYPES OF MAGAZINES

Generalizations about the content, style, and appearance of magazines are danger-ous because so many variations exist among the more than 11,000 periodicals being published. That is the figure (11,090, to be exact) given in the *IMS/Ayer Directory of Publications* in 1985, as distinguished from listings of newspapers with general circulation. Not all appear in magazine format, however; quite a few are tabloid or regular newspaper size. No more than 600 can be classified as general interest magazines. In contrast, more than 3000 specialized business and trade publications are published, as well as 1300 in the field of religion and about 270 agricultural periodicals, to list three major subfields. Not included in these figures are almost 10,000 industrial, or company, publications designed for employees, customers, stockholders, dealers, and others. Most of these are issued in maga-zine format.

Although all magazines share certain basic problems of production and distribu-tion, their editorial content and advertising are of many hues. Even trying to group them into categories becomes difficult because inevitably there is overlapping, and a few magazines almost defy classification. Most magazines fall into the following general categories.

General Family Interest

Two mass circulation magazines, *Reader's Digest* and *TV Guide,* lead this group. *Reader's Digest,* begun in 1922 by DeWitt and Lila Wallace as a pocket-size compilation of nonfiction articles, is the centerpiece of a giant publishing business. It is a well-staffed monthly, blending informative, inspirational, and entertaining nonfiction. In 1986, in order to eliminate subscriptions expensive to acquire and retain, *Reader's Digest* dropped 1.5 million copies from the 17.75 million circulation base that it had guaranteed to advertisers since 1971. Accord-ing to publisher Richard F. McLoughlin, a steady decline in its newsstand sales, a problem for many other magazines as well, was at the root of the decision. "All newsstand sales are down, and ours is no exception," McLoughlin told *Folio* magazine. "They've declined by an average of 600,000 per year over the last five to six years. That means we had to bring in 500,000 to 600,000 incremental [additional] subscriptions to maintain the rate base, and those subscriptions are very expensive to get."

Reader's Digest thus abdicated its position as the largest circulation magazine in the United States to *TV Guide,* a Walter Annenberg-family publication, whose circulation even so had dropped from 19.5 million in 1980 to 16.8 million in 1986. *Reader's Digest,* however, with more than 10 million circulation in other countries, continued to outsell all other magazines in the world and at the same time maintain its substantial annual advertising income.

Television's diversion of advertising revenues from general family interest periodicals spelled the doom of such formerly great magazines combining nonfiction and fiction as *Collier's* and the *American,* which ceased publication in the 1950s, and the *Saturday Evening Post.* After being abandoned as a weekly in 1969, the latter was reinstituted as a monthly "nostalgia" publication. In the 1970s, confronted with a lack of advertising and rising postal rates, the enormously successful weekly picture magazines *Life* and *Look* also disappeared. *Life,* however, reappeared as a monthly with 1.6 million circulation by 1986.

Into the void created by the loss of these magazines came *National Geographic,* established in 1888 as a travelog journal that blossomed out as a slickly edited, superbly illustrated monthly with a current circulation of 10.7 million. It absorbed some of the displaced photojournalists. Others from *Life* and *Look* found their way to the Smithsonian Institution, whose *Smithsonian* magazine, founded in 1970, soared beyond 2.1 million circulation by 1986. *Ebony,* founded in 1945 by John H. Johnson as a black picture magazine, had a comfortable 1.7 million circulation in 1986.

News Magazines

Close behind these magazines in general family appeal are weekly publications designed to summarize the news and provide added depth and interpretation that newspapers cannot give. They publish articles on news situations, examine headline personalities, and discuss trends in such diverse fields as religion, labor, sports, art, and the environment.

John H. Johnson (left) *is the publisher of* Ebony *and* Jet, *which are magazines geared toward the black reader. Johnson's company, Johnson Publications, is based in Chicago. With him are actor Bill Cosby* (center) *and the Rev. Jesse Jackson.* (AP/Wide World)

The present leaders are *Time,* with 4.8 million circulation, *Newsweek,* near 3 million, and *U.S. News & World Report,* a more specialized journal, with about 2 million circulation. *Jet* has 815,000 circulation among black readers.

Henry R. Luce's formula for *Time* was to organize and departmentalize the news of the week in a style "written as if by one man for one man," whom *Time* described as too busy to spend all the time necessary to peruse the other media. The magazine developed a large research and library staff, as well as its own good-sized newsgathering organization, to supplement the news services. Begun in 1923, *Time* helped to drive the older *Literary Digest* out of business with this approach. *Newsweek* appeared in 1933, with an almost identical format. *U.S. News & World Report,* which grew out of a combination of two of David Lawrence's publications in Washington, hit its stride in the late 1940s.

It should be noted that the news magazines offer their readers both news and opinion. *Time* makes no attempt to distinguish between the two functions, intermingling opinion and editorial hypotheses with straight news. *Time* said it wanted to be "fair," not objective or even impartial. *Newsweek* injects less opinion into its columns and offers separate editorial opinions written by commentators.

Sophisticated Writing Quality

Possibly the most distinctive of American magazines has been the *New Yorker,* founded in 1925 by Harold Ross and carried on from 1951 to 1987 by William Shawn. E.B. White long conducted its "Talk of the Town"; it has had writers of the quality of James Thurber, Wolcott Gibbs, A. J. Liebling, and Frank Sullivan; artists such as Helen Hokinson, Peter Arno, Otto Soglow, and Charles Addams. It also gives its one-half million readers—along with the cartoons, whimsy, and fiction—penetrating "Profiles" and lengthy, incisive commentaries on public affairs. The magazine was acquired in 1986 by Samuel E. Newhouse, Jr., head of a family-owned publishing empire that includes 29 newspapers, the Condé Nast magazines, and Random House book publishers. In 1987 Robert A. Gottlieb, president and editor-in-chief of the Alfred A. Knopf publishing firm, a Random House subsidiary, was named as the magazine's third editor in 82 years.

Esquire, founded in 1933 by Arnold Gingrich, ran the top bylines of American writing: Wolfe, Hemingway, Faulkner, Steinbeck, Capote, Mailer, Talese. It had 1 million readers but faltered and was sold in 1977 to Clay Felker. In 1979 the magazine was acquired by Phillip Moffitt and Christopher Whittle, who had achieved remarkable success with their 13-30 Corporation, a Knoxville, Tennessee, publisher of student giveaway magazines. *Esquire* retained most of its enviable stable of writers, and by 1986 circulation exceeded 700,000 with a 65 percent male readership. In that year Whittle and Moffitt, both not yet 40 years of age, ended a 20-year business partnership that had begun when they were students at the University of Tennessee. Their assets were divided into two corporations, Whittle Communications and the Esquire Magazine Group. At year's end the Hearst Corporation purchased *Esquire,* and the American Express Publishing Corporation bought the group's six-month-old magazine, *New York Woman.* Moffitt announced plans to write full time.

Quality Magazines

Two quality literary magazines, *Harper's* and *The Atlantic,* both about 135 years old, veered toward nonfiction and public affairs several decades ago. Harold Evans, former editor of the *Sunday Times* and then the *Times* of London, served as editor of *The Atlantic* from 1984–1986, with circulation rising to about 435,000. Carl Navarre, a Chattanooga, Tennessee, businessman, bought the magazine in 1986, whereupon Evans resigned and eventually joined Condé Nast Publications to develop new magazines. Gary L. Fisketjon became the new editorial director. In 1983 *Harper's,* with a circulation hovering around 300,000, underwent a change in format, content, and appearance after the rehiring of its former longtime editor, Lewis Lapham.

The bimonthly *Saturday Review,* a fixture in literary circles for 35 years under former editor Norman Cousins, returned to its original strong emphasis on the arts in the early 1980s but has struggled to remain alive. The venerable *Vanity Fair,* however, achieved a remarkable comeback, mainly in the arts and literature field. Founded in 1859, the magazine was merged with *Vogue* in 1936 but was reestablished in 1983; three years later its circulation had soared to 400,000.

Also ranking high in quality of writing are a growing number of city, state, and regional magazines, aimed at sophisticated, mostly young-adult audiences. *New York,* founded in 1968, had such talented writers as Tom Wolfe, Jimmy Breslin, Judith Crist, and Gloria Steinem. (Steinem's 1972 creation, *Ms.,* began in *New York*'s offices and became the leading magazine of the feminist movement, with almost one-half million circulation.) *New York*'s highly regarded publisher, Clay Felker, lost financial control of the magazine and also of *Village Voice,* another haven of 1960s-style new journalists; both were acquired by Rupert Murdoch. The circulation of *Village Voice* approached 440,000 in 1986.

Texas Monthly was established in 1973 as an iconoclastic, investigative-style magazine. In 1986 its circulation approached 290,000 and its readership was estimated at 1 million.

Opinion Magazines

Seeking new readers and advertisers in the conservative political and social climate of the 1980s, two magazines noted for their combative, left-of-center opinions, *Mother Jones* and the *New Republic,* in 1986 developed new marketing approaches and instituted changes in editorial content. The circulation of *Mother Jones,* published nine times each year by the Foundation for National Progress, in San Francisco, had dropped to 150,000 from 227,000 in 1981. Under the new editorship of Michael Moore, former editor and publisher of an alternative newspaper, *Michigan Voice, Mother Jones* continued its role as a muckraking, investigative journal. Its marketing staff, however, began seeking national image-making corporate advertising. Jeff Dearth, publisher of the *New Republic,* with circulation nearing 100,000, said that, "without prostituting our editorial," (altering its liberal stance) the magazine would seek "to reflect some of the new thinking and turmoil that's happening in the Democratic party." At the same time the weekly magazine

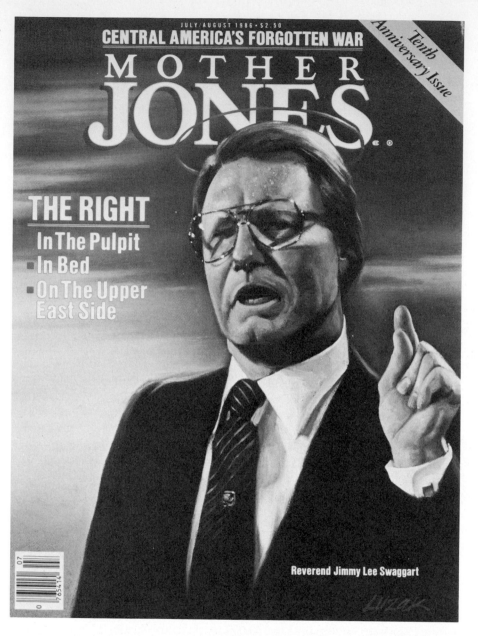

sought new subscribers in the Washington, D.C., area along with advertisers wishing to target policymakers on Capitol Hill. New designs accompanied the new approaches of both magazines.

Among other leading magazines of opinion are William Buckley's conservative *National Review;* the *Nation,* well over a century old; and Erwin Knoll's *The Progressive.* A number of other opinion magazines also continue to struggle for attention, notably Bruce Brugmann's vigorous *San Francisco Bay Guardian.*

When 16 prominent writers were asked in the late 1970s to name the publications on which they depended most for their insights, an *Esquire* article reported that the *New Republic* drew the most votes (four). Obtaining three endorsements each were the *Nation, Washington Monthly, New Yorker, New York Review of Books,* and the *Wall Street Journal.* Cited twice were *Commentary, Economist, Catholic Worker, Seven Days, Psychology Today, International Journal of Psycho-Analysis, Public Interest, Village Voice,* and *National Review.*

Women's Interest Magazines

The traditional women's magazines known as the Seven Sisters *(McCall's, Ladies' Home Journal, Woman's Day, Family Circle, Good Housekeeping, Better Homes and Gardens,* and *Redbook)* maintain their appeal, with circulations ranging from 4 to 8 million. The average age of their readers is 42.

These magazines, however, are being challenged by more recently established publications aimed at specialized, younger audiences and presumably representing a major shift in the women's market. They include *Glamour, Mademoiselle, Self,* and *New Woman,* for young women; *Working Mother* and *Parents,* for women with children; *Savvy* and *Working Woman,* for career-oriented women; *Seventeen,* for the teenager; and *Essence,* for black women. Of these publications *New Woman, Mademoiselle,* and *Self* have circulations exceeding 1 million. *Cosmopolitan,* under the editorship of Helen Gurley Brown, has proclaimed a new sexual freedom for its women readers and attained a circulation of 2.8 million.

The sensationalized *National Enquirer* (4.1 million), *The Star* (3.3 million), and *National Examiner* (1 million) also are aimed at women buyers. Although printed in newspaper format, in their feature content these publications more nearly

Specialized publications such as these are building strong circulations and are challenging traditional women's magazines such as Ladies' Home Journal. *(Grunnitus Studios)*

resemble magazines. Sold mostly at supermarket checkout counters, the weekly publications have been noted for their "hoked-up" headlines; medical, science, and parascience stories; revelations about celebrities, usually TV stars; and first-person testimonials of an inspirational nature.

Faced with the increasing number of libel suits brought against publications and the competition from televised celebrity shows and from magazines such as Time Inc.'s highly successful *People* (circulation 2.8 million) featuring news of celebrities, the *National Enquirer* turned increasingly in the mid-1980s to reader "service" stories such as how to cope with cancer and how to care for pets. Although circulation declined from 5 to 4.5 million during a three-year period, largely because of a price advance to 65 cents, the publication's advertising revenues steadily increased.

Men's Interest

Two magazines, *Playboy* and *Penthouse*, fall within the top 15 in circulation among sexually oriented publications intended for men (euphemistically dubbed "gentlemen's sophisticates"). *Playboy*, established by Hugh Hefner in 1953, approached 7 million circulation, but has since declined to 3.9 million. *Penthouse* had 4.6 million circulation in 1980, but has since fallen to 2.7 million. *Oui, Club, High Society, Genesis, Gallery,* and *Cheri* also have suffered heavy circulation losses.

Publishers attributed the decline largely to the increase in sales to dealers of prerecorded adult-oriented videocassettes. According to *Adult Video News,* a sex film industry publication, about 1700 sex videos were produced in 1985, as compared with 400 in 1983. The cassettes constituted about 15–18 percent of the total of 53 million cassettes purchased by dealers in 1985, an increase of about 22 million in one year.

The increased cost of the magazines, to about $3.50 and $4, was viewed as another factor.

Readers also faced increased difficulty in purchasing the magazines. For well over two years an outspoken minority of customers bombarded chain drug and convenience stores with letters and phone calls, threatened boycotts, and picketed some establishments, protesting, in particular, the sale of *Playboy, Penthouse,* and *Forum.* Most of the complaints were fueled by the Rev. Donald Wildmon's National Foundation for Decency and the Rev. Jerry Falwell's Liberty Foundation (formerly the Moral Majority).

The chains weighed the protests against annual sales each of up to $3 million and $4 million. In 1986, however, after additional surveys indicated an increase in the minority of customers who felt the magazines should not be sold, even wrapped and behind counters, People's Drug, Southland Corporation, and several other major chains removed the magazines from their shelves. Others followed upon receipt of a letter from the Attorney General's Commission on Pornography, labeled censorship by civil libertarians and publishers, suggesting that they might be cited in the commission's report for distributing pornography. The report is discussed in Chapter 24.

Of a nonsexual nature in the men's interest category, but increasingly attractive

John Lennon
November 9, 1967

Tiny Tim
July 6, 1968

The Beatles
October 26, 1968

Elvis Presley
July 12, 1969

Woodstock
September 20, 1969

Kent State
June 11, 1970

Muhammad Ali
March 18, 1971

The Beach Boys
October 28, 1971

Jane Fonda
May 25, 1972

Mick Jagger
July 6, 1972

Richard Nixon
September 27, 1973

Prisoners of War
March 28, 1974

Evel Knievel
November 7, 1974

Led Zeppelin
March 13, 1975

David Bowie
February 12, 1976

Star Wars
August 25, 1977

The Sex Pistols
October 20, 1977

Bob Dylan
January 26, 1978

The Blues Brothers
February 22, 1979

Bette Midler
December 13, 1979

John Lennon, Yoko Ono
January 22, 1981

E.T.
July 22, 1982

Eddie Murphy
July 7, 1983

MTV
December 8, 1983

Bruce Springsteen
December 6, 1984

David Lee Roth
April 11, 1985

Live Aid
August 15, 1985

Rock and Roll Hall of Fame
February 13, 1986

Madonna
June 5, 1986

Pee-wee Herman
February 12, 1987

Rolling Stone, *created as a San Francisco underground paper, specializes today in coverage of the rock music world.*
(From *Rolling Stone* magazine, by Straight Arrow Publishers, Inc., © 1987 Fallon McElligott. All rights reserved. Reprinted by permission.)

to women, are a half-dozen magazines of 1.5 to 2.8 million circulation: *Sports Illustrated, Outdoor Life, Field and Stream, Popular Science, Popular Mechanics,* and *Home Mechanix.*

Special Interest Magazines

The hundreds of periodicals intended for special audiences form a very large segment of the magazine industry. Some are little known to the general public because they are infrequently displayed on the newsstands; others fall in major circulation categories.

The latter type includes the "shelter" magazines about family living, headed by *Better Homes and Gardens, Southern Living, Country Living,* and *Sunset;* farm magazines such as *Farm Journal* and *Successful Farming;* such science interest publications as *Scientific American, Discover,* and *Omni;* youth-oriented magazines such as *Boys' Life, Scouting, Junior Scholastic,* and *American Girl;* travel guides such as *Travel & Leisure;* and such diverse publications as *Psychology Today, Popular Photography,* and *Outside* (recreation).

The movie and TV fan magazines form still another special interest area. Others include trade and technical journals, professional and scientific publications, and publications intended for readers with hobbies such as model railroading or stamp collecting. Religious magazine publishing is an influential and important field. There are denominational and nondenominational publications, the largest of which—*Presbyterian Life, Catholic Digest,* and *Christian Herald*—circulate to hundreds of thousands of readers. The *National Jewish Monthly* serves 200,000 families. The bimonthly, *Modern Maturity,* founded in 1958 and distributed to members of the American Association of Retired Persons, has a circulation that has soared above 13.5 million.

New computer magazines proliferated during the early 1980s, bringing the total of such trade and consumer publications to about 200. *Personal Computing* led the way with circulation exceeding 500,000 and advertising priced at more than $12,-000 per page. *Creative Computing* and *Compute!* had circulations of 200,000 or more. Other leading magazines included *PC Magazine, Byte, PC World, Compute! Gazette, Run,* and *Family Computing.* As computer sales declined in the mid-1980s, however, the advertising revenue base shrunk to a level that could not support so many publications. As a consequence, and because readers could not absorb so much printed material, almost 100 of these magazines ceased publication and media analysts predicted the survival of only about 50.

Sunday Supplement Magazines

The Sunday magazine field experienced its greatest shakeup in history in 1985. The Gannett Company, Inc., purchased *Family Weekly,* a 32-year-old supplement distributed by about 360 newspapers, mostly in small cities. The magazine was renamed *USA Weekend* and redesigned along the lines of *USA Today,* with more but shorter stories, more color, and more pages than its predecessor. Concern that distributing *USA Weekend* would promote the sales of *USA Today* to their detriment led, in part, to more than 100 newspapers with 5 million circulation switching to *Parade*. The circulation of that 44-year-old magazine, formerly distributed mainly by 135, mostly large, newspapers, was thus boosted to more than 30 million. By 1987 its circulation had reached 31.6 million.

During that same period of realignment, however, the new *USA Weekend* signed up several major dailies including the Chicago *Tribune,* Denver *Post,* Des Moines *Register,* Dallas *Times Herald,* and Houston *Post,* and announced a circulation total of about 13 million. In 1987 the publication was carried by more than 285 newspapers.

The realignment followed a decline of approximately 30 percent in national advertising revenues by most Sunday magazines from high-profit years of 1979–1983, according to Sterling Dimmitt, president of Metropolitan Sunday Newspapers, Inc. The national advertising sales firm represents 46 of the 51 independently edited local Sunday magazines, with circulation exceeding 21 million.

At the same time, having lost much advertising support, the Indianapolis *Star* and the *Arizona Republic* in Phoenix ceased publication of their magazines and the Atlanta *Journal* and *Constitution* reduced the number of pages of its magazine, purchased *Parade,* and inserted the local magazine into the national supplement. Even so, the Los Angeles *Times* brought out a new Sunday magazine billed as a "home delivered weekly shaped on an entirely new newspaper concept—in its consumer size, far-ranging content, and brilliant color." These were confusing times, indeed, for the supplement field in this period when Sunday newspapers were growing: 144 new Sunday papers begun since 1975, representing a 22.5 percent increase, and a 12.6 percent increase in Sunday circulation, more than 6.5 million, despite the demise of several metropolitan papers with Sunday editions.

Meanwhile, the New York *Times* magazine, with an editorial staff of 50, maintained its position as the editorial and profit-making flagship of locally produced Sunday magazines. In 1985 the magazine grossed $109 million in advertising revenue, compared with $198 million for *Parade,* according to the Publishers Information Bureau.

Retail Store Magazines and Supplements

A number of giant retail chains followed the lead of the Great Atlantic and Pacific Tca Company (A&P) and began publishing their own magazines in the 1980s, complete with feature stories and outside advertising. Termed *magalogs,* because they combine features of both magazines and catalogues, the publications have helped build customer loyalty and defray the high cost of direct-mail marketing.

Neiman Marcus's *NM,* a quarterly begun in 1982 as *Imprint,* showcases the store's merchandise but also includes such editorial material as fiction by W. Somerset Maugham and an article on Perth, Australia, which appeared in a 1986 issue, along with advertisements of products not carried by the store.

Among other such magalogs are K mart's American *Lifestyles,* of which a million copies were placed on sale at 78 cents each in its stores and an additional 2 million copies mailed free as a marketing test in late 1986; *Geoffrey's Toys R Us Magazine,* with 300,000 copies on sale by Toys R Us, Inc., at 99 cents each; and Waldenbooks's *Kid's Club,* with its 200,000 copies containing games and articles along with advertising.

Harrods, the London department store, sells its own magazine on American newsstands at $5.50. A recent issue contained nearly 200 glossy pages of advertising with a smattering of editorial content.

A new genre of Sunday newspaper advertising supplements also continued to grow. In order to reduce the heavy cost of advertising in newspapers in 13 states, Macy's store in San Francisco began producing its own advertising magazine in 1981. Macy's then started a preprinted magazine, with some editorial content, for all of its stores. Dayton Hudson not only began distributing its *Today* advertising supplement through newspapers but also started a glossier, high-fashion magazine for its employees.

Retailers point out that both the magalogs and advertising supplements help them project their own image, reduce advertising costs, and cut through what they term the clutter of the approximately 10 billion catalogues mailed each year.

The Business Press

The fastest-growing magazine field, known as the *business press,* contains more than 3000 publications and is divided into two segments. One consists of magazines termed *horizontals* because their target audiences consist of readers in many fields of business rather than just one industry. They include national magazines such as *Fortune, BusinessWeek, Forbes,* and *Nation's Business* as well as a rapidly expanding array of regional, state, and local publications. They report developments in all aspects of the business world in much greater depth than that provided by broadcast networks and stations and by newspapers (except the *Wall Street Journal*). The much larger segment consists of magazines known as *verticals* because each covers one industry. They provide a steady flow of news, feature stories, and other information especially tailored for readers in their respective industries. Well-known examples are *Iron Age, Women's Wear Daily, Medical Economics,* and *Oil and Gas Journal.* The trade association representing both segments is the Association of Business Publishers, formerly known as the American Business Press.

The business press has grown significantly since World War II, especially during the last 15 years, a period characterized by mergers and acquisitions. So fierce is the competition and so rich the rewards that, whereas a major publication could be started in the 1970s for $200,000 to $500,000, today the cost ranges from $2 million to $5 million.

The largest firm, Harcourt Brace Jovanovich, publishes 127 magazines and newsletters and also produces or sponsors more than 25 trade and consumer shows and conventions. The second largest, McGraw-Hill, publishes 54 magazines and 43 newsletters (some in a joint venture with a Japanese firm), and also operates 18 newswires and information services. Other large groups include Cahners Publishing, Chilton (owned by the American Broadcasting Companies), Penton Publishing International, Thomson, and Technical Publishing (a subsidiary of Dun & Bradstreet).

Almost half of the business press consists of *controlled-circulation* publications,

AVERAGE CIRCULATION IN LEADING BUSINESS PRESS FIELDS IN 1984

Rank	Field	Circulation
1	Medical	2,982,975
2	Data management	1,611,874
3	Industrial products and design engineering	1,484,511
4	Electronics	1,370,281
5	Business and consumer services	1,308,931
6	Nursing	1,154,363
7	Aerospace and aviation	792,168
8	Architecture and building	735,413
9	Retail management	533,744
10	Food service	463,453
11	Telecommunications	458,103
12	Finance and investing	418,789
13	Chemicals	409,519
14	Automotive industry	357,964
15	Education	322,890
16	Metals	253,615
17	Marketing	181,421
18	Apparel	86,102

SOURCE: *Folio* magazine estimates. Courtesy of Folio Publishing Corp.

sent without charge to readers who are active buyers of the product and service advertisements that they contain. The remainder, except for a relatively small number sold on newsstands, are sent to subscribers at prices ranging from about $40 to almost $400 per year. The success of these publications is linked closely to the industries upon which they report; for example, magazines serving such fields as oil and gas, computers, steel, and farming recently have lost circulation because of financial setbacks in those industries. Nevertheless, the *trades,* as they are known, with total circulation exceeding 70 million, produced 1.8 million pages and received $3 billion in gross advertising revenues in 1985, according to William G. O'Donnell of the Association of Business Publishers. America's "best-kept media secret," as one publisher put it, is indeed a thriving field of journalism.

Company Publications

These are magazines published by corporations for distribution to their employees, stockholders, and customers, usually without charge. Their purpose is to present the company's policy and products in a favorable light and to promote a better sense of teamwork and belonging among employees. They are known also as industrial magazines; the term "house organ" was once widely used for these publications.

This field of industrial publishing has made large advances as corporations have become more conscious of their public relations. Many of these company publications are edited by people who are widely experienced in general magazine work and who have been given ample funds to produce magazines of sophisticated appearance and high-grade editorial content. More and more companies are realizing that they must hire professional people and set their standards to compare with general magazines on a broad basis. As one leading industrial editor, a veteran of general magazine staffs, expressed it: "No longer can the mail clerk or the personnel manager be regarded as an authority in the field of industrial editing. The emphasis definitely is on editing—and on journalism." Some university graduates move directly into industrial editing. In many such publications, articles of general interest, unrelated to the company's products, are included, and company propaganda is kept at a very subdued level. Some large corporations, in fact, publish a number of magazines intended for customers, stockholders, and employees. For example, the International Harvester Company and the Ford Motor Company publish some two dozen employee magazines each at different plants. Some of the more elaborate company publications, intended to reach the public as well as employees, have circulations above 1 million.

Company publications are of many sizes and shapes, and it is difficult to say at any given time how many of them qualify as magazines. Many appear in newspaper format. One recent estimate put the combined circulation of major company periodicals above 100 million. American business and industry invest more than $600 million a year in almost 10,000 publications with some 16,000 editors and staff members.

Desktop Publishing

The new phenomenon known as *desktop publishing* has enabled editors and publishers in recent years to produce at relatively low cost thousands of specialty magazines and newsletters, as well as books, newspapers, brochures, manuals, reports, and many other types of printed materials.

With only a personal computer, software, hard-disc drive, and a basic laser printer, one operator can write (or edit copy provided by others), set type, prepare artwork, and lay out an entire publication. The result is camera-ready copy that can be sent to a printer to be reproduced in hundreds or thousands of copies.

The method saves the larger cost and the time-delay of having a publication produced either by a huge typesetting machine that assembles pieces of metal type into columns, which are printed on paper as galley proofs, or a bulky photocompositor that projects type characters onto photosensitive film or paper. The columns are cut to size and pasted, with accompanying artwork, on cardboard layout sheets called mechanicals and then printed photographically.

Desktop publishing got its big boost early in 1985 when Apple Computer's Laserwriter plain-paper printers were made available and then received further impetus a few months later when Aldus introduced its Apple Macintosh-compatible Pagemaker software. Other manufacturers followed with hardware and software of their own.

Accelerating the adoption of the new equipment was its relatively low cost of about $10,000, tens of thousands of dollars less than the cost of a traditional phototypesetting machine. One early user prepared a trade magazine for 60 cents a page, whereas a professional typesetter would have charged from $4 to $6 a page. Another produced a book at the cost of about 30 cents a page, as compared with professional typesetting charges ranging from $10 to $30 a page.

The new method lacked the quality and flexibility of traditional typesetting. Viewed closely, the images were not quite as sharp as regular type, and professional machines offered a greater choice of typefaces. But when extremely high-quality type was desired, do-it-yourself typesetters could use a personal computer to set type on an expensive typesetting machine, paying the owner on an hourly basis for the privilege.

Desktop publishers, using a wide variety of type styles and sizes, prepare the text and headlines and then, with the aid of a handheld "mouse" or other pointing device, expand or reduce the copy, arrange it into columns, and decorate the computer page with rules and other embellishments. The finished product then is fed into a nearby laser printer that produces camera-ready copy.

Among the first magazines produced in such a fashion were *Balloon Life, Hawaii, Western Horse, Professional Locksmithing,* and *Vintage Motorsport.* Do-it-yourself magazines also appeared, including *Publish!* and *Desktop Publishing.* A number of books were published on the subject.

By giving computers a function both dazzling and practical, desktop publishing pumped new life into the computer industry. One market analyst predicted that the market for the equipment would reach $5 billion by 1990.

HOW MAGAZINES ARE MARKETED

The magazine industry obtains its revenues from circulation and advertising, built upon strong editorial content. For decades publishers sold each copy to the reader for far less money than it cost to produce it, making their profit through the sale of national and regional advertising. During recent years, however, the rising costs of paper, printing, payrolls, and home and newsstand deliveries greatly increased subscription and single-copy prices. Consequently, as reported in 1980 by *Folio,* a trade magazine for magazine publishers, readers paid $3.32 billion during a preceding measured year (46 percent of total revenues) as compared with $3.95 billion spent by advertisers (54 percent). Thus, as readers now provide nearly half of net income, the publishers' onetime reliance upon advertising revenue to pay most of the costs of producing and distributing magazines has diminished considerably. *Folio* termed this development the most important change in magazine economics in recent years.

Folio examined more than 12,000 magazines and 6,000 publishing companies, and thoroughly analyzed the 400 largest magazines (by gross sales), representing 94 percent of the entire industry. It found that total gross sales for these 400 amounted to $7.27 billion, with subscribers spending $1.74 billion and single-copy purchasers $1.58 billion, the latter increasingly at checkout counters and family reading centers in supermarkets throughout the country (see Figure 8.1.).

Figure 8.1 shows how magazine expenses are allocated. Total magazine indus-

PRIMARY SOURCES OF MAGAZINE ADVERTISING REVENUE

	Percent
Automotive	11.1
Business and consumer services	9.4
Toiletries and cosmetics	7.8
Tobacco	7.6
Food	7.0
Mail order	6.5
Apparel	5.1
Computer, office equipment and stationery	5.0
Travel, hotels, and resorts	5.0
Beer, wine, and liquor	4.9

SOURCE: Publishers Information Bureau. Courtesy of Magazine Publishers Association. These 10 product categories accounted for almost 70 percent of all magazine advertising revenue in 1985.

try circulation fell just short of 350 million copies per issue, or approximately 7.7 billion copies annually. Of the 350 million copies, 197 million were sold by subscription, while the remainder was divided between newsstand (99 million) and free and controlled circulation. *TV Guide* alone accounted for more than 1 billion copies sold during the year.

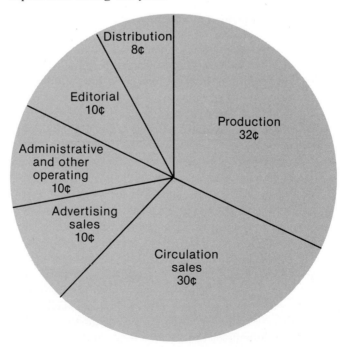

FIGURE 8.1
Magazine Industry costs: The expense dollar. (Source: Price Waterhouse study for Magazine Publishers Association, 1985. Courtesy of Magazine Publishers Association.)

In all, more than 469,000 advertising pages were published by the top 400 magazines studied.

A survey of these magazines reported by *Folio* in 1985 revealed that total revenues had increased beyond $12 billion per year and the number of advertising pages had swelled well beyond one-half million.

With consumer and advertiser interest in magazines high, and the population growing, between 250 and 350 new magazines are announced each year, according to *Folio.* Observers say the odds are ten to one that a magazine will fail, with much depending upon skilled management and the extent of capitalization. ("It depends upon who's starting it," one magazine investor said. "If a *Time* has a child, the odds are much shorter, maybe two to one.") *Viva, New Dawn,* and *Sassy* are among recent casualties.

Since hundreds of magazines, as well as other media, compete for advertising dollars, successful publishers must convince advertisers that the purchase of space in their pages is a good investment. This proof is based mostly on circulation figures. Magazines must show either very large mass distribution figures among a general readership or a firmly established circulation among the special interest groups to which their publications appeal editorially.

These economic principles have a powerful influence on the shape of the entire magazine industry. A magazine must be designed for appeal to a well-defined segment of the population, such as outboard boating enthusiasts or members of a fraternal order, or it must possess such broad interest that it will attract huge numbers of general readers.

Approximately 70 magazines have circulations of more than 1 million, as compared with only about 50 in 1980. The rising population makes big publishers hopeful of even greater circulation figures in the years ahead. The death of one-half dozen or so mass circulation magazines created the false impression that hard times had hit the magazine field. Circulation figures and other evidence, such as record revenues, show that this is not the case. Many individual magazines have suffered because of changing public tastes; shifting marketing conditions, including increased production costs and postal rates, the latter causing some to consider alternative delivery systems; and the loss of much advertising by mass circulation magazines to cable television. On the whole, however, the magazine field remains healthy.

Hundreds of small magazines operate profitably year after year by concentrating on their special fields. Since advertising rates are based mostly on circulation, many advertisers cannot afford to buy space in magazines with circulations in the millions, on which the rate for a single black-and-white advertising page ranges from $30,000 to $60,000 and for color from $40,000 to $75,000. Instead, they spend their money in publications they can afford and that offer them an audience especially receptive to their products. To counteract this, some large magazines offer advertising space on regional or fractional split-run bases, and this practice accounts for some 20 percent of total magazine advertising revenues.

Magazines are sold by two principal methods, *single-copy* sales on newsstands and *mail delivery* copies to subscribers. Circulation is one of the most costly and complex problems a magazine publisher faces. Copies of each issue must be distributed nationwide and must be on sale by fixed dates each week or month. Copies unsold when the publication date for the next issue comes around must be discarded at heavy loss. Newsstand sales of magazines are handled through news wholesalers. Intricate arrangements and deals are made to ensure good display at outlets, since many sales are made on impulse as the buyer walks past the colorful array on the racks. This makes attractive cover design and provocative, attention-getting titles and sales catchlines on the covers extremely important.

As previously reported, the largest magazine publisher today in terms of total income (about $3 billion annually) is Time Inc. *Time* made its appearance in the early 1920s with a condensed, opinionated style of news presentation. The company's picture weekly, *Life,* held top place among all magazines in gross advertising revenue from the 1950s until the shifting of many of its advertisers to television caused its collapse in 1972. *Time* then held that position until surpassed by *TV Guide.* Time Inc. also publishes *Fortune,* devoted to the business world; *Sports Illustrated; Life,* revived in 1978 as a monthly, with 1986 circulation exceeding 1.5 million; and, among others, *Southern Living, Money,* and *People* (see Chapter 21).

The Hearst magazine group is affiliated with that newspaper publishing family's empire. The group includes such large and profitable properties as *Good Housekeeping, Cosmopolitan, Harper's Bazaar, Esquire, Popular Mechanics, Sports Afield,* and *House Beautiful.* Its group also includes magazines in motoring and sailing, leisure, and other fields.

Other major groups include the McGraw-Hill trade publications, headed by *BusinessWeek;* the McCall Corporation, with *McCall's* and *Redbook;* Meredith Publishing Company, with *Better Homes and Gardens* and *Successful Farming;* the Johnson Publishing Company, with *Ebony, Jet,* and *Tan;* and the Condé Nast publications, *Glamour, Vogue, Mademoiselle, Gentleman's Quarterly,* and *House and Garden.*

Unlike newspapers, a large majority of magazines do not own their own printing facilities. The editors and advertising staffs prepare each issue in the office and then send the material to a commercial printer who holds a contract to produce the magazine. In fact, a few large printing houses with high-speed color presses do the printing for most of the major national magazines. This freedom from the heavy initial investment in printing equipment enables new publishers to start magazines with limited capital; however, unless the new venture embodies an attractive basic idea or angle, and is well edited, the printing and circulation bills can soon exceed the adventurous newcomer's capital.

EDITORIAL CONTENT AND OPERATION

The editorial operation of magazines varies greatly, depending upon the size, type, and frequency of the publication. Generally, editorial staffs are relatively small. A magazine selling 4 million copies can be prepared editorially by a smaller staff than the one needed to put out a newspaper that sells one-half million copies. This is possible because much of the material published in some magazines is written by freelance writers, either on speculation or on order from the editors. These writers are paid fees for their work and do not function as members of the staff.

The magazine editor's job is to decide what kinds of material to publish, arrange to obtain it, and then present it in a manner pleasing to the reader's eye. Most editors work from a formula; that is, each issue contains specified types of material in predetermined amounts. Articles and stories are selected for publication not only on their merit but for the way they fit the formula.

The editor has a staff of assistants to screen freelance material, work with writers, think of ideas, and edit the material chosen for publication. One staff member arranges attractive layouts and chooses the covers. On many magazines a substantial portion of each issue is written by staff members.

The skillful, imaginative use of photojournalism has contributed heavily to the acceptance gained by many magazines in recent years. Combining technical efficiency with an appreciation of the aesthetic and the dramatic, the photojournalist is an able communicator with a camera. Only a few magazines have their own staffs of professional photojournalists. Freelance photographers, often working through agents, provide most of the pictures. Rates range in excess of $300 per day for black-and-white pictures, $400 for color, and $500 for cover shots. Picture editors make assignments and select the photos wanted for publication.

A key part of most magazine operations is the editorial conference, a session in which the editors discuss the forthcoming issue, make decisions on the material to be used, examine proposed layouts, and agree upon projects for future issues. In order that assignments may be made, projects generally are planned months in advance of publication.

The news magazines operate somewhat differently. All their content is written by staff members, who are responsible for designated categories of material and for specific assignments, somewhat like a newspaper. Bureaus around the country and staff members abroad usually submit material ordered from the home office; the material is then rewritten and condensed to fit the available space. Magazines also lean heavily on press association material. News magazines operate on a rigid schedule in order to put the latest information on the newsstands throughout the United States.

Most magazines have at their command large amounts of freelance material submitted by writers who hope to "strike it lucky" and sell their work for a substantial sum. As most editors will testify, a relatively small amount of the unsolicited material unloaded on their desks by the mail carrier each day ever reaches print. Not that it necessarily is badly written or devoid of fresh ideas, but much of it does not fit the magazine's purpose. The problem for the freelance writer is to have the right manuscript in the right editorial office at the right moment—not an easy task. Professional writers usually submit their articles in outline form or offer just a brief proposal called a *query*.

Since editors have found that they cannot depend upon unsolicited freelance material to fit their individual needs, they go in search of what they want. They assign article ideas to writers they know, and then work with them until the manuscripts have the desired flavor and approach. Or the idea might be assigned to a member of the staff and developed in the same manner.

Very few writers in the United States, perhaps only 250 or 300, make a living as full-time freelance magazine writers, but thousands try to join them. Although an established writer may be paid from $1000 up per article, the uncertainties of the craft are many and the number of big money markets is relatively small. Most of these full-time magazine writers work on assignment, being commissioned by editors who know and like their work to prepare articles on ideas proposed by the editors or ideas approved by them. In many cases freelance writers use agents to sell their output to editors on a commission basis. The agent functions to a degree as an adjunct of the editorial staff by channeling worthwhile stories to appropriate magazines. The better-known agents are quite selective about the authors they will handle, and having a well-known agent is a helpful endorsement for a writer.

Much of the contributed material published in magazines is written by writers who do freelance work on a part-time basis as a sideline to their regular occupation. Newspaper reporters, other mass media people, teachers, attorneys and other professionals, and anyone with a flair for writing try their hands at freelancing with varying degrees of success.

There are hundreds of places where magazine material can be sold. *Writer's Digest* and *The Writer* provide information about specific magazine markets. Competition to place articles and fiction in the mass circulation magazines is intense, and the material purchased must be excellently written and extensively researched. Preparation of a major magazine article requires so much skill and time that the work for the major general magazines is done largely by the small group of full-time professionals and staff members. However, the part-time freelancer can hit even the biggest magazines with short material, such as anecdotes, personal experiences, and humor. With a little luck and a lot of perseverance, a writer can sell numerous articles to smaller magazines and specialized periodicals. However, the pay in these smaller markets is not high; it ranges from $50 for a 2500-word article or up to about $500 for a short story. Rates of payment for the confession-type magazines are 3 to 5 cents a word. At the upper end of the scale, where the competition is intense, the mass circulation magazines pay from $1000 to $3000 or higher for an article. The rates are flexible because the editors will pay extra if they consider that the material is exactly right for them or if the writer has a well-known name worth publicizing on the cover. One of the best ways for the newcomer to break into the market is to submit short-item filler materials, for which many magazines pay $10 or more.

JOB OPPORTUNITIES IN THE MAGAZINE INDUSTRY

The magazine industry provides interesting, stimulating, and generally well-paid jobs for thousands of men and women. On some periodicals the editorial staff members do extensive writing, handling special departments and articles; on others, the editors are engaged mostly in selection and editing of submitted material.

Historically, magazines have offered greater opportunities for the woman editorial worker than have newspapers traditionally staffed by men. The percentage of staff positions held by women is greater and the opportunity for advancement to high editorial positions has been much brighter. Women associate editors, managing editors, and editors-in-chief are not uncommon.

Robert E. Kenyon, Jr., longtime executive director of the American Society of Magazine Editors, points out that entry-level editorial jobs are hard to find unless applicants are well qualified. Says Kenyon:

> Entry-level jobs are in editing, not in writing. Too many aspirants in magazine journalism assume their first tasks will be in writing. That is not so. Your first magazine job is more likely to be in editing; that is, you will be reading proof, reviewing unsolicited manuscripts, checking facts, doing research for articles to be written by others, writing headlines, subheads, picture captions—but not cover lines. You can also expect some gofering chores. If you are lucky—and quite good—you might do an occasional column or a short by-lined piece. Writing assignments come along later, maybe.

Kenyon recommends that journalism majors take as many skill courses (reporting, writing, and editing) as possible. They should involve themselves deeply in campus journalism, having responsibilities as a senior editor of the college newspaper or magazine. In addition, internships or jobs should be spliced between course work. Liberal arts majors, Kenyon observes, should assume even greater responsibilities in campus journalism, internships, or jobs than journalism majors.

Selling a magazine some articles or stories also can open the door for jobs. The very fact that the editor buys the material indicates that he or she approves of the writer's work. Personal contacts developed in this editor-writer relationship sometimes lead to staff positions.

Large magazines draw many of their staff members from the trade magazines and company publications, much as metropolitan newspapers hire reporters who have had training on smaller dailies. The mechanical techniques of magazine editing and design are complex and can best be learned by experience on smaller publications.

Industrial magazines are among the finest training grounds for magazine workers. This is a rapidly expanding field, as more and more corporations realize the value of issuing a periodical for customers, employees, salespeople, stockholders, and other groups the management wishes to inform or impress. These are divided into *internal* publications, for distribution within a company, and *external* ones, which go to nonemployee readers. Many are combinations of these approaches. The type of distribution influences the kind of material published and to some extent the size of the staff. The best available estimate puts the number of editorial employees on company publications at around 15,000. Although many of these publications are prepared by a single editor with clerical help, the more elaborate ones have a staff of six or eight editors. They use the same techniques of design, multicolored artwork, and editorial presentation as those employed by the better-known consumer magazines.

External publications are usually published by manufacturers who hope for repeat sales of products of relatively high price. Automobile manufacturers are among the most lavish publishers in this field; magazines such as *Ford Times,* more than 80 years old, are widely circulated to maintain contact with users and to promote sales and service.

Many fraternal and nonprofit organizations also publish magazines in order to maintain the bond with their members or supporters. Such periodicals as *American Legion* and the *Rotarian* publish a rather broad range of general articles that their editors consider of interest to their readers, and interweave promotional and fraternal material about the sponsoring organization.

Work on specialized magazines, both of the industrial magazine and trade varieties, sometimes requires technical knowledge in such fields as engineering, electronics, and chemistry. It is natural for a young person seeking a job to enter whatever trade field seems particularly interesting. No matter what technical knowledge may be necessary, however, the fundamental requirement in all magazine work is a sound knowledge of the English language. With this foundation and a willingness to work hard at learning the rudiments of a specialized field, the aspiring trade journal or industrial editor can progress steadily. A knack for simplifying technical material for the general reader is a desirable asset. College courses in economics are valuable in almost any kind of magazine work because so much of the material printed in magazines deals in some way with the operations of American business. Many schools offer industrial and technical courses to help students prepare for industrial journalism.

Salaries

Editorial managers of consumer and business magazines earned an average salary of $52,240 in 1986, according to the second annual survey conducted by *Folio* magazine. At $84,101 the average salary of managers of the top 400 revenue-producing magazines was considerably higher than the $49,112 average paid to the editorial managers of other magazines.

Editors earned an average salary of $52,240; managing editors, $39,088; senior

THE TOP MAGAZINE MONEY MAKERS

These ten magazines led all others in the United States in total advertising revenues in 1986, according to the Publishers Information Bureau:

Magazine	Revenues (In Millions)
Time	$344.8
TV Guide	$318.1
People	$267.7
Sports Illustrated	$247.4
Newsweek	$238.4
BusinessWeek	$166.6
Good Housekeeping	$145.0
Family Circle	$141.6
Better Homes and Gardens	$129.8
Woman's Day	$123.5

editors, $43,536; associate editors, $26,594; copy editors, $23,549; and art directors, $42,326. Salaries were higher in the Northeast, the center of magazine publishing, than elsewhere.

About three-fourths of the 457 professionals responding in the survey reported that they had the option of participating in a deferred compensation (pension or profit-sharing) plan. Annual bonuses averaged $13,150 for editorial managers; $7,353 for editors; $2,809 for managing editors; $2,366 for senior editors; $1,612 for associate editors; $622 for copy editors; and $3,872 for art directors.

Folio reported that working on a top revenue-producing magazine can mean more money for editorial managers, editors, managing and senior editors, and art directors, but it seems to make no difference for those lower on the masthead. Male editors and art directors earned about $10,000 more annually than females with the same titles.

The position of copy editor, often the starting point for college graduates, was marked by an average salary of $17,637 for those within their first three years of employment. Copy editors with four to ten years' experience averaged $24,526, while those more experienced earned $29,484.

These salaries carry with them a substantial amount of job uncertainty. If a magazine begins to lose advertising support, frequently one of the first corrective moves is to change editors, even though the fault may not lie in the editorial department at all. When a magazine is struggling to work out a new formula to regain readership, it may try several editors before finding one who can do the job. The pay offered to college graduates as beginners is in line with that offered by other media.

Salaries in the industrial magazine fields are somewhat lower, but the job security is better. A survey by the International Association of Business Communicators disclosed that in 1982 the average salary of its member publication editors was $22,900, with assistant editors averaging $17,475.

Editorial and business offices of most large national magazines are in New York and other eastern cities. Trade publication headquarters are situated throughout the United States, depending in part upon the market being served. There are numerous editorial links between magazine and book publishing, and the movies as well. Some magazine material eventually finds its way into book form and even into films, one example being the article, "The Urban Cowboy." This leads to some movement of editorial workers from magazines to book publishing firms and occasionally back in the other direction.

Other types of magazine jobs also can be rewarding. These include such tasks as working with the art director or editor; circulation and advertising promotion, sales, and research; and production, including work with the printer. There are fewer applicants for these jobs than for writing and editing positions.

A LOOK AHEAD

The flexibility that magazines enjoy in catering to the specific interests and needs of their readers and advertisers forecasts their generally steady growth in the years ahead. Demographic, geographic, psychographic, lifestyle, and just about every special interest can be targeted. Demographic editions, for example, can be sent exclusively to readers in high-income areas so denoted by zip codes. Regional and city magazines can concentrate advertising in the most profitable markets.

Studies have shown that magazine reading is strongest among 18–44-year-old readers, the college-educated, professional/managerial people, and those with household incomes of $30,000 or more. The continued strong acceptance of magazines thus can be postulated by studies predicting that, while from 1980 to 1990 the total U.S. population is expected to grow by 10 percent, the college-educated portion will increase 42 percent and households earning $25,000 or more (in constant dollars) annually will increase 74 percent.

Those are the consumers of mass circulation magazines that advertisers most want to reach. Consequently, more and more magazines likely will follow the lead taken by *Reader's Digest* and *McCall's* in 1986 in eliminating from their subscription lists millions of subscribers expensive to gain and to retain. Thus they can offer advertisers both reduced space rates and a more easily targeted body of better-educated, high-income subscribers than would otherwise be provided.

Book Publishing

Read a Good Book Lately?

From work on magazines such as *Good Housekeeping* and the *Ladies' Home Journal,* to sex-oriented *Cosmopolitan,* to writing sensual novels of which *I'll Take Manhattan* is her most recent, right into American living rooms with TV miniseries.

That's the career path that New York City native Judith Krantz has followed in becoming one of the world's most popular novelists.

Houston homemaker Karleen Koen took a more direct route. Imagining the life of an heiress in eighteenth-century England and France, she read more than 400 works about the period, wrote a novel, and mailed the manuscript to a New York literary agent whose name she saw in a writer's magazine. *Through a Glass Darkly,* her first literary effort, appeared on the New York *Times* best-seller list in 1986.

Krantz and Koen are among several dozen authors whose works have helped propel publishers of hardcover books right into the mass market paperbound business, instead of selling the reprint rights to paperback publishers as they once did.

Movie, television, video—even audiotape—tie-ins are acquainting millions with the works of such authors as Jean M. Auel *(The Mammoth Hunters),* James A. Michener *(Texas),* and Garrison Keillor *(Lake Wobegon Days),* not to mention such nonfiction giants as *Iacocca,* the autobiography of Chrysler's president, which sold well over 2.5 million copies during the first two years.

Eight paperback originals by John Jakes have sold more than 40 million copies. The combined hardcover and paperback sales for his two most recent novels, *North and South* and *Love and War,* exceed 5 million copies.

The lure for these writers? Overwhelming cash. Random House paid Koen an advance of $350,000 for hardcover rights, reported to be a record for a first novel. Krantz already is a multimillionaire, as is Jakes, who was paid a reported $4.3 million by Random House for a novel yet to be written. His *California Gold* is scheduled for publication in 1989.

*B*ooks are an essential ingredient in our lives, providing knowledge and entertainment for people of all ages and stimulating our creative imaginings.

In the United States books are produced by approximately 1750 publishing houses, spread throughout the country but situated mainly in New York City, Boston, and Philadelphia.

Publishers gross more than $10 billion in sales each year. Trade books—those marketed to the general consumer and sold mainly through bookstores—provide the largest immediate gross returns. Well over $1 billion in each category is garnered through purchases of professional books, college texts, and textbooks sold for use in elementary and secondary schools. Libraries buy books of all these types.

During recent decades the mass market paperbound book has been a publishing phenomenon, paralleled by the rise of major bookstore chains with outlets primarily in shopping malls. Audiocassettes, videocassettes, and computer software represent rapidly growing markets. Most publishing houses are owned by giant conglomerates, and bottom-line financial considerations dictate almost all publishing decisions. Tie-ins of trade books with the movie, television, and video industries are common.

In this chapter we explore the changing world of book publishing, relate how books are made and sold, and discuss the job opportunities in writing, editing, designing, promoting, advertising, marketing, selling, and other aspects of the business. ◆

THE ROLE OF BOOKS

Books are a medium of mass communications that deeply affects all our lives. Books convey much of the heritage of the past, help us understand ourselves and the world we live in, and enable us to plan for the future. They are a significant tool of our educational process. They stimulate our imagination, and they provide entertainment for people of every age.

The nation's current educational, business, and social life could not survive long without books. Judges and attorneys must examine law tomes and their computerized indices continually; doctors constantly refer to the repositories of medical wisdom and experience; government officials must be aware of all the ramifications of new legislation. Teachers and students find in textbooks the vast knowledge of history, philosophy, the sciences, the arts, literature, and the social sciences accumulated through the ages. People in every walk of life read to keep abreast of a fast-changing world, to find inspiration, relaxation, and pleasure, and to gain knowledge. Books explain, question, and interpret nearly every aspect of life.

The literary record has been one of the hallmarks by which each succeeding world civilization has been measured: the works of Plato and Aristotle, for example, both reflected and refined the quality of life in Greece. These philosophers and others of their time had no books, but created them for *us.* Social historians have long examined creative literature as well as the factual records of a civilization in their efforts to reconstruct the life of the people of a particular time and place. In the United States today the finest published fiction has a reverberating impact upon our society. The ideas and techniques employed by fiction writers have an enormous effect on theater, movie, and television scripts. Many outstanding productions result from the book publisher's enterprise in encouraging and promoting both new and established authors. Creative writing enhances most of the art forms by which our civilization will one day be judged.

Whether they are paperbacks or hardcover volumes, books provide a permanence characteristic of no other communications medium. Newspaper reporters and radio-television commentators address a large audience, but their materials quickly disappear. Videocassettes, audiotapes, recordings, motion pictures, and microfilm may deteriorate through the years. Magazines, especially those printed on high-quality paper and bound into volumes, may have extremely long lives, but most get thrown out with the trash. If cared for properly, however, books, such as the superb copies of the Bible produced by Gutenberg in the fifteenth century, last virtually forever.

For the mass communicator, books perform several important functions. They

Rachel Ward and Richard Chamberlain in a scene from a movie adapted from Colleen McCullough's best-selling book, The Thorn Birds. *(Courtesy of Warner Bros. Television Distribution, Photo Trends)*

not only serve as wellsprings of knowledge but, through translation and reprinting and through conversion to movies, television productions, and live performances, convey vital ideas to millions of people throughout the world. In publishing itself the mass communicator may find a rewarding outlet in writing, editing, and promoting the distribution of books.

Journalists such as Tom Wolfe, Jimmy Breslin, Gay Talese, and Anthony Lewis have written books that vastly increased the audience for their reports, and each has made an impact on the world of ideas that almost invariably accompanies the creation of a widely read book.

In the wake of news events that command great attention, some paperbacks are rushed into print. *Terrorism: How the West Can Win,* the Tower Commission report of the so-called Irangate scandal, and books dealing with the invasion of Grenada are examples. Even so, because of the relative slowness of writing, editing, and publishing a manuscript, books lack the immediacy that other media enjoy in conveying their messages. What may be lost in timeliness is often more than compensated for by the depth of coverage and analysis and by the care that editors and writers take in checking facts and rewriting copy for maximum effectiveness. This sustained, systematic exposition of a story or an idea (with the reader's opportunity to reread, underscore, and study at leisure) is afforded only by books.

THE CHANGING BOOK PUBLISHING INDUSTRY

By dollar volume, book publishing is a dwarf among American industrial giants. It makes up only a tiny fraction of the nation's economy. Approximately one of

Paperback books about major news developments sometimes appear on sales racks only days after the event. Assistant manager Richard Haas stocks shelves of the Doubleday bookstore in New York with copies of the Tower Commission Report, which Bantam Books produced less than 48 hours after the document was released in Washington. (AP/Wide World)

every three of the approximately 1750 publishing houses, employing about 65,000 persons, is situated in New York City, Boston, and Philadelphia. In recent years, however, many new firms have been established on the West Coast and in the South. In all, the industry grosses almost $10 billion in sales each year.

Categories of Books

Approximately 90,000 books are published in the United States each year. The major divisions of the industry include:

- *Trade books,* marketed to the general consumer and sold mainly through bookstores and to libraries.
- *Religious books,* including Bibles and hymnals.
- *Mass-market paperbacks,* sold mainly through newsstands and chain retail stores.
- *Professional books,* such as medical, technical, legal, scientific, and business works.
- *Book clubs,* actually a marketing channel for books issued by other publishers.
- *Mail-order publications,* created to be marketed by direct mail to the consumer, frequently as part of a continuing series related to a particular topic.
- *University or academic presses,* nonprofit adjuncts of universities, museums, and research institutions, mainly concentrating on scholarly or regional topics.
- *Elementary and secondary textbooks* (called elhi or school textbooks), hard- or soft-cover texts and manuals, maps, and other items for classroom use, mainly sold in bulk to school districts.
- *College textbooks,* hard- or soft-cover volumes and audiovisual materials; the texts are sometimes similar to trade books.
- *Standardized tests,* for schools, colleges and universities, and industry.
- *Subscription reference books,* mainly sets of encyclopedias sold through the mail or door-to-door, as well as dictionaries, atlases, and similar works.

As Figure 9.1 shows, four categories of book publishing produced more than $6.3 billion in sales during 1985. Trade books, with more than a 50 percent increase from 1981 to 1985, led the way, followed in order by professional books, elementary and secondary school (elhi) texts, and college texts.

College textbooks had been the third most productive category for years, but their unit sales increased by only 4 percent as compared with a 51 percent increase in unit sales of used texts during this same period. One reason is the substantially higher price of a new college text, up 50 percent during the period—35 percent higher than the nation's Consumer Price Index, according to the Follett Corporation of Chicago. Sharply increased production and marketing costs, as well as the fact that bookstores return to the publisher about one of every six new texts, are among reasons for the advance. College bookstores achieve an average operating profit of 10 percent from the sale of used books (sales that mean zero profits for publishers and authors), whereas, according to the Follett study, college stores

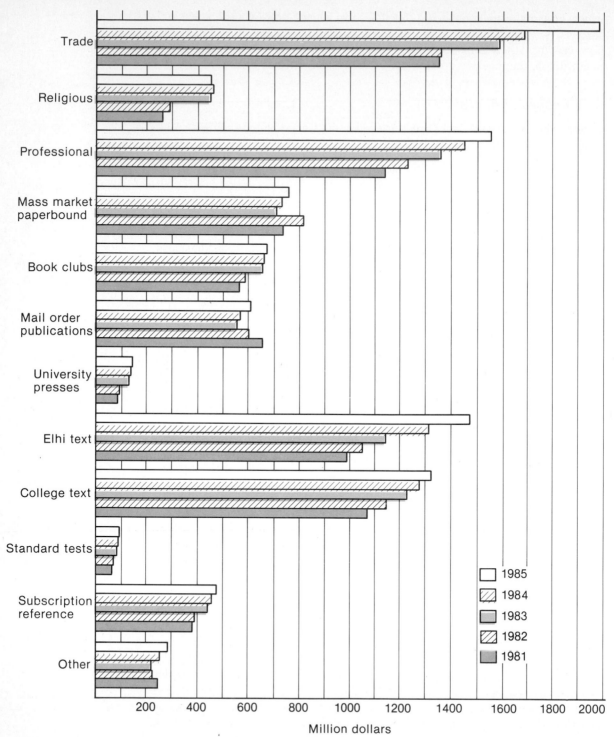

FIGURE 9.1
The 1981 to 1985 book publishing industry sales by division. (Source: Data courtesy of the Association of American Publishers.)

actually lose about 3 percent from the sale of new texts. Dealers buy used texts from the stores and from professors (almost always complimentary copies sent by publishers) and ship them across the country to meet demand. In order to give college stores flexibility in setting prices of new texts, a number of publishers, beginning with Harper & Row in 1980, instituted net pricing (the cost of the book to the store) for new college textbooks instead of establishing the retail sales prices themselves.

In the nonprofit field the sale of publisher-originated audiovisual materials and computer software more than doubled during the five-year period, to a total of almost $200 million. Audio programs, pitched at the myriad number of home cassette players, car audio systems, and Walkmans, showed marked increases. The product ranged from audio versions of popular books such as *Lake Wobegon Days* (some read on the tapes by their authors) to tapes on how to lose weight, stop smoking, or become a better manager. Videocassettes, mostly rented rather than sold by stores, offered an equally wide range of choices. Firms other than book publishers also produced tapes. Waldenbooks and B. Dalton, for example, commissioned the production of private-label audiocassettes. Mitch Deutsch, president of Warner Audio Publishing, which acquired B. Dalton in 1985, predicted a billion dollar audio industry by the end of the decade (see Chapters 12 and 15).

Distribution Channels

Books are marketed through six main channels: (1) retail stores; (2) college stores; (3) directly to consumers through mail order, book clubs, and door-to-door sales to individuals; (4) libraries; (5) schools and institutions; and (6) in miscellaneous fashion to industry, government, foundations, and research institutions. In addition, more than $6.4 million in books from U.S. publishers are sold annually in more than 140 other countries where English is read. Translations provide additional income. Canada accounts for about 25 percent of this total (see Chapter 25).

Although book publishers constitute one of the few consumer industries that sell many products directly to users, most sales are made through wholesalers and jobbers, who stock the goods, mostly trade books, of many publishing houses and sell them locally and regionally. Wholesalers also sell nationally to retailers and through independent distributors, known as IDs, who supply retail outlets with mass market paperbacks and magazines as well.

A phenomenon of recent years has been the rise of big bookstore chains such as Waldenbooks and B. Dalton Booksellers. In 1972 the four largest chains accounted for about 11½ percent of all trade book sales in the country. By 1986, however, the two largest chains alone sold more than a third of all trade books and mass market paperbacks. The figure continues to rise. There are now more than 850 Walden stores in operation, with annual sales exceeding $360 million. Walden's closest competitor, B. Dalton, has well over 775 stores and sales of $375 million a year. These stores, often located in shopping centers and malls, employ supermarket strategies, including computerized inventory control and ordering systems. Major factors in the industry are discount chains such as Crown, which sells mostly trade books, and Barnes & Noble, which handles mostly trade books but texts as well.

The R. R. Bowker Company recently listed more than 12,000 book outlets of all kinds in the United States. They included 6700 that handle new books; 900 department stores; 2900 college bookstores; 7300 stores that sell paperbacks; 1700 that carry law, medical, technical, and scientific titles; 4000 religious-book sellers; 3000 that stock juvenile books; 1300 rare-book dealers; and 1000 dealers of secondhand books.

Technological Improvements

New technology is used in book publishing houses to reduce costs and improve customer service. Some firms will accept author manuscripts in computer disc form. Computer-formatting devices are widely used to prepare manuscripts prior to typesetting, providing, among other benefits, easier access to the product for storage and retrieval.

Few publishing houses print their own books. They rely on the more than 900 major printing and composition establishments in this country, a third more than the number in 1970. An increasing amount of four-color work and even the complete manufacture of books, however, is being assigned to printers in other countries where costs are lower (see Chapter 25).

The recent trend to laser printing technology is expanding through use of a technique identified in smaller printing operations as desktop publishing (see Chapter 8). In 1986 Avon Books produced the first rack-size mass market paperback from reproduction copy typeset on plain paper, thus significantly reducing composition costs. Observers viewing the type through a magnifying lens could discern no differences in character sharpness from type produced by the traditional phototypesetter.

In another development, leading mass market paperback publishers are printing Universal Product Code (UPC) bars on title pages. When processed by electronic scanners, UPC speeds order fulfillment and the handling of returns. Publishers anticipate the day when the International Standard Book Numbers (ISN), which now appears on copyright pages and on the spines or back covers of books, will be scanned by optical character recognition (OCR) equipment to help publishers and booksellers record and control inventory.

Ownership Developments

A seemingly relentless trend toward concentrating the ownership of individual publishing houses into ever-larger corporate organizations began in the 1960s. As part of inexorable economic trends that have transformed much of American business during the last century, and also because of near-confiscatory personal inheritance taxes, many privately owned companies have been converted into publicly held corporations and they, in turn, often have become absorbed into huge conglomerate organizations.

Today, with a handful of giant companies controlling much of the industry, a new and more complex corporate and financial environment has replaced the former leisurely and often inefficient atmosphere and practices of the major firms. Today's publishing decisions are based almost entirely upon bottom-line financial considerations.

Nowhere have these consolidation and management trends been more apparent than in the mass market paperback field. Formerly, as consultant Carolyn Anthony has pointed out, publishing was divided into two camps: on one side, those that produced hardcover books and sold them through bookstores; on the other, mass market paperback houses that did cheap reprint editions of hardcover books and sold them through many other outlets in addition to bookstores. The staggering sums paid to hardcover houses by the reprinters (for example, $3.2 million for Judith Krantz's *Princess Daisy*), and hardcover firms' recovering the rights to successful books when the paperback license expired, produced a change. Many mass market houses either disappeared or found their lines, or identities, absorbed into other firms. Today many paperback houses are producing their own hardcover editions, and a number of hardcover publishers are publishing their own rack-size paperback editions, using the facilities of mass market paperback organizations for manufacturing and distributing. Like banks in the 1980s, they have become providers of one-stop services, able to publish and sell in all formats.

In the mass market paperback field in particular, management people of a new breed now build images, plan marketing, and set production and performance standards. Their work is closely akin to that of advertising people, TV producers, talk show hosts, and Hollywood producers and packagers. Literary agents remain the power brokers, and publishing decisions are increasingly made with movie, television, video and audio subsidiary earnings in mind as well as the author's ability to "hype" a book on television talk shows.

Contending that many authors of artistically worthy works that lack immediate commercial appeal are being excluded from publication and that the conglomerates also threaten the lives of the remaining independently owned companies through unfair business practices, the Authors Guild, representing more than 5000 professional writers, unsuccessfully sought relief in the late 1970s from the Federal Trade Commission. The Association of American Publishers, representing more than 300 member companies accounting for about 85 percent of all books published in the United States, called these charges extreme and distorted. Instead, said industry spokespersons, the publishing industry was, in fact, "amazingly diverse, flexible, and open," with good books never in more plentiful supply and authors never more numerous or better rewarded. Mergers, they asserted, are an absolute necessity to keep publishing financially sound.

Among other problems facing the industry in the late 1980s, censorship will be discussed in Chapter 24 and the international marketing of books, including the extensive foreign piracy of American copyrighted works, will be discussed in Chapter 25.

Literacy

The shocking extent of illiteracy in the United States is a growing concern among book, magazine, and newspaper publishers; librarians; educators; and much of the informed public. The United States ranks 49th in the world in literacy, according to the United Nations Educational, Scientific, and Cultural Organization (UNESCO). The Association of American Publishers, representing the book industry, reports that as many as 20 to 27 million American adults are functionally illiterate (unable, for example, to read a soup can label or to read to their children); 40 to 49 million are marginally illiterate (with the reading abilities of fifth graders). Half of American children will not finish high school, and the illiteracy rate is growing by approximately 2.25 million each year.

Among other reasons for lack of reading ability, industry spokespersons point to the enormous amounts of time devoted to television (an average of more than seven hours daily per household) and to the popularity of videocassette recordings, citing predictions that Americans by 1990 will own an estimated 50 million VCRs. Concern also is voiced over the sale of items other than books, including VCRs, in bookstores and other consumer outlets.

The literacy problem is being attacked on a number of fronts. They include programs of the Library of Congress, National Commission on Excellence, American Book Awards, Literacy Volunteers (which has established a literacy hotline providing information on instructional reading programs), television network programs encouraging reading, publishers, and booksellers (B. Dalton Booksellers, for example, has committed $3 million for a national literacy initiative.) Federal support has been minimal, but many states and local school boards are encouraging reading; the California Department of Education, for example, allotted 20 percent of its $66 million budget for 1986–87 to enable schools to purchase contemporary and modern classics.

An encouraging note was sounded in 1986 when a Gallup national survey disclosed that about one teenager in five reported the purchase of a book within the past seven days, a proportion similar to that found among adults. Teenagers with college-educated parents were buying twice as many books as those whose parents had less formal education. Paperbacks, by far, were most popular. In addition, industry sales in 1985 of both hardcover and paperbound trade (popular) books increased an average of 20 percent over sales the previous year.

STEPS IN BOOK PUBLICATION

All books begin with an idea germinated by the author or by an editor employed by a publishing house. If the author has an idea for a nonfiction book, he or she generally prepares a précis and perhaps several sample chapters and submits them to a literary agent or publisher. Generally, unless the author is well known, the entire manuscript of a novel must be submitted. If it is the editor's idea, the editor seeks out the writer who can best develop the book based upon the concept.

Publishing houses vary in the number and level of responsibility of the editors they employ. In general, however, an acquiring editor works closely with an author in the development of a manuscript, and may also shepherd the work through various business and production stages. The editor must keep abreast of matters of public taste and interest and be able to intuit the types of books that will find markets in the years ahead. Reference, technical, and textbook editors who deal with specialized subject matter often employ professional critics. Trade book

A textbook editor prepares an outline for a new book.

editors, especially those dealing with fiction, are less likely to employ outside advice.

A common fallacy held by each summer's crop of job applicants in book publishing is that a publisher or an editor is simply a person of taste who sits waiting for hungry authors to arrive with best-selling manuscripts. But book publishing is like an iceberg. The part that shows, mainly books that are reviewed in mass media journals and magazines, often touted on TV talk shows, and sold in general bookstores, constitutes only about 8 percent of the total dollar volume in books. For every editor who breaks bread with Norman Mailer or Shirley McLaine, there are hundreds who edit reference books or work with college and school textbook authors. For most publishing houses, the unsolicited manuscript is rarely publishable, as many disillusioned beginning writers can testify.

Manuscripts accepted for publication are turned over to copyeditors, who may rewrite considerably as well as search for grammatical, spelling, and punctuation errors. They corroborate facts, correct discrepancies in style, and perhaps help cut the copy to a predetermined length. The copyeditor must also coordinate entries in the bibliography with the citations in footnotes (if the book has them); ensure that chapter headings correspond to tables of contents; relate pictures, tables, charts, and the like to the text; query the author when necessary; read the proofs (material returned from the compositor), including indexes; check corrections made by the author in the proofs; and in general ascertain that the text is as accurate as possible.

The production department, which may consist of from three to two dozen or more persons, normally serves as the book publisher's liaison with the compositor and printer. Highly specialized employees oversee the production process. They design the book, including selection of the type, and oversee preparation of the cover and jacket; produce or commission art work, if necessary; estimate length; select the paper; and order the typesetting, printing, and binding. Every book presents an individual problem and every stage of production must be worked out carefully in advance, the schedule often requiring a full 12 months to complete.

At the time the book is contracted, plans are made for its marketing and sale. The marketing department, increasingly more important in this competitive industry, helps to determine the direction and the form of advertising and promotion, with the acquiring editor acting as supervisor. Marketing also monitors the information to be sent to the salespeople. Trade sales representatives are called together usually twice a year for conferences involving the entire list of books being prepared for sale. In accordance with the advertising and promotion budget established for the book, based on anticipated sales, media are selected and advertisements and dealer aids, such as posters, circulars, and mail enclosures, are prepared.

The trade publicity department writes and mails news releases, arranges author interviews on television and radio and other personal appearances, sends copies of the book to reviewers, announces the publication of the book in trade magazines such as *Publishers Weekly,* arranges for exhibits at conventions attended by booksellers, and works in other ways to promote sales. The primary responsibility of the publicity department is to establish a climate of acceptance for the new book by employing every possible means at hand.

General sales representatives, calling on major bookstores, visit the largest stores perhaps 15 to 20 times a year. These persons normally work on salary or commission or a combination of the two, and sometimes carry the lines of two or more publishing houses. In addition, some sales personnel call on booksellers on behalf of jobbers and other wholesalers.

College textbook sales representatives, employed by the publishing house, perform a distinctly different function. Calling on the nation's college and university professors, they make certain that their clients are acquainted with or receive examination copies of textbooks appropriate to the courses the professors teach. Textbook salespeople seldom, if ever, sell directly to bookstores. They must hope that the professors they visit, who usually have freedom of textbook selection, will give them a share of business via the college bookstores. Sales representatives also act as manuscript scouts, since most college textbooks are written by college professors.

Hundreds of elhi school textbook agents work through state, county, and city adoption systems. Most school textbooks and audiovisual materials are written and prepared by the staff at a publishing house with professional advisers and teachers.

There are many other aspects of the production and sale of books not covered in this sketch of publishing. It is an intricate, fast-paced business, and many years of practical experience are required to learn the ground rules.

HOW THE MASS COMMUNICATOR FITS IN

The kinship of book publishing activities to those of other mass media should be apparent. Writing and editing must be done, as well as copyediting and proofreading; illustrating and designing; printing; marketing, advertising, and publicizing; distributing and selling. The editor must have shrewd insight into what interests the public, and when. The book editor identifies with the tastes and needs of various segments of the book-buying population, just as the newspaper city editor maintains a sense of rapport with the newspaper's readers.

Book publishing is a step removed from the operations of some of the other media, which continually deal with a mass audience. Books are often read by highly selective groups. Yet work in other mass communications fields can provide an ideal background for the responsibilities of book publishing.

Writers for newspapers, magazines, and radio-television, for example, inevitably gain insights that can be drawn upon to advantage at the book editor's desk. With their attention to craft, they can quickly spot good or poor writing in a manuscript. Their experience in rewriting the work of others can help strengthen weak spots in a manuscript. As journalists they have learned to respect facts and to insist upon documentation. Familiar with the principles of style and grammar, they can effectively supervise the work of copyeditors and proofreaders. Experience gained from having worked with printers and other craftspeople will help keep production costs at a minimum. As media reporters or editors, they have drawn paychecks from profit-making organizations. Their appreciation of sound business methods will help them deal with authors who may be unfamiliar with the business world.

The knowledge of graphics that mass communicators obtain in school or on the job will be of use in ordering printing for a book and supervising the production of its cover and jacket. Advertising staff people can draw upon this same knowledge of typography, as well as other journalistic skills, in preparing direct mail folders, posters, and advertisements for print media. They will find that the same principles of copy, layout, illustration, color, and selection of paper and ink apply in the preparation of advertisements for new books.

Skills gained in journalism or public relations courses, or in previous practice, should enable book publishing employees to plan and carry out effective promotional campaigns, including writing news releases and other materials and maintaining contacts with the media.

JOB OPPORTUNITIES IN BOOK PUBLISHING

Many college graduates begin their careers in the trade editorial offices of book publishing firms. Often they are assigned the task of reading and making initial judgments about the merits of unsolicited manuscripts that arrive with great frequency. Some become copy and proof editors and research facts in encyclopedias and other reference works. As their judgment is corroborated by senior editors, they are assigned greater responsibilities. Editorial assistants usually start at about $14,000 a year. Successful senior editors earn $30,000 to $50,000 a year.

Young people who enjoy travel may choose to become sales representatives of the college textbook divisions of publishing houses. Their starting salaries generally range between $13,000 and $18,000 annually. All their business expenses are paid while they are on the road. With sales bonuses experienced representatives may earn $30,000 or more in a year. Some men and women enjoy lifelong careers as sales representatives or managers. Others move into the office, where they most likely will put their road experience to work in the editorial, sales, advertising, marketing, or production departments. Eventually they may become department managers, later perhaps officers or directors of the company, with salaries in the $70,000 to $100,000 range. Hard-headed business acumen is essential for such advancement.

While some people, as noted, ascend the publishing ladder as editors, others move into marketing and publicity jobs. They write news and feature copy, help plan marketing campaigns, prepare advertising materials, compose jacket blurbs, arrange radio and television personal appearances and lecture tours, and otherwise exercise ingenuity in promoting the sale of books. For these services they may be paid from $14,000 to as high as $30,000 annually. Hundreds of persons freelance as copyeditors, indexers, and proofreaders at home, earning between $6 and $13 per hour. Most of them have had previous in-house experience.

The book manufacturer and the publisher employ production managers, whose responsibility it is to see that all elements of a book are in the right place at the right time. They are the liaison between the manufacturer and the publisher. In addition to the production staff, both publishers and manufacturers employ estimators, designers (both freelance and staff), schedulers, and general management people, most of whom have had technical school training or printing plant experience.

Qualifications

A good education, intelligence, talent in communicating with people, excitement about books, and an ability to keep abreast of the latest developments in many phases of life, particularly in the area of one's specialization, are prime characteristics of a good editor. One need not—and probably should not—be a creative writer. Persons with highly individual ideas and taste are unwilling to remain anonymous and to play second fiddle to authors with quixotic personalities. The good editor has the capacity to deal in a calm, unruffled fashion with everyone, including the occasional prima donna whose genius or near-genius and ability to attract a large reading public may spell the difference between profit and loss in a publishing year. A sound grasp of the fundamentals of business practice is essential in today's financially oriented publishing business. Companies are looking for bright young people who know how to use computer terminals, analyze profit-and-loss statements, make decisions based on hard evidence, and become acquainted with the market in a short time.

Whether one wishes to become a general editor, a copyeditor, a designer, a sales representative, an advertising specialist, or a marketing and promotion person, the college graduate who aspires to a career in book publishing will profit by an education, as well as experience, in mass communications. He or she should seek to acquire a sound background in a major discipline—in literature, history, languages, the natural and social sciences, or philosophy—in fact, in any of the areas of knowledge that comprise a liberal arts education. The aim is to learn to think, find information, and acquire the ability to solve problems and make decisions. Professional education will not be overlooked, for the insights, skills, and fundamental knowledge gained in classrooms and laboratories of a school of mass communications should prove of inestimable value throughout one's career.

PART THREE

The Electronic and Film Media

Growth of Radio,

Television, and Film

News From a Haystack

Hans Von Kaltenborn spent 50 years in broadcast news, pioneering as a Brooklyn local news announcer in 1922 before becoming a CBS commentator in 1930. His clipped, high-pitched, precisely accentuated tones became familiar to all Americans as he covered the Nazi era, translating Hitler's tirades and serving as CBS anchor-commentator during the 1938 Czech crisis ending with the Munich Pact. He was always dignified, always cool, no matter how tense the drama.

But in Spain in 1936 his yen for dramatic news at least ruffled his dignity. He discovered that a French farm jutted across the border into the midst of the Loyalist-Franco Civil War battle for the city of Irun. The farmhouse had a telephone line.

Kaltenborn's engineer ran his line out from it to a haystack, where the CBS microphone could pick up the whining of bullets and explosions of artillery shells. Not content with remote control, Kaltenborn elected to burrow into the haystack, between the battle lines.

But when he told CBS New York what he had for the radio network, he was told, "Stand by. Too many commercial programs just now. Will call you later."

Twice his transmission lines were cut by bullets. The French engineer crawled out and made repairs. Late in the afternoon the go-ahead came, but the Bordeaux relay engineer had gone out for an *apéritif*. Finally at 9:00 in the evening Kaltenborn was on the air with 15 minutes of battle description and sounds of whining bullets and crashing shells.

The battlefield broadcast caught the imaginations of listeners and radio people. Kaltenborn won a Headliners Club award for spending several hours in a haystack, plucking straws from his hat and coat and staying dignified as best he could.

*T*he first news event shown on film to a theater audience was the Corbett-Fitzsimmons heavyweight prizefight of 1897. The first dramatic radio newscast incorrectly called the outcome of the 1916 presidential election. David Sarnoff's RCA experimental station's first live telecast was of a 1938 fire. All familiar subjects!

Radio's story is told first, beginning with the inventions by Marconi of wireless telegraphy and by Dr. Lee De Forest of the vacuum tube. Network radio began in 1927 with Sarnoff's NBC and William S. Paley's CBS. World War II broadcasts of Hans Von Kaltenborn and Edward R. Murrow made radio history.

Enter television, whose first experimental broadcasts were in the 1930s. World War II suspended the industry; at its end coaxial cable and microwave relays made transcontinental telecasting possible by 1951. The networks carried history in the making; their countless viewers also laughed with Archie Bunker and the cast of "M*A*S*H."

David Wark Griffith's 1915 *Birth of a Nation* was the first film epic. His pioneering filmmaking was matched by Mack Sennett and Charlie Chaplin. The "talkies" arrived in 1927 and for two decades, before entertainment patterns changed, as many as 90 million Americans went each week to the movie houses to see such triumphs as *Gone with the Wind, It Happened One Night,* and *Citizen Kane.* ◆

NEWS TAKES TO THE AIR

Public interest in news made it natural for people to use any new medium of communication—the telegraph, the telephone, the underseas cable, the wireless, the motion picture film, radio broadcasting, telecasting and cable, and the communications satellite—to hurry the news to waiting eyes and ears, or to bring news events directly to distant audiences.

The telegraph, the telephone, the cable, and the wireless were nineteenth century inventions that could speed the transmission of messages to waiting newspaper editors and printing presses. The motion picture film became a competitor that could bring to audiences in theaters a visual portrayal of such an exciting event as the Corbett-Fitzsimmons heavyweight prizefight of 1897—the first news event shown on film. Soon excerpts of films of news events were put together into newsreels, which were a part of the standard fare of the movie palace of the 1920s. But the time lag before a newsreel could be shown kept it from being more than an incidental competitor for the newspaper. Interpretive films like Time Inc.'s *The March of Time* of the 1930s and the development in that decade of the techniques of the documentary film—*The Plow That Broke the*

Plain and *The River* were notable examples—foreshadowed the impact that film would have on other news media once it had the means to reach the public directly, which television later provided. In the meantime news took to the air through the magic of radio.

The first news broadcast in the United States is generally credited to Dr. Lee De Forest, who in 1906 invented the vacuum tube that made voice broadcasting possible, the next step beyond Guglielmo Marconi's transmission of dot-and-dash messages through wireless telegraphy in the 1890s. On November 7, 1916, the New York *American* ran a wire to De Forest's experimental station at High Bridge, New York, so that the "father of radio" could broadcast to a few amateur radio enthusiasts the returns from the Wilson-Hughes presidential election. Like the *American* and other newspapers misled by the early returns from that closely contested election, De Forest signed off with the statement that "Charles Evans Hughes will be the next president of the United States."

The inventive and engineering resources of wireless and radio were subsequently needed for military purposes during World War I, and private broadcasting was banned until 1919. Even then, few saw the possibilities of mass radio listening. One person who did was David Sarnoff, the son of a Russian immigrant family who got his start as a Marconi wireless operator. When three big companies of the communications and electric manufacturing industries—Westinghouse, General Electric, and American Telephone & Telegraph (AT&T)—pooled their patent rights interests in 1919 and formed the Radio Corporation of America (RCA), Sarnoff became RCA's sparkplug and eventually headed both RCA and its subsidiary, the National Broadcasting Company. His active career extended to 1970.

It was a Westinghouse engineer, Dr. Frank Conrad, who offered the first proof of Sarnoff's contention that people would listen to radio. His broadcasts of music in Pittsburgh in 1919 stimulated sales of crystal sets and led Westinghouse to open KDKA on November 2, 1920, as the first fully licensed commercial broadcasting station. The featured program consisted of returns from the Harding-Cox presidential election, one whose outcome was more easily predictable. The station got its vote results from the obliging Pittsburgh *Post.*

Other newspapers were more directly involved in broadcasting. One, the Detroit *News,* broadcast news regularly beginning on August 31, 1920, over an experimental station that was to become a regular commercial station in 1921, WWJ. Others quick to establish stations included the Kansas City *Star,* Milwaukee *Journal,* Chicago *Tribune,* Los Angeles *Times,* Louisville *Courier-Journal,* Atlanta *Journal,* Fort Worth *Star-Telegram,* Dallas *News,* and Chicago *Daily News.* By 1927 there were 48 radio stations owned by newspapers, and 97 papers presented news over the air. The publishers thought radio newscasts stimulated sales of newspapers—and subsequent events proved them correct.

ENTERTAINMENT. But despite these evidences of concern for news, radio's pioneers were more intent on capturing the public's interest by entertaining it than by informing it. Dramatic news events and on-the-spot sports coverage combined both objectives. News summaries themselves remained infrequent in the 1920s because they excited little advertiser interest, because radio itself did not collect news, and because news merely read from the newspaper sounded awkward and dull on the air. Meanwhile, in 1921, KDKA broadcast accounts of prize fights and major league baseball games. The next year, AT&T's New York station, WEAF (now WNBC), used phone lines to bring to its listeners the Chicago-Princeton football game from Stagg Field. By 1924 an estimated 10 million Americans heard presidential election returns; there were 3 million sets that year, and the number of stations had grown from 30 in 1921 to 530. Twenty-one stations from New York to California joined in a March 1925 hookup to broadcast President Calvin Coolidge's inauguration.

The Networks Emerge

The development of networks was vital for radio's progress. In early 1924 the Eveready Battery Company bought time on 12 stations for its Eveready Hour performers—the first use of national radio advertising. By 1925, AT&T had organized a network headed by WEAF with 26 outlets, reaching as far west as Kansas City. RCA, Westinghouse, and General Electric had a competitive network led by WJZ, New York, and WGY, Schenectady. In 1926 the big companies reached an agreement under which AT&T would retire from the broadcasting business and in return would control all forms of network relays. RCA, Westinghouse, and General Electric bought WEAF for $1 million. They then formed the National Broadcasting Company as an RCA subsidiary. The station group organized by AT&T and headed by WEAF became the NBC Red network at the start of 1927,

Dolly the elephant rehearses a "song" at Madison Square Garden for radio broadcast of the Ringling Brothers Barnum and Bailey Circus over WJZ New York in 1925. Such novelty shows were frequent during the early days of radio. (Library of Congress)

while the group headed by WJZ became the NBC Blue network. Regular coast-to-coast network operations began that year. Sarnoff emerged in full control of RCA and NBC in 1930 when Westinghouse and General Electric withdrew under pressure of an antitrust suit.

Only seven percent of the 733 stations operating in early 1927 were affiliated with NBC. Some rivals organized a network service with the support of the Columbia Phonograph Record Company in 1927; financially reorganized the next year under the control of William S. Paley, it became the Columbia Broadcasting System. CBS bought WABC (now WCBS) in New York as its key station and by 1929 was showing a profit. In 1934 it had 97 station affiliates, compared with 65 for NBC Red and 62 for NBC Blue.

FCC's ROLE. Passage of the Radio Act of 1927 strengthened the two big networks, since the number of stations on the air was reduced by the new Federal Radio Commission to avoid interference in receiving programs, and a group of about 50 powerful "clear-channel" stations was authorized. By 1938 all but two of the clear-channel stations were either network-owned or affiliated. And although only 40 percent of the 660 stations then in operation were network-affiliated, they included virtually all those licensed for nighttime broadcasting. The two independent clear-channel stations, the Chicago *Tribune*'s WGN, and WOR, New York, formed the loosely organized Mutual Broadcasting System in 1934 but found competition difficult. Mutual's complaints to the Federal Communications Commission (the regulatory body was renamed in the Communications Act of 1934) brought about the sale by NBC in 1943 of its weaker Blue network to Edward J. Noble, who renamed it the American Broadcasting Company in 1945.

The growth of the networks after 1927, and their success in winning advertising revenues, made radio a more disturbing challenger to the newspaper industry. Radio's increasing interest in broadcasting news and public affairs also provided competition. In 1928 Republican Herbert Hoover and Democrat Alfred E. Smith took to the air, spending $1 million on campaign talks over NBC and CBS networks that reached many of the nation's 8 million receiving sets. That year the press associations—Associated Press, United Press, and International News Service—supplied complete election returns to the 677 radio stations. Radio's success in covering that bitter presidential election whetted listeners' appetites for more news broadcasts. In December KFAB in Lincoln, Nebraska, responded by hiring the city editor of the Lincoln *Star* to produce two broadcasts daily of what it called a radio newspaper. Other stations developed similar programs, and as the Great Depression deepened after October 1929, the public became even more interested in news. By 1930, KMPC in Beverly Hills, California, had put ten reporters on the Los Angeles news runs.

The Radio–Newspaper War

A bitter war then broke out between radio and newspapers over the broadcasting of news. Newspaper advertising revenues were sharply contracting as the nation moved toward the 1933 depression crisis. Radio, however, as a new medium was winning an increasing, if yet small, advertising investment. Why let radio attract with news broadcasts listeners who would become the audience for advertisers' commercials, asked some publishers. This argument gave more weight to public interest in news than it deserved, considering the demonstrated interest in listening to such entertainers as Amos 'n Andy, Jack Benny, Walter Winchell, the Boswell sisters, Rudy Vallee, Kate Smith, and the stars of the radio dramas. But after both 1932 political conventions were aired on coast-to-coast networks, and after the Associated Press furnished 1932 election returns to the networks to forestall the sale of United Press returns, the American Newspaper Publishers Association cracked down. The press associations should stop providing news to radio; broadcasting of news should be confined to brief bulletins that would stimulate newspaper reading; radio program logs should be treated as paid advertising. There were dissenters to this approach, but after a majority of AP members voted in 1933 for such restrictions, all three press associations stopped selling news to radio stations. Radio now had to gather its own.

The Columbia Broadcasting System set up the leading network news service with Ed Klauber and Paul White as directors. CBS opened bureaus in leading United States cities and in London and developed a string of correspondents. Hans Von Kaltenborn and Boake Carter, already CBS commentators, did daily news broadcasts. Kaltenborn, a former Brooklyn *Eagle* managing editor, had started broadcasting in 1922 and had joined CBS in 1930 to become the first of a long line of radio commentators. NBC organized a less extensive news service headed by Abe Schechter. Local stations got their news from the early editions of newspapers, despite AP court suits to stop the practice.

A compromise was soon proposed. This was the Press-Radio Bureau, which would present two five-minute newscasts daily on the networks from news supplied by the press associations. Bulletin coverage of extraordinary events would also be provided. In return, the networks would stop gathering news. The bureau began operating in March 1934, but was doomed to quick failure. Stations wanting more news bought it from five new agencies that jumped into the field, led by Transradio Press Service. A year later UP and INS obtained releases from the Press-Radio Bureau agreement and began selling full news reports to stations. UP began a wire report written especially for radio delivery, which AP matched when it began to sell radio news in 1940. The Press-Radio Bureau stopped functioning in 1940; Transradio closed in 1951.

ENTERTAINMENT. Radio, meantime, was developing a blend of entertainment and news. The trial of Bruno Hauptmann in 1934 for the kidnap-murder of the Lindbergh baby attracted more than 300 reporters, including many with microphones. Listeners were bombarded by more than 2000 Press-Radio Bureau bulletins. President Roosevelt's famed "fireside chats" and the presidential nominating conventions and campaigns were major events. In December 1936 the entire world listened by shortwave broadcast as Edward VIII explained why he was giving up the British throne for "the woman I love." Kaltenborn, Boake Carter, Lowell Thomas, Edwin C. Hill, and Gabriel Heatter were the public's favorite news commentators. Ted Husing and Clem McCarthy were the leading sports announcers. America's top radio entertainment favorites in 1938 were Edgar Bergen and his dummy Charlie McCarthy, Jack Benny and Mary Livingston, Guy Lombardo and his orchestra, Kate Smith, the Lux Radio Theatre and "One Man's Family" dramatic shows, George Burns and Gracie Allen, Eddie Cantor, Don Ameche, Nelson Eddy, Bing Crosby, and announcer Don Wilson. But before the end of the year it was Kaltenborn who stole the laurels as the world stopped all else to listen to news of the Munich crisis, which brought Europe to the brink of war.

RADIO COMES OF AGE

Radio fully met the challenge of diplomatic crisis and world war that began with Adolf Hitler's annexation of Austria and ultimatum to Czechoslovakia in 1938. Beginning with a patched-together but striking coverage of the Munich crisis, the radio networks expanded their news reporting and technical facilities tremendously during World War II. At the station level newscasts took a place of prime importance.

In 1937 CBS sent a then unknown Edward R. Murrow to Europe as news chief. For an assistant he hired William L. Shirer, who had been working for the just-closed Universal Service, a Hearst-owned press association. Like the others, they did human interest stories and cultural programs for shortwave broadcasts that were rebroadcast by United States stations. Then came Hitler's invasion of Austria and the *Anschluss*. Murrow hurried to Vienna. On March 12, 1938, the first multiple pickup news broadcast in history went on the air. Shirer spoke from London, Murrow from Vienna, and newspapermen whom CBS had hired gave their impressions from Berlin, Paris, and Rome. The pattern was set for radio's coverage of the fateful 20 days in September, beginning with Hitler's demand that the Czechs cede him the Sudetenland and ending with the Munich Pact. Key staff members such as Murrow (who went on to become television's best-known commentator and director of the United States Information Agency) and Shirer (author of *Berlin Diary* and *Rise and Fall of the Third Reich*) bore the brunt of the effort, reinforced by the best of the United States newspaper and press association correspondents.

THE MUNICH CRISIS. American radio listeners heard news broadcasts from 14 European cities during the Munich crisis period. Beginning with the plea for support made by President Eduard Beneš of Czechoslovakia on September 10, 1938, and Adolf Hitler's challenge to the world two days later from Nuremberg, listeners heard the voices of Chamberlain, Goebbels, Mussolini, Litvinoff, and Pope Pius XI. Such broadcasts were not new, but the intensity of coverage was. CBS devoted 471 broadcasts to the crisis, nearly 48 hours of air time; of these, 135 were bulletin interruptions, including 98 from European staff members. NBC's two networks aired 443 programs during 59 hours of air time. On climactic days these efforts kept the air alive with direct broadcasts, news summaries, and commentaries by the news analysts.

In his "Studio Nine" in New York City, Kaltenborn spent the 20 days catnapping on a cot, analyzing the news reports, and backstopping the CBS European correspondents with hours of analysis and commentary. It was Kaltenborn who provided the translations of Hitler's fiery oratory at the Nazi rallies, and who later predicted what diplomatic steps would follow. He made 85 broadcasts, many of them lengthy commentaries, during the three weeks. A few times he carried on two-way conversations with Murrow, Shirer, and other European correspondents. The CBS "European News Roundup," usually a 30-minute show from three or four points, was matched by NBC after two weeks. Heading NBC's European effort was Max Jordan, who had a 46-minute beat on the text of the Munich Pact, which he broadcast from Hitler's radio station. He relied especially on M. W. Fodor of the Chicago *Daily News* and Walter Kerr of the New York *Herald Tribune* in Prague, Alistair Cooke in London, and leading press association reporters. Mutual had only John Steele in London and Louis Huot in Paris, and used their occasional broadcasts, cabled news, and shortwave pickups to augment the regular press association news flow.

American listeners felt the brutal impact of Hitler's demands when Jordan and Shirer spoke from microphones inside the Berlin Sportpalast, against a background of hysterical oratory and frenzied Nazi crowd reaction. They were grave when they heard Murrow describe war preparations in London, relieved when Kaltenborn predicted that Chamberlain, Daladier, Mussolini, and Hitler would find a peaceful solution at Munich. Although they devoured columns of type, it was radio that brought them a sense of personal participation in what they realized was the world's crisis, not merely Europe's.

NEWS OF WAR. By the summer of 1939 Murrow had a four-man staff: himself, Shirer, Thomas Grandin, and Eric Sevareid, a young newsman who was also to become a leading television commentator for CBS. When German troops marched into Poland, Americans tuned in their radios to hear Prime Minister Chamberlain announce that Great Britain was at war. Bill Henry of CBS and Arthur Mann of Mutual became the first front-line radio reporters. Radio news staffs expanded, and eyewitness broadcasts made history. James Bowen of NBC described the scuttling of the German battleship *Graf Spee* off Buenos Aires. Shirer of CBS and William C. Kerker of NBC reported the surrender of the French to a strutting Hitler in the railroad car at Compiègne. Radio brought news of Dunkirk, of the fall of Paris, Winston Churchill's stirring oratory. And in August 1940, Murrow's "This Is London" broadcasts made the Battle of Britain come home to his American audience. His graphic descriptions of bomb-torn and burning London, delivered in a quiet but compelling manner, did much to awaken a still neutral United States to the nature of the world's danger.

The first news of Pearl Harbor reached Americans by radio bulletins that shattered the Sunday quiet of December 7, 1941. A record audience listened the next day to President Roosevelt's "day of infamy" war message to Congress. Radio newsmen, using mobile units and tape recordings, joined the coverage of American forces in the Pacific and Europe. There were many memorable broadcasts: Cecil Brown of CBS reporting the fall of Singapore, Murrow riding a plane in the great Berlin air raid of 1943 and describing it the next night, George Hicks

Edward R. Murrow, shown here on a rainy London street in 1941, first won fame as a broadcaster with his CBS radio reports on the German bombing blitz of the British capital. He opened each report with a slow and solemn, "This . . . is London." (UPI/Bettmann Newsphotos)

of ABC recording a D-Day broadcast from a landing barge under German fire. Network reporters made broadcasts and recordings, filed cables, and competed on equal terms with press association and newspaper correspondents.

The demand for news seemed inexhaustible. In 1937 NBC had devoted 2.8 percent of its total program hours to news; in 1944 the figure had risen to 26.4 percent. CBS in 1945 spent 26.9 percent of its network time on news and sports. Variety shows still ranked highest in audience size—those of Jack Benny, Fibber McGee and Molly, Bob Hope, Edgar Bergen and Charlie McCarthy, and Fred Allen. Dramatic shows and popular music were next. But four of the leading programs in listenership in 1944 and 1945 were news shows: CBS commentator Lowell Thomas, *The March of Time,* Mutual's emotional Gabriel Heatter with his human interest commentaries, and the irrepressible Walter Winchell. As the war drew to a close, radio expressed the sorrow of the people by devoting three days of programming solely to solemn music and tributes to the late President Roosevelt.

RADIO'S POSTWAR EXPANSION

The war years were exceedingly prosperous ones for radio. Total annual revenue more than doubled between 1937 and 1945, and income on revenues increased from 20 percent to 33 percent. When the FCC returned to peacetime licensing procedures in October 1945, there were 909 licensed commercial standard (AM) radio stations. Sixteen months later there were approximately 600 new stations and the number of communities with radio stations had nearly doubled. By 1950 there were 2086 AM radio stations on the air and 80 million receiving sets.

Frequency modulation (FM) broadcasting, done experimentally beginning in 1936, was represented by 30 stations on the air in 1942, when wartime necessity brought a freeze in new construction and licensing. In the postwar years many AM stations took out FM licenses, and the number of FM stations on the air in 1950 reached 743, a figure that proved to be a high for the ensuing decade. Few of the FM stations were operating independently and giving audiences the selective programming that later was to characterize FM broadcasting.

Radio newspeople, somewhat to their surprise, found listener interest in news sustained during the postwar years. Sponsors, who by 1944 had elevated news and commentaries into third place behind dramatic and variety shows in sponsored evening network time, kept up their interest in news at both network and local levels. The established stations had in many cases developed their own newsrooms during the war, with personnel to prepare both general news summaries and local and regional news shows. The newly licensed stations, often without network affiliation, found news one area in which they could compete. Indicative of the trend was the founding in 1946 of an association of radio news directors, now known as the Radio Television News Directors Association.

RADIO'S COMMENTATORS. Among the network commentators, Edward R. Murrow began his "Hear It Now" program for CBS, where he was joined by his wartime associate Eric Sevareid. H. V. Kaltenborn, who left CBS in 1940, became NBC's leading commentator. Radio listeners who sat glued to their sets all night in 1948, wondering whether President Harry Truman had upset Thomas E. Dewey in the presidential voting, found Kaltenborn one of the first to realize that Truman's popular vote lead would hold up in electoral college totals. ABC had Raymond Gram Swing, one of the finest of the war era commentators. It also obtained Elmer Davis, who had replaced Kaltenborn at CBS before becoming director of the Office of War Information. Davis won high praise for his postwar reporting, his dry humor and telling barbs, and his ability to get at the heart of complex and confusing issues. NBC scored with public affairs programs from the United Nations during 1946 and 1947. The networks and some local stations also offered documentary programs that analyzed important social issues in a semidramatic format.

But television was casting its shadow over radio. Television's breakthrough year was 1948, the one in which the value of time sales for the national radio networks reached an all-time high. Competition among the four networks was already intense, and the vogue for program popularity ratings as a means of snaring sponsors led to such devices as the "giveaway" program featured by 1948 radio. The smaller stations found plenty of local advertising revenues in newly exploited markets, fortunately, and after 1947 radio had more revenue from local advertisers than from network advertisers. The networks were already shifting their attention to television, and station owners were seeking television licenses until the FCC instituted a four-year freeze so that comprehensive plans for television broadcasting could be worked out. In the meantime CBS forecast the fate of network radio when it made its famed 1948 talent raid on NBC to capture such stars as Amos 'n Andy, Jack Benny, Burns and Allen, Edgar Bergen, and Bing Crosby for future television shows. While network radio dwindled in favor of music, news, and sports programming, radio continued to expand as an industry. By 1987 there were 10,076 radio stations—4867 AM and 5209 FM—and an estimated 489 million radio sets.

TELEVISION ARRIVES

Experimental television broadcasting in the United States began in the 1920s. The scientific advances that preceded actual broadcasting stretched back over a century in the fields of electricity, photography, wire transmission, and radio. Early television experimenters used a mechanical scanning disc that failed to scan a picture rapidly enough. The turning point came in 1923 with Dr. Vladimir Zworykin's invention of the iconoscope, an all-electric television tube. Zworykin, then a Westinghouse scientist, soon joined RCA, where he developed the kinescope, or picture tube. Other leading contributors were Philo Farnsworth, developer of the electronic camera, and Allen B. Dumont, developer of receiving tubes and the first home television receivers.

There were experiments in wire transmission of pictures during the 1920s that were to lead to the founding of AP Wirephoto in 1935. One of the researchers, H. E. Ives of AT&T, sent a closed-circuit television picture from Washington to New York in 1927. The next year General Electric's WGY began experimental telecasting. In 1930 NBC began operating W2XBS in New York; in 1939 it became the first station to offer regular telecasting schedules. Large numbers of people first saw television that year at the New York World's Fair. Commercial broadcasting was authorized by the FCC in 1941, but the wartime freeze on nonmilitary equipment sales left only six pioneer stations on the air. Among them were the first commercially licensed stations, NBC's WNBT in New York, and WCBS-TV in the same city. The two big radio networks thus had their entries into television broadcasting.

Because of postwar equipment shortages and industry uncertainties, it was 1948 before television could achieve a significant place among the media. In the meantime RCA's image-orthicon camera tube had appeared, to enhance the possibilities of live pickups, and AT&T was busily extending the coaxial cables that preceded the microwave relay for transcontinental broadcasting. During 1948 the number of stations on the air increased from 17 to 41, and the number of sets in use neared a half-million. Cities with television increased from 8 to 23, and the arrival of the coaxial cable and network programming stirred a city's excitement much like the arrival of the telegraph a century before. Cities along the Atlantic coast from Boston to Richmond saw and heard the 1948 political conventions and the Metropolitan Opera. Television's first great star, Milton Berle, stepped before the cameras for NBC in 1948, as did Ed Sullivan for CBS.

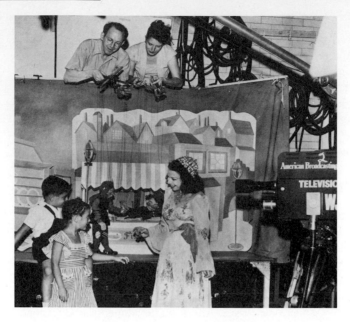

Ireene Wicker, a radio star known as the Singing Lady, conducts a pioneer television show for children for the American Broadcasting Company in 1948, the year commercial television began to gain popularity. (Library of Congress)

FCC's TV POLICY. Then, in the fall of 1948, came the FCC's freeze on additional station authorizations, which lasted until June 1952. During that time the FCC worked out a comprehensive policy for telecasting designed to give all areas of the country equitable service. In the interval only 108 stations were eligible for broadcasting. A few failed, but many became firmly established. The number of sets in use rose to 15 million. The transcontinental microwave relay was completed in 1951, and on September 4 the first coast-to-coast audience saw the Japanese peace treaty conference in San Francisco. NBC also offered the first telecast of a World Series and the first regular coast-to-coast sponsored program, the "NBC Comedy Hour."

The FCC's 1952 plan called for more than 2000 channel assignments to nearly 1300 communities. To do this, the FCC extended telecasting from the established very high frequency channels (numbered 2 through 13) to 70 more ultrahigh frequency channels (numbered 14 through 83). There were more than twice as many UHF as VHF assignments, and in addition 242 channels were reserved for educational television stations. But different equipment was needed to tune a set to UHF and VHF stations, and the established pattern of set-making and broadcasting was VHF. The FCC did not require set makers to include both UHF and VHF tuning until 1964; in the meantime UHF languished. In a 1953 decision the FCC ended a long controversy over color telecasting in favor of the RCA compatible system permitting reception in either black and white or color.

Television's great "gold rush" came during 1952 and 1953, with the end of the freeze. Among the networks, NBC and CBS were well along in their transition from emphasis on radio to emphasis on television. ABC merged with Paramount Theatres in 1953 and took a third-ranking position in television. Mutual did not attempt to enter television; a Dumont network gave up the attempt to compete nationally in 1955. That year there were 439 stations on the air and 33 million receivers. By 1960 there were 533 stations and 55 million receivers. By 1987 there were 1000 commercial stations (454 of them UHF), plus 297 noncommercial stations. There were more than 125 million sets covering 98 percent of the homes in the United States. Television surpassed radio and magazines by 1955 in total advertising revenues and a year later passed newspapers as the number one national advertising medium, although newspapers continued to lead in total advertising thanks to their top-heavy position in the field of local advertising.

TELEVISION AND THE NEWS

Television's first efforts at news shows too often consisted of newsreels supplied by the United Press and Acme Newspictures and still pictures shown while the on-camera announcer read the script. But television newspeople, equipped with mobile units and magnetic tape, gradually overcame the problems of developing news shows with live film and sound. During the first decade of telecasting, they did far better with on-the-spot broadcasts of major news events, public affairs programming, and documentaries.

In 1951 Edward R. Murrow turned from "Hear It Now" to "See It Now" for CBS. NBC's early morning "Today" show with Dave Garroway, a mixture of news and entertainment, opened in January 1952. That year network viewers saw an atomic blast at Yucca Flats, the political conventions, and a heavyweight championship prize fight. An estimated 60 million Americans saw President Eisenhower inaugurated in 1953. Television audiences next followed live broadcasts of the McCarthy-Army hearings, which resulted in the Senate's censure of the Wisconsin senator, and watched a parade of gangsters before Senator Kefauver's crime subcommittee. Crucial United Nations sessions went on camera. At least 85 million Americans saw one of the "Great Debates" between John F. Kennedy and Richard M. Nixon in 1960, with the presidency at stake. President Kennedy opened some of his news conferences to live telecasting in 1961 and used television extensively at the height of the Cuban crisis in October 1962. An estimated 135 million people saw some part of television's coverage of John Glenn's orbital space flight in 1962.

MOURNING FOR KENNEDY. If proof were needed of television's ability to report great events, it came on November 22, 1963, when President Kennedy was assassinated in Dallas, Texas. Within minutes the networks began a four-day vigil ending with the burial at Arlington. Many heard the first bulletins on radio, then rushed to watch the unfolding drama and hear news summaries on television. A survey of audiences in New York City showed that TV viewing rose from 25 percent to 70 percent on Friday after the assassination reports became known. Viewers saw the new president, along with Jacqueline Kennedy and the casket, returning to Washington. They went with the cameras into the White House, saw the Sunday ceremonies at the Capitol. Sunday viewers on NBC (the only network "live" at the precise moment) saw Jack Ruby lunge forward in a Dallas police station to shoot fatally the alleged assassin, Lee Harvey Oswald, and heard re-

*President John F. Kennedy is
laid to rest in Arlington
National Cemetery. The
funeral climaxed three days
of mourning during which
the nation was bound
together by television as
never before. (UPI/Bettmann)*

President John F. Kennedy is laid to rest in Arlington National Cemetery. The funeral climaxed three days of mourning during which the nation was bound together by television as never before. (UPI/Bettmann)

porter Tom Pettit describe the incredible event. Viewership in New York homes jumped to 80 percent as all the networks ran and reran their film. On Monday the funeral of President Kennedy drew a 93 percent viewership figure, the highest known level in television history. The nation agreed that both television and radio had reported the four days magnificently.

With full involvement of American troops in Vietnam after 1965, the ugliness of the indecisive war was brought into American living rooms by television news crews. Public reaction against the war led to President Lyndon Johnson's decision to retire from the 1968 election race—an announcement made live to a Sunday evening television audience. There were even greater public shocks in 1968: the assassinations of the Rev. Martin Luther King, Jr., and Senator Robert F. Kennedy and the turmoil and rioting accompanying the Democratic convention in Chicago. In each event television played a major news coverage role.

CAMERA ON THE MOON. In July 1969, however, television played a happier role when it brought to a worldwide audience the flight of Apollo 11 and direct transmission of the pictures of mankind's first steps on the moon. Viewers saw black-and-white pictures originating from the moon for five hours, including two hours with the astronauts on the moon's surface. Some 125 million Americans saw the climactic nighttime broadcast, and a satellite network carried the pictures to an eventual audience estimated at 500 million. Truly a "See It Now" triumph of immediacy, the pictures from the moon gave all viewers a sense of participation in a great feat of exploration.

CBS. After Murrow departed CBS in 1958, Walter Cronkite became that network's leading personality. A United Press war correspondent, Cronkite joined

CBS in 1950 and became the star of many of its documentaries, including "Eyewitness to History" and "CBS Reports." He took over the major CBS news program from Douglas Edwards and transformed it into a 30-minute dinnertime show in the fall of 1963, with Eric Sevareid as commentator. Mike Wallace, Dan Rather, Morley Safer, and Harry Reasoner made the documentary "60 Minutes" a "top ten" show. Rather succeeded Cronkite on the evening news show in 1981 and after hitting his stride, ranked first in the weekly ratings without interruption for more than four years. Among the CBS correspondents were Lesley Stahl in the White House and Charles Kuralt as a roving correspondent.

NBC. NBC's top stars were two seasoned newspapermen, Chet Huntley and David Brinkley, whose mixture of news and comments between 1956 and 1970 made them a top-ranking television team. When Huntley retired in 1970, John Chancellor emerged as the chief NBC newscaster, with Brinkley continuing to contribute his wry commentaries. Tom Brokaw became the evening show anchor in 1982 with Chancellor in a supporting commentary role. Frank McGee, Barbara Walters, Brokaw, and Bryant Gumbel and Jane Pauley were hosts of the morning show in turn. An early woman correspondent was Pauline Frederick of NBC at the UN; two NBC stalwarts were Irving R. Levine in Europe and Edwin Newman in Washington.

ABC. With fewer resources, ABC kept pace by offering such topflight commentators and news anchors as John Daly, Frank Reynolds, Howard K. Smith, and Barbara Walters, who came from NBC in 1976 and continued to excel in interviewing famous personages. ABC's fortunes began to turn upward in 1979 when Ted Koppel began his "Nightline" broadcasts following the local newscasts at 11:30 P.M. EST. Koppel focused first on the Iranian hostage crisis, blending late-breaking news with live interviews by satellite of newsmakers, politicians, correspondents. Crisis followed crisis; Koppel also developed programs treating domestic social

Ted Koppel casts a skeptical glance at a guest on his provocative ABC "Nightline" show before pouncing with a hard question. (Laurel Luth)

and political problems. Peter Jennings scored successes as the evening anchorperson after 1983, and by 1986 ABC had caught up in the ratings. ABC's White House team was Ann Compton and the colorful Sam Donaldson, known as "Jumping Sam" as he leaped into the air to shout questions at a retreating President Reagan on the White House lawn.

CNN. Cable News Network became a competitor in 1980, when Ted Turner launched it with profits from his Atlanta superstation, WTBS. Beating back similar cable competition, Turner also began CNN Headline News, with news on a 30-minute cycle. CNN scored some reporting beats and had veteran Daniel Schorr as a commentator. It reached 80 percent of cable subscribers.

PBS. Favored by serious followers of the news was the one-hour show produced for Public Broadcasting Service by Robert MacNeill and Jim Lehrer. They first won attention as PBS anchors for the Watergate hearings and began their hourlong program in 1983 with Charlayne Hunter-Gault and Judy Woodruff (formerly of NBC) as staff reporters.

SATELLITES. News by satellite became television's most sensational achievement of the 1960s. The successful launching of AT&T's Telstar on July 10, 1962, permitted the first live transmissions between the United States and Europe. These were "staged" shows of only a few minutes' duration, but they thrilled TV audiences. RCA's Relay carried pictures of events surrounding the Kennedy assassination to 23 nations. Howard Hughes' efforts to launch a satellite that would achieve a fully synchronous orbit (an orbit and speed that keep the craft directly over one point on earth) met success with Syncom III in 1964. Four such satellites, equally spaced around the world, could provide television coverage to all inhabited portions of the planet.

The Communications Satellite Corporation, formed by Congress in 1962 to unify the U.S. effort, put Early Bird into synchronous orbit in 1965, then followed with the (International Telecommunications Satellite Organization's) Intelsat II series in 1966 and 1967, and the larger Intelsat III series in 1968 and 1969. After the Intelsat IV satellites followed between 1971 and 1973, no fewer than 150 ground facilities located in 80 countries were connected to a greatly expanded television facility whose social and political potential remained to be realized. Impact was great, however; the 1978 World Cup soccer matches were seen by 1 billion people, a new all-time audience total. Intelsat grew increasingly independent of the United States Comsat enterprise and launched its own Intelsat V series beginning in 1980. With message capacity doubled for each orbiting satellite, there were decreased costs and increased transmissions, including news and pictures at an almost commonplace level.

TELEVISION AND ENTERTAINMENT

The period from the end of World War II to the present has been one of turmoil and indeed revolution in the world of visual entertainment. Television's sudden emergence as a major home entertainment medium affected all other media, but particularly radio and motion pictures. In the years after 1948 the aerial became a fixture atop almost every roof; inside the living room the TV screen grew from 7 inches in diagonal to 12, to 17, to 21, and in some cases to 24 inches. During the first years of television's popularity, at least, the presence of such free entertainment had a profound effect on American social habits. Some families planned their day's activities so that they could be at home for favorite programs; that gastronomical phenomenon, the TV dinner, was marketed to be eaten by families sitting in partially darkened rooms with eyes focused on the screen. Gradually, audiences became more selective, but the average set still remained on for more than six hours each day.

PROGRAMMING PROBLEMS. Having captured a very large portion of the entertainment-seeking audience, television found many serious problems. Program directors discovered that, operating as they did many hours a day, the television stations devoured good program material faster than it could be created. The writing and producing talent drawn into the television industry simply could not conceive enough fresh material of broad general appeal to fill the stations' program time.

As a result, the mass of television programming offered to the public was uneven in quality. Much of it was trite, inane, and repetitious. The critics denounced it vehemently, with good reason. Yet every week, at least during the winter months, a selective viewer could find many hours of literate, provocative, informative, and frequently very entertaining programs. Some of the best were the "spectaculars" or "specials" originated by Sylvester (Pat) Weaver for NBC to break the monotony of regularly scheduled series. The cost of these lengthy and star-studded productions also could be spread to several sponsors.

Television programming suffered from two major difficulties: (1) the tendency of many program directors and sponsors to underestimate the intelligence of the audience; and (2) a severe case of overexposure—too many hours of program time in relation to the amount of good-quality program material, even when old Hollywood movies were added to the fare.

New program ideas quickly attracted imitators. The public was subjected to cycles of entertainment, a number of programs similar in nature. For two or three seasons in the late 1950s, quiz programs were extremely popular; these gave away fantastic amounts of money to contestants who made the correct replies to many kinds of questions. But the public began to grow weary of these giveaways, and when revelations of unethical assistance to some contestants were made, most of the quiz programs disappeared from the air. Western programs, a modification of the Western movie or "horse opera" that long was a standard item in the motion picture industry, came into vogue. Soon the obvious tales of the Old West were exhausted, and producers took to exploring many ramifications of life, transferred to a Western setting. In some cases they took classic fiction plots and reworked them as Westerns. At the peak of the Western craze, so many of these "oaters" (as the industry called such horse pictures) were being shot around the overcrowded Hollywood outdoor locations that the casts of competing shows had to wait in line for turns to perform their heroics before the camera.

TELEVISION STARS. Milton Berle was television's first great star, going on the air for NBC in 1948. During the medium's first decade, the top audience ratings went to variety shows and comedies. Holding steady places for several years each were Berle, Groucho Marx, Ed Sullivan, and Arthur Godfrey. "I Love Lucy," starring Lucille Ball, held its first-place rating for five years. Then, in 1958, came the Westerns, led by "Gunsmoke," and in 1959 half the top ten shows were action-filled, bullet-punctuated tales. "Wagon Train" took top honors for four years, then gave way to "Bonanza." A public outcry against violence contributed to a decline of the Westerns in the late 1960s and the rise to number one ratings of the "Smothers Brothers Comedy Hour" and "Laugh-In." Situation comedies such as "Gomer Pyle," "The Andy Griffith Show," and "Julia" ranked high. Perennials such as Bob Hope, Dean Martin, and Lucille Ball kept their ratings.

The 1970s saw the demise of the Westerns ("Gunsmoke" in 1975) and the rise of family programs, led by "All in the Family" and "The Waltons." Shows featuring minorities also appeared, such as "Chico and the Man" (Mexican-American) and "Sanford and Son" (black). "M*A*S*H" kept the Korean war years alive for an 11-year span ending with the most widely watched single show in history. The "Mary Tyler Moore Show" and its spinoffs were comedy successes, along with Carol Burnett's variety show and "Lou Grant." ABC finally got top rating with "Laverne & Shirley," "Happy Days," the 1976 Olympics, and a 1977 smash hit, "Roots," tracing black history for eight nights for a new top audience of 130 million. ABC continued with its controversial "Masada" miniseries in 1981, examining the Jewish heritage in Israel, and its 1983 miniseries "The Winds of War," which raised the all-time audience figure to 140 million persons.

CBS set the pace for a rash of series about families with twisted lives and romances when it built "Dallas" into an international attention-getting epic. The 1981 "Who shot J.R.?" segment had a 76 share of U.S. homes watching television that evening, a record exceeded by one share by the final episode of CBS's "M*A*S*H" in 1983. (The television rating system is discussed in Chapter 13.) The "Dallas" villain, J.R., and a host of imitations were still in vogue in the late 1980s. But in 1985, five years of effort by Grant Tinker to put NBC into the top ranking among the networks paid off, thanks to viewer response to the warm-hearted Bill Cosby family show and to the glitter of "Miami Vice."

Not all television entertainment was keyed to audience ratings. The educational program "Omnibus" was a rewarding contribution of the 1950s; so was "Playhouse 90." There were such artistic productions as "Peter Pan" and "Victoria Regina." Leonard Bernstein and the New York Philharmonic orchestra played for appreciative television audiences. Walt Disney's "Wonderful World of Color" even made the top ten lists of the 1960s. PBS contributed its own and BBC's artistic fare. Such shows, combined with the news and documentary programs, gave television some claim to a role more socially useful than the casual entertainment role identified by critics as a "vast wasteland."

THE RISE OF THE MOTION PICTURE

The motion picture preceded radio and television as an entertainment medium. The illusion of movement created by the motion picture projector, and the sense of reality felt by a viewer of the film, made "going to the movies" a popular activity for Americans by the 1920s and kept them going in great numbers until 1950. The history of film and of the golden years of Hollywood is briefly recorded here.

Inventors worked steadily on the motion picture concept after Peter Mark Roget (of *Thesaurus* fame) advanced his theory of "persistence of vision" in 1824. Roget contended that the human eye retains an image for a fraction of a second longer than it actually appears. Thus a series of still pictures printed on a ribbon of celluloid film, and projected at 16 or 24 frames per second, will create the illusion of continuous motion.

The work of Joseph Nièpce and Louis Daguerre in France created a photographic process that enabled Eadweard Muybridge and John D. Isaacs to use 24 cameras to conduct their famous 1877 demonstration of the gait of a galloping horse. "Magic lantern" shows became commonplace on lecture circuits. George Eastman's marketing in 1888 of his Kodak camera, which used a roll of film, enabled Thomas A. Edison and his assistants to develop a 50-foot "peep show" in a 4-foot box called the kinetoscope. Louis and Auguste Lumière and Charles Pathé in France and Robert W. Paul and William Friese-Greene in England were simultaneously creating moving pictures. The first public showing in a theater in the United States, using Edison's improved Vitascope, occurred in 1896. *The Great Train Robbery,* Edwin S. Porter's eight-minute film of 1903, was the first to tell a unified story, utilizing camera angles, film editing, and parallel development of story themes. It was also the first of untold Westerns to follow.

THREE FILMMAKERS. In the second decade of the twentieth century, three men led in the rise of filmmaking. One was David Wark Griffith, a director at Biograph, which ranked with Pathé and Vitagraph as leading picture-making companies in New York. In 1915 Griffith produced *The Birth of a Nation,* the first American film "epic," a 12-reel film that took nearly three hours to show. The story was of a victimized Southern family, told in a setting of Civil War battles, renegade blacks, and Ku Klux Klansmen. While controversial, the film's emotional impact, and its excellence in filmmaking artistry, gave it a permanent place in motion picture history.

Mack Sennett, also a graduate of the Biograph studio, made a major imprint on film history. In 1912 he founded the Keystone Film Company in Los Angeles. A master of slapstick, he created the Keystone Kops, starred comedienne Mabel Normand and frozen-faced Buster Keaton, and discovered a young English actor named Charlie Chaplin.

Chaplin rose to fame with *The Tramp* (1915) and *Shoulder Arms* (1918). In 1919 he joined with Griffith, Douglas Fairbanks, and Mary Pickford to form the United Artists Corporation so they could control their own careers and earnings. Chaplin used pantomine to tell the story of "the little fellow" who never fitted in. He captivated his audiences with his tramp's costume and orchestrated mannerisms in *The Kid* (1921), *The Gold Rush* (1925), and *City Lights* (1931). He was the wistful little tramp who set a dinner table for guests who never came or who shuffled off into the night. He also projected messages to his audiences in *Modern Times* (1936), rebelling against the assembly line and industrial system, and in *The Great Dictator* (1940), satirizing totalitarianism.

A silent movie being filmed. Note the "plus four" knickerbockers and loud checked sox worn by the director, kneeling. Performers used broad gestures to express their feelings, because the audience could not hear their words. (Culver)

Hollywood was producing three-quarters of the world's films in the early 1920s at studios named Fox, Metro-Goldwyn-Mayer, Paramount, Warner Brothers, Universal, and Columbia. Its producers were Sam Goldwyn, Thomas Ince, Louis B. Mayer, Jesse Lasky, and William Fox. Its stars included comedian Harold Lloyd, horseman William S. Hart, actresses Lillian Gish and Gloria Swanson, and "The Sheik," Rudolph Valentino, whose 1926 death brought hysterical mourning. In 1923 Cecil B. De Mille made *The Ten Commandments,* which competed with a Western epic, *The Covered Wagon.* Greta Garbo, Marlene Dietrich, and Maurice Chevalier came from Europe along with directors Ernst Lubitsch and Erich von Stroheim. Two notable war films were *What Price Glory?* and *All Quiet on the Western Front.*

THE "TALKIES." The "talkies" arrived in 1927, when Al Jolson sang "Mammy" in *The Jazz Singer.* The addition of the sound track doubled weekly movie attendance from 46 million persons in 1925 to 90 million in 1930. In the Great Depression years the movie houses offered double bills, even triple bills, for as little as a quarter, and warmth for the underpaid and unemployed. Humor was an antidote for the Depression; it was provided by Mae West, W.C. Fields, the Marx Brothers, Carole Lombard, and the *Thin Man* duo of William Powell and Myrna Loy. Frank Capra directed Clark Gable and Claudette Colbert in the 1934 smash hit, *It Happened One Night.* The decade of the Thirties closed with Gable playing Rhett Butler to Vivian Leigh's Scarlett O'Hara in *Gone With the Wind,* the Civil War story that held first place in the list of movie box-office successes from 1939 until 1965.

The art of animation was revolutionized by Walt Disney, whose teams of artists produced Mickey Mouse and Minnie, the Three Little Pigs, Donald Duck, and

Clark Gable and Vivien Leigh in a romantic scene from Gone with the Wind, *one of the most famous motion pictures ever made. Released in 1939, the film is still being shown on television a half century later.*

other favorites between 1928 and 1933. *Snow White and the Seven Dwarfs* (1937) followed. The 1930s featured lavish musicals, gangster films, and a succession of child stars, led by Jackie Coogan, Shirley Temple, and the team of Mickey Rooney and Judy Garland. Garland attained stardom in the 1939 version of *The Wizard of Oz.*

Ranked among the top motion pictures ever made is *Citizen Kane,* filmed by Orson Welles in 1941 as a psychological study of publisher William Randolph Hearst. It reflected exciting experimentation, particularly in the technique of narration. Director John Ford's production of John Steinbeck's *The Grapes of Wrath* in 1939 set another standard for examination of significant social issues. Audiences of the 1940s saw Humphrey Bogart and Ingrid Bergman in *Casablanca,* Katharine Hepburn in sophisticated comedies with Cary Grant and Spencer Tracy, and melodramatic performances by Bette Davis and Joan Crawford. William Wyler's *The Best Years of Our Lives* was a 1946 postwar hit. Alfred Hitchcock had come to the United States in 1940 after making *The 39 Steps* (1935) in England, foreshadowing his thrillers of the 1950s, *Rear Window* and *Vertigo.*

Hollywood had become a symbol of high living, sex, and sin; its stars had fan clubs and endless publicity. Some indulgences were detrimental to careers, as in the cases of "Fatty" Arbuckle, Mabel Normand, and Wallace Reid in the 1920s. The studios named Postmaster Will H. Hays to be their czar, as head of the Motion Picture Producers and Exhibitors of America. The Hays Office wrote a 1930 production code that restricted moviemakers, along with city and state censors and the 1934 Legion of Decency movement. Nevertheless the movies prospered until the impact of events in the 1950s (see Chapter 14).

Radio

Martians Invade New York

The radio announcer's voice is tense, frightened. "This is the most terrifying thing I have ever witnessed!" He is looking at a space ship from Mars that has smashed a huge crater in a field outside Grovers Mill, New Jersey, with a flash visible for several hundred miles.

Out of the red-hot craft crawl vile, bearlike creatures. Firing heat-ray guns, they slaughter local residents who have rushed to see the intruders.

From coast to coast, radio listeners become panic-stricken at the news bulletins.

The Martians raise a towering tripod machine whose heat rays wipe out 7000 hastily deployed U.S. Army troops. More space vehicles land to swell the attacking force.

Relentlessly the creatures in their deadly tripod machines march toward New York. . . .

The date was October 30, 1938—before television, before space movies, and during war scares in Europe. Radio demonstrated that night what a tremendous impact it has on the American mind.

Orson Welles and his Mercury Theater on CBS were performing a modernized version of the H.G. Wells novel, *The War of the Worlds,* with the dramatic setting switched to New Jersey. Thousands of listeners took the broadcast literally. They fled into the streets, trying to escape invaders who existed only in a radio script. Hospitals treated people for hysteria.

A banner headline in the New York *Daily News* the next day proclaimed: "FAKE RADIO WAR STIRS TERROR THROUGH U.S."

*R*adio is almost everywhere—at home, in the automobile, at the beach, on the street. For every person in the United States, there are approximately two radio sets. In some foreign countries ownership is nearly as high. This abundance of receivers makes radio perhaps the most pervasive of all the mass media.

Satellite transmission as a means of distributing programs, recently adopted by networks and syndicates, has opened a new era for radio. By providing stations with additional sources of material, this form of transmission is changing the style of programming that has existed since radio went through its post-television upheaval in the 1950s. Fresh elements are available to strengthen the traditional broadcasting of recordings interspersed with chitchat by disc jockeys.

In this chapter we look at how the radio industry operates and the economics involved. We trace the spectacular rise of FM broadcasting compared to the older AM method and see how stations try to develop special "personalities" aimed at closely focused, specialized audiences.

One section discusses the role of radio news—how it is prepared and broadcast, its strengths and weaknesses. As in chapters on the other media, we discuss job opportunities and career paths available in radio. ◆

A CHANGING MEDIUM

Radio's pervasive impact on American life is due primarily to its immediacy and flexibility. It is present almost everywhere: the mail carrier walks a route with a transistor fastened to the mail bag, the crowd on the beach listens to a singing group, the carpenter on a roof nails shingles in time to a rock beat. There are half a billion radio sets in the United States.

Most radio programs consist of recorded music, usually the pop-rock variety, interspersed with news, sports, talk, commercials, and relatively little dramatic or intellectual content. Although radio offers generally undistinguished fare, it obviously has broad popular appeal. While cynics describe much radio programming as that of an on-the-air jukebox with commercials, in fact radio not only provides mass entertainment but serves a vital function as a swift disseminator of information.

Because of its diversity of programming, radio offers something for virtually everyone. Urban commuters tune in for freeway traffic reports, farmers for livestock prices, families for lists of school closings when winter storms hit the northern states. Radio is quicker than any other communication medium in providing such service material. The bulk of radio listeners, however, tune in their sets to be entertained—and have strong, widely varied tastes in what they wish to hear.

Radio's capacity to serve the nation as a channel of instant communication in an emergency, and the cultural impact its outpouring of music has, especially on the nation's youth, are two principal aspects of its role in contemporary American life.

Having survived one basic change during the 1950s, when television replaced it as a medium for general entertainment, radio today is in the midst of another major evolution. This has been brought about by satellite transmission of radio signals, to be discussed later in this chapter. The recent removal of many federal regulations controlling operation of radio stations also influences the reshaping of programs.

As a commercial industry, radio is uneven. Many of the approximately 8800 commercial stations on the air are flourishing, with strong staffs and generous profits. Hundreds of others with low power and limited audience potential scramble to stay alive, hunting constantly for a magic programming formula to increase their share of the listeners and bring in greater advertising revenue. Three of every 10 American radio stations lose money. Stations in the cluttered radio spectrum are as varied as vehicles in a crowded parking lot where glossy limousines stand bumper-to-bumper with dented, aging compacts and muddy pickup trucks. All function but with vastly differing images.

Radio stations range from extremely strong, clear-channel, 50,000-watt transmitters whose signals can be heard for hundreds of miles to low-powered noncommercial stations with a range of only a few miles. While many stations operate under joint ownership with television stations, hundreds of small ones are unaffiliated with television or other media. In metropolitan areas competition among radio stations for audiences has created a jungle. Approximately 65 stations broadcast in the New York metropolitan area, for example; Chicago has about 50.

For several years in the 1950s and early 1960s, radio floundered under the shock of television's visual competition. Then industry leaders began to realize that radio has several advantages over television in the competition for listeners. Chief among these is mobility, brought about by development of the small transistor radio. One can either listen to a program attentively or have the music playing as background with almost a subliminal effect. Millions of people drive with their car radios turned on. Radio stations outnumber television stations approximately eight to one, providing a broad choice of programs to hear around the clock. Hardly a square mile exists in the United States—this applies to most other countries, too—where the sound of radio cannot be heard.

Every radio station must hold a license from the Federal Communications Commission (FCC), authorizing it to broadcast on a specified band with designated power, at certain authorized hours. If the government did not allocate the wavelengths in this manner, the broadcast spectrum would become a chaotic jumble of sound as station signals overlapped and the strong stations overpowered the weak. Station licenses must be renewed every seven years.

For several decades radio operated under strict federal regulation of its procedures. Station owners chafed at the limitations and the paperwork burden the government imposed on them. Finally, in 1981, came partial deregulation by the FCC.

The commission removed its requirements that stations must (1) devote a portion of their air time (8 percent for AM, 6 percent for FM) to nonentertainment programming, (2) restrict the number of minutes in each hour devoted to commercials, and (3) keep detailed program logs in their public files. Requirements for license renewal were greatly reduced; however, if challenged, a station must still defend its performance in dealing with the needs of its community, presenting reasonable evidence to support its case.

In making this decision, the FCC majority emphasized its belief that competition in the marketplace would exercise sufficient control over behavior of the stations.

The Growth of AM Radio

Radio transmissions are of two types, amplitude modulation (AM) and frequency modulation (FM). AM transmitters send their signals high into the air, while FM consists of "line-of-sight" (horizon) broadcasting. AM came into existence first; until after World War II, almost all commercial stations were AM outlets.

President Carter once recalled to a group of broadcasters his boyhood days on a farm in Georgia that had no electricity, and how the family gathered outdoors at night to hear a radio hooked up to the battery of his father's automobile. The music, drama, comedy, and political talk they listened to opened the world to them, as it did to millions of other persons when mass listening to radio began to develop after World War I.

From a fascinating novelty in the early 1920s, radio grew swiftly into an essential element in family life. At first, listeners used earphones and brought in programs by meticulously moving a "cat-whisker" wire across a crystal. Many sets were homemade; equipment in the broadcasting stations was almost as amateurish. On certain nights local stations would remain silent so listeners could tune in

Silent film stars Mary Pickford and Douglas Fairbanks aboard the S.S. Paris in mid-Atlantic listen in the wireless room to a 1921 broadcast from the American mainland. (Library of Congress)

distant stations. Call letters of stations east of the Mississippi River were designated to start with the letter W, those west of the Mississippi with a K. Two pioneer exceptions were KDKA in Pittsburgh and KYW in Chicago. When the loudspeaker was developed, radio's place in the living room was assured.

Families were transported in their imagination to far-off places by clever use of sound effects. As the Lone Ranger and Tonto rode off in pursuit of bandits, the hoofbeats of their horses echoed from the loudspeaker, made by studio technicians drumming a half-dozen toilet plungers on pebbles. When Sergeant Preston of the Royal Canadian Mounties stalked killers through the snow with his dog King at his side, listeners thought they heard King's heavy breathing; what they actually heard was an actor panting into a megaphone close to the microphone.

As network programming expanded, listeners developed habits similar to those exhibited by television audiences today. They planned their activities so they would be home for the weekly broadcasts of their favorite shows. They set aside time every day to listen to the observations of the commentators and the emotional sufferings of the soap opera casts. Although radio performers at work were only disembodied voices to the listeners, their physical features became nationally known through newspaper and magazine publicity and public appearances.

The first glimmerings of radio's future disc jockeys came during the 1930s, when a few stations offered "Make Believe Ballroom" programs. During those shows an announcer played records and pretended to be broadcasting from a ballroom, simulating the live performances of orchestras broadcasting from hotels and nightclubs that were a staple of local and network radio programming. Expanded from terse telegraphic reports, play-by-play descriptions of baseball games in distant cities were simulated by imaginative studio announcers, including a young Midwestern sportscaster named Ronald Reagan.

The Growth of FM Radio

When FM broadcasting began to develop, the industry treated it as a minor novelty. Few sets were equipped to receive FM signals. Those AM stations that also had FM licenses regarded them as a sideline of little consequence or potential. The poor relation has grown tremendously, however, and now dominates its onetime big cousin. Surveys show that 71 percent of the radio audience listens to FM, only 29 percent to AM. Between the mid-1970s and mid-1980s, the FM share of the audience increased 38 percent. Today more FM stations are on the air (5209) than AM stations (4867). FM's appeal is exceptionally strong to younger listeners—81 percent of the 12- to 24-year-old audience listens to FM. AM stations primarily reach listeners above age 50, serving 56 percent of that group. The role of FM will continue to grow, especially since the FCC in 1984 decided to proceed with a plan to license 1000 or more new FM stations.

AM stations have longer range and in most cases greater power than FM stations, but are subject to static interference. In some instances government regulations require them to reduce their power or sign off at sundown to avoid conflict with other station signals, which carry farther at night. FM stations can be heard only for relatively small distances but are virtually static free and transmit

U.S. BROADCASTING STATIONS

Type of Service	Stations on Air
Radio	
Commercial AM	4867
Commercial FM	3946
Educational FM	1263
Total radio	10,076
Television	
Commercial VHF	546
Commercial UHF	454
Educational VHF	110
Educational UHF	187
Total television	1,297
Low power television	
VHF LPTV	247
UHF LPTV	163
Total LPTV	410

SOURCE: *Broadcasting,* January 31, 1987.

music with greater fidelity in stereophonic sound. Investment in FM stations is generally smaller. Most of the highly profitable AM stations are situated in large urban centers.

At first, FM stations played semiclassical or classical recordings without commercial interruptions. Stations with both AM and FM licenses often transmitted their AM programs on FM, as well as in simulcasts, just to keep the FM signal on the air at virtually no cost.

Gradually, broadcasters and advertisers became aware that FM could be an effective commercial medium. New sets for homes and automobiles were built with both AM and FM bands. Hundreds of additional FM channels were authorized. Many FM stations took on much the same mixture of advertising and entertainment heard on AM stations.

From the advertiser's point of view, FM is attractive because stations can target the content of their broadcasts to audience segments with special listening interests. While individual FM station audiences are usually smaller than those hearing AM programs, use of demographic studies enables the FM stations to shape their programs for specific age ranges and listening preferences. This technique is called *narrowcasting.* Thus an advertiser may choose a station that features progressive rock, to reach the young liberal audience with a message, or one that plays softer, easy-listening music, to appeal to an older, more conservative group with different purchasing desires. Because of their larger audiences, AM stations cannot specialize to the degree that FM stations can. Some still cater to a mixture of tastes, staying in the middle of the road musically. FM stations as a whole program music, while AM stations stress news, talk, and information.

Tangible evidence of FM's huge strides is found in the prices purchasers will pay for an FM station. By the mid-1980s, FM outlets that once were money losers were being sold for as much as $12 million because buyers saw in them potentially strong profits. One Los Angeles area FM station recently was sold for a record $45 million. To capitalize on the trend, stations that operated AM and FM stations under the same call letters changed the FM letters to something entirely different and set up the FM channel as a separate advertising and program entity. AM stereo transmission, offered by a growing number of stations in the late 1980s, may offset the FM trend somewhat as the number of outlets increases. Growth of AM stereo has been delayed by confusion about which of four available systems is most desirable. Two Japanese companies, Sony and Sansui, were developing a chip that would enable listeners to hear any of the four systems. The FCC has steadfastly refused to select one system as the standard, maintaining that the decision should be made in the marketplace.

RADIO PROGRAM STYLES

As radio recovered from the shock of television's arrival, which stole its general entertainment program structure, a new style of programming developed. This consisted in large part of recorded popular music, interspersed with commercial messages, and the mixture tied together by the chitchat of a disc jockey. Except for brief hourly newscasts and some sporting events, radio networks became insignificant. Stations did their own programming, including syndicated material— often with guidance from, if not outright control by, outside consultants concerning the musical selections they should play. This is contemporary radio as most Americans know it: pop music, mostly of the rock variety, brief news, frothy talk, frequent commercials, and sports. But, as we shall see, a change has begun.

The talking that a disc jockey does between records helps to create a station's

A radio disc jockey broadcasts a program, surrounded by racks of tape cassettes, record turntables, program logbook, tape recorder, and other tools of his craft. (© Hall, Stock, Boston)

personality and bring it closer to its listeners. Lonely listeners in particular come to regard favorite disc jockeys as companions. Many station managers urge their DJs to publicize local events and thus to develop an atmosphere of community involvement by the station.

A disc jockey's on-the-air job is to package several hours of record playing in a lively manner, so that it seems to the listener to have recognizable form. Usually the disc jockey's broadcast time is listed under the performer's name as, say, the Jim Nelson Show. Jim Nelson does not simply introduce the records and read the commercials. He gives traffic reports, announces the time and temperature, offers free tickets and gifts as promotional tie-ins with advertisers, and chats on the air with listeners who call in. Since his voice is the only tool with which to sell personality, Jim Nelson cultivates a tone that is easily recognizable—jovial, confidential, aggressive, or theatrical—whatever is effective.

The art of the DJ is specialized. The peppy "morning drive time" announcer has techniques to hold listeners' attention as they arise and drive to work; the noon-time performer's style is more leisurely; then the late afternoon "drive time" announcer adopts a style for listeners who are driving home from work. DJs who broadcast in the lonely after-midnight hours develop rapport with their listeners by using a confidential, intimate tone. Automobile audiences are especially important to radio, because they are captive within the confines of their cars and are somewhat compelled to pay attention to the commercials. This is not true of listeners in other circumstances, who may turn their radios on to provide half-heard background companionship.

USE OF PLAY LISTS. Radio stations exploit Americans' tendency to value numerical superiority by playing tunes that are ranked as the Top Forty of the current week. The ranking of records in descending order from the week's number one favorite is done by trade publications such as *Billboard* and *Cash Box,* based on sales in stores. Indeed, in this age of specialization, separate Top Forty lists are compiled for contemporary-rock, country-western, and soul single-record categories, and for albums of multiple selections.

Some stations follow the Top Forty lists so dogmatically that they will play only those songs. A few have reduced their play list even further, to the Top Thirty, having their DJs play the same few tunes again and again. Their theory is that when a record is a hot new favorite, listeners want to hear it repeatedly. Constant on-air exposure of a song that has just reached the lower rungs of the Top Forty ladder helps it to climb to a higher position. Some stations vary the Top Forty diet by interspersing "golden oldies" and "extras."

Radio and the recording industry are tied together in a relationship of convenience and mutual need. Radio depends upon the record manufacturers for a constant flow of new material to broadcast. The recording industry must have exposure of its products to promote their sale, and radio play to bring new recordings to the attention of potential purchasers. The relationship between radio and recording companies will be examined more closely in Chapter 12.

Program directors usually strive for a special *sound* that will make their stations distinctive. Often this means broadcasting music of a special type. A station may air only country-western, hard rock, or reggae and soul, hoping to build a loyal following from devotees of the genre. Or it may stress a blending of styles, such as folk rock, and emphasize the play of albums rather than single records. Extremes in specialization are found most often in urban FM stations. The easy-listening format of heavily stringed background music, sometimes called wallpaper or Pablum music, is heard on FM. Only a handful of stations, mostly FM, play classical music. Religious programs, many of them syndicated, are frequent fare on smaller stations.

The abundance of program variations offered by American radio stations is apparent from this list of formats used by the National Radio Broadcasters Association in taking surveys: adult contemporary, urban contemporary, country, religious, easy listening/beautiful music, contemporary hit radio, album oriented rock, news talk, classical, oldies, soft rock, ethnic, and big band/nostalgia.

Year after year, adult contemporary has been reported as the most programmed format, usually followed by country and contemporary hits, with album-oriented rock strong on FM stations.

Automated radio has made large gains, as station managers try to reduce expenses by eliminating some of their on-the-air personnel. These stations broadcast packaged taped programs obtained from syndicates, hour after hour, or material delivered by satellite from a central program source. The closely timed tapes contain music and commercials, along with the necessary voice introductions and bridges. They have spaces into which a staff engineer can slip local recorded commercials. By eliminating disc jockeys in this manner, a station keeps its costs down but loses the personal touch and becomes a broadcasting automation. For example, one leading syndicator, Satellite Music Network, provides more than 625 stations with their choice of seven different 24-hour music formats that include news and live disc jockeys playing records.

Program rigidity imposed by slavish adherence to Top Twenty or Top Forty playlists and the upsurge of computerized automation have caused some concern both within the industry and outside. A rock station in Albuquerque sounds almost identical to one in Indianapolis or Boston. What once had been a highly personalized medium seems to have lost some of its distinctive character. This trend upset a Tennessee country music disc jockey who called himself Captain Midnight. He wanted to play what he liked, playlist or no playlist, but management said no. So the captain nailed shut the door to the control room. Management personnel had to pry it open, and shortly thereafter Captain Midnight was fired.

In making up the list of songs a station will play each week, its program and music directors consult several nationally published music tipsheets and listen to sales pitches from record company promoters pushing new releases. Then, typically, the local directors talk to the station's programming consultant by phone. The consultant keeps a close watch on what is being played in each popular format in numerous cities. The resultant playlist decisions on each station thus reflect national patterns. That is why a cross-country motorist hears the same songs on rock stations in half a dozen states, and the same country tunes. The music that local radio stations offer in the various formats to a considerable extent shapes the taste of American listeners, rather than reflecting it.

QUESTIONS OF CENSORSHIP. As radio pours out rock-pop sounds and DJ chatter, it inevitably runs up against questions of censorship. Lyrics of contemporary records frequently allude to drugs and sex, at times in terms so frank that broadcasting them to a general audience may be questioned. Stations may refuse to air certain selections. Even so, parents occasionally express shock at what their children are hearing on radio. Some radio announcers, professional and amateur, go beyond conventional boundaries of good taste in emphasizing their points and demonstrating their right of free expression. Although the Communications Act of 1934 prohibits the Federal Communications Commission from censoring broadcast matter, the "dirty words" issue reached the U.S. Supreme Court under a special set of circumstances in the late 1970s. In the George Carlin case, the court banned the use of seven specific words during daytime broadcasts, when children were most likely to be listening. Radio station managers have the responsibility for monitoring what their stations broadcast and of dealing with public objections. The topic is discussed further in Chapter 24.

THE SATELLITE ERA ARRIVES

Traditionally, radio stations have obtained most of their entertainment material from recordings donated by record companies, tapes or discs purchased from syndication firms, and network programs sent over expensive land telephone lines. Transmission by satellite has opened broad new sources of program material to stations on an economically feasible basis. While changes in programming wrought by the new technology will be gradual, it is apparent that stations wishing to improve their broadcasts can obtain the material with which to do so.

Satellite transmission is sparking a revival of radio networks. Such a network can save up to 60 percent in transmission costs, compared to landline expense, and deliver music and talk of higher fidelity, focused on narrowly defined audiences. The major radio networks have switched to satellites; so have numerous syndication firms. By using multiple satellite channels, a network can feed special regional interest material to pertinent stations without interrupting its general network programming. A broadcasting company can send one type of target-audience material to a group of affiliates at the same time it is sending different special interest material to another group. For example, ABC operates seven different special interest networks. Drama, live rock and classical concerts, national call-in talk shows, health and psychology programs, more sports and news commentators are among the programs offered to stations via satellite by the expanding networks and syndicate packagers.

Stations are responding to the increased attractiveness of the networks. Approximately 4000 stations had network affiliations in the 1980s, up about a third in a four-year period. Advertising income is rising, too, partly because radio costs substantially less than television. Another result of the network revival is development of more nationally known radio personalities.

In pretelevision days, radio was organized in blocks of 15, 30, and 60 minutes. This changed to staccato 3-minute music periods during the post-television era. A swing back to longer time blocks may be another result of satellite delivery.

Years will pass before the full impact of satellite transmission is felt on radio, but it has opened the door for fresh ideas, new program sources, and larger audiences.

NEWS COVERAGE

When an event of tremendous national or global significance occurs, such as a presidential assassination or a great natural disaster, news of it is delivered faster by radio than by any other medium. Radio's programming flexibility enables news bulletins to go on the air immediately. During a hurricane, tornado, or other continuing crisis, radio is invaluable in delivering information and instructions over a wide area.

Unfortunately, routine daily news reporting on radio frequently fails to achieve a similar high standard. Some of the larger AM stations are noted for the scope and excellence of their local news operations and national affairs reporting, but many AM and FM station managements regard news as a costly nuisance. Radio stations operating under joint ownership with television stations tend to have better-quality newscasts than those without TV ties. Staff-prepared news stories are broadcast on both outlets, and often TV news reporters do some radio broadcasts. About 5000 radio news operations exist in the United States, some of them serving joint AM-FM station organizations.

Approximately 21,000 radio news jobs exist nationwide, according to surveys made by Professor Vernon A. Stone of the University of Missouri for the Radio Television News Directors Association. Annual turnover in staff membership at stations is nearly 40 percent, so many job openings occur.

Hundreds of stations offer their listeners little more than rip-and-read news summaries that their announcers take from the news service machines. All stations have pronunciation guides that announcers are supposed to use, though some do not, and it is evident that they have not read the copy before going on the air. The news service summaries are headline coverage of national and world news. At many smaller stations coverage of local news consists primarily of stories rewritten from the local newspaper or obtained from police sources, plus announcements of meetings or events submitted by community organizations. Local news reports are especially sparse on weekends.

In contrast, some large city stations use an all-news format, broadcasting news summaries, commentaries, and sports 24 hours a day. Close to them in style are the "talk" stations that broadcast discussions, commentaries, and live phone-in conversations between announcers and audience.

There are wide differences in types of news broadcasts. Some announcers deliver the news in strident, excited tones, a fashion sometimes referred to as the "town crier syndrome." This occurs especially on rock and roll stations, whose managements believe that their young audiences are not interested in news at all. Newscasts designed for this audience emphasize soft items about life styles and rock stars, instead of heavier, hard news about world and national affairs.

Stations affiliated with one of the four traditional national radio networks in the United States—NBC, ABC, CBS, and Mutual—or with one of the other networks that develop from time to time, offer brief hourly network news summaries. The networks supplement these with five-minute news commentaries and other examinations of news situations in more depth. Using these services and the audio *actualities* offered from the scene of the news by national, regional, and state networks and syndicates, an alert station with an able news director can keep its listeners well abreast of state, national, and foreign news. Hundreds of stations, however, still have no network affiliation.

News staffs are expensive to maintain; yet without enough reporters, a station cannot cover the police, municipal, school, and other beats fundamental to comprehensive newsgathering. As a result, many small stations tend to abandon all but the most cursory local news coverage to the television stations and newspapers. Some FM stations offer news only during the morning commuting "drive-time" hours.

While this minimizing of news is regrettable, it is also understandable. The financial resources of many radio stations, especially in small cities, are sparse because the revenue they generate from a limited market is not great. If they invested heavily to build a large, competent news department, the effort might wipe out the annual profits. So a small station may try to do the best it can afford to with a news director and possibly one assistant. The news director also may have other on-the-air responsibilities. The management of a lucrative station that gives little more than lip service to news coverage because it does not find such programming profitable could be considered more open to censure.

A continual turnover among news directors tends to weaken the quality of radio news. Many of these directors move rapidly from job to job; this shuffling undercuts the consistency of news coverage. Just as they are becoming well acquainted with local names, politics, and community background, news directors often depart. They may step up the career ladder to a larger station; perhaps they leave because of disputes with station management; quite frequently they leave in frustration over budget restrictions. A recent survey by the Radio Television News Directors Association showed that the median tenure of radio news directors was less than two years. Forty-nine percent held their jobs a year or less, while only 6 percent held the same position for more than ten years. According to the survey, the greatest turnover occurred in areas of 250,000 to 1 million population. Although this turnover creates frequent job openings, the goal of reliable, enterprising news coverage suffers.

Closely linked to news on radio is sports. Sometimes the news director carries the title of sports director as well, or may also be a disc jockey. For example, a help-wanted advertisement published recently in a broadcasting trade journal read: "Small market adult contemporary AM needs morning drive announcer to jock and anchor news block." Play-by-play reports of baseball and football games attract large radio audiences.

THE ECONOMICS OF RADIO

Radio stations have only one thing to sell, and that is an inventory of time, intangible and perishable. The majority of each hour a station is on the air is devoted to entertainment and information. The rest is cut into small segments and sold to advertisers as commercials. A station's financial success depends on the number of commercials it sells each day, and the prices it can charge for them, based on the size of its audience. When a station broadcasts a network program containing commercials, the network pays to the station an agreed-upon fee.

In the older days of radio, before television, sponsors commonly bought 15- or 30-minute portions of air time during which their commercials alone appeared. Today, stations fill the hours with brief spot commercials paid for by many different advertisers.

This practice of scheduling commercials at such frequent intervals influences the recording industry; it holds the length of its popular song releases to about three minutes. Between these brief segments of music the disc jockey can work in two or three commercials, keeping a staccato pace to the program and accommodating many advertisers. The heavy loading of AM programs with commercials turned many irritated listeners to FM stations. However, many FM stations now follow the same practice of loading their air time with commercials.

A station's sales staff seeks to convince clients that radio is an effective medium on which to spend advertising dollars and that its station is the place to spend them. Having achieved this objective, the sales staff works with the advertiser to select the programs and times of day best suited for the client's commercials. The station's rate card shows the price it charges for commercials at different hours, depending upon the size and type of audience it reaches at those times. Combinations of time slots and prices can be agreed upon. When a station has difficulty selling its available commercial minutes and its income is suffering, it may go "off the rate card" and make cut-rate deals giving advertisers special bargains, such as including one or several free commercials.

Sales representatives stress demographics, to show an advertiser the size and nature of the audience that can be reached. This information includes income, education, occupation, ethnic background, marital status, and buying behavior. Program and sales directors are especially anxious to reach the audience of young adults born after World War II. At the middle of the 1980s their median age was 37; they were a group with ample income, young children, and strong purchasing desires.

A station cannot identify and count every listener in the way a newspaper can determine its audience by the number of copies sold each day and the addresses of its subscribers. Thus, radio depends upon surveys and polls, along with statistical research. The Arbitron rating service provides information to many stations. Researchers for large stations also make contact with a limited number of individuals, by telephone or mail, or in person, then project the results to cover the entire population of the station's listening area. The return addresses on cards and letters the listeners send to the station in response to a gift offering made by a disc jockey can be analyzed by researchers.

The primary advantage that radio offers to advertisers compared with television is lower cost, both for air time and for preparation of the commercials. Radio is more flexible, too, in time availability and the speed with which it can accommodate new advertising copy. Radio, however, lacks the visual appeal that helps television sell goods.

In one form of broadcasting, taxpayers rather than advertisers underwrite most of the operating costs. This is National Public Radio (NPR), a not-for-profit organization based in Washington, D.C., that supplies programming, largely of a cultural and informational nature, to more than 200 noncommercial radio stations. NPR receives its operating funds from the federal government through the Corporation for Public Broadcasting, from annual station membership fees of about $200 each, and from supplying technical services. Member stations receive about 50 hours of programming each week, most of which is produced at NPR headquarters. "All Things Considered" has been one of the most popular NPR programs. After nearly going bankrupt in 1983, NPR cut back its program services and staff sharply. American Public Radio, which grew out of Minnesota Public Radio, is a competitor of NPR with about 275 affiliates, 98 percent of which are also NPR members. APR does no producing of its own but distributes programs created by stations.

JOB OPPORTUNITIES IN RADIO

Success as a performer in radio depends heavily upon the kind of vocal personality the individual projects. If it is vibrant and distinctive, a voice the listener will remember, the beginning performer has a much better prospect of advancing to the large stations. A performer's physical appearance is of no importance except in occasional public appearances, but a lively, friendly personality is usually evident in a person's voice.

Voice quality, however, is not enough. Professional coaching can improve vocal technique and confidence, but it cannot create intelligence and a good command of English. Successful radio newscasters, talk-show hosts, and disc jockeys have quick minds and an ability to articulate their thoughts smoothly in ad lib situations.

The advice for a person beginning a career in radio is much the same as that for newspapers: start small. Basing his opinion on his surveys for the news directors association, Professor Stone has stated, "In summary, a college graduate who wants to start out doing air work or getting out on the scene of news stories is advised to seek a first job in a radio market of less than 1 million population or a TV market smaller than the top 50."

Most young people begin work at low-powered radio stations, then move to larger ones as they gain experience. In addition to reading and reporting news, they may fill in as disc jockeys during weekends and night hours. Not only must beginners acquire confidence and a sense of timing, but they must learn production techniques and the fundamentals of radio engineering. At small stations some announcers sell advertising during their off-air hours.

The Stone survey in 1985 found radio newscasters earning an average salary of $13,000 with wide variations between small stations and major ones. The lowest salary on each staff in the national survey averaged $11,700.

Sales is an attractive, well-paying aspect of radio work. A successful salesperson needs several attributes: ability to write a commercial that attracts the listener's attention and sells the product or service, skill at preparing and explaining research material that will convince a prospective client to advertise on this particular station, and detailed knowledge of the station's programming in order to place specific commercials in the most suitable time positions. Work in sales leads to executive positions on the business staff, including that of station manager.

Announcers on small stations may function at times as station engineers. This task involves at least a rudimentary knowledge of electricity and knowing what meters to read and what switches to turn to keep the station on the air.

The ability to write radio news copy and advertising messages is important. As in television writing, the basic technique is to compose conversational English that rings true to the ear. Such writing avoids complex and inverted constructions, and uses simple, declarative sentences and broken phrases in the manner in which people normally talk. Also, it uses repetition more heavily than writing for print does, especially for commercials.

Job applications for on-the-air personnel normally include demonstration tapes. A prospective employer wishes to hear the vocal styles of applicants in order to screen the candidates and select a few for personal interviews. Samples of writing style may be requested as well.

Women have a large and growing role in radio, especially in news. They comprise nearly one-third of the newspeople in radio, according to a 1985 survey by Professor Stone. On 21 percent of commercial radio station staffs, they serve as news directors. These figures are dramatically higher than those in the early 1970s when women on the air were a novelty.

The growth of minority representation on radio news staffs has been much slower. According to the Stone survey, minorities in 1985 formed 9 percent of the radio news work force and provided only 3 percent of the news directors. Minority newspeople tend to be employed at stations in major markets that have large staffs. (A discussion of employment in the media for minorities and women appears in Chapter 24.)

High among the career goals of radio personnel are the positions of program director, news director, and station manager. Salaries for these posts vary widely according to the size of the station and the experience of the individual. For example, the Stone survey showed the median income of radio news directors in major markets to be $27,456. In urban areas a news director for a major station earns well above the median. Big-city disc jockey stars have incomes of $100,000 or more, depending upon the agreements they have with station managements. A popular air personality attracts advertisers willing to pay higher rates in order to have their messages on the show, and the performer may earn extra fees from personal appearances. The classified advertising columns of *Broadcasting* magazine provide a guide to job opportunities and requirements in radio.

Recording

12

"The Boss" Turns Them On

His album "Born in the U.S.A." sold 8 million copies. In less than a day 236,000 tickets were purchased for four concerts in his native New Jersey. Bruce Springsteen was the newest king of rock and roll.

Youthful American and foreign audiences screamed when Springsteen strode on stage with his guitar. President Reagan invoked his name while campaigning in New Jersey for re-election. The Pennsylvania House of Representatives passed a resolution designating him "The Boss of Rock and Roll."

The onetime long-haired college dropout became a multimillionaire. One Springsteen recording after another hit the Top Ten spots on the charts.

These are the rewards for recording musicians who attain superstardom. Adulation and luxury await them if their songs, exuberant personalities, and musical styles catch the public's unpredictable fancy.

Just as Bruce Springsteen did, most rock musicians perform first in amateur bands and scramble for bookings in small clubs. They send demonstration tapes to recording companies, hoping for commercial release. And they dream of becoming another Elvis Presley or Michael Jackson or Madonna or Prince.

Only a few are that good or that lucky. Most of the others make a few records, then disappear from view.

*S*old by the millions and played on the air incessantly, recordings are not only a form of popular entertainment but a channel for expression of opinion as well. Songs deliver the messages of love and protest, most often to a rock and roll beat.

Because popular tastes are ever-changing, the recording business is risky and full of surprises. Some music personalities develop huge followings that endure, while others soar to prominence, then disappear almost as quickly.

This chapter explains how the recording industry functions. It examines the sudden popularity of the compact disc. Also, it discusses the close ties between those who produce recordings and the radio stations that play them, as well as the influence of music videos upon the marketing of records.

Among other aspects examined are the threat of home recording to the producers, and the appeal of rock festivals.

Concert tours to college campuses and large cities by recording stars are another method of dramatizing popular music. We show how these tours are organized and take a backstage look at the methods and economics of a typical campus concert. ◆

THE POWER OF POPULAR MUSIC

The impact of popular recordings on the public consciousness is insufficiently recognized as a means of mass communication. Records, tape cassettes, and, increasingly, compact discs form crucial channels of communication in the youth culture. Through them, desires, anger, ideas, attitudes, and fads spread around the country and across the oceans.

The electric guitar does not yet rank with the typewriter or word processor as a tool for distributing ideas. However, the recordings, music videos, and stage performances of such stars as Tina Turner and Prince have a strong impact on youthful thinking. For teenagers in particular, rock musicians often become role models.

"Hot" individual performers and groups rise from obscurity to international renown almost overnight, sometimes on the basis of only one or two recordings. They sing fervently of youth's yearnings for love, freedom from restraints, popularity, and peace. The voice of protest and defiance is prominent in the lyrics. The music is vibrant, beat-driven, insistent—and usually loud.

Unorthodox ideas and uninhibited language that challenge codes of conventional social conduct have found an audience through recordings. In earlier years musicians were prominent in the anti-Vietnam war movement. Today their voices are

British rock star Steve Winwood kisses the Grammy award he received as the best male pop vocalist of 1987 for his hit song, "Higher Love." He received a second Grammy that night when "Higher Love" was named record of the year. (AP/Wide World)

raised in the antinuclear campaign, the environmental crusade, and the women's movement.

Some people regard popular music lyrics as seductive propaganda for a hedonistic attitude toward life that encourages the use of drugs and casual sexual relationships. (Questions of sex and good taste are discussed in Chapter 24.)

Although popular music is heavily oriented toward teenagers and young adults, other types of recordings have devoted followers, mostly among somewhat older groups. Heartbroken country singers with their plaintive laments sell millions of records. Jazz, blues, classical music, and the sweet saxophone sounds of the big bands lure recording customers to the cash register.

THE COMPACT DISC

Already stimulated by the recent popularity of music videos on television, the recording industry is enjoying a surge of enthusiasm for a revolutionary form of recorded music, the compact disc.

For decades purchasers could buy recorded music in only one form, the vinyl record. Then the more portable tape cassette appeared; it constitutes nearly 60 percent of the prerecorded music market. Now purchasers may obtain recordings in three forms—vinyl, cassette, and the new compact laser disc, called a CD. How much of the recording market the compact disc will take over cannot be determined yet, but its popularity is growing so rapidly that it already has made a major impact on this always volatile form of communication.

The digital laser disc coated with plastic is slightly less than five inches wide and extremely durable, easy to transport, and convenient to store, requiring only a fraction of the space occupied by a 12-inch long-playing vinyl record. Between one and two hours of music are contained on the single playing surface of a CD. Sound reproduction of the compact disc is far superior to that of the other recording methods. Digital recording involves the coding of sound waves into binary digits etched on the disc surface. As the disc is played in a small machine, a laser beam "reads" the digits and translates them into sound.

Compact discs appeared on the market in mid-1983. The cost of the playing machines and the discs was too high for the average music purchaser, and availability was limited. Less than one million discs were shipped to stores that year by the record manufacturers.

In 1984, as enthusiasm developed, manufacturers produced 5.8 million discs, a six-fold increase. In 1985 the boom was on, and buyers purchased 18 million discs. Manufacturers could not keep up with the demand. During the two-year period, the cost of a compact disc player fell from about $1000 to $200, and the retail price of a disc declined from the $15–$25 range to $10–$15. Further price reductions were probable. From only a handful of selections available in 1983, buyers soon had their choice of more than 4000 CD releases, popular and classic. Record companies dug into their files of master recordings to reissue earlier selections in compact disc form and produced new music in all three types of recording. In a typical recent weekly listing of bestselling albums in *Billboard,* 17 of the 20 were issued in compact disc form, as well as in tape and vinyl.

Record industry executives predict that, until CD prices decrease further and the availability of portable and automobile CD players increases, tape cassettes will remain the primary format for use out of the home. Compact discs are expected to cut heavily into vinyl sales but will not entirely replace traditional records soon because millions of music lovers own expensive stereo record players they will hesitate to discard.

Still another recording method, the digital audio tape, appeared in the late 1980s. The DAT cassette is smaller than the familiar audio tape cassette, fitting into the palm of the hand, and produces a sound equivalent to the compact disc. Also, it can be used to copy prerecorded music, which the compact disc cannot.

Despite the excellence of its sound, its compact flexibility, and its home recording capability, features of great interest to consumers, American and European recording companies delayed putting the digital audio tape on the market. They feared that it would harm the compact disc sales boom and increase home and illegal commercial taping. Under pressure from Japanese manufacturers, however, digital audio tape began to appear in 1987. How heavy its ultimate impact on the recording industry will be is uncertain.

MUSIC VIDEOS

An electronic phenomenon of the 1980s, the *music video* has greatly increased the impact of rock music in particular by bringing its vivid sights and sounds to television. Other forms of popular music are receiving similar, if less abundant, exposure on the home screen.

The music video is a taped performance, usually three to five minutes in length, in which a popular recording group plays a song while its members or other performers act out the song's story or meaning. Some videos have a narrative thread. In others, the pictures merely create an atmosphere or a mood. These hybrid sound-and-sight mini-movies have found a swiftly growing audience. Among other effects, they are changing the marketing of recordings. They introduce new acts and new songs. Also, they project contemporary pop music to an entirely new audience, the stay-at-home television viewers who are not traditional purchasers of recordings or tickets to concerts.

Created as a promotional device to sell recordings, the video has taken on a life of its own—an art form, its enthusiasts call it.

Cable television music programs, especially the Music Television Network (MTV), are the primary outlet for video releases. MTV plays rock music videos 24 hours a day. The visual portion may be a videotaped excerpt from a live performance by the group or it may be conceptual—a piece of fantasy, drama, or comedy, often using computer graphics and animation. These videos are introduced, disc-jockey fashion, by a new kind of performer called a *veejay*.

Virtually every important recording made today has a video version. These usually cost about $40,000 to make, with occasional ones running as high as $250,000. Producers regard this expense as a good investment in most instances because the appearance of an attractive new video on television has an immediate impact on record sales. Approximately 1500 music videos a year are produced in the United States.

Recording companies provide videos to stations, frequently without charge, and urge their use in the same way they "push" recordings at radio stations. Since many radio stations play as few as 30 songs, repeating them again and again, new recording releases have difficulty in getting air time. MTV has 24 hours a day to fill, however, and gives air time to little-known groups and unknown selections. In the cable television field, in which scores of entrepreneurs are hunting a successful formula, MTV has gained a large and devoted following. Aware of MTV's impact, other networks and stations are packaging similar music-and-visual services, often playing country-western and other categories of music that MTV does not offer.

Critics express concern about the effect of music videos, with their emphasis on sex and violence, upon the predominantly teenage audience that watches them. A study by five researchers—Richard L. Baxter, Cynthia De Riemer, Ann Landini, Larry Leslie, and Michael W. Singletary—analyzed 62 MTV music videos with this concern in mind. Their findings, published in the Summer 1985 issue of the *Journal of Broadcasting & Electronic Media,* included these observations:

> Music video sexual content was understated, relying on innuendo through clothing, suggestiveness, and light physical contact rather than more overt behaviors. . . .
>
> The study's results indicate, however, that sexually oriented, suggestive behavior is portrayed frequently in music videos. Questions regarding the impact of this portrayal on adolescent socialization, peer relationships, and modeling are raised.
>
> The frequency of instances of violence and crime content also merits further attention. . . . The most frequently coded content elements were physical aggression, not the use of weapons, murder, or sexual violence. Violent action in music videos often stopped short of the fruition of the violent act.

Clearly, the addition of a provocative visual element accentuates the sexual and violent aspects already present in numerous rock music recordings.

Robert W. Pittman, president, views the programming of MTV Networks, Inc., as answering the desires of what he calls the "television generation." He told the 1986 convention of the American Society of Newspaper Editors, "They [today's youths] don't require a narrative line to take in information or entertainment. They readily respond to more elusive sense impressions communicated through feelings, mood, and emotion."

RECORDING: A VOLATILE INDUSTRY

Making and marketing recordings is a large and volatile industry, far less structured than the print media, radio, and television. Approximately 1200 American companies produce as many as 700 million records and tapes each year, according to figures supplied by the Recording Industry Association of America (RIAA). Many of these companies are small, some handling only one performer or category of recordings. More than 95 percent of the recordings sold in the United States are made by the 55 companies belonging to RIAA. The industry's gross sales in a typical year are around $4 billion, an estimate based on listed retail prices of records; net sales are difficult to ascertain because of price discounting and heavy returns of unsold records.

Success in the industry depends upon one's ability to exploit the quicksilver changes in public taste, indeed, to stimulate those changes through the production of new sounds and the promotion of fresh performing groups and individuals. The pursuit of novelty in sound and performance style is endless. Although half a dozen large companies dominate the industry and concentrate enormous promotion and sales efforts on their big-name stars, it is still possible for an unknown performer recorded by a minor studio to attain overnight fame with a record that catches the public fancy. The hope that lightning will strike in this manner keeps thousands of performers struggling along in obscure night spots, trying to assemble enough material and money to make a demonstration tape that will convince a producer to offer them a contract.

This is a business for quick-witted individuals who can recognize trends, make deals, take risks for the "big buck"—those who know how to practice the art of "hype," the tricks of providing an exciting buildup for the performers they are selling. They must be able to sense which performers have the magical ability to stir audiences, while others of equal musical skill do not. An industry built on such an ephemeral base inevitably contains an element of chaos.

Electronic recording techniques using tape, developed in and after the late 1950s, provide great flexibility in making recordings. No longer is a studio recording session a simple act of a group or an individual singer performing a piece of music before a microphone. Now a record is an intricate melding of several taped sound tracks into a master recording. The skill of the studio sound mixer is as important as the ability of the performers. The use of electronic musical instruments expands the variety of sound effects achievable.

Rock and roll's first spectacular star was Elvis Presley, a young Tennessee truck driver who made his first amateur record in 1954, was heard on a Memphis radio station, and quickly became a national, even international phenomenon. By the time he died in 1977, at 42 years of age, Presley had become a legendary figure,

This view of a recording studio shows the intricate electronic equipment needed to produce a popular record. (Farrell, Courtesy Mix Magazine)

leaving an estate of $15 million derived from the sale of more than 500 million records. His death touched off mass mourning. Years after his death, Presley remains a cult hero and sales of his records continue to be high. Thousands of visitors tour his mansion in Memphis, spending large sums on Elvis ashtrays, scarves, statuettes, and other souvenirs.

Although rock and roll began in the United States, many of its most popular groups came from Great Britain. The exuberant Beatles made a spectacular American tour in 1964, followed by the more arrogant Rolling Stones, who proclaimed and practiced a life style involving drugs, violence, and blatant promiscuity. Country-western music, always popular on small-town radio stations in the West and South, has enjoyed a strong growth in national popularity since the late 1970s. "Crossover" blends of rock, folk, and country have emerged, producing such stars as Kenny Rogers and Dolly Parton, while the more traditional ballad singers such as Frank Sinatra and Barry Manilow remain popular. Bruce Springsteen, Madonna, Lionel Ritchie, and Michael Jackson were among the big-selling stars of the middle and late 1980s.

The American public was jarred into realization of the impact rock and folk music had on its young listeners by what happened on a muddy farm near Bethel, New York, during a humid August weekend in 1969. Known as the Woodstock Music and Art Fair, this three-day marathon performance by rock and pop stars drew an amazing throng of 400,000 people who swarmed around the grounds in an unfettered demonstration of independence from their parents' social norms. The participants camped out in the fields, sang, drank, swam in the stream, used drugs, listened to the bands on the stage, and talked defiantly against the Vietnam War. Three persons died of drug overdoses and hundreds were treated for drug

illnesses. The crowd itself was as much an event as the music it had come to hear. Woodstock became the historic symbol of the counterculture. Rock festivals patterned after Woodstock became a part of American life, even though many other manifestations of the youthful revolt dwindled into the greater conformity and conservative political trend of the 1980s.

RECORDING AND RADIO

Producers of popular recordings have four principal ways to introduce their new numbers to the public: "play" on the radio, advertising in youth-oriented publications, live concerts by performing groups, and music videos on television. The most important of these is radio. Without it, the mass marketing of discs and cassettes would collapse.

Not only do record distributors provide copies of their new products to radio stations free of charge, but their promotion staff members try to encourage the stations to play them. If a new record is introduced on a major Top Forty station in a metropolitan market, listeners in search of something fresh will buy it in the stores. Industry trade magazines and tip sheets report that the record is "hot" in that city. By telephone calls and personal visits, promoters spread the word and cajole stations in other cities to add the song. If it catches on, sales flourish in those cities also, and onto the Top Forty charts it goes.

With commercial success of a record so dependent upon radio exposure, promoters sometimes resort to unethical tactics to obtain air play. The result has been the recurring *payola* scandals. In its simplest form payola is under-the-counter payment of cash to a radio program director or disc jockey to play certain records frequently. Payola may take more subtle forms as well, such as free trips and other favors paid for by a record company. Another device is including the radio decision makers in profits on "backdoor sales," an industry racket. Stacks of new records are slipped out of the normal commercial distribution system and given to a radio executive or disc jockey; that individual sells them at a reduced price to a retail music store and pockets the proceeds. It should be emphasized, however, that most radio personnel reject such practices.

A federal law makes undercover payments for playing records a crime, punishable by a $10,000 fine and a year in prison. When fresh rumors of payola surfaced in 1986, alleging use of drugs as payments and ties between record promoters and organized crime, a Senate investigating subcommittee undertook a probe of the industry.

In the dizzy promotional milieu of the recording world, a valuable accolade for an album or a single recording is to be certified "gold" by the Recording Industry Association of America. This means that an album has sold 500,000 copies and a single record 1 million. To be declared "platinum," an album must sell 1 million units and a single 2 million. A standard album has 10 songs on one long-playing disc. In 1985, a relatively weak sales year, 65 albums won the platinum award and 138 the gold. At their lowest point in 20 years, single-song records produced only nine gold awards, three of them to Madonna. Competition is so intense and production costs so high that 75 percent of the records produced fail to earn a satisfactory profit for their creators.

THE "FREE" MARKET

Although they sell huge quantities of recordings, record producers are angry about unknown millions of recordings made annually from which they and the performers collect no income. These either are taped by amateurs for personal use or "bootlegged" at cut rates by professionals who evade payments of royalties. The simplicity of electronic copying makes this situation possible.

When moderate-priced home recording machines came onto the market, the industry uttered cries of corporate pain. Rather than purchase recordings of a new song they hear on the radio, many owners of home recorders tape the music from a broadcast. The cost of blank tapes for home recording is less than that of records and cassettes. Or, after one person purchases an album, half a dozen friends may make tapes of the music from it, eliminating portions of the album they dislike. Even worse, from the recordmaker's point of view, are rental stores. A person may rent a popular new album overnight for a modest fee; the renter and friends may tape the album's contents before returning it to the store.

Alarmed by loss of sales from these methods, music recording companies joined videotape producers in shouting, "Unfair!" They pressed a suit all the way to the

U.S. Supreme Court, requesting a decision that such home recording was illegal. The Court ruled in 1984 that home videotape recording of television shows does not violate copyright regulations (see Chapter 13), a decision that affected the music recording industry similarly. The two groups continued to ask Congress for a law requiring the manufacturers of blank tapes to pay them a fee for each tape sold, as compensation for lost recording sales.

The appearance of small personal cassette machines has created the phenomenon of men and women walking city streets, jogging, cycling, and riding on buses with small headsets covering their ears. Tuned out from the world around them, even though surrounded by people, they listen to taped music and conversation that sometimes is packaged in cassette "magazines." Often they listen to home-recorded tapes.

THE CONCERT CIRCUIT

Groups and individual performers in the pop-rock world whose records have sold well enough from radio exposure to earn them a reputation frequently capitalize on this achievement by doing live concert tours. These tours stimulate sales and build the performers' followings.

An intricate public appearance circuit has developed. Famous stars play the circuit of arenas in cities and on university campuses that seat 10,000 or more people. Performers with a growing reputation, but who are not yet at the top, are booked into smaller houses that seat 2000 to 5000. If the touring performer demonstrates drawing power at this level, a promoter may risk booking the act onto the arena circuit. Another way in which a group promotes itself is to perform as the opening act in a big-name show. Opening-act performances are

The tightly packed crowds at rock concerts are able to hear the music well through complex, expensive sound systems. (Albertson, Stock, Boston)

watched closely by promoters. If the openers please the crowds—not an easy task, before a restless, often boisterous throng waiting impatiently for the main act—promoters may finance the act on a tour as a headliner on the small-house circuit.

Always a high-risk enterprise because of the heavy operating costs involved, the concert business suffered during the recession of the early 1980s, then revived. The number of touring acts was reduced, and some tours by well-known groups were financial failures. Nevertheless, tour appearances by such groups and individuals as Bruce Springsteen, Kiss, Kool and the Gang, Rolling Stones, Fleetwood Mac, David Bowie, and Barry Manilow drew immense crowds at high ticket prices.

A look backstage at a concert given by a famous rock group in a university arena seating 12,000 provides an insight into the live concert business.

The promoter of the concert takes the principal financial risk. If the house is full, he or she can make a generous profit. If the act fails to draw well, the promoter takes a financial beating. The five-member rock group booked into this arena has received a guarantee of $25,000 for its performance, plus a percentage of gross ticket sales. On this night the arena grosses $80,000, so the star group leaves town with payment in excess of $40,000. Grosses of more than $100,000 for a single performance in very large arenas were relatively common before the music industry suffered a severe slump beginning in 1979.

The basic rent the promoter has paid for the arena is $4000, plus several thousand dollars more in a percentage of the total ticket sale amount and fees for cleanup, ticket selling, security, and other services. Also, the promoter has paid $5000 to a specialty firm to set up the group's bulky sound and light equipment. Four semitrailers are needed to haul this equipment, which represents an investment of more than $100,000. While the headline acts take in immense sums, they have heavy expenses for travel and equipment.

The setup for the night's performance starts at 8 in the morning and continues all day as carpenters, electricians, and sound technicians build the stage sets. Uninvolved with all of this, the star act flies into town aboard its private airplane in the late afternoon. At the airport the group is met by the two chauffeured limousines specified in its contract to be available at all times. The performers stay at the best hotel in the city, and dine on the special menus their contract demands. Traveling pop-rock stars enjoy luxuries and the attributes of wealth most of them hardly dared dream about as children, yet many complain about life on the road because of the physical drain they feel from their nightly high-decibel, high-energy shows, and constant travel.

Altogether, more than 50 persons are involved in staging the night's performance—the headline group and the opening act, managers, publicity people, and stage and setup crews. The majority of the crowd, as on most nights, range in age from 16 to 25, with many 14-year olds and some audience members near 30 years of age.

Concert performances are often videotaped; portions of the tape are used as videos on television, as explained earlier. At some concerts the tape is played simultaneously on huge screens—a boon to customers in the far back rows.

JOB OPPORTUNITIES IN RECORDING

Young people who wish to enter the popular music business for careers in management or writing have no clear path to follow. Some management personnel are drawn from the ranks of former performers; knowledge of electronics, sales, and marketing is more valuable than traditional training in mass communication processes. Most pop-rock songs performed by groups today are written by a member of the group or its entourage. One nontechnical, nonmusical type of job opportunity is in the promotion department of record producers and distributors, advertising new recordings and performers and urging radio and television stations to play specific new releases. Those individuals best suited for such work are extroverted, personable, and aggressive, with enthusiasm for and knowledge of contemporary music.

Television

A TV Drama Flops

The breezy *Variety* headline tells the story: Capone's Empty Vault a Goldmine.

Once the Prohibition-era gangster Al Capone and his Chicago mob lived in arrogant luxury in the Lexington Hotel. Now, 50 years later, the abandoned hotel was being torn down.

Wreckers found sealed rooms in the cellar. Rumors swept the city that the vaults contained bodies of gang victims. Or a huge cache of money. Or secret records of Capone's illegal deals with politicians and police.

A Chicago station arranged to show the opening of the vault on live television. Stations in 180 other cities joined in.

A commentator dramatically built up the excitement and showed old films of Capone to the nationwide audience. Then workmen blasted their way into the walled-up rooms and found—absolutely nothing. Apparently the rooms had been used for coal storage.

The promoters were jubilant, nevertheless, because the show drew a phenomenal audience. In Chicago 73 of every 100 turned-on TV sets were tuned to it. Other cities reported heavy viewing. Sponsors bought 13 national commercials on the show at nearly $100,000 each.

What attracted the audience? Mystery? Suspense on live TV? The so-called glamour of the gangster era? TV programming specialists have yet to figure out the answers to those questions.

*O*f all the mass communication methods, television has the most impact on our lives. Ninety-eight percent of American homes have TV sets, and those sets deliver entertainment, news, and advertising into the average home more than seven hours a day.

Television has expanded dramatically through the recent growth of cable television. Transmission of programs around the country by satellite, and their delivery to the home TV screen by wire rather than over the air, have opened dozens of additional channels for viewing.

The world of television is constantly in flux as new technologies and programming ideas develop. This chapter explains what is happening and may happen. First, we discuss the general role of television and its influence on contemporary life. We see how a television station operates, look at the battle among the networks for audiences, and examine how television covers the news.

Other areas explored include the way TV shows are rated, the role and performance of public television, and the emergence of cable television as a major force in communications—its programming, its economics, and the competition it encounters from the video industry. The chapter includes a survey of job opportunities in television, especially for women and minorities. ◆

THE EXPANDING WORLD OF TELEVISION

The viewer reclining in his easy chair aims a hand-held remote control switch at the darkened television screen across the room and pushes a button. The screen comes alive with brightly colored individuals cavorting in a situation comedy. Laughter from a prerecorded sound track fills the room.

At his side the man's wife shakes her head, no. He pushes the button, again and again. Click . . . click . . . click. Rapidly the selection process runs through the standard 12 channels of the TV set. Snippets of a baseball game, a toothpaste commercial, a police drama, a game show, a beer commercial, and a 1950s movie flash onto the screen.

Still dissatisfied, the man clicks onward through the supplementary channels visible because the set is hooked up to cable television—an evangelist pleading for contributions, a national news summary, a health talk show, a local volleyball tournament, two undecipherable globs of color representing additional pay cable services the couple doesn't purchase, a championship soccer game from Europe. Finally, the channel selector brings in the start of a popular R-rated movie on Home Box Office, one shown recently at a local theater. Husband and wife nod in agreement and settle back to watch it, uncut and uncensored.

Similar scenes occur in millions of American homes every evening. The profusion of programming made possible by cable delivery of programs in place of over-the-air reception by antenna, satellite transmission, and computer technology is altering television spectacularly. And more changes are coming. Even the most astute futurist hesitates to define all the ways in which television sets will be used in the 1990s.

A great many American television set owners still do not have access to the visual abundance the new technology provides. The heavy expense of building cable systems in urban areas and the political problems of distributing operating franchises have delayed the spread of cable television. Relatively limited in scope until 1975, cable's expansion is now swift. By 1987 cable service had been installed in about 48 percent of American homes, with new connections being made every month. However, the growth of pay channels on cable TV—those such as Home Box Office and Showtime, for which the set owner pays an extra charge beyond the basic cable fee—has been slowed by competition from home video (see Chapter 15).

The television industry today is divided into two primary areas: (1) Free *over-the-air television,* in which advertisers pay the cost of the programs; and (2) *cable television,* in which viewers pay monthly fees to receive programs. A third, growing but still minor, form of program delivery is *pay-per-view,* in which the subscriber pays fees to see special extra programs of unusual merit.

The competing forms of television are not mutually exclusive. Broadcast television and cable television overlap directly to the extent that viewers receive the programs of the broadcast networks and some independent over-the-air stations as part of the basic cable package they purchase. Anxious to obtain a foothold in cable, the broadcast network companies have developed various forms of financial participation in cable programming.

THE IMPACT OF TELEVISION

The power of television to shape contemporary life is astounding. What viewers see and hear influences their attitudes, their manners, their speech, and often their daily habits.

Television is not content to cover athletic events. It dictates the hour at which they take place and when the game action will halt for commercials. The World Series, for generations an afternoon event, now is played on cold October nights, to the acute discomfort of players and crowds, so that networks may sell their commercials between innings at prime-time rates. National political conventions are staged and timed like theatrical performances to lure a TV audience. Protest demonstrations that would pass almost unnoticed gain national exposure when a television news crew arrives and photographs protesters shaking their fists at the camera. In the home, the program listings influence meal- and bed-times. Parents may use the TV set as a babysitter, relieved that it keeps the children quiet, and too often unconcerned about the ideas and images they are absorbing. According to A. C. Nielsen statistics, the average American family watches television 7 hours and 10 minutes per day.

Although television has been a force in American life for some 40 years, a large

The ABC series "Amerika," a fictionalized account of life in the United States after a Soviet takeover, stirred controversy during its broadcast on seven consecutive nights in 1987. Cindy Pickett and Robert Urich, left, play a couple trying to make their marriage work in the face of radical social change. Wendy Hughes, center, plays a woman who has built a political career for herself under the Soviet regime. Her son, Keram Malicki-Sanchez, is at right. (AP/Wide World)

percentage of viewers have not yet developed a discriminating attitude toward it. In its finest hours—coverage of the explosion of the space shuttle Challenger and the assassination and funeral of President John F. Kennedy, to cite two examples —television with its enthralling visual immediacy gives its audience a feeling of participation far more powerfully than any other medium. Each season, a limited number of dramatic programs such as Alex Haley's series, "Roots," and ABC's "The Winds of War" and "Amerika," rise above the tightly packaged limits of commercial television, stirring viewers' emotions. ABC's drama, "The Day After," depicting the effects of a nuclear bomb explosion in the Kansas City area, drew a huge audience and stirred a national debate on nuclear policy in late 1983.

Television's spokespersons cite a long list of distinguished accomplishments. But these are almost obscured in the daily TV grist. The monotonous succession of game shows, soap operas, reruns of old movies, inane situation comedies, and violent police shows, interrupted relentlessly by commercials, becomes an opiate for some adults, an escape from the reality of daily life while purporting to be reality. It is an artificial reality: in the television world, hardly anyone grows old, even the poor are well dressed, the private detective hero always finds a parking place, and the emotional impact of tragedy is blunted by the bouncy, cheerful toothpaste and laundry detergent commercials that follow it.

In 1961, when Newton N. Minow, then chairman of the Federal Communications Commission, labeled much of television programming "a vast wasteland," he drew praise from critics and criticism from TV industry leaders. In his speech he said:

> You will see a procession of game shows, violence, audience participation shows, formula comedies about totally unbelievable families, blood and thunder, mayhem, vio-

lence, sadism, murder, western bad men, western good men, private eyes, gangsters, more violence, and cartoons. And, endlessly, commercials—many screaming, cajoling and offending. And most of all, boredom.

Twenty-five years later, in 1986, John J. O'Connor writing in the New York *Times* recalled Minow's description, then commented:

> Yet, while getting bigger and more pervasive, and periodically laying claim to accomplishments of unquestioned value and stature, the television landscape remains essentially and distressingly the same as that described by Minow. Substitute "disease of the week" movies for the westerns, and the picture is still all too familiar. . . . As one analyst after another has pointed out over the decades, commercial television is in the business not of creating programs but of supplying audiences to advertisers who generally do not want their potential customers to be unduly upset.

As long as measurements of audience size—the ratings—determine whether a program stays on the air and the cost of commercials in it, the quality of television programming will continue at approximately the same level. Networks rarely risk showing a notably innovative program, because if it fails to attract a large audience, the price the network can charge for commercials in it must be reduced. So they play safe. Year after year they present the same familiar types of programs whose audience ratings, and hence advertising revenue, are predictable. (The rating system is discussed later in the chapter.)

THE MONEY ROLLS IN

Television yields large profits for the three primary American networks, the American Broadcasting Company (ABC), the Columbia Broadcasting System (CBS), and the National Broadcasting Company (NBC), and the owners of most of the 1000 commercial stations. Television stations are of two types: *VHF* (very high frequency), and the less-powerful *UHF* (ultra high frequency). In 1980 the FCC instituted technical changes that are adding hundreds of low-powered, short-range television stations in both VHF and UHF bands. The money rolls in because advertisers have found that commercials on TV sell merchandise in such enormous quantities that they will pay very high prices for air time to broadcast those commercials. This is not surprising, since there is at least one television set, and often more, in 98 percent of American homes.

Broadcaster Advertisers Reports, a private research firm, reported that total television advertising income in 1985 was $19.1 billion, of which the major networks received $8.3 billion.

A survey by the National Association of Broadcasters reported that in 1982 the typical American television station had a profit margin of 23.3 percent. Margins of 25 percent or more were not uncommon.

The elaborate Liberty Weekend celebration in New York harbor marking the reopening of the Statue of Liberty on July 4, 1986, illustrates the profit potential of network television. ABC paid $10 million for exclusive rights to telecast the official festivities, sharing with other networks only a few segments of the 17½-hour program during which President Reagan and Chief Justice Warren Burger

25 YEARS OF BROADCASTING

	1961	1985
Combined pre-tax profits of the three major networks	$267,960,000*	$1,034,000,000
Women network correspondents (three major networks)	3	54
Annual budget, CBS News	$75,000,000	$250,000,000
Households with TV	47,200,000	85,900,000
Households with cable	725,000	34,740,300
Average salary, anchorperson in top-25 market	$40,580	$115,860
Average salary, TV news "star" in top-25 market	$272.000– 363,000	$800,000– 2,500,000

*All 1961 figures stated in 1986 dollar values
SOURCE: *Columbia Journalism Review,* 25th Anniversary Edition, November/December 1986

appeared. In return for this investment, ABC sold $30 million of advertising and made a profit of approximately $16 million.

When CBS televised the 1987 Super Bowl game between the New York Giants and Denver Broncos in Pasadena, the game was seen by an estimated 122.6 million viewers. The network used some $10 million of electronic equipment including 14 cameras, one of them operating from a blimp, and had a staff of about 150 persons at the Rose Bowl. It charged advertisers $1.2 million for a one-minute commercial. To cash in even further, CBS staged a two-hour pregame show. Special announcers were assigned to game telecasts fed to Great Britain and Ireland.

This is television at its most grandiose. If a few wry voices ask, "All this, just for a football game?" television leaders reply that the Super Bowl is not merely a game, it is a "great American spectacle"—a spectacle spawned by television.

Televising the Olympic Games also produces mind-boggling figures. After making a large profit from televising both the Winter and Summer Games in 1984, for which it paid combined rights fees of $316.5 million, ABC paid $309 million for rights to only the 1988 Winter Games at Calgary. After intense bidding, NBC won the rights to the Summer Games at Seoul for a base payment of $300 million plus a split in advertising revenues that could bring the total fee to $500 million. Thus fees to televise the 1988 combined games had a potential of exceeding three-quarters of a billion dollars.

With amounts of this magnitude at stake, it is understandable that making a profit dominates the thinking of television executives. Indeed, their readiness to risk huge sums makes possible the televising of such spectacular events. Critics recognize this fact but contend that commercial television has a social obligation

Televised sporting events are popular entertainment for viewers in homes and bars. A TV cameraman zeroes in on a major league baseball game at Fenway Park, home of the Boston Red Sox. (© Herwig, The Picture Cube)

to temper its drive for profits by providing audiences occasionally with stimulating cultural and intellectual fare. Caught in a fierce competition to be "Number One," network decision-makers only rarely break away from their slavish adherence to the ratings to do so.

HOW A TELEVISION STATION OPERATES

Unlike the printed media and the commercial motion picture industry, a television station gives its product away. Anyone possessing a television set may watch hour after hour of programs free of charge. The station, of course, must earn money to cover its high cost of operation and return a profit. It does so through the sale of commercial advertising time.

Examination of the operation of a successful TV station of medium size, affiliated with one of the three major networks, shows how American television functions. In most respects this station is typical of many in the United States, although it has a considerably larger news operation than many of its size.

The station is headed by a general manager. Reporting to the manager are four major department heads—chief engineer, program director, news director, and sales manager. The head of the production department reports to the program director. The promotion director is closely linked to the sales department but also reports to the program director.

Although it is on the air 24 hours a day, the station creates only about three or four hours of programming in its own studios, mostly local news. The rest is obtained from the network and from independent suppliers of filmed shows. To do this job, the station has a staff of nearly 100 people, plus eight to ten part-time employees. Some of the latter are local college students who usually help with live show production. The station offers a full hour of local news, weather, and sports at the dinner hour preceding the evening network news program, and another 30 minutes of news in the late evening and at noon. During the week it presents other local background news and discussion programs. Twenty-five people of varying degrees of experience comprise the news staff.

The necessary income with which to operate the station is obtained from three primary sources: the network, national spot commercials the station puts on the air during station breaks, and local and regional commercials. One widely held misconception is that an affiliate station pays the network for the national programs it puts on the air. The reality is just the reverse.

In 1984 the FCC voted to raise its ownership limits of 7 AM stations, 7 FM stations, and 7 TV stations to 12 of each and to abolish the limits in 1990. Under congressional pressure the FCC later postponed raising the TV ceiling to 1985. At that time the commission approved the limit of 12 TV stations provided that collectively those stations served no more than 25 percent of the nation's viewing households (UHF stations were counted as serving only one-half of the TV homes within their markets). In addition, the FCC stated that a company could own 14 stations in each of the AM, FM, and TV categories if two each were subsidiaries controlled by minorities.

Network-owned stations are known in the trade as O and Os; in addition, each major network has about 200 affiliated stations. An affiliate contracts with a network for the exclusive right to broadcast in its coverage area all programs distributed by the network. It also has the right to refuse to broadcast any network program. Rejections occur when the station believes its audience will find a particular program objectionable, or when it prefers to use that block of air time to broadcast a program it originates on its own, or obtains from another source. In practice, most affiliates broadcast more than 90 percent of the network programming. When a network plans to present a controversial program, it transmits the show in advance to the affiliates on a closed circuit; the station executives then decide whether to use it.

With certain exceptions, the network pays the station to air a network program; the price is based on the size of the station's market. In our example the station's compensation is approximately $800 per hour in prime time. The network pays the station 30 percent of its card rate. During an hour-long show, most of the commercials are put on the air by the network, which receives all the income from them. However, station break slots in which the local station inserts its own commercials, either national or local, are left open. The local station keeps all the revenue from these spots.

Thus it follows that the larger the number of affiliates carrying a show, the larger the network's audience and the greater the amount of money it can charge an advertiser that places a commercial on the show. Television advertising rates are based on the cost of reaching 1000 viewers. That is why there was great concern in the industry when in 1977 national ratings services revealed that both daytime and nighttime viewing had declined after almost two decades of an almost continuous rise. Changing demographic patterns of the viewing audience were among several factors cited as the possible reasons for the decline, which continued into the 1980s.

To supplement network and local programming, stations obtain programs from other sources as well, under varying financial arrangements. A common example of this is the syndicated show, such as the Phil Donahue interview program. The station purchases the show from a syndication firm for a flat, negotiated fee. All commercial time slots are open for local commercials. If the station's sales staff is effective, it fills those spots with high-paying sales messages. A variation of this involves barter. The station receives the program without charge, and the program organization provides no compensation. Half the spots in the hour-long program are sold nationally by the organization. It keeps all this income, from which it covers the expense of preparing the show. The other half of the commercial slots are reserved for the local station's own commercials.

In recent years a combination of barter–purchase has come into vogue in program syndication. That is, a syndicator will sell a program to a station but retain one or two 30-second positions to sell to national advertisers. This arrangement permits the station to obtain expensive syndicated programming at less cost,

Talk show hostess Oprah Winfrey interviews an audience member in Cumming, Georgia, about racial attitudes in all-white Forsyth County. She took her program there after an antisegregation march in the county drew national attention. (AP/Wide World)

without having to give up as much inventory as it would in the traditional barter arrangement.

Still another variation is the network show provided to an affiliate without the usual compensation from the network. Enough local spots are left open during the program for the station to profit satisfactorily. The "Today" show and Sunday professional football broadcasts are examples of this arrangement. The audiences for these broadcasts are so large that, in these instances, a local station can afford the noncompensation arrangement.

Occasionally, a station will replace a network program in prime time with a nonnetwork program that it considers exceptionally important or more lucrative. This action often angers loyal audiences of the preempted program, so it is done infrequently. The Billy Graham evangelistic crusade, for example, will purchase consecutive evenings of prime time, for which it pays the station more than the $800 hourly network rate. This is a good financial arrangement for the station because it receives full income for the hour and at the same time appeals to the portion of the viewing population that finds the Graham message inspiring.

THE BATTLE OF THE NETWORKS

Close Watch on Ratings

The three principal general networks are in such a battle among themselves to attract viewers, and the advertising dollars they bring, that the weekly ratings report of their standing is a popular news story in the newspapers, but not on the network news programs.

For years CBS was the consistent overall winner, then ABC took over the top position in the late 1970s with a group of youth-oriented comedies and innovative sports programs. ABC's hit shows in turn grew old and tired, and in 1985 NBC, long in last place, surged ahead to become the highest-rated network in prime time. It achieved this level by aiming shows at the numerically large younger adult audience, whose strong buying power is especially attractive to advertisers.

The immensely popular "Bill Cosby Show," built around the family of a young urban professional couple, led the NBC list, along with the sophisticated comedy "Cheers"; the slick police show "Miami Vice," which featured rock music with its plot; "Family Ties," a situation comedy; and "Golden Girls," a comedy about three older unmarried women and the razor-tongued mother of one who share a house. The common denominator of these shows was clever writing and appeal to liberal-minded audiences, including far more specific sexual references than were permitted a few years earlier.

CBS had a major success in "Murder, She Wrote," an hour-long mystery in which a quite mature woman plays the main role in plots designed to attract relatively youthful audiences. A group of glossy, emotional soap operas including "Dallas," "Dynasty," and "Falcon Crest" dominated the dramatic category in the late 1980s. These, too, reflected the general loosening in depiction of moral standards evident in prime-time television during the decade.

Although cable television has cut substantially into the networks' share of the total TV audience, as we shall discuss later, and videocassettes played on home TV sets have diverted other viewers, network audiences during the evening hours remain huge. Between 70 and 75 percent of the total television audience watches the networks at that time. As an indication of this fact, a show attracting only 10 million viewers usually is considered a failure and cancelled.

With satellite transmission commonplace, still a further challenge to the networks has come from the growing power of independent TV stations—that is, stations without network affiliation. Independents are increasing in number and in audience-pulling power. Program packagers using satellites put together *ad hoc* networks of independent stations to show specific one-time programs. Instead of existing on programming crumbs left over from the networks, some independents now offer first-run made-for-television movies, miniseries, and sports in prime time that draw viewers away from the networks. The provocative words "world premiere" have begun to appear in promotional advertising for such independent offerings.

Creation of an additional regularly scheduled national network became a logical, if financially risky, step in the late 1980s after major deals brought groups of television stations under the same ownerships as important sources of filmed material. Rupert Murdoch became the first entrepreneur to launch such a network with formation in 1986 of Fox Broadcasting Company, based on six large TV stations that he owned. Fox began its original programming and movie presentations in 1987 (see Chapter 21).

Entertainment on Television

With fanfare, every September the major networks put their fall lineup of prime-time entertainment shows on the air. Each new program is publicized as a sure winner, yet relatively few survive through the winter. Many vanish after the first 13-week programming cycle, some after only two or three episodes. Since the network executives know that this will happen, they are continually ordering replacement programs to be tossed into the breach.

The networks do not produce the entertainment programs they show, although at one time they did so. They halted the practice after Justice Department suits charged that they were operating a monopoly. Instead, the shows are created by independent production companies, which sell first-performance rights to the networks. After their network showing, episodes of a program may be syndicated —that is, leased for rerun showing—by the production firm to independent stations and cable networks. The major networks are forbidden by the federal government to hold a share of the syndication profits in a program or to do any syndication themselves. Their strenuous efforts to get this ban changed have been unsuccessful.

Enormous amounts of money are involved in the fight between the networks and production firms over rerun rights. Syndicated reruns of such popular series as "Happy Days" and "M*A*S*H" are worth $100 million or more.

After a network agrees to use a program idea proposed by one of the production firms, or commissions a firm to develop a program from an idea the network

John Forsythe and Joan
Collins engage in an
emotional scene during an
episode of "Dynasty," a
primetime soap opera
favorite of the 1980s.
(Sabine Shooting Star, Photo
Trends)

provides, the relationship between producer and network is close (Figure 13.1). The network supervises the stories used and has the final word on casting. Its censors must approve the scripts. Among the largest entertainment film producers are MTM, Inc., Lorimer Productions, MCA TV, Aaron Spelling, and motion picture companies including Twentieth Century-Fox, Paramount, Universal, and MGM.

The odds against any specific program being placed on a network schedule are enormous. In the process of program development, on which millions of dollars are spent every year, the network staffs study audience demographics, programming and advertising sales goals, and the programming desires of affiliated stations. They weigh proposed program ideas in this light. For example, in a recent season one network examined 2500 program ideas, studied scripts for 150 of them, and underwrote production of 37 pilot films. Out of this mass the network actually obtained 9 new programs, most of which did not last beyond this first season. Occasionally, a network will show a pilot film it has made, but never developed into a series, as a single free-standing program.

The hour at which a program is shown, and the nature of the programs the rival networks put on the air against it, may be the deciding factor in its survival. Like generals maneuvering their battle forces, network program executives move the programs on their lists around from time slot to time slot. On the offensive, a programmer may place a promising new show at a time when the competition's offerings are weak, giving it favorable audience exposure. As a defensive act, a well-established program may be shifted into a slot opposite a popular show on another network, in the hope that it will siphon off some of the rival's rating. It is common practice to have a new show follow an established hit, to pick up the lead-in audience, viewers who watched the previous show, then decided to take

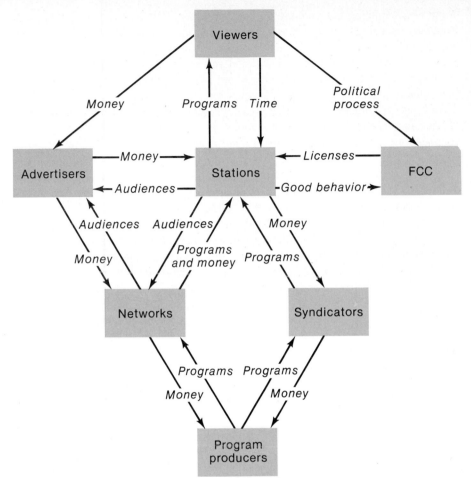

FIGURE 13.1
Organization of the television industry. (Source: Reprinted by permission from *Television Economics* by Bruce M. Owen, Jack H. Beebe, and Willard G. Manning, Jr. (Lexington, Mass.: Lexington Books, D.C. Heath and Company, 1974.)

a look at the new show, rather than get up and turn the dial. Another device is to *hammock* a show, placing it between two hits. Concentrating a group of a network's best shows, especially comedies, on the same night of the week is often done; executives hope that the combined impact of their high ratings will enable the network to claim that it "owns" that particular night in the relentless network warfare. The ploys used in programming are myriad. If one of them raises the rating of a show in trouble or reduces the rating of a rival network's hit, the maneuver is hailed as a success even though some viewers are irked because their comfortable routines have been disturbed.

Those who conceive and produce programs watch constantly for "spinoff" possibilities—that is, taking a character from one situation show and building a new series of programs around that character. An example is "Benson," an ABC comedy. The minor role of Benson, the sardonic butler in the zany, sexy series "Soap," was played so effectively by Robert Guillaume that in the following season he was made the star of his own show, in which he was the major domo in the home of a bumbling but well-intentioned governor. TV series often are derived from movies, using the same characters and settings. "M*A*S*H," the immensely popular military hospital series on television, was a spinoff from the motion picture of the same name. After the series ended an exceptionally long run on CBS, the network put some of its familiar characters into a civilian setting and called the new spinoff series "After MASH," which had only a short life.

Analysis of listings discloses that on a day-long basis the entertainment portions of television programming on most stations consist predominantly of game shows, soap operas, talk shows, old movies, and reruns of former network situation comedies. In some cases stations show old episodes of a series while new episodes still are appearing on a network, as was the case with "Love Boat." Rarely do locally created entertainment programs get on the air.

In a sense the networks are victims of their own success. Executives know the kind of programming that sells and, as explained earlier, rarely deviate from it. The year after year of predictable formula programming has a ripple effect throughout television because much air time on independent stations is filled with reruns of programs that have finished their first-run life on the networks. By breaking away from this monotony of network fare, operators of cable channels have an opportunity to attract viewers with innovative programming. Unfortunately, however, at times some of their offerings seem like clones of the standard network output.

Once television and the motion picture industry were such rivals that the film studios would not allow their stars to appear on TV, even on talk shows. Then the studios realized how much money they could make by selling their backlog of old films to television. Now the two industries are closely tied financially and in the production of material. Much of what we see on TV is filmed on Hollywood sound stages. Movie producers make their films knowing that they may also be aired on television. Many films are made specifically for original showing on TV, using camera techniques suitable for the small screen and dramatic development carefully paced for the insertion of commercials. This has led to the miniseries. Instead of telling a story in one long piece, as a feature motion picture does, the producer packages the story into segments that can be shown on television on several successive nights, a technique reminiscent of the Saturday afternoon serials of the early movies.

Another recently developed type of TV entertainment is the docudrama. This form takes the facts of an actual event, such as the mass murders of Atlanta children, and adds fictional scenes and situations to create a more dramatic story. Such blending of fact and fiction is condemned by social critics as a rewriting of history that creates false conceptions and perverts the truth. Yet use of the docudrama persists.

Rating the TV Shows

When a network claims that 30 million viewers saw a show, it is obvious that the viewers have not been counted one by one. Television viewership is determined by monitoring the viewing habits of a small, scientifically selected sample, then extrapolating the percentage results into nationwide statistics. Although these projected statistics have built-in potential for error, television producers and sales people quote them as though they are completely accurate. The fact is that the viewing preferences of a few American families determine the national ratings for a show.

Two firms provide most of the ratings reports, the A. C. Nielsen Company and Arbitron. Arbitron specializes in monitoring local TV markets. Programs are dropped or renewed, executives keep or lose their jobs, and advertising revenues rise and fall, depending upon what the "Nielsens" and Arbitron ratings reveal. These reports give two kinds of data about a show, its *rating* and its *share.* The rating of a show is the percentage of all households having TV sets that viewed the particular program. Nielsen placed the number of television-owning households in 1986 at approximately 85.9 million. Thus, according to Nielsen calculations, a show with a rating of 20 was viewed in 17.1 million homes, a fact an advertiser is anxious to know. The share figure is based on the number of households having their sets turned on at a given time. The show with a rating of 20 has a 31 share; that is, 31 percent of the sets turned on at that time were tuned to it. The share figure measures a program's popularity against other shows on the air at the same time. The networks believe that, to be called successful, one of their shows must have at least a 26 share:

For years Nielsen obtained its information by placing 1700 small electronic boxes in homes chosen by sampling techniques, whose household members' identities were secret. Each box, wired to every TV set in the house, recorded details of each set's use—when it was turned on and to what channel. A computer-dialed telephone call from the Nielsen center in Florida to each of the homes in the sample automatically collected this information twice a day.

In order to ascertain the age and sex of viewers, and to learn how many household members are watching television, Nielsen runs a supplementary service in which 2400 participating household members complete weekly diaries for each quarter-hour of viewing.

Seeking more accurate information about individual viewers, Nielsen in 1986 tested a measuring device called a "people meter." Developed by the competing AGB Research Group, this device is a small hand-held instrument with eight numbered buttons, each for a family member. Users feed their sex and age information into the people meter. Individual viewers are supposed to punch in when they begin watching and punch out when they leave the room. The people meter may become the primary tool in the measuring process despite opposition to it from the networks and some stations. This opposition arose when early tests of the people meters recorded fewer people viewing network TV than the original Nielsen system reported.

Critics of television and its manner of measuring its own success emphasize that, huge as the viewership figures are, many people watch very little television. They argue that an important difference exists between having a TV set turned on and watching the program attentively. Surveys indicate that many persons turn on a set primarily for the companionship the voices and pictures provide as background for their other activities. Les Brown contended in the New York *Times* that one-third of the households owning television sets in the United States account for two-thirds of the actual watching.

Nielsen announced plans early in 1987 to depend entirely upon people meters for measuring national audiences, beginning with 2000 meters in the 1987–1988 TV season and increasing to at least 4000 meters the following year. For measuring local audiences, it continued to use a combination of boxes and diaries.

Arbitron, a subsidiary of Control Data Corporation, also reported plans to switch from diaries to people meters, and the AGB Research Group, a British-based firm, made aggressive efforts to capture some of Nielsen's business.

NEWS ON TELEVISION

Television newscasts are the primary source of news for a large percentage of Americans and virtually the only source for many of them. Yet, as leaders of the television industry concede, most TV news programs are only a headline service with pictures but little depth. The restrictions of time, the fight among stations and networks for audience ratings, and the concern of news producers about the short attention span of many viewers have created programs that make audiences aware of news developments but only skimpily informed about them.

Robert MacNeil, co-host of the MacNeil-Lehrer News Hour on public television, contends that the assumptions behind many TV news programs are that "bite-sized is best, that complexity must be avoided, that nuances are dispensable, that qualifications impede the simple message, that visual stimulation is a substitute for thought, and that verbal precision is an anachronism."

Writing in the *Christian Science Monitor,* Rushworth M. Kidder reaches much the same conclusion: "Television, unlike print, favors movement over stillness, simplification over complexity, specificity over abstraction, personality over conceptualization, and the present over both the past and future."

Despite the shortcomings cited by these and other critics, annual surveys by the Roper organization have found that a large percentage of those questioned regard TV news as more believable than newspapers. Frustrated newspaper editors, who argue that they provide more comprehensive stories than television does, wonder how such an attitude can be so widespread.

The explanation lies in the three-fold advantage television news has over newspapers:

1. Its ability to tell stories visually from the scene of the action, making viewers feel as though they are at the scene themselves.
2. The ease with which viewers can receive the news. Reading a newspaper story requires more concentration than watching a news item on television.
3. The fact that TV news is delivered by attractive men and women whose carefully nurtured personalities create an aura of intimacy impossible in print reports and only partially achievable in radio news. For many viewers, the TV messenger who brings the news has more impact than the news itself.

In weighing these criticisms of television news as essentially a headline service, one must remember that many purchasers of newspapers merely scan the headlines; "bite-size" TV news stories satisfy their limited appetites for news as much or more than newspaper headlines do. Those individuals who desire to learn *why* things have happened almost always must supplement TV news viewing by reading printed accounts.

Knowing the impact of television news, political leaders from the White House down plan their actions and time their statements in an effort to obtain 30-second appearances on evening news shows. The impressions formed by these brief glimpses strongly influence the opinions Americans develop about their leaders, many of whom they never see in person or listen to at length. President Reagan, guided by public relations advisers, is especially skillful in creating an image of amiability through carefully controlled "photo opportunity" appearances on network news programs. He gained an unexpected public relations benefit during one televised appearance in the White House press room in 1987. For almost 20 seconds three network anchors simultaneously shouted questions. Some observers termed the spectacle a "feeding frenzy" caused by Reagan's infrequent news conferences and interview opportunities.

For extended coverage of Congress in session, viewers of many cable systems can watch live coverage of the House and Senate on C-SPAN, the Cable Satellite Public Affairs Network.

TV NEWS MAKES PROFITS

Television news programs are a hot commercial property, the source of much profit to networks and local stations. Critics both inside and outside the industry complain that the drive for profit has influenced the content of news programs negatively by injecting entertainment razzle-dazzle, such as "happy talk" chit-chat among members of a broadcasting team and selection of stories more for the visual excitement of on-the-scene tape footage available than for the intrinsic merit of the stories.

Osborn Elliott, dean of the Columbia University Graduate School of Journalism, warned against this trend at a recent awards ceremony. He asserted that broadcast journalists "feel the wash of an accelerating tide away from news business and toward just plain show business. News divisions, which once may have enjoyed some kind of special standing within their companies, may now be perceived as just another chicken in the corporate hothouse, to be stuffed or starved as may serve the corporate purpose."

These criticisms and concerns must not obscure the fact that, on occasion, television news coverage is superb.

When stories are big enough, the networks provide quick and frequently very perceptive special reports as supplements to the breaking news coverage. CBS has had spectacular success with its "60 Minutes," an hour-long investigative and interview show in which veteran correspondents develop several stories each week in considerable depth. The other networks have offered similar programs, notably ABC's "20/20." Occasionally, but less frequently than in the past, the networks show documentary programs. And at times the network evening news programs focus in unusual depth on a single topic, developing the background.

Local stations, too, can rise to moments of drama in notable fashion, as for example when a light airplane carrying two men crashed into a high power electric

Mike Wallace interviews Sam Hall, right, an American arrested as a spy and imprisoned by the Nicaraguan government, for the popular CBS program, "60 Minutes." Others in the picture are "60 Minutes" staff members. Later Hall was released from prison in Managua, where this interview occurred, and returned to the United States. (AP/Wide World)

transmission line in Southern California at night. The plane, dripping gasoline, hung from the power line upside down 90 feet in the air, held precariously to the wire by its propellor and one wheel. While television cameras recorded the floodlit action for two hours, rescue crews rode high cranes up to the dangling plane and stabilized it by running ropes from its struts up to a mobile hook overhead. Firemen then removed the two men feet first from the plane's cabin onto the top of a high-rise fire ladder.

Television news coverage is unmatchable in such situations. Its problems arise in the handling of mundane day-to-day news.

News show producers dread "talking heads" on the screen—that is, anchorpersons reading items from the teleprompter minute after minute—so much that they sometimes use inconsequential videotaped stories from the field merely because they show movement. Local news programs are the worst offenders in this respect. On some stations, almost any group that organizes a protest march, waving banners and shaking fists when the TV cameras arrive, can get air time. Far too often the programs air the protesters' complaints without including response from the organization or individual being attacked, a serious breach of objectivity in news coverage.

IMPORTANCE OF PERSONALITY

So important is personality for TV newspersons that on-camera people may hold or lose their jobs on the basis of measured physiological response by sample audiences.

TV journalists chosen to anchor news programs—to read news items and introduce stories from the field—are particularly subject to personality testing and

Dan Rather, anchor of the CBS Evening News, confers at his desk before beginning a broadcast. (© Webb, Magnum)

shaping. Self-assurance, charm, a resonant voice, and the ability to ad-lib smoothly are key ingredients. Walter Cronkite, longtime anchor on the CBS Evening News, projected such an avuncular presence that one survey found him to be the most trusted man in the United States. The chief anchors at the three general networks —Dan Rather at CBS, Tom Brokaw at NBC, and Peter Jennings at ABC—reached their positions against fierce competition because of polished personalities that generate confidence in those who watch them.

The nation received an inside glimpse of how television anchorpersons are chosen and molded in 1983 when Christine Craft sued station KMBC-TV in Kansas City after it dismissed her as its anchor newscaster. She charged that station management told her she was being hired for the job because of her journalistic abilities. But when she was dismissed, the management told her she was "too old, unattractive and not deferential enough to men." Trial testimony told how the station had called in a specialist to alter her image by changing her hair, makeup, and wardrobe. When asked for his list of qualifications for an anchorperson, the station's general manager testified that he "would put appearance at the top of the list."

A jury, finding in Craft's favor, awarded her $500,000 in damages for fraud and told the judge that they believed sexual discrimination had taken place. The judge ruled later that no sexual discrimination had been involved and overturned the $500,000 award for fraud as excessive, ordering a new trial on the fraud issue. The jury in the second trial awarded Craft $325,000, but that award too was overturned. The Supreme Court refused to hear her case, thereby depriving her of victory and the $325,000. After an extended absence from the air, Craft resumed work in 1986 as co-anchor at a Sacramento, California, station.

The battle for audience supremacy in news programs among the three traditional networks is ferocious. In addition, their combined monopoly on national and world news coverage has been challenged from two directions.

First, Ted Turner's Cable News Network (CNN) with its 24-hour coverage has emerged as a fourth major television news source (see the discussion later in this chapter). Second, numerous major stations around the United States are extending coverage in their own shows beyond local areas by use of satellite transmission. They dispatch correspondents to distant news events, exchange stories with other stations, and operate mobile satellite uplink vans in the field, either on their own or in cooperation with their affiliated national networks. More than 50 television stations have their own news bureaus in Washington, concentrating on local angles. Thus development of *satellite newsgathering* (trade talk calls it *SNG*) has opened large additional sources for TV news content.

MASS NEWS COVERAGE

The upsurge of almost-instant transmission facilities has added to the mob-scene news coverage of big events that many observers find distasteful. When President Reagan met the Soviet leader Mikhail Gorbachev at Geneva, Switzerland, in 1985, the four American networks alone sent 425 correspondents, producers, writers, and support staff to cover the event. This throng, plus TV crews from other countries, radio crews, and print correspondents and photographers created a huge pack of journalists—more than 3000—scrambling for the relatively few crumbs of genuine news that the participants handed out. Both heads of state consciously played up to the banks of cameras.

At Geneva, organizers of the event at least had time to prepare facilities for the media army. When a tragedy occurs and the television crews and other newspeople swarm in, they often trample lawns, invade the privacy of individuals, and virtually take over the area. Little of this is apparent to TV viewers, but it creates anger and bitterness in its wake.

Behind the smooth delivery of each anchorperson is a large staff of writers and tape editors. At the networks, they number in the hundreds. The executive producer of a network show decides which taped reports from correspondents will be used. The writers prepare the "tell" stories, those brief summaries that the anchorperson reads, perhaps with drawings or other graphics on the screen to illustrate them, as well as the lead-ins with which the anchorpersons introduce the taped field reports.

Preparation and delivery of local news programs resembles the network method, on a smaller scale. In a survey taken for the Radio Television News Directors Association in 1985, Professor Vernon A. Stone found that a typical television network affiliate station in the top 25 markets had a full-time news staff of 65 plus one part-time worker. So did some major independent stations. At the other end of the spectrum, the typical small independent station had one full-time and one part-time news employee; 30 percent of the independents had no one working in news.

The median TV news staff nationwide consisted of about 18 full-time and 2 part-time workers. At small stations, where many beginners break in, a staff member may be reporter, tape editor, writer, and anchorperson as well.

PUBLIC TELEVISION

Viewers who prefer more educational and cultural programs than commercial TV usually offers can find them on the approximately 300 nonprofit (noncommercial) public television stations operating in the United States. Their programs are presented without commercial interruptions.

These nonprofit stations obtain operating funds from several sources, including government grants, underwriting grants from large corporations trying to build a good public image, foreign partners in coproduction, and public subscriptions. Well over $50 million a year is contributed by the public to the nonprofit stations. A federally funded organization, the Corporation for Public Broadcasting, established by Congress in 1967, provides money for production and distribution of programs through the Public Broadcasting Service (PBS). For many years PBS relied on government funds for 25 percent of its income. By 1985, however, income from donors had grown, and the federal share had dropped to $136 million—15 percent. In almost all other countries public broadcasting is assured an annual income produced by a tax on each television and radio set.

In a controversial experiment, nine public television stations accepted commercial advertising for a 15-month period during the early 1980s. After assessing public reaction and financial results, a federal task force recommended that Congress continue to forbid commercials on public television. The task force proposed, however, that companies be allowed to air "enhanced underwriting" messages. Critics complain that some of these messages mentioning brand names and slogans look exactly like advertisements on commercial television.

Some of the programs seen on PBS are created in production centers at seven noncommercial stations or at the Children's Television Workshop. Numerous others are imported, often from Great Britain. Indeed, PBS is sometimes accused of being more concerned with depicting Victorian and Edwardian England than contemporary American life. This is because of the resounding success of the "Upstairs, Downstairs" series in particular and other English imports about those eras shown on "Masterpiece Theater," the best known of PBS adult programs. "All Creatures Great and Small" is another highly popular British import.

Among the strengths of the public broadcasting system are its intelligent and stimulating programs for children, of which "Sesame Street" is the best known. Science programs such as "Nova" and Carl Sagan's "Cosmos" attract older children along with an adult audience. The MacNeil-Lehrer news report, expanded to a one-hour program in 1983, is applauded for in-depth examination of major news developments.

Some observers believed that the varied programming of cable television would destroy public television. Quite the opposite has happened. Public broadcasting's audience has grown, primarily because many public stations whose UHF signals were weak and fuzzy now are carried into homes by cable, with much improved reception.

Despite the excellence of some of its programming and the audience PBS has developed, there are doubts that public television works as well as it should. A recent report by the second Carnegie Commission on the Future of Public Broadcasting recommended that the government spend large additional amounts to improve it. Pressures to balance the budget and the Reagan administration's negative attitude toward funding for public television made this proposal meaningless.

The PBS objective of educating and enlightening its viewers, about 85 million each week, has led to criticism that it reflects a liberal bias. A $5.6 million, 13-part series, "Viet Nam: A Television History," shown in 1983, won wide acclaim as a comprehensive and balanced piece of work. It came under attack, however, and in 1985 the network ran an hour-long rebuttal produced by the conservative organization, Accuracy in Media. In 1986 a nine-part, $3.5 million series, "The Africans," told the continent's story from an African point of view. Because of its showing and that of a previous documentary, "Guatemala: When the Mountains Tremble," 60 members of Congress demanded an investigation of whether PBS had become "a forum for propaganda." In that same year some stations refused to air a documentary, "Seeing Red: The Stories of American Communists," on grounds that it gave "a warm view of communism."

Bruce L. Christensen, PBS president, defended the broad scope of programming. "Public TV," he stated, "is the electronic embodiment of the ideals and goals that we hold dear, that we, through our democratic government, reach for every day: pursuit of knowledge and understanding, tolerance and support for minority groups and perspectives, freedom to challenge accepted truths."

The most frequent criticisms of public television are that its programs are dull at times, elitist in tone, and intended only for the well-educated upper middle class; that it is not sufficiently innovative; and that a cumbersome management bureaucracy impedes its progress. A public opinion poll taken for the Public Broadcasting Service and made public in 1980 revealed that while PBS has broad public support in principle, its broadcasts draw a somewhat limited audience. Public television attracts only one-seventh of the median weekly viewing accorded to commercial TV.

The most frequent negative attitude stated in the poll was that public television spends too much air time on fund raising. Of greater potential importance was the second most frequent criticism, that public television could mean government control over what viewers watch because of the federal subsidy it receives.

The Public Broadcasting Service's independence in programming was severely tested in 1980 when the Mobil Corporation, one of its major underwriters, publicly condemned the PBS decision to show the British program, "The Death of a Princess." The film dealt with the public executions of a Saudi Arabian princess and her commoner lover, for adultery. The Saudi Arabian government was so enraged when the film was shown in Great Britain that it temporarily expelled the British ambassador. Mobil at that time had a heavy financial interest in the Saudi Arabian oil industry. The State Department and the Saudi government also asked that the show be canceled. Despite the pressure, PBS showed the production; only seven of its then 240 affiliates failed to carry the program.

According to the PBS survey, "Viewers perceive many valuable assets and only few drawbacks in public television's existence, yet their allegiance to PTV does not run deep. Despite the credit that public television receives for its cultural broadcasts and its service to children, less than a third of our respondents say that it would make a great deal of difference to them if there were no public television at all. Others might feel a sense of loss if PTV were to go out of business, but their responses indicate that their sense of loss would not be great."

In short, the American public regards public television as a welcome alternative, to which it turns for specific programs or when it is tired of commercial fare, but does not accept public television as a primary source of TV viewing.

CABLE TELEVISION

Effect on Networks

A set owner who subscribes to cable television receives two forms of program service: (1) the transmissions of nearby broadcast television stations, brought to the home by wire instead of antenna reception, generally with greater fidelity, and (2) original programming.

It is the abundance and variety of original programming—everything from a 24-hour news broadcast and championship fights to soft pornography movies—that has made cable TV such a booming business. As more and more of the United States becomes wired for cable reception, the traditional broadcast television networks are losing a substantial portion of their viewers. Instead, many in the audience are watching cable programming.

During prime-time evening hours in the early 1970s, the three national networks were watched by most of the viewers. Then came the cable boom. The percentage of network viewers shrank from an all-time high of 93 percent in 1978 to 77 percent in 1984–85. Trying to put a good face on their problem, network executives contend that the networks will continue to reach approximately as many viewers in 1990 as they did in 1982, in terms of absolute numbers, because of the increase in population and the larger number of sets in operation. Network executives were encouraged by a small gain in the network audience during 1986.

By 1987 cable television had grown to the point that 7800 systems were in operation. Entering approximately 48 percent of American television homes, the systems served 41.5 million subscribers—perhaps 116 million people—in 20,000 communities (Figure 13.2). Another 700 franchises had been approved but not built. As these franchises came into operation, and new franchises were granted, the number of homes reached by cable increased each month.

Although new metropolitan systems offered as many as 100 channels to viewers, the majority of systems provided only 12 channels. Reconstruction and enlargement of the older 12-channel systems were costly for their operators, but many were making the change to increase service capabilities.

In its early days cable television had a simpler role and much smaller significance than it does today. Because rugged terrain interferes with over-the-air transmission of television pictures, a method was devised in 1949 to carry TV signals by cable into regions with poor reception. The first Community Antenna Television

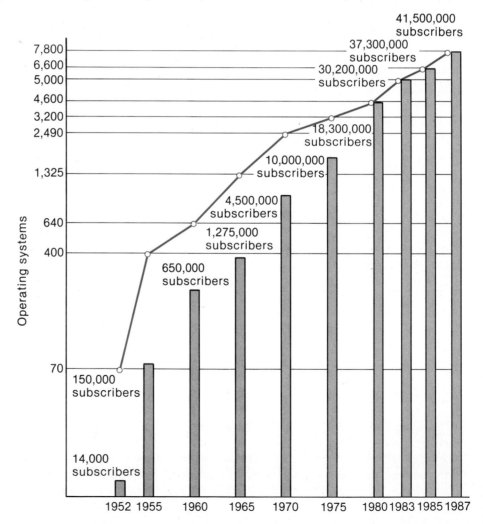

FIGURE 13.2
Growth of the cable TV industry in the United States as of January of each year. (Sources: Figures for 1952 to 1974: *Television Factbook,* services vol. no. 44 [1974–1975 ed.]. Figures for 1975: National Cable Television Association. Figures for 1978: *Television Factbook,* services vol. no. 47 [1977–1978 ed.]. Figures for 1980: Television Digest, Inc. Figures for 1983, 1985, and 1987: *Broadcasting/ Cablecasting Yearbook.*)

(CATV) systems were constructed in the hills of eastern Pennsylvania and Oregon. Only three to five channels were provided in early CATV operations. In the intervening decades, technical improvements have revolutionized the TV-by-cable concept. From being a fill-in service of limited capacity, cable television has become such an extensive source of entertainment, information, and personal convenience service that its full scope is not yet realized, let alone developed for general use.

The growth of cable television is inextricably tied to development of satellite transmission. The cable boom began in 1975 when Time Inc. leased space on a communication satellite to distribute its Home Box Office service, mostly motion pictures at that time, to participating cable system operators. After being plucked from the sky by earth receiving dishes, Home Box Office programs were fed over local cable systems and could be viewed by set owners willing to pay extra for the service. A special connection on the set made viewing of the HBO scrambled signals possible.

Quickly, other cable program producers came into being and distributed their offerings by satellite. Since all television sets manufactured after 1972 were required to have at least 20 channels, sufficient positions existed on them to receive numerous additional programs. In the late 1980s approximately 40 national cable television program services of varying duration and character were being offered.

Prominent among the entrepreneurs who brought innovation to cable television was Ted Turner of Atlanta. Turner beamed the signal of his Atlanta television station, WTBS, to a satellite, then back to cable systems around the country. Suddenly, this local UHF station was seen nationwide, becoming known as a superstation. The baseball games of the Atlanta Braves turned up on screens from coast to coast. Two other powerful local stations, WGN-TV in Chicago and WOR-TV in New York, did the same, giving the country three superstations.

Turner then took another adventurous step. Challenging the three broadcast networks, he established his Cable News Network (CNN). This 24-hour service has its own staff of correspondents and editors, feeding news and background information by satellite to cable and over-the-air viewers around the clock. Slowly, as its audience grew, CNN became a significant force in news coverage. Turner supplemented his first channel with a second, CNN Headline News. Late in 1983 Cable News Network purchased its rival, Satellite News Network, for $25 million, thereby increasing its audience and prestige. Turner also sought to provide or exchange programs with station operators in other countries. Operating at a profit, CNN is carried into 34 million homes. It reaches 80 percent of all cable subscribers. (See Chapter 21 for more about Turner.)

The Economics of Cable Television

The harsh reality is that the cable television industry, despite a rapidly growing audience and a proliferation of services, has failed so far to be profitable for many of the companies involved in making and distributing its programs. Some firms have lost large amounts, and a few have abandoned their efforts. CBS Inc. shut

Newscasters for Cable News Network check their scripts before a broadcast. CNN, established by Ted Turner, has become an important force in television news, challenging the coverage of the three general TV networks. (Taylor/Sygma)

down its CBS cable channel, a source of innovative, nonstereotyped programming, after losing $40 million during its first year of operation. At the time Cable News Network purchased Satellite News Network, the latter was losing money at the rate of $50 million a year.

For operators of cable systems that distribute programs by underground cable or aboveground wire, installation costs are extremely high. Underground installations in heavily built-up metropolitan areas run as much as $100,000 a mile. Obviously operators of urban systems must collect large monthly fees from subscribers to offset this investment. Installation cost is the principal reason that arrival of cable service in major urban areas has lagged behind that in smaller cities. In the competition between cable system operators for franchises in major cities, the municipal governments often demand that the successful bidder provide as many as 100 channels, including two-way and public-access channels, studios, and other supplementary services. For this reason ownership of cable systems falls increasingly into the hands of wealthy corporations with resources to meet the start-up costs. In the jargon of the industry a company owning several cable systems is known as an MSO (multiple-system operator).

Certain cable networks obtain their income by selling advertising in their programs. Others charge local cable systems a fee, usually 10 or 15 cents, for each subscriber served. Some do both.

One fact is certain about cable television economics: Cable system operators must look for their profits to the sale of pay television services supplementing the basic cable package. Cable services are sold on an add-on basis. First comes a basic package of stations for a fixed monthly fee; then come additional fees for as many supplementary services as the system offers and the subscriber is willing to purchase. This is known as *tiering.* The supplementary services are known collectively as *pay cable,* a slight misnomer since the subscriber already is paying to obtain the basic service.

Under a long-standing Federal Communications Commission rule, each cable system had to carry the programming of all broadcast television stations within its area. The U.S. Court of Appeals threw out this "must-carry" rule in 1985 because it violated the First Amendment rights of cable systems to select their own programming. The FCC then adopted a temporary compromise rule, effective until 1992, that cable systems must carry a minimum number of local broadcast stations, the number depending upon each system's size. Under this rule most systems may choose which stations they will carry. A court test of this narrower rule was undertaken. The ruling may cause extensive realignment of the offerings of some systems as they replace duplicated or little-viewed channels with new programming. Approximately 40 basic and pay cable services are available to local systems by satellite.

Adoption by Congress of the Cable Communications Policy Act of 1984, giving system operators the right to set their fees at any level they choose from 1987 on, also is causing changes in the economic structure of cable TV.

Here is how the tiering system works, as exemplified by a typical California system at the outer fringe of the Los Angeles area. The set owner's options and costs are these:

1. *Ordinary over-the-air television.* Free, but reception of most stations is fuzzy because of nearby mountains.
2. *Basic cable package.* $9.40 per month. The viewer receives 12 channels, including the three general broadcast networks, a public television station, two local area stations, a Spanish station, and Los Angeles independent stations. All these are available over the air, but reception of most is poor.
3. *Expanded cable package.* $4.95 per month. Eleven additional channels including MTV, video rock music; C-SPAN, Congress and public affairs; ESPN, 24-hour sports; Prime Ticket, Southern California sports; Nickelodeon and Arts, programming for young people and of a cultural nature; USA, sports and variety; CNN Headline News: CBN, Christian religious programming; Lifetime, fitness, fashions, relationships, and public affairs; Nashville, country music; and a public access channel.
4. *Pay channels.* Six channels available at $12.95 each. The customer may order one to six of these, receiving a $2 discount if a second channel is taken. Total cost for all six, $51.80. Included are HBO, Showtime, Cinemax, The Movie Channel, Disney Channel, and Galavision in Spanish. These channels offer movies, specials, family entertainment, music, and series.

Thus an obsessive television watcher who wants access to everything available in the area, 29 channels, can run up a monthly cable bill of $90.05. The bill for a commonplace "buy" of basic and expanded services, plus one pay channel, is $27.30.

In practice, viewers reach a saturation point with such a multiplicity of channels and pay little attention to some they receive. A Nielsen survey has shown that in households with 20 or more available channels, only one-third of the channels are watched for ten minutes or more a week. Households receiving pay cable service generally watch more television than noncable or basic cable households, perhaps partly to get their money's worth.

When a cable system offers 50 or more channels, this channel clutter is immensely accentuated. Either the viewers split their watching time into many fragments or they ignore much of the programming their sets can bring in. Surveys suggest that most viewers with a wide choice of channels available concentrate their television watching on four or five channels.

Cable systems offering a range of tiered services, such as the one described, face problems of cancellations by subscribers who, after a period of curiosity and try-out, lose interest and drop some services. Also, there is the problem of "churn"—households canceling one supplementary service in favor of another.

As cable television moved through its second decade of growth, these critical questions still were unanswered:

How much television will the public watch and pay for?
Is the technical ability to supply programs greater than the public's desire to see them?
How many people actually want 50 or 100 channels, and can the industry supply programs for that many?
How much does home video viewing cut into the use of pay cable channels?

ADVERTISING ON CABLE TELEVISION. This is a source of revenue sought by many cable companies. So far, the income it has produced for most cable system operators and producers of programming has been inadequate, but some television specialists believe the potential is large.

About 40 percent of the nation's cable systems accept advertising on their local origination channels. Large national advertisers have been slow to use cable because its audience is so fragmented that they have difficulty in reaching the mass viewers they need. They complain also about lack of information concerning cable audiences. Most cable systems receive less than 5 percent of their gross revenue from advertising. Because the showing of feature-length movies uncut and uninterrupted is a selling point to cable viewers, such pay cable offerings are not chopped up for commercials. In 1986 Home Shopping Network reported that since its inception in 1981 it had delivered 18 million packages to 500,000 buyers.

Cable has developed new-style, longer commercials called *infomercials.* Instead of the hard-sell message of 30 seconds duration so common on broadcast television, the well-done infomercial 5 to 7 minutes long delivers information about the product's purposes and demonstrates its applications. Because cable programming is more flexible in its timing than broadcast television's rigid 30-minute pattern, it can absorb these infomercials of uneven length.

Programs on Cable Television

Persons who have watched only broadcast television and almost never go to the movies get a shock when they first view cable television. They see nude scenes and hear language that astounds them. They wonder, how can such things be shown on the family television screen?

In the answer lies an important point about the difference between broadcast and cable television. Because broadcast television is distributed on the public airwaves, it is subject to such restrictions as the Federal Communications Commission chooses to impose. Cable television is not.

In addition, the broadcast networks traditionally have sought to avoid public criticism, in particular organized pressure from self-proclaimed morality organizations that might affect their advertising income. When the broadcast networks show R-rated theatrical-release motion pictures, they edit them carefully to remove offensive language and nudity. Cable channels show the films uncensored. Their operators contend that the programs come into the home by invitation and the subscribers pay to obtain them. If subscribers dislike the pay channels that show so-called adult fare, they are free to cancel them. Opponents of such openness attempt to curb it by urging municipalities to file charges under local or state obscenity laws against cable operators who show material such as the Playboy programs. These efforts have had little success. The issue of how much, if any, authority local governing bodies have to censor cable television programs has been debated in Congress. Efforts to legislate controls either at the local, state, or federal levels undoubtedly would be challenged vigorously in court.

Aware that such adult programming contributes to cable's popularity, the broadcast networks have loosened their own standards gradually—intensifying sexual situations in comedy series, for example—to test public reaction and determine what today's limits of acceptable on-screen conduct are.

Dominating pay cable entertainment programming is Home Box Office with 14.5 million subscribers. Showtime is second with 5.4 million. Both networks show recent theater-release motion pictures, often before the broadcast networks do; taped concerts by popular entertainers; and special events. Recently, they began production of their own motion pictures, as well as comedy and drama series that usually are more free-swinging in content than the traditional broadcast series.

In addition to these mass audience approaches, cable television uses the *narrowcasting* method, producing programs aimed at specialized audience segments. The Playboy network with soft pornography programs and the Financial News Network use this approach. Local-origin programming also uses narrowcasting. Such specialization should increase as the number of channels grows.

Home Satellite Reception

Backyard receiving dishes that pulled satellite transmissions of entertainment and news programs out of the air directly onto their owners' TV screens were a frequent sight, especially in rural areas, by 1985. Owners of these dishes received free a wealth of shows for which subscribers to cable systems paid substantial fees. In addition, they could watch dozens of transmissions not intended for public viewing, such as the unedited "backfeeds" of network reporters' stories from the field to network headquarters. This is called *direct broadcast satellite* (DBS).

Doubts about the legality of this practice were removed when the 1984 cable policy act of Congress specified that dish owners were permitted to receive signals free for their private viewing. Many bar and hotel owners ignored the ban on commercial use, however, in effect stealing the signals. A sales boom for dishes developed, with approximately 1.5 million in use in early 1986.

Then, suddenly, much of the "free ride" ended. Tired of giving away its product to dish owners, HBO began scrambling its satellite signal. To be viewed on earth, the signal must first move through an expensive descrambler. Other program originators followed suit; soon much of the most desirable programming was scrambled, although dish owners still could capture numerous unscrambled signals of secondary interest.

The major cable networks developed marketing plans under which dish owners using descramblers could see shows by paying monthly fees similar to those charged by the cable systems. Sales of satellite dishes fell precipitously.

Efforts to launch a direct broadcast satellite system (DBS) using greater power and small reception dishes, with programming chosen especially for its viewers, met initial failure, but DBS proponents continued to search for a successful formula.

Two other forms of programming in limited and still largely experimental use are:

1. *Local-access channels.* Some large cable systems set aside one or more channels for use by local groups and individuals. Although the results often are amateurish, existence of such outlets is socially valuable.
2. *Two-way channels.* These permit their viewers to "talk back" in at least limited form. By use of a special home terminal unit, the viewer can give instant "yes," "no," or "undecided" responses to questions asked by an announcer on a two-way channel and take quizzes. They also may play interactive games. The QUBE two-way system was first introduced in Columbus, Ohio, in 1977. Six years later, in 1983, the QUBE service was expanded into a satellite-distributed network serving seven Midwestern and Southwestern cities. In 1984, however, after heavy financial losses, the network operation and some local QUBE programming were ended.

News on Cable Television

As a purveyor of news, cable has many intriguing possibilities, but by the late 1980s few of these had grown much beyond the experimental stage. On a national level Cable News Network had emerged as an important challenger of the three traditional broadcast networks. The local-origin news situation was far less well defined.

The terms *electronic publishing* and *the electronic newspaper* evoke fascinating visions. Because newspapers are the principal newsgathering institutions in every city, they are the logical source of news for distribution on cable. Their data banks are waiting to be tapped. Some imaginative observers rather glibly predicted that distribution of news by cable, along with local classified and display advertising, would be a death blow to printed newspapers. A few years hence, these enthusiastic seers predicted, the electronic newspaper read on the home screen would replace the familiar one of newsprint.

Scores of newspapers leased channels on local cable systems, on which they offered news in various forms. As a whole, at least in the early days, these news channels had difficulty in finding an audience.

By the mid-1980s it was obvious that newspapers in print form would survive, because many people desire to receive news in greater depth than cable television news provides. News stories shown at length in blocks of text on a screen tend to turn away viewers, so brevity dominates most cable news just as it does over-the-air newscasts. The extent of the public's desire to receive news by cable remains uncertain but seems to have limits. Only a few of the newspapers that ventured into cable news were making a profit, and some had dropped out. Yet experimental development of new systems for news delivery suggests that this uncertain picture may improve, perhaps impressively.

The simplest method of news delivery on local cable television is called *character-generated text.* This consists of brief news summaries in text block form on the screen, along with weather, time, and temperature reports. The news usually comes from a local newspaper, plus news service items. Classified and display advertising are shown, too, as a source of revenue. Colorful graphics can be inserted; soft background music accompanies the text.

More elaborate and expensive to produce are a newspaper's *video news* programs. Local newscasts with newspaper material, using an anchorperson and staff reporters, frequently direct from the newsroom, are a standard feature. Public affairs shows, local sports, and feature programs often are presented as well, depending upon how heavily the newspaper wishes to commit its resources to cable. Advertising frequently is included.

Among the most ambitious news services on cable television by a newspaper is that of *Newsday* on Long Island. This one-way service operates 24 hours a day, delivering textual news summaries and other information, brightened by graphics, plus live programs of events sponsored by the newspaper. Formerly *Newsday* presented daily live news programs but dropped them because of inadequate advertising support. The channel carries classified and display advertising, including infomercials.

These two forms of news presentation share a basic element: They are one-way systems, from program creator to viewer, in which the content of the cablecast is controlled entirely by the sender. Viewers receive these news programs without extra charge as part of their basic cable service.

Other Transmission Methods

Two more sophisticated methods of cable information delivery now under development, with a few experimental systems in existence, may enlarge cable's role as a news medium. They are *teletext* and *videotex.*

TELETEXT. This one-way service transmits text news, graphics, advertising, and service information over a cable channel or over the vertical blanking interval of a standard television signal. The vital difference is that teletext adds the element of *viewer selectivity.* Viewers have special keypads. By punching certain keys, they can call up on the screen the type of news or information they desire, chosen from an index shown on the screen. Hundreds of pages of material are in the electronic bank, awaiting the viewer's selection. Each page is kept up-to-date.

A viewer may, for example, wish a current report on stock market prices. He or she can call up the stock pages immediately without having to wait for other news and information to scroll past first. Teletext viewers pay for the service. Usually they are billed according to the number of pages they call up.

One unanswered question about teletext is both economic and psychological: Will enough viewers be willing to pay a substantial price to receive on the screen information that in considerable part will be available to them in print when the next edition of the newspaper is delivered? To be profitable for its operators, teletext must have quite heavy usage by those who receive the service.

VIDEOTEX. This more complex and expensive system provides viewers with *two-way interactive* service. Using either cable or telephone lines, the viewer can connect the home television terminal to a central computer and either call up a broad range of news and information or conduct business transactions.

Broadcasting magazine illustrates the difference between teletext and videotex with this example: "A teletext service might allow a user to access [call onto the screen] an airline's schedule, but a videotex user could not only access that schedule but also make his reservation, transfer money from his bank account to pay for the ticket, then buy a new wardrobe for his planned trip—all without leaving his seat."

The videotex customer is charged for the amount of use made of the system. Videotex has been called the Cadillac of cable information systems and teletext the Chevrolet. Although several major corporations have spent millions of dollars in developing videotex systems, participation by consumers and advertisers has been disappointing so far.

Two major operators of videotex systems, the Times Mirror Company and Knight-Ridder Newspapers Inc., closed their Gateway and Viewtron projects in 1986 because of heavy losses. Representatives of the two companies agreed that their subscribers were more interested in exchanging messages with each other electronically than in receiving news.

Videotex has failed as a news medium in the United States because of public apathy. Experience shows that it is not an alternative to newspapers, as once was thought possible. It does have a role, perhaps eventually a substantial one, in providing special services such as banking and commercial transactions and certain categories of limited-interest information.

Although videotex failed to arouse much public interest, shopping at home by cable television became popular in the late 1980s through the Home Shopping Network and similar services. The home viewer sees merchandise on the screen, then orders by telephone using a credit card.

SATELLITE MASTER ANTENNA SYSTEMS (SMATV). These operate as cable television systems do, with one exception. The ordinary cable system obtains a local government franchise to serve an extended area, while an SMATV system operates only on private property such as an apartment building complex or mobile home park. The system distributes programs only within the confines of its private property zone, picking up signals directly from satellites.

Low-power Television (LPTV). As mentioned earlier, recent FCC rulings make possible new low-power television stations permitted to relay TV signals and to originate programming. These stations have secondary status with power too low to interfere with existing UHF and VHF stations. Their role is to serve small areas and supplement present television programming. About 410 low-power stations were on the air in 1987, half of them in Alaska.

Videoconferencing. By using temporarily leased satellite circuits, companies can hold press conferences or business meetings at one site and have them seen and heard at numerous points, perhaps in several countries. Two-way telephone connections, or even two-way satellite transmissions, allow participants at distant points to respond to those at the point of origin. Use of videoconferencing (also known as teleconferencing) is growing steadily.

JOB OPPORTUNITIES IN TELEVISION

Young people hoping for careers in television may find them in three areas: on-the-air performing in news and entertainment programs, production, and sales and business management.

Starting one's career at a small station is almost essential. Competition for jobs is intense, so most stations of medium and large size usually hire persons with experience. A beginner should not shun an opportunity to take what appears to be a menial job; getting a job on the "inside" is what counts. Numerous high-ranking executives of the networks started their careers in entry-level jobs.

Approximately 19,000 jobs exist in the news departments of American commercial television stations. Constant turnover occurs as individuals advance in their careers from small stations to larger ones.

Women today hold about one-third of those jobs, according to the Stone survey. They occupied the news director position at 75 stations in 1985, up from 32 six years earlier. The survey found female representation among news directors to be much greater at independent stations than at network affiliates, 29 percent to 8 percent. Women anchored news programs at 9 of every 10 network affiliate stations and nearly half the independent stations, comprising 36 percent of all TV anchorpersons.

Members of minority groups held 14 percent of the television news jobs in 1985. Of the minority newspersons, 62 percent were black, 27 percent Hispanic, 9 percent Asian American, and 2 percent Native American.

(A discussion of employment in the media for minorities and women appears in Chapter 24.)

In the news department the first level in a small station is that of a beat or general assignment reporter. Beginners have a few on-the-air appearances with news stories. As they develop a screen personality and prove to be accurate and

A female television camera operator photographs a female newscaster. Women hold a solidly established position behind the camera as well as in front of it. (Houtchens-Kitchens, The Picture Cube)

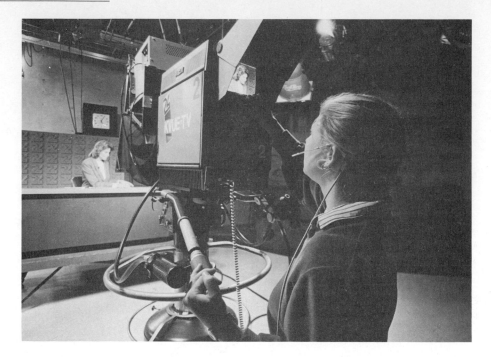

dependable, the news director may allow them to sit in as weekend or vacation relief anchorpersons on a local news show. The top job in news at a station is held by the news director, the person who makes the assignments and decides which stories will appear on the air. Becoming a news director is a desirable career goal. The median annual salary for a news director in 1985 was $35,360. When an applicant seeks a position on a larger station, the videotapes of on-the-air performances that he or she submits will play a critical part in the prospective employer's decision. A nationwide study by three University of Illinois researchers disclosed that broadcast newspeople change jobs more frequently than those in any other news occupation.

Jobs on news staffs of the networks go to people who have learned their trade at individual stations over a period of several years. Salaries of station TV news personnel are generally comparable to those paid by newspapers. They vary widely depending upon size of the station and the market. Network salaries are high, as are those for top-level reporters on metropolitan stations, some of whom receive more than $100,000 per year if they project that nebulous but vital star quality. Dan Rather, the CBS anchor, reportedly makes $2.5 million a year, and other network anchors receive as much as $1 million dollars or more annually. However, only a handful of stars at each network are in the highest pay range. The average network correspondent starts at $80,000 or more; the three major networks among them have approximately 200 on-air personnel.

Another major job on a TV station staff is that of the program director, who handles programming policy and scheduling. This job requires detailed knowledge of network and syndicated program operations, as well as an understanding of tastes and interests among the audience the station serves. The upward route to this job is usually through the production or business staffs, rarely through the news department. The production department puts together locally produced shows and commercials, giving beginners an opportunity to work behind the cameras with cue cards, timing signals, and props, and also in the control booth. Directors and producers of individual programs usually rise to those positions along this path.

On the business side, novices eventually may become account executives selling commercial time. To do this well, the salesperson needs technical knowledge of TV operations, understanding of the station's audience characteristics, and skill to match up the time spots the station has to sell with the needs and budgets of potential advertisers. Another important factor is the salesperson's ability to present effectively to a potential client his or her station's advantages over competing media. The promotion manager's role is to publicize programs that the station will present and build a friendly public image for the station through community service endeavors.

At the top of the hierarchy is the station manager, who usually has had experience both on the air and in production. Managers of larger stations may earn in excess of $100,000 a year.

Growth of cable television has brought fresh job opportunities. Cable news services run by newspapers tend to select their staffs in part from newsrooms, while hiring technical specialists from broadcasting. Qualifications for various types of cable news jobs are essentially the same as those for similar work in traditional broadcasting. For artistically inclined persons, the cable industry provides job opportunities in preparation of illustrations, graphs, and other artwork for use in news and advertising.

A LOOK AHEAD

Delivery of entertainment and news to television screens grows ever more complex. First, cable delivery supplemented over-the-air TV, then videocassettes arrived to claim a share of viewers' time. Although rented or purchased programs on videocassettes are not actually televised, home video is an essential part of the contemporary viewing equation because it appears on the same TV screen as the other systems do. (Video is discussed in Chapter 15.)

The fight for viewers' time, already sharp, will intensify. Broadcast television has suffered substantial losses to cable; in turn, cable is losing an undetermined share to home video. Eventually viewers' preferences will stabilize, but not before cable and video have demonstrated more clearly the scope of what they can offer.

As discussed earlier, the nature of over-the-air programming probably will remain much as it is today. Perhaps the chief pressure on it for change comes from cable programming, which has not yet reached its full potential for providing challenging, innovative shows. Already the more liberal social and moral standards applied on cable TV have forced broadcast television to loosen its restrictions on sexual situations, and the bombastic arrival of rock music videos on the MTV cable channel quickly led to rock music shows and the use of the music videos' quick-cut photographic techniques on over-the-air stations.

For cable television, a critical problem is audience fragmentation. It provides so much programming on so many channels that few of its programs reach mass audiences—"mass" at least in terms of broadcast network audience size and the demands of major advertisers. Much fine programming is seen by relatively small audiences. The very diversity that cablecasting has brought to television tends to keep away from it national advertisers who need large audiences for their messages.

No conclusive answers to long-debated questions about television's impact on the fabric of society and on the lives of individuals are likely to emerge soon, if ever.

- Does televised murder and mayhem, when watched hour after hour, induce violent behavior in juvenile and adult viewers?
- Does TV news with its emphasis on brevity and personality provide sufficient substance to inform the electorate adequately?
- Do the unrealistic glossy, simplistic solutions, and implausible plots of many TV shows cause viewers to believe in an artificial dream world dangerously at odds with their own daily lives? Indeed, has television become an opiate that lulls some viewers into mental stagnation and dulls their lives?
- Or, just the opposite, does television enliven dull lives and provide welcome escape from depressing realism?

The questions are many, the answers subjective and difficult to document. The one obvious truth is that television, ever more pervasive, shapes contemporary politics, news coverage, the form and timing of public events, the nature of family life, and, in many respects, the quality of our national thinking—remarkable power for a medium whose critics, often with good reason, dismiss much of its programming as "mindless."

The Film

Disastrous Movie Gamble

The grandiose Western film cost $35 million. It ran 3 hours and 39 minutes at its New York City preview in November 1980. The critics denounced it. United Artists withdrew it from circulation. The ''unqualified disaster,'' as one critic called it, destroyed the studio. Its name was *Heaven's Gate*.

Michael Cimino, fresh from winning an Academy Award for *The Deer Hunter*, which he wrote and directed, set a budget of $11 million to make *Heaven's Gate*. Filming on location in Montana, he spent with a profligate hand in pursuit of a masterpiece. In one scene, he shot 53 versions of Kris Kristofferson shaking a bullwhip at a mayor. Altogether Cimino exposed nearly 1.5 million feet of film, about 220 hours of viewing.

United Artists recut the film into a 2½-hour version and released it nationally a year later to a brief, lackluster audience reception.

Then the studio wrote off *Heaven's Gate* for a loss of $44 million, including the money spent to promote it. Badly shaken, United Artists was sold to the rival MGM studio.

For a detailed account of the dealing, personality clashes, inflated egos, and complicated finances involved, read *Final Cut* by Steven Bach, published in 1985. Bach supervised *Heaven's Gate* for United Artists and was fired as a result.

*W*hen motion pictures are mentioned, the automatic word association is "Hollywood." The mass entertainment films symbolized by that word are in fact only one aspect of filmmaking, although by far the largest and best publicized. Foreign films, documentaries, experimental pictures, and sponsored films also make their contributions to the motion picture as an artistic medium and an immensely powerful form of mass communication.

In this chapter we examine all these elements of the motion picture industry —their roles, techniques, audiences, and trends.

Since Hollywood pictures are best known, we look first at how modern American entertainment filmmaking functions. We see how it defines its audiences, with dominant youth orientation; the economics involved; the close ties between motion pictures and television; and the effects of the electronic explosion on production and distribution of "the movies."

After that, we discuss foreign films, experimental and documentary pictures, film criticism, and the purpose and impact of sponsored films. The latter are provided free by commercial firms, government agencies, and nonprofit institutions to explain their work and advocate their causes.

The chapter closes with a look at job opportunities in filmmaking. ◆

THE ROLE OF MOTION PICTURES

From the capture of a moving image on a strip of film was born a form of communication that, surmounting language barriers, soon carried visual messages to the remote places of the world. When sound was later added, the motion picture became an even more powerful mass medium for entertainment and the transmission of ideas. Today, in its many forms, film projects reality and the illusion of reality on theater screens, on television sets in millions of homes, in school classrooms, and on building walls in isolated villages.

As motion picture critic Stanley Kauffmann observes, "Film is the only art besides music that is available to the whole world at once, exactly as it was first made." And film, like opera, can be enjoyed despite the viewer's ignorance of the language employed in the dialogue or narration. Kauffmann contends, "The point is not the spreading of information or amity, as in USIA or UNESCO films, useful though they may be. The point is emotional relationship and debt." To understand this observation, consider the Russian entertainment film *The Cranes Are Flying* (1957), a romantic drama of life and death, of love and loss, set in the years 1941 to 1945 and played by Russian actors against a Russian background. If one empathizes with the young lovers, sharing their anguish at war and separation and their desire for peace and reunion, the viewer has been drawn into an emotional relationship with the characters that makes it impossible to view all Russians as unfeeling puppets, solely committed in thought and deed to advancing the communist state.

Although the advent of sound tended to nationalize film and reduce film's claim to being an international art as in the days of the silent movie, the popularity of foreign films in America and the even more widespread distribution of American films in foreign markets demonstrate the primary role played by a film's visual elements, and the lesser importance of language as a communications device. In fact, when a motion picture is subtitled for distribution in a foreign market, the subtitles convey little more than one-third of the dialogue. Yet the meaning of the film is seldom, if ever, impaired, and its beauty is often enhanced.

The film *Years of Lightning, Day of Drums* (1964), made for the United States Information Agency (USIA), illustrates the lesser role played by verbal language in motion pictures, even in a nontheatrical film. Approximately 40 percent of the film uses neither dialogue nor narration. Designed as a tribute to John F. Kennedy and as a vehicle to bolster confidence that the work Kennedy had begun would continue after his death, the film presents the six facets of the New Frontier, interlacing such programs as the Alliance for Progress, Civil Rights, and the Peace Corps, with sequences depicting the funeral. These funeral sequences are largely wordless, with the sound track carrying natural sound: the heavy footsteps of the marchers, the more staccato hoofbeats of the horses, and the steady, muffled drumbeat. Yet no words are necessary during these sequences. Assembled from stock footage, *Years of Lightning, Day of Drums,* by sharing Kennedy's death with the foreign viewer, shares his political achievement and America's aspirations.

A note of warning: *Film is probably the most powerful propaganda medium yet devised.* As a consequence, its potential for aiding or injuring civilization is enormous. In addition to supplying a verbal message through dialogue, narration, or subtitles, the film provides an instantaneous, accompanying visual message—supplying the viewer with a picture to bulwark what has been learned through language. Thus the imagination need not conjure a mental image to accompany the words; the viewer leaves the theater complete with a concept and its substantiation. If a picture is worth 1,000 words, a picture together with three or four carefully chosen words is worth 10,000 words. Makers of television commercials know this; so does anyone who has ever thought carefully about this compelling and contemporary medium of communication.

VIDEOCASSETTES AND SATELLITES

Motion pictures today are far more readily available to viewers worldwide than ever before. Satellite transmission of films, both in the United States and abroad, brings them to home television screens. Films distributed in videocassette form, for viewing on videocassette recorders in homes and other nontheatrical settings, are a phenomenon of the 1980s.

Indeed, the remarkable growth of the video industry is causing deep shifts in the marketing of motion pictures and in their content as well. The interlocking relationships between the motion picture and video industries are examined in Chapter 15 and the distribution of American films and television programs abroad in Chapter 25.

In the minds of most Americans, mention of motion pictures conjures up Hollywood and the mass entertainment films it produces. But Hollywood, like so many of the pictures it turns out, is largely an illusion. Aspiring young men and women who are drawn there, hoping to become movie stars, find the storied corner of Hollywood and Vine to be merely a dingy, noisy commercial intersection. Actually "Hollywood" film production is spread across a wide portion of the Los Angeles area, through many other states, and indeed around the world. Yet the fable of a tightly knit Hollywood community persists, and so does the misconception that the world of film consists almost entirely of the slick, carefully contrived, mass-marketed pictures associated with it.

The motion picture has other significant facets—as an art form, as a purveyor of information, and as a channel of international cultural exchange—that we shall examine. First, because of their popular impact, we shall look at Hollywood and the films that bear its imprint.

THE ENTERTAINMENT FILM

Hollywood: 1945–1965

The late 1940s found "old" Hollywood at the peak of its prosperity. With World War II ended, the market for Hollywood films was huge worldwide. Television had not yet developed as a rival medium of mass entertainment. The major studios churned out a flow of movies, from low-budget B films to big-name epics, using the actors they kept under contract. They were assured of distribution for their products through the theaters they owned, under the block-booking system (to be discussed later in this chapter).

During 1949, more than 90 million tickets were sold weekly in American movie houses, compared with 21 million in 1968. In 1949 the major studios—among them Metro-Goldwyn-Mayer, Twentieth Century-Fox, Columbia Pictures, RKO, and Warner Brothers—released 411 new motion pictures. By the early 1960s their annual output had decreased to barely 200. Still administered by the people who established them, the major companies offered such entertainment films as the horror-thriller *The Beast With Five Fingers* (1946) and the slick romantic comedy *June Bride* (1948), along with provocative and candid films such as *The Best Years of Our Lives* (1946) and *Crossfire* (1947), to a receptive and apparently uncritical American audience.

Then, around 1950, two developments staggered the motion picture industry. Television rocketed into prominence; millions of families watched free TV shows at home instead of making one or two trips a week to the neighborhood movie house. The second blow to the old order came from the federal courts. Bowing

U.S. MOVIE ATTENDANCE

	Tickets Sold	Population
1946	4,100,000,000	137,165,000*
1962	1,080,000,000	179,323,000†
1965	1,032,000,000	193,526,000‡
1970	921,000,000	203,810,000
1975	1,033,000,000	213,200,000‡
1980	1,022,000,000	226,549,000
1985	1,056,000,000	237,839,000‡

*1940 census
†1960 census
‡official estimate
SOURCES: Motion Picture Association of America, Bureau of the Census.

to government pressure and a lawsuit charging them with restraint of trade, the major studios signed consent decrees in which they agreed to sell their chains of theaters and to end the practice of block booking. In doing so, they lost the automatic outlet for the pictures they made. Instead of arbitrarily booking their pictures—good, bad, or indifferent—into hundreds of theaters, the moviemakers were required to sell pictures on their merit, one by one. With their audiences shrinking because of TV, the theater operators did not want to show the shoddy "program" films being ground out. The result was a severe reduction in the number of pictures made, leading to the death of the contract player system, under which a studio paid a performer a salary and assigned him or her to whatever picture it desired. Studios that did not sign the consent decree because they owned no theaters at the time, or came into existence later, began to buy theaters in the late 1980s to guarantee outlets for their movies.

Hunting for ways to save itself, Hollywood made drastic alterations in its films, both in appearance and in content. The great change in appearance came with the introduction of the wide screen, which has been called the most significant innovation in film technology since the advent of sound. Since the pictures on early TV sets were so small, the massive scope of the wide screen was intended to entice audiences away from their living rooms and into the theaters. Until the appearance of the first wide-screen motion picture, *The Robe* (a $5 million Cinemascope film produced and distributed by Twentieth Century-Fox in 1953), the standard screen shape had been a rectangle 20 feet wide and 15 feet high; this represents a ratio of 4 to 3, or 1.33 to 1—a proportion determined by the width of the film, and going back to Thomas Edison and the Kinetoscope. Cinemascope settled its widescreen proportion at 2.55 to 1. Regardless of trade name, most new screens are at least twice as wide as they are high.

Initial critical reactions to the wide screen were mixed, with some filmmakers

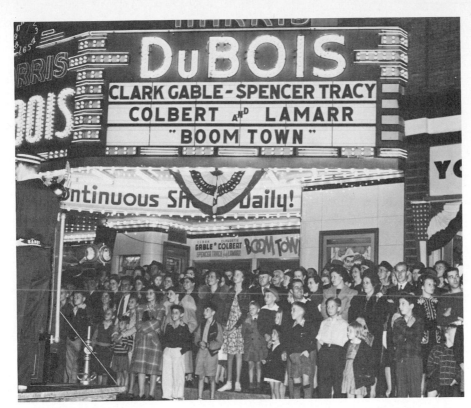

Movies drew attendance during the 1940s never since equalled. Fans crowded theaters to see such glamorous stars as Clark Gable, Spencer Tracy, Claudette Colbert, and Hedy Lamarr. Theaters in large cities offered continuous all-day showings. Boom Town *was released in 1944.* (Library of Congress)

insisting that the new screen size signaled the end of the closeup and rendered established directorial and cutting techniques ineffective. In time, however, the advantages and possibilities of the wide screen became apparent to filmmakers, who have used its inclusiveness to achieve a naturalness and spontaneity, and its new dimensions to experiment with new kinds of visual compositions and new uses of the closeup.

In response to the wide screen and as a further effort to bring the American public back into the movie theaters, Hollywood began to produce longer and more expensive movies with casts of thousands and an abundance of well-known stars. Often, best-selling novels or successful dramas that called for copious action and spectacle provided the story for these productions—as in *Raintree County* (1957), *El Cid* (1961), and *Cleopatra* (1963).

As a further lure to their audience, the filmmakers lowered the censorship barriers of their self-imposed Production Code and made pictures about topics and situations they knew would not be shown on the home TV screen. *The Moon Is Blue* (1953) depicted adultery and *The Man With the Golden Arm* (1956) opened up the subject of drugs. In 1956 revisions in the code also permitted depiction of kidnapping, prostitution, and abortion. Soon, other movies portraying narcotics addiction, such as *Monkey on My Back* (1957) and *The Pusher* (1959), and films involving prostitution, such as *Butterfield 8* (1960) and *Girl of the Night* (1960), were released bearing the Motion Picture Seal of Approval. Although the new freedom of subject matter resulted in the creation of a few artistic successes, Hollywood quickly managed to create new clichés from the once-forbidden subject matter at its disposal.

At first, the Hollywood studios tried to shun television, hoping that it was merely a novelty. However, they soon changed course. Hollywood executives decided to do business with the new electronic medium, recognizing a potential for immense profits. Television needed a continuing supply of programs, and the studios had masses of material available: the old movies stored in their vaults. The studios sold rights to this backlog of films to the TV networks and individual stations for high prices—a windfall not anticipated when the movies were made. Between 1955 and 1958, Hollywood sold almost 9000 pre-1948 feature films to television, and by 1960 the major studios were vying with each other for sale of films produced after 1948. This bonanza for the studios began a relationship of interdependence between them and television that continues to grow.

Although Hollywood studios profited from old work in this manner and created a fresh source of income by renting out sound stages and equipment to TV companies shooting television series, the major studios' basic business of making movies continued to dwindle. Foreign films found increasing popularity in the United States and American experimental filmmakers gained attention, but the traditional Hollywood film, lavishly produced, lost much of its audience appeal. The audience itself was changing. It grew more sophisticated and was weary of shallow, innocuous fare. By 1965 box-office receipts in the domestic market had fallen to barely half what they were in 1946, despite such smash hits as *Dr. Zhivago* and *The Sound of Music,* with Julie Andrews. Even the appearance of directors of the caliber of Alfred Hitchcock, Otto Preminger, and Joseph Mankiewicz, and of stars such as Elizabeth Taylor, Doris Day, Cary Grant, Rock Hudson, Burt Lancaster, and Marlon Brando did not help. Stars alone did not draw large audiences. Three studios—RKO, Republic, and Monogram—stopped production entirely. Approximately 6000 movie houses closed their doors.

HOLLYWOOD TODAY

Motion pictures made in Hollywood dominate the world market today, as always, but both the films and the industry that produces them are far different from what they were in the early 1960s. After floundering, Hollywood has found a profitable new course. The box-office income in the domestic market, the United States and Canada, reached an all-time high of $4.03 billion in 1984—this compared to only $1.2 billion in 1953. However, a sharp drop followed in 1985; admissions that year fell 11 percent to 1.056 billion tickets sold. In 1986 box office income showed a slight increase over 1985, but ticket sales declined again. Inflation, which has pushed the average ticket price above $3.50, was partially responsible for the high prices of the 1980s. Examination of the list of all-time box-office champions shows that all the top ten were released during or after 1975, when inflationary dollars produced high figures in all forms of business.

Perhaps the most fundamental difference between old and new Hollywood is that with a few exceptions, notably the Walt Disney studio, moviemakers have stopped producing films intended for the traditional family audience. They concentrate instead on a youthful audience. A study by the Motion Picture Association of America shows 54 percent of movie theater audiences to be under age 25 and another 31 percent between 25 and 39. Only 15 percent of all moviegoers are age 40 or older. The over-40s stay home to watch television and, more recently, videocassettes.

Since the target audience is more liberal in its attitudes toward sex, profanity, and violence than the older age categories, and since the target audience is also more fascinated by fantasy, and more rebellious against the social and political establishment, film producers choose stories and ways of telling them that cater to its tastes.

In Alan Alda's 1986 comedy *Sweet Liberty,* about the making of a movie based on an historical novel, the novelist protests the way the director distorts the script. Cynically, the director explains that to succeed with a youthful audience a film must do three things: defy authority, destroy something, and have actors take off their clothes.

The power structure of Hollywood has been altered radically. The generation of movie moguls—men such as Louis B. Mayer, Samuel Goldwyn, Harry Cohn, Adolf Zukor, the Warner brothers, and Darryl F. Zanuck—is gone, and so is the way in which they ran the industry. In their day a major studio created a story, arranged financing for it, cast it with performers from its roster of contract players, and filmed the story on its back lot, which housed standard sets such as a Western cowtown or a Manhattan street. Then it booked the movie into the theaters it controlled. Its overhead was tremendous, especially the salaries of stars under contract.

Today, a large percentage of Hollywood films are independent productions. This is the era of the package deal, in which the outside talent agent or producer has in a sense replaced the old-time studio czar. Independent companies avoid excessive overhead investment by having neither costly studios nor large production staffs.

Independent producers came to prominence during the 1950s as the once-awesome power of the big studios diminished. Some of the independent production companies were formed by the stars themselves—among them Burt Lancaster, Frank Sinatra, Kirk Douglas, and Bob Hope. One advantage for them was that, by incorporating, the stars could take part of their income from the films they made in the form of capital gains, rather than as straight salary from the studios, which would be subject to much higher personal income tax rates. In itself, the independent production company was not a new commodity in Hollywood. But the independent producer had never made any significant inroads in the Hollywood system until the 1950s. At that time the major studios, having involved themselves in fewer productions, began increasingly to finance and then distribute films made by an independent production company. Gradually, therefore, the studios began to function like United Artists, which had been started in 1919 as a releasing company without studio facilities.

By accepting the lesser roles of financier, promoter, and distributor, even at

Film crew and actors take a break during the shooting of Apocalypse Now, *Francis Ford Coppola's motion picture about the Vietnam war, released in 1979.* (Millinaire/Sygma)

times leasing their own facilities to the independent production companies, the major studios relinquished artistic control over the films they were underwriting. Control passed to the independent producer, creating a situation that allowed a film to have a style impressed upon it by those who created it, rather than by a studio boss who would oversee a dozen or more films simultaneously.

Variations of the independent production system exist. Some independent companies handle their own distribution instead of paying a major studio organization to do so for them. They also do their own filming without ties to a major studio, frequently on location in the United States or abroad. Others rent production facilities from a large studio. An independent company's success depends not only upon the popularity of the film that it produces, but also on the financial deals it

MOTION PICTURES MADE BY U.S. PRODUCERS

	1976	1978	1980	1982	1983	1984	1985	1986
Major studios	82	80	103	85	120	130	105	161
Independent producers	92	123	106	99	129	188	225	354
Total	174	203	209	184	249	318	330	515

SOURCE: Compiled by *Variety,* 1986.

can arrange. Although they do not see their names on the marquees, accountants and deal makers keep the wheels of Hollywood turning.

Hollywood filmmaking has always been influenced by trends and fads. An exceptionally successful picture almost automatically draws imitators and leads to sequels. For example, Sylvester Stallone's *Rocky* was followed by *Rocky II, Rocky III,* and *Rocky IV.*

"BLOCKBUSTER" PICTURES

A major trend in recent years has been toward the spectacular "blockbuster" picture, of which the space fantasy films with their awesome special effects have been notable. The four biggest all-time box-office attractions are space adventures: *E.T. The Extra-Terrestial, Star Wars, Return of the Jedi,* and *The Empire Strikes Back.* Usually made at very high cost, these films are designed to attract large crowds for weeks or months, especially in urban theaters. The economics of distribution are weighted by the distributors in such a way that a theater operator must keep showing the same film for many weeks in order to make much money on it.

Films emphasizing sexuality, horror, and rock music—all with strong youth orientation—are other contemporary favorites of both filmmakers and audiences. So are violent, chauvinistic films with simplistic story lines, epitomized by the Sylvester Stallone pictures *Rambo: First Blood Part II* and *Rocky IV,* both highly profitable and both criticized by the Soviet Union for their vehement anti-communism. Only an occasional picture with historical or social significance, such as *Gandhi,* breaks the pattern. Emphasis is on escapist entertainment, resulting in what critic Pauline Kael has called the "infantilization of movies of the '80s."

During the second half of the 1980s, however, certain producers, sensing a change in the market for movies brought about by the video boom, began to make films that appealed to the more traditional tastes of older stay-at-home users of videocassette recorders. Examples are *Murphy's Romance,* with James Garner and Sally Field, and Alan Alda's *Sweet Liberty.*

RATING SYSTEM. Application of the rating system has been liberalized with regard to nudity, obscene language, and violence; films that once would have been rated X are now rated R. This permits people under the age of 18, even small children, to attend if they are accompanied by their parents. Some theater owners do not enforce the R admission restriction. Because films with a G (general audience) rating often fare poorly at the box office, producers may include gratuitous profanity and violence in the films to require that they have a PG (parental guidance) rating. The rating PG-13, added in 1984, urges special caution for attendance of children under 13. As proof of how the industry ignores the innocuous G films, of the 452 pictures released during the heavy production year 1985, only eight carried G ratings (see Chapter 24).

Before embarking on a movie, producers analyze audience tastes and makeup with a variety of research projects. They have found, for example, that persons

MOVIE RATINGS SCORECARD

The Motion Picture Association of America began its rating system for movies in November 1968. Between then and early 1986 the MPAA gave ratings to 7004 films. A tabulation of these ratings shows how heavily producers have injected violence and sex into their pictures.

Rating	Number of Films	Percentage of Total
Restricted (R)	3135	45%
Parental Guidance (PG)	2551	36
Parental Guidance, 13 years and under*	91	1
General audience (G)	886	13
X-rated†	341	5

*Category established 1984.
†Films made for showing in adult theaters usually are not submitted for MPAA ratings.

who have attended college are more than twice as likely to see movies as those without a high school diploma. These well-educated persons are more willing to accept violent sexual films if they can be convinced that the pictures in question contain socially significant themes.

ECONOMICS OF FILMMAKING

Anyone in Hollywood hoping to produce a popular movie is guided by a few economic rules of thumb. Production of the movie will be very expensive. The average major film costs about $16 million, up to the point where the final master negative is complete and ready for release. Much of this money is borrowed, at high rates of interest. Another $7 to $10 million will be needed to cover costs of promotion and distribution. Standard Hollywood wisdom is that a movie breaks even, or should, when the maker collects two and a half to three times its negative cost. Roughly one film in seven makes money at the box office, although recently some have been turned from losers into winners by the additional revenue from videocassette sales. Leasing films for showing on television is another major source of supplementary revenue.

Behind the performers, there is a costly phalanx of off-screen personnel: producers, directors, writers, camera operators, editors, stunt men and women, script consultants, script personnel, costumers, set designers, wardrobe assistants, prop men and women, lighting technicians, makeup artists, carpenters, actors' agents, painters, publicists, and the sales staff. One cause of the huge overhead is the high degree of unionization among motion picture personnel. Few industries are so

ALL-TIME BOX OFFICE CHAMPIONS

These 10 motion pictures are the largest revenue producers in film history, based on film rentals in the United States and Canada markets.

E.T. The Extra-Terrestrial (1982)	$227,960,804
Star Wars (1977)	193,500,000
Return of the Jedi (1983)	168,002,414
The Empire Strikes Back (1980)	141,600,000
Jaws (1975)	129,961,081
Ghostbusters (1984)	128,216,446
Raiders of the Lost Ark (1981)	115,598,000
Indiana Jones and The Temple of Doom (1984)	109,000,000
Beverly Hills Cop (1984)	108,000,000
Grease (1978)	96,300,000

SOURCE: Compiled by *Variety,* the show business publication, as of January 1, 1987.

highly structured; there are rigid restrictions on the duties each worker may perform and the kinds of physical properties he or she may touch.

As the movie industry has changed, the old picture palaces have been replaced by hundreds of new, small cluster theaters, in which different pictures are shown simultaneously in two or more relatively small auditoriums that one enters through a central lobby. Often these theaters are located in shopping centers. Despite competition from television and home video, a record number of more than 20,000 motion picture screens are in use today in the United States.

WHAT HAPPENED TO *ENEMY MINE*

A look at the fate of a recent science fiction movie, *Enemy Mine,* reveals how the filmmaking system functions and the enormous financial risks involved. *Enemy Mine,* a story about the developing tie between a fighter pilot and his one-time enemy alien, was budgeted to cost $17 million when filming began in Iceland and Budapest in spring of 1984. Disputes arose on the set and the early portions of film were unsatisfactory, so 20th Century-Fox stopped production after spending $9 million.

The studio hired a new director. He discarded all the film his predecessor had shot, moved the filming from Budapest to Germany, built new sets, and had experts spend five months in redesigning the latex makeup worn by Louis Gossett, Jr., in his role as the alien. Throughout the changeover, the studio paid interest on the $9 million in wasted money, all borrowed.

By the time *Enemy Mine* was released in 703 theaters nationwide just before Christmas 1985, 20th Century-Fox had spent more than $40 million on it—$33 million on production and more than $7 million on promotion and distribution.

Accountants calculated that the movie's maker–distributor had to receive more than $80 million from box-office sales to break even. (A distributor receives in rental fees from theaters about 50 percent of what moviegoers pay at the box office.)

Advertising and promotion to launch *Enemy Mine* was intense. On opening day, the studio published full-page advertisements in 43 large newspapers. That evening it purchased 30-second commercials which appeared almost simultaneously on the three major television networks in what is called a "network roadblock." Also, it shipped 3500 promotional "trailers" to theaters and mounted large displays in 164 major shopping malls.

Some critics praised the film, others disliked it. Unfortunately for the movie's owners, the public developed little enthusiasm for *Enemy Mine.* It did lackluster business during Christmas week, a prime time at the box office, and its earnings drifted downward after that. During the first two crucial months after release it grossed only a small fraction of the receipts needed to break even and disappeared from *Variety*'s weekly tabulation of the current 50 top-grossing films. After three months, *Enemy Mine* had been relegated to bookings as second feature at drive-in theaters. Its final loss probably exceeded $30 million.

These figures are in sharp contrast to two massive box-office successes issued a few months earlier. *Ghostbusters* cost $32 million to make and earned $128 million from domestic ticket sales. *Beverly Hills Cop* starring Eddie Murphy cost $14 million and took in $108 million. In addition, both pictures collected large amounts from foreign releases, videocassettes, and other ancillary sales.

TIES WITH TELEVISION

In an earlier era the producer and director made a motion picture with only one audience in mind: viewers in a theater. Financial success or failure depended upon the number of theatrical admissions it attracted. Today the realities are different. Much of the income a movie generates is from nontheatrical sources, especially television and videocassettes.

Once separate camps suspicious of each other, the motion picture and television industries are drawing closer and closer together. Ownership of the major filmmakers' libraries of movies, a rich source of material for television programming, has been the goal of recent massive multimedia ownership deals (see Chapter 21). Home Box Office, the giant of pay cable television, produces films of its own and helps to finance others so it can have exclusive material to show home viewers who buy its services. Its major competitor, Showtime, does the same thing. Videocassette marketing firms have begun to produce their own low-budget movies for sale or rental to home video consumers.

Those who control a new film have several ways to collect income from it. They manipulate the sequence of its appearance on various outlets to generate the largest sums possible. A common sequence is to release the film initially in first-run movie houses; second, on videocassettes for the home audience; third, on pay-per-view television, in which the viewer pays a special added fee to see the new picture; fourth, on regular pay cable television, in which the viewer sees it as a part of basic cable service for which he or she pays a monthly fee; and fifth, on free television.

Knowledge that a movie will be shown on the small home screen as well as the large theatrical screen influences the way in which it is shot. Differing closeup techniques and camera angles are considered. So is plot development, to permit breaks for commercials at convenient intervals. Television has long borrowed program ideas from motion pictures. For example, the enormously popular TV series, "M*A*S*H," was derived from the earlier movie of the same name. Recently, the process has worked in reverse; motion pictures borrow ideas and material from television shows and blow them up into big-screen productions—more evidence that the two industries are inextricably tied together.

Motion pictures often derive their titles and stories from books and magazine articles. A classic example of the former is Margaret Mitchell's big novel of the Civil War, *Gone with the Wind,* still revived on television periodically decades after its original appearance. The film *Urban Cowboy* was developed from an *Esquire* magazine article. Usually, when a movie is adapted from a book, the film producer and book publisher work together on promotional tie-ins such as a reissue of the book in paperback form to coincide with the release of the film.

THE INTERNATIONAL MOVIE. Part of the life style that characterizes the new Hollywood involves the international movie. A step toward internationalization occurred in the 1950s. The independent producers, not being shackled to particular film studios, made movies in Europe and other foreign locations in order to profit from cheaper labor costs and national subsidies, to use authentic locales, and to please the movie stars themselves who, by establishing residence in a foreign country, at that time could avoid paying United States income tax on money earned while working abroad.

An international movie is not the output of the film industry of a single foreign country; it is a melange of performers, production concepts, and scenery from several countries. To cite one example, most of the filming of the Home Box Office made-for-pay-TV film, *The Far Pavilions,* was done in England, with location shots made in New Delhi and Jaipur, India. Featured in the cast were three English performers, an Italian, an Egyptian, and an American.

The mobility of contemporary moviemakers has been aided by certain technological developments. Lightweight cameras and sound recording equipment, as well as ministudios capable of being airlifted, are allowing movie producers to set up shooting wherever whim and geography dictate.

The many film festivals prevalent today are additional evidence of the internationalism of the film industry. Festivals in Cannes, Berlin, Venice, San Sebastian, New York, Moscow, Montreal, Cork, Chicago, and Mexico City have provided showcases for films from every nation and a meeting site and marketplace for actors, directors, writers, and producers.

International aspects of filmmaking and distribution are discussed in Chapter 25.

The Vietnam film, Platoon, *won an Oscar for best picture in 1987 for its harsh, unrelenting portrayal of that conflict. Charlie Sheen and Keith David had prominent roles.* (Photo Trends)

THE FOREIGN FILM

Italy

If Hollywood chose to ignore, by and large, the realities of the post-World War II world, that was not true of Italian filmmakers. Responding to the grim reality of war-torn, impoverished Italy, Roberto Rossellini directed *Open City* (1945)—the first important film shot in a style that was quickly dubbed by the critics as *neorealism.* Combining stock newsreel footage with his own film (shot chiefly on the streets of Rome and scratched to resemble newsreels), Rossellini depicted the hardships endured by Italians during the Nazi occupation and their courageous resistance. To heighten the authenticity gained by the use of actual locations and natural lighting, he employed only a handful of professional actors whom he encouraged to ad-lib, and chose ordinary Roman citizens as supporting players. Although none of these techniques in isolation was new, they had not been used so successfully together before; and *Open City* became, as the film historian Arthur Knight has said, "the key film in the entire neorealist Italian revival."

Equally as personal and visually intense, and equally as concerned with social realism, are two early films by Vittorio De Sica. In *Shoeshine* (1946), De Sica portrays the lives of a group of homeless Roman boys involved in the corrupt underworld of the Italian black market. *Bicycle Thief* (1947) treats the relationship between a father (played by a factory mechanic) and his son (played by a Roman newsboy) who together try to beat insurmountable odds occasioned by unemployment, poverty, and corruption.

In more recent years, amid a rash of conventional and often sensationalist films, the work of two masterful directors emerged. Described as "second-generation realists," Federico Fellini (*La Dolce Vita,* 1960; *8½,* 1962; *Juliet of the Spirits,* 1965; *Satyricon,* 1970; *Amarcord,* 1974; *Fellini's Casanova,* 1976) and Michelangelo Antonioni (*L'Avventura,* 1959; *La Notte,* 1960; *The Red Desert,* 1964; *Blow-Up,* 1966; *The Passenger,* 1975; *Suffer or Die,* 1979) have little in common except a compulsion to use the surfaces, rituals, and hidden recesses of contemporary existence as theme and subject matter, and a proven ability to use improvisation as an effective cinematic technique.

In 1983, however, for the first time in the 50-year history of the Venice Film Festival, no Italian film won a prize. In evaluating what they termed "the virtual disintegration of the Italian cinema," some critics charged "unimaginative state agencies" with turning down the best scripts—those that take a thoughtful approach to real life—in favor of those with more popular themes. Director Gianfranco Caligari lamented "a generation that opts for the easy road of aping the masters rather than the dangerous one of original thought." Scriptwriter Cesare Frugoni charged that huge salaries paid to actors impoverished other parts of the industry. Franco Bruno, chairman of the General Association of Italian Film, said directors were to blame for producing "pseudo-intellectual, whining, self-pitying movies that tell their stories in an incomprehensible way." As one result, American films captured 38.5 percent of ticket sales in Italy in 1983, up from a third in 1982, whereas attendance at Italian movies declined.

Only 90 Italian films were produced in 1985, mostly of the hardcore and softcore pornography variety. Critics, however, commented favorably upon a handful of important films, including Ettore Scola's *Macaroni,* Federico Fellini's *Ginger and Fred,* and Nanni Moretti's *Mass Is Over.* Beset with videocassette film piracy and the growth of home video, the industry began a large-scale promotion campaign, urging Italians to view "Cinema in Cinemas." At the same time, the industry lobbied for an unlimited tax shelter system, virtual elimination of nationality quotas affecting talent and technicians, and favorable treatment of Italian and European Economic Community films and TV programs within a pending broadcasting act.

France

During 1958 and 1959, the New Wave erupted on the French film scene, with Francois Truffaut's *Les Quatre Cents Coups* and Alain Resnais' *Hiroshima Mon Amour* winning awards at the 1959 Cannes Film Festival. Other films that heralded the New Wave were Claude Chabrol's *Le Beau Serge* (1958), Louis Malle's *Les Amants* (1958), and Jean-Luc Godard's *Breathless* (1959). Although heterogeneous and resistant of labels in the manner of all creative artists, these New Wave directors do share many cinematic ideals as well as an outlet for these ideals in the influential film journal *Cahiers du Cinema.* Truffaut, Godard, and Chabrol had been film critics in the early 1950s, and they continued to write about the cinema. Describing his own procedures, Truffaut has said:

> I start with a very imperfect script, in which there are certain elements that please and stimulate me. Characters that strike some chord of response in me. A theme that lets me "talk about" something I want to film. As I work I find I am eliminating all the scenes of story transition and explanation. So it can happen that when the film is done, it is

completely different from what it was proposed to say in the first place. The shooting of the film is that sort of adventure.

In *Breathless,* Godard took his camera onto the Paris streets. Using a hand-held Arriflex and a three-page script outline by Truffaut, Godard allowed the camera to follow the actions and reactions of Michel (a small-time gangster, played by Jean-Paul Belmondo) and his American girl friend (played by Jean Seberg), depicting a life devoid of logic or purpose.

Although the New Wave dissipated itself (by 1964, Cannes was denigrating the very movement it had applauded five years earlier), these films and their directors made great and irrevocable contributions to cinema art. In particular, these lasting contributions are the imaginative and free camera work that characterizes New Wave films, the encouragement of a liberated acting style dependent on improvisation and self-portraiture rather than on self-conscious or stagey performance, the fanciful use of silent film techniques, the absence of conventional plotting and continuity, and a movement away from a cinema grounded in literature and drama to one that uses the strengths of the film medium to make its own powerful, highly cinematic statements.

Documentary filmmakers Jean Rouch and Mario Ruspoli led a brief *cinéma vérité* (direct or spontaneous) creative movement during the 1960s. Later, a second wave of young directors unsuccessfully pressured the government for greater support of experimental films. Gangster, comedy, and erotic films were the chief commodities into the 1970s, accompanied by a boom in pornographic movies. In the mid-1970s the government offered tax incentives to exhibitors of quality films and imposed heavy taxes on X-rated productions. Movie attendance continued to languish, dropping to an eight-year low in 1985. For the first time that year French films drew smaller audiences than English-language features, mainly American films supported by some British imports. New tax shelters again were introduced in an effort to revive the industry.

Great Britain

Room at the Top (1958) was the first in a remarkable series of outspoken realistic British films to gain widespread critical attention. Soon, motion pictures such as *Saturday Night and Sunday Morning* (1960), *A Taste of Honey* (1961), *The Loneliness of the Long-Distance Runner* (1962), *A Kind of Loving* (1962), *Billy Liar* (1963), *Morgan* (1966), *The Leather Boys* (1963), and *This Sporting Life* (1962) had established the reputations of their directors—Karel Reisz, Tony Richardson, John Schlesinger, Sidney Furie, Lindsay Anderson—and the significance of the British feature film. Describing their work as "free cinema," these directors brought to the screen a penetrating social realism focused on the English working class, preparing the way for the Beatles (who themselves are featured in Richard Lester's *A Hard Day's Night,* 1964; and *Help!,* 1965) and the ascendancy of Liverpool over Pall Mall.

American financial interests, however, largely withdrew support of British films when the U.S. tax laws changed, and by 1980 fewer than half the number of movies were being produced in the United Kingdom than a decade earlier. Only 14 feature films were made in 1981, compared with nearly 100 each year in the early 1950s. The number of cinema admissions has declined 60 percent during the last decade, to about 65 million. The success of the award-winning *Chariots of Fire* (1982) and *Gandhi* (1983) sparked a small revival in films produced for the international market, and the number of films produced mainly for British television increased. Noteworthy was the release in the United States in late 1985 of Hugh Hudson's *Revolution,* a $22-million re-creation of the Revolutionary War told from both American and British perspectives.

People's Republic of China

Although encumbered by outdated technology, movie studios in the People's Republic of China produce about 150 films per year. Most lack synchronized sound. In 1986 almost 1000 feature films had been made since the reopening of the industry in 1977 at the end of the Cultural Revolution. Almost all the provinces have studios; two in Beijing are said to be the largest in Asia. In contrast with Hollywood stages, where dirt is brought in to cover wooden floors when needed, the Beijing studios have dirt floors over which wood is placed as required. After the movies receive government approval, as many prints as requested are sent to the provinces; there is no bidding.

Urban admission prices range from 17 to 25 cents; tickets in rural areas cost 10 cents. Five days is considered a long run, with the average exhibition extending from three to five days. Showings begin at 8 A.M. The spread of black-and-white television sets has reduced the size of audiences, and further erosions are anticipated with the advent of color and videocassettes. Most films reflect topical social problems and are aimed at young people, who comprise more than 70 percent of moviegoers. A veteran of 30 years of filmmaking, Xie Jin is the country's most famous producer.

Soviet Union

Film production in the Soviet Union not only is nationalized, but the work of individual studios such as Lenfilm, in Leningrad, and Mosfilm, in Moscow, is closely supervised by a specially designated state committee. Not unexpectedly, therefore, many Soviet feature films have either implicit or explicit social messages such as the strongly chauvinist *They Fought for Their Country* (1975). But there are also films that focus on personal crises and solutions, including *I'm Twenty* (1965) and *Confession of Love* (1978), as well as adaptations of literary classics such as Grigori Kozintsev's *Hamlet* (1964) and *King Lear* (1972).

Russian film production is decentralized; about 50 percent of the films are made in the Soviet Union's 15 constituent republics. A few foreign films are imported from the Eastern Bloc. Western films are viewed only by the supervising committee or small, privileged audiences at Moscow's Illusion Theater.

Sweden

For more than three decades Ingmar Bergman has been Sweden's dominant director, acclaimed both at home and abroad. Beginning with his *Illicit Interlude/ Summer Interlude* (1950) and extending to the 1983 release, *Fanny and Alexander,* Bergman has used film to explore such abstract and eternal problems as the meaning of life and death (*The Seventh Seal,* 1956), the nature of truth (*The Magician,* 1958), and our tragic inability to communicate (*The Silence,* 1963, and *Cries and Whispers,* 1972). Many critics view Bergman as a cinematic Dostoyevsky or Shakespeare; others see him as too literary and too closely linked to high culture. A review in *Film Quarterly* described *Fanny and Alexander* as "lush, sprawling, flowing," with Shakespearean characteristics.

The Swedish film industry's difficulties during the last decade have included a technicians' strike, Bergman's self-exile, and a feud between the film and television industries, which was resolved. As in most countries, financial difficulties persist. About 20 to 25 films are produced annually.

Japan

The Japanese film has become known to audiences throughout the world largely through the work of Akira Kurosawa, who was 76 years of age in 1986. Like Sweden's Ingmar Bergman, Kurosawa depicts elemental problems and passions, using highly stylized, historical settings to underscore the timelessness of his themes. *Rashomon* (which won the Academy Award for Best Foreign Film in 1951) concerns the nature of truth, while *Throne of Blood* (1957), like *Macbeth,* after which it is patterned, depicts the breaking down of morality through greed.

With *Ran* (meaning chaos in Japanese) Kurosawa re-established himself in 1985 as one of the world's foremost directors. *Ran,* loosely adapted from *King Lear,* depicts children warring against their father in strife-torn 16th century Japan. It was Kurosawa's 27th film and the most expensive in Japanese history, costing more than $11 million. *Time* magazine termed the director's films "both rousing and cerebral, endowed with heart and brains, muscle and spirit, spleen and vision." Directors such as Peter Bogdanovich, Steven Spielberg, and John Milius acknowledge Kurosawa's strong influence on their movies.

Other serious Japanese filmmakers include Shohei Imamura, who in 1983 won the Golden Palm Award at the Cannes Film Festival with *The Ballad of Narayama,* picturing the Japanese concept of God in a world of robots, computers, and riches. Sex and violence have been the dominant themes of films in Japan, where television is blamed for a decline in movie attendance from the peak year of 1958. About half the films shown in Japan are imported, most of them from the United States.

Australia

During recent years the Australian film industry has attracted international attention for its high-quality productions. *Breaker Morant* drew critical praise in the early 1980s. *A Town Like Alice* was a serialized hit on European television,

and the PBS Masterpiece Theatre offered it to American television audiences in 1983. That same year *A Man From Snowy River,* hailed for its cinematic techniques and breathtaking scenery if not for its plot, packed American movie houses. In 1985 Mel Gibson's *Mad Max III: Beyond Thunderdome* and Anthony Buckley's *Bliss,* the latter a black comedy of an advertising executive's descent into a living hell, achieved modest financial success, but critics found little to praise in Australian cinema production that year. *"Crocodile" Dundee,* however, was an American triumph in 1986.

India

India has the world's largest film industry. Well over 700 films are produced annually in approximately 15 languages at the major studios in Bombay, Madras, and Calcutta. Hindi and South Indian cinema predominate. Although the films serve largely as escapist fare, the best are produced with style. Recent box office successes include *Sholay* ("Flames"), which ran for six years in Bombay; *Ram, Teri Ganga Maili* ("Rama, Your Ganges Is Dirty"); and *Coolie.* Music is a vital part of the typical film, as are stunts, fight sequences, and melodramatic situations.

The Art Cinema—the Indian New Wave—is best illustrated by the internationally acclaimed work of Satyajit Ray, whose work, however, has failed to succeed commercially in India. Other notable filmmakers in this genre include Shyam Benegal, a favorite at British film festivals; Govind Nihalani, who made a stunning debut in 1982 with *Aakrosh* ("Silent Cry"); Sai Paranjpye, who produces both commercial and artistic successes; Aruna-Vikas, a husband and wife team; and Mrinal Sen.

As in many other countries, the advent of video has dealt a severe blow to the industry through piracy. Many filmmakers now produce movies primarily for the TV screen.

AMERICAN EXPERIMENTAL FILMMAKERS

While Hollywood producers during the 1940s and 1950s persevered on a chosen course, determinedly oblivious to innovations in European filmmaking, a segment of the American moviegoing public was well aware of their importance. Excited by the new techniques and possibilities for film, dismayed at the impersonality and inanity of most Hollywood movies, and aware that film is as much an art form as the novel, dance, or painting, numerous young Americans turned to film to give shape to their feelings and ideas, as their predecessors (and many of their contemporaries) had chosen the more conventional vehicles of drama, fiction, poetry, painting, and sculpture.

Much of the credit for publicizing and organizing the work and aesthetic doctrines of America's experimental filmmakers goes to Jonas Mekas, himself a filmmaker, in addition to having served as editor of *Film Culture,* occasional film critic for the *Village Voice,* and organizer of the Film Makers' Cooperative and Distribution Center. In describing his own work and that of other independent filmmakers, Mekas said:

> Our movies come from our hearts—our little movies, not the Hollywood movies. Our movies are like extensions of our own pulse, of our heartbeat, of our eyes, our fingertips; they are so personal, so unambitious in their movement, in their use of light, their imagery. We want to surround this earth with our film frames and warm it up—until it begins to move.

Of extreme importance to the experimental filmmakers is the unambitiousness and intensely personal nature of their films, as described by Mekas. In many instances desire and budget dictate that the film be the result of one person who functions as producer, director, cameraperson, editor, and often distributor. The actors are often friends, and usually nonprofessionals. Most films are done on 16 mm. And, as in the New Wave films, there is an absence of chronological continuity and carefully plotted story lines, along with considerable use of improvisation and emphasis on spontaneous action and reaction rather than upon stagey performance.

As the New Wave is a convenient rubric that lumps together highly individualistic directors, so the New American Cinema Group—"a free organization of independent filmmakers dedicated to the support of the men and women giving their vision to the filmic art"—is a convenient label, embracing filmmakers with divergent purposes, talents, and methods. But, like the New Wave directors, the New American Cinema Group shares an outlet for its views, the magazine *Film Culture,* and evinces a common hatred and a common enthusiasm. As the French directors rebelled against film's prior dependency on literature and rejoiced in the cinema as an art form with its own aesthetic, so the New American Cinema rebels against all that is unimaginative, standardized, and hopelessly phony about Hollywood and celebrates, too, the film as an art form.

Among the more notable experimental filmmakers are Jonas Mekas *(The Brig, Diaries, Notes, and Sketches, Reminiscences of a Journey to Lithuania),* Stan Van-DerBeek *(Mankinda, Skullduggery, Summit, Breathdeath),* Stan Brakage *(Dog Star Man, Window Water Baby Moving, Scenes from Under Childhood),* Bruce Conner *(A Movie, Cosmic Ray, Liberty Crown),* Kenneth Anger *(Scorpio Rising, Inauguration of the Pleasure Dome),* Gregory Markopoulos *(Twice a Man, Seren-ity, Ming Green),* Charles Boultenhouse *(Handwritten, Dionysius),* Shirley Clarke *(The Connection, Skyscraper, The Cool World),* Paul Morrissey *(The Chelsea Girls, Trash),* and, of course, the late Andy Warhol *(Empire, Sleep).*

The many purposes and styles of American experimental films range from social criticism using documentary techniques to embodiments of the subconscious through surrealism and myth to psychedelic experiments with light and color. At their best, the films of the avant garde are exciting, fresh, sensitive, and fully able to transmit their maker's vision. At their worst, they are very bad indeed—as bad as the worst products of any art form—as trivial and boring, for example, as the worst Hollywood movie.

Image-oriented artists also have turned to video productions in recent years, finding primary outlets on public and cable television and comparing their work in video festivals. They include Nam June Paik, who has done dozens of videos for public broadcasting stations WGBH-TV, Boston, and WNET-TV, New York; Ed Emshwiller, provost of the California Institute of Art and artist-in-residence for WNET-TV; Peter Campus, New York, combining fantasy and reality; and Stephen Beck, National Center for Experiments in Television, San Francisco, first to suggest use of the Dewey decimal system in visual image-making.

FILM CRITICISM

As film's potential for personal and artistic expression was realized, and as its capability for being more than a cheap entertainment medium was understood, an accompanying aesthetic developed to explain and analyze the form and content of motion pictures. Vachel Lindsay's *The Art of the Moving Picture* (1915) and Rudolf Arnheim's *Film* (1933) are early examples of enlightened film criticism. Later, James Agee achieved even greater acclaim.

Good film criticism, like good literary criticism, serves two functions: (1) It explicates the work at hand, and (2) it elevates the public taste. The first function is the more obvious. As film techniques have become more complex, as film has probed deeper into human sensibility and experience, and as films have become identifiable as the work of individual directors who use personal symbols in the manner of contemporary poets and novelists, effective film criticism seeks to explain this heightened complexity by clarifying techniques, images, and relation-ships of time, place, and character.

The second purpose is perhaps best explained by Walt Whitman's often-quoted remark that great audiences make great poets. An audience knowledgeable about film history and techniques is in a position to recognize the second-rate, the false, the vacuous, the film that appears to be saying something but in reality says nothing, and the slick directorial tricks that attempt to hide the untrue. Great audiences make great poets (filmmakers) because they provide a need and a receiving ground for great poetry (films); they inspire the poet (filmmaker) to create a great film by providing a reason for being that transcends the individual's physical identity. Advances in film technology and subject matter have occurred and will continue to occur because film artist and film audience have become knowledgeable together.

At its best, good film criticism is informative, expanding the reader's knowledge by relating the film at hand to other works of a particular filmmaker, or to other films of similar or dissimilar genre; it respects the film and glories in its potential being realized; it bears the stamp of its creator's mind by possessing a distinctive style; it bridges epochs and nations by linking past with present achievement regardless of country of origin.

In all this, the film critic must be distinguished from the film reviewer, who serves a reportorial function. Whereas the film critic seeks to analyze and explain, the film reviewer seeks to ascertain the merits of a particular film with the intention of warning audiences against an inferior, boring, or morally degrading film, or touting those films with a high entertainment value. Gene Shalit has served this function in his frequent reviews on NBC's "Today" show. For the most part, movie reviewers write for the daily papers and preview and describe films on television; they seldom go beyond the value of amusement as a criterion.

In contrast, film critics generally write for magazines such as *Film Quarterly, Cahiers du Cinema* (available in an English edition), *Film Culture, Sight and Sound, New Yorker,* and *Esquire.* Stanley Kauffmann in *New Republic* and Arthur Knight and Hollis Alpert in *Saturday Review* have written weekly pieces that combine previewing a film with deeper, more thoughtful, analysis. A few other well-known American film critics are Andrew Sarris, Pauline Kael, Wilfrid Sheed, Jonas Mekas, Molly Haskell, and John Simon.

THE DOCUMENTARY FILM

In both England and America the documentary film came of age in the 1930s through direct patronage by national governments, and matured, still under government auspices, during the troubled years of World War II. Perhaps this is not surprising, as a documentary's purpose is always partially social—setting forth public and private crises and victories, showing us where humanity has been and what, inevitably, humanity will become unless proper action is taken.

In England the earliest documentaries are associated with the Empire Market Board (EMB) Film Unit, headed by John Grierson. Grierson's first documentary, *Drifters* (1929), filmed on location on the North Sea, portrays the daily existence of the herring fishermen. When the EMB Film Unit was shifted to the General Post Office in 1933, Grierson and the film unit continued the production of quality documentaries, including *Weather Forecast* (1934), *Song of Ceylon* (1934), *Coal Face* (1935), *Night Mail* (1936), and *North Sea* (1938). "By the time the war broke out," Arthur Knight writes, "the British documentary movement—headed by men like Paul Rotha, Stuart Legg, Basil Wright, Harry Watt, Alberto Cavalcanti, Arthur Elton and Edgar Anstey—had achieved a worldwide reputation and inspired scores of directors outside England to attempt documentary movements in their own countries."

In America the Depression and the New Deal gave rise to a remarkable series of documentaries produced under the auspices of the Farm Security Administration. As noted in Chapter 13, the most famed were two produced by Pare Lorentz: *The Plow That Broke the Plains* (1936) and *The River* (1937).

World War II gave impetus to increased documentary film production, ranging from training films for United States service personnel to informative films for a civilian population needing instruction in wartime procedures. As well, Hollywood directors such as John Huston, William Wyler, and John Ford began making films for the military. *San Pietro* (1944), *Memphis Belle* (1944), and *Battle of Midway* (1944) are memorable documentaries filmed on and around World War II's battlegrounds.

In England the documentary filmmakers, now working under the aegis of the Ministry of Information, also turned their attention to wartime subjects, producing films such as *London Can Take It* (1940), depicting London during a Nazi air raid; *Target for Tonight* (1941), documenting an air force bombing mission; and *Desert Victory* (1942), an account of the North African campaign.

Basic to many recent documentaries is a problematic cinema technique known as *cinéma vérité,* spontaneous cinema, or direct cinema, as mentioned previously. Cinéma vérité applies to film that uses the camera to record reality in an unbiased and unmanipulated way. In presenting the essence of a situation, the director does not work from a preconceived shooting script, and, for all intents and purposes, does not direct—if by directing one means organizing and controlling what happens before the camera. By making use of the new lightweight cameras and recording equipment, the filmmaker goes into the field where he or she, and camera, act as witnesses and scribes. The intent is to provide either minimal or no interpretation and to retain the spontaneity and natural characteristics of the actual event.

In practice, documentary films exhibiting pure cinéma vérité are hard to find. Either consciously or unconsciously, most filmmakers impose an interpretation on their subject matter with in-camera editing, or editing after the film has been made. Others "edit" reality before any filming occurs by carefully selecting the persons and objects to be photographed and only then applying cinéma vérité filming techniques. For example, *Chronique d'un Eté,* by Jean Rouch and Edgar Morin, shows evidence of rather stringent preshooting editing, although the most effective parts of the film result from the characters behaving in ways that could not have been predicted beforehand.

In contrast, *Showman* and *The Beatles* provide good examples of pure cinéma vérité. Directed and produced by Albert and David Maysles, these films have been criticized for their superficiality. But, the Maysleses contend, their vow has been to avoid interfering with the subject during filming; any superficiality, therefore, is inherent in the subject and is inevitably part of the truth that the film depicts.

Robert Drew, Richard Leacock, Donald Pennebaker, and Gregory Shuker have produced many outstanding documentary films under the label The Drew Associates. *On the Pole* depicts the ambitions, anguish, and ultimate failure of an Indianapolis race-car driver named Eddie Sachs. *Primary* concerns the Hubert Humphrey–John F. Kennedy primary contest in Wisconsin. *Crisis* depicts the Robert Kennedy–George Wallace fight over the token integration of the Alabama schools. *The Chair* is about an effort to prevent a young black from going to the electric chair. *Jane* is a portrait of Jane Fonda on the opening night of an unsuccessful play.

Other notable documentaries include Lionel Rogosin's *On the Bowery,* filmed on location in New York City, and Frederick Wiseman's controversial *Titicut Follies, High School,* and *Hospital.* Still others are Allan King's *Warrendale,* which concerns the treatment of emotionally disturbed children, and Frank Simon's *The Queen,* on a beauty contest for transvestites.

In recent years television has provided a ready market for documentaries. A fine example of a television documentary, and one that also makes use of cinéma vérité techniques, is *Royal Family,* produced by a consortium of BBC and England's independent television companies and shown on American television. Richard Cawston served as producer-director, working with an eight-person crew throughout nearly a full year of shooting 43 hours of film. Cawston has attributed the success of this film to the royal family's willingness to talk without restraint, ad-libbing in front of the cameras, with the knowledge that Queen Elizabeth and Prince Philip had the right to veto any sections they found unacceptable in retrospect. "I decided it could be done only with some sense of humor and with a sort of cinéma vérité technique," Cawston has said. "Therefore, nothing was really rehearsed. We would discuss beforehand what would happen, and then simply shoot it. It worked out very well."

Contemporary documentaries made for American commercial television rarely have the political and social impact of earlier programs such as CBS's "The Selling of the Pentagon" and NBC's "Pensions: The Broken Promise." However, "60 Minutes" on CBS-TV, an hour show consisting of three or four shorter documentary-style sequences, has won top ratings, outdrawing popular entertainment shows, and has started a trend toward magazine-type "minidocumentary" shows, many of which are built around personalities and trivia. ABC-TV sought to match the success of "60 Minutes" with "20/20" and NBC-TV offered "Real People."

Arthur Knight has conjectured that, in the near future, regional filmmakers may be celebrating their regions through film as, traditionally, novelists, poets, and musicians have done. Certainly, the field for documentary production is wide open. Invariably, it seems, truth is stranger and more interesting than fiction. As a purveyor of facts and feelings, as a conveyor of an increasingly important photographic reality, and as a molder of public opinion, the documentary film is a powerful force in modern communications.

THE SPONSORED FILM

The term *sponsored* is used as a catch-all description for the thousands of films made for showing to industrial and sales groups, schools and universities, government and community organizations, the armed forces, and professional and religious groups.

A commercial entertainment film is made to earn money at the box office; a sponsored film is created to inform or influence viewers on a special topic. Usually, sponsored films are shown free to audiences. Production and distribution costs are borne by the sponsor, whose cause, whatever it may be, is advanced by showings of the picture. In theatrical films advocacy is uncommon and when present is incidental to the primary purpose of box-office profit. In sponsored films it frequently is the primary purpose. Such advocacy may promote a commercial product or may urge such noncommercial goals as better health practices and in-plant safety.

While not widely publicized, this area of production is booming. It presents substantially greater opportunities than does Hollywood for newcomers with skill and creativity. About 600 established producing and marketing firms for sponsored films operate worldwide; numerous others, often not much more than one-person operations, exist on the fringes. Federal and state governments make many such films.

The creativity and production quality of sponsored films frequently is exceptional, to the point that some have won Academy Awards for short subjects. A few large corporations have released pictures using IMAX 70-mm film, which can be projected on screens up to 75 feet high and 100 feet wide with spectacular effect.

One outstanding example of ingenuity is the General Motors film *Ballet Robotique*. Filmed in a Chevrolet plant, the short picture explains how automatic machines have changed automobile production. This cleverly edited film shows robots at work, with their actions coordinated to music performed by the Royal Philharmonic Orchestra. Not a word of narration is used.

Nontheatrical filmmaking is heavily financed by American industry, which has found in this type of motion picture a highly effective means of presenting its purposes, methods, and achievements. Approximately 15,000 nontheatrical films are produced each year. Most are on 16-mm film, the standard size for projection by small and portable machines. A few of the more elaborate are made on 35 mm, some even for wide-screen projection. This total includes some 9400 business and industrial pictures, 1900 government films, 1700 educational films, 250 for medical and health use, 300 for community organizations, and 150 religious films. Nearly $1.7 billion is being spent annually to produce these films and for other audiovisual aids, such as filmstrips, slides, and equipment. Some sponsored films are released in videocassette form.

The price of making and distributing a good company film averages $200,000, with some major productions exceeding $500,000. As many as 200 prints are made for some films to satisfy the demand. The average total audience for such a film is estimated to be 1.5 million. Many educational and instructional films are produced on far smaller budgets, some of them only a few thousand dollars, and are shown to more limited audiences.

Production of educational and informational films began with the development of the 16-mm portable projector in 1923. At present more than 750,000 projectors are in use in the United States, mostly in schools and businesses, but also in clubs, libraries, homes, and churches. There are 2600 film libraries in the United States, distributing 16-mm films. *The H.W. Wilson Educational Film Guide* lists more than 20,000 films that can be borrowed.

Although a few films include "hard-sell" material, most sponsor messages are subdued, often consisting of little more than name identification and discreet image-building. Perhaps the most widely viewed company film ever produced, still in free distribution after more than 25 years and seen by more than 200 million people, barely mentions the sponsor's name. This is *The Mayflower Story,* about the 1957 transatlantic voyage of *Mayflower II,* a replica of the pilgrims' ship. A moving company, Aero Mayflower Transit, owns and distributes the picture. The only commercial mention is a brief shot showing cargo from the little wooden vessel being loaded into company vans, plus a one-sentence credit line at the close. Nevertheless, the name association with the adventurous ship has brought much business to the moving company.

JOB OPPORTUNITIES IN FILM

Breaking into commercial entertainment filmmaking requires technical knowledge, a creative flair, and often a stroke of good luck. Since the major studios and independent producers make only about 500 films a year, their need for writers, directors, producers, and other innovative talent obviously is limited. Work on production of television shows and commercials is another goal for properly trained beginners. As just described, sponsored films offer another, broader, point of entry into the industry.

Competition for jobs is intense. Approximately 900 U.S. colleges and universities offer film or television courses; a survey in 1980 by the American Film Institute reported 35,000 students enrolled in these courses. Three film schools in the Los Angeles area—University of Southern California, UCLA, and the American Film Institute—are especially popular because of their proximity to Hollywood production. Only 98 graduate students were admitted to the UCLA cinema school out of 800 applicants in a typical recent year. Total enrollment at the USC film school averages 600. An increase in the number of films being made and the heavy emphasis on youth-oriented movies recently have led Hollywood producers to hire a larger number of writers directly from these and other film schools.

Women have had an especially difficult time breaking into motion picture production, but the situation is improving slowly. A few such as Martha Coolidge, Joan Tewksbury, and Amy Heckerling have reached the top as successful directors of feature pictures; others are earning attention as directors in television. At the craft level, women gradually are pushing through the traditionally all-male union barriers to work as camera operators, lighting specialists, and assistant directors. Others are successful as writers.

By working first in television or sponsored films in minor jobs, or making self-financed personal films, women can accumulate examples of their skill to use in seeking higher level positions. Prospects are better with independent movie producers than at major studios. The organization, Women in Film, helps aspirants find jobs.

For those who break into salaried jobs, the pay compares favorably with that in other mass communication industries and professions, and almost limitless financial returns may be achieved by highly creative, productive, and lucky individuals. In no area of mass communications is success less predictable and the potential rewards greater.

Video

"Let's Rent a Movie"

A cardboard cutout of Rambo stands guard, his machine gun pointed at the cashier. Brightly illustrated boxes resembling book jackets line the shelves.

This is video a la carte. In the store, as in thousands more across the country, home viewers rent or buy videocassette movies for their evening's entertainment.

A mishmash of films awaits their choice, a catch-all collection of new movies and old ones. Recent hot box office favorites mingle with long-vanished pictures dragged from studio vaults to satisfy the enormous appetite of the home video audience.

Strange shelf-mates appear: *Cattle Queen of Montana,* an almost forgotten 1950s Western starring Ronald Reagan, stands next to *Clockwork Orange,* a controversial sex-and-violence shocker. The Orson Welles classic, *Citizen Kane,* rubs shoulders with *Creepers,* a horror film whose box proclaims, "It will make your skin crawl." Alongside the memorable *High Noon* with Gary Cooper and Grace Kelly (1952) is the sleazy *Hellcat Female Mud Wrestlers,* whose skin is too slippery to crawl.

On nearby shelves are stacked hundreds of X-rated films even the most liberal cable television channel won't show. A few how-to information videotapes are available, too.

That is video: something for everyone, to be viewed at home in privacy. Owners of videocassettes cheer it. Theater owners hate it.

*F*irst came the half-inch-wide videotape. Then came the videocassette recorder, a machine into which the tape is inserted. When the recorder was attached to a television set, and a button pushed, the pictures captured on the tape appeared on the TV screen with sound. Thus was born the video industry, the newest and fastest-growing form of mass communication.

Some commentators call the system "home video," because the choose-it-yourself programming it provides is viewed primarily on television sets in the home. Others call it "a-la-carte" video because users rent or buy movies and other prerecorded tapes in stores and take them home for viewing.

This chapter examines the enormous growth of the video industry—how it developed, how its marketing system operates, and how it has reduced attendance at movie theaters and slowed the growth of pay cable television.

The recording of TV programs for later replay and the viewing of popular movies on tape at home are the principal uses of the videocassette recorder. However, the video industry increasingly provides other forms of taped programming such as self-help, child guidance, education, books on videotape, and political information. We shall discuss these uses and explore unanswered questions facing the swiftly expanding world of video. ◆

VIDEO BURSTS FORTH

Suddenly, in the 1980s, the public's fancy turned to a new method of mass communication called *video,* made possible by a compact electronic machine, the *videocassette recorder* or VCR.

Use of VCRs has opened enormous sources of entertainment and information for viewing in the home. By attaching these machines to television sets, viewers can watch material contained on prerecorded videotapes they have rented or purchased. They can automatically record programs from television and cable channels for replay later at their convenience. And they can show their own homemade videotapes.

This almost unlimited abundance of material, much of which gains entry into the home only through the VCR, has a potential role well beyond video's immediate popularity as a purveyor of Hollywood movies. Its possibilities as an educator and persuader are still being explored.

Video is a hybrid of more traditional methods of communication. The name itself, which derives from the Latin word *vidēre* (to see), was used originally to describe the visual portion of broadcast television. Now it has taken on a life of its own. Video uses the equipment of television to show products of the motion picture industry. Because video offers the same movies as pay television, often sooner and more cheaply, it has cut heavily into the growth of the cable television industry. The tapes video stores rent and sell are packaged to resemble books and increasingly contain material transferred from books (see discussion later in this chapter).

Yet video is more than a borrower. A body of original material available only on videocassettes is growing steadily, going direct from the creator to the home viewer. This is where the most intriguing potential of video lies.

For viewers, video is alluring because it enables them to watch what they wish, when they wish, and to view their favorite tapes over and over again. They can do so in the privacy and comfort of their homes. With video, users control their own viewing without being subjected to the dictates of television programmers.

Convenient for individuals and families as this capability is, it has created a problem whose scope is not yet clear—a decrease in communication with others. In many homes family members expand their heavy daily time commitment to watching television by spending additional hours viewing home video. Those who sit in isolation at home, receiving their impressions of the world primarily from packaged electronic entertainment, lose community awareness and personal contact with individuals outside the family circle.

Participation in such group activities as going to the movies is an expression of the gregarious instincts of people. Mingling with others stimulates the mind, broadens perceptions, and provides impressions that help to form independent opinions and shape living styles. If carried to excess, the habit of being an isolated electronic viewer has a negative effect on the individual and on the process of societal communication.

HOW THE MARKET GREW

Videotape has been in existence as an alternative to film since the late 1950s. For years, however, its use was restricted to professional applications such as shooting news stories for television and making TV commercials. The videocassette recorder, introduced in 1976 and purchased originally by viewers and electronic enthusiasts who could afford it, came into extensive use around 1980 as prices fell. Television fans absent from home when their favorite programs were broadcast discovered the advantage of taping those shows on a VCR. Also, they liked the idea of preserving programs in a video library.

Innovative entrepreneurs wondered, would VCR owners also play videotaped versions of popular movies if they could rent or purchase the tapes? The marketers obtained rights to a few motion pictures and some films no longer covered by copyright restrictions, converted the movies to videotape form, packaged the tape cassettes attractively, and offered them to the public.

The result was spectacular. By 1984 sales of videocassette recorders skyrocketed. During 1985 approximately a million VCRs were sold each month in the United States, and by 1987 trade sources estimated that more than one third of American homes had VCRs. Jack Valenti, president of the Motion Picture Association of America, who watches the video industry closely because of its impact on the movie business, has predicted that 50 to 60 million videocassette recorders will be operating in the United States by 1990. That total is approximately double the number of VCRs in use when he made the prediction early in 1986.

The boom was stimulated by a U.S. Supreme Court decision in 1984 stating that Americans are legally entitled to videotape shows and movies from television for personal use. With a mass market thus hastily created, producers of VCRs and videotapes scrambled to fill the demand. Similar upsurges in popularity of video occurred in Great Britain, on the European continent, in Japan, in the Middle East, and in other areas around the world.

There was a product and a demand. But no obvious sales outlets for videotapes existed in the traditional pattern of American retailing. This void did not last long as video shops blossomed in every city. Supermarkets and department stores installed video departments. By 1986, some 20,000 video rental shops were operating in the United States, roughly the same number as the total of movie screens in the country.

MOVIES IN THE LIVING ROOM

Family shopping lists now include a new element: "Luv, when you go to the market for the eggs and bread, pick up a movie for tonight. Get something exciting and sexy."

Hollywood has penetrated the home, a presence that has altered family life and jarred the motion picture industry. Families have found a new way to entertain and inform themselves; film producers are marveling at their good luck in falling into such a rich new source of income. Yet as they count the dollars rolling in, the producers have a lurking worry. Will the growing popularity of movies at home become so great that eventually many theaters may be forced to close from lack of business?

Theater attendance fell during the middle and late 1980s, simultaneously with the upsurge of videocassette recorder sales. How much of this decline was due to the VCR upsurge and how much was the result of the generally poor quality of new pictures released during the period was debated within the film industry. Most analysts put the majority of the responsibility on the VCRs.

The trade publication *Variety* summarized the trend bluntly: "Forty percent of the films that will be viewed in America in 1986 will be seen on a videocassette recorder. 'VCR dates' are rapidly replacing 'let's go to the movies' as a teenage courting ritual. Teenagers reduced their film attendance by 20 percent in 1985 and tripled their VCR rentals."

The growing home audience has begun to influence the films Hollywood turns out. For years producers concentrated on flashy, sexy, shallow films for the teenagers and young adult customers who were dominating theater audiences. In 1986, however, some astute filmmakers began to issue pictures with greater thematic depth and a higher level of performance aimed at the over-30 age audience sitting at home with their VCRs. Having lived through earlier filmmaking revolutions caused by the advent of sound, color, and television, the industry faced a complex task of adapting its thinking and production to an audience gathered at home in small groups as well as to one assembled in large darkened theaters.

Sex-oriented movies, the outright X-rated pornographic pictures as well as softer R-rated ones, are big attractions in video. Renting or purchasing porn films for home viewing can be done at video stores, although some do keep their X-rated films in semi-enclosed areas restricted to customers aged 18 and over. The availability of pornography in the parlor has caused a widespread closing of adult movie theaters from lack of business and a dropoff in street sales of magazines featuring nude photographs. *Playboy* has attempted to offset this loss by issuing monthly videocassettes of its nude centerfold Playmates simultaneously with their appearance in the magazine.

Of course, movies have been coming into homes for more than 30 years over the broadcast television channels, and more recently over cable television. Movies shown on regular TV are interrupted by commercials, however, and often reduced in length to fit broadcast requirements. Although movies on pay channels are uncut, uncensored, and free of commercials, on any given evening the choice of films is limited.

Even when VCR owners record broadcast TV movies for later replay—an action called *time-shifting*—they can avoid the commercials by "zapping" them with the fast-forward switch that skips over them. This practice disturbs advertisers, who see their expensive messages being blacked out by the audience.

HOW THE INDUSTRY OPERATES

"Going to the movies" at home is easy for VCR owners. They rent or purchase tapes, pop the cassettes into the VCR, and watch the film on the television screen. Behind this simple act, however, is a complicated system of marketing that continues to evolve as the potential of the video field becomes better understood.

Film producers sell the video rights to their pictures to distributors, many of which are divisions of major motion picture companies. A distributor prepares the videotape version of a movie, packages it, and sells copies through wholesalers to the retail video shops. The shopkeeper either sells copies of the film to customers or rents them for a daily fee. As competition has intensified and the supply of available films has multiplied, rental prices have dropped as low as 99 cents a day for nonprime pictures. The film producer usually receives nothing from the rental fees.

At first moviemakers and distributors set high sale prices for videocassettes of their films, around $80 a copy. This price remains in effect for many major new releases. In 1983 Paramount broke new ground by selling the slam-bang adventure movie *Raiders of the Lost Ark* for $24.95, and the mass marketing rush at lower prices was on. *Beverly Hills Cop,* a comedy starring Eddie Murphy, became the first picture to sell more than a million cassettes.

Rentals exceed sales of movies to retail customers seven to one, but this margin may narrow if the producers offer a larger selection of films at reduced prices.

By 1985 sales revenue for moviemakers from videocassettes was second only to their income from theater showings. Films that had lost money or barely broken

A customer decides which motion picture videotape to rent for playing at home on a videocassette recorder. Thousands of video stores opened during the mid-1980s to rent or sell tapes when the VCR won swift acceptance as a home entertainment machine. (Strickler, Monkmeyer)

even in theaters became profitable with income from video sales. Some actually earned more from cassettes than from the theater box office. Some enthusiastic business observers predicted that by 1990 video income for the entire industry would match or exceed box office revenue.

VIDEO INFLUENCES FILM PRODUCTION

Financially, the home video market significantly affects the planning and production of today's movies. Often video rights to a picture are sold by the producer before the cameras roll and help pay for the film's production. The Sylvester Stallone blockbuster *Rambo* is an example of this system. When it was released in video early in 1986, a million-dollar promotional drive heralded its appearance in video stores.

By 1986 the major distributors, enthralled by the profit potential, began applying high-powered promotional techniques to selling videocassettes of big movies. The promotions were similar to those employed for original theatrical releases. CBS-Fox Video, largest of the distributors, conducted a $2 million advertising campaign for the video version of the space adventure *Return of the Jedi*.

With VCR owners hungry for tapes to view, motion picture studios and television show producers dug deep into their files for old material to package and release. Hundreds of long-forgotten movies returned to life. Adventure series, situation comedies, and collections of music videos that had disappeared from the television screens were resurrected and distributed as videocassettes. In fact, a two-hour videotape of the popular NBC police show "Miami Vice" appeared while the TV series still was running in network prime-time.

To learn how large the loosely organized supply of video material had become, the National Video Clearinghouse took a survey in late 1985. It found 40,111 video titles on the market, of which 8,575 were theatrical movies, enough to fill 18 months of around-the-clock viewing time. The other titles included an array of training, sales, educational, inspirational, and similar special-interest material. As many as 400 new titles a month were being issued.

The raid on the motion picture libraries largely depleted the backlog accumulated for 50 years or more. In the latter portion of the 1980s, theatrical releases were mostly of recent films.

While producers enjoyed their bonus profits, theater operators grumbled because home viewing cut into their income. Their particular complaint was about the "window," the length of time between the original release of a movie to theaters and its subsequent release for home viewing. Filmmakers established a six-month window, and a survey by the National Association of Theatre Owners showed that this time span was being quite well observed. Many theater operators contended, however, that the period for exclusive showing should be longer. Movies generally are released in cassette six to eight months before they are shown on the pay cable channels.

Moviemakers in turn complain about widespread pirating of their films, especially in foreign countries. Highly organized rings of pirates make illegal videocassette prints either by gaining possession of a theatrical print or taping the movie as it is shown in a theater. The videotapes are shipped around the world.

A leader of the Motion Picture Association of America's anti-piracy campaign reported that unauthorized videotapes of major new American movies are distributed in Thailand within four days after the movies open in the United States. A trace put on the film *Rocky IV* showed that after the pirated version reached Thailand, copies with local subtitles were sent from there to Malaysia and Singapore; from Singapore copies went to Jordan, then to Turkey, where Turkish subtitles were substituted and copies sent to Turkish workers in Germany. Some producers place a secret marking code on each theatrical print in an effort to find where the thievery occurs.

VIDEO'S OTHER ROLES

Video is best known for entertainment, through the showing of movies and television programs. Because their potential is still being tested, the roles of video as educator, stimulator of psychological and physical self help, and commercial and political persuader are even more provocative.

The National Video Clearinghouse survey reported that slightly more than 20 percent of video viewing time was spent watching nonentertainment tapes. As releases of movies on tape began to slow, an upsurge in special interest tapes become evident, with material drawn from a wide range of fields. Often these informational tapes are viewed in meeting rooms by professional, student, community service, and other groups concerned with the particular subject matter.

SELF-HELP AND HOW-TO TAPES

Jane Fonda scored the first mass market success in nonentertainment video with her "Jane Fonda Workout" videotape. In thousands of homes, muscles ached and pounds vanished as viewers dutifully followed the aerobic exercises of the svelte actress. Four more Fonda workout programs followed.

Julia Childs, the gourmet cook, lured some of those pounds back onto hips and thighs with her videotaped cooking demonstrations, also a hit in early video.

The following sample of self-help tapes indicates the range of material available:

"How to Legally Ax Your Taxes," a 90-minute explanation of how to save money on income taxes, sold for $39.95 through advertisements on television news shows.

"Bring Out the Best in Your Children" and "Create Success from Disappointment," inspirational self-realization tapes designed for home and office use by business executives.

"Wok Before You Run," a comedy cooking videotape.

"Running Great with Grete Waltz," in which the Norwegian woman marathon star gives training tips and a demonstration of long-distance running methods.

Already famous as actress and political activist, Jane Fonda won a large new following with release of her exercise routines on videotape. Jane Fonda's Workout *was among the first big-selling how-to videotapes to reach the videocassette recorder market. Later she made follow-up versions. (Shapiro/Sygma)*

"Mr. Boston Official Video Bartender's Guide," an hour-long video presentation in which bartenders from famous bars demonstrate their techniques.

CHILDREN'S PROGRAMS

Inevitably called *kid vid,* more than 2000 video titles for children were on the market by 1987. Although many were cartoons from the movies and television, as well as such entertainment films as the classic Disney movies, a large and growing body of material is designed to instruct young viewers. Usually the information is delivered in an entertaining manner.

Examples of informational videocassettes for children include:

"Draw and Color Your Very Own Cartoons Along With Uncle Fred."

"Bill Cosby's Picturepages."

"Strong Kids, Safe Kids," a lesson in avoiding abuse of children by strangers, starring Henry Winkler and cartoon characters. Taking advantage of the stop-start feature of videocassette recorders, Winkler at several points tells his juvenile viewers, "Stop the tape now and talk to your mom or dad."

"America," a lesson in American history teaching the dangers of war given by Kurtis Blow to a classroom of ethnically mixed children. Footage of historical figures and scenes flashes on a video screen behind Blow as he sings.

EDUCATION

The use of videotape as a teaching tool is obvious, and its appearance in the classroom, in study at home, and before professional groups is expanding.

A frequent criticism of the televised or videotaped classroom lecture is that students cannot interrupt with questions, as most instructors permit them to do in live lectures. This difficulty has been overcome in some classes by having instructors or teaching assistants stop the tapes at critical points for questions and discussion.

At Stanford University, for example. 27 graduate engineers from the Hewlett-Packard electronics firm completed a semester-long course in computer science in two weeks by using VCR tapes of lectures by eminent engineering scholars. A graduate student tutor answered questions during halts in the tape.

At the Bloomington campus of Indiana University, a troublesome campus problem, sexual harassment, was examined in a videotape that was sold to other universities at cost. On the tape female students described problems they had faced, and a panel discussed ways in which to deal with harassment. The U.S. Department of Education underwrote the production.

Closely related to education is use of videotapes in legal proceedings. Approximately 40 states permit cameras to record courtroom action; also, numerous judges will accept carefully prepared videotapes of depositions, reconstructions of incidents, and summaries of a plaintiff's case. Such taping can save the courts' time. Often it is expensive, however, and critics are concerned that affluent plaintiffs who can afford the expense may have an advantage over opponents who cannot.

Use of videotaped testimony by child victims in molestation cases, in order to spare them the psychological ordeal of testifying in open court, has been sharply debated by the legal profession. Some attorneys contend that this method is unfair to defendants because their attorneys lack adequate opportunity to discredit the children's testimony in face-to-face questioning. Trial judges face a delicate problem of balancing the welfare of child witnesses against the rights of defendants.

BOOKS

The wedding of book publishing (printed words and still pictures) to video (spoken words and moving pictures) has taken place, but the partners are uncertain how the marriage will develop. Stakes are high, but many persons involved in the world of books are unenthusiastic about the pairing. Because viewing and listening require less mental challenge than reading, they worry that children will fail to develop reading skills and adults will allow theirs to stagnate.

Simon & Schuster became the first major publishing house to enter the video market, in 1984, with taped versions of books, especially of the how-to variety. The publishing house also created new material for video, including a 45-minute tape made in association with the American Cancer Society titled "How to Quit Smoking."

At the juvenile level, the producer of the popular Little Golden Books, Western Publishing, issued several of its volumes for small children in videocassette versions.

Experiments in marketing book videotapes through bookstores have been made, with varying results. Publishers have searched their backlists for titles that might effectively be converted to video form.

During the second half of the 1980s, numerous public and academic libraries have added videocassettes to their services. Public libraries circulate cassettes of popular movies just as they do books, except that the loan periods are shorter. About 70 percent of the libraries surveyed by *Library Journal* reported circulating cassettes free to users; others charged fees comparable to those of commercial video stores.

Some librarians are less than pleased about providing this service, although it draws patrons who did not previously use a library. They complain about the lack of good educational titles in videocassette form and point out that cassette borrowers primarily want entertainment films. One unhappy librarian told *Library Journal,* "The predominance of public preference is for slash-and-scream movies. It is more like a supermarket than a library."

ADVERTISING AND PUBLIC RELATIONS

Whenever a large audience exists, advertisers ask themselves, "How can we get our messages to this group?" Their entry into video has been cautious. Recognizing that hard-sell commercials included on entertainment or informational tapes probably would turn away a large portion of viewers, advertisers have used a soft approach comparable to that seen on public television. They attempt to deliver a message and gain awareness without creating resentment.

One example of this method is the video version of the popular book *Eat to Win* by Robert Haas. The Red Lion restaurant chain partially financed the tape. In return, some scenes were shot in a Red Lion location and an understated Red Lion commercial message appeared at the beginning. Another method is a home video instructional cassette about using video cameras, "How to Shoot Like a Pro," cosponsored by Sony Corporation. Brief mentions of two Sony cameras and visual references to the company occur in the tape. Such "sponsored" videos probably will become more common. New ground was broken in 1987 when a commercial for Diet Pepsi was inserted at the beginning of the video version of the popular Paramount film, *Top Gun*.

POLITICS

Delivery by videotape of political messages on the home screen and to selected groups is a form of advocacy so new and experimental that its power is undetermined. When a political argument can be made effectively in visual form, the potential appears strong.

The most provocative early use of videotaped politics took place in California during the 1986 re-election campaign of state Supreme Court Chief Justice Rose Bird. A drive to oust the justice developed because she had led the court in reversing dozens of death sentence convictions, often on narrow technical grounds. The anti-Bird campaign was led in part by a group of ultraconservative state legislators and special interest organizations.

This group produced a 28-minute videotape including graphic descriptions of several murder cases in which the death verdicts were overturned. The tape quoted a county prosecutor about the court: "It's the laughing stock of the United States."

The sponsoring group announced that it was distributing up to 10,000 copies of the tape to video rental outlets, libraries, private individuals, law enforcement officials, and community organizations. Production expense was $30,000 plus the cost of the cassettes, a relatively moderate investment in the high stakes maneuvering of California politics.

On television, political advocacy is subject to the Fairness Doctrine, which gives the criticized party the right to respond to attacks made in news stories and editorials. Whether they realize it or not, TV viewers are conditioned by that ruling to expect even-handedness on the TV screen and tend to give high believability to what they see.

It is doubtful that a commercial television station would sell time for a tape like that against Rose Bird. Yet recipients of the anti-Bird tape were free to watch it unchallenged and unanswered on those same TV screens.

The anti-Bird video contained an important error of fact, asserting wrongly that one convicted murderer whose case was overturned was "a free man," when actually he was in jail awaiting retrial. The sponsors promised to correct the error in later distributions of the tape. When the police chief of Lodi showed the video to a mandatory departmental training session, the police union publicly protested that the officers had been used as a captive audience for political purposes. A spokesperson for Bird contended that showing the videotape under such circumstances raised serious legal and ethical questions.

After Bird's defeat in the election, political strategists debated how effectively the videotape had influenced voters, how well it was distributed, and how its rather heavy-handed approach could be refined for future political use.

Printed campaign material comes into homes in similarly unrestricted form, but the known free distribution of printed matter often causes recipients to discount some of its political claims.

UNANSWERED QUESTIONS

The explosive growth of video inevitably has created unanswered questions of a social nature, as well as commercial and technical ones, some of them partially concealed by the excitement surrounding the form.

Will excessive watching of electronic material in private isolate viewers from normal participation in the affairs of society? At a time when almost fanatical involvement in single-purpose political and social causes strains our national fabric, the retreat of large numbers of individuals into static nonparticipation could seriously undercut the breadth of citizen action that traditionally has brought balance to the democratic system of government.

Will dependence upon packaged electronic visual material for entertainment and instruction deprive children and adults alike of the desire to read? The amount of illiteracy already is distressingly high in the United States, for a country so richly endowed, and millions of people are almost functionally illiterate, barely able to conduct the simple business of everyday life. This situation will become worse if today's children are lured away from the stimulation and pleasure of reading by a surfeit of visual material that requires minimal mental exertion to watch.

Will public interest in video decrease as the novelty wears off? Wary electronic specialists remember the sensational growth, then the abysmal collapse, of the video game market. That episode probably is not relevant to the whole field of video; the diversity of material it provides and the convenience of home viewing and taping are strong supporting forces. Although VCR sales may slow as demand is met, industry specialists foresee continued growth throughout the late 1980s until more than 50 percent of American homes would have VCRs in the early 1990s.

Will the technical conflict be solved? Purchasers of VCRs have been confused because two conflicting types of machines have been on the market, Betamax and the much more popular VHS, and tapes made for one cannot be played on the other. Still a third type, the 8mm video cameras and recorders, reached the market in late 1985. They use videocassettes about as small as the familiar audiocassettes, and an international agreement has set uniform standards for their production.

The most popular early form of 8mm equipment has been the so-called camcorder, a lightweight (about four pounds) combination of camera and videotape recorder that films home movies on a cassette and also can be connected to a television set to record programs for replay. Adoption of the 8mm format was limited in the years immediately after its introduction by its cost and by the small number of prerecorded movies and informational tapes available in 8mm size.

Some electronics experts believe that 8mm equipment ultimately will replace both Beta and VHS systems, while others see it more as a supplement than a replacement.

Will marketing methods improve? Retail video shops carry a relatively small range of tapes for rent or sale, predominantly popular movies. Persons wishing to obtain specialized videotapes often have difficulty in doing so. Catalogs, direct mail offers, and television commercials are in use as marketing methods.

Can a system of audience measurement be devised? Statistics are available on sales and rentals of videotapes, and the Nielsen service samples the amount of time VCRs are used each month to record programs from television channels. Detailed information is not available, however, on the crucial question of how frequently the prerecorded commercial tapes and home-recorded TV shows are actually watched by viewers. One estimate, offered by Valenti, was that the average household with a VCR watched prerecorded movies and playbacks of home-taped television programs six hours a week. Although such estimates are loose at best, clearly the use of home video occupies a portion of a family's time previously devoted to other activities. Lack of detailed, reliable audience data discourages some commercial interests from entering the field.

THREE TRENDS

To summarize, the field of video is so new that even persons deeply involved in it hesitate to describe the shape it will take during the next decade. Three trends, however, seem to be fairly certain:

- The number of homes with videocassette recorders will continue to grow. Predictions within the electronic industry that 50 percent of American homes will have a VCR by the early 1990s appear to be reasonable.
- Original programming—that is, material created especially for VCR viewing as contrasted with repackaged movies and television shows—will increase markedly.
- Use of videotape cassettes for educational, sales, and promotional purposes, still in its infancy, will take creative new forms. Men and women who can develop ingenious ideas for video content and marketing have exciting possibilities for success.

Photographic and

Graphics Communications

Electronic Wizardry

Two Egyptian pyramids in a color photo were too far apart. An artist waved a magic wand. Presto! One pyramid moved nearer the other. The result: A perfect cover picture for the February 1982 issue of *National Geographic.*

The sky over the Atlantic Ocean was dark in an AP color photo of the Challenger shuttle explosion in 1986. Presto! In several newspapers the sky appeared bright blue.

In both instances the magic wand was the pointing device on a computer. By touching any of the thousands of tiny *pixels* on a screen an operator may easily move, clone, delete, or combine objects with others. Colors may be changed, physical features altered, people removed or added.

It's a frightening new world for people who have always felt they could trust what they saw in a photograph. And it raises questions about the inherent credibility of photojournalism.

"This new technology has the potential of undermining our faith in photography as a reflection of reality," Edward Klein, editor of the New York *Times Magazine,* told *Folio* magazine.

Newspaper editors and photographers interviewed in a survey agreed that they would never alter a news or documentary picture. But they disagreed on whether feature section photo-illustrations and advertising photos could be changed. Use of the new technology is being closely monitored.

"I'm never going to move a pyramid," declared Jackie Green of *USA Today.* "I'd rather move the photographer. . . ."

*T*he advent of electronically operated cameras accompanied a surge in the use of striking and informative graphics in the newspaper, magazine, television, video, and movie industries during the 1980s. The computer was the primary transforming agent.

Swirling, bouncing three-dimensional and other special effects brought new excitement to many movies and videos and to television commercials and logos.

Digitized photographs and art work, as well as textual materials, were sent around the world in seconds. Computer operators learned that they could effect almost any changes to the images on their screens. At the same time many major newspapers improved their visual appearance through expanded use of graphics and color.

Modern still photography, and the motion picture as well, had come into being a hundred years earlier. The invention of small cameras in the 1920s enabled photographers to take many pictures, rapidly, in low-level lighting conditions. Picture magazines flourished. Other inventions, including magnetic videotape, new cameras and lenses, laser technology, and digital processing, transmission, and storage, brought photocommunication to its present stages.

In this chapter we trace the development of photography and photojournalism, describe modern techniques in both photography and graphics, and relate the opportunities and working conditions of visual mass communicators. ◆

THE VISUAL DIMENSION

Photographic communication has grown dramatically in recent decades as a key mode of mass communication. It was joined in the 1980s by exciting new forms of graphics communication in the print media, television, video, and motion pictures. Together they offered a greatly expanded visual dimension for readers and viewers, achieving in the print media strong impact through color, description, and detail, and in television, video, and the movies dramatic new three-dimensional art forms and other special effects.

The art of telling a story with still and motion pictures, and with graphs, maps, and other such devices, developed centuries later than the technique of telling it with words. Photographic equipment was relatively slow to become available, and those who used visual techniques needed time to develop the editorial methods of photo and graphics communication. The rapid development of new technologies, particularly in the 1980s, and of comprehension of how to use these sophisticated new tools, however, has made pictorial and design creations a fundamental mode of mass communication.

Photojournalism for newspapers and magazines developed rapidly during the 1930s, keyed by the development of the 35-mm camera and the birth of the picture magazines *Life* and *Look*. Film was first used in the motion picture theater to provide entertainment, news, and documentaries. In the mid-1950s film was joined by videotape, which gradually became the dominant ingredient of televised news, public affairs, and documentary communication. Photojournalism thus has expanded in concept and function and today is part of the larger field known as *photographic communication,* which serves advertising and other purposes as well.

Fewer than 150 years elapsed from the moment when the first photographic image was produced until a fascinated world watched astronauts Neil Armstrong and Edwin Aldrin transmit a live television picture from the surface of the moon. In that century and a half the growth of photography as a medium of communication was spectacular. But in the years following 1969, the image became even more important both in print media and on the screen. A new wave of picture agencies gave newspapers and magazines searching and revealing visual reporting and spectacular, compelling, on-the-spot coverage. Presidential elections hinged on the perceptions Americans gained from television screens—images rather than words. New graphics art forms enhanced movie and television presentations. And by 1986 individual Americans, according to industry sources, were taking as many as 12 billion pictures a year.

HOW PHOTOGRAPHY DEVELOPED

Pioneering Photography

Joseph Nicéphore Nièpce, a retired French lithographer, began searching for a method to capture the photographic image in 1813. Three years later he is believed to have succeeded in producing a negative image, but he could only partially

Still and television photographers crowded into an assigned space cover a news story. Such concentrations, joined by similar throngs of reporters, sometimes cause complaints about "pack journalism." (Franklyn/Sygma)

fix the image after exposure—that is, desensitize it to light. In 1826 he made a photograph on a pewter plate showing a view from his workroom window. He called this process Heliographie (sun drawing).

Photography took a significant step forward with the creation of the Daguerreotype by another Frenchman, Louis Jacques Mandé Daguerre, in 1839. In this process an invisible (latent) image was developed by using mercury vapor. The exposure time was reduced from eight hours to 30 minutes, giving photography a practical application. The Daguerreotype process had three major limitations: (1) The image could be only the size of the plate in the camera; (2) the image was unique in itself and could be duplicated only by reshooting; and (3) the image was a *negative,* coated on a mirrored metallic surface, so a viewer could see it as a *positive* only if the mirror reflected a dark background.

Many of the early photographers were artists. Among them was Samuel F. B. Morse, inventor of the telegraph, who learned the new process from Daguerre himself in Paris. Daguerre spent almost a year demonstrating the technique to artists and scientists. Morse sent back to the United States a description of the process, which was widely published in newspapers. He is credited with making the first Daguerreotype portrait in America when he photographed his family in 1839.

Wet Plates

Another important approach to photography was the collodion wet plate process, developed in 1851 by Frederick Scott Archer, an English sculptor. The process required the coating of a glass plate with a light-sensitive solution that had to be kept wet until exposed in the camera and processed in a darkroom. Very sharp paper prints could be made from a collodion negative. A photographer could use this process outdoors to record exposures of only ten seconds to a minute, a spectacular improvement in photographic speed. The photographer was required, however, to work from a portable darkroom on location.

It was with this wet plate process, so clumsy by modern standards, that Mathew Brady and his assistants produced magnificent photographs of the Civil War. He sent out 20 teams of photographers, led by Timothy O'Sullivan and Alexander Gardner, who followed the Union soldiers onto the battlefields and into their bivouacs. The Brady team's photographs have preserved for posterity a fascinating record of the war. For the first time, photography proved its value as a news medium.

Flexible Film and New Cameras

The next leap forward, opening the door for modern photography, came in 1889 when the Eastman Kodak Company, headed by George Eastman, introduced a transparent film on a flexible support. Creation of this film made the motion picture possible. It increased the picture-taking possibilities for still photographers, too; they could use smaller cameras and were no longer burdened with heavy glass plates.

In 1912 the famous Speed Graphic press camera, which was to become the workhorse for news photographers for a half-century, was introduced. The small camera came into use in America in the 1920s. Ernst Leitz's Leica, a German camera using 35-mm film, was followed by another German make, the Rolleiflex, a larger 2¼ × 2¼ camera. Both remain popular in professional circles today, along with Japanese and other cameras.

The small camera freed the photographer from carrying bulky film or plate holders. It enabled him or her to operate less obtrusively, to take 36 pictures in rapid succession, and to use the fast lens to take pictures without flash in low-level lighting situations. The pictures were thus less formal, more candid, and honest. A German lawyer, Dr. Erich Salomon, who declared himself to be the first photojournalist, began using such a camera in 1928, photographing European nobility. Two other Europeans who influenced the development of photojournalism were Stefan Lorant, who edited German and English illustrateds, and Alfred Eisenstaedt, a West Prussian, who moved from the Berlin office of the Associated Press to become one of *Life* magazine's first photographers.

Color photography became a commercial reality when the Eastman Kodak Company announced development of its Kodachrome color film in 1935. In the same year the first motion picture in Technicolor, a high-fidelity color process, was presented on the American screen.

Two more fundamental breakthroughs in photographic equipment followed World War II. In 1947 Edwin H. Land introduced the Polaroid system for producing a positive black-and-white print 60 seconds after exposure. Soon this time was reduced to 10 seconds. Then in 1963 a 50-second Polaroid color print process opened new avenues for amateurs and professionals alike. The second of these breakthroughs, as previously stated, came in the mid-1950s: the recording of moving pictures on *magnetic videotape*. This was an electronic approach; all the other advances in the photographic process had depended on chemistry. Electronic photography will be discussed later in this chapter.

Early Newspaper Photography

From a mass communications viewpoint, taking good photographs in the 1860s was not enough: a way had to be found to reproduce them in newspapers and magazines. Woodcuts had been used in the Civil War period, but they were slow to produce, expensive, and not exact. A direct photographic method was needed.

This was achieved by two men working separately, each of whom developed a *halftone photoengraving* technique. Frederic Eugene Ives produced a halftone engraving in his laboratory at Cornell University in June 1879, and Stephen Horgan published a photograph "direct from nature" in the New York *Daily Graphic* in March 1880. By the mid-1890s halftone engravings were appearing in supplemental inserts of the New York newspapers, and in 1897 the New York *Tribune* was the first to publish a halftone in the regular pages of a high-speed press run.

During the early years of the twentieth century, pictures in newspapers generally were used singly, to illustrate important stories. The newspaper picture page, making use of special layouts and unusual picture shapes, was developed during

World War I. A major new force in American journalism, the *picture tabloid,* came into being shortly after World War I. In these newspapers with their small page size and flashy makeup, designed to appeal to street sale readers, the photograph was given the dominant position, often overshadowing the text of the news stories. The tabloid front page usually consisted of a headline and a dramatically blown-up news photo.

The New York *Daily News* began publication in 1919, followed by Hearst's *Daily Mirror* and Bernarr Macfadden's *Evening Graphic.* Intense picture competition among these three New York tabloids led at times to the publication of photographs that violated many people's sense of good taste. The *Evening Graphic* illustrated major stories with faked composograph (pasted together) photos, and the *Daily News* shocked readers by printing a full-page photograph of the electrocution of murderer Ruth Snyder. Of these three original New York tabloids, only the *Daily News* survives, still sharply edited but less flamboyant and less a "picture" paper than in its earlier days.

During the 1920s, when the picture newspapers were flourishing, experiments were carried out in transmission of a photographic image by wire and by radio. The first American photos sent by wire were transmitted from Cleveland to New York in 1924. A decade of development passed before the Associated Press established its Wirephoto network on January 1, 1935. Distribution of newsphotos by wire enabled newspapers across the country to publish pictures from other cities only a few hours after they were taken.

The Picture Magazines

The expanded interest in all forms of photographic communication in the 1930s led Time Inc. to establish the weekly picture magazine *Life* in November 1936. *Life* was patterned after photographic publications developed in Germany and England. In 1937 the Cowles organization established *Look,* published every other week and more feature-oriented than *Life,* with less emphasis on news. *Look* ceased publication in 1971 and *Life* followed in 1972. (*Life* was revived, first through special issues and then as a monthly with 1.6 million circulation in 1986.)

Both *Look* and *Life* emphasized editorial research and investigation preceding assignment of photographers to all but spot news stories. Photographers were well briefed as to the significance of a story before arriving on the scene to begin interpreting it with their cameras. In that sense photographers on the two magazines controlled a mind-guided camera.

From the mid-1930s into the 1960s a small group of well-known magazine photographers contributed to the development of the photographic essay and interpretive picture story. Dorothea Lange's sensitive images of America's condition during the Great Depression stand as examples of still photography at its finest. So also do the pictures of Margaret Bourke-White and photographs by Gordon Parks, whose creative abilities transcended the photographic medium to include writing, musical composition, and Hollywood film. During this period Henri Cartier-Bresson, a French photojournalist, defined the *decisive moment,* and Robert Capa demonstrated how the still camera could record the reverberations of war. David Duncan's word-and-picture reports of the Korean War have been matched only by his equally powerful Vietnam War magazine stories and photograph books.

The Picture Agencies

When the great photographic teams developed at *Life* and *Look* dissolved in the wake of the financial crises that forced the closing of the two magazines, there was a slump in photojournalism in America. Some of the photographers and editors migrated to the *National Geographic,* which became a center of photographic communication in the 1970s under the guidance of Robert E. Gilka as the director of staff photographers and freelance assignments. Its circulation was 10.2 million in 1986. Even more spectacular was the rise of the *Smithsonian* magazine. Founded in 1970 by the Smithsonian Society, in Washington, it had more than 2 million circulation in 1986. Edward K. Thompson came from *Life* to make *Smithsonian* a superb example of photographic communication. A highly sophisticated and expensive entry was *Geo,* founded in Germany and introduced in America in the early 1980s.

But none of these publications gave an outlet for the on-the-spot news photography that had made *Life* and *Look* so memorable, and which was still seen in *Paris-Match* and other European picture magazines. The news services, networks, and picture agencies such as Black Star were at work, but falling short of the tradition of the 1950s and 1960s.

Filling the gap in the 1970s and 1980s was a group of new picture agencies, strongly European based, devoted both to photojournalism and to high-level action news photography. One was Contact, developed by Robert Pledge and including such photographers as Eddie Adams, David Hume Kennerly, Annie Leibovitz, and David Burnett. Another was Sipa, French based and represented in the United States by international picture agencies such as Black Star and its director, Jocelyne Benzakin, with Charles Steiner and Maggie Steber as leading photographers. Gamma, a European leader directed in New York by Jennifer Coley, scored with Matthew Naythons's Guyana suicide story photos. Sygma, Paris based, had Elaine Laffont in New York as director. All had crews of photographers available for assignments on contract with *Time, Newsweek,* and the revived *Life.* Their picture essays were marketed at high prices; Naythons's Guyana pictures earned $250,-000 for Gamma.

Motion Pictures

In 1891, only two years after Eastman's development of flexible film, Thomas A. Edison developed the kinetoscope, thereby laying the foundation for the motion picture (see Chapter 10). The kinetoscope was a motion picture projector designed to show still pictures in rapid succession to produce the visual illusion of motion on a screen in a darkened room.

The Lumiere brothers presented the first public performance of a motion picture for pay in the Grand Cafe of Paris in 1895. Edison made jerky, primitive motion pictures of President William McKinley's inauguration in 1896, Admiral Dewey at Manila in 1898, and McKinley's speech in Buffalo, New York, shortly before his assassination in 1901. William Randolph Hearst personally took motion pictures of action in Cuba during the Spanish-American War. These early efforts showed the motion picture's potential as a recorder of history. Exhibition of commercial motion picture films began with regularity about 1900.

Edison's pioneer efforts at recording news events on film led within a few years to creation of the *newsreel,* a standard short item on virtually every motion picture theater program for half a century until the faster news coverage of television drove the last one out of business during the 1960s. The first regular newsreel series is credited to the Pathé "Journal" of 1907. Among the familiar newsreel names in American theaters were Pathé, Fox Movietone News, Metrotone, and International Newsreel.

The *documentary* film, a more elaborate method of recording the lives and activities of real people, had its start in 1922. Hired by a New York fur company to film the life of an Eskimo family, Robert Flaherty overcame great technological difficulties in the Arctic climate to produce *Nanook of the North.* From this film developed the documentary tradition that has given filmmaking some of its finest products.

During the Depression years Pare Lorentz produced *The Plow That Broke the Plains* for the Farm Security Administration (FSA) in the same spirit of the FSA team of photo documentarians who, under the guidance of Roy E. Stryker, made more than 272,000 negatives and 150,000 prints of the United States and its dustbowls and migratory workers. Lorentz's 1937 film, *The River,* visualized the problems of erosion in the Mississippi River basin with more power than his previous documentary had.

A third form of factual storytelling on film, halfway between the newsreel and documentary, was *The March of Time,* a weekly *news magazine of the screen.* Started by Time Inc. in 1935, it played for 16 years. At its peak in the late 1930s and the early years of World War II, it was seen by audiences of nearly 20 million per week in more than 9000 American theaters. Louis de Rochemont, the producer, used real events and actors, skillfully blended, to present an interpretive account of an event in relation to its background.

When television became a commercial force in the late 1940s, the tools and techniques developed by the motion picture industry were adopted for presenting news on television. A motion picture camera was relatively small and portable, and film shot at news events could be shown on the television screen. Until remote telecasting became technically practical, visual presentation of on-the-spot news had to be done with motion picture film, but this medium has been almost entirely replaced by videotape.

The television documentary became an established part of the networks' programming. Some outstanding examples have been CBS's "The Selling of the Pentagon" and its "Hunger in America," done in the tradition of Edward R. Murrow's earlier documentary, "Harvest of Shame"; NBC's documentary on chemical and biological warfare, "The Battle of Newburgh," shown on its "White Paper" series; and a religious documentary, "A Time for Burning," aired over many educational stations. CBS's "60 Minutes" and ABC's "20/20" reflect another documentary trend. Under the tyranny of the ratings system, the number of documentaries on commercial television declined during the 1980s.

THE ELECTRONIC REVOLUTION

As the photographic world moved from its mechanical and chemical base into the electronic era, a multitude of inventions and new processes strongly affected individual photography and the field of mass communications.

Cameras

New technological devices greatly increased the sale of 35-mm cameras in the latter part of the 1980s. The models could do everything—load the film, wind it to the next picture, set the exposure, focus, and unwind the film. These automatic features relied heavily on sophisticated electronic circuits and motors built into the camera. Everything was electronic except the film, and that was soon to change.

Eastman Kodak introduced a new line of cameras, recorders, and accessories that adapted the television set to a range of new roles. The set serves as a screen for viewing photographs and home movies made with a videotape camera; a substitute for the darkroom that makes prints electronically; a movie lab for adding sound to home videotape and creating programs that mix still and video pictures; an electronic family album or picture archive of still and video motion pictures; a utilizer of the floppy disc; and a source of near-instant still photographs.

Sony perfected its new Mavica (MA-gnetic Vi-deo CA-mera) system. Images are recorded on miniature diskettes by analog video, not digital, means. (The *analog* method uses changes in electrical voltages to create sound and pictures; *digital* devices translate signals into binary and decimal notations.) No processing is required. Users slip the diskette into a viewer for display on a TV monitor, after which a printer can produce a color picture in about a minute. The images also may be transmitted over phone lines anywhere in the world.

A number of other companies produced cameras capable of these or other new electronic operations.

The Electronic Darkroom

The global news services for many years have conducted and sponsored research into the making and transmission of photographs, as well as news stories and other materials, by digital means. A breakthrough occurred in the late 1970s when Bell Laboratories invented an electronic chip capable of recording images electronically.

As research accelerated, the Associated Press introduced its *electronic darkroom.* Under the system a picture can be sent electronically to the AP's offices or directly to the print and broadcast media. There, under a system known as *image processing,* an editor can crop (by maneuvering horizontal and vertical lines on the screen) and enlarge or reduce the desired portion. The photo also can be

Shown is driver Mert Littlefield of Buena Park, California, in a car crash that took place during a qualifying run in the N.H.R.A.'s 24th Annual Winternationals in Pomona, California, in February 1984. This photograph demonstrates the use of laser technology that enables the Associated Press to transmit photographs almost immediately. (Courtesy of Associated Press)

enhanced by brightening or darkening certain portions and can even be combined with other photos to produce composite pictures. The refining of the image can be carried on at the level of the individual *pixel,* the tiny dot that by the multi-thousands comprises the image.

The ease with which minute or wholesale digitized portions of a photo may be altered, or the picture combined with others, has raised the specter of the future loss of credibility for all published photos. Sheila Reaves, a visiting lecturer at the University of Wisconsin at Madison, conducted the survey mentioned in the vignette preceding this chapter. Concluded Reaves: "Will readers be able to make distinctions between a newspaper's handling of feature photography and news photography as easily as some editors do? If not, newspapers may risk losing the public's trust in all photography."

In 1987 United Press International introduced its Pyxys system, using satellites and electronic workstations to deliver and manipulate digital information. The system transmits pictures, sound, and text in digital form to newspapers and to television and radio stations, and also is an electronic darkroom for processing pictures.

At the same time, Reuters installed a computer-based electronic darkroom, aimed at its 400 picture service subscribers and others. Plans called for the eventual delivery of pictures directly into newspaper pagination systems. Pagination is the process of making up an entire newspaper page on a videoscreen, ready for transmission to a printing plate.

By the late 1980s an increasing number of newspapers were using electronic darkrooms to process both news service photos and those received from their own photographers in the field using portable picture-transmission machines. Some editors found that they could publish pictures made from videotapes of television broadcasts.

PRINCIPLES OF PHOTOGRAPHY

Four Dimensions

A photograph reproduced in a newspaper, magazine, or book is a two-dimensional representation of a subject that originally had four dimensions: length, width, depth, and existence, and perhaps movement through time. Moreover, the printed image in almost every instance differs in size from its original model. Frequently it is a black-and-white representation of a subject with many colorful hues. The photographic communicator must master the technique of condensing these dimensions and conditions into a space having only length and width.

Photography is capable of high-fidelity reproduction of very fine details and textures. A skillfully made photograph can communicate the essence of tactile experience. It can be controlled to represent a subject in various perspectives, determined by the photographer as he or she selects a particular lens and the camera-subject relationship for the picture. Black-and-white photographs provide the photographer almost unlimited control in representing the original subject in shades of gray and the extremes, black and white. Thus the photographer's technical skill and mental attitude influence the picture that is taken. Two persons photographing the same subject may produce widely dissimilar pictures.

Since photography relies upon a lens to form a clear, sharp image and a shutter to control the length of time during which light strikes the sensitive film, two additional visual qualities are unique in photographic communication. As the lens aperture is opened or closed to allow varying amounts of light to strike the film, a change occurs in the depth of field, that is, the area in front of and behind the subject that appears in sharp focus. The photographer may render only the subject sharp, with details in foreground and background blurred to reduce their importance. Or, by controlling the aperture size of the lens, an entire scene may be rendered in sharp focus, from the nearest to the farthest object shown.

By selecting a shutter speed for a picture, the photographer begins control over the fourth dimension, time. He or she may use a long exposure, in which case a moving subject might blur in the finished photograph, or a very short exposure time to "freeze" a moving subject at a precise instant. Having determined a shutter speed for the effect desired, the photographer must decide which moment to capture out of the millions available. The French photojournalist Henri Cartier-Bresson refers to this act as determining the *decisive moment.*

Still Pictures

Photographic communication for the printed page may be in the form of a single picture; or it may be a *series,* a *sequence,* or a *picture story.* The series of pictures can be distinguished from the sequence by noting that the series is generally photographed from more than one viewpoint and has been made over a relatively long period of time. The sequence is a group of pictures made from the same viewpoint and generally covering a very short period of time, such as a group of pictures on the sports page of a Sunday newspaper showing stages of a sensational touchdown run. Most picture magazines today present picture series rather than picture stories; the latter are the most complex form of photographic communication in the print media, requiring logical visual continuity built upon a well-researched idea. Excellent examples of the picture story include W. Eugene Smith's "Spanish Village" and David Duncan's "This Is War," both published in *Life* during the 1950s. In book form, Edward Steichen's *The Family of Man* has been widely acclaimed as a photo essay.

In attempting to re-create the essence of an event, photographic communicators feel the need to couple their pictures with some sort of "sound track." They use the written word in the form of captions, headlines, and overlines. When one looks at a picture and reads its word accompaniment, one's eye serves two sense functions. While it studies the image, it functions as a normal eye; when it begins reading words, the eye functions as an ear, picking up the sound track. This reading and seeing occur through time, thus further developing the fourth dimension in a two-dimensional photograph.

Wilson Hicks, for many years executive editor of *Life,* contributed in the introductory chapter of Smith Schuneman's *Photographic Communication* a definition of the photojournalistic form. In its simplest unit it is *a blend of words plus one picture.* Words add information the picture cannot give, and the picture contributes a dimension the words cannot. When the two have been blended, there emerges a greater meaning for the reader than could be received from either words or picture separately. Hicks suggests that this blend develops a communicative overtone.

Moving Pictures

Although the characteristics of the still photograph apply to motion picture film and television magnetic tape, both of which are sequences of still pictures, there are important distinctions about the moving picture as a medium. Films and videotapes reproduce natural movement and sound, two elements extremely difficult to communicate in still photography. Moving picture communicators in addition have as their most important tool creative control over the fourth dimension, time. An audience viewing a message on film or tape is captive to the communicator in terms of pace, emphasis, and rhythm. A reader can spend as much or as little time as he or she chooses in studying a picture, and can do it whenever desired, returning later for another look. When one is a member of an audience in a motion picture theater or in front of a television screen, one does not have these options unless a home viewing device is being used.

The producer of film and videotape is concerned with the continuity, the sequence of images. He or she knows how to use the "establishment" shot at the beginning of a particular scene and medium shots and closeups to continue the action, adding variety and emphasis. During the shooting and editing of film or tape, photographer and editor concern themselves with such visual techniques as screen direction, cutaways, cover material, reverse angles, and sound effectiveness. Film may be shot as silent footage, with a narrator adding description later in a studio, or it may be shot with natural lip-sync (synchronized) sound. Electronic videotape recording is used in place of film for most stories and commercials on television. The first moon pictures sent back by Armstrong and Aldrin were an example of live presentation of moving pictures produced electronically without film or tape.

FUNCTIONS OF PHOTOGRAPHERS AND EDITORS

Photographs are used, just as are words, to inform, persuade, and entertain users of the mass media. Their effectiveness depends upon how well they are taken by the photographer and how well they are assembled for presentation to the audience by the editor. Each medium has special problems of picture presentation that require special knowledge and experience. Television is not radio with a picture of the announcer added; there is an important visual dimension. The still photograph is not decoration as it was in the newspaper and magazine early in the twentieth century. The development of candid photography with its quick, intimate glimpses of subjects off guard gave photojournalists exciting new possibilities by permitting them to avoid the stilted aspect so common in older pictures with slower cameras.

Daily newspaper photographers perform one of the fundamental tasks in photojournalism. On a typical day they receive three or four assignments, usually to events fairly close to the office. They most likely will use a staff car, equipped with a two-way radio. The editor has written an assignment sheet describing the event and what is wanted, and perhaps has discussed the job in detail. On many newspapers, photographers use their own equipment, for which the publication pays a monthly depreciation allotment; on others, they use office-owned cameras.

Once at the scene, the photographer will make a number of pictures, gathering names and important caption material. Back at the office, the film will be processed, either personally or by a laboratory assistant, and finished prints delivered to the editor. On most assignments, only one of the pictures taken will be published; in fact, frequently none will be printed because of space limitations or the development of later, bigger news stories.

A photographer on a general magazine staff works on more elaborate projects than does the daily newspaper staff member, often taking several weeks or even months to complete a single job. Assignments at times range far from home. The photographer is well briefed by researchers concerning the background of the story, and receives large research folios for "homework." On a major assignment the photographer will shoot from 1000 to 5000 images, sending them in "takes" to the editors, who keep the photographer posted on how the work has turned out. After all this effort, 12 to 20 of the pictures most likely will appear in print.

USA Today employs more than 580 freelance photographers, who receive precise technical instructions for each assignment. The newspaper transmits about 100 color photographs in an average week and processes approximately 1000 rolls of color film each month. Transmission time of a color photograph is three-and-a-half minutes by telephone wires and 30 seconds by satellite.

Major television stations use eyewitness news crews, reporting live during news broadcasts from the scene of a major news event. In metropolitan areas the stations compete with helicopter coverage, with one standard assignment being the tracing of traffic snarls on the freeways. The local television station news photographer works in a manner similar to that of his or her daily newspaper colleague. The TV photographer has four to six assignments a day, usually travels in a radio-equipped staff car, and carries lightweight videotape camera equipment. The photographer takes notes ("spot sheets"), including the names of those appearing in various scenes. Camera operators may work alone, with a reporter, or with a full crew to handle lighting and sound. After their return to the station, the tape is edited and a script is written. Increasingly, however, TV footage is being transmitted direct from the field via satellite.

With so much more film and tape being shot than can be used either in print or on the air, the role of the editor is essential. The editors of tape, film, and still pictures have three functions: to procure the picture by assigning staff photographers, buying material from freelancers, and subscribing to syndicate services; to select the pictures to be used; and to present them in an effective manner. Once the raw material has been obtained, the editor makes a selection from the entire take submitted. In the print media the editor must crop and scale the pictures to emphasize their most interesting aspects and to work them into a layout. In television the editor is concerned with juxtaposition effects from scene to scene and with time considerations. The presentation each editor puts together represents a blending of pictures and words, a designing of space and time.

Beginning in the 1970s, photocommunication students increasingly turned to advertising illustration as both a challenging and potentially lucrative area. It offered many opportunities for freelance photographers in metropolitan areas with substantial numbers of advertising agencies and company headquarters. Visual communication conferences devoted program time to trends in advertising illustration and graphics.

JOB OPPORTUNITIES IN PHOTOGRAPHIC COMMUNICATION

Qualifications

Stimulating opportunities await young people who decide to enter the photographic aspect of mass communications. The work at times is exciting, and always interesting; each day brings new assignments that give the photographer room for creative expression and the use of professional techniques.

Anyone contemplating such a career should be healthy and possessed of physical stamina because the work can be dangerous on assignments such as fires and riots, and the hours frequently are irregular. The photographer must carry equipment and guard it against loss or damage. Both physical and emotional exhaustion may affect a photographer involved in a long, difficult assignment.

Career photographic communicators also should have initiative, energy, and creative motivation. A degree of aggressiveness is necessary, but it should be tempered by thoughtfulness. Visual imagination is essential—the ability to see various interpretations of a subject in a given visual form. Photographers should have an interest in design and the knack of examining pictures for each one's special qualities. They must be curious about the world around them and have an

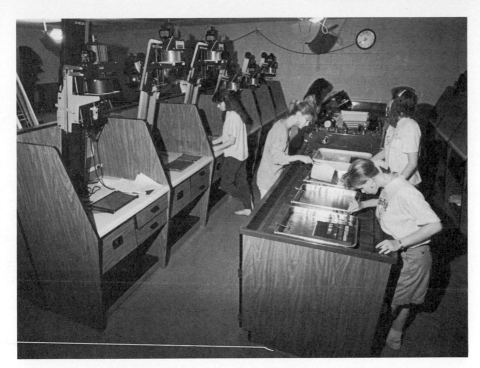

Student photographers at work in a large laboratory. (Courtesy of Henry W. Grady School of Journalism and Mass Communication, University of Georgia)

ability to mix with people. Being able to sketch scenes and individuals roughly is an important asset, but by no means a requirement.

Photographic communicators should have a good general education. About one-fourth of their studies should be spent in learning how to relate general knowledge to the discipline of photocommunication. Those who plan to work in the news and information function of the mass media should take courses in basic reporting, editing, law and history of the press, and graphic design and typography. In photography courses they must develop foundations in both the technical and visual dimensions of the medium. Their courses should include both still and motion photography, both black-and-white and color. Attention to the picture story, the documentary film, and advertising illustration is all-important. They should study the history of film and photography and also take courses in basic design.

Technical qualifications include an understanding of the photographic medium in terms of optics, lighting, color theory, and photographic processes, which include basic photochemistry and physics. With the growing importance of electronics in nearly all areas of photographic communication, an understanding of electronic theory is desirable.

Earnings

A college graduate with photographic skills may start on a daily newspaper at from $10,000 to $13,000 per year. An experienced newspaper photographer, with five years or more on the job, may earn from $17,000 to $30,000 annually in large cities. The starting salary for a college graduate photographer on a local television station will vary from $9,000 to $12,000; after five years the range is $14,000 to $22,000. A staff photographer for a general or specialized magazine can expect to earn $10,000 to $15,000 in early career years. The salary may rise rapidly, faster than in newspaper or television work. Top professionals on *National Geographic* earn as much as $50,000.

Some photographers prefer to freelance: that is, to work for themselves and sell their pictures to clients either directly or through picture agencies. The agencies take a commission of 25 to 35 percent of the selling price of the pictures. A freelancer also may work on contract, under which a magazine guarantees an agreed-upon earning in return for a commitment to be available to it on call. A freelancer usually begins as a staff photographer, then branches out after establishing a reputation and a group of clients. Freelance photographers can earn around $40,000 a year if very successful, although they start much lower in their early years. To be a successful freelancer, one must have good business sense and know how to market pictures as well as take them. The American Society of Magazine Photographers sets minimum rates for its members. The rate exceeds $350 per day plus expenses.

THE GRAPHICS EXPLOSION

Innovative uses of the computer have transformed aspects of television, video, and the movies into a kaleidoscope of movement and illusion and helped convert many newspapers, magazines, and books into intriguing, highly informational, and well-designed publications. So-called desktop publishing, discussed in Chapter 8, has been a factor. Color, long resplendent in film and television, has found increasing use in the print media.

The Print Media

Confronted with an upsurge in the use of striking graphic displays in television, music videos, videocassette recordings, magazines, billboards, and *USA Today,* a large number of newspapers during the 1980s hired designers, trained their staffs to work with them, and began using computers and picture-scanning systems in much more creative ways, turning once-somber pages into attention-getting and much more immediately informative displays.

"Indeed, the entire appearance of many newspapers is being redesigned from coast to coast," wrote staff writer David Shaw in the March 13, 1986, issue of the Los Angeles *Times.*

> New typefaces. More drawings and charts and graphs. More news summaries and "chronologies" of major events. Fewer stories on the front page. More (and bigger) photographs. Wider (and fewer) columns on a page. A more complete index. New headline and byline styles. Front-page "teasers" referring to stories inside the paper. Provocative quotations lifted out of a story and displayed separately, in larger type, to catch the reader's eye and lure him into the story itself.

As early as colonial days a few design elements, consisting of drawings carved into wood blocks, dressed newspaper pages. The drawings were interspersed among the columns of type, especially in advertisements. At times the thin wedge-shaped strips of metal (called *rules*) that separated the type columns were turned over to produce heavy black lines. An example is the famed Tombstone Edition of Philadelphia's *Pennsylvania Journal and Weekly Advertiser* that protested the Stamp Act of 1765.

In later decades large wood drawings, often based upon photographs, embellished the pages of newspapers, magazines, and books. Larger, wider headlines came into use, followed, as previously mentioned, by photographs that could be printed through use of the halftone process. Pulitzer's New York *World* and Hearst's New York *Journal* made profuse use of both pictures and drawings. During much of the twentieth century the use of print graphics was much more subdued. Notable exceptions included the Jazz Journalism press of the 1920s and the highly ornamental picture pages and rotogravure sections displayed in newspapers mainly during the 1920s, 1930s, and 1940s.

The New York *Herald Tribune* in the early 1960s was the first newspaper to convert the number of columns on certain pages from eight to six. The newspaper also is credited with using good-quality color on a daily basis. During the 1970s other newspapers experimented with new approaches to the presentation of news and pictures. The movement gained substantial impetus when the New York *Times* redesigned some of its pages and sections in the latter part of the decade.

In contrast with the mainly black-and-white photo and long-story coverage of the flash fire that killed three astronauts aboard the Apollo I spacecraft 18 years earlier, scores of newspapers provided striking, colorful coverage of the explosion of the Challenger space missile in 1986. The newspapers published large color photographs, drawings, charts, and chronologies in orderly newsmagazine style in special sections or on consecutive, carefully designed, often advertising-free, pages. It was a dramatic testament to the arrival of the print graphics revolution.

News Services and Syndicates

Although computer and traditional pen, pencil, and brush artists on a countless number of newspapers and the newsmagazines produce all sorts of maps, graphs, and other visual presentations, many graphics are provided by the news services and syndicates.

The Associated Press and United Press International accelerated their transmission of graphics during the latter half of the 1980s. In 1987 the AP began a graphics retrieval service, called AP Access, that swiftly delivers original, camera-ready art to its members. The service, available to AP LaserPhoto members with Macintosh computers and a modem, features computer-to-computer digital transmission, original quality art, 24-hour telephone retrieval of graphics, constantly updated weather maps, camera-ready copy for reproduction, the ability to edit text and manipulate type faces and other images, and the ability to store graphics locally for future use. Both the AP and UPI offered a wide range of charts, maps, photo color separations, and feature packages.

Group-owned newspapers not only exchanged graphics but received many from their headquarters' artists.

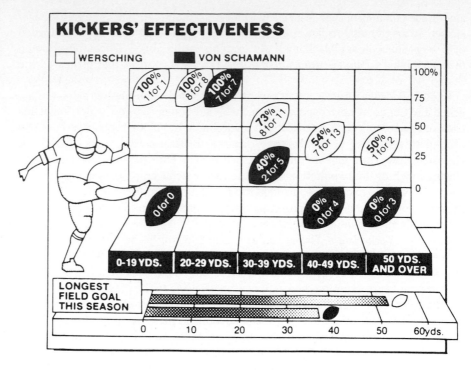

KICKERS' EFFECTIVENESS

□ WERSCHING   ■ VON SCHAMANN

| | 0-19 YDS. | 20-29 YDS. | 30-39 YDS. | 40-49 YDS. | 50 YDS. AND OVER |

Wersching: 100% 1 for 1; 100% 8 for 8; 73% 8 for 11; 54% 7 for 13; 50% 1 for 2

Von Schamann: 100% 7 for 7; 40% 2 for 5; 0 for 0; 0% 0 for 4; 0% 0 for 3

LONGEST FIELD GOAL THIS SEASON
0 10 20 30 40 50 60yds.

Syndicates provided similar services. Among them were Tribune Media Services, of the Chicago *Tribune,* with more than 350 subscribers in 1986; InfoGraphics, with 200 clients; and the Newspaper Enterprise Association.

Newspapers producing their own graphics were aided by such companies as Computer News Graphics, which offered a stand-alone computer graphics system enabling newspapers to create and manipulate graphics and store them for later use. The database included such elements as a world mapping system, drawings of civilian and military vehicles and aircraft, flags of every nation, and sports and corporation logos as well as symbolic logos to illustrate topics such as terrorism, war, and economics. The system was developed in partnership with the AP.

Television, Video, and Film

The use of computer animation, three-dimensional, and other special effects became commonplace during the 1980s in the production of movies, television programs and logos, videos, and commercials. Three-dimensional colorful objects now bounce or fly around screens at will.

A computer operator, for example, enters a 3-D design of a building, then tours its interior while it rotates on its axis. Another blends 3-D animation with two-dimensional effects, flying a 3-D object over a giant two-dimensional logo or rotating a large 3-D logo over an entire city. The possibilities seem endless in creating in Americans, as one observer put it, "a sweet tooth for eye candy."

It was a Frenchman, George Melies, however, who produced the first special effects movie, *A Trip to the Moon,* in 1902. Over the years techniques were improved in such landmark films as *King Kong* (1933) and Stanley Kubrick's *2001: A Space Odyssey* (1968). Industrial Light & Magic (ILM), the special effects division of George Lucas's Lucasfilm, Ltd., broke new ground with the first of the three *Star Wars* epics in the late 1970s.

In 1982 electronic animation dramatically occupied a full 53 minutes of Walt Disney Studio's 96-minute *Tron,* thrusting the protagonist via laser beam into the flowing grids of a vast computer system. Handmade backdrops and miniature objects abetted computer magic in such ILM-assisted films as Steven Spielberg's *Raiders of the Lost Ark.* Boss Films Corporation created the special effects for *Ghostbusters* and *Poltergeist II.* Lucas's *Captain Eo,* a 17-minute, 3-D musical science-fiction movie starring Michael Jackson, won high praise in 1986 for its spectacular effects. Allowing the imagination to run wild, these and other movies have enormously expanded the limits of storytelling.

By 1987 computer-created Max Headroom, a talking head on a TV screen, became a multimedia megastar with a cable-TV series seen in 20 countries, a multimillion dollar advertising contract with the Coca-Cola Company, two best-selling books, and a line of merchandise. Actually an actor (Matt Frewer) whose image is manipulated by electronic trickery, Max Headroom originated in 1982 in a Music Television (MTV) video seen in Great Britain.

Computers also have been put to work converting old black-and-white movies such as George M. Cohan's *Yankee Doodle Dandy* into modern four-color versions. Critics, including the 800-member Directors Guild of America, termed the practice "a mutilation of history."

In 1986 scientists at the Massachusetts Institute of Technology produced a three-dimensional image that appeared to float in space to demonstrate the creation of the first free-standing hologram. Using lasers, computers, a mirror, fiber optics, and special film, the scientists generated a solid-looking image of a nine-by-four-inch green Chevrolet Camaro that seemed to be suspended four feet from the projector. As discussed in Chapter 1, future holographic development is necessary before movie audiences will view and "touch" such images seemingly only a short distance in front of them.

FUNCTIONS OF ARTISTS, DESIGNERS, AND EDITORS

As increasing attention was paid to a newspaper's appearance during the latter half of the 1980s, a new era of teamwork among reporters, editors, artists, photographers, and designers gradually came into being on major newspapers.

During most previous decades, it was word-conscious, nonvisually-oriented subeditors who more often than not laid out the portions of pages allotted to them by the advertising department. Often scant attention was paid to the dynamic possibilities inherent in the proper interplay of white space, body and headline type, color, photos, and other illustrative material to capture the reader's eye. On many papers photographers held second-class status in decisions about the taking and play of pictures, and artists were used mainly to retouch their work, accentuating lines and airbrushing unsightly backgrounds from pictures, and for other illustrative purposes. Such a situation is still true on many newspapers.

During the 1970s some newspapers hired specialists full-time or as consultants to redesign type faces and improve the overall appearance of their pages. The advent of computer technology, including pagination, heightened the movement. But disagreements frequently arose. Some designers, with no journalistic background or training, proposed display ideas incompatible with production deadlines.

At a number of major newspapers today, however, graphics personnel and photographers meet with editors to plan immediate and future coverage and presentation. Under this new arrangement major newspapers have (1) a top editor committed to the importance of attractive design, (2) a staff designer with authority and a title, generally "assistant managing editor for graphics"; (3) an ongoing design review; and (4) a practice of treating artists and photographers as partners in the journalistic process rather than as a mere service department.

Such changes occur slowly, however, and it must be pointed out that the functions of these personnel remain much as they have been in the past on the majority of American newspapers.

Magazines always have been design leaders; consequently, many magazines underwent major redesigning in the 1980s. Amid an equally fierce competition for sales, designers of books achieved even greater prominence, especially in the creation of striking covers. One publisher, Zebra Books, even introduced a hologram as a logotype to identify its historical romance titles. With computers replacing pen, pencil, and brush, designers also achieved increased recognition in creating new forms of movie credit "crawls" and television logos.

OPPORTUNITIES FOR GRAPHICS DESIGNERS AND ARTISTS

Increased demand for graphics designers and artists has produced a shortage in the field. Visual imagination, of course, is essential. A relatively small number of graphics specialists are produced by schools of journalism and mass communication. Most designers learn their techniques in schools and departments of art or at institutions such as the School of Visual Arts in New York City.

Designers aiming for newspaper employment should acquire a knowledge of journalistic practices since at many papers they will be called upon to help make editorial decisions. Some journalism and mass communication students with a flair for design seek jobs in the field, one relatively new area being the preparation of advertising for use by videotex catalogue merchandisers. A large number of newspaper and magazine editors acquire expert visual capabilities through years of experience in planning and laying out pages, by attending seminars, and by studying design at nearby colleges and universities.

On most newspapers the salaries of artists compare favorably with those of reporters. The competitive market is such, however, that graphics directors command much higher salaries. As discussed in Chapter 8, the art directors of consumer and business magazines in 1986 earned an average annual salary of $42,326, almost as much as that paid senior editors and higher than the salaries of managing, associate, and copy editors. The salaries of art directors employed by advertising agencies, as discussed in Chapter 17, ranged in 1985 from $25,500 to $39,600.

The Persuasive Professions

Advertising

"Match MTV or Die"

"Surrealistic pictures . . . incredible choreography . . . special effects . . . music, music, music.

"Am I talking Pat Benetar videos, am I talking Mick Jagger, Huey Lewis?" asks Stanley Becker, executive creative director of the Dancer Fitzgerald Sample advertising agency.

"No. I'm talking Apple, I'm talking GE. I'm talking Nike. I'm talking Levi's, Coke, Dodge. I'm talking a whole kit and caboodle of commercials that seem to take their cue from MTV."

Music video has taken over much of the creative advertising world. Incredible graphic effects combine with rock music to evoke patriotism, romance, or a particular lifestyle. In only a half-minute, for example, the viewer identifies Levi jeans with living in New York lofts, strutting down streets, and falling in love.

"It's gotta be entertaining, it's gotta grab the viewer," says Josef Lubinsky, writer of music for the compelling, mood-soaked Levi's 501 jeans commercials. "You can't say, 'Look here, this is a widget' any more. You have to make the widget fly into space and come back down."

Many such commercials now grab emotions rather than feed information, which print media can provide. Why? Competition from cable television and videocassette recorders. Upgraded remote controls that allow viewers to "zap" commercials or switch to another channel.

Most of all, however, it is because advertisers spend more than $20 billion each year for all types of television presentations. The new wave of video commercials helps keep them happy.

*A*dvertising is indelibly woven into the fabric of our society. It is credited with raising our standard of living, lowering unit costs of mass-produced goods, providing information, and helping new firms enter the marketplace. Some forms of advertising may irritate us, but without it we would pay far more for most of the mass media that we enjoy.

Advertisers of goods, services, and ideas spend approximately $95 billion in the United States each year. Well over 400,000 people are employed in the industry, and close to 1 million others hold jobs related to advertising. In recent decades advertising by U.S. companies in other countries has increased substantially with the spread of American business internationally.

Advertising is monitored by the industry, mass media, consumer groups, and some government agencies in an effort to eliminate deceptive and unfair advertisements and commercials.

In this chapter we describe the development, function, and regulation of the industry, as well as the job opportunities and range of salaries available to those who enter the field. ◆

THE ROLE OF ADVERTISING

Advertising plays a unique and central role in the American economic system. Along with other forms of marketing communication, it helps to sell ideas, goods, and services. As a large part of the environment in which we live, advertising both reflects and affects our very life styles and thus plays a substantial social role. And, particularly since the advent of television, advertising figures prominently in our political decisions.

The American Marketing Association defines advertising as *any paid form of nonpersonal presentation and promotion of ideas, goods, or services by an identified sponsor.* Thus, advertising is distinguished from publicity in that the medium using publicity does not receive payment for its use, and the sponsor is not always identified.

Advertising has become a workhorse that serves many communication needs of society, including needs other than goods and services. Business firms, labor unions, government agencies, and political leaders, among others, are successfully employing advertising to inform and persuade preselected audiences about major issues.

Americans live in an advertising environment. A Harvard study in the late 1960s indicated that the average adult was potentially exposed to 500 advertisements per day from television, radio, newspapers, and magazines. Add to that billboards, direct mail, such specialty items as book matches and ballpoint pens, and other types of advertising, and the amount to which one is exposed is increased. The figure currently quoted in advertising circles is much higher: 1800 potential exposures each day. No one sees that many, of course, and the figure is impossible to verify. But it does indicate the huge competition for attention that characterizes the field. Without advertising, most Americans would not be able to afford the cost of broadcast programs, newspapers, and magazines; even specialty items, now distributed so freely, would bear a price.

Stanley E. Cohen, an authority on consumer-government relations as well as on advertising-government relations, stated the following in the April 30, 1980, issue of *Advertising Age:*

> It is hardly strange that advertising has become a focus for so much attention. It comes uninvited into the home. Sometimes volunteering useful information, often probing into hidden feelings and yearnings. Sometimes subtle, sometimes harsh. Often useful. Occasionally brash and offensive. It brings championship football into the living room but breaks the spell as the action nears the climax. It provides TV programs which keep children occupied on rainy afternoons, but it encourages them to want a multitude of things, some of which don't especially appeal to their parents. It encourages contributions to a multitude of causes; pleads the diverse viewpoints of politicians, causes and special interests. It exercises a powerful, but undefined, influence on the life cycle of products and companies, ringing in the new, while silently marking the passage of the old.
>
> Name a problem and someone will almost surely find a way to link it to advertising, whether it is the wasteful use of energy, changing moral standards, bad eating habits, or the poor quality of TV programming. For advertising is a communications tool which influences our attitudes toward products, companies, lifestyles, and public issues. Advertising helps determine which styles are fashionable, which resorts are "in," what music we hear, which public figures are our next folk heroes.

It is estimated that advertisers in the United States now spend well over $100 billion each year, compared with $1.69 billion spent in 1935, according to census reports. As the nation's gross national product (GNP) has risen above 3.3 trillion, advertising expenditures have kept pace, ranging beyond 2.3 percent of the GNP each year. Advertising, with its marketing aids of sales promotion, product design, point-of-purchase displays, product publicity, and public relations, thus plays an obvious role in the growth of the nation's economy.

Table 17.1 shows how U.S. advertisers allocated their expenditures to the various media during 1985, as compared with 1984. Newspapers led the way, followed by television, direct mail, and radio, in that order (excluding miscellaneous). In addition to the purchase of print space and air time, the expenditures include commissions to advertising agencies as well as the art, mechanical, and production expenses that are part of the advertisers' budgets for each medium. *Spot* refers to commercials obtained by local broadcast stations. The top ten national advertisers in 1985, in order of their expenditures, were Procter & Gamble, General Motors, Sears, Roebuck & Co., Beatrice, R. J. Reynolds Industries, Philip Morris, AT&T, Ford, K mart, and McDonald's.

Because so many other factors contribute to purchasing decisions it is difficult

TABLE 17.1   U.S. Advertising Expenditures by Medium in 1985

Medium	1984 Millions of Dollars	1984 Percent of Total	1985 Millions of Dollars	1985 Percent of Total	Percent Change
Newspapers					
National	3,081	3.5	3,352	3.5	+8.8
Local	20,441	23.3	21,818	23.0	+6.7
Total	23,522	26.8	25,170	26.5	+7.0
Magazines					
Weeklies	2,224	2.5	2,297	2.4	+3.3
Women's	1,209	1.4	1,294	1.4	+7.0
Monthlies	1,499	1.7	1,564	1.6	+4.3
Total	4,932	5.6	5,155	5.4	+4.5
Farm publications	181	0.2	186	0.2	+3.0
Television					
Network	8,526	9.7	8,285	8.8	−2.8
Spot	5,488	6.2	6,004	6.3	+9.4
Cable (national)	492	0.6	637	0.7	+29.5
Local	5,084	5.8	5,714	6.0	+12.4
Cable (local)	80	0.1	130	0.1	+62.5
Total	19,670	22.4	20,770	21.9	+5.6
Radio					
Network	320	0.4	365	0.4	+14.0
Spot	1,197	1.3	1,335	1.4	+11.4
Local	4,300	4.9	4,790	5.1	+11.4
Total	5,817	6.6	6,490	6.9	+11.6
Direct mail	13,800	15.7	15,500	16.4	+12.3
Business papers	2,270	2.6	2,375	2.5	+4.6
Outdoor					
National	562	0.6	610	0.6	+8.3
Local	310	0.4	335	0.4	+8.3
Total	872	1.0	945	1.0	+8.3
Miscellaneous					
National	8,841	10.1	9,551	10.1	+8.0
Local	7,915	9.0	8,608	9.1	+8.8
Total	16,756	19.1	18,159	19.2	+8.4
Total					
National	49,690	56.6	53,355	56.3	+7.4
Local	38,130	43.4	41,395	43.7	+8.6
Grand total	87,820	100.0	94,750	100.0	+7.9

SOURCE: Prepared for *Advertising Age* by Robert J. Coen, McCann-Erickson Inc. Reprinted courtesy of *Advertising Age* 57:30 (May 12, 1986).

to measure the effectiveness of any single advertising campaign, and it has not been possible to determine the overall impact of advertising on the marketplace. For decades, economists generally ignored advertising and its influence on the economy. Today, many maintain that advertising people have not proved their claims of advertising's value to society. Writing in the April 30, 1980, issue of *Advertising Age,* Dr. Richard H. Holton of the University of California at Berkeley, an authority on marketing and economic development, says that the proponents of advertising would like to have economists agree on at least four points:

> First, because of advertising, *the country's gross national product is greater and the standard of living is higher than they would otherwise be.* Advertising creates generic demand as well as demand for individual brands and thus assists in the marketing of more and better products. So advertising creates jobs, the argument runs, and provides us with a greater variety of products, while the quality of goods is improved over time in part because of advertising.
>
> A second argument put forth by advertisers is that *advertising plays a major role in informing the consumer so that more intelligent choices are made in the marketplace.* Thus advertising aids the competitive process.
>
> A third rationale for advertising is that *the firm's cost of production per unit of output is lower because advertising increases demand for the firm's output.* Thus substantial plant economies or economies of scale are achieved; fixed costs are spread over a larger number of units of output. So advertising leads to a more efficient use of resources in the economy.
>
> Finally, advertising's proponents ask economists to recognize that because of advertising, *new firms have an easier time entering the market than would be true if advertising were restricted or prohibited.* Advertising helps the new firm, or the firm with a new product, take on the giants in the industry and carve out a niche in the marketplace. Thus, advertising, again, is pro-competitive.

Since the 1950s, with better data on advertising, the refinement of analytical techniques, and the introduction of the computer, economists have seriously studied the economics of advertising. The results have been inconclusive, but Holton asserts that economists today are much more likely to have a balanced view of advertising than before these inquiries were undertaken.

HOW ADVERTISING DEVELOPED

Early Beginnings

Advertising is as old as civilization itself. In the ruins of ancient Egypt, explorers have found papyrus posters offering rewards for the return of runaway slaves. In the ruins of the Roman city of Pompeii, archaeologists have discovered political advertisements painted on walls along streets bearing such entreaties as, "Vote for Cicero, the friend of the people." However, until the advent of mass selling in the nineteenth century, advertising played only a minor role in the conducting of business. In early Greek and Roman days, signboards were placed above the doors of business establishments, and town criers proclaimed that merchants had certain wares for sale. These were merely means to attract customers to a shop, however; in contrast with modern advertising and sales techniques, the display of merchandise and personal selling were depended upon to make the sale.

After the invention of movable type accelerated printing in the mid-fifteenth century, handbills, posters, and then newspapers were used in increasing quantities to advertise products. Advertisements appeared in early American newspapers, but the volume did not grow to sizable proportions until trade began to flourish in the metropolitan centers in the early days of the republic. Almost all selling was local until about 1840, when the development of railroad transportation enabled industry to send its products to consumers who lived far from the manufacturing plants. National advertising resulted as business people used both magazines and newspapers to broaden their markets.

The first advertising agency in the United States was organized by Volney B. Palmer circa 1840. His agency, and those that followed his, did not prepare copy but served primarily as publishers' representatives. By 1860 approximately 30 agencies were selling space for more than 4000 American publications. Since there were no public lists of these publications and no way of substantiating circulation claims, the agents could manipulate the buying and selling of space to substantial personal advantage.

In 1869, however, George P. Rowell began publishing *Rowell's American Newspaper Directory,* a rather complete list of newspapers, together with careful estimates of circulation. The same year F. Wayland Ayer and his father founded N. W. Ayer & Son, Inc., to buy space in the interest of clients rather than to sell it for newspapers, and the agency began its continuing directory of all periodicals in 1880. Soon other agencies were started along professional lines of providing planning and space buying services for their clients. There was an upsurge in the use of pictorial art in advertisements, and the nation began to be conscious of the first widely quoted slogans such as Ivory Soap's "99 44/100 Per Cent Pure" and "It Floats," Eastman Kodak's "You Press the Button—We Do the Rest," and "Good Morning, Have You Used Pears' Soap?"

Early in the Twentieth Century

As newspaper and magazine circulations increased and new technological advances were made, at the turn of the century advertising developed new slogans, better copywriters and artists, and improved methods of analyzing products, media, and markets. Because much advertising was deceptive and grossly exaggerated, a strong movement to regulate advertising was begun in the 1910s. This involved both federal and state laws and control systems initiated by responsible advertising leaders. (The history of this movement is described later in this chapter.)

The advent of radio and a steady improvement in the techniques of advertising, such as copy-testing, the study of psychological appeals, and plans for integrated campaigns, characterized the 1920s. Advertising fought to hold its own during the depression years of the 1930s against both the near-paralysis of business and organized consumer objections to improper practices. During that decade, advertisers increasingly used research methods, such as readership studies and audience measurement.

ALBERT D. LASKER

Known as "the father of modern advertising," Albert D. Lasker did more than anyone else to change advertisements from dull lists of items for sale into what he called "salesmanship in print."

At the age of 18, the Texan began work in 1898 with the Lord and Thomas advertising agency in Chicago, which he later acquired.

From about 1900 to 1940, when American industry produced a cornucopia of new products, many became household words because of the advertising campaigns that Lasker ran for them after creating the first copywriting department in an advertising agency.

Lasker was a gregarious, loquacious, emotional man with a subtle mind. An instinctive psychologist, he and his creative team produced catchy advertising headlines and slogans. Among the latter were "Keep That Schoolgirl Complexion" for Palmolive soap and "Reach for a Lucky Instead of a Sweet," which probably did more to convince women to smoke than any other promotional effort by the tobacco industry.

Lasker helped to develop the use of test markets, sampling, and the distribution of coupons. Words meant much more to him than pictures, so the agency paid little attention to graphics.

At one point during the 1930s the agency purchased 30 percent of all radio network time on behalf of its clients and packaged many of the most famous evening comedy and dramatic shows as well as afternoon soap operas.

After more than 40 years in the business, Lasker closed the agency and transferred most of its clients to the newly created Foote, Cone & Belding agency. He then turned to philanthropies and art collecting. He died in 1952, a legend among his peers and one of the most influential shapers of modern mass communications.

Advertising Council

During World War II, the War Advertising Council was established by advertising agencies, media, and advertisers as a voluntary contribution to the war effort. So successful was the council in promoting the sale of war bonds, donation of blood, rationing, and the like, it was continued as the Advertising Council, Inc., headquartered in New York. This private, nonprofit organization conducts more than 30 major public service campaigns each year pertaining to such matters as health and safety, education, the environment, the disadvantaged, consumerism, the economy, and community and international projects.

During the past four decades Smokey the Bear has told Americans that forest fires cost them money as well as the loss of recreational facilities and the natural beauty of the country ("Smokey Says: Remember, Only You Can Prevent Forest Fires!"). More recent council campaigns have borne slogans such as: "Thanks to You It Works for All of Us: The United Way," "Take a Bite Out of Crime," "A Mind Is a Terrible Thing to Waste," and "If the Press Didn't Tell Us, Who Would?"

Major American advertisers provide volunteer coordinators. The agencies rotate in conducting the campaigns, and the media offer free time and space for the ads. Each year the media donate more than $800 million in time and space in support of these campaigns. Urging Americans to participate in the 1980 census consumed almost $38 million in such donations. The media's total dollar contribution since 1942 has exceeded $14 billion.

After World War II

The booming economy after World War II produced rapid growth in all areas of advertising. Staffs were enlarged, branch offices of agencies proliferated, and small agencies formed networks to provide reciprocal services for their clients across the country. Television—described by industry leaders as the most important development affecting advertising in the twentieth century—accelerated the trend toward larger agencies because it increased the complexities of advertising. Television arrived at a most opportune time, for advertisers were introducing hundreds of new products and consumers were eager to learn their merits. Advertisers turned increasingly to research to provide facts about their products and services and to discover the motivations of consumer markets.

During the 1960s and 1970s, advertising was confronted with the staggering task of helping to move into the hands of consumers an unprecedented volume of manufactured goods. Periodic recessions made this task more difficult. More money was entrusted to advertising personnel, and their responsibilities mounted. Management demanded more efficient methods of measuring the effectiveness of advertising as distinguished from other marketing functions. Many large agencies went public—that is, converted their proprietorship to shares that were traded and priced on the stock market. In order to generate greater profits for principals and stockholders, some agencies diversified into side businesses, such as retail stores and product manufacturing.

The computer, long used for the common chores of accounting and billing, came into more sophisticated use, providing the breakouts and analyses necessary for sound manufacturing and marketing decisions. As information increased, the computer helped management, advertising, and marketing people understand the new world of product proliferation, market segmentation, automated distribution, population shifts, and the profit squeeze. National and international computer networks were established by large agencies using high-speed data transmission telephone lines, satellites, and other communications facilities. The computer was used to analyze consumer surveys, to assist in media buying, to help in predicting the effectiveness of one media plan as opposed to another, to calculate television program cost efficiencies in relation to client objectives, and in numerous other ways. By 1986 about half of the members of the American Association of Advertising Agencies depended on computers to handle basic agency chores and other functions, including the sharing of information by all departments within those agencies.

Increasingly large amounts of money were allocated to marketing and advertising research. The emphasis on research resulted from high entry costs into markets, high costs of new product development, market failures, the rapidly changing marketing environment, changing life styles of consumers, and the urgency of having more information for decision making. Companies found it necessary to involve specialized outside consulting groups as well as their own in-house groups to analyze the changing market. As a consequence, independent research groups increased threefold throughout the United States during the 1970s.

Creativity

As an increasing number of advertising specialists drew upon their imagination and instinct, grounded in experience and research, to produce attention-getting print and broadcast messages, a widely discussed "cult of creativity" swept the industry. Early examples included the highly entertaining creations of satirist Stan Freberg for Jeno's Pizza and Chun King products and popular Braniff, Avis Rent-a-Car, Volkswagen, and Benson & Hedges advertisements. Later came the television commercials of Clairol's Herbal Essence Shampoo, launched with an anima-

Television commercial being filmed. Outside shooting requires careful control of lighting. (Kopstein, Monkmeyer)

tion technique that included warm humor; Morris the 9-Lives Cat commercials; and those portraying the Keebler elves. Humor began playing a larger role in slice-of-life commercials as consumers became more sophisticated and more critical of their portrayal in advertising. Many new agencies were established as the most creative advertising personnel went into business for themselves.

Some advertising people decried the extensive use of wit and humor, contending that it might be entertaining but that it does not always help to sell goods and services. Because of the business slowdown during the 1975 and 1980 recessions, many commercials of a humorous, awareness, and image-building variety gave way to "hard-sell" advertisements. "Less emphasis on showmanship, more on sellmanship" is the way one observer put it. The influx of business school graduates steeped in the case-study approach to marketing was credited with some of the resistance to off-beat, innovative approaches.

Creativity returned in force during the 1980s as advertisers vied for the attention of consumers whose attention was splintered among over-the-air and cable television, videocassette recordings, and a myriad of other media and leisure-time pursuits. Striking print and video graphics augmented the novel approaches of creative advertising people, as illustrated in part by the vignette that opens this chapter.

Eroticism characterized the print and broadcast commercials of Calvin Klein, the designer whose suggestive series of underwear ads first appeared in 1982. ("Nothing comes between me and my Calvins," cooed the then-15-year-old beauty Brooke Shields.) Erotic advertising sold everything from after-shave lotions to exercise machines. Nostalgia for the 1950s was the theme of advertisers who turned to black-and-white television to attract attention in the color-dominated medium.

Humor was everywhere. Dancing raisins sing "I Heard It Through the Grapevine." Men waddling in penguin costumes buy Coors' Colorado Chillers. In a "time machine" commercial a man heads back 100 years in time inadvertently holding a can of Pepsi; as he moves through time Coke and Pepsi dispensing machines come into view but the Coke machine slowly disappears and a Coke delivery truck and bottling plant suffer the same fate. On a radio commercial a woman offers Laughing Cow cheese from France as a snack for her husband in bed and declares: "Then he ate all 10 mini-cheeses and said it was the best treat he ever had in bed. So I smacked him."

Cycles in Advertising

Many observers have noted the apparent trends that have characterized advertising during the post-World War II decades, all of them continuing today.

1950s: THE PRODUCT ERA. For the Ted Bates agency Rosser Reeves sought the "unique selling proposition" for each product: "Wonder Bread builds strong bodies 12 ways." "Rolaids absorb 47 times its weight in stomach acid." David Ogilvy, founder of Ogilvy & Mather, offered finely crafted ads for products such as Hathaway shirts, Schweppes tonic, and Rolls Royce motor cars. Leo Burnett, founder of the so-called "Chicago school," ascertained the "inherent drama" of each product and sold it in folksy, down-to-earth style or created figures such as the Jolly Green Giant and the Marlboro Man.

1960s: THE IMAGE ERA. Setting the dominant tone, William Bernbach brought together creative teams at Doyle Dane Bernbach agency to combine words and images in memorable campaigns such as those for Avis Rent-a-Car ("We're number two, but we try harder") and the Volkswagen Beetle ("Think small").

1970s: THE ERA OF COMPARATIVE ADVERTISING. Manufacturers and marketing people have always sought to identify in the public mind the unique position of their products in the marketplace. The advertising door to this practice, known as *positioning,* was opened wide in 1972 when the Federal Trade Commission strongly advocated the use of comparative advertising—naming the competing product(s) instead of referring to "brand X" or bleeping the names. The FTC

BIG BUCKS FOR STAR POWER

Celebrities sell soft drinks, beer, personal computers, even underwear on television—but not for peanuts. Celebrity endorsement fees in 1985 totaled $240 million, according to industry estimates, about four times the figure calculated 10 years previously. The stars appeared on about 20 percent of all commercials.

Michael Jackson garnered the biggest contract ever in 1986—a whopping $12 million for three Pepsi commercials over a three-year period. The pop star's first series for Pepsi in 1984, at a fee of $4.5 million, was judged a key factor in soaring sales of the soft drink.

Among other stars, Bill Cosby earned $3 million for 10 E.F. Hutton ads. Don Johnson picked up $1 million for a series of Pepsi spots, and George C. Scott, Joan Collins, Larry Hagman, Joe Montana, and Burt Lancaster received fees from other advertisers ranging from $300,000 to $750,000.

Those estimates were made by Mark Lacter, correspondent for the San Francisco *Chronicle,* after interviews with Hollywood sources.

Until Sir Laurence Olivier appeared in a TV commercial for Polaroid in the early 1970s, the stars avoided such endorsements, fearful of being branded as having sold out their artistic integrity. Clint Eastwood, Burt Reynolds, Barbra Streisand, and Mary Tyler Moore still are holdouts.

Joining the right celebrity with the right advertiser is the key, advertising executives say. Karl Malden, star of yesteryear's TV series, "Streets of San Francisco," is still viewed as the perfect celebrity to warn viewers not to leave home without their American Express travelers' checks.

reasoned that the direct comparison of brands provides additional information for consumers and thereby increases competition. By the mid-1980s comparative advertisements, based on objective data or subjective tests, accounted for 35 percent of all television commercials. Pepsi announced it had found that "more people prefer Pepsi to Coke" and mounted "the Pepsi Challenge." Coke's Max Headroom competed with Pepsi's Michael Jackson. The confrontations also included Schlitz versus Michelob, and Whopper versus Big Mac.

With only mixed results, some injured defendants mounted counter-campaigns. Others sought relief from the networks, the National Advertising Division of the Council of Better Business Bureaus, the FTC, and the courts, the latter under provisions of Section 43(A) of the Lanham Act, which prohibits "any false description or representation . . . of any goods or services." In 1986 a federal appeals court awarded U-Haul a record $40 million from the rival Jartran rental company on the basis of false advertising. Many leaders contended that comparative advertising, with its attendant litigation and negative publicity, was harming the industry. Nevertheless, the practice grew.

1980s: THE ERA OF TARGET ADVERTISING AND MARKETING, AND OF ADVOCACY ADVERTISING. Carrying positioning a step further, advertisers began marketing more by how their products—fast foods, soft drinks, and automobiles, for example—fit into different lifestyles than by dwelling on specific details of the products. Often this "targeting" was based not on customary demographics but on psychographics—the grouping of people by values and lifestyles as well as by age, sex, and income. Intensive research, including a wide variety of tests, studies, and interviews, formed the basis of the campaigns.

Advocacy advertising, in which corporations run paid ads that take sides on important issues, became popular. In the historic case of *First National Bank of Boston* v. *Bellotti,* the Supreme Court in 1978 had stated that the government may not limit the range of issues upon which a corporation may express itself. The Court, however, did not define the outer boundaries of such expression. When the broadcast networks, because of their access policies, refused to carry commercials telling their side of the energy story, major oil companies inserted their advertising messages in newspapers and magazines. Other corporations used print advertising to respond to what they considered unfair treatment in such network programs as "60 Minutes" and "20/20."

CURRENT TRENDS IN ADVERTISING

The advertising industry is seeking to cope with a number of changes taking place in the field. Among them are the following:

1. Advertisers on television have been increasingly concerned about the growth of cable and the number of independent stations that, coupled with the heavy use of videocassette recorders, have splintered the audience for conventional TV programming and advertising. Ascertaining the number of persons who view commercials has become difficult. Not only are VCR users not watching TV programs available at the time but, with the aid of the fast-forward button, they

A NUCLEAR WEAPONS TEST BAN

For you, for us — for the world

LET'S GET IT DONE AMERICA

The Nuclear Test Ban Committee
Hämeentie 6 A 10
00530 HELSINKI
FINLAND

Mr. Reagan — Be The President Who Turns The Tide!

THE VERY FUTURE OF THE WORLD IS AT STAKE.

Sweden is a small neutral country with strong emotional bonds to the United States. Many of our ancestors emigrated to your country during the turn of the century when times were hard in Sweden. We therefore find it extra painful to criticize a country with which we have such strong ties, but considering the gravity of the situation we can no longer be silent.

THE WORLD'S RESOURCES MUST NOT BE USED FOR THE VERY DESTRUCTION OF THE WORLD.

The world needs its natural resources for development and the wellbeing of all people. Your nation is strong and rich. This gives you special opportunities to contribute towards these goals, whereas the arms race is not only extremely wasteful, it also increases the risk of a nuclear holocaust by accident.

In memory of our late Prime Minister, Olof Palme, and for the future of the children of the world, SWEDES SAY:

"HALT NUCLEAR TESTING NOW"

WE NEED A SYSTEM OF COMMON SECURITY WITHOUT NUCLEAR WEAPONS.

As long as nuclear weapons exist, there can be no security for the world. The International Christian Conference for Life and Peace, held in Sweden in 1983, declared itself to a resolute effort for the total elimination within a specified time period of nuclear weapons. Similar demands have been voiced by many different representatives of world opinion.

A HALT TO NUCLEAR WEAPONS TESTING IS FIRST STEP AWAY FROM A NUCLEAR WAR.

The world welcomed your summit meeting with General Secretary Gorbachev last year and the affirmation of your determination to achieve early results in the negotiations on space and nuclear arms. We however, that no concrete measures have as yet been agreed to "prevent an arms race in space and terminate it on earth."

In particular we ask:

- SIGN THE "OLOF PALME AGREEMENT" proposed to you and Mr Gorbachev by the Center for Defense Information for a one-year moratorium on nuclear weapons testing and for a beginning of the negotiation of a comprehensive test ban treaty.
- ACCEPT THE OFFER OF THE FIVE CONTINENT PEACE INITIATIVE (Argentina, Greece, India, Mexico, Sweden and Tanzania) to assist in verifying any halt in nuclear testing. Such assistance could include on-site inspection as well as monitoring activities both on US and USSR territories and in their own countries.

We appeal to you as well as to Mr. Gorbachev:

TAKE THE STEP — START ON THE ROAD TO AVERT A NUCLEAR WAR. LET THE COMING
SUMMIT MEETING BECOME AN HISTORIC TURNING POINT. BE THE PRESIDENT WHO TURNS THE TIDE!

This appeal has also been signed by 155 local organizations (religious, political, trade unions, etc.) and by 5,838 individuals. The money for the advertisement has been paid by those organizations and individuals who signed the advertisement (and exclusively by them). The appeal has been organized by

The Swedish Peace Movement's Working Group
for a Nuclear Test Ban
c/o The Swedish Peace Council
Packhusgränd 6
S-11130 Stockholm
Phone 01146-820084.

For further information on ending all nuclear explosions in the United States and the Soviet Union, and copies of the "Olof Palme Agreement", write to:

Center for Defense Information
1500 Massachusetts Ave., N.W., Washington, D.C. 20005; Tel.: 202-862-0700 Telex: 904059 WSH (CDI)

often "zap" unwanted pieces of the programming, such as commercials. Moreover, the advent of the 15-second commercial has increased commercial clutter.

In an effort to overcome the resulting lack of viewer attentiveness, a number of advertisers have turned to *blockbuster* commercials. These spots, frequently running to 90 seconds or even two minutes, are especially notable for their high production values and high visual impact. These commercials, however, have compounded the already escalating cost of TV commercial production, which rose 90 percent between 1981 and 1986, bringing pressure on agencies to trim expenses.

2. Full-service advertising agencies have been losing business through the creation of "in-house" agencies by their clients and through competition from so-called boutiques, the creative-only shops that provide work on an a la carte basis. Many companies have set up their own agencies primarily to plan and buy the placement of their advertising. Battling back, most big agencies have become, in effect, one-stop shopping centers. They have added such services as direct marketing (mail operations on which almost half of all advertising dollars are spent), public relations (some agencies have acquired public relations firms), sales promotion and package design, and dealer aids and sales-meeting assistance.

3. The almost constant shifting of clients from one agency to another in about 20 percent of the industry achieved an even higher proportion in 1986–1987 with the establishment of a number of global mega-agencies through mergers (to be discussed later in this chapter).

4. The search for bright recruits to the field was intensified in an effort to refresh and replenish the industry's more than $16 billion pool of advertising talent, even in the face of relatively severe employment cutbacks.

Despite the problems in this mercurial, exciting business, however, few deserted it, and the level of earnings, although declining because of industry problems, remained generally high.

CRITICISMS OF ADVERTISING

Because advertising is so much a part of our lives, criticisms are rampant. Some of the more common complaints and the replies that have been made to each of them are:

1. *Advertising persuades us to buy goods and services we cannot afford.* Persuasion is present, but never coercion; it is up to each of us to exercise self-control and sound judgment in our purchases.
2. *Advertising appeals primarily to our emotions, rather than to our intellect.* Since all of us are motivated by emotional drives, it is only natural that advertisers should make such appeals. Again, a cautious buyer will avoid obvious appeals to the emotions.
3. *Advertising is biased.* This, too, is natural; all persons put their best foot forward in whatever they say or do. Being aware of this bias, we can discount some of the superlatives used in advertising.
4. *Advertising involves conflicting competitive claims.* But advertising is "out in the open," never hidden as are some forms of propaganda, and we can decide for ourselves.
5. *Advertising is unduly repetitious.* This is because the public is essentially a passing parade, not a mass gathering; there are always new users whom the

appeal has never reached. Slogans such as "It Floats" have sold goods successfully for generations.

6. *Much advertising is vulgar, obtrusive, irritating.* Actually, only a handful of advertisers employ poor taste in their appeals; their excesses damage the higher standards of many other advertisers. The very nature of radio and television, whose commercials cannot easily be turned off, accounts for much irritation; this complaint is seldom voiced in relation to printed advertising, which may be ignored.

Other criticisms are directed toward advertising by those who fear that their very lives are being manipulated by clever and unscrupulous Madison Avenue word wizards whose sole objective is to sell goods, services, and ideas regardless of the social consequences. These critics are generally persons who resist classification among the masses to whom most advertising is directed. Their intense desire to think and act of their own volition in an increasingly monolithic world leads them to attack advertising—"mass" by its very nature—at every turn, with little thought of the inevitable consequences of a society in which advertising is unduly shackled.

Some opinion leaders consider advertising to be almost devoid of ethics. Frederick Wakeman's 1946 bestseller, *The Hucksters,* spawned a series of antiadvertising novels. Advertisers and the broadcast industry shared blame for the rigged quiz shows and the disc jockey payola scandals of the late 1950s, the latter emerging again as a problem in the 1970s and 1980s. The image of the earnest young-man-about-Madison Avenue complete with gray flannel suit, attaché case, sincere smile, and lavish expense account was not one to inspire confidence. Set against the background of yesterday's patent medicine quackery, extravagant advertising, and the doctrine of *caveat emptor* (let the buyer beware) and today's allegations of misleading drug advertising, the bill of indictments is devastating.

Add to this the question of good taste in broadcasting—the jarring loudness of some commercials, the so-called insulting and obnoxious advertisements, the cramming of multiple commercials into segments of broadcast time, and the clutter and length of some TV program credit crawls—and it is perhaps understandable that some critics of advertising have grown so heated in their denunciations. "TV is a series of tasteless and endless interruptions," cried one critic. "The people are tired of being screamed at, assaulted, and insulted by commercials," exclaimed another.

Some years back, Morton J. Simon, Philadelphia lawyer and author, cited six principal reasons for unfavorable government and public attitudes toward advertising. Five of the reasons are still valid:

1. *Advertising is a horizontal industry.* It cuts across almost every business and service, so an attack on any industry almost always includes advertising.
2. *Advertising represents a lot of money.* It spends billions of dollars annually, and some persons view these funds as apparently untaxed and outside the grip of government (a complaint expressed by many Third World countries in their quest for a New World Order of Communications).
3. *Advertising lives in a glass house.* By its nature, it cannot hide its sins.

4. *The gray flannel suit image is pervasive.* Many consider that advertising people live lavishly and improperly on tax-deductible expense accounts (a view that led to President Carter's attack against the "three-martini lunch" as a tax-deductible business expense).

5. *Advertising is not constitutionally protected.* Some persons in government believe that advertising is somehow tainted by its commercial purpose and therefore is not protected by the First Amendment; its legal status has still not been made wholly clear.

Simon also pointed out that advertising has rarely lobbied; in the last decade or so, however, advertising interests have maintained a Washington lobby to further their interests.

REGULATION OF ADVERTISING

Business people and consumer groups alike agree that advertising should not be dishonest or misleading and that it should provide pertinent information for the public. At issue is the question of how much regulation is reasonable and necessary. Historically, federal and state laws and self-regulation by the industry have provided the control mechanisms, with laws serving in the primary role. The first legal restraint was a postal fraud law enacted more than 100 years ago, designed to ensure that persons ordering goods from mail-order catalogues received what the catalogues promised. During the progressive reform era after the turn of the century, business abuses, including the gross exaggerations and misleading claims of some advertisers, prompted a flurry of actions supported both by consumer groups and by various advertising organizations determined to elevate the ethics of the advertising business. They included the following:

1. Many states, beginning in 1911, enacted a model Truth in Advertising law proposed by *Printers' Ink,* a magazine formerly published for advertising people. State controls, however, were weak, so pioneer advertising leaders supported federal legislation to deal with interstate advertising.

2. Advertising organizations adopted codes of behavior, and some publications established guidelines for accepting or refusing advertising. The *Good Housekeeping* Seal of Approval is a notable, more recent, example of evaluations of advertising by magazines.

3. The first Better Business Bureau was organized in 1913. Bureaus have since been established in major cities across the nation to promote ethical practices and to help consumers with problems.

4. The Audit Bureau of Circulations, a nonprofit organization making unbiased periodical audits and statements concerning a publication's circulation, was established in 1914.

5. Congress enacted the Federal Trade Commission Act of 1914, establishing the agency (FTC), which steadily increased the extent and nature of its regulation of advertising until the 1980s.

In 1931 the Supreme Court ruled that the FTC could restrict deceptive advertising only if it could show that such advertising injured competition. With the passage of the Wheeler-Lea Act in 1938, however, the FTC was given a clear-cut mandate to deal with advertisements that deceived consumers. In the 1950s the FTC—well before the Surgeon General's warning condemning cigarette smoking —challenged the use of cigarette advertising slogans that implied that smoking was harmless. In addition, the agency attacked "bait and switch" advertising, misleading discount offers, misleading use of the word "free," extravagant claims for indigestion products and headache remedies, and other such practices.

The first serious attempt at self-regulation of advertising occurred in 1952, when the National Association of Broadcasters (NAB), through the operation of its Code Authority and accompanied by threats from the Federal Communications Commission that it would take action if self-regulation failed, established sets of advertising and program standard guidelines for radio and television stations. The NAB code's professional staff began clearing commercials prior to their airing, and the networks, operating independently, began reviewing commercials for truth, taste, and fairness to children. It was a major undertaking; each year NBC, for example, processes about 16,000 commercials.

In 1982 the U.S. District Court for the District of Columbia ruled that parts of the NAB television code, relating to the number and length of commercials within certain time periods, violated the Sherman Antitrust Act. In response the NAB immediately suspended *all* its broadcasting code activities.

Dr. Lynda M. Maddox of George Washington University and Dr. Eric J. Zanot of the University of Maryland a year later evaluated the effects of the action. Their findings concluded that: (1) Pre-clearance of commercials for cholestoral-related products and advertising to children had disappeared, with the burden of regulating children's commercials partially assumed by the children's unit of the National Advertising Review Board, a trade-sponsored, self-regulatory body; (2) the major networks revised their clearance standards, incorporating many of the NAB standards; (3) a larger burden was placed on agencies that regulate on a case-by-case basis after the commercials have appeared, notably the self-regulating agency and the FTC (although "in this era of deregulation the FTC is not predisposed to take any action on this matter"); and (4) the NAB did not seem anxious to reformulate the code because of possible legal repercussions and administrative expense. The researchers concluded that "some changes in the regulation of false and deceptive advertising have occurred in the short run; it is possible more will occur in the long run."

Another wave of consumerism occurred during the 1960s, led by the Ralph Nader organization and other activist groups. Regulatory agencies were accused of operating more in favor of the industries they were supposed to supervise than for the public. An American Bar Association task force, established at the request of President Nixon, urged that the FTC "get tough" or be abolished. As a consequence of these demands, the agency vastly enlarged its operations. Among other actions, the FTC began to require factual substantiation of advertising as well as factual disclosures in future ads and, in some cases, corrective statements to offset previous misstatements. In the belief that consumers would benefit if advertisers argued with each other in their ads, the FTC, as previously discussed, vigorously urged comparative advertising. The agency asked the FCC to require the airing of countercommercials, particularly regarding those addressed to children, so that consumer groups could reply to advertising claims. The FCC declined to do so, however, contending that such action would amount to "a tortured or distorted application of Fairness Doctrine principles." Even broader powers were extended to the FTC through the Moss-Magnuson Act of 1975.

By the 1960s more than 20 federal agencies, including the Internal Revenue Service and the Securities & Exchange Commission, had taken steps to regulate advertising. More than 12 states had begun to tax advertising. In 1966 Congress passed the Fair Packaging and Labeling Act, covering food, drug, and cosmetics packages. A Department of Commerce program to reduce the proliferation of package sizes followed. In 1968 came the Truth in Lending Act requiring disclosure of the annual interest rate on revolving charge accounts. It was still permissible to use the phrase "Easy Credit" in an ad, but if specific language such as "$1.00 down and $1.00 a week" were introduced, the annual interest rate had to be stated. Congress banned the broadcasting of cigarette commercials in 1971.

In that same year the advertising industry sought to forestall further legal action with a two-tiered system of self-regulation. A permanent professional staff working within the structure of the Council of Better Business Bureaus began receiving complaints from the public and from business, and to do its own monitoring. In addition, a National Advertising Review Board was created. Fifty persons, including ten public members with no advertising connections, were designated to consider complaints in five-member panels throughout the country. The board considers about 400 complaints each year. Although no penalties are imposed, findings are published. Legal complications have arisen, however, including lawsuits in Colorado and Louisiana that have chilled the enthusiasm of many volunteers and caused insurance companies to withdraw liability protection for advertisers. Nevertheless, the industry continues to support the review system.

The direct mail industry in 1971 began cooperating with postal authorities in a plan enabling recipients of direct mail advertising to have their names removed from mailing lists. Guidelines of ethical business practice in the industry were established in 1978.

In numerous governmental hearings, industry leaders strongly defended the social and economic values of advertising. They warned that imposing broad restrictions on all advertising because of the misleading or deceptive content of some would destroy the integrity of the marketing process and the need to foster public confidence in the free enterprise system—which some people saw as the real target of the most militant consumer advocates. The House of Representatives blunted the consumer drive in 1978 when it defeated a bill to establish an Agency for Consumer Representation.

Responding further to business complaints of too much government interference, in 1980 Congress passed legislation subjecting FTC regulations to two-house congressional veto and limiting the agency's public participation funding. The FTC's children's advertising inquiry was allowed to proceed, but any new rule would have to be published in full in advance and such inquiries would have to be based on charges of false and deceptive, rather than simply unfair, advertising. Because the broadcast industry had instituted reforms that the FCC incorporated into a policy statement, broadcasters continued to resist any further FTC restrictions involving children's advertising on television.

The FTC's wings were also clipped in a Supreme Court decision in 1976 overturning a Virginia ban against prescription-drug advertising and flatly asserting First Amendment protection for "commercial speech." "Speech is not stripped of First Amendment protection merely because it appears in the form of a paid advertisement," wrote Justice Harry Blackmun. However, in the landmark decision, *Virginia State Board of Pharmacy* v. *Virginia Citizens Consumer Council,* the Court pointed out that commercial speech is different from other types of expression and may be regulated under certain circumstances.

In fact, the Supreme Court ruled in 1986 that states may ban advertisements for products that have "serious harmful effects" on citizens. At issue was a Puerto Rican law that authorized gambling casinos but prohibited casino owners from advertising their establishments on the island. They were permitted to run advertisements on the U.S. mainland with the hope of attracting tourists. The Court upheld the law by a 5-to-4 margin. "The particular kind of commercial speech at issue . . . may be restricted only if the government's interest in doing so is substantial," Justice William Rehnquist wrote for the Court majority.

The decision was criticized by the American Newspaper Publishers Association and other groups that contend that no advertising ban should be placed on any legal product or service. It was hailed as a victory, however, by the American Medical Association and other groups attempting to ban print cigarette advertising.

THE SIZE OF THE ADVERTISING FIELD

In the United States

More than 400,000 persons are employed in all phases of advertising in this country. This estimate by industry spokespersons includes those who create or sell advertising for an advertiser, medium, or service, but not the thousands behind the scenes such as printers, sign painters, and clerical workers. Manufacturing and service concerns employ the largest number of advertising workers. Next in order are the mass media, including radio, television, magazines, outdoor, direct mail, and transportation advertising departments. Following them are retail establishments, advertising agencies, wholesalers, and miscellaneous specialty companies.

In addition, it has been estimated that approximately 1 million persons fill jobs related to advertising. They include paper salespeople, representatives of media, advertising, printing, and typography companies, and others. Of the approximately 20,000 newcomers attracted into the advertising business each year, about 1500 are hired by the advertising agencies directly from college, although this number diminishes considerably during periods of economic recession.

The approximately 700 members of the American Association of Advertising Agencies (4As) place about 75 percent of all agency-placed advertising in the United States. There are thousands of other agencies, however; the U.S. census counted 8000 agencies in 1977, but industry sources generally put the figure at about 5000. Young & Rubicam led all other agencies in income derived from U.S. advertising in 1985, more than $340 million. The next nine agencies reported U.S. income ranging from $269 million to $481 million. They were the Ogilvy Group, Ted Bates Worldwide, BBDO International, J. Walter Thompson Company, Foote,

Cone & Belding Communications, D'Arcy Masius Benton & Bowles, Grey Advertising, Leo Burnett Co., and Saatchi & Saatchi Compton Worldwide. Part of the agencies' increased income resulted from the more efficient use of personnel. Not long ago an average of four employees handled $1 million in billings, but the figure today stands closer to one. (*Billings* are the cost of advertising placed through an agency.)

International Advertising

United States advertisers, agencies, and advertising personnel have been engaged in international advertising for decades. By the late 1980s, however, the volume had swelled to unprecedented proportions, buoyed by the worldwide movement, particularly in Europe, not only to enlarge the number of mainly government-controlled broadcast media, including cable, but also to open many more of them to advertising. Computerized, digital transmission of programming, advertising, and business data via satellite made communication much faster and less expensive than in the past. Ever-increasing competition with foreign products accelerated American marketing efforts.

Giant corporations such as IBM World Trade, Exxon, Coca-Cola Export, General Motors, and Monsanto, long in the international field, were joined by countless other companies seeking their share of the world market. As one consequence, U.S. investment in foreign plants soared to more than $60 million. IBM, one of the largest multinational firms, can be cited as an example of foreign country operations. IBM conducts business in more than 120 countries, receiving more than one-half of its corporate gross income from sources outside the United States. The IBM payroll supports about 150,000 employees engaged in non-U.S. operations. Almost all non-U.S. employees are nationals of the countries in which they work.

Advertising agency mergers of unprecedented magnitude rocked the advertising world, both nationally and internationally, in 1986. In the wake of several years of consolidations of giant manufacturing corporations, three of the top global agencies—BBDO International, the Doyle Dane Bernbach Group, and Needham Harper Worldwide—formed a holding company, Omnicom Group, to handle about $6 billion a year in billings.

Shortly thereafter the firm's new position as the world's largest advertising agency was taken by England's Saatchi & Saatchi Company, the largest agency in Europe, when it acquired America's third largest agency, Ted Bates Worldwide, for $450 million. Saatchi & Saatchi/Ted Bates Worldwide thus had annual billings at that time of $7.5 billion.

Additional mergers shocked the advertising world in June 1987. Strengthening its position as one of the top three agencies in the world (along with Dentsu of Japan and Young & Rubicam of New York), Saatchi & Saatchi merged its Saatchi & Saatchi Compton with its DFS Dorland Worldwide, creating the largest agency in New York. The new entity was named Saatchi & Saatchi Advertising Worldwide.

Five days later the JWT Group, the world's fourth largest advertising agency, agreed to be taken over by the WPP Group, a small British marketing company, at a price of $566 million, the largest sum ever paid for a company of that kind. In the JWT Group were the J. Walter Thompson Company; MRB Group of three research firms: Hill & Knowlton, a leading U.S. public relations firm; and Lord, Gelier, Federico, Einstein.

British firms thus owned three of the five largest U.S. agencies: Saatchi & Saatchi, Ted Bates, and J. Walter Thompson. The other two companies in that category were Young & Rubicam and Ogilvy & Mather.

The mergers climaxed a trend begun in 1954 by advertising enterpreneur Marion Harper when McCann-Erickson acquired Marschalk & Pratt. Harper acquired agencies all over the world in building the Interpublic Group of Companies' empire. It was the J. Walter Thompson Company, however, that pioneered in global agency operations, having opened its first overseas office in London in 1889. During the mid-1980s, the Thompson company, ranked fifth in 1985 billings, had more than 5600 employees in 80 or more offices in 25 countries. McCann-Erickson Worldwide, with more than 70 full-time service offices in 27 countries, ranked among the top 10 in total billings.

Because most advertisers are unwilling to do business with an agency that serves a competitor, a large number of clients, including one that ended a relationship of more than half a century, shifted to other agencies as a result of the mergers. The new mega-agencies relied on the concept, pioneered by Interpublic and now used by many of the largest agencies, that separate agency subsidiaries would operate under a holding company management, presumably with no contact among the different arms. Within three months in 1986 the mega-agencies lost more than a half-billion dollars in accounts, but counted on recouping their losses and gaining much more new business by providing a global presence for the increasingly large number of corporations expanding their foreign operations.

In addition to London-based Saatchi & Saatchi Advertising Worldwide, large advertising agencies have been developed in a number of other countries, most notably in Japan and others in Europe. For the most part the agencies were modeled after those in the United States, where they continued to garner accounts. The Japanese agencies Dentsu, Hakuhodo, Asatsu, Daiko, and Dai-Ichi Kikaku are among the world's largest.

Smaller U.S. agencies operate overseas in four ways: through subsidiaries, of which they own part or all of the stock; through exclusive affiliations; through account affiliations with overseas agencies that may also work with other American agencies; and through export media, such as *Reader's Digest* and *Vision*. The fourth method is often used along with any of the other three.

International advertising is discussed further in Chapter 25.

Advertising agencies acquired public relations firms in increasing numbers during the 1970s and early 1980s. By mid-1986 no fewer than 16 of the 50 top U.S. public relations firms were advertising agency subsidiaries. Burson-Marsteller led the list, followed by Hill and Knowlton and Carl Byoir & Associates as the three firms with the largest net fee incomes. A few months later Hill and Knowlton, a JWT Group subsidiary, acquired both Gray and Company Worldwide Communications and Carl Byoir & Associates to regain from Burson-Marsteller the distinction of being the industry's No. 1 firm. Because of the absence of other sizable, independent public relations firms, analysts expressed the opinion that the U.S. merger movement was at or near its end.

WHAT ADVERTISING PEOPLE DO

Advertising people disseminate messages through purchased space (print) or time (television and radio), or through expenditures in other media, in order to identify, inform, and/or persuade. How some of these people accomplish this objective can be described by examining briefly the roles they play in agencies, in advertising departments of the mass media, in retail store and company advertising departments, and in the planning of a national advertising campaign.

Advertising Agencies

An agency first studies its client's product or service to learn the advantages and disadvantages of the product itself in relation to its competition. It then analyzes the present and potential market for which the product or service is intended. Taken into consideration next are the distribution and sales plans of the client, which are studied with a view toward determining the best selection of media. A definite plan is then formulated and presented to the client.

Once the plan is approved, the agency staff writes, designs, and illustrates the proposed advertisements or prepares the broadcast commercials; contracts for space or time with the media; produces the advertisements and sends them to the media with instructions; checks and verifies the use of the ads; pays for the services rendered and bills the client; cooperates in such merchandising efforts as point-of-purchase displays; and seeks to measure results.

Who are the persons who perform these services? The answer varies since advertising agencies range in size from small operations to full-service agencies employing 1000 persons or more. The executive heads of an agency usually are people who have proved they can achieve results for clients through print, broadcasting, and other media and who are capable of procuring new business for the agency. These executives may be organized into a plans board, giving general direction to such departments as research, planning, media, copy, art and layout, television production, print production, traffic, merchandising, checking, and accounting.

The key persons in servicing an account—that is, in providing a liaison between the agency and the client—are the account executives. These executives must have a general knowledge of all phases of advertising, merchandising, and general business practices, as well as the ability to be creative in solving a client's special advertising problems and in planning campaigns. Account executives call on the agency's various departments for assistance and correlate their efforts in behalf of clients.

Copy and art chiefs are responsible for the actual creation of advertisements. Copywriters are salespeople, inventors, interpreters, and perhaps artists, but always competent writers. Art directors are salespeople, inventors, interpreters,

perhaps writers, and sometimes producers, but also are visually oriented persons who usually can draw. They see to it that all the visual elements come together at every phase of the work from rough layouts to finished ads. They supervise every aspect from the graphic approach to selection of type. For television, they begin by making a storyboard, the series of pictures representing the video portion of the commercial. Often they help choose the film techniques, music and other sounds, and models.

From the moment an ad is designed and written to the time it actually appears in magazines and newspapers or on billboards, it is in the hands of the print production people. They are up-to-date on typography, printing, photoengraving, electrotyping, and allied crafts and processes. They know what is practical for reproduction and help to guide the creative departments in planning their work. They buy graphic arts services and materials and see assignments through to completion.

Because so many agency functions, including copy, art, production, and media, are involved in the same assignment—that of producing a single ad or commercial or an entire campaign—it is vital to keep everyone working smoothly and on schedule. Planning the flow and timing of all the work is the function of traffic control. Whether the project is large or small, traffic sees that all do their parts on time in order to meet deadlines and publishers' closing dates.

The marketing research department gathers the facts that make it possible to solve sales problems. Research findings provide vital intelligence for the agency. Facts—for instance, about what type of people use a product and why—may help to provide creative people with the central idea for an advertising approach. Or media people may plan an entire advertising campaign based on research about the way consumers read certain magazines or which television programs they watch. Most agencies depend upon their clients for the majority of their marketing information.

Media people select and buy print space for ads and air time for commercials. They get many of the facts and figures from the research department. They must know the tones and attitudes of magazines, the psychological environments of TV shows, and the editorial tone of any given newspaper. From daily and weekly newspapers, national magazines, business magazines, radio and television stations, outdoor posters, and direct mail lists, they choose the most effective combinations for each advertisement and product. And they must be able to stay within a budget.

In 1984 many newspapers adjusted their mechanical formats and billing procedures, under an expanded Standard Advertising Unit system, so that the resulting conformity would make it easier for agencies to place national advertising in papers throughout the country.

Agencies also have people who handle such matters as sales promotion, merchandising, public relations, fashion, home economics, and personnel. Then too, like other firms, agencies need comptrollers, secretaries, general office workers, bookkeepers, and billing clerks. (Figure 17.1 shows a typical organization chart.)

Most of an agency's compensation comes in the form of commissions received from the media in which the advertisements appear. This usually is 15 percent of the medium's national rate; if the advertising space or time costs $1000, the agency collects that amount from the client and pays the medium $850. These commissions account for 75 to 80 percent of the agency's gross income. In addition, the agency bills the client for actual costs incurred in preparing the advertisements, such as for typography, photostats, filmed commercials, artwork, and any special services, plus a service charge—usually 17.65 percent. For example, if these costs amounted to $1000, the agency would bill the client $1000 plus 17.65 percent, or a total of $1176.50. After all expenses have been met, the agency usually winds up with a 2 to 3 percent net profit on its gross income each year. Verification that the advertisements have been used by the media is accomplished by the national Advertising Checking Bureau.

Advertising Departments of Mass Media

All the media employ space or time sales personnel and almost all engage national sales representatives to obtain advertising for them. Let us consider several actual newspaper and radio operations.

One newspaper publishes both morning and evening newspapers with a combined circulation of 38,000. The combined retail advertising staff consists of six sales representatives and a retail manager. Advertisements handled by the department comprise 70 percent of the newspaper's total advertising volume, the remainder being in classified and national.

Each salesperson services between 75 and 100 accounts, ranging from department stores to small shops. Unlike the practice on large newspapers, these

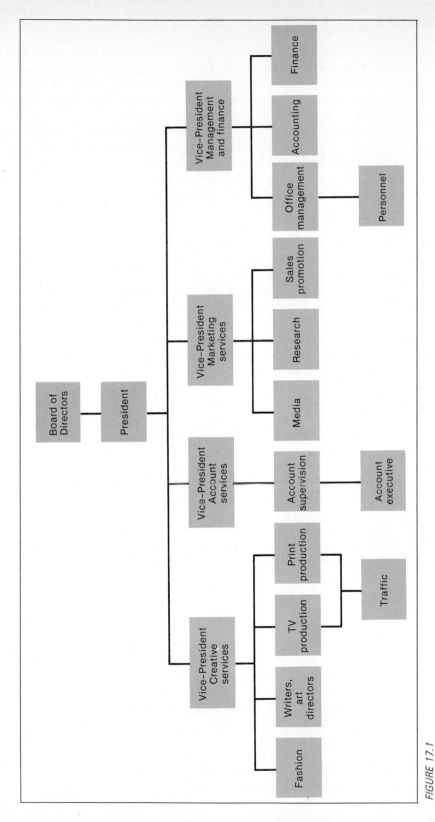

FIGURE 17.1
Full-service advertising agency organization chart.

salespeople are not assigned to specific territories. After calling on the business firms that have accounts with them, they prepare semicomprehensive layouts using artwork from one of several advertising layout service books. The layouts are then sent to the offset composing room. Proofs are delivered to any retailer placing an ad that contains 15 or more inches of space.

These salespeople work from 8:30 A.M. to 6 P.M. five days a week. Each salesperson is required to produce at least one "speculative" layout each week. They are paid a base salary plus commission, and annual incomes range from $12,000 to $14,000. Commissions are paid when the amount of space sold at the same time the previous year is exceeded, and in connection with the 15 or so special editions (such as "back-to-school") printed each year, as well as color ads and departmental sales contests.

In contrast, 32 salespersons are employed by a nearby morning, evening, and Sunday newspaper selling more than 350,000 copies primarily in a 15-county metropolitan area. Each must serve accounts only in a specified district. If the ad is too elaborate for the salesperson to prepare, the newspaper's art department lends assistance. After the typed copy and artwork are arranged on the dummy ad, it is printed on a proof sheet exactly as it is to appear in the newspaper. The salesperson checks the ad and may send it to the customer for signed approval before it is printed. These salespeople work in air-conditioned, carpeted offices with easy access to a covered parking lot. They earn commissions above their base salary if they produce more sales than their monthly quotas.

A nearby 1000-watt medium-market AM station employs four salespeople. Among them is the commercial manager who doubles as station manager but spends most of her time calling on accounts. One salesperson also announces occasional play-by-play sports broadcasts. The station owner handles all national accounts as well as a dozen local ones. People on the sales staff earn $12,000 to $14,000 annually in commissions. The commercial manager receives a salary, plus 15 percent of the collections on her own accounts and a graduated percentage of the sales volume of the entire staff.

A copywriter prepares the commercials and the station announcers tape them. The spots are played over the telephone for client approval before being aired. The traffic manager then schedules them on cartridge tapes ("carts"). Many of the commercials also are aired on the station's 5200-watt FM station.

All advertising personnel provide fresh, up-to-date information about the markets that their newspaper, magazine, or station covers and about the "pulling power" of the medium itself. These facts are provided regularly by their own research and promotion departments or by national trade associations or bureaus.

Most magazines deal directly with national advertisers or indirectly through national representatives. As is true with the other media, copywriters, artists, and production, promotion, and merchandising personnel supplement the sales force. And there is a similar ladder of promotion to executive positions.

Retail Store Advertising

Retail firms employ more than 80,000 persons in their advertising departments. These range from one-person staffs to those employing dozens of persons. In a large store the advertising manager works closely with sales promotion and marketing specialists. In one large Chicago department store, the staff consists of a copy chief, production manager, and proofreader; an art director and assistant art director, together with six layout artists, five "finish" artists, and two apprentices; and five copywriters, people with a high degree of creativeness who specialize in women's and children's apparel, men's apparel and accessories, and home furnishings. In addition, two copywriters are assigned to the basement store and the suburban store. Other journalistic personnel may be found in the public relations and publicity office and in the radio-television division preparing special product demonstrations. Mary Wells Lawrence, a talented copywriter and founder of her own successful agency, started at the retail copy department level.

Those charged with planning a store's advertising must be familiar with all aspects of the market, consumer behavior and attitudes, and such factors as product images and characteristics. The steps normally taken in planning a campaign include these: (1) setting a sales goal or budget, based to a large extent on sales the preceding year; (2) deciding how much advertising is needed; (3) determining which products or services to promote and when; and (4) preparing a day-to-day schedule. Store displays and other merchandising efforts are coordinated. The volume of sales produced during each advertising period is carefully monitored to determine the probable success of the advertising and to help in future planning.

Industrial and Trade Advertising

The public is well aware of consumer goods advertising. We see and hear advertisements almost every moment of the waking day, and often advertising jingles course through our minds even as we sleep. Not so with industrial and trade advertisements, for they are not addressed to the general public. *Industrial* advertising is employed by producers of industrial goods, such as steel, machinery, lubricants, packaging, and office equipment, in order to sell these products to other industries. *Trade* advertising is employed by the producers and distributors of branded and nonbranded consumer goods in order to reach the retailers and wholesalers of consumer goods. They, in turn, sell these goods to their own customers.

The industrial or trade advertising department may employ only one person, the advertising manager, or may employ as many as 400 or more persons. The typical department, however, employs about six. These are likely to include the advertising manager, a secretary, a writer, perhaps an artist, and one or two persons engaged in marketing research, media evaluation, or production work.

The department handles inquiries and prepares catalogues and technical data sheets, direct mail, exhibits, and sales promotion materials such as slide films, videos, movies, and props for sales meetings. It may engage in market research, but most departments obtain market data without charge through business paper research services.

Almost all industrial and trade advertising departments employ outside agencies to handle trade advertisements. More than half the advertising placed in business publications comes from general agencies. Others identify themselves as industrial advertising agencies, although most of them also handle consumer goods advertising. They specialize in industrial, technical, scientific, commercial, and merchandising products and services. A few agencies confine themselves to such fields as financial or pharmaceutical advertising.

The industrial agency is most likely to emphasize the services of account executives who work directly with the client, write copy, and make media-buying analyses and decisions on their own. There is a minimum of creative direction by an overall planning board. Between 20 and 50 percent, or more, of industrial agency income is derived from fees rather than media commissions. This is because commissions are limited, generally amounting to only $150, often even $25 or $50, per insertion. And an agency may be called upon to prepare between 50 and 100 different advertisements each year per $100,000 in annual space expenditures. With costs for research, layout, merchandising, and public relations running high and commissions low, the charging of supplemental fees for these services is a necessity.

National Campaigns

Selecting appropriate media for a particular advertising campaign demands great business acumen and reliance on research studies. If an advertiser decides to use magazines as a vehicle, for example, the class or group, such as women's interest magazines, must be chosen, and then the specific publication, such as *McCall's,* must be selected. The size of the advertisement and the frequency of publication also must be determined. Similar choices must be made for all the media to be employed.

Rarely has so much depended upon the success of a national marketing, advertising, and promotional campaign as that which heralded the introduction of the all-new, front-wheel-drive, fuel-efficient "K" cars of the Chrysler Corporation in 1980. The company had just suffered its most dismal year economically and psychologically, marked by near bankruptcy and the need for federal loan guarantees, coupled with a national recession and resulting poor sales. In addition, the company, and others, had been portrayed as builders of "gas guzzlers," products out of step with a market that demanded fuel economy. The success of the "K" car and the success of the corporation were inseparable.

Advertising strategy thus focused upon a "prelaunch" effort designed to create awareness and interest in the cars and also to establish Chrysler's credentials as a marketer of economical, front-wheel-drive products, and upon the designated "launch period" devoted to fixing the divisional names, Dodge Aries and Plymouth Reliant, in the public mind and to accomplish the distinctive marketing objectives assigned to each division.

Television and Sunday newspaper supplements were selected for the preannouncement campaign. Commercials 30 seconds long were run throughout the five-day miniseries, "Shogun," which reached about one-third of all television households and more than 50 percent of the viewing audience. This was followed by the insertion of eight-page, four-column advertisements in *Parade, Sunday, Family Weekly* (now *USA Weekend*), and other supplements carried in more than 500 newspapers reaching about 70 percent of all American households. Research disclosed that public awareness of the "K" cars rose from 23 to 40 percent during the one-week period.

The two divisions then announced their specific lines of three models each. Strategy called for positioning the Plymouth Reliant as a product with a broad national appeal—a family automobile designed to meet the needs of most new-car buying households as either a primary or secondary car. The Dodge Aries was positioned at the other end of the spectrum as exciting, youthful, and fun to drive —a stylish performance car, as contrasted to a sensible family automobile. The positioning objectives were followed in the creative and media executions for the product lines, with the Reliant featured as a four-door sedan and the Aries as a high-styled two-door vehicle.

Media were selected to correspond with the overall image objectives of each division. The Reliant's commercials were placed on a television schedule making heavy use of news-oriented programs such as "60 Minutes" and "20/20," reflecting the sensible car image. The Aries, on the other hand, was positioned in programming oriented to action-adventure and sophisticated comedies, such as "M*A*S*H," "The Dukes of Hazzard," "Vega$," and "The Tonight Show with Johnny Carson." The same separation was carried over into the magazine medium. The Reliant appeared in such magazines as *TV Guide, Reader's Digest, Fortune, Scientific American,* and *Money,* while the Aries made use of *Car & Driver, Motor Trend, Road & Track,* and *Hot Rod.*

Image building was reinforced with Chrysler President Lee Iacocca's proclaiming on TV commercials that "Yankee ingenuity" had produced cars with room for "six Americans" designed to "challenge the imports"—"the American way to beat the pump"—and with red, white, and blue as the colors in the advertisements and in materials provided to dealers.

Numerous promotions characterized the public relations aspect of the campaign. In one, the "K" cars were exhibited in front of K mart stores throughout the nation in connection with a public drawing that gave away some of the new models.

Few advertising and promotional budgets are this extensive. The procedure, however, is the same in each: the judicious expenditure of an allotted sum in a carefully coordinated campaign involving research, marketing, advertising, and public relations, and using every medium necessary to accomplish the specific objective.

JOB OPPORTUNITIES IN ADVERTISING

Men and women with a wide variety of interests and talents qualify for careers in advertising. As the American Association of Advertising Agencies puts it:

> Whether your career interests lie in marketing or management, design or decimals, psychology or public service, fashion or finance, computers or copywriting, people or

products, ideas or imagery, the medium or the message, personnel or photography, communications or commerce, sales or show business, math or music, graphics or global markets, packaging or printing, research or retail promotion, television . . . or you name it . . . the multifaceted world of advertising offers opportunities to get involved in all these areas—and more.

The advertising world is made up of people who have creative, analytical, selling, or management abilities. Successful advertising people are said to be constructive, adaptable, and eternally curious. They must be constructively optimistic because they are called on to originate ideas and to initiate action—to visualize in full operation something that has not yet been started. They must be adaptable because of the infinitely varied problems and the different types of persons they meet almost daily. And they must have an unceasing interest in people and things and the operation of business in general and the industry in particular. They must keep abreast of developments in advertising and remain keen and interested students in many fields throughout their careers.

Imagination, foresight in sensing trends, the ability to reason analytically, a sense of humor, and a sense of form are characteristics of advertising people that are frequently cited. Also emphasized is a broad general education in the liberal arts, obtained either in conjunction with the offerings of schools of communication or commerce or entirely in the humanities, social sciences, or sciences. Generally, professional preparation in advertising opens doors most quickly.

Young persons with talent and ability rise rapidly in the advertising field. More than one-fifth of the agencies that belong to the American Association of Advertising Agencies (4As) are run by executives who were less than 40 years of age when they stepped up to the chief executive's chair.

Women play important roles in nearly every phase of advertising. Industry reports indicate that about 50 percent of all agency employees are women, and almost one-third of the total are professionals. About one-half of the trainees brought into agencies from university campuses are female. Many women graduates go to work immediately as copywriters for agencies and for department stores and other companies. A number of women sell space and time for the media, with most newspapers employing virtually all women for desk jobs in their classified advertising departments.

A number of national advertising campaigns have been masterminded by women functioning as account executives. The advertising directors of some of the largest department stores are female, and women have also achieved success as media buyers for agencies. More and more women are being made vice-presidents of agencies, and a number of very successful women now head firms of their own.

Although surveys indicate that men still hold most of the key positions in the jingle-composing field, a half-dozen or more women have established formidable reputations there. For example, the music production company headed by Susan Hamilton handled "The Burlington Look" and Dr Pepper's "Most original soft drink." Anne Bryant composed such memorable jingles as Mountain Dew's "Hello, sunshine" and "Reach for the sun," and "Don't say beer, say bull" for Schlitz.

Ginny Redington, in the $100,000 per year income bracket, scored with McDonald's "You, you're the one."

Minorities are gaining increased footholds in advertising and allied industries. One survey revealed that minorities accounted for about 7 percent of professional positions and about 20 percent of nonprofessional jobs in the 4As agencies. The board of directors of the 4As, stating that "it is vital to seek out, recognize, and employ the best talents available wherever they may be found," has supported a successful summer internship program for minority professional candidates as well as basic courses for creative people and government-connected programs for nonprofessionals.

Numerous career opportunities are also available in other advertising and related areas such as *direct marketing, outdoor* (billboards), *business papers, specialty, sales promotion, trade shows, premium and incentive,* and *point-of-purchase.*

Rewards, both financial and psychological, come quickly for those who are imaginative and quick-thinking, can work under pressure, and have a bent for solving problems. About one-half of the people in a typical agency, for example, are professionals or executives. The sharing of ownership and profits with these key employees is practiced more often in advertising agencies than in most businesses.

SALARIES

A biennial survey by Rubel and Humphrey, a management consultant firm with headquarters in Northfield, Illinois, revealed that salaries paid to advertising agency employees in 1985 had increased considerably more than the 7.9 percent rise in inflation from 1983 in all except two of seven categories of agency size (ranging from $150,000 to $43 million in annual gross income). During the previous two years salary increases had surpassed inflation by almost 15 percent. The average salaries paid to employees in 12 job functions in seven agency size groups are shown in Table 17.2. It is apparent that the higher the annual gross income of an agency, the greater is the overall salary scale. The survey also disclosed that the total compensation paid to chief executive officers, including deferred compensation, executive bonuses, and profit-sharing, ranged from $78,000 to $378,000, with the average at $178,000.

As their skills and experience increase, advertising specialists generally find that they possess knowledge for which there is great demand. In moving from one agency to another, often taking accounts with them, they naturally move into higher pay brackets. A somewhat similar promotion situation is true in media and company advertising departments. The top advertising executives of newspapers, magazines, other media, and client companies generally earn about two-thirds of what their counterparts with the agencies receive. Other factors, however, such as security and fringe benefits, often more than make up for the lower salaries.

In the general magazine field, advertising directors earn from $15,000 to $60,-000, depending mostly on circulation. Business paper advertising managers earn from $15,000 to $40,000. Advertising managers for newspapers are paid about the

TABLE 17.2 Larger Agencies Pay More: Average Annual Salaries Paid for 12 Functions in 1985 (in thousands of dollars)

Function	Agency Size Group (annual gross income)						
	$150,000–$450,000	$450,000–$750,000	$750,000–$1,500,000	$1,500,000–$3,000,000	$3,000,000–$6,000,000	$6,000,000–$15,000,000	$15,000,000–$45,000,000
Account supervisor/Group head	$36.8	$40.7	$46.4	$52.7	$64.6	$60.4	$ 57.1
Account executive	25.0	27.6	28.8	31.0	33.5	33.8	34.6
Creative cirector	35.4	44.7	52.8	60.5	84.9	78.1	115.5
Art director	25.5	27.4	26.0	32.0	30.4	35.7	39.6
Copy chief/Copy supervisor	33.6	32.9	37.1	40.4	50.6	56.1	67.7
Copywriter, senior	22.4	21.5	27.8	31.9	38.4	40.2	48.7
Media director	29.0	26.9	29.2	36.8	42.9	56.7	77.7
Media buyer	16.3	15.9	18.2	17.7	18.2	20.4	21.4
Print production manager	23.8	21.1	26.2	30.4	33.7	36.7	46.1
Traffic manager	14.3	15.8	17.8	20.1	19.8	27.7	24.6
Head of accounting	22.4	21.7	26.5	27.8	33.6	39.6	49.1
Office manager	18.9	18.1	20.2	22.7	24.1	30.7	38.3
Average for 12 listed functions	$25.3	$26.2	$29.8	$33.7	$39.6	$43.0	$ 51.7
Percentage increase from preceding group	—	3.6%	13.7%	13.1%	17.5%	8.6%	20.2%

SOURCE: Courtesy of Rubel and Humphrey, Inc.

same. Commercial managers for radio and television stations earn from $10,000 to $35,000.

Beginning salaries in both print and broadcast media and in company advertising departments for college graduates average $12,000, whereas those possessing master's degrees are paid average starting salaries in excess of $14,000. Once they have proved their worth, qualified advertising people generally move upward rapidly.

Public Relations

How "Big Boy" Was Saved

Chubby Big Boy in checkered overalls, holding a hamburger aloft, appeared to be doomed. He had been the restaurant chain's trademark for 50 years. But company officials decided he was old-fashioned—"just too silly and outdated for today's public," one of them told *Public Relations Journal.*

Before discarding Big Boy, however, his owners, the Marriott Corporation, decided to ask the public's opinion.

Ballots were distributed at the 835 Big Boy restaurants. Television commercials announced the voting. Response was so great that Marriott hired a public relations company, Rogers & Cowan, to handle the contest.

The PR firm gave $5000 to Hollywood High School in Los Angeles for permission to stage a pep rally for Big Boy on its campus. Students painted signs demanding that he be kept. A band played, cheerleaders cavorted, people shouted. The major news services covered the rally with feature stories.

Rogers & Cowan transmitted videotaped scenes from the rally by satellite to approximately 700 television stations for use in their news shows.

Johnny Carson mentioned the voting repeatedly on his TV show. Columnist Erma Bombeck wrote about it. Demonstrations by students for Big Boy were organized outside the restaurants.

Four million ballots were cast 7-to-1 to keep Big Boy. Today he is far better known than ever before.

*P*ublic relations is a rapidly growing field of communications that has evolved into an essential link in much of the world's industrial, political, social, and mass communications network.

Some of its elements—publicity, persuasion, and press agentry—are as old as civilization itself. But as a recognized function in business and other areas of activity, public relations dates back only to the start of the twentieth century.

Public relations may be defined as the planned and organized effort of a company or institution to establish mutually beneficial relationships with its various publics. In its most efficient form it advances the interests of a company or institution and those of society as well.

In this chapter we describe the various facets of public relations, outline its historical development, and discuss the qualifications and opportunities for those seeking a career in the field. ◆

A NEW FIELD

Public relations is one of the fastest growing fields in communications. It is estimated that as many as 125,000 persons are employed in various kinds of public relations jobs, with an increasing number at high levels of management. More are being attracted every year from the mass media and from among graduates of journalism and public relations sequences in mass communication schools. As society becomes more complex—and the need for effective relationships between the numerous institutions and the individuals they serve becomes more essential —the field of public relations is likely to continue its steady growth.

The term *public relations* means many different things to different people. It has been used to include a wide range of activities from legitimate attempts at persuasive communication to the bribery efforts of unscrupulous lobbyists. In its best and narrowest sense, public relations is *the planned and organized effort of a company or institution to establish mutually beneficial relationships with its various publics.* Publics, in turn, may be defined as the various groups of people who are affected by—or who can affect—the operations of a particular firm or institution. Each public is bound together by a common interest vis-à-vis the organization.

Thus, for a manufacturing corporation, such publics would include employees, stockholders, citizens of the community in which it is located, dealers who handle its products, and the ultimate purchasers or users of its products. Similarly, for a hospital, these publics may include its professional staff, its employees, its patients and their families, the citizens in the community in which it is located, and its financial supporters.

Although many persons tend to consider public relations and publicity as synonymous terms, it should be obvious that more than effective communication is required to initiate and execute a sound public relations program. Effective public relations programming begins with the establishment of equitable policies by management. The essence of these policies must be explained, in varying forms of communication, to those who work for the organization or who represent it, and to the interested public. In short, communication must explain the policies and actions of management, but the policies and actions must support the words. Finally, the responses of these publics to what the organization says and does must be reflected back to management so that—with recommendations—appropriate adjustments may be made in policies and operations.

Public relations has been defined by *PR News,* a weekly newsletter in the field, as "the management function which evaluates public attitudes, identifies the policies and procedures of an individual or an organization with the public interest, and plans and executes a program of action to earn public understanding and acceptance." In recent years, managements have tended to look toward their public relations executives for a continuing analysis of social, economic, and political trends that may have an impact on the operations of the business or institution so that future problems may be avoided or alleviated. In this capacity the public relations people may be required to evaluate developments in such areas as consumer activism, the environmental protection movement, and government responses to minority problems. The practice is known as *issues management.*

James F. Fox, a New York public relations consultant and a past national president of the Public Relations Society of America, says that the public relations executive in business also must "lay claim to the title of company futurist, mastering the calculus of long-range forecasting: economic indicators, technological assessment, social indicators, political trend analysis." He adds: "We must be prepared to alert management to the early-warning signs of social change and advise how to cope with them."

In such areas public relations practice—at its best—affords genuine opportunities for meaningful service to society. As this function develops more fully, the value of public relations people to management and the social significance of the public relations function will offer even greater opportunities to those who wish to follow a public relations career.

The student who desires a successful career in corporate public relations (the largest area of public relations practice) or who desires to be a member of a public relations firm serving business clients should be committed to the private enterprise system. But, beyond this, the proper exercise of the public relations function in corporate management offers opportunities for improving the profit system and making it work more effectively to serve society. Thus, careers in corporate public relations may provide compensations for idealistic persons beyond the relatively good salaries and fringe benefits.

In other areas of public relations work—for nonprofit organizations (health and welfare groups, educational institutions, etc.) and for government—similar personal, psychological compensations will also be experienced among those public relations practitioners who are dedicated to social service.

Left: Employees and their families came first when The Coca-Cola Company celebrated its 100th birthday in Atlanta in 1986. Hundreds entertained at a party preceding the weeklong series of events heard their work praised by the company's chairman. A Rose Bowl-type parade climaxed the celebration. (Courtesy of The Coca-Cola Company)

Right: Three public relations campaigns coincided when the Hands Across America organization, seeking funds for hungry and homeless Americans, entered a float in an Atlanta parade celebrating The Coca-Cola Company's 100th birthday in 1986. Logos of the company and Citicorp., principal sponsors of the fund drive, appeared on the float. More than 300,000 lined the downtown parade route. (Courtesy of The Coca-Cola Company)

HOW PUBLIC RELATIONS DEVELOPED

Early Beginnings

Although the concept of public relations as a systematic social activity, and the term itself, were not recognized until the first decades of the twentieth century, its more elementary functions of publicity, persuasion, and press agentry are as old as civilization itself.

Archaeologists have discovered evidences of political communication, such as painted messages, in ruins of ancient civilizations. Just as thousands of communicators publicized the Olympic Games in Los Angeles in 1984, so did their predecessors promote the first contests in Greece. Caesar's *Commentaries,* glorifying the emperor, and the four Gospels of the New Testament represented other forms of publicity and persuasion. As Peter G. Osgood, president of the public relations firm, Carl Byoir & Associates, remarked, "St. John the Baptist himself did superb advance work for Jesus of Nazareth."

In colonial America Samuel Adams and other agitators achieved a propaganda triumph in helping persuade the colonists to revolt against Great Britain. Their tools included a staged event, the Boston Tea Party, widespread publicity accorded the so-called Boston Massacre, and exhortations published in pamphlets and newspapers.

As the first presidential press secretary, former newspaperman Amos Kendall adroitly counseled and publicized Andrew Jackson. Those opposing Jackson glorified Davy Crockett as a frontier hero in order to draw political support from the rough-hewn politician.

When the nation expanded into the plains territories and states, almost every town was heralded as "the garden spot of the West" in pamphlets and newspaper copies sent back East and to Europe to attract settlers.

Throughout the nineteenth century, proponents of such causes as women's rights, prohibition, freedom of the slaves, and antivivisectionism employed publicity to maximum effect. The play and book, *Uncle Tom's Cabin,* for example, dramatized the plight of some of the slaves.

As a wave of industrialization, mechanization, and urbanization swept the nation after the Civil War, the public became concerned about many aspects of big business, including concentrations of wealth and control. In 1888 the Mutual Life Insurance Company sought to improve its image by employing newspaperman Charles J. Smith to write press releases. A year later Westinghouse Corporation created what is said to be the first in-house publicity department. In 1897 the term *public relations* was used, perhaps for the first time, by the Association of American Railroads.

Press Agentry

Nineteenth-century America also experienced the rise and popularity of press agentry, whose modern counterpart is found, among other places, in the *hyping* of movie and television stars, books, magazines, and the like, through shrewd use of the media and other devices. Press agents attracted thousands to the touring shows of Buffalo Bill and his sharp-shooter Annie Oakley, made a legend of frontiersman Daniel Boone, and promoted hundreds of other personalities, politicians, and theatrical performers with remarkable success. Today's press agent, usually called a publicist, rarely resorts to the outright fabrications that characterized the oldtime promoter.

Phineas T. Barnum was the great showman of the century. He was the master of what historian Daniel Boorstin has termed the *pseudoevent,* the planned happening that occurs primarily for the purpose of being reported. Barnum brought pleasure to thousands of people deprived of today's innumerable opportunities for entertainment—people who longed to be entertained, whether deceived or not.

Barnum provided the attractions and he and his own corps of press agents, headed by Richard F. "Tody" Hamilton, contrived immense buildups, planted "news" stories and letters in the press, and prepared advertisements containing gross exaggerations. Much of the public loved it, and made Barnum a wealthy man.

The Connecticut-born showman employed the public relations technique known today as third-party endorsement when he induced London society leaders and even royalty to view the midget "General" Tom Thumb; when he drew opinion leaders to the performances of Jenny Lind, billed as "the Swedish nightingale," by arranging for donation of part of the proceeds to charity; and when he persuaded the clergy to attend plays in his American Museum in New York City at a time when such performances were considered by many to be wicked.

Because of the exaggerations that characterized oldtime press agentry such as Barnum employed, today's public relations practitioners strongly disassociate themselves from the practice and chafe under the heritage of distrust that persists among many journalists. Yet, in much more restrained fashion, the scheduling of pseudoevents and the hyping of celebrities and products do constitute one, albeit relatively minor, phase of public relations activities today.

Twentieth-Century Developments

The first publicity firm, known as the Publicity Bureau, was established in Boston in 1900, with Harvard University as one of its clients. Within the decade a number of other such bureaus were established. Among them was the office of Ivy Ledbetter Lee and George Parker.

IVY LEE. Lee, a Princeton graduate and former newspaper reporter of business activities, soon branched out on his own to offer the first public relations counseling service. It was Lee's belief that much of the public's antipathy toward business at that time—an antipathy exploited by the muckrakers (publications and writers who exposed corruption and exploitation)—resulted from the fact that most businesses operated in secrecy and most business people would not discuss their policies or operations with the public.

Such was the case with the anthracite coal industry, which hired Lee in 1906 during a strike. Lee persuaded industry leaders to change their policy and release information to the public. Retained by the Pennsylvania Railroad Company after a rail disaster, Lee again was successful in changing management policies. Reporters were taken to the scene of the accident and given full information, after which the company received fairer press comment than on any previous such occasion.

Lee was hired by John D. Rockefeller, Jr., in the wake of the vicious strike-breaking activities known as the "Ludlow Massacre" at the Rockefeller family's Colorado mining operation. By arranging photographic and feature story coverage of the activities and generous philanthropy of the family over a period of several years, Lee gradually changed the public's image of the Rockefellers.

Among other counseling activities, Lee persuaded the Pennsylvania Railroad to beautify its stations, got the American Tobacco Company to install a profit-sharing plan, and persuaded the movie industry to stop its inflated advertising and form a voluntary code of censorship. Lee, who died in 1934, is remembered for four important contributions to public relations:

1. Advancing the concept that business and industry should align themselves with the public interest.
2. Dealing with top executives and carrying out no program unless it had the active support and personal contribution of management.
3. Maintaining open communication with the news media.
4. Emphasizing the necessity of humanizing business and bringing its public relations down to the community level of employees, customers, and neighbors.

PUBLIC RELATIONS IN WORLD WAR I. Another dimension was added to the public relations concept during World War I, when the Committee on Public Information was established by the federal government under George Creel, a former newspaper reporter. The committee conducted a massive and successful publicity campaign to mobilize the American public behind the war effort.

The values of such massive communications efforts were impressed upon those who worked with Creel, and some of them became pioneers in the establishment of public relations firms designed to conduct similar campaigns for private clients. They included Edward L. Bernays, who in 1923 coined the term *public relations*

counsel to describe a function that was to become the core of public relations, and Carl Byoir, whose firm, previously mentioned, became highly successful.

EDWARD L. BERNAYS. In 1922 Walter Lippmann published his classic treatise, *Public Opinion,* in which he pointed out how people are moved to action by "the pictures in our minds." When it was followed in 1923 by publication of Bernays' book, *Crystallizing Public Opinion,* widespread attention was drawn to the subject of opinion formation. Bernays taught the first public relations course, at New York University, and spent the rest of his life counseling companies and individuals, writing books, and lecturing (in 1987, at age 95, he was still conducting seminars).

Bernays aptly theorized that if the public relations practitioner has the responsibility for explaining management's policies and actions to the public, then the public relations specialist should also have a voice in advising management on the formulation of its policies and the development of programs affecting the public. Although some managements still have not recognized this aspect of public relations practice, in many of America's largest corporations today the public relations executive is a vice-president who participates in boardroom discussions and has strong influence on the development of management policy.

Bernays helped Procter & Gamble sell soap and heightened interest in art by promoting national interest in children's soap sculpturing. He helped publishers sell books by persuading contractors to build book shelves in new houses. Many other such examples could be cited. Perhaps his greatest counseling feat, in the service of General Electric and Westinghouse, was attracting worldwide attention in 1929 to the fiftieth anniversary of Edison's invention of the electric light bulb.

OTHER PIONEERS. Among other notable public relations pioneers have been the following:

- Benjamin Sonnenberg, who proposed that the Texaco Company counter unfavorable publicity received after negotiating an oil deal with Hitler by sponsoring performances of the Metropolitan Opera Company on radio. The series, begun in the late 1930s, still continues.
- Rex Harlow, probably the first full-time public relations educator, who began teaching a public relations course on a regular basis in 1939 as a professor at Stanford University. Harlow founded the American Council on Public Relations that same year, and later founded the *Social Science Reporter* to demonstrate how social science findings directly benefit the practice of public relations.
- Arthur Page, former vice-president of the American Telephone and Tele-

Edward L. Bernays, frequently called the "father" of public relations, began counseling clients in the 1920s. He was still active in the field during the late 1980s, lecturing and writing in his mid-90s.

graph Company, who advocated the philosophy that public relations is a management function.

- Paul W. Garrett, whose 25-year career as public relations counselor for the General Motors Corporation, beginning in 1931, was a model for corporate public relations practice.
- Earl Newsom, who worked behind the scenes (issuing no news releases and holding no news conferences) to bring public and press recognition to Henry Ford II after he assumed command of the Ford Motor Company.
- Leone Baxter and her husband Clem, credited with establishing the first *political* campaign public relations firm in the United States. Among their first clients on a national level were Dwight Eisenhower and Richard Nixon. In 1986 Leone Baxter remained an active public relations consultant in San Francisco with an impressive array of corporate, government, and trade association clients.

In addition, no survey of the development of public relations would be complete without mention of the inventor Henry Ford, who staged events and solicited by mail customer opinions of his Model-T car; President Theodore Roosevelt, who exploited the news media in building his image as a trustbuster, Rough Rider, and Bull Moose; and President Franklin D. Roosevelt, the master of the radio "fireside chat" in communicating with the public.

BEHAVIORAL TECHNIQUES. A major dimension was added to the public relations concept in the 1930s with the development of modern public opinion and marketing survey techniques by George Gallup, Elmo Roper, Claude Robinson, and others. This development provided a tool by which public relations counselors and executives could achieve some degree of objective measurement. Public opinion measurement techniques are still far from perfect and their results subject to error, but they have become more reliable as the result of refinements over the years. Public attitude surveys have become a standard tool of public relations practitioners.

PUBLIC RELATIONS IN WORLD WAR II. During World War II the federal Office of War Information (OWI), headed by journalist Elmer Davis, enlarged upon the public relations practices of the previous Creel Committee. A number of the people who worked with Davis became public relations leaders after the war. The OWI was the forerunner of the U.S. Information Agency, established in 1953 "to tell America's story abroad."

THE MATURING OF PUBLIC RELATIONS. Public relations developed rapidly after World War II. By 1950 an estimated 19,000 people were employed, and major corporations had departments that included community relations, product publicity, motion pictures and exhibits, employee publications, news bureaus, and industrial economics. By 1960 the figure had risen to more than 30,000, and by 1987 it had swelled to approximately 157,000 people, an increase of 60 percent over the 95,000 employed in 1974.

Although the initial thrust of this expansion occurred in business and industry, it was followed by further development of organized public relations programs in many other kinds of institutions, including public school systems and universities, hospitals, nonprofit health and welfare organizations, and even the military.

Federal law prohibits the employment of public relations people by U.S. government agencies, but essentially the same function is carried out by "information officers." The Army, Navy, and Air Force all have designated public information officers especially trained in military public relations policy at service schools or who have been sent for the same purpose to universities with good public relations programs.

The latest refinement in public relations practice, as mentioned earlier, is the idea that the public relations executive should be the monitor of social, economic, and political trends that may affect the business or institution he or she represents. Thus, contemporary public relations, when practiced at the optimal level, involves four general responsibilities:

1. Continuing analysis of the social, economic, political, and human environment in which the business or institution operates in order to anticipate developments and provide a basis for advice to management.
2. Counseling management on the development of policies and operations to develop sound relations with the various pertinent publics.
3. Communicating essential information about managerial policies and practices, products, and services to the concerned publics.
4. Evaluating the results against the stated objectives to learn what was done right, what was done wrong, how much progress was made, and how to perform more productively the next time.

Government agencies issue an immense amount of public information. This advertisement by the U.S. Government Printing Office offers a free catalogue listing nearly a thousand of the most popular books sold by the federal government.

KEEP UP IN A CHANGING WORLD

Take advantage of the wealth of knowledge available from your Government. The U.S. Government Printing Office has just produced a new catalog. It tells about the most popular books sold by the Government—nearly 1,000 in all. Books on business, children, energy, space, and much more. For a **free** copy of this new catalog, write—

New Catalog
Post Office Box 37000
Washington, D.C. 20013

In short, the public relations function today—as foreseen in some of its important aspects by Ivy Lee, Edward L. Bernays, and others many decades ago—helps correlate the private interests of management with the overriding interests of various publics to facilitate the development of the particular organization. No public relations program can succeed if the private interests of the business or institution run counter to the interests of its publics. Only when the private and public interests are effectively correlated can an organization expect to have a healthy environment in which to operate. As an adviser and an expert communicator, both to management and its publics, today's public relations executive helps to bring about this correlation.

PUBLIC RELATIONS AND THE MASS MEDIA

Public relations at its best has a unique relationship with the mass media. The communicative function of public relations practice has become an inextricable part of the mass communications network in the United States. It is not too extreme to state that, without the contributions of tens of thousands of public relations communicators, the print and broadcast media would not be nearly as accurate or as well rounded in content as they are.

Consider, for example, that no newspaper—not even the New York *Times* or the *Wall Street Journal*—nor any magazine, news service, or broadcasting station or network can afford to support a staff large enough to have experts in every field of human endeavor. Even the largest media rely upon the public relations persons representing companies and institutions to provide the expertise, the background, and the explanations and translations from the language of the experts to the language of the lay person that enable journalists to write about complex and arcane subjects with understanding. The smaller papers and the smaller news staffs of the broadcast media are even more dependent on public relations people for this kind of help. In one sense, then, public relations practitioners provide a necessary link between the media and many specialized areas of activity in our society, a link that the media usually could not afford to provide for themselves.

Inasmuch as public relations people also are responsible for presenting their companies and institutions in the best possible posture, the question may arise as to whether this situation leads to abuse of the channels of public communication. The answer is that, although admittedly it is possible for public relations people occasionally to take advantage of the media, over the long range it is imperative that public relations communicators establish their integrity with media people. Public relations people cannot risk ending their usefulness by duping journalists. Most journalists recognize this fact, and over a period of time come to know which public relations people can be trusted. Thus, mutually honest and beneficial relationships can be developed.

Although public relations people are dependent to a considerable extent on the mass media in their communications activities, public relations communications are not limited to the mass media. Public relations staffs and counselors develop many specialized (or controlled) forms of communication, such as printed booklets or periodicals; exhibits; and motion pictures, slide films, and other audiovisual presentations aimed at specific publics. In this area also, public relations com-

National and state foresters wage a constant public relations campaign to acquaint the public with the danger of forest fires. Smokey the Bear is the symbol of one of the Advertising Council's most successful public service efforts. (Forsyth, Monkmeyer)

municators are influenced not only by their innate sense of honesty but also by the knowledge that their long-range effectiveness must be built on a reputation for integrity.

JOB OPPORTUNITIES IN PUBLIC RELATIONS

Opportunities for employment in beginning jobs are plentiful for those qualified to practice public relations; in fact, hundreds of entry-level jobs, such as those with charitable organizations, hospitals, and small business firms, are filled each year by people with less than desirable preparation for their tasks. Many graduates are hired directly out of school, while others find employment shortly thereafter. Some, however, must be prepared to work in geographical areas or fields of public relations that are not their first choices. This is true, of course, for college graduates in many other fields; it is the time-honored path followed by many as they begin their careers.

As previously stated, corporations employ the greatest number of practitioners; a recent survey disclosed that 85 percent of the 1500 largest corporations have public relations or communications departments. Some, such as General Motors and U.S. Steel, employ scores or hundreds of people in numerous subdepartments specializing in different areas of public relations or in differing communications techniques. Thousands of smaller business firms employ only a few public relations people each.

About one-third of the large companies retain external public relations counseling firms. The number of such firms has mushroomed since World War II, and today there are well over 1500. Like an advertising agency, a public relations counseling firm may serve a number of clients on a fee-plus-expenses basis. Such firms range in size from those with only one practitioner and a secretary to complex organizations with 2000 or more employees.

The public relations counseling firm often is in a position to offer a more objective point of view about a company's or an institution's problems than the internal public relations department. The counseling firm also can provide extra staff to supplement the internal staff during periods of intensified activity and to provide experts in certain fields that may not be represented on the internal staff. In large counseling organizations separate departments may specialize in newspaper publicity, placing clients on television talk shows, developing and placing magazine articles, producing audiovisual presentations, developing special programs intended for educators, and so on.

Many thousands of practitioners are employed in the approximately 4000 national trade and professional associations, as well as in some of the 40,000 or more state, regional, and local associations of the same types. A community's chamber of commerce is one example; others are the Institute of Life Insurance and the American Hotel and Motel Association. Some of these organizations have extensive public relations staffs with budgets of several million dollars.

The thousands of nonprofit organizations comprise a sizable market for public relations talent. They include the following (with examples): (1) social service agencies (American Red Cross), (2) health agencies (American Heart Association), (3) most hospitals, (4) religious organizations (Southern Baptist Convention), (5) welfare agencies (Salvation Army, government offices), (6) cultural organizations (museums, symphony orchestras), and foundations (Ford Foundation, hundreds smaller).

Entertainment and sports organizations require constant promotion. Performers such as country music singers and rock groups, and the managers of exhibition halls in which they appear, need promotional help. Every major professional sports team has staffs engaged in promotion. The careers of most movie and television celebrities hinge on successful public relations efforts.

Tourism and travel constitute a growing market requiring promotion.

Colleges and universities—even the smallest—employ thousands of practitioners. They may be found in public relations offices operating general news bureaus; writing, editing, and designing internal and external publications; producing broadcast materials; preparing audiovisual presentations; taking photographs; and so on. Others, in alumni and development offices, are engaged in somewhat similar activities, with an emphasis on fund-raising. Still others promote the work of individual schools on campus, such as agriculture, engineering, and medicine.

Public and private schools on the elementary and secondary levels comprise perhaps an even larger educational marketplace for graduates.

Public relations is an attractive field for women. About 48 percent of the members of the Public Relations Society of America are female, as are three of every four members of the Public Relations Student Society of America. Women comprise 62 percent of the membership of the International Association of Business Communicators. Some women have reached top-level positions and more will do so soon. During a 1985 poll by *pr reporter,* a weekly newsletter, 40 percent of

This typical publicity photograph showing actor Kevin Dobson playing with pets available for adoption was issued to promote Pets Are Wonderful (PAW) Month. Publicists create such artificial "months" and "weeks" to obtain attention for their causes in the print and electronic news media. (PAW Council)

all public relations practitioners who responded were female, almost double the percentage in 1978. Nearly 77 percent of the respondents were women, and women constituted almost 66 percent of those between 30 and 34. (The salary findings of the poll will be reported later in this chapter.)

There are two types of public relations people in these jobs: *generalists* and *specialists.* The generalists, a definite minority, are usually at the executive or managerial level. They are responsible for analyzing problem situations, developing programs to resolve these situations, participating in management-level discussions of policy, and supervising the implementation of programs. The specialists, much greater in number, are the experts in various techniques of communication and in the specialized areas of public relations practice. These men and women work under the direction of the generalists. The specialists write news releases and speeches, prepare booklets, answer inquiries from the press, arrange press conferences and special events, develop audiovisual presentations and educational materials, and so on. Most public relations careers start at the specialist level—for example, in product news release writing or employee publications writing. After the individual gains experience and shows promise of generalist potential, he or she moves to a higher level.

Overall, the growth of public relations jobs since World War II has been spectacular. Prospects for well-trained and competent public relations people continue to be promising. As more and more companies and institutions compete for public understanding and support, as more and more managements recognize the values of—and the utter necessity for—effective public relations efforts, the demand for competent practitioners will continue. As a matter of fact, today there are more top-level public relations opportunities than there are experienced and competent persons to fill them.

Typical Public Relations Careers

Consider a university communications graduate who goes to work for a public utility, such as the regional telephone company, after preparing for publishing, broadcasting, public relations, or advertising work. He becomes a member of the three-person magazine staff. The next assignment is in the company news bureau, preparing stories for the hometown newspapers in cities where the company operates—stories about personnel changes and promotions in the local telephone office, about the retirements of employees, about service changes resulting from the AT&T breakup, and so on. He is working at the "tool" level, using his journalistic skills but not making policy, although he attends staff meetings of the public relations department at which policy is discussed. The graduate is being indoctrinated in company policy and procedures, and is beginning to understand the total nature of the company operation.

Next the graduate may be sent to the community relations section, where he is more of an "idea" person. He consults with the local office manager in a town where customer attitude survey studies have shown dissatisfaction with service or misunderstanding of billing procedures and rates. They decide that they need better employee communication and arrange group meetings; they coordinate donations to local charities, attend civic functions, and encourage employee volunteerism; they check to see if local managers are making effective use of company films that can be shown to civic groups; they plan an institutional advertising series in the local newspaper that will explain the company's costs and needs for revenue if the town is to have the best possible telephone service; and they plan other measures by which the firm can show responsiveness to community attitudes.

Next the young communicator returns to employee relations work, perhaps as editor of a magazine or as an information specialist who develops manuals and programs for the use of supervisory management. He attends employee meetings as a consultant, and suggests ways in which employees may become more interested in the company's financial problems. He may help run orientation sessions for higher supervisory personnel in which the public relations objectives of the company are explained. Why should a local manager spend time working with the local newspaper editor? How should he go about becoming a news source? Why should the manager belong to the Rotary or Kiwanis club? The employee relations specialist tries to relate the total public relations program to the personal interests of employees.

There are other assignments. If he has had advertising experience, the public relations man may be placed in charge of institutional advertising. If he has had training in sampling procedures and statistical methods, he may take charge of a customer attitude survey and its interpretation, or he may head the audiovisual section and handle films, slides, and pictures. He may return to the news bureau as director in charge of the major company stories. He may edit the company's

Magazines published by companies for their customers or employees, such as this Polaroid publication, often are expertly edited with high-quality graphics. (INSTANTS Magazine, courtesy of Polaroid Corp.)

WINTER 1986 $2.50

Instants

THE MAGAZINE OF POLAROID INSTANT PHOTOGRAPHY

NEW YEAR'S COLORS IN SAN FRANCISCO'S CHINATOWN

HOLIDAY NIGHTS ON THE PASEO DEL RIO

SOLVING THE MYSTERIES OF FILM CHEMISTRY

annual report for a time and do shareholder relations work. He may become a policy adviser, preparing speeches for the company president, writing a manual explaining the public relations policies of the company, or working with various executives on long-range planning. He may in time become assistant director of the department. And finally he may become vice-president in charge of public relations, a member of the company's management group. Or, he will remain in a median-level assignment, rounding out a comfortable and satisfying career as a telephone company officer who serves the community and other employees in a specialized staff role demanding technical journalistic skills and policy-making ability.

Another example might be a young journalism graduate who is not certain whether she wishes to do newspaper work, but who has acquired an understanding of journalistic routines through her classes and summer work on a newspaper. She is more interested in magazine writing and layout and begins as assistant editor of a company employee magazine. One year later she becomes editor. Later she marries and decides to relinquish full-time employment but still work professionally. She finds that the local hospital needs someone to edit its staff bulletin, handle the printing of occasional brochures and reports, and represent the hospital with the local media when newsworthy events take place. She is able to advise the hospital administrator on both printing matters and news policy and develops interesting stories of value both to the hospital and to readers.

A third example might be a five-year veteran of metropolitan newspaper work who is offered a position with a major automotive company. She starts in information work, moves on to employee relations, and becomes assistant director for a major branch plant. Three years later she is transferred to Detroit, and becomes assistant manager in the company's public relations department. She decides instead to enter a public relations counseling firm, and becomes an account executive for one specializing in automotive clients. At age 40 she is a vice-president of the firm and receives as high a salary as a major executive of a large metropolitan daily.

These are only three examples of an infinite variety of career possibilities in public relations. It is hardly necessary to point out that the highest salaries are earned by those who reach the executive level and who are capable of analyzing problems, advising on policy, planning programs, and administering large staffs and budgets.

Qualifications

There was a time when public relations people were hired away from the communications media. Many top-level executives in public relations today began their careers as journalists. Their development as public relations people was the result of on-the-job training, usually on a trial-and-error basis. That they succeeded is a tribute to their intelligence, their adaptability, and their willingness to keep learning throughout their careers. This generation is now retiring. Although many employers still look to the media for recruits, more and more are seeking recent college graduates to fill beginning jobs in public relations departments.

More than 350 colleges and universities provide some instruction in public relations. Schools of journalism and mass communications offer the greatest number of public relations degree programs, although they have been joined in recent years by an increasing number of speech communication departments. As pointed out in Chapter 20, most business schools teach public relations only as a theoretical unit within management programs but do not provide the instruction essential for specialized work in the field.

Students who achieve undergraduate degrees in public relations are most readily employed; those who then obtain master's degrees in communications, business, or a related field such as economics, sociology, psychology, or another liberal arts area, find greater opportunities. Thirty undergraduate programs in public relations had been accredited by the Accrediting Council on Education in Journalism and Mass Communications, the official accrediting agency, by 1986.

Many other journalism and communications majors, as well as those from traditional liberal arts programs, are being employed in beginning public relations jobs—provided they have the vital ability to write and speak well. One of the few things that experienced practitioners agree upon is that the primary qualification for anyone wishing to succeed in the field is the ability to articulate: to write clearly and with facility and to express oneself well orally. No one can hope to succeed in public relations without the ability to use words effectively. Words are the basic tool of the practitioner. To be successful, he or she must have an intimate understanding of language.

Both research ability and creative ingenuity are important. Practitioners must know how to dig out the facts and then have the imagination to make the most of those facts by applying innovative approaches and fresh ideas toward the accomplishment of their evaluation, planning, and communication efforts.

Practitioners also need the ability to empathize with other people, to anticipate and understand their points of view. In the managerial structure the public relations executive bears the responsibility for estimating how a particular policy or action on the part of management will be greeted by the publics affected. More than intuitive ability is necessary here. Whatever inherent abilities practitioners may have in this area of human understanding should be supplemented by background education in the social sciences, so that their estimates of human reactions will be more than mere guesses. Of course, in many situations, when the magnitude of the problem justifies such research, practitioners will supplement their own interpretation of the situation with formal surveys of public opinion and attitudes.

A group of public relations executives recently listed the following, in descending order, as "very important" attributes for job seekers: ability to write, speaking skills, professionalism, maturity, poise, appearance, grade-point average, social graces, part-time work, college credit internship, recommendations, and work on campus media.

In today's competitive employment situation, students no longer may enjoy the luxury of waiting until graduation to acquire experience. Unless they build up a portfolio through internships, work on campus media, part-time jobs, or club or class campaigns experience, many likely will not find employment soon after graduation.

Salaries

Public relations professionals in the United States earned a median annual salary of $43,000 in 1985, according to a survey by *pr reporter*. Salaries reported by 830 persons ranged from $10,000 to $200,000. The respondents were subscribers of the newsletter and members of PRSA and the Canadian Public Relations Society. Canadians reported a median salary of $48,000.

Although salaries increased about $3000 over those in 1984, for the first time in the 21-year history of the poll the median salary dropped $1000 over that for the preceding year. The decline was attributed to demographics—the departure from the field of a number of male practitioners, the highest paid in the field. Staff additions took place at a far lower level and consisted mostly of women. The median salary for women stood at $35,000.

Women between the ages of 25 and 29 earned an average of $2300 more than men of that age group, but men's salaries were higher in all other age categories. The figures reflect the fact that most female practitioners have been named to their present jobs more recently, have been employed by their present companies for fewer years, and have less public relations experience than most male respondents.

Newcomers to the corporate and agency public relations field in 1986 were paid a median salary of $15,300, according to an annual survey of journalism and mass communication school graduates conducted by the Dow Jones Newspaper Fund. This figure compares with the $14,700 paid by advertising agencies, $13,900 by daily newspapers, and $12,600 by radio and television stations. Salaries were higher in the Northeast and on the West Coast. As a general rule, a job with a profit-making corporation, an industry association, or a counseling firm pays a higher salary than a job with a nonprofit educational institution, government agency, hospital, or charitable institution. Nevertheless, the kind of rounded experience that one gains in some of these lower-paying jobs can be valuable later.

PROFESSIONALISM IN PUBLIC RELATIONS

Like journalism and advertising, public relations is not—and cannot become—a profession such as medicine and law. Practice in these latter fields requires legal state certification following years of educational preparation and the passing of examinations. Under the First Amendment no one can be prohibited from engaging in an occupation based upon freedom to speak and to publish. Nevertheless, journalists and advertising and public relations people attain varying degrees of *professionalism,* in the broader sense, through the preparation, skill, and practice that distinguishes them from amateurs in these fields. Such professionalism normally is characterized by a high degree of independence, a sense of responsibility to society, and an adherence to recognized ethical and other standards that supersedes their loyalty to an individual employer.

The 13,850-member Public Relations Society of America certifies the professionalism of practitioners through a program of accreditation. To become an accredited member of the society, a person must have at least five years of experience in public relations practice or teaching, must have two sponsors who will testify as to integrity and ability, and must pass written and oral examinations.

The PRSA accreditation program, instituted in 1965, has been a major step toward professionalizing the field. To be an associate member of PRSA, one need have only one year's experience in the field. For students who have just earned their college degrees and who have been members of the Public Relations Student Society of America, there is an associate form of membership in PRSA. The student organization, sponsored by PRSA, has chapters in more than 120 colleges and universities. More than 78 percent of its approximately 4300 members are female.

Additionally, PRSA, the International Association of Business Communicators (IABC), and the public relations division of the Association for Education in Journalism and Mass Communication have worked to improve and standardize the curricula for programs of public relations studies at the bachelor's and master's levels. PRSA and IABC also have developed a code of professional standards for the practice of public relations. Although parts of the code are phrased in general terms, such as requiring practitioners to adhere to generally accepted standards of accuracy, truth, and good taste, other clauses and interpretive supplements deal with specifics. For example, a PRSA member cannot represent conflicting or competing interests without the express consent of both parties, nor can the member reveal the confidences of present or former clients or employers.

In 1986 the national PRSA president, Anthony M. Franco, a Detroit counselor, signed a consent order with the Securities & Exchange Commission after he was accused of improper insider trading on a client's stock. Although signing such an order signifies neither guilt nor innocence, the resulting publicity caused Franco to resign from the PRSA presidency and, several months later, his membership in the organization while the PRSA board of directors was considering suspension or censure based on violations of the PRSA code of ethics. Because of the resignation, the board no longer had jurisdiction over Franco and could not make a decision regarding possible violation.

Despite the embarrassing situation of a national president's resigning for possible unethical conduct, in the opinion of a number of PRSA members the incident revealed that the code of conduct does have meaning and that the judicial process, although somewhat cumbersome, does provide a method of removing unethical practitioners from the organization. Members also pointed out that PRSA is the only professional communications organization with an established grievance procedure that can lead to the suspension and censure of a member for illegal or unethical professional activity.

The Foundation for Public Relations Research and Education, which was established in 1956 with the support of the society but is now independent, seeks to advance professionalism through grants for research studies, publications, and sponsorship of a quarterly, the *Public Relations Review.*

The other organization for public relations practitioners, IABC, had approximately 12,000 members worldwide in 1986. IABC describes itself as "a professional organization for writers, editors, audiovisual specialists, managers, and other business and organizational communicators." The association sponsors student chapters at universities and has developed its own accreditation program. About 10 percent of IABC members hold the accredited business communicator (IABC) rating.

Approximately 1500 of its members are in Canada, where the Toronto chapter, with more than 400 members, is IABC's second largest. Other chapters outside the United States in 1986 included those in the United Kingdom, the Philippines, Hong Kong, and Belgium.

The International Public Relations Association (IPRA) was organized in 1955 as an individual membership society for public relations professionals with international interests. IPRA has well over 700 members in more than 60 countries and is seeking further expansion. Every third year it sponsors a World Congress of Public Relations, which attracts 600 or more practitioners from the United States and Europe as well as from countries in Latin America, Africa, the Near East, and the Far East, where public relations is also growing rapidly.

International public relations is also discussed in Chapter 25.

Thus, although public relations still suffers some stigma as a result of the occasional misuse of the term, it has come a long way from the time when the practitioner was scorned by colleagues in journalism as a "flack." Nevertheless, public relations still has a long way to go before it achieves the distinction of becoming a genuine profession. Today, at the very least, it is an essential link in much of the world's social, political, industrial, and mass communications network.

PART FIVE

Research and

Education

Mass Communications

Research

Measuring Public Opinion

The Gallup Poll has become a familiar American—and, indeed, world—institution through which the science of public opinion measurement is identified in the public mind. George H. Gallup was a pioneer not only in opinion polling, but also in the development of reader-interest measurement techniques for the print media and for use in marketing.

While he was a young instructor in journalism at the University of Iowa, Gallup devised a method for calculating the amount of attention by readers to various items in a newspaper through interviews with selected persons representing various classes among the audience. Using this application of random sampling principles, he did reader-interest studies for the Des Moines newspapers and national periodicals.

Through patient refining of his sampling techniques, Gallup broke new ground and worked out a system for determining the opinions of a total group from interviews with a small number of persons. In 1935 he left teaching and launched his American Institute of Public Opinion in Princeton, New Jersey.

Fate smiled on Gallup. Before 1936 the highly respected *Literary Digest* had been successfully predicting the outcome of presidential elections by making unscientific telephone calls. That year the *Digest's* straw poll predicted that Republican candidate Alf Landon would defeat President Franklin D. Roosevelt. Gallup came up with a prediction giving Roosevelt 54 percent of the vote. Even so, he was 6.5 percent short of measuring the avalanche of New Deal votes that buried Landon 531 electoral votes to 8 and swept the *Digest* into oblivion.

Gallup came to grief in 1948, along with rival pollsters and other political experts, when he failed to predict President Harry Truman's upset victory over Republican Thomas E. Dewey. Assuming that Dewey was certain of victory, Gallup measured only small samples during the summer and fall, adding them together cumulatively. He thus missed the sharp swing to Truman late in the campaign. The lesson was learned, and since 1952 the Gallup Poll has been off an average of only 1.2 percent in national election predictions.

Actually, election predictions were not George Gallup's most important contribution. The *Gallup Opinion Index* gives access to the results of hundreds of poll questions on political and social issues of national importance. And guiding the marketing of products is undoubtedly more rewarding financially.

*M*ass communications research has been a rapidly developing graduate studies field since the 1950s, and the products of the graduate schools of journalism and mass communication have taken their places in the research departments of newspapers, advertising agencies, broadcast networks and stations, public relations firms, magazines, and other mass communications organizations. In this chapter we review the specific types of research involved.

Mass communications research is the scientific study of the mass communication behavior of human beings, usually in current situations calling for the gathering of primary quantitative information about the audience. It also includes study of the media, the communicators, and the contents of their messages.

There has been extensive research into the four aspects of the communication process described in Chapter 3: the communicator, the message, the channel, and the audience. In doing such studies researchers use the basic methods of the behavioral sciences: survey research, field studies, and field experiments.

Specific fields of specialization include the readership and listener or viewership studies conducted by individual media or commercial firms, graphics research for the print media and advertising copywriting, market research for advertising purchasers, public opinion research to determine attitudes and predict actions, content analysis of media material, and the processes and effects research described in Chapter 3. ◆

THE NEED FOR RESEARCH

The enormous growth of the various forms of mass communication in the twentieth century has resulted in an increasing need for better knowledge of the processes and effects of mass communication. The complex mass media system has produced a need for research not only among practicing communicators, but also among policymakers, consumers, and various social groups. Many of the problems and criticisms to be discussed in Part Six, for example, have led to research questions. Consequently, a core of specially trained research persons has risen to search for and supply this knowledge.

Much of the mass communications research conducted today attempts to answer the questions of broadcasters, advertising specialists, and other communicators. The magazine or newspaper editor, for example, needs to know things such as: How many persons read my publication? (Typically, each copy has several readers so the total audience may be something quite different from the total circulation.) What kinds of persons read my publication? (The New York *Times,* for example, is intended for a different audience from that of the New York *Daily News;* the audience of *Fortune* is almost completely different from that of *Peo-*

ple.) How am I doing as an editor? Am I printing the kinds of things my audience wants to read about? Are my stories easy to read or hard to read? How can I improve the content of my publication? How can I improve the presentation of this content in terms of layout and typography?

There was a time when an editor could know many of these things by personal contact with the people in the community or area. By informal means, through experience, the editor developed a rough idea of the composition of the audience and how well the publication was liked. This unsystematic, informal, intuitive method no longer is adequate for the modern communicator for several reasons:

1. *The increasing number of communications media.* In the present-day community the average person has access to many media—local and out-of-town newspapers, a number of television and radio stations, cable, video, and hundreds of magazines, books, and films.

2. *Increasing competition among the media for the attention of the public.* Since no individual has enough time to read or listen to all the media, or even to pay attention to all the output of just one medium, this means a small fraction of the available output will be selected, and the rest ignored. This leads to intense competition among the different media to capture as much of the public's time and attention as possible—obviously, the newspaper or magazine or station that succeeds in satisfying the needs of the public, and whose messages are interesting and easy to absorb, will get a good share of public attention. Those that do not succeed in doing this will eventually fall by the wayside.

3. *The increasing number of people in the audience.* An editor or broadcaster reaches from several thousand to several million readers, viewers, or listeners, and the tendency is constantly toward reaching larger audiences. No communicator can possibly have personal contact with everyone in the audience and knowledge of all their varying needs, likes, dislikes, and opinions.

4. *The changing tastes of the public.* People are becoming better educated and more sophisticated; they travel more, know more about the rest of the world, and are constantly developing broader interests through exposure to more communications from outside their immediate environment. Any communicator's audience is in a state of continuous turnover and interest change. Decisions cannot be based on what was known to be true ten years or five years or even one year ago.

These are all good reasons why the effective communicator—whether advertising copywriter, editor, or broadcaster—can no longer rely on hunches and intuition alone to capture and hold the attention of the public. As Harry Henry says in *Motivation Research:* "There are examples, of course, of 'hunch-merchants' who hit on successful ideas with enormous success, and finish up as classic case histories. But no case histories are written up of the 99 equally self-confident but not so lucky venturers whose only spell of glory is in a brief trip to the bankruptcy courts."

In the face of all these changing requirements, then, just how do modern mass communicators get the precise information they need to make their media successful? They turn to communications research, a specialty that has grown up in the past four decades, to help answer some of the questions they do not have the time or training to answer for themselves. The communications researcher is just one member of the team of writers, editors, artists, advertising persons, and others working together to help a medium do its job, which is to transmit information, opinion, and entertainment to a mass public. Or the researcher may be a scholar in a university setting whose main objective is that of adding to our general knowledge of the communication process.

Modern communicators also face criticism and questions about their role in society. For example, do TV commercials in children's programs mislead or take advantage of young viewers? Is there any relationship between television programming and violent behavior? Do news media distort the news? Such questions often lead to research that is as important as that of describing the changing tastes of the public. Thus, although the media need research telling them how to compete with one another and how to serve their audiences, they also need answers to broader questions about their role in modern society. Much research of this type is being conducted in schools of journalism and mass communications.

WHAT IS COMMUNICATIONS RESEARCH?

A broad definition of research is simply "careful investigation," or a diligent inquiry into any subject. This broad term would include almost any kind of study—the literary scholar who reads all of Shakespeare's works, the biographer who finds out all he can about a famous woman, or the historian who compiles a history of American newspapers.

Mass communications research, however, has taken on a somewhat more specialized meaning. First of all, it is usually (though not always) considered *behavioral* research—the study of human beings (rather than inanimate or nonhuman objects). It is a branch of the behavioral sciences, which include psychology, sociology, and anthropology.

Thus we see that it is also *interdisciplinary* research; that is, it borrows the tools and knowledge of various other fields of study that will help in the understanding of mass communications problems. It does not confine itself to any particular point of view, theory, or subject matter. It may borrow from linguistics, general semantics, philosophy, economics, or any other discipline that might help communications effectiveness.

It is *scientific* research since it uses scientific methodology in solving communications problems. As in any science, its intent is to explain, predict, and control. In achieving this end, its methods must be objective (as opposed to subjective) and systematic (as opposed to unsystematic). Although most mass communications research is done on specific problems, the goal—as in any scientific field— is to formulate general principles and theories that can bring about more effective communication. Being scientific, it is, of course, also *quantitative* research. Random sampling methods, the laws of probability, and mathematical statistical techniques all help to make more precise and meaningful the findings from any particular investigation.

It is generally *primary* research rather than secondary. That is, the mass communications researcher customarily gathers new and original information rather than relying on printed source material. This is not always the case, however, since one may, for example, have to consult year-by-year statistical figures gathered in the past by other researchers in order to spot a trend over a period of time.

Of course, the subject matter of communications research is communication. More specifically, it is concerned with mass communication, the communication behavior of large numbers of people, particularly those who make up the audiences for the different media. Other groups may be studied, too, of course—newspaper reporters, news sources, magazine editors, or public relations specialists, for example. In order to understand the behavior of groups, however, it is usually necessary first to understand individual behavior.

To summarize the definition of mass communications research: It is the scientific study of the mass communication behavior of human beings, usually in current situations requiring the gathering of primary quantitative information. It also includes the study of the communicators, their media, and the content of their message.

This is not the only definition that might be legitimately applied. It leaves out other kinds of important research being done in the field of journalism and mass communications (historical, literary, biographical, legal, economic, international aspects), which are discussed in Chapter 20 on mass communications education; editorial research of the "fact-checking" variety; and the creative synthesizing of ideas and research findings. It also includes some topics that might be claimed by other disciplines. It is, however, a reasonably comprehensive definition of the specialized type of mass communications research that has grown up in recent decades.

AREAS OF COMMUNICATIONS RESEARCH

The volume of communications research has grown in recent years as an increasing number of scholars have been attracted to the subject. Two trends have accompanied that growth. The breadth of communications research has grown as scholars with varying interests have delved into different areas—those of political communication, consumer interests, and media economics, for example. And the depth of communications research has increased as scholars taking different avenues have tended to specialize within one area or another. Consequently, communications research could be divided in a number of ways. One approach is to categorize research within the four aspects of the communication process described in Chapter 3: the communicator, the message, the channel, and the audience. Extensive research has been done in each area.

Communicator Research

One way to improve communication is to find out what kinds of people are best suited for the role of communicator and what factors affect communicator performance. We need to know the essential characteristics of good reporters, editors, and advertising people, among others, so that the proper training may be offered to future professionals. Even the most professional communicator, however, may be unaware of some of the factors affecting performance. In one study it was found that stories resulting from assignments by editors were more accurate than those originated by the reporter or stemming from coverage of general meetings. Another study disclosed that news personnel with "supportive images" (more establishment oriented than others) reported so-called good news more accurately than bad news, whereas those with critical images of society did a more accurate job on bad news. Communicators increasingly are using sophisticated tools such as the computer to analyze complex problems. How will journalists adjust to the new demands placed upon them in the era of cable? How are reporters performing with the new technologies? These are questions for communicator research studies.

Message Research

The effects of different forms of the same message may be compared through variations in style, length, degree of difficulty, and the like, with attention paid to comprehensibility, interest, and attention value. We often vary our personal conversations as to complexity and word usage in terms of some determination of the sophistication of the intended receiver. With scientific content analysis we can easily determine the relative degree of difficulty of any message, and we can make inferences about the intent of the communicator as well.

Channel Research

The channel through which a message is transmitted is closely related to the effectiveness of the message. This is due in part to the differing characteristics of the various media, which perform the functions of informing, interpreting, entertaining, and selling differently from one another. By their character, content, style, and geographic coverage, media, to a great extent, are able to select their desired audiences. Advertisers are especially interested in determining which media can best deliver their messages and in knowing something about the people who comprise the potential audience of a medium. In face-to-face communication, we often use facial expressions—a smile, for example—to much greater advantage than a flow of pleasant words.

Audience Research

The majority of communications research ultimately is concerned with mass media audiences. Communicators need to know the behavior, interests, tastes, attitudes, and opinions of the people whom they seek to reach. Advertisers must know the number and description of people in a medium's audience so that they may reach the right kind of person for their products. For example, a baby food manufacturer may want to learn which of two magazines with equal circulations has the greater number of young parents. Publishers and editors require audience information so that they may select editorial content that fits their readers' needs.

The reading interests of young newspaper readers are quite different from those of older readers. More recently, researchers have gone beyond simply describing the audiences of mass media. In some studies researchers are seeking to determine the motivations for media use; in others the goal is to determine the gratifications people derive from using the media. Still other scholars are focusing on children of different ages, trying to learn how children understand what they see and hear on television. Specialists in political communication are examining how people use the media to follow candidates and their campaigns. One type of research focuses on the relationship between the media's inventories of campaign issues and the personal lists of readers and viewers.

The overall goal is to find out how mass communications affects audiences, just as we individuals need to know how our words affect other individuals with whom we communicate. The object of mass communications is to affect human behavior and attitudes. The object of communications research is to find out how and to what degree human behavior and attitudes are affected by mass communications.

COMMUNICATIONS RESEARCH METHODS

Communications research uses the same basic research methods as other branches of the behavioral sciences. Depending upon the needs of the researcher, any of the following methods may be applied to practically any problem.

In *survey research* the scientific sample is studied to gather demographic information or sociological facts as well as psychological information—opinions and attitudes. As opposed to the status survey, which produces an inventory of facts, survey research gathers both factual information and the opinions of subjects. Thus, the researcher is able to talk about the relationships among variables—for example, the relationship between educational level and media usage, or between sex and opinion in regard to a particular political candidate.

A similar method, but one in which independent and dependent variables are related and hypotheses tested, is the *field study.* In a third method, the *field experiment,* the independent variable is introduced by the researcher in an environment in which considerable control of extraneous variables is possible; the field study is ex post facto. In both the field study and field experiment an attempt is made to establish causal relationships between independent and dependent variables. The most closely controlled method of study of causal relationships is the *laboratory experiment,* in which all except the independent variable to be studied are eliminated.

The survey is frequently used to determine relationships between demographics and mass communication behavior, as in determining the relationships of sex and age to television program viewing. An example of a field study is a case in which it is hypothesized that the grade performance of school children has a stronger and more consistent relationship to the extent of usage and comprehension of mass communications than do other variables in the school and home environment. In a field experiment one might designate two groups or communities that are similar in relevant characteristics and introduce variables, such as two forms of advertising of the same new product, to determine which form of advertising is more conducive to the purchase of the new product. Both the field study and the field experiment are difficult to control because variables other than those studied may affect the measured or dependent variable without the researcher's being able to know what really happened.

The laboratory experiment provides the best opportunity for control of variables since the researcher can be nearly certain that the causal variable introduced actually brings about the measured effect. For example, using two equivalent or matched groups, the researcher might present a message in oral form to one group and in written form to the other. If a standard test then demonstrates that comprehension was consistently higher for the oral message group than for the written message group, one could be reasonably certain that the oral message was more easily understood by people such as those in the two groups.

EXAMPLES OF COMMUNICATIONS RESEARCH

Research is used by every kind of communicator—newspaper and magazine editors and writers, television and radio personnel, advertising and public relations experts, government information specialists, book publishers, and film producers. Some research has immediate utility in that it can be applied by changing the content or layout. In a sense this can be called *feedback* research, since it is one way in which members of the audience may inform the editor or broadcaster what they like or dislike. In readership studies subscribers indicate what they prefer to read; in graphics research readers disclose what types of displays they find most attractive; in advertising research readers indicate which ads are most effective; in public opinion research the public relates how it feels about a medium; and in content analysis the communicator learns how much print space or broadcast time is being devoted to various kinds of stories. Other research, such as that dealing with the processes and effects of mass communication, also provides important information for communicators. While it may have less immediate application, it is of great concern to policymakers, critics, social groups, and other consumers.

Readership Studies

Sometimes called reader traffic studies, these tell the editor how many and what kinds of people have read each item in a publication. For example, story A had 40 percent readership whereas story B had 10 percent, picture A had 37 percent readership whereas picture B had 12 percent. Such information, gathered by trained personnel in personal interviews with representative samples of readers, provides a check on editorial judgment. It is useful to the editor in following trends of audience interest, in evaluating effects of typographical makeup and display of stories on readership, in deciding which of several syndicated features should be retained or dropped, and so on. Effectiveness of various types of advertising also can be studied.

Similar research is conducted on television and radio programs. The various rating services determine how many sets were tuned in to each of a number of programs, how many people were listening to each set, and what kinds of people they were. One TV-radio research service gets its information from an electronic device permanently attached to the television or radio sets of a sample of households. Another rating service makes personal telephone calls to homes while programs are on the air. Another method uses diaries. In 1987 the A. C. Nielsen Company began using "people meters" to measure national TV audiences.

Graphics Research

Typography, layout, and makeup fall within the area called graphics by the print media. By experimentation with different methods of presentation, the researcher can tell the editor what the most effective means of presentation of a given item is. A book publisher or magazine or newspaper editor may choose to test audience preference for one kind of typeface as compared with another; the use of one large illustration instead of several smaller pictures; or the effectiveness of a news item published in an area two columns wide and 5 inches deep, as contrasted to the same item set in one column 10 inches deep. Much research has been done on the legibility of typefaces and aesthetic preferences for them.

Advertising people, too, are strongly interested in graphics research. Which ad gets across the most information—an ad with a big picture and a little text, or a little picture and a lot of text? Such research may be accomplished by split runs in the publication, so that the alternatives are presented to two different samples of readers whose reactions then can be compared after a readership survey, or by experimentation with a relatively small group of persons before publication of the ad.

Graphics research has its parallel in the broadcasting media. Research can tell whether three minutes of commercial time are most effective at the beginning of a program, at the end, or spread through it. Or it can tell whether, on a radio newscast, a summary of headlines at the start of the program will increase interest in the news items that follow.

Advertising Research

The various media and almost all advertising agencies conduct advertising research to help them in their job of persuading people to buy. *Market* research has been carried on since the start of the century and was the forerunner of other public opinion research. It includes consumer surveys on potential markets for new products, dealer studies, customer attitude surveys, and studies of effectiveness of brand names and package designs. Media use by advertisers is determined in part by market research results, and various media seek to point out their usefulness by undertaking market research studies for particular advertisers' products. *Copy* research includes analysis of advertisement readership studies, pretesting of advertisements, evaluation of printed advertisement campaign effectiveness, and graphics. In broadcasting, commercials and programs may be tried out on small samples of listeners by means of response-recording devices. The same is true of films.

Public Opinion Research

All communicators are interested in knowing the state of public opinion about themselves or their medium. Publishers want to know how the public feels about their newspapers, magazines, or books. Broadcasters and film producers are equally sensitive to public approval. Public relations and advertising specialists want to know if they have succeeded in creating a favorable image for their companies or products in the public mind. Surveys of attitudes held by specific customer groups, and by the public in general, give them some answers.

Communicators are interested in public opinion from an additional viewpoint— that is, public attitudes toward social and economic issues, government officials and their policies, and important events. The familiar national polls conducted by George Gallup, Louis Harris, Elmo Roper, and others offer a check on prevailing opinion. And since public opinion is news in itself, the polls are sold to many media units; in addition, some media conduct their own polls and report the outcomes as news stories. Large companies subscribe to opinion survey services as a part of their public relations programs. Government also uses public opinion research —the United States Information Agency has a survey research division whose sole function is to measure public opinion toward the United States in other countries and the effects of our various foreign information programs, including the Voice of America. Politicians are constantly using public opinion surveys to gauge campaign progress and important issues.

Content Analysis

Much can be learned about a publication merely by studying its content. (This falls somewhat outside the definition of behavioral research.) Content analysis provides a clue to an editor's or writer's intentions and to the kind of audience a publication or broadcast attracts. Combined with readership studies, it gives clues to what people want to read about. This form of research can be especially valuable when more precise kinds of research are inappropriate or unavailable. For example, a content analysis of German wartime broadcasts gave the Allies useful clues to the enemy's war strategy. An analysis of Soviet cold war propaganda helped the United States government in the formulation of its own propaganda, since it revealed the themes that were currently being stressed and enabled us to combat them.

Processes and Effects Research

What are the effects of mass communication? For many years this question directed the work of scholars interested in mass media processes. The model of communication outlined in Chapter 3 provides the elements, with arrows indicating that the major flow is from communicator to message to audience. More recently, researchers have noted that the model is theoretical: TV viewers and newspaper readers are not just passive agents reacting to what they see and read. As explained in that same chapter, research scholars have sought to determine what people seek in the media, what happens when they use the media, and what they get out of them. The more complex perspectives recognize that people have varying interests, biases, and needs that they "take with them" to the media. At the same time, other researchers have chosen to work with families, groups, and communities rather than with individuals. The following are a few examples of current trends in mass communication research.

1. *Community media systems.* One vein of research has focused on the role of the mass media in communities. Editors, broadcasters, and other communicators act as "gatekeepers," deciding what information community residents will receive about various issues. Are there differences in the types of information conveyed by communicators in small as contrasted to large communities? One study suggests that editors in smaller, more homogeneous communities tend to avoid controversial issues and concentrate on more positive, socially supportive information. Editors in larger communities, which have organized interest groups and more mechanisms for handling disputes, distribute more conflict information and are more likely to stress opinion leadership.

2. *Information diffusion.* People are provided with an abundance of information by the mass media, and technologies developing with the cable systems are accelerating this "information explosion." In coping with this barrage, people must be selective. They learn things from the mass media, but not necessarily the same things, nor the same amount. For example, those who use more of the print media —newspapers, magazines, and books—tend to be more knowledgeable than those who rely mainly on radio and television for their information.

3. *Media socialization.* Adults do not suddenly appear with full-blown reading, viewing, and listening habits. They acquire these habits through many years and under the influence of many factors. One approach to understanding the development of communication behavior is called socialization research. Scholars try to specify the social origins and processes by which people learn and maintain reading and viewing habits. In a sense they are turning around the question of effects and asking what leads to use of the mass media. Researchers taking this perspective have found varying TV viewing patterns among children from different family environments. In families in which children are encouraged to explore new ideas and to express them openly, children spend far less time with TV and pay more attention to news and public affairs programs when they do watch. By contrast, in families placing greater emphasis on obedience and social harmony, children spend the most time with TV of any group and their interest is concentrated on entertainment rather than on news and public affairs programs.

4. *Children and television.* Parents, broadcasters, government regulators, and others have been concerned with violence shown on television. This has led to a large number of studies trying to determine whether there is any relationship between watching TV violence and real acts of violence. Do children use the violent characters shown on TV as models for their own behavior? How do children understand the violence they view on the TV screen? These are among the questions researchers are asking. Obviously small children have more limited capacities than adults for understanding the world around them. For example, do children under the age of seven have difficulty relating the different parts of a plot

A 2-year-old child watches "Mr. Rogers" on the family television set. Most children see hundreds of hours of TV shows before they start school. Researchers conduct elaborate studies, seeking to determine the good and bad effects of such exposure. (Weisbrot, Stock; Boston)

sequence? This has implications for their TV viewing, since they may be unable to connect the punishment accorded a TV murderer with the criminal act or the motive.

5. *Agenda-setting function.* For years, researchers have been interested in the relationship between media use and attitude change. More recently, studies have focused on information and the new cognitions acquired from the media. An example of this trend is the notion of an agenda-setting function of the press, which was explored in Chapter 3. The view is that the media often may not be successful in telling people what to think, but they have considerable success in telling people what to think about. Studies here, for example, look at the relationship between the agenda of political campaign issues set by the media and the personal agendas of the audience.

6. *Motives, uses, and gratifications.* As noted in Chapter 3, researchers are delving into the motives people have for using the mass media and are trying to identify the uses and gratifications associated with newspaper reading, TV viewing, cable use, and the like. In one study readers relied on the newspaper for help in deciding how to vote in a nonpartisan election. In another study people who had switched to a four-day work week started watching TV programs that had direct application to activities planned for expanded weekends. Other researchers, particularly those for cable systems, are examining the different things people seek in the media—specific information, a chance to relax, favorite programs, and so on.

The preceding examples demonstrate the range of communications research today. Each area has implications for communicators. For example, editors may want to rethink their coverage of political candidates if their readers' issue agendas are not closely linked with a newspaper's campaign coverage. Media consumers also need to understand how communication works, and much of the research discussed helps to provide that information.

One of the most satisfying aspects of communications research is in doing original, imaginative thinking and investigation. Creative researchers try to think of different ways to do a particular communications job and then test the alternatives to see which is the most effective. They critically analyze the long-standing traditions and accepted practices of the media and then test these tricks of the trade to see if they are really the most effective ways to communicate. They devise new and original research techniques and methods to solve particular problems. They keep abreast of developments in related disciplines such as psychology and sociology, applying the findings and theories from those fields to communications problems. Creative communications researchers also make valuable contributions to theory and practice in those related disciplines. They both borrow from and contribute to other areas of knowledge.

A glance through a few issues of journals such as the *Journalism Quarterly,* the *Journal of Communication,* and *Public Opinion Quarterly* will reveal some of the directions that mass communications research now takes. Although some of the questions or problems explored do not differ greatly from those explored 40 years ago, the emphasis now is on the use of more scientific methods of studying those questions. Earlier expressions of subjective opinion by communications experts are being subjected to scientific scrutiny and the "folklore" of the media is being tested.

JOB OPPORTUNITIES IN COMMUNICATIONS RESEARCH

Research is being conducted in every kind of communications and business enterprise today. All the media are engaged in research to some degree: newspapers, magazines, radio, television, cable, publishing houses, film producers. So are the supporting agencies: press associations, advertising agencies, public relations firms, specialized commercial research firms. Further, manufacturers of consumer and industrial products, retail and wholesale business firms, the federal government, and colleges and universities are engaged in communications research.

Surveys have revealed that four of every five U.S. companies have a department (one person or more) engaged in market research, which almost always includes some form of communications or opinion research in its activities. Even among the smaller firms—those with sales under $5 million annually—three of every five have a research department. Advertising agencies are the most avid users of research; more than 90 percent of all advertising agencies in the United States have a research department. And the large publishing and broadcasting organizations employ researchers.

Naturally, the larger the firm, the more likely it is to have a research department. However, both the larger and the smaller firms frequently turn to commercial research firms, whose sole business it is to conduct research for outside clients. Most medium-sized and large cities in the country today have at least one commercial research firm, and the number of such firms is increasing yearly. Many of these firms serve clients on a national basis, and a few conduct research in foreign countries. Some of the largest are the Opinion Research Corporation of Princeton, New Jersey; International Research Associates and Alfred Politz Research of New York City; A. C. Nielsen Company in Chicago; and Field Research, on the West Coast.

Advertising agencies tend to have larger research staffs than other kinds of businesses; the largest agencies employ an average of 50 persons in their research departments. Large publishing and broadcasting firms average four research employees, but a few have departments more the size of those in the agencies.

How high is the salary for a worker in communications research? Because of the extensive amount of advanced training and specialized knowledge required, researchers are well paid compared with other mass communications personnel. A person who has a master's degree and who has specialized in research may expect a starting salary of $18,000 per year. The more advanced student in communications research—who has completed most or all of the training necessary for a doctoral degree—may initially command $25,000 per year. These figures vary, of course, with location and size of the firm. With experience, communications research specialists may rise in salary to $50,000 or higher. Research analysts exceed the $20,000 level.

Opportunities for advancement in mass communications research are good because of the expansion taking place in the field. Not only can research be a rewarding and satisfying vocation in itself, but it also serves as a stepping-stone to other kinds of work, both in the creative and business aspects of communications. One example is Dr. Frank Stanton, who started in research and became head of the Columbia Broadcasting System. Two others are A. Edward Miller, who became publisher of *McCall's,* and Marion Harper, Jr., who became head of McCann-Erickson advertising agency.

Another excellent opportunity for researchers exists in schools of journalism and mass communications. More and more universities are adding communications researchers to their staffs, both to do research and to teach and train students in the skills involved. In addition, such schools often contract to do research for the media or for civic and government agencies. A doctoral degree is usually considered a requirement for such a faculty position.

TRAINING FOR RESEARCH POSITIONS

Until just after World War II, most scientifically trained researchers on mass communications problems came from psychology and sociology. The importance of research as a specialty has since led some of the nation's leading schools of journalism and mass communications to set up graduate programs in quantitative scientific research methods.

In some of these schools mass communications research is offered as just one of several communications fields graduate students may elect in their courses of study; in others the entire graduate program is devoted to courses in behavioral research theory and methodology, with a minimum of emphasis on the communications aspect. In almost all, however, the research specialization requires a sampling of appropriate courses drawn from several different disciplines and heavy emphasis on statistics and scientific method courses.

A typical graduate program calls for a major in mass communications with a minor in psychology, sociology, or statistics. Various other departments—anthropology, philosophy, economics, political science, speech communication, marketing, to name a few—may also figure in the program to a lesser extent, depending on the individual interests of the student. Some individuals prefer to major in social psychology or sociology and minor in mass communications.

It is considered desirable—though not necessary—for graduate students in communications research to have professional experience in one or more of the mass media. The first wave of communications research Ph.D.s—those receiving degrees in the 1950s—almost without exception had practical journalism experience as newspaper reporters and editors, radio news personnel, and so on. The value of a practical journalism background lies in the greater awareness of crucial communications problems, a better knowledge of the questionable assumptions of the trade, and a more critical perspective based on an understanding of journalistic processes and folkways.

It should be emphasized, however, that prior journalistic experience is not a requirement, but merely helpful for the person interested in mass communications research. He or she can acquire knowledge of the media and of journalistic techniques in journalism courses and in postdegree professional work. It should be noted, too, that the only distinction between the graduate program of a mass communications researcher and that of the less specialized behavioral scientist is the former's preoccupation with mass communications as the subject matter of the research; in practice, the student may engage in almost any kind of social research.

Education for

Mass Communications

20

"Why Is My Introductory Class So Large?"

If you are a student in a large college or university, or even in some smaller ones, you may wonder why your introductory mass communications class is large. Some of the reasons:

- *Budget.* The funds allocated to your department or school very likely are based upon the total number of student credit hours in classes taught by the unit's faculty. Substantial enrollment in one or more beginning classes makes possible the limited number of students in *skills* courses, generally no more than 15.
- *Core courses.* In most departments and schools *all* pre-majors and majors must take one or more such courses as necessary groundwork for advanced classes. This class may help you select a major.
- *Guest speakers.* Large classes generally are more suitable vehicles than small ones in attracting outside lecturers.
- *Nature of the course.* The introductory mass communications class generally attracts students from a number of other disciplines.

So, enjoy your class! Millions of other students have followed this same path in acquiring knowledge that has helped them either as practitioners in, or consumers of, the mass media, which affect *all* our lives.

$\mathcal{T}$he education required for careers in journalism and mass communications is provided, for the most part, by the several hundred colleges and universities in the United States that offer degree programs in the field. Community college and secondary school programs contribute heavily, as do also the hundreds of four-year institutions that offer such courses but not a mass communications degree.

Some media hire graduates of strictly liberal arts programs, but not so frequently as in past decades before journalism and mass communications schools strengthened and enlarged their programs, attracted heavy enrollments, and maintained a strong liberal arts component in the total education of their students.

Professional and industry groups and foundations support journalism and mass communications education in many ways. Since 1945 practitioners and educators have nourished an accreditation process that has helped improve the quality of many schools. Numerous educator organizations aid in the total effort.

In this chapter we discuss the historical development of such programs, review some of the problems, and delineate channels that lead to specialized careers, both as practitioners and as teachers in secondary schools, community colleges, and four-year and graduate-level institutions. ◆

THE ROLE OF EDUCATION

Informing, persuading, and entertaining the public are difficult tasks. Few succeed as mass communications practitioners without grasping at least the essentials of the broad areas of knowledge that comprise a college education. Society is so complex, its specialties so numerous, and its varying relationships so involved that only a person with intelligence and a comprehension of many facets of human activity can begin to understand the meaning of processes and events. Without such understanding, reporting, for example, may not only be superficial but actually dangerous to the future of a democratic nation.

Some exceptional individuals acquire a broad education without attending college. But for most of us the only certain path to acquiring knowledge about our world lies in formal courses of instruction in the social sciences, the natural sciences, and the humanities. Here we discover the precise methodology of the researcher and the scientist and the skills of the writer or artist; we have guided access to the accumulated wisdom of the ages; we learn what people have considered to be the good, the true, and the beautiful; and we study the behavior of human beings, both as individuals and in their relationships with others.

Obtaining such a basic education has special importance to communicators. For one thing, they are exposed to areas of thought and criticism that give them opportunities to become cultured persons of discrimination and taste in their own right. From these experiences they should be able to acquire a working knowledge of society and a sensitivity to its many problems that will enable them to exercise the type of forthright citizenship so essential in our democracy. If their exposure to the processes of education has been productive, they will be enabled, in the words of Cardinal John Henry Newman, "to see things as they are, to go right to the point, to disentangle a skein of thought, to detect what is sophistical, and to discard what is irrelevant."

Education, however, assumes an even greater importance to future communicators. Almost every bit of knowledge that they acquire in college, from a study of the love life of an oyster to Thorstein Veblen's views on "conspicuous consumption," eventually seem to become grist for the mill as they report and interpret the kaleidoscopic nature of life in the most practical of working assignments,

CHANNELS OF EDUCATION FOR MASS COMMUNICATIONS

Students desiring to equip themselves for careers in mass communications may follow several avenues toward reaching their goal. The most common method is to enroll either directly, or through transfer from a community college, into an institution offering a four-year program leading to a degree in a field of journalism and mass communications. Approximately 300 colleges and universities in the United States provide such courses of study. A number of these institutions have established separate administrative units (colleges, schools, divisions) for their journalism and mass communications instruction. Most units, however, are housed in liberal arts colleges.

In either case students typically take no more than 25 percent of their course work in journalism and mass communications. The remainder is spread throughout the social sciences, humanities, and natural sciences, as well as business, physical education, and other studies, in accordance with the institution's requirements for both breadth and depth of study in the various areas of learning. In effect, students elect a major specialization in professional studies that gives them instruction in basic communication skills and in courses that relate journalism and mass communications to society. They do this just as other students elect a major concentration in geography, political science, or languages—and they are no more specialized in one subject than are these others.

Many practitioners in mass communications are college graduates who have pursued noncommunications majors in liberal arts institutions. Some media employers seek out such students, in the belief that their backgrounds best equip them for full development within their organizations. It seems more reasonable, however, that students who acquire both professional and general liberal arts education while enrolled in journalism and mass communications schools will be better prepared for professional work and will be employed more readily. This latter point has been corroborated by numerous surveys of employment patterns. For example, it has been found that journalism graduates comprise more than 80 percent of the new news-editorial employees hired by daily newspapers each year.

Mass communications educators know about this heavy dependence of the media upon their graduates through the operation of their placement offices. Employers rely upon the schools to recommend applicants for both beginning and advanced positions and almost always make calls directly to the school rather than to the college's general placement service. A large journalism and mass communications school receives several hundred requests each year from newspapers, news services, radio and television stations, magazines, advertising agencies, companies and agencies seeking advertising and public relations personnel, and others desiring graduates with communications skills.

Many students are introduced to mass communications fields through study in community colleges and in the more than 500 four-year institutions in the United States that offer some journalism and mass communications courses but not a full major. Some students work on the campus newspaper, yearbook, and radio and television staffs or find part-time employment with a newspaper or broadcast station while still in school. Many eventually find jobs in communications or related areas. Secondary schools provide beginning courses and media work for thousands of other students.

During recent years advertising has become an increasingly popular field of study. Fairly new programs in media management also have attracted a number of students. Much of the background they need is offered through schools of business. In many universities a cooperative arrangement exists so that, regardless of the degree sought, these students obtain their specialized courses in both business and communications areas. The communications major must learn the principles of sound business practice; the business major must become familiar with the peculiar problems and structure of the branch of the communications industry he or she proposes to enter. During the 1980s, however, business schools became so popular that mass communications students encountered difficulty in enrolling in their courses.

Public relations also has risen to prominence as a career sought by thousands, and extensive public relations degree programs are offered in many schools. Others offer only one or two courses in the subject along with classes in additional journalism and mass communications areas. Few business schools offer separate courses in public relations, although they incorporate course units emphasizing the theory and overall knowledge of public relations essential to successful management. Mass communications schools seek to offer the student both this background and the instruction necessary for becoming a practitioner in public relations.

In the broadcast area students desiring careers in performance and production usually concentrate on courses in radio, television, and speech. Those desiring to become radio and television newscasters and writers combine journalism, speech, and broadcast performance and production courses. Some headed for sales, promotion, public relations, and management positions major in business with allied instruction in broadcast courses. Television production and performance students generally take as much work in theater and dramatic literature as possible. There are other variations. Common to all these career paths, however, is a strong background in the liberal arts.

Courses in cinema are offered by many broadcast, speech communication, theater arts, and education schools and departments. They range from a single film appreciation course in some institutions to multiple courses in writing, performance, production, history, and aesthetics leading to a film major in others. The

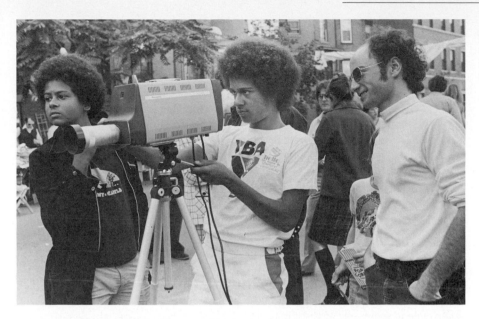

Students learn the techniques of mass communications through such "hands-on" experience as operating a camera. (© 1976, Hamlin, Stock, Boston)

University of Southern California, UCLA, and New York University are among the several dozen institutions emphasizing film study.

Combination programs involving two or more departments or schools enable many students to specialize in such areas as agricultural, home economics, and science communication.

Serving an internship while in college has become a key to rapid placement upon graduation. During the 1980s mass communications schools reported heavy increases in the number of available internships, offered throughout the year as well as during the traditional summer months. Cooperative programs, under which students alternate periods of employment and college study, registered enrollment increases in some schools.

In an effort to identify talent at the college level, the Dow Jones Newspaper Fund has awarded more than $1 million in intern scholarships since 1960.

HOW COMMUNICATIONS EDUCATION DEVELOPED

Journalism, a comparative fledgling among university disciplines, gained its foothold in college curricula early in this century. Formal education for journalism was inevitable in the face of the steadily increasing complexities of the twentieth century, which demanded better-trained personnel on American newspaper staffs. General Robert E. Lee first proposed a special college education for printer-editors. That was in 1869, when the general was president of Washington College, now Washington and Lee University, in Virginia. Little came of his proposal. Other early attention was given to printing instruction, such as that beginning at Kansas State College (now Kansas State University) in 1873.

In 1904 the first four-year curriculum for journalism students was organized at the University of Illinois, and journalism instruction began the same year at the University of Wisconsin. Four years later the first separate school of journalism was founded at the University of Missouri by an experienced journalist, Dean Walter Williams. In 1912 the Columbia University School of Journalism, endowed with $2 million from Joseph Pulitzer, opened its doors. By that year more than 30 colleges and universities were offering courses in journalism.

The first courses were largely vocational in nature as pioneer teachers in the field endeavored to prepare college students for careers on newspapers, then the primary medium of mass communication. During the 1920s, however, emphasis on technique lessened and curricula began to reflect an increasing interest in the social, ethical, and cultural aspects of journalism. Dr. Willard G. Bleyer, director of the University of Wisconsin School of Journalism until his death in 1935, is credited with leading the movement away from a preoccupation with technique. Also influential was exposure to methods of teaching the social sciences that journalism instructors were receiving in graduate programs. Courses in the history and the ethics of journalism became popular, and they were followed by studies of the newspaper as a social institution, of the interpretation of current affairs, and of public opinion.

These courses, together with those dealing with foreign news channels and legal aspects of the press, heightened respect for journalism as a discipline among other college teachers. At the same time, graduates from journalism departments were earning a grudging acceptance from curmudgeons of the editorial offices who, as Horace Greeley put it, learned their journalism through eating ink and sleeping on the exchanges. Teachers began to offer courses to prepare students for careers in newspaper management, advertising, photography, radio, and other such specialized fields. While recognizing the importance of the humanities and the natural sciences in the total educational program of their students, teachers came to achieve the closest working relationships with the social sciences.

As both the breadth and depth of subject matter in journalism increased, master's degrees were offered. In 1935 the Pulitzer School at Columbia restricted its year's course to those holding a bachelor's degree, and the Medill School of Northwestern University established a five-year plan for professional training in 1938. Graduate study for journalism majors developed at a rapid pace after World War II, as the schools themselves and some of the media units began to urge advanced study in both journalism and the social sciences. Many of those who obtained master's degrees entered journalism teaching, but increasing numbers spent the five years of study in preparation for professional careers.

At the doctoral level most graduate schools that recognized journalism instruction followed the lead of the University of Wisconsin in providing a minor or a double minor in journalism for candidates who generally majored in fields such as history or political science. The University of Missouri, however, awarded the first degree of Doctor of Philosophy in journalism in 1934, and by the 1940s other programs were under way. Some were based on strong supporting emphasis in the social sciences. In 1987 the Ph.D. degree in mass communications was offered at 21 universities. Some Ph.D. recipients entered the communications industry or other research areas, but most became faculty members.

The growth of the philosophy that journalism and communications schools should develop research scholars capable of critical analysis of the media and their social environment coincided with the rise of television and the increased importance of departments of speech communication and radio-television in providing preparation for broadcast careers. New, integrated instructional units emerged, a few merely for administrative convenience, but most devoted to the serious study of communication as the common denominator linking several academic areas of study. For example, Michigan State University brought its speech communication, journalism, advertising, and broadcast instruction together into a College of Communication Arts, with a research unit at its center. The University of Texas at Austin similarly combined its speech communication, radio-television-film, journalism, and advertising programs into a School of Communication. The trend continued into the mid-1980s, when Pennsylvania State University established a School of Communications composed of journalism and advertising programs offered by the former School of Journalism, the telecommunications major in the Department of Speech Communication, and the communication studies major formerly offered by the journalism school and the speech communication department.

ORGANIZING FOR HIGHER STANDARDS

Because of their diversity of interests, mass communication educators find teaching, research, and public service inspiration and assistance through membership in a number of regional, national, and international organizations. They include the Association for Education in Journalism and Mass Communication, Speech Communication Association, International Communication Association, Broadcast Education Association, American Academy of Advertising, Popular Culture Association, and many others.

The Association for Education in Journalism and Mass Communication (AEJMC), founded in 1912, consists of more than 2000 members in the United States, Canada, and more than 20 other foreign countries. Membership is open to university, community college, and secondary school educators; journalism and mass communication practitioners; and students.

The association conducts annual and regional conventions and conferences, offers a job placement service, administers several grant and scholarship programs, and publishes the following periodicals: *Journalism Quarterly, Journalism Educator, Journalism Monographs, Journalism Abstracts, Journalism Directory,* and *AEJMC News.*

Members concentrate on specialized areas of interest through 14 divisions: advertising, communication theory and methodology, history, international communication, law, magazine, mass communication and society, minorities and communication, newspaper, public relations, qualitative studies, radio-television journalism, secondary education, and visual communication.

About 50 professional, trade, and other educational groups support AEJMC through membership in a Council of Affiliates.

Two administrator organizations, the American Association of Schools and Departments of Journalism, organized in 1917, and the American Society of Journalism School Administrators, founded in 1944, joined in 1984 to form the Association of Schools of Journalism and Mass Communication (ASJMC). Its headquarters and those of AEJMC are maintained at the University of South Carolina at Columbia.

Accreditation

The two remaining organizations—AEJMC and ASJMC—have representatives on the Accrediting Council on Education in Journalism and Mass Communications (ACEJMC), with headquarters at the University of Kansas. The agency is formally recognized by the Council on Postsecondary Accreditation and the U.S. Office of Education for accreditation of programs for professional education in journalism and mass communications in institutions of higher learning in the United States. The 32-member council, which convenes semiannually, also includes three persons representing the public and representatives of the following organizations:

American Advertising Federation
American Newspaper Publishers Association
American Society of Magazine Editors
American Society of Newspaper Editors
Associated Press Managing Editors Association
Broadcast Education Association
California Newspaper Publishers Association
Inland Daily Press Association
International Association of Business Communicators
International Newspaper Advertising and Marketing Executives
National Association of Broadcasters
National Conference of Editorial Writers
National Newspaper Association
National Newspaper Publishers Association
National Press Photographers Association
Public Relations Society of America
Radio Television News Directors Association
Society of Professional Journalists, Sigma Delta Chi
Southern Newspaper Publishers Association
Women in Communications, Inc.

The council publishes two booklets each year. One states the accrediting standards and lists schools that have achieved undergraduate and graduate (master's degree) professional accreditation. The other booklet describes procedures in preparing for an accreditation visit. In recent years the council has phased out its accreditation of sequences of study and now accredits the entire journalism unit when more than 50 percent of its students are enrolled in accreditable programs and the unit meets ACEJMC standards. Almost 90 schools have received unit, graduate, and/or sequence accreditation.

From its organization in 1945 through the 1985–1986 academic year, ACEJMC called upon schools to maintain a ratio of 25 percent in professional journalism and mass communication courses and 75 percent in liberal arts courses. Beginning with the 1986–1987 academic year the council decreed that of 120 semester hours students shall take no more than 30 credit hours (25 percent) in journalism and mass communications courses, 65 outside the school in liberal arts, and the remaining 25 in other subjects, also outside the school. These latter hours may be in liberal arts subjects, but many students use them for background courses in such areas as management and marketing, required in certain journalism and mass communication degree programs. The loosening of the 75 percent liberal arts requirement created a controversy, particularly involving the newspaper industry.

Schools are visited every six years upon invitation of the institution's chief administrator. In preparation for the visits, schools submit a detailed report, including the results of a self-study, which provides information about such matters as governance, budget, curriculum, faculty, instruction, student advising and records, equipment and facilities, public service, employment of graduates, and minority and female representation among both students and faculty.

Teams of educator and practitioner members spend almost three days at the schools, inspecting records and facilities, visiting classrooms, and talking with students, faculty members, key administrators, and (normally by telephone) nearby professionals. Recommendations of the team lead to eventual accreditation, provisional accreditation (if deficiencies are expected to be corrected within one year), or denial of accreditation by the council.

Communication Associations

The Speech Communication Association (SCA), founded in 1914, consists of teachers and administrators at all educational levels, speech scientists and clinicians, media specialists, theater artists and craftsmen, communication consultants, students, and industry representatives. Primary publications are *The Quarterly Journal of Speech, Communication Monographs, Critical Studies in Mass Communication,* and *Communication Education,* as well as the newsletter *Spectra,* an annual directory, a bibliographic annual, and convention abstracts. Its divisions are forensics, instructional development, interpersonal and small group interaction, interpretation, mass communication, organizational communication, public address, rhetorical and communication theory, speech and language sciences, and theater. Administrators of speech communication departments are organized as the Association for Communication Administrators.

The International Communication Association (ICA), formed about 35 years ago, brings together academicians, other professionals, and students whose interest is focused on human communication. Publications are *The Journal of Communication, Human Communication Research,* and a newsletter. Its divisions are information systems and interpersonal, mass, organizational, intercultural, political, instructional, and health communication.

The Broadcast Education Association publishes the *Journal of Broadcasting & Electronic Media* (formerly the *Journal of Broadcasting*), as well as *Feedback.*

The Council of Communication Societies brings together leaders of the ICA, SCA, American Business Communication Association, American Forensic Association, American Medical Writers Association, American Translators Association, Industrial Communication Council, Society for Technical Communication, and Society of Federal Linguists. The council publishes a news digest and a communication calendar.

A COMMUNICATIONS EDUCATION NEVER ENDS

It is a truism, of course, to point out that a college diploma, or its equivalent in individual attainment, is only the beginning of a lifetime of education. This fact holds great validity for those who embark on careers in mass communications. Every aspect of human experience and emotion can become their concern; the world changes and so must their ability to understand and interpret those changes.

People who want to develop to their fullest potential in the field of mass communications cannot neglect their reading, both fiction and nonfiction, and the selective viewing of films, televised documentaries, and the like. Just as a physician peruses periodicals to keep abreast of advances of knowledge in medicine, so must the communicator read journals in communications and allied fields. These include research journals such as *Journalism Quarterly, Public Opinion Quarterly,* and the *Journal of Communication;* trade journals such as *Editor & Publisher, Broadcasting,* and *Advertising Age;* and general interest professional journals such as *Nieman Reports, Quill,* and *Columbia Journalism Review.*

Maintaining active membership in organizations that seek to improve their crafts also is the mark of the professional communicator. Highly stimulating to many communicators are the conferences and literature of the groups previously listed as supporting journalism and mass communication accreditation, as well as state and local associations and the news services.

Many media people return to college for regular courses as well as for continuing education activities such as institutes, workshops, and forums. The Dow Jones Newspaper Fund has sent well over 7000 high school and junior college journalism teachers back to college for special summer training in advising school newspapers and teaching journalism. Several hundred newspaper persons have been selected by the Nieman Foundation for a year's study at Harvard University. The American Press Institute and the Poynter Institute for Media Studies provide seminars. The Southern Newspaper Publishers Association sponsors both public affairs and newspaper skills seminars. Other such activities available to mass media personnel are described in the last section of chapter 24.

MASS MEDIA TEACHING IN THE SECONDARY SCHOOL

There are more potential openings for teachers of journalism in the secondary schools of the United States than in any other field for which journalism training provides preparation. The best estimates are that approximately 45,000 senior and junior high school publications—newspapers, magazines, and yearbooks—are issued regularly. More than 1 million students work on these publications, which cost collectively around $85 million per year. About 175,000 students are enrolled each year in journalism courses offered at approximately 5000 high schools. Many others learn the principles of radio and television production in classes and activity clubs, and in working with cable outlets in their communities.

A phenomenon of the last decade or so has been the establishment of thousands of high school courses designed to acquaint students with the operations of the mass media and to consider the effects of mass communications on their lives. These courses, offered through language arts, speech, journalism, and other departments, were one of the principal causes of the steady growth in mass communications enrollments in colleges and universities before their leveling off in the mid-1980s.

Secondary school journalism can be traced to the founding of the first known high school paper, the *Literary Journal,* in 1829 at the Boston Latin Grammar School. It was not until 1912, however, that the first known class in high school journalism was started in Salina, Kansas. Secondary school journalism matured during the 1930s and 1940s as school boards, superintendents, and principals noted its educational value.

Those who have taught high school journalism over the years speak with genuine enthusiasm about the satisfaction they have derived from teaching journalism classes and advising school publications and broadcast clubs. For one thing, they enjoy having many of their school's brightest students on their publication staffs; frequently the highest ranking group of students in the English placement tests is assigned to the teacher producing the school paper. These imaginative and creative youngsters are stimulated by writing for print. Many of them go on to other fields of study at the universities, but some become the prize students of journalism or communications schools and eventually take their places in professional work. The school paper, the annual, and broadcast clubs are major activities at the high school level; this gives their advisers additional prestige as teachers.

Some prospective teachers major in journalism and mass communication and minor in an area such as English or the social sciences, meanwhile acquiring sufficient hours in education courses to qualify for certification. Others major in education and take first or second minors in journalism and some other field. Still others major in English or language arts and take as many journalism courses as they can work into a four-year program. All realize that they most likely will be teaching only one or two courses in journalism, with the balance of their instructional assignments in another subject.

About 30 percent of the states, however, have no specific journalism certification requirements, and about the same percentage grant certificates upon the completion of fewer than 15 semester hours of college journalism courses. Only about 40 percent require the equivalent of a minor in journalism. Many principals, superintendents, and state education officials resist journalism certification efforts so they may have a freer hand—to the detriment of journalism education—in making assignments.

Journalism As Basic Education

The downgrading of journalism courses as the equivalent of English instruction began in many states immediately after the National Commission on Excellence, citing "a nation at risk," in 1983 called for massive educational reform. In one part of its report the commission recommended that students be required to take four years of English, with no mention of newspaper journalism as an acceptable substitute for a portion of this instruction. In some states high school counselors began informing students that journalism was no longer acceptable credit in gaining admission to colleges and universities. Some schools discontinued journalism instruction.

In 1984 the Journalism Education Association (JEA), the primary organization for high school journalism teachers, established a Commission on the Role of Journalism in Secondary Education. Groups providing financial support included the Gannett Foundation, Dow Jones Newspaper Fund, American Association of School Photographers, and several yearbook companies. A series of research studies and national conferences was begun.

In 1986 Professor Jack Dvorak of Indiana University reported the results of a study that found that college freshmen who had been on the staff of a high school newspaper or yearbook earned "significantly higher" scores in 10 of 13 academic categories than those without such experience. The study, conducted in cooperation with American College Testing (ACT), examined 19,249 college students who completed their freshman year in 1984.

Another Dvorak study disclosed that high school journalism sparks interest in journalism and mass communications as a career. Students who had high school publication experience were found to be four times as likely to choose the field as a college major and career goal.

On another front, the association prepared a list of qualified teachers to nominate as members of teams representing the five agencies that accredit secondary schools.

Meanwhile, strong resolutions of support were voted by the Association for Education in Journalism and Mass Communication, American Society of Newspaper Editors (ASNE), National Council of Teachers of English, and other organizations. Typical of the resolutions was the following: "Resolved, That the ASNE encourage the acceptance into the English curricula of journalism course work which focuses on the collecting, writing, and editing or the interpretation and evaluation of news and information, that these courses are recognized as academic and taught by a trained journalism teacher." At the JEA national convention in 1986 the commission ended its two-year study with the recommendation that credit for secondary school journalism be equivalent to that for other language arts courses and that journalism be an essential component in the high school curriculum.

Organizations

Several organizations issue publications and guidebooks for teachers and students and conduct critical services providing professional evaluation and ratings of school media. They include the National Scholastic Press Association at the University of Minnesota (affiliated with JEA), Columbia Scholastic Press Association at Columbia University, and the Catholic School Press Association at Marquette University. They publish, respectively, *Trends, School Press Review,* and *Catholic School Editor.*

Also providing services are the Future Journalists of America, at the University of Oklahoma, and the Student Press Service and Student Press Law Center, both in Washington, D.C. The latter three times each year publishes *The Student Press Law Center Report,* summarizing current controversies over student press rights, particularly those involving censorship, libel law, and the liability of high school publications.

Quill and Scroll, the international honor society for high school journalists, with headquarters at the University of Iowa, publishes a magazine bearing the society's name. The American Scholastic Press, Wheatley Heights, New York, provides a critiquing service only.

Regional associations, such as the Southern Interscholastic Press Association, with headquarters at the University of South Carolina, and state associations also provide services. Another teachers' organization, in addition to JEA, which publishes *Communication: Journalism Education Today,* is the Columbia Scholastic Press Advisers Association, publisher of the *CSPAA Bulletin.*

TEACHING JOURNALISM IN THE COMMUNITY COLLEGE

Hundreds of opportunities for teaching journalism are available in community colleges throughout the United States.

Fifty-nine percent of the 936 community colleges that responded to a survey conducted by Professor Frank Deaver of the University of Alabama offer some courses in journalism. Most often these courses include introduction to mass communications, beginning newswriting and reporting, news editing, and photography. Two-thirds of the courses serve as laboratories for student publications— newspaper, magazine, or yearbook. In most of these two-year colleges the journalism program is designed to encourage these student publications and to give basic preparation for students planning to major in journalism or communications at four-year colleges and universities. A number of community college educators state that their primary purpose is to acquaint students with the mass media and to teach them to become discerning news and opinion consumers so that they will be better able to carry out their responsibilities as citizens. In some community colleges enough advanced instruction is available to prepare graduates to take jobs with the media.

Two-year college educators are organized as the Community College Journalism Association, an affiliate of the Association for Education in Journalism and Mass Communication. Members meet several times each year to discuss curriculum, teaching methods, and new technology. In California, more than 60 two-year and city colleges belong to the Journalism Association of Community Colleges. The typical degree of the two-year college educators is the M.A., earned by 75 percent. Many serve as advisers to student publications or as college publicity directors.

THE FOUR-YEAR COLLEGE AND UNIVERSITY LEVEL

Journalism and communications faculty members at the university or college level are engaged in three major activities: teaching, research, and service. Most of them have one or more specialties in the journalistic techniques, acquired through their own professional experience with the mass media. Among these fields are reporting, news editing, magazine writing, radio and television news, typography and graphic arts processes, advertising, public relations, news photography, film, critical writing, broadcast programming and production, and editorial writing. Teachers usually start at this techniques level, but they are well advised to be equipped for teaching and research in one or more of the scholarly fields of interest. They should be interested, too, in performing services for the mass media with which the school or department is in close contact and in spending much time offering advice to students who turn to them for guidance and stimulation.

Those who aspire to the top ranks of university or college teaching in journalism and mass communications usually seek master's degrees in the field. They then undertake study toward the Ph.D. degree in a college or university that offers either a major or a minor in the subject and that has a journalism and communications faculty of graduate school caliber. Some prefer to minor in journalism or communications and to do their major doctoral work in political science, history, psychology, sociology, economics, speech, American studies, or another related field. Others enter universities that award Ph.D. degrees in journalism or communications.

Not all college journalism and mass communications faculty members need to undertake doctoral work. Some with sound professional experience and specialized abilities in fields such as reporting, graphic arts, news photography, weekly journalism, or radio and television writing, production, and programming find employment at the master's degree level. There have been shortages of qualified teachers in the advertising and broadcast media fields, particularly.

Opportunities for scholarly teaching, research, and publication are almost unlimited. Many aspects of the history of communications remain to be explored, despite the fact that this area traditionally has been a favorite one for professors. The literary aspects of journalism constitute another little-plowed field. Important studies of the relationships between the press and society, and of the conflicts between press and government, await future scholars. Only a start has been made on penetrating studies of the economics of the mass media. Advertising offers wide opportunities for advanced study and research projects of both basic and applied character. As explained in Chapter 19, the fields of mass communications theory and research, of public opinion and propaganda, and of other studies allied to the behavioral sciences have barely been opened by scholars. Particularly, there is a need for interpretive analysis of scientific findings and quantitative data by those who can relate what the researchers have found to the everyday problems of the mass media. The processes of international communication and the study of foreign journalism have become more important in recent years also, with relatively few faculty members qualified to do advanced teaching and research in the field.

Offering assistance to the publications adviser at the junior college and college level are the Associated Collegiate Press (ACP), companion organization of the National Scholastic Press Association (NSPA), and College Media Advisers (CMA), formerly known as the National Council of College Publications Advisers. The ACP and NSPA issue guidebooks and other publications for college publications staffs and maintain critical services for newspapers, annuals, and magazines. The Student Editors Association was organized in 1983 to support and promote college publications programs.

Salaries for communications teachers in colleges and universities run somewhat above the average for some other disciplines because of the competitive bidding from the mass media for the services of those who are preparing for teaching careers. University and college salaries have improved substantially in recent years, and those who reach professorial status may look forward to nine-month salaries running from $25,000 to $40,000 or more. These figures, however, still are substantially lower than those for professors in such fields as computer science, business, and economics, and for persons employed in industry. There also are opportunities for additional income from summer teaching, summer refresher work in the media, consultantships to advertising agencies and other groups, research projects, book publication, and other activities.

PART SIX

Criticisms and Challenges

Who Owns the Media?

Mixed Company

Can you determine what the following groups of mass media and commercial products have in common?

1. The *Times of* London, Twentieth Century-Fox film studio, the Boston *Herald,* television station KTTV in Los Angeles, *New Woman* magazine.
2. Home Box Office, Book-of-the-Month Club, *People,* Little, Brown & Company book publishers, *Progressive Farmer.*
3. Paramount Pictures, Simmons mattresses, Simon & Schuster book publishers, Catalina swimsuits, Madison Square Garden.
4. *Newsday,* television station WVTM in Birmingham, Alabama, *Sporting News,* H.M. Gousha Company road maps, Harry N. Abrams art books.
5. *USA Today,* Lou Harris Poll, *Pacific Daily News* in Guam, Mediacom Inc. billboards in Canada, Des Moines *Register.*

The answer: *Each* group is a portion of a large mixed bag of properties owned by a *single* huge corporation. The list provides a glimpse at the tremendous concentration of mass media in the hands of a relatively few conglomerate giants.

The owners: (1) Rupert Murdoch; (2) Time Inc.; (3) Gulf & Western, Inc.; (4) Times Mirror Company; (5) Gannett Company, Inc.

*A*merican mass media are part of the free enterprise system, privately owned and operated for a profit without the controlling hand of government and political party ownership that restricts the media in many countries.

Until relatively recently, ownership of American print media was noted for its diversity. Most newspapers were owned by the families that established and developed them. Radio and television stations similarly had a broad mixture of individual ownership, as did book and magazine publishing firms.

A great change has occurred in the past 25 years. The rush toward group and conglomerate ownership that has swept through the entire fabric of American business has significantly altered control of the mass media.

By the late 1980s more than two-thirds of American newspapers were under group ownership. Media observers fear that some of the papers' traditional individuality will be lost when operating orders are given by distant corporate headquarters.

Recent huge financial deals combining television and motion picture companies, and the explosive growth of conglomerate corporations controlling both media and nonmedia subsidiaries, have completed the transformation of media ownership into the realm of massive business ventures.

In this chapter we discuss the causes and significance of this multiple-ownership trend. ◆

PRODUCTS OF FREE ENTERPRISE

The owners of broadcasting stations, newspapers, and other mass media outlets expect them to earn a profit, an expectation that many of them fulfill handsomely. Some outlets, however, although important to the audiences they serve, have difficulty in providing a return on the investments their owners have made in them. The annual profit figure is not the sole motivation driving many media managers, who think also of their responsibility to provide the truth and serve their communities, but the necessity to survive in a competitive market makes profitable operation vital.

Even most of the noncommercial radio and television stations get into the money scramble because they must find financial grants and underwriting gifts to keep them on the air. So the demands of the marketplace influence and often determine the decisions of those who distribute the printed and spoken word: which books to publish, what type of films to produce, what kind of programs to televise, what size each day's newspaper should be.

In this respect the American concept differs from that of many parts of the world. The federal government neither finances nor operates any of the media in this country, although it assists some noncommercial stations with subsidies. Nor do the political parties underwrite daily newspapers to enunciate their point of view. An American broadcasting station or publication survives only if it provides a product its audience likes and manages its finances prudently.

Contrast this to the practice in Europe, for example, where it is commonplace for many television and radio networks to be owned by the government. In many countries, especially communist-governed ones, newspapers are published by the government, with the censorship and manipulation of news such control implies.

Because the United States is so vast and its population so diverse, American media have historically and proudly lacked uniformity, both in content and ownership. Newspapers born as the frontier moved westward were the products of individual enterprise, reflecting the views of the editor-proprietor. So were the magazines. Book publishing for decades was largely controlled by individuals, families, or partnerships. When commercial radio came into being, stations were established by a potpourri of owners anxious to play with the new toy, among them newspaper executives, automobile dealers, manufacturers, and amateur engineers who could scrape together enough money for the primitive equipment needed. Licenses for television, when that medium's turn came, were obtained in many instances by companies already involved in radio. Thus the American media truly consisted of many thousands of voices, often highly individualistic.

Frequently these individual proprietors were more concerned with exercising influence in their communities than with drawing the last dollar of profit from their operations. Since they answered only to themselves or to small groups of private stockholders, they were free to function in that way.

A tremendous change from this pattern of diversified, uncoordinated ownership has taken place during the past 25 years. In the print media, group ownership has replaced this multiplicity so dramatically that by 1987 only 27 percent of the nearly 1700 American daily newspapers—not quite 450—still were independently owned. The rest had been taken over by group ownerships of various sizes. A *newspaper group* is usually defined as two or more dailies in different markets under common ownership. At one time several newspapers under common ownership were frequently called a "chain," but preferred contemporary usage is "group."

Since these groups in many cases also own radio and television stations, magazines, and specialty publishing firms, and have acquired cable television franchises and networks as well, their control over the totality of American media voices has become enormous. Concentration of ownership power arouses fears of excessive conformity. Critics perceive the danger that the large corporate owners may manipulate the content of their media outlets for selfish purposes, or at least defend the status quo in order to protect their own and other large corporate interests. They note uneasily that the National Broadcasting Company's television and radio networks, one of the country's basic sources of news, are now owned by the General Electric Company, a mammoth manufacturer of defense equipment with close contractual ties to the Pentagon. These critics foresee the possibility that opposition voices and unorthodox ideas could be stifled by conglomerate ownerships. (A *conglomerate* ownership is a corporation owning companies in several different fields of endeavor.)

In reality, the possibility that a community could be forced to depend upon a single corporate source for its news is almost nonexistent. Much competitive news delivery is available to its citizens through other media voices, including radio and television newscasts, neighborhood newspapers, magazines, and newspapers published in nearby larger cities.

MASSIVE MEDIA DEALS

As the 1980s entered their second half, a tumultuous churning in the ownership of American mass media took place. Billion-dollar deals transferred ownership of television stations, cable TV systems, motion picture studios, two major television and radio networks, and metropolitan newspapers from one corporation to another.

Media entities widely regarded as invulnerable semi-public institutions, because they had been household words for so long, were swallowed by corporate raiders. Spinoffs, buyouts, and trades of media units, financed by enormous borrowing, have created an ownership structure of almost baffling complexity.

The primary result of this Wall Street jockeying is greater concentration of media ownership in fewer hands.

Traditional dividing lines between the ownerships of various media categories have been wiped out. Newspapers, television and radio stations, magazines, book publishers, cable television systems, motion picture studios, videocassette production firms, and makers of recordings have been tossed into a gigantic financial grabbag, to be plucked out and assembled in various combinations that adventurous entrepreneurs conceive as lucrative.

INCREASE IN MEDIA VOICES

	1959	1965	1970	1975	1977	1981	1987
Commercial TV stations	520	672	690	709	725	864	1000
Educational TV stations	43	115	182	242	258	292	297
AM radio stations	3377	4058	4269	4436	4502	4729	4867
FM radio stations	776	1301	2471	3571	3743	4350	5209
Daily newspapers	1755	1763	1761	1768	1762	1745	1674

SOURCES: FCC, *Broadcasting* magazine, *Editor & Publisher* magazine, compiled in *Les Brown's Encyclopedia of Television.* 1987 figures as of Jan. 31.

Vivid and disturbing evidence of the rush to conglomerate ownership of the media is found in the following series of ownership deals made within a hectic 15-month period during 1985–1986:

• Rupert Murdoch expanded his already large international holdings of newspapers and television properties by purchasing the 20th Century-Fox Film Corporation for $575 million. Then he bought six metropolitan U.S. television stations from Metromedia Inc. for $1.55 billion. These purchases gave him control of 93 publishing, broadcasting, and other operations internationally.

Possession of the movie company's library containing hundreds of films, plus its production facilities for making new movies and television series, provides Murdoch with abundant material to show on the Fox Broadcasting Company television network he formed in 1986, based on the six stations. He also shows the films on his European satellite TV network based in Great Britain.

Murdoch's media empire at that point also included newspapers in five American cities and three American magazines. Under a Federal Communications Commission ruling, he was given two years in which to sell his money-losing New York *Post* and his profitable Chicago *Sun-Times* because he had acquired TV stations in those cities. (The FCC's ownership rules are explained later in this chapter.) Spreading his American activities even further, Murdoch in 1987 purchased Harper & Row, Publishers, Inc., thus acquiring an important position in book publishing.

In his native Australia, Murdoch owned 11 newspapers, a television station, and two magazines. He became an American citizen at the time of his multiple television station purchase but retained his Australian properties.

His four British newspapers, including the historic *Times* of London, control 30 percent of the entire British newspaper circulation. In early 1986 he defied a violence-ridden strike by the London printers unions, which insisted upon continuing the wasteful, outmoded "hot metal" printing processes long abandoned in the United States, and successfully opened an electronic publishing plant with new employees. He also owns three magazines and two book publishing houses in England.

Rupert Murdoch, a controversial Australian publisher who became an American citizen so he could own U.S. television stations, has built an international mass communications conglomerate of newspaper, television, motion picture, and book publishing companies. (AP/Wide World)

Murdoch told an interviewer that by using his new British plant he would increase his annual cash flow in that country by $80 million—a fortunate thing for him, because he assumed a debt of nearly $3 billion to acquire his American movie and television properties.

The lurid and often irresponsible content of some Murdoch newspapers has subjected him to condemnation by many critics.

• Capital Cities Communications, Inc., a large proprietor of newspapers, radio, and television stations, purchased the American Broadcasting Companies for $3.5 billion. This purchase included the ABC television and radio networks and owner-operated stations, and magazines, as well as video and film production facilities and distribution organizations.

Because of geographic duplication between Capcities (as it is known) and ABC stations, under the FCC rules the merged company had to spin off some of its broadcast properties to nine different purchasers. The Washington *Post,* which also owns *Newsweek* magazine, purchased 53 cable television systems from Capcities for $350 million.

• Already the owner of Cable Network News and the satellite-distributed TV superstation WTBS in Atlanta, Ted Turner plunged into Hollywood, buying MGM/UA Entertainment Company for $1.5 billion. He then sold the United Artists (UA) portion of MGM/UA to Kirk Kerkorian, former principal owner of MGM/UA, for $470 million.

Turner bought the renowned movie company in order to own its film library containing movies, including such classics as *Gone With the Wind* and *The Wizard of Oz.* He planned to show them on WTBS and possibly organize a cable TV entertainment network built around them.

The MGM/UA purchase put Turner $2 billion in debt—"more than some smaller Third World countries, and I'm pretty proud of that," he told a Swiss audience. Later Turner sold the MGM studio property and production facilities for $490 million but retained his real objective, the film library. He also sold one-third of the stock of Turner Broadcasting for $550 million to a group of cable operators, but retained management control.

Just before his MGM/UA purchase, Turner tried in vain to take over the Columbia Broadcasting Company. He came close enough to give CBS management a bad scare.

A few months later, after an intensive power struggle, CBS management came under control of financier Laurence Tisch, who owned nearly 25 percent of network stock. With the support of William S. Paley, the network's octogenarian founder, Tisch instituted rigid cost-control practices.

Turner became a focus of international attention in 1986 when he committed $35 million to sponsor the Goodwill Games in Moscow jointly with the Soviet government, gaining additional stature as an innovative promoter.

• General Electric Company purchased RCA Corporation, including its prime property, the National Broadcasting Company, for $6.3 billion. The deal included the NBC television and radio networks and NBC owned-and-operated stations in major U.S. cities. Also involved were electronic mail, videotex, satellite transmission, and other communication services.

Thus within a few months two of the country's three primary networks, ABC and NBC, changed ownership and the third, CBS, nearly did.

• The Gannett Company, Inc., largest of the newspaper groups, became even more gigantic through three major purchases. It bought the Des Moines *Register* and its group of small subsidiary newspapers for $200 million. A short time later it paid $717 million for the Detroit *Evening News,* the country's ninth largest newspaper, along with its four small subsidiary daily papers and five television stations. Within weeks it added the Louisville *Courier-Journal* and its affiliated operations for another $300 million.

Gannett then arranged to spin off three TV stations to Knight-Ridder Newspapers, Inc. for $160 million.

When the shuffling was finished, Gannett owned 93 newspapers including the national daily *USA Today,* the newspaper magazine supplement *USA Weekend,* eight television stations, 16 radio stations, a nationwide billboard company, a motion picture studio to produce TV films, and the Lou Harris polling organization.

And Gannett's hunger for acquisitions was not yet satisfied. Late in 1985 its chairman Allen Neuharth was asked, "Where would you like to see Gannett 10 years from now?" He replied, "Bigger and better."

• The Tribune Company, best known for its two metropolitan newspapers, the Chicago *Tribune* and New York *Daily News,* paid $510 million for a single independent television station in Los Angeles, KTLA. The company indicated plans to organize a network of independent TV stations and needed an outlet in Hollywood.

Because of FCC restrictions, the Tribune Company then sold its Los Angeles newspaper, the *Daily News,* to Jack Kent Cooke, a cable television, real estate, and sports owner, for $176 million. (The Tribune Company's growth is discussed in more detail later in this chapter.)

These Tribune maneuvers illuminated the frantic escalation of media prices during the fast-and-loose shopping spree. For his $176 million Cooke obtained the *Daily News* circulation of 150,000. Only two years earlier, in 1983, Murdoch had

TEN LARGEST U.S. MEDIA COMPANIES

	Media Revenues
Capital Cities/ABC	$4.06 billion
CBS Inc.	3.22 billion
Time Inc.	3.10 billion
General Electric	2.96 billion
Gannett Company	2.73 billion
Times Mirror Company	2.24 billion
Advance Publications (Newhouse)	2.20 billion
Dun & Bradstreet	1.93 billion
Knight-Ridder Newspapers	1.88 billion
Tribune Company	1.77 billion

SOURCE: *Advertising Age,* June 29, 1987.

obtained approximately five times as much circulation when he purchased the *Tribune*'s arch-rival Chicago *Sun-Times* for $90 million, thought at the time to be a high price. Three years later Murdoch sold the *Sun-Times* to an investment group for $145 million.

• Times Mirror Company, parent of the Los Angeles *Times,* purchased the Baltimore *Sun,* the Baltimore *Evening Sun,* and two television stations for $600 million in cash from the A.S. Abell Company. The announcement was made only one day after the Hearst Corporation closed Baltimore's other daily newspaper, the *News American,* because of excessive losses. Shortly thereafter, Times Mirror sold the Dallas *Times Herald* for $110 million and the Denver *Post* for $95 million, and bought *Broadcasting* magazine for $75 million in cash.

• MCA Inc., the parent of Universal Pictures and Universal Television, purchased the satellite superstation WOR-TV serving New York from Gencorp Inc. for $387 million. MCA wanted a New York outlet on which to show the movies and TV shows it makes.

• Westinghouse Electric Corporation sold its Group W network of 140 cable television systems to Time Inc. and four other investors for $2.1 billion. Westinghouse made a $500 million profit on the cable system sale.

$18 BILLION TURNOVER

Such a series of massive media deals, tumbling on the heels of each other, confuses media consumers. How can TV stations and newspapers be worth so much? Added together, these transactions total approximately $18 billion.

Taken as a group, these transactions convey a fundamental message: the ultimate decision-making power over large portions of American broadcasting operations and newspaper publishing rests in distant corporate executive offices and board rooms. The day of the small local media owner with an independent and sometimes cantankerous voice is vanishing. Even weekly newspapers are being brought under group ownership as the number of daily paper targets for acquisition dwindles. The psychological atmosphere of ownership has changed.

Pointing out that the strength of television news often is blamed for the circulation and advertising difficulties of newspapers, the influential trade magazine *Advertising Age* commented editorially:

> Yet, we wonder if the problem isn't exacerbated by the bottom-line focus that can often distort a corporate mission, even in the newspaper business, where highly individualistic, sharply opinionated publisher-owners used to hold sway. Increasingly, the business is being dominated by the large public newspaper groups, which gobble up local papers at an alarming rate. . . .
>
> How much hope is left for the dissemination of diverse, or offbeat, opinions? TV already is feeding the public a homogenized news diet; just monitor the three nightly network newscasts if you have any doubts about this.
>
> It's sad to see print journalism traveling this same route as the entrepreneurial companies sell off their proud possessions.

Group managements emphasize that individual newspapers in their organizations retain local editorial control. Nevertheless, local executives operate under group management norms and formulas, many of which improve the papers' economic efficiency, and are inevitably drawn, perhaps without being fully aware of it, into group conformity.

The consolidation trend seems likely to continue, limited only by the willingness of corporations to pay huge prices for desirable properties. Apparently the big will grow bigger. Conglomerate managements headed by nonmedia people increasingly will enjoy the power and prestige of media ownership, as well as the profits.

The Reagan presidency, under which the land rush of major media buyouts occurred, made no effort to block them. Neither the Justice Department, which initiates anti-trust procedures, nor the Federal Communications Commission, which regulates the broadcasting industry, challenged the acquisitors.

Television viewers and newspaper readers usually do not detect glaring changes in what they receive immediately after their favorite stations and newspapers are sold. Critics, however, fear that the mountainous debts incurred in these purchases, and the pressures by stockholders and bankers to make the risks pay off, have enshrined money-earning as the dominant factor in management decisions, resulting in severe cost-cutting in operational budgets at the expense of socially valuable products.

Broadcasting magazine summarized the concerns in a worried editorial:

> Many of the deals put together to take over broadcast empires—or to defend against such takeovers—are so burdened with borrowing that management may be forced to cut to the bone—or near it—just to meet the debt service. One of the first casualties is likely to be public service, or cultural programming, or any other category of broadcast operation that doesn't return more than it takes out, or that may take a while to do so.

The following portions of this chapter will examine how conditions developed to make possible transactions such as the above.

THE NEWSPAPER GROUP PHENOMENON

Control of more than two-thirds of U.S. daily newspapers no longer rests in the home communities in which they are published. It is held by corporate headquarters of the groups that gobbled up independent newspapers with a voracious appetite during the 1970s and 1980s. Most of the dailies remaining under local ownership are in the under-50,000 circulation class.

Preceding the surge of group ownership, and contributing to it, was the rise to predominance of "one-newspaper cities." This results from the death through economic attrition of second and sometimes third newspapers in a city. Today, fewer than 30 American cities have fully independent, competing dailies. Critics fear that, in a city with one daily newspaper, the publication will print only the news and opinion it wants its readers to see, leaving out or deemphasizing stories that might embarrass the publisher and his or her friends, or run contrary to the paper's political position. On the other side, there are frequent instances in which a monopoly publisher, sensitive to the charge, has made extra effort to provide the city with more extensive, deeper news coverage than was previously available in a competitive situation.

Closely connected is the charge that advertisers dictate a newspaper's coverage, or at least exercise veto power over certain kinds of stories that might damage their trade. Numerous episodes exist to document this complaint, in which stories went unreported because an advertiser requested that they be dropped. Yet many newspapers consistently reject such pressures, rebuffing all attempts to have stories suppressed.

Organizations and readers who do not want to hear the truth also at times exert extreme, unpleasant pressure against newspapers in revenge for stories they print. In Texas, the Fort Worth *Star-Telegram* lost 1200 subscribers and endured vitriolic attacks from the Bell Helicopter Corporation, a hometown company, other business firms, and Bell employee unions because it published articles disclosing a long-standing fault in the construction of Bell helicopters. This fault had contributed to crashes in which about 250 military servicemen had died. A blue ribbon military-civilian panel subsequently confirmed the newspaper's findings, and 600 Army helicopters were grounded for repairs. The *Star-Telegram* won a Pulitzer Prize for the series.

Similarly, when the Lexington *Herald-Leader* disclosed years-long illegal payments to University of Kentucky basketball players by school boosters, the newspaper was attacked vehemently for "disloyalty" to the school. The *Herald-Leader* received bomb threats and angry petitions, and lost 369 subscribers. The editor's home was festooned with toilet paper. This paper too won a Pulitzer Prize.

Publication of columns called "Action Line" or some similar name, in which the newspaper acts as its readers' problem-solving agent, often causes it to print facts that show its advertisers in a poor light. The completeness of a newspaper's coverage of controversial issues and sensitive stories depends largely upon the moral courage and journalistic integrity of those who run it.

So many newspapers have ceased publication in competitive markets, especially in the metropolitan field, that fewer than 2 percent of daily newspaper cities and 5 percent of weekly newspaper towns have competing newspaper ownerships. Nevertheless, the total number of daily newspapers has remained fairly stable for more than two decades because new newspapers have begun publication, especially in areas of fast population growth around the fringes of metropolitan centers. Usually these newspapers are without competition in their cities of publication but face heavy inroads in circulation and advertising from nearby large-city papers.

While the presence of two daily newspapers in a city gives readers the benefit of rival coverage effort, a substantial argument exists on the other side. One strong newspaper in a city, if the publisher and editor are conscientious persons sensitive to their responsibilities, often can provide better news coverage and community service than two weaker ones. Also, a financially strong paper may be more willing to attack entrenched and harmful interests in a city because it can absorb the financial retaliation aimed at it.

The chief immediate reason for the disappearance of newspapers is the constantly rising cost of production. The wages of those who write, edit, and print the newspapers; taxes; the cost of newsprint and gasoline for the delivery trucks —these and many other expenses have risen precipitously. This has led publishers to raise the sale prices of their newspapers and their advertising rates, attempting to keep the newspapers profitable. In cases where a newspaper's hold on its readers and advertisers is not strong, or where its area of distribution loses population at the same time that radio, television, and competitive newspapers cut into its circulation and advertising revenue, the salvage effort fails and the paper must cease publication. This has been especially true among some papers in Northeastern metropolitan areas, whose inner cities have become depressed areas.

The Newspaper Preservation Act was passed by Congress in 1970 after lively controversy within the newspaper industry. This act created exemptions in the antitrust law, so that a struggling newspaper might join forces with a healthy publication in the same city. The newspapers were allowed not only to operate joint production facilities but to combine business departments and have joint advertising and circulation rates. Their editorial departments remained separate. An argument for the measure is that it would preserve a second newspaper voice in the city. Publishers who testified against it, especially those from aggressive suburban newspapers, asserted that it would increase the trend toward monopoly.

Size of Newspaper Groups

The acquisition trend reached the stage in which large groups were buying out small ones, thus increasing their holdings at a wholesale rate. In the late 1980s twelve groups had aggregate weekday circulation of more than 1 million copies each. These organizations published more than 45 percent of the newspaper copies sold daily in the United States and more than one-half of those sold on Sunday.

Although the Gannett Company with its 93 newspapers plus broadcasting stations and other properties far outpaces it financially, the little-publicized Thomson Newspapers Ltd. owns and operates nearly as many U.S. daily newspapers, 92. It also owns 39 Canadian dailies. Most of Thomson's newspapers are small, in the 10,000–25,000 circulation range. The family-controlled Thomson group, based in Canada, operates with a profit margin above 30 percent. Second to Gannett in group circulation is Knight-Ridder Newspapers, Inc., whose 27 dailies and nine nondailies include several major metropolitan newspapers.

Ownership of a newspaper group, supplemented by radio and television stations, can be extremely profitable. In 1985, for example, Gannett reported net earnings of $253 million, Times Mirror earned $237 million, and Knight-Ridder $132 million. Pretax profits of all American and Canadian newspaper publishers average about 18 percent.

To illustrate the money-making potential, let us look at the spectacular financial success stories of two newspaper organizations. Both began as family enterprises based on a single property. By purchasing and starting other newspapers, and creating or purchasing electronic outlets and subsidiary operations, they grew into extremely lucrative groups. The value of their holdings came to light when they chose to sell stock to the public after decades of being privately held.

For more than 130 years, the Chicago *Tribune* has been an influential institution in that city, with current daily circulation above 750,000.

Until its recent public stock sale, the Tribune Company was privately owned by 378 stockholders, who held its existing 7393 shares. Principal ownership was held by the Medill-McCormick family. The company also owns the New York *Daily News,* founded by Joseph M. Patterson, a Medill descendant and cousin of Col. Robert R. McCormick, the publisher who ruled the Chicago *Tribune* for many years until his death.

At the time it went public in 1983, in addition to these metropolitan giants the company had six other daily newspapers, three in Florida and three in California. Also, it owned 20 weekly newspapers and shoppers in Florida, Illinois, and California. In addition, it had four television stations, including WGN in Chicago and WPIX in New York; six radio stations; a newsprint company; full or partial ownership of 10 cable television franchises; and the Independent Network News television service. On top of all that, it owned the Chicago Cubs baseball team in the National League.

How much was all this worth? To get the shares down to manageable size for trading on the New York Stock Exchange, the company split each privately held share 4799 to 1. The opening trading price for a new share was $26.75, making the value of an original share $128,373. Thus anyone who had owned a mere 8 shares of the original 7393 was a millionaire. The residuary trust of the late Colonel McCormick held 1412 original shares, making its value about $175 million. The price of a Tribune public share had soared by 1986 to $78 from the opening $26.75 in 1983.

In contrast to the Tribune Company, whose key properties are two huge metropolitan dailies, Park Communications concentrates its ownership of newspapers and stations in small cities. Its 23 daily newspapers in 12 states have average paid circulation of less than 10,000 each. Yet its financial statement shows how profitable a shrewdly operated group ownership can be even when handling such low-volume units.

Roy H. Park began the group by purchasing a television station in North Carolina in 1962, and he started to buy newspapers in 1972. After a swift buildup of properties, the company went public in 1983.

In addition to the 23 small dailies, Park Communications at that time had 18 nondaily newspapers, 27 controlled circulation weekly shoppers, 7 television stations, and 14 radio stations. It also was seeking licenses for low-power television stations.

Park personally owned all 1400 shares of common stock in the company at the time it made its public offering. For marketing convenience, each of the 1400 shares was split 6000 to 1, making his holding of new stock 8.4 million shares, each valued at $19. One original share thus was worth more than $100,000. Park's original 1400 shares had a value of approximately $140 million. Less than two years after it went public, Park split its shares again, 3-for-2.

Not all group operations are so wealthy, of course, but these examples illustrate why ambitious companies have acted so aggressively to buy up newspapers.

Why do owners of independent newspapers succumb to the lures of group corporations and surrender ownership that in some cases has been in their families for more than a century? The answer lies primarily in a bedeviling economic headache for them, caused by the federal income tax and inheritance tax laws, compounded by inflation. The individual publisher who heads a family-owned newspaper, and who perhaps owns a majority of the stock, faces the distressing fact that upon death the inheritance taxes will be so high that any heirs may be forced to sell their stock in order to pay them. Because of the income tax laws, the family members cannot afford to receive high dividends from the paper's comfortable earnings. The family newspaper plant is growing obsolete and needs new electronic and press equipment in order for it to remain profitable. Yet inflation has made the price of that equipment extremely high, and the cost of borrowing money for it frightens the publisher.

Along comes a group publishing corporation whose stock is publicly owned. By using part of its profits to purchase additional newspapers, the corporation reduces the federal income taxes it otherwise would be required to pay. It has additional tax advantages and financial resources not available to the individual owner and never faces an inheritance tax problem. Thus it can offer the perplexed individual owner an extremely lucrative price for the newspaper; the publisher and other family stock owners may receive large cash payments which, after payment of capital gains tax, they may place in tax-free municipal securities. The publisher and heirs in turn are made financially secure instead of facing the likelihood of a forced sale of the paper for inheritance taxes. So the publisher sells to the highest bidder, after running up the price as far as possible. Competition among purchasers is intense. When the family owners recently put up for sale one small Midwestern city daily, 14 companies sought to buy it.

Quarrels among the younger generations of publishing families, and the desire of some family members to obtain cash for their stock holdings, also cause the sale of newspapers. Such a dispute among members of the Bingham family in Kentucky led to the sale of the distinguished Louisville *Courier-Journal* in 1986 to Gannett, highest bidder in an intense competition among giant groups.

As a result of these circumstances, the prices at which newspapers are being

Robert Maynard is the first black publisher of a metropolitan daily newspaper, the Oakland Tribune. *Behind (left to right) are company directors Shirley Temple Black; Nancy Hicks Maynard, the publisher's wife; and Warren Lerude.* (Courtesy of John Harding, *Time* magazine.)

sold approach the astronomical. Newspapers with less than 10,000 circulation bring prices of $5 million and $6 million.

The sale price of a newspaper depends upon several factors. These include its pattern of profits, circulation, extent and vigor of its competition, condition of its physical plant, and its advertising volume. As a rule of thumb, a prosperous big-city newspaper without competition usually sells for about twice its annual revenues, while one involved in an intense competitive battle may sell for about half its annual revenues, as did the *Sun-Times.*

One aspect of this buying splurge that has attracted federal investigators of monopoly business practices is the manner in which the Newspaper Preservation Act is used to the advantage of large group owners. In 1986, group owners had acquired partnership status in 19 of the 22 joint publishing situations, and thus the antitrust exemptions there. Proponents of legislation to curb monopoly practices regard this as perversion of the act's intent.

A primary difference between contemporary newspaper groups and the newspaper chains of an earlier era, of which the Hearst newspapers under the personal direction of William Randolph Hearst were an example, is the local editorial autonomy generally practiced today. In Hearst's heyday, his newspapers from coast to coast looked almost alike with the same screaming headlines, heavy typography, and crowded front pages. They took the same editorial positions on national issues and played up Hearst's personal campaigns, such as antivivisection.

Group managements today as a rule permit each newspaper to have an individual appearance and personality and to set its own editorial policy. Thus newspapers under the same ownership may be liberal or conservative, Democratic or Republican, and support different candidates for national public office. Such diversity is practiced by most group ownerships largely in order to alleviate disapproval of absentee ownership among local readers and advertisers.

CROSS-MEDIA OWNERSHIP

While examining the media transactions earlier in this chapter, we saw how a single company often owns outlets in several media fields. Although its origin and primary interest may lie in newspapers, for example, a company may own television and radio stations, and perhaps magazines as well. Or a broadcasting group may also own newspapers or have an ownership stake in a motion picture studio. This is called *cross-media ownership.*

To cite a prominent example, the Times Mirror Company began with one small daily newspaper, the Los Angeles *Times,* in the 19th century. Today the company stands 139th among *Fortune* magazine's 500 largest U.S. industrial companies, has annual revenue of about $3 billion, and owns numerous subsidiaries inside and outside the media fields. It has eight additional newspapers in Connecticut, Colorado, Maryland, and New York. Also, it has three television stations and 50 cable TV systems serving 300 communities in 15 states.

In the print media field Times Mirror publishes *Popular Science, Outdoor Life, Golf,* and *Ski* magazines, the *Sporting News,* and law, medical, and art books. Moreover, it manufactures computer software and owns Learning International, a maker of electronic educational systems. Through other subsidiaries it produces programs for its cable companies, manufactures newsprint, and owns 25 percent of Tejon Ranch Company, a huge oil, cattle, and farming firm.

Still another aspect of the intricate ownership structure in today's mass media is control of media outlets by conglomerate corporations that do not spring from media origins. Their top leaders are not television people at heart, or newspaper people, or movie people; they are financial management people who look at their media properties in the same way they do their factories: to determine how much profit each can contribute to the conglomerate balance sheet or how much gain they might achieve by selling it. Creative and news-oriented people within the ranks of the mammoth cross-media corporations also often complain that their top-level company leaders hold the same far-away, emotionally uninvolved attitude. Bigness inevitably breeds remoteness. It is difficult to relate conglomerate ownerships such as General Electric and Gulf & Western Industries, Inc. to the day-by-day problems of media operation.

Indeed, Gulf & Western provides provocative evidence of the strange bedfellows a conglomerate can assemble for its media properties.

By purchasing Prentice-Hall, a major book publishing and magazine house; Simon & Schuster, an eminent general publisher; and Allyn & Bacon, a textbook publisher, the conglomerate claimed to have created "the nation's leading book publishing company" with annual revenues exceeding $500 million. It also owns one of Hollywood's largest motion picture and television studios, Paramount Pictures.

These media endeavors must compete for the attention of top management with other Gulf & Western operations of far different types. The corporation operates Madison Square Garden, the New York sports arena, and it makes Simmons mattresses, aircraft and automobile parts, bikini bathing suits, hospital furniture, and panty hose. People who need money to buy these and other items may borrow it from the conglomerate's Associates First Capital subsidiary.

Nine of the ten paperback houses that publish 90 percent of the paperback books in the United States are owned by conglomerates.

Excessive concentration of power over what Americans read, see, and hear is a specter that frightens many observers of the mass media. Traditionalists who feel a mystique about the media, and sense an aura of personal relationship between them and the public, are disturbed to see publications and stations bought and sold coldly like factories or truck lines, based on the balance sheets of accountants.

Contending that 50 giant corporations control the majority of all major American media, Ben H. Bagdikian, in his book *The Media Monopoly,* views this concentration of power as a danger to the free flow of information. He points out that large media companies often have interlocking memberships with other corporations on their boards of directors. This, he asserts, tends to reinforce the big business mind-set at upper management levels of the media firms.

"The degree to which the parent corporation controls the content of its media subsidiaries varies," he states. "The most powerful influence, possessed by all, is the power to appoint media leaders. It is a rare corporation that appoints a leader

PROPERTIES OWNED BY TIME INC.

Magazines *Time,* with four international editions; *Sports Illustrated, Fortune, People, Money, Life, Asiaweek, Southern Living, Progressive Farmer, Creative Ideas for Living, Southern Living Classics.*

Books Little, Brown & Co., general publishers; Time-Life Books, sold primarily by mail; Book-of-the-Month Club, Inc., Oxmoor House, Scott Foresman, textbook publishers.

Cable television Home Box Office, a pay-cable program network that distributes motion pictures, coverage of sporting events, and other features nationwide; Cinemax, a movie network; one-third ownership of USA network; American Television and Communications Corporation, which serves cable TV subscribers with 451 franchises in 30 states plus an interest in British cable systems; and Manhattan Cable Television, operating in the southern portion of Manhattan.

Motion pictures Time-Life Films, Inc., partner in Tri-Star Pictures, maker of theatrical and television films.

Video Partner in Thorn EMI/HBO Video to distribute home videos.

Recordings Time-Life Records, which produces and markets records, primarily by mail order.

Along with these media operations, Time Inc. manufactures paper and cardboard products, furniture, printing inks, and wrapping tape. It also engages in land development and contracting and sells marketing information about supermarket product movement.

considered unsympathetic to the desires of the corporation. And when it feels threatened by law, public opinion, or the marketplace, no corporation will permit a subsidiary to harm the parent. Real independence for a media subsidiary is, at best, a disposable luxury."

Leaders of the group ownership movement depict it in benign terms. They assert that it brings greater efficiency to the publications and stations taken over, through application of skillful management techniques, infusion of fresh capital, and use of bulk purchasing power. Group operation frequently increases a newspaper's profits. So far, those who watch the trend with distrust have failed to produce evidence that any conglomerate attempts to present a unified point of view through the cross-media voices it controls or uses them in unison to promote a political or social cause. Yet they sense potential danger. They fear what might happen in the future, in different political and economic circumstances. The concern sometimes expressed that stockholders of a public corporation may try to

TEN LARGEST U.S. NEWSPAPER COMPANIES IN CIRCULATION*

	Daily Circulation	Sunday Circulation
Gannett Company, Inc.	5,827,662	5,360,861
Knight-Ridder Newspapers, Inc.	3,831,968	4,635,478
Newhouse Newspapers	3,034,836	3,758,194
Times Mirror Company	2,714,155	3,431,497
Tribune Company	2,641,655	3,476,767
Dow Jones & Company, Inc.	2,514,466	404,833
The New York Times Company	1,744,932	2,305,458
Scripps Howard	1,640,035	1,669,972
Hearst Newspapers	1,582,485	1,948,472
Thomson Newspapers Inc., United States	1,539,286	983,728

*Figures are average for six months ending September 30, 1986
SOURCE: American Newspaper Publishers Association 1987 statistical summary, from Morton Research, Lynch, Jones & Ryan, Audit Bureau of Circulations.

influence the editorial policies of the media units their company owns seems to have little foundation. Stock ownership is so widely diffused as to make such pressure difficult to organize. Profit, not editorial influence, is the usual corporate goal.

The extremely high prices at which media entities are sold, and the rising operating costs, increasingly squeeze out small entrepreneurs from media ownership, including a growing number of weekly newspapers.

LIMITS ON BROADCAST OWNERSHIP

Two changes in long-standing Federal Communications Commission rules limiting ownership of television stations have contributed to the furious spree of buying and selling. One increased the number of stations a single owner could possess. The other canceled the requirement that an owner who buys a station must hold it for at least three years before reselling. This change opened the door for quick in-and-out deals.

Attempts to halt the expansion of newspaper groups by imposing government restrictions on newspaper ownership run up against the freedom of the press guarantee in the First Amendment. However, efforts to extend First Amendment protection to broadcasting have not yet succeeded. Therefore, the federal government may prevent excessive ownership of radio and television stations through use of the licensing authority of the FCC. The FCC decides what level constitutes "excessive." Following the deregulation philosophy of the Reagan administration, the FCC in recent years has reduced government control of broadcasting both in ownership and operational procedures.

The principle underlying this licensing authority is that the public owns the airwaves, that the number of broadcasting channels technically available form a limited national resource that needs to be regulated by the government. Opponents of regulation argue against this principle. They contend that the spectrum of airwaves exists whether it is used or not, and only when it is enhanced by the use of broadcasters and others does it have any value to the public. In support of their argument, they cite the fact that when Congress passed the Radio Act of 1927, it specifically deleted a declaration of public ownership that had been passed by the House of Representatives.

In 1953 the FCC put a limit on the number of radio and television stations any company could own. The restriction was known popularly as the 7-7-7 rule. It permitted a single company to own or control only seven AM radio stations, seven FM stations, and seven television stations; only five of the television stations could be the more powerful VHF stations. In practice, for economic operating reasons corporations rarely own the maximum number of stations permitted. The FCC in 1984 relaxed controls on ownership, raising the limit on single ownership to 12 AM and 12 FM stations. Ownership of 12 television stations by a single company was permitted in 1985, providing that the owner's stations do not reach more than 25 percent of American households with TV sets. Thus the old 7-7-7 rule became a 12-12-12 rule. The argument for permitting greater ownership was that since 1953 the number of television stations had grown from 199 to 1303, AM radio stations from 2458 to 4805, and FM stations from 686 to 5066.

No limitation exists on the number of cable television franchises a company can operate, although efforts to impose a restriction have been discussed in Congress.

The FCC also enforces a one-to-a-market rule, whose goal is to prevent a company from owning more than one type of medium in a market. The rule states that a newspaper cannot own and operate a television or radio station serving its home community, nor can a radio station own a television station in the same market. Yet in many cities we see radio and television stations under the same ownership; indeed, numerous cases exist in which the local newspaper owns both a local radio station and a local television station, seemingly in contradiction to the FCC rule. These multiple-media combinations are legally permissible because they were "grandfathered"; that is, they were exempted from the FCC restrictions because they were in existence when the rules were imposed. When a grandfathered combination is sold in the future, the new rules apply, requiring a separation of ownership.

That is why the Tribune Company had to sell the Los Angeles *Daily News* after it purchased the Los Angeles television station and why Rupert Murdoch was ordered to sell the Chicago *Sun-Times* and New York *Post* within two years after buying TV stations in those cities. Interestingly, both Tribune and Murdoch decided that owning the television stations was more important to them than owning the newspapers.

License Renewal Threats

Radio and television stations must periodically satisfy the federal government that they are using the electromagnetic spectrum assigned to them in a manner that meets federal standards. FCC policy specifies that when a station comes up for renewal of its license, which occurs every five years for television and seven years for radio, it must demonstrate that its programming "has been substantially attuned to the needs and interests of the community it serves."

A period of uncertainty about FCC policy on license renewals occurred in the early 1970s, after the commission denied renewal of the license of station WHDH-TV, Boston, and awarded it to a competing applicant in 1969. The Boston decision encouraged the filing of competing applications against a number of major licenses, without success. Under current practice, a station that performs responsibly can anticipate license renewal but must provide evidence at each renewal time that it is doing so.

MINORITY GROUP REPRESENTATION AND OWNERSHIP

Blacks, Hispanics, and other minority groups have brought strong pressures to bear against the media in recent years. They seek a larger, more favorable role on the air, both in the number of minority performers and the elimination of false, stereotyped images of minority individuals. Progress has been made. For example, a large increase is evident in the number of black performers in television commercials. However, on a more significant level, serious examinations of problems facing minorities have been shown more frequently on television recently—problems arising from history, economic injustices, and contemporary social attitudes. Among these presentations are "Roots," which made a tremendous impact on the American consciousness; "The Vanishing Family—Crisis in Black America," "Holocaust," "I Remember Harlem," "Playing for Time," and "The Women's Room." Some productions, such as "The Bill Cosby Show," provide an excellent showcase for actors from minority groups to display their talents. Some stereotyping still exists, but gradually it is being reduced through a sharpened awareness on the part of those who control television programming. Organized groups that focus attention on these evidences of stereotyping also help to promote more balanced programming.

Stations must demonstrate their efforts toward equal treatment of the races and sexes as part of their license renewal applications.

Efforts by minorities to obtain ownership of large newspapers, as well as television and radio stations, have advanced more slowly largely because of heavy financial requirements. Among newspapers, Robert Maynard became the first black publisher of a metropolitan daily when he and associates purchased the Oakland, California, *Tribune.* Minorities own only about 2 percent of American radio and television stations.

Private and governmental efforts have been made to improve the situation. Until 1986 the FCC gave special tax breaks to broadcasters who sold their stations to minority purchasers, making such deals easier to consummate. During the Carter administration, the government undertook a program to promote minority ownership, one aspect of which was to have the Small Business Administration make loans to broadcasters. The National Association of Broadcasters created a nonprofit Minority Broadcast Investment Fund, whose goal was to raise $45 million in contributions to be used for direct loans and loan guarantees to minority owners. The National Radio Broadcasters Association has a program for its members to help minority workers learn station-operating techniques. A National Black Network was created in radio with the goal of its members owning a full complement of AM and FM stations, along with the possible purchase of cable television franchises.

Credibility:

Media and Government

Promoting Credibility

In 1971 the Seattle *Times* became one of the first papers in the country to send accuracy-check questionnaires to the subjects of news stories. Over the years, more than two-thirds of the forms have been returned to the *Times,* where they have been circulated among reporters and editors. The responses have provided the basis for corrections, clarifications, and follow-up stories—and have made the news sources happy. For the record, the percentage of returned forms saying stories were completely accurate, including headlines, has ranged from a low of 60 percent to a high of 78.9 percent.

The Pittsburgh *Post-Gazette* offers minority readers a special outlet for expressing their opinions on race-related matters. The column, "Black on Black," runs each Wednesday. When the column began in 1984, the paper had to solicit contributors, but two years later it was filled with good-quality pieces.

The Tucson *Citizen* ran a special series, "New Pueblo," examining the city's quality of life, its problems, and its future. Reader feedback was presented in a four-page follow-up section and in nine additional pages over three weeks.

These and 202 other practical approaches to heighten reader trust were published by the American Society of Newspaper Editors in a 1986 credibility project.

*T*his chapter opens with a review of several major studies of press credibility and public support for the media, made during the mid-1980s. These show a more substantial public support of the media, in terms of believability, than many journalists had estimated; they also show shortcomings in press performance that fan criticism. Most important, they show that the "watchdog" function of the press is highly regarded; 67 percent of survey respondents said press criticism keeps leaders from doing things that should not be done, while only 17 percent thought press criticism keeps leaders from "doing their job."

If the role of the press is to serve the governed, not the governors, as Justice Hugo L. Black declared, then the self-assigned role of the press to act as censors of the government is vitally necessary in a democracy. In the past three decades there has been a credibility duel between government and the press, with the public alternating its support between a particular president and the media.

Violence at home and stalemated wars abroad brought credibility gaps for both president and the media, who played the unhappy role of the bearers of bad tidings. Lyndon Johnson retired from public life in 1968 when the Vietnam War brought bitter national debate. Richard Nixon, caught up in the dissent of the times among youths and minorities, became enmeshed in the Watergate scandal that brought about his 1974 impeachment and resignation. Things went little better for Gerald Ford, who lost his 1976 election bid to Jimmy Carter; Carter in turn was brought down by the national frustration at enduring the long Iran hostage crisis. During Ronald Reagan's two terms hostility exhibited by the government toward the press neared an all-time high. ◆

MEASURING PRESS CREDIBILITY

Four major studies of press credibility and public support for the media were published in the mid-1980s, presenting much fresh data and offering extensive analytical interpretation.

The most elaborate was a depth study titled, *The People and the Press,* commissioned by the Times Mirror newspaper publishing group and carried out by the Gallup Organization. It involved focus group interviews and a pilot study, two national interviewing surveys reaching 3100 respondents in their homes, and follow-up interviews with 2100 of them. Gallup utilized rarely employed segmentation analysis involving factor analysis and cluster research to help solve enigmas in measuring public reactions to media.

Another major national study was conducted by the Minneapolis-based MORI Research, Inc. for the American Society of Newspaper Editors (ASNE) titled, *Newspaper Credibility: Building Reader Trust.* This study used focus group discussions and a nationwide representative telephone sample of 1600 adults, of whom 1002 later answered an extensive mailed questionnaire and read back their answers in telephone interviews. A total of 284 questions were used.

In addition, the MORI researchers did a separate study for the Associated Press Managing Editors Association (APME) involving a 153-question survey answered by 1333 journalists from 51 newspapers selected randomly. Analyzing the credibility gap perceived by many journalists as existing between them and readers, it was titled, *Journalists and Readers: Bridging the Credibility Gap.* The ASNE's Credibility Committee produced *Newspaper Credibility,* a guide with 206 practical approaches to heighten reader trust.

A fourth major contribution was made by the Gannett Center for Media Studies, which published *The Media and the People,* a 50-year review of the literature reporting polling and research findings about media credibility, including the studies described above.

The Times Mirror study offers several conclusions that run counter to the conventional wisdom concerning public opinion and the nation's press. If credibility is defined as believability, it says, then there is no credibility crisis for the nation's news media. Nor are journalists' concerns that public perceptions characterize them as inaccurate and arrogant folk borne out by the data. But the study offers cautions. Overall measures of favorability reveal a reservoir of public support that is wide, but not deep. The public appreciates the press far more than it approves of news media performance. Its marks for believability are good, not excellent. Its approval is asymmetrical; critics are more critical than supporters are supportive. But, says the Times Mirror study, emphatic public appreciation of the press's watchdog role against the government and an inherent desire to get the news are two factors washing out dissatisfactions with press performance.

ASNE's study gives more weight to the dissatisfactions, and warns that newspapers have a credibility problem: Three-fourths of all adults have some problem with credibility of the media; one-sixth express frustration with the news media. The study found that newspapers and television have very similar credibility ratings. With percentages for newspapers listed first, they were: high, 32, 30; medium, 43, 43; low, 25, 27. The Times Mirror cluster studies showed similar results: 70 percent of people falling within positive orientations, 30 percent among the negative. Of the latter, half were bitter or vociferous critics, a figure similar to the ASNE's frustrated group. When controversies arise about the role of the media, or the press becomes pitted against the government, it is the voices of the critical minority that are loudest.

Respondents to the Times Mirror study were asked to rate news organizations and people on a scale of 1 to 4, the top ranking going to those found to be believable for all or most of what they say. Table 22.1 shows some of the results. All ten news personalities and ten news institutions, with the exception of one of each, have a rating above 80 percent when figures for those saying "believable" and "highly believable" are combined. This is the wide reservoir of public support! Walter Cronkite, longtime CBS anchorman, ran away with the votes, as he always has done in polls.

White House correspondents ranked lower than anchorpeople. Sam Donaldson of ABC had a believability total of 79 percent and high believability score of 30, while Diane Sawyer of CBS had ratings of 80 and 28. The man they interviewed, President Ronald Reagan, was rated highly believable by 28 percent of the respondents but his total believability score was only 68—well below that of the media.

The believability rankings showed fairly similar totals for television and newspapers, but newspapers trailed in the highly believable category. Part of the reason was the perceptions people had of newspaper performance. Table 22.2 gives positive attitudes of the public toward newspaper people and negative attitudes toward newspaper organizations.

While 55 percent of respondents said newspeople got the facts straight, 34 percent said they were often inaccurate. Forty-five percent said newspapers were politically biased in reporting. The Times Mirror study showed that some readers who had high regard for the press as an institution were among the most severe critics of press performance.

The APME study of newspaper journalists uncovered strong degrees of uneasiness, especially among senior editors, about media and the public trust. The survey reported journalists thought their newspapers were more credible and

TABLE 22.1 Believability Rankings

News Institution	Highly Believable	Total for Believability	News Personality	Highly Believable	Total for Believability
Wall Street Journal	45	87	Walter Cronkite (CBS)	57	92
Reader's Digest	40	81	Dan Rather (CBS)	44	89
Cable News Network	38	84	McNeil-Lehrer (PBS)	43	83
Local TV news	36	85	Ted Koppel (ABC)	41	88
Time	35	85	Peter Jennings (ABC)	40	90
National TV news	34	87	John Chancellor (NBC)	39	89
Newsweek	31	86	David Brinkley (ABC)	38	90
Radio news	30	84	Tom Brokaw (NBC)	37	88
Local daily newspaper	29	84	Mike Wallace (CBS)	35	83
National influential newspapers (grouped)	25	78	Barbara Walters (ABC)	30	78

TABLE 22.2 Public Attitudes Toward Newspapers

Attitudes Toward Newspaper People: % Favorable		Attitudes Toward Newspapers: % Unfavorable	
79	Care about quality of work	73	Invade people's privacy
78	Fair to President Reagan	60	Too much bad news
72	Highly professional	55	Try to cover up mistakes
55	Get the facts straight	53	Favor one side (biased)
52	Stand up for America	53	Often influenced by powerful

accurate than the ASNE study found the public thought they were. Journalists almost unanimously agreed that their own credibility was a public problem. Efforts to improve their press performance could only help in the maintenance of media standards.

Journalists were disappointed by the lack of public knowledge, and also public interest, in issues considered vital to the press. Only 45 percent of respondents to the Times Mirror survey could identify the First Amendment or the Bill of Rights as providing for freedom of the press. And 75 percent said libel law should be the same for public officials and private citizens, which would be a sharp setback for aggressive journalism. Generally the public response as measured in the surveys showed an indifference to both the operations of the press and the issues that concern it.

THE BARKING WATCHDOG. In 1987 the Advertising Council began a public service advertising campaign designed to increase public awareness of the First Amendment. The council was to provide about $25 million in free print space and broadcast time during the five-year Project Watchdog, a campaign by the Society of Professional Journalists, Sigma Delta Chi (SPJ, SDX). The society sought almost $400,000 to meet production costs during the first year and about $1.2 million for the entire campaign.

The New York-based advertising agency Lowe Marschalk Inc. developed the campaign at the request of the council, with the theme, "If the press didn't tell us, who would?" The advertisements were accompanied by either a Washington box number or an 800 telephone number. Persons seeking more information receive a brochure explaining the history of the First Amendment and what it means. Their names and addresses are being computerized, sorted by zip code, and sent to SPJ, SDX professional chapters for use in inviting people to town hall-type public events in their areas.

The campaign will extend to the bicentennial celebrations of the U.S. Constitution in 1988 and the Bill of Rights in 1991. The Watchdog name was adopted from a speech by Alan Barth, former editorial writer for the Washington *Post*. Barth drew an analogy between the press and a barking watchdog. He said, "If you want a watchdog to warn you of intruders, you must put up with a certain amount of mistaken barking. Some extraneous barking is the price you must pay for his service as a watchdog."

RESIDUAL PUBLIC SUPPORT. In one area the public already stands solidly on the side of the press. When the issues involve the rights of news organizations versus the rights of the government, the public usually sides with the press. As the Times Mirror survey concludes:

> The public says "no" to formal censorship and says "no" to prior restraint. The public says "no" to the government requiring fairness in news coverage. The public says "no" to the government requiring equal advertising time on television or space in newspapers for political candidates. And the public says "yes," emphatically, to publishing a story such as the Pentagon Papers [to be discussed in this chapter].

Seventy-nine percent of respondents agreed with this statement in an ASNE study: "I may not be happy with everything the press does, but if the government tried to close down a newspaper and stop it from publishing, I'd be upset enough to do something."

Much of the remainder of this chapter illustrates how these attitudes have worked out during the last three decades.

GOVERNMENT AND PRESS: A CREDIBILITY DUEL

The mass media during the era of Vietnam and Watergate came under the most severe attacks from the public and the federal government since the days of the Revolution and the Civil War, when patriots eliminated the newspapers they did not like by destroying the printing offices where they were published. The public, frustrated and bewildered by rapidly changing social and technological conditions, an unpopular war, and the emotional bombardment caused by near-total and near-instant mass communication, tended to blame the mass media for many of their problems. The federal government, always an adversary because of the constitutional role of the press in a democratic society, capitalized on the growing feeling of disenchantment with the media and engaged in a credibility duel characterized by both direct and indirect assaults.

It was a situation ripe for demagogues. A cult of disbelief had grown steadily since the days of Senator Joseph McCarthy's treason charges and the Republican party's 1952 election slogan of "Communism, Corruption, and Korea." A credibility gap between president and public developed for John F. Kennedy, and widened dramatically for Lyndon Johnson and Richard Nixon.

But another credibility gap, between the media and the public, emerged. There was much bad news that people did not want to believe, much reality that they did not want to have exist: the Bay of Pigs, the Berlin Wall, the assassination of a president, the Vietnam War, racial riots in big cities, college campus riots, the assassinations of Robert Kennedy and the Rev. Martin Luther King, Jr., the collapse of victory hopes in Vietnam, the secret bombing of Cambodia, the My Lai massacre, Kent State, sexual permissiveness and obscenity out in the open, and an inflation-depression. Blaming the source of the bad news—the press—became popular.

Some people did not believe the president; some did not believe the press; some believed neither. And both the president and the press encouraged people not to believe the other. In late 1972 Richard Nixon appeared to have the upper hand. Reelected with 61 percent of the vote, the president stood triumphant. But the ever-widening political conspiracy known as Watergate had already begun its course. At first dismissed by the White House as "a third-rate burglary," it developed into a major constitutional crisis. When it was over, 61 individuals and 19 corporations had been charged with violations of federal laws; 18 members of Nixon's administration had pleaded guilty or been convicted, including two cabinet members and four of his closest Oval Office associates; and the president had resigned in disgrace, joining his vice-president, who had resigned a year earlier rather than face bribe-taking charges.

The credibility of the media had been substantially restored, along with that of the Congress and courts. "A President has been deposed, but the Republic endures," wrote one editor. Obviously, however, the long duel between press and government had been costly to both institutions. In the 1980s the cult of disbelief was still strong; President Ronald Reagan and his spokespeople openly attacked the patriotism of the press in retaliation for its questioning of his administration's dogmas in domestic and foreign policy.

VIOLENCE AND WAR

Violence and war occur all over the world. But no country welcomes the use of violence in its own social situations and neighborhoods, and nothing is more frustrating to a nation than an unsuccessful, costly war. Americans in the decade of 1965 to 1975 were subjected to violence at home and a stalemated war abroad; both widened the public credibility gap.

Vietnam, Cambodia, and Laos

Few Americans knew where these countries were when the first U.S. military advisers arrived in Saigon in 1955. Step by step, America descended into what David Halberstam, then of the New York *Times,* aptly called a quagmire, which was to swallow up one president and help destroy another.

By 1963 the most perceptive members of the U.S. press corps in Saigon were challenging the assumptions of the American intervention, but they were prophets without honor in their own country. The assassination of strong-man Ngo Dinh Diem opened the door to U.S. domination of South Vietnamese affairs; the number of "advisers" had grown to 16,300 at the time of President John F. Kennedy's death. Lyndon Johnson responded to the Gulf of Tonkin incident by instituting bombing of North Vietnam and sending 180,000 more troops during 1965. The number rose to more than one-half million, but no victory was forthcoming. Instead, the Vietcong humiliated the U.S. command with its Tet offensive of early 1968, which reached the gates of the American embassy.

Public confidence in the war leadership collapsed. President Johnson, before he retired from public life, instituted peace talks in Paris that were to drag on for five years. Antiwar sentiment surged through the American youth and spread more widely. President Nixon's plan for "Vietnamization" of the war also included its widening into Cambodia in 1970. By the end of 1971, more than half the U.S. military force had been withdrawn, but there were 50,000 U.S. personnel dead. The country was divided almost evenly in its attitude toward the war, which eventually would end in total victory for those the United States had opposed.

The press, which had to report these events and analyze American policy and strategy, heavily supported the war until 1968. Then many more voices were raised for peace. Television, which had for the first time brought the battles and the brutalities of war into the family living room, was not thanked for its effort. Americans did not want to hear about or see search-and-destroy missions, burnings of villages, the dead civilians of the My Lai massacre, and saturation bomb-

ings. The majority wanted Nixon's "peace with honor," and the tragedy continued to unfold.

City Riots and the Kerner Report

Television was caught up in another credibility gap during the 1960s. It has been considered by many observers to be a primary cause of the so-called revolution of rising expectations among America's disadvantaged peoples. Both the programs and the commercials aired on television held out a better way of life for minority groups without changing the reality. Unfulfilled expectations built up angry frustrations that erupted into the ghetto riots of Los Angeles, Newark, Detroit, and other cities. America's affluence, of course, was also reflected in movies, radio, newspapers, and other media; undoubtedly, too, there were other factors contributing to the social unrest. But television, the medium most often used by minority groups, had made an impact that could not be denied. Before big-city riots, television had covered the suppression of civil discontent in the South, principally at Little Rock, Arkansas; Selma, Alabama; and Oxford, Mississippi. A new level of awareness and indignation had spread throughout the rest of the country.

Many public officials criticized television for its thorough coverage of the disturbances. It was alleged that the mere arrival of a TV camera crew on the scene of a demonstration often set off crowd action that had not occurred before. The National Advisory Commission on Civil Disorders, with Governor Otto Kerner of Illinois as chairman, also criticized the news media, including television, for incidents in which it felt bad judgment had been displayed and material treated in a sensationalistic manner. But on the whole, the commission found, the media had tried hard to present a balanced factual account of the riots in Newark and Detroit in 1967. Errors in many cases were attributed to false police reports.

The Kerner Commission, however, indicted the mass media for failing to communicate to their predominantly white audience "a sense of the degradation, misery, and hopelessness of living in the ghetto" as well as "a sense of Negro culture, thought, or history," thus feeding black alienation and intensifying white prejudices. With few black reporters and fewer race experts, the report charged, the media had not seriously reported the problems of the black community. Pointing out that fear and apprehension of racial unrest and violence are deeply rooted in American society, coloring and intensifying reactions to news of racial trouble and threats of racial conflict, the commission asserted that those who report and disseminate news must be conscious of the background of anxieties and apprehension against which their stories are projected.

The news media admitted that they had not properly prepared the American people for an understanding of social unrest. Through television documentaries, radio and TV "talk" programs and interviews, in-depth newspaper and magazine articles, and the like, the media explored the issues and sought solutions. Efforts were intensified to recruit black and other minority reporters. But public support of the black movement dwindled.

STUDENT DEMONSTRATIONS AND CHICAGO, 1968. As student unrest spread across the nation with disruptions at the University of California at Berkeley, Columbia University, and Kent State, coverage of the disorders by the mass media was criticized both by proponents of "law and order" and by the protesters themselves. A segment of the public, greatly disturbed by what it saw and read, complained that television was being used by the demonstrators for purposes of propaganda against the war and the conventional social fabric. Furthermore, it was alleged, news coverage of the occupancy and burning of buildings and especially of counteraction by police or the National Guard provoked similar disturbances on other campuses.

On the other hand, student militants and their supporters complained that the mass media, which were part of the establishment they hated, failed to focus on the root problems of the disorders and thus to help the public understand the issues involved. They saw scant evidence that the media were bringing before the public such matters as the universities' tie-ins with the military, their heavy involvement in investments, the role of ROTC on campus, and depersonalization of campus life. A hard core of militants sought to tear down the entire social structure, whereas most students merely desired changes in some patterns of national life. When the antiwar and protest movements coalesced in the campaign of Senator Eugene McCarthy for the 1968 Democratic presidential nomination, many of these students went to Chicago as delegates and workers for McCarthy. The militants also went seeking to tear apart the political fabric by provoking street rioting. This they accomplished. Altogether, it was a tension-filled four days without precedent, as one TV network described them, "either in the history of American politics or in the experience of American journalism."

The National Commission on the Causes and Prevention of Violence asked

Chicago attorney Daniel Walker to study the convention disturbances. Walker's staff took statements from 1410 eyewitnesses and participants and had access to more than 2000 interviews conducted by the FBI. The report described both provocation and retaliation. The provocation "took the form of obscene epithets, of rocks, sticks, bathroom tiles, and even human feces hurled at police by demonstrators," some planned, some spontaneous, and some provoked by police action. The retaliation was "unrestrained and indiscriminate police violence on many occasions, particularly at night," with reporters and photographers singled out for assault, and their equipment deliberately damaged. The final report of the commission in December 1969 said the Chicago police used "excessive force not only against the provocateurs but also against the peaceful demonstrators and passive bystanders."

Although the Walker Report disclosed that no fewer than 70 broadcast and print reporters and camera operators suffered injuries at the hands of the police, scant attention was paid to this fact by an uneasy public. CBS correspondent Eric Sevareid found the public's reaction obvious:

> Over the years the pressure of public resentment against screaming militants, foul-mouthed demonstrators, arsonists, and looters had built up in the national boiler. With Chicago it exploded. The feelings that millions of people released were formed long before Chicago. Enough was enough: the police *must* be right. Therefore, the reporting *must* be wrong.

THE GOVERNMENT ATTACKS

It was in this setting of a frustrating war, big-city riots, student demonstrations, radical militancy, and sex-drugs-pornography permissiveness that Richard Nixon became president. Beaten narrowly in 1960, apparently out of politics after losing the California governorship in 1962 and telling the press "you won't have Dick Nixon to kick around any more," he had rebounded into the political vacuum caused by the Goldwater debacle of 1964, Lyndon Johnson's retirement, and the assassinations of John and Robert Kennedy.

Hubert Humphrey, his campaign left in shambles by the Chicago convention, which alienated both conservative-minded voters and the antiwar intellectuals, ran a hard race but failed because he lost all the Southern and border states except Texas. Nixon received 43.16 percent of the popular vote; Humphrey, 42.73; and Alabama Gov. George Wallace, 13.63. The Democrats won both houses of Congress; indeed, Nixon was to become the first American president never to carry at least one house with him.

Richard Nixon's personality remains to be fully dissected, but he was clearly a loner, instinctively distrustful of others, a hard-nosed politician who nursed resentments into hatreds and insisted upon taking revenge. Feeling intense political isolation as a minority president and determined to win reelection in 1972, Nixon assumed that he had to attack his enemies, especially the media. He would coalesce his conservative support by continuing the Vietnam War until peace could be won "with honor," by blunting the black movement through the issue of unpopular school busing, and by taking roundhouse swings at those he hated—

political radicals, student militants, Eastern establishment intellectuals, and influential large daily newspapers such as the New York *Times* and Washington *Post,* which he regarded as "soft" on social and political issues.

The president asked his top aides 21 times in one month in 1969 (mid-September to mid-October) to counter what he regarded as unfavorable media coverage, according to an internal White House memo made public in 1973. The memo recommended harassment of unfriendly news organizations by the Internal Revenue Service and the antitrust division of the Justice Department.

Nixon's 21 requests covered CBS, NBC, and ABC. One singled out Dan Rather, CBS White House correspondent. Among other targets were political columnist Jack Anderson, and *Time, Life,* and *Newsweek.* Nixon's associates proved responsive to his antimedia mood.

The Agnew Criticisms

The spark for a steadily growing conflagration of public debates, pressures against the media, and proposed and actual regulatory action by numerous agencies of government was touched off by Vice-President Spiro Agnew in November 1969. In two speeches he declared that the networks and newspapers with multiple-media holdings exercised such powerful influence over public opinion that they should vigorously endeavor to be impartial and fair in reporting and commenting on national affairs. Specifically, Agnew criticized network managements for employing commentators with a preponderant Eastern establishment bias and for failing to provide a "wall of separation" between news and comment. A similar liberal bias, he implied, affected the policies of the Washington *Post* and its other media holdings, and those of the New York *Times.* Because Agnew referred to the dependence of broadcast stations on government licensing, although disclaiming any thought of censorship, some observers saw in his remarks an implied threat to the freedom of broadcasters to report and comment freely on public affairs.

Never before had a high federal official made such direct attacks on those reporting and commenting on the news. A research study by Dennis T. Lowry comparing random samples of newscast items reporting administration activities for one-week periods in 1969 and 1970 bore out the contention that the criticisms generated by Agnew had significantly affected the newscasts in the direction of "safe" handling.

The Pentagon Papers

When the New York *Times* began in June 1971 to publish a series of news articles summarizing the contents of a 47-volume study of the origins of the Vietnam War, the "Pentagon Papers case" erupted. The study had been ordered by Defense Secretary McNamara, as a "History of the U.S. Decision-Making Process on Vietnam Policy" and had been made by a group from the RAND Corporation.

The study was historical and revealed no military secrets or strategy, but it was highly explosive in terms of political and diplomatic interest. As a Supreme Court justice put it, the Pentagon Papers were also highly embarrassing (to Kennedy, Johnson, and Nixon administrations alike).

Executives of the *Times* decided that it was in the national interest to report the documentary evidence that had come to their hands, even though it was stamped "top secret," as was the widespread custom in the government. A team of *Times* staff members led by managing editor Abe Rosenthal and reporter Neil Sheehan labored for three months to prepare the series.

When the first story appeared, Attorney General John Mitchell asked the *Times* to stop the series. The newspaper refused, and the Nixon administration went to court to seek a prior restraint order forbidding further publication. The government obtained a temporary restraining order but was refused a permanent one. It engaged in a second duel in the courts with the Washington *Post* and met increasing resistance from the Boston *Globe* and other newspapers dismayed that prior restraint had been invoked.

The case finally reached the Supreme Court, which by a five-to-four order continued the temporary prior restraint order, a shocking setback to the free press concept. The newspaper lawyers then avoided a historic showdown on the absolute nature of the constitutional ban on prior restraint and argued only that the government could not prove any involvement of national security in the banned publication. To this, the Supreme Court agreed, six to three. The Court said, "Any system of prior restraints of expression comes to this court bearing a heavy presumption against its constitutional validity." It was hoped that, as with the John Peter Zenger case, the Pentagon Papers case would not be repeated; that is, no president would again seek to impose a prior restraint upon the press, as had been done in 1971 for the first time in the history of the nation. The political sensitivities of the case made the Nixon administration pause in seeking criminal indictments against any newspaper editors or reporters involved in the Pentagon Papers disclosures, although it moved against Daniel Ellsberg, accused of taking the secret papers from the files.

Why did Nixon and his staff pursue this issue so relentlessly? Because the New York *Times* and Washington *Post* were involved; because Ellsberg represented the liberal intellectual element; because the majesty of the executive branch of the government and the presidency had been challenged on an issue they called "national security." And because, as FBI director William Ruckelshaus testified in May 1973, Nixon had instituted a wiretapping search to plug what he termed "security leaks" to the press as early as May 1969. Between then and February 1971, the FBI had wiretapped the telephones of four reporters and 13 government employees, mostly members of the National Security Council (this episode involved Secretary of State Henry Kissinger). One of the wiretaps recorded Ellsberg's voice.

When the FBI finally balked in 1971, the tapes were delivered to White House aide John Ehrlichman. Nixon then set up his own special investigative group, the infamous White House "plumbers," who were to implicate the CIA in their efforts. One of their jobs was to "get Ellsberg," and in July 1971 the White House unit obtained CIA "logistical support" in planning a September break-in at the office of Ellsberg's Los Angeles psychiatrist.

All this proof of White House subversion of the FBI and CIA came to light in May 1973 at the Los Angeles trial of Ellsberg and Anthony J. Russo for the Pentagon Papers theft. The CIA director admitted the facts in a memorandum to the U.S. district court, and Judge W. Matthew Byrne dismissed the case against Ellsberg and Russo, citing government misconduct. Nixon's zeal thus ensured Ellsberg's escape from prosecution. In July 1974 four members of the White House staff (Ehrlichman, Charles Colson, Egil Krogh, and Gordon Liddy) and two ex-CIA men were to be convicted on conspiracy charges or for the actual break-in.

CBS and "The Selling of the Pentagon"

Of the networks, the Columbia Broadcasting System especially drew the hatred of the Nixon staff. Dan Rather, White House correspondent, dueled with the president throughout the entire Watergate period and endured Nixon's sarcasm. Daniel Schorr and Marvin Kalb were harassed by White House-inspired investigations. Kalb was one of those who was wiretapped. (So was columnist Joseph Kraft; and joining these newsmen on the celebrated White House "enemies list" were columnist Mary McGrory and the managing editor of the conservative Los Angeles *Times,* Ed Guthman.)

It was not surprising, then, that CBS and its then president, Frank Stanton, should be involved in a major freedom of the press case in 1971. The program was "The Selling of the Pentagon," which had aroused anger both in the White House and in the Congress. At issue was Congress' right to legislative inquiry versus broadcasters' rights under freedom of the press. A contempt citation was recommended by the House Commerce Committee when the network refused to supply all its "out-takes," or unused pieces of film and tape, used in the production of the controversial documentary. The award-winning investigative report had contended that the Department of Defense was spending millions of dollars promoting both its activities and political points of view. In reply to a subpoena, Stanton stated: "If newsmen are told that their notes, films, and tapes will be subject to compulsory process so that the government can determine whether the news has been satisfactorily edited, the scope, nature, and vigor of their newsgathering and reporting activities will inevitably be curtailed." The House, by a vote of 226 to 181, declined to cite Stanton and the network for contempt.

Nixon's Effective Use of Television

There was a positive side to Richard Nixon's involvement with the media. In the wake of his disastrous television debate with John F. Kennedy in 1960, he assiduously studied the medium. He loosened up, learned to joke about himself in televised interviews, and whenever possible utilized staged situations (convention press conferences with selected members asking questions, political speeches before controlled small audiences, person-to-person interviews) rather than rough-and-tumble news conferences.

Most effectively of all, he used television in live news-making situations in which no journalists were interposed between him and his audience. His visits to the Soviet Union were a television success. And his imagination-catching trip to mainland China was a triumph.

Such was Nixon's style. He did not like the regular White House press conferences. Instead, he relied upon prime-time requests for direct talks to the television audience. During their first 1½ years in office, according to one careful count, Eisenhower had made 3 such requests, Kennedy 4, and Johnson 7. Nixon made 14 his first 18 months, and his final talk from the Oval Office the night he resigned the presidency was his thirty-seventh.

Nixon's use of television in the 1972 campaign was faultless. He selected controlled audiences for backdrops, avoided confrontations with his Democratic opponent, and capitalized on his foreign affairs leadership. The luckless George McGovern, plagued with controversies over his running mate, Thomas Eagleton, and supported only by a loose confederation of political minorities—women's rights advocates, big-city intellectual liberals, blacks, young people—caught the media criticism while the Nixon campaign rolled on toward a nearly clean sweep of electoral votes.

WATERGATE AND THE MEDIA

If the president and his Oval Office advisers had been able to see ahead, they would not have become involved in Watergate. But they had assumed since 1969 that they would be fighting for their political lives in 1972 as minority party leaders against a strong Democratic party candidate—a Kennedy, a Muskie, a Humphrey. And they had put in motion a plan that could not be halted when a McGovern appeared on the scene.

That plan involved the harassment of the media, the creation of an enemies list, the raising of a $60 million fund for the Committee to Reelect the President that often involved illegal pressure upon corporations, the creation of a "dirty tricks" group that sabotaged Democratic presidential candidates (notably Edmund Muskie), and the use of the IRS, FBI, and CIA to discourage political opponents and check on possibly vulnerable Democrats (notably Edward Kennedy).

It also had involved the creation of the White House plumbers group, whose talents were used against Ellsberg in 1971 and who now were to bring the Nixon administration to disaster. It was June 17, 1972; the target was the offices of the Democratic National Committee in the Watergate building complex, including that of Chairman Lawrence O'Brien; the apparent goals were to find interesting materials and to "bug" the O'Brien office in the hope of developing compromising tapes that could be used against the Democrats.

Disaster struck. The five men on the job bungled it; a watchman called the police; within two or three days the trail was leading from the plumbers back to their White House sponsors. The Washington *Post* assigned two youthful reporters, Carl Bernstein and Bob Woodward, to follow that trail. More experienced men might have faltered, but instinctively executives of the *Post* and its still obscure team of reporters sensed that an incredible story was in the making.

What the Tapes Finally Revealed

The twists and turns of the Watergate story can best be understood by first knowing the ending. What became referred to as "the smoking gun"—positive proof of President Nixon's participation in the Watergate conspiracy and consequent criminal obstruction of justice—did not publicly emerge until 780 days after the break-in. Four days later, Nixon was on his way to exile in San Clemente.

The president's entire defense had been built around his claim that he had not known about the Watergate problems until March 21, 1973, when his counsel, John Dean, told him there was "a cancer on the Presidency." Many dents were made in this defense, but the smoking gun was missing until the story's end.

It was the tape of June 23, 1972, conversations in the Oval Office. Why Nixon had taped his private conversations, and why the tapes survived to bring down his administration, remain topics for speculation. From the time a presidential aide revealed their existence in July 1973, a tense struggle developed over them. An incredibly detailed presidential daily diary, recording minute-by-minute his conversations, had readily been made available to investigators and the media. It proved to be the key to the tapes. There were three conversations listed for June 23 between the president and H. R. Haldeman, his chief of staff.

After losing an 8–0 Supreme Court decision on custody of the tapes, Nixon had no recourse but to release the June 23 tape and others. Nixon acknowledged in an accompanying statement that he had withheld the contents of the tapes from his staff and his attorneys despite the fact that they contradicted his previous declarations of noninvolvement and lack of knowledge of the Watergate coverup. Six days after the break-in, the tape related, Nixon and Haldeman had developed and put into operation a plan to have top CIA officials tell the FBI to stay out of investigations of the Watergate break-in for national security reasons. Thus the employees of the Nixon reelection committee and White House staff members involved might escape detection.

There were other tapes, which revealed the attitude of the Nixon administration toward the media. The Washington *Post* obtained this censored portion of the September 15, 1972, tape from the House Judiciary Committee:

PRESIDENT The main, main thing is the *Post* is going to have damnable, damnable problems out of this one. They have a television station—
DEAN That's right, they do.
PRESIDENT And they're going to have to get it renewed.
HALDEMAN They have a radio station, too.
PRESIDENT Does that come up too? The point is, when does it come up?
DEAN I don't know. The practice of non-licensees filing on top of licensees has certainly got more . . .

PRESIDENT That's right.

DEAN . . . more active in the, this area.

PRESIDENT And it's going to be goddamn active here.

Three months later, four application challenges had been filed against two Florida television stations owned by the *Post* interests by a number of Nixon friends and supporters. As Kenneth Clawson, White House communications officer, put it to the Los Angeles *Times* later: "I separate out TV from the print media when it comes to criticism. Newspapers are privately owned, but we all have a piece of TV's ass and we're entitled to do something—although I'm not sure exactly what—if it offends us."

How the Media Fared with the Watergate Story

The Washington *Post* had led in Watergate coverage from the beginning. Its reporting team, Carl Bernstein and Bob Woodward, was backed by publisher Katharine Graham and executive editor Benjamin Bradlee. The *Post* was first to uncover the CIA connection; first to link the break-in culprits with White House sponsors; first on August 1, 1972, to print the proof that a $25,000 check donated to the Committee to Reelect the President had ended up in the Watergate conspirators' defense fund (Haldeman had informed Nixon about this slipup on June 23). On October 10, the *Post* broke its major story, which won a Pulitzer Prize, identifying the Watergate affair as one of massive political spying and sabotage.

But few were following in the *Post's* footsteps. Press critic Ben Bagdikian calculated that of 433 Washington-based reporters who could in theory have been assigned to the Watergate story when it broke in the fall of election year 1972, only 15 actually were. Of some 500 political columns written by Washington pundits between June and Election Day, fewer than two dozen concerned Watergate.

Media critic Edwin Diamond found that during the seven-week preelection period beginning September 14, CBS devoted almost twice as much evening air time to Watergate as its competitors (CBS, 71 minutes; NBC, 42; ABC, 41). Half of the NBC and ABC stories were less than a minute in length. Because of media inattention, the Gallup Poll found in October 1972 that only 52 percent of Americans recognized the word *Watergate*.

The Watergate break-in trial began in Judge Sirica's court in January, 1973, and attention increased with guilty pleas and convictions. A bombshell exploded in March when James W. McCord wrote Sirica a letter saying he and the other six arrested men were only agents for higher authorities. The Los Angeles *Times* contributed its first major newsbreak, linking counsel John Dean and Jcb Magruder to the break-in; the *Post* followed with the names of former Attorney General John Mitchell and Charles Colson (all four eventually pleaded guilty or were convicted of conspiracy).

Watergate was now the consuming news story. Seven out of ten Americans listened on April 30, 1973, as President Nixon announced the resignations of his key aides, Haldeman, Ehrlichman, Dean, and Attorney General Kleindienst; 41

percent gave him a positive rating, 36 percent, a negative rating. Gallup now found 83 percent had heard of Watergate, but more than half thought it was "just politics." The Senate Watergate Committee with Sam J. Ervin, Jr., as chairman began televised hearings on May 17; soon "Senator Sam" became a household character. Magruder and Dean made confessions and major charges against the White House in June testimony. At first the public split evenly (38 to 37 percent) on whether to believe Nixon or Dean; by April 1974, it found Dean more believable (46 to 29 percent).

Vice-President Agnew's resignation on October 10 after pleading no contest to a charge of income tax evasion, based on a court-submitted record of extensive bribe-taking, shocked the country. Attorney General Elliot Richardson accepted plea bargaining because the Watergate crisis pointed to the need for a new vice-president—Gerald Ford. The Washington *Star,* a rock-ribbed Republican paper, took honors on the Agnew exposé.

The crisis over the tapes now began to consume the Nixon administration. Judge Sirica's demand for their surrender had been upheld by the court of appeals; Nixon countered with a plan to submit transcripts only. Special prosecutor Archibald Cox was summarily fired when he objected, and others resigned from the Justice Department in what became known as the "Saturday night massacre." A spontaneous wave of protest swept the country; Nixon hastily appointed a new special prosecutor and handed over the requested tapes. But some of them were missing and one had the famed 18½-minute gap blamed on secretary Rose Mary Woods' "stretch" for the telephone (Sirica found it was a deliberate erasure).

The ultraconservative *National Review* and the Detroit *News* now ran editorials calling for Nixon's resignation. They were joined by Time Inc., whose magazines had three times endorsed Nixon for president; by the Denver *Post;* and by the New York *Times.* Public opinion, as reflected in the Gallup and Harris Polls, also began to shift. Everybody had now heard about Watergate; the number who believed Nixon's story that he had no knowledge of the break-in or coverup had dwindled to 15 percent; more Americans thought Nixon should resign than wanted him to stay (47 to 42 percent).

The indictments for the Watergate coverup conspiracy came on March 1, 1974. The grand jury gave Judge Sirica a sealed envelope about Richard Nixon; on June 5, his longtime supporter, the Los Angeles *Times,* revealed that the president had been named an unindicted coconspirator with Haldeman, Ehrlichman, Mitchell, and others. (The trial ended with four convictions on January 1, 1975.)

The story now came to a rapid end. Nixon released a massive mound of tape transcripts on April 29. The Chicago *Tribune* flew advance copies supplied them by the White House home in an airplane; had its editorial board read them; published them in full; and editorially announced, "We are appalled." The *Tribune* then called on Nixon to resign or be impeached.

The House Judiciary Committee on July 24 began its televised debate on the impeachment articles. The hearings were conducted at the highest levels of democratic processes and did much to reassure the huge television audience that honesty and decency could still prevail. All 38 members had their say. There were 21 Democrats and 17 Republicans. Six of the Republicans joined the Democrats to seal Nixon's doom. On July 27 the committee voted 27 to 11 to impeach the president for obstruction of justice; it followed with two more articles charging abuse of presidential powers and contempt of Congress. Its report was still before the House when the President resigned on August 9, 1974, but became a permanent record.

The editorial words of the Los Angeles *Times* on August 7, written in the wake of reading the June 23, 1972, transcript, offer a fit closing:

> No one can read those conversations between Richard Nixon and H. R. Haldeman without anger—anger at these men whose arrogance let them, with such apparent ease, abuse trust, pervert the system of government and breach the law in a voracious bid for more power. . . .
>
> Mr. Nixon has brought dishonor to the Presidency—dishonor and disgrace. He has broken his oath of office. By his own admission, he has committed felonious crimes. He is not fit to remain the President. . . .
>
> We ourselves especially feel the betrayal of Mr. Nixon. This newspaper has supported him in his candidacy through a political career that we have more often cheered than criticized. As recently as 1972 we had supported his bid for reelection.

Too few newspapers were as forthright and candid as this conservative leader of American journalism in enlightening their readers.

What of the public's thanks to the press? Generally the press came out ahead. It could thank the House Judiciary Committee for so handling its hearings that public belief in the charges against Nixon—and in the media that had reported those charges—had been greatly enhanced. The polls showed in August 1974 that only 33 percent of Americans thought Nixon should be granted immunity (as he was the next month by President Ford), while 58 percent said he should stand trial. But in June 1974, in answer to a question asking opinion about the amount of space and time devoted to Watergate, 53 percent said "too much," as against 30 percent "about right" and only 13 percent "too little." The messenger was still only sometimes appreciated.

PROBLEMS OF PRESS CREDIBILITY

While many Americans in the last three decades viewed the mass media as "too liberal," despite their predominantly conservative ownerships, liberals and young activists saw the media as unresponsive, obtuse, and largely irredeemable as instruments for illuminating the root issues of social unrest. As a result, they turned to underground newspapers, discovered ways in which to use the media for their own ends, and increasingly sought government intervention with which to gain access.

Many intellectuals viewed the mass media with disdain for catering to mass tastes. Public officials generally resented the press' role of "watchdog" for the public's interests. Specialists in most fields complained that reporting of their activities often was oversimplified or erroneously stated. Many persons felt that the media conspired with other elements of the establishment in withholding the truth of events. And many newspeople themselves dissented through publication of at least 20 critical journalism reviews. In addition, the media were caught in the public mood of distrust for almost all institutions, including business corporations, the church, educational institutions, and government.

A number of groups and individuals took up Vice-President Agnew's assault against what was considered to be biased and often inaccurate reporting of national issues and events, primarily by the Washington press corps, the New York *Times,* the Washington *Post, Newsweek, Time,* CBS, NBC, and, to a lesser extent, ABC.

Among them were two "nonpartisan, nonprofit" organizations, Accuracy in Media, Inc. (AIM) and the American Institute for Political Communication (AIPC). AIM investigated complaints of serious error in news reporting, such as those alleged in the CBS documentary, "The Selling of the Pentagon"; statements on defense spending made by NBC newsman David Brinkley; and New York *Times* articles about the Vietnam War. The American Institute for Political Communication began a series of studies in 1971 which, it reported, revealed "a significant degree of bias" in television news coverage of the 1972 Democratic presidential primary ("pro-McGovern") and the Vietnam War ("anti-Nixon").

In addition to numerous magazine articles and newspaper columns, a spate of books appeared with similar contentions of media pollution. They included Edith Efron's *The News Twisters,* Arnold Beichman's *Nine Lies About America,* and James Keogh's *President Nixon and the Press.* In reaction to the criticism, the networks commissioned extensive studies of their own news practices and specifically examined the programs that were the subjects of the Efron and AIPC charges. Independent scholars in each instance questioned the methodology and the objectivity of the studies resulting in the anti-media charges.

Journalists Serving the CIA

The public's faith in the journalist as an independent gatherer and interpreter of the news, free from any connection with government, was diminished in 1977 with revelations that many American news personnel, in the decades after World War II, had served as salaried intelligence operatives for the Central Intelligence Agency (CIA) while also performing their duties as reporters.

Watergate reporter Carl Bernstein, after an extensive inquiry, said more than 400 American journalists had secretly carried out assignments for the CIA. The New York *Times* stated that between 30 and 100 journalists were paid for such work.

The *Times* reported that more than 50 news organizations, owned or subsidized by the CIA, had spread pro-American views as well as propaganda and lies in ways that often made Americans and foreigners the victims of misinformation. In addition, the *Times* reported, at least 12 full-time CIA officers had worked abroad as reporters or noneditorial employees of American-owned news organizations, in some cases having been hired by the news organizations whose credentials they carried.

Some reporters freely acknowledged that they had exchanged information with the CIA, maintaining that, during the era of the Cold War with the communist world, cooperation between journalists and the CIA represented both good citizenship and good craftsmanship. CIA officials, who saw nothing untoward in such relationships, said the agency had cut back sharply on the use of reporters since 1973, primarily as a result of pressure from the media, but Bernstein insisted that some journalist-operatives were still posted abroad.

In 1980, Admiral Stanfield Turner, director of the CIA, told the American Society of Newspaper Editors in convention that in three separate instances since 1977 he had personally approved the use of journalists for secret intelligence operations. Replying to sharp criticism by editors, Turner said that the journalists had not in fact been utilized as operatives, but he insisted on reserving the right to employ them in future emergencies.

Presidential Endorsements

The support given by newspapers on their editorial pages to presidential candidates has been another source for charges of political bias. Figures compiled by *Editor & Publisher* magazine explain why. Historically, the majority of daily newspapers giving support to a presidential candidate has been on the side of the Republican party.

In 1980 President Jimmy Carter was endorsed by newspapers with 21.5 percent of the polled circulation, compared with 48.6 percent endorsing the Republican challenger, Ronald Reagan, and 4.4 percent supporting independent candidate John Anderson. In this "campaign of frustration" newspapers with 25.5 percent of the polled circulation were uncommitted. Reagan's support was the lowest recorded in the poll for a Republican except in 1964. But four years later President Reagan rebounded to 51.6 percent of the polled circulation. Democratic party contender Walter Mondale received 21.3 percent with 27 percent uncommitted. Mondale, however, had the editorial support of such elite newspapers as the New York *Times,* Washington *Post,* Boston *Globe,* Philadelphia *Inquirer,* St. Louis *Post-Dispatch,* Milwaukee *Journal* and Louisville *Courier-Journal.* Critics cited this as evidence of press bias.

In 1976 President Gerald Ford was endorsed by newspapers with 62.2 percent of the polled circulation. Jimmy Carter's 22.8 percent was the best for a Democrat since 1940 except during 1964. Newspapers with 15 percent of the polled circulation were uncommitted. But President Richard Nixon had the endorsement of 753 daily newspapers in his one-sided reelection victory in 1972, whereas only 56 supported Senator George McGovern, *Editor & Publisher* reported. In terms of the percentage of the polled circulation, Nixon had 77.4 percent to McGovern's 7.7 percent, with the remainder making no endorsement. This was Nixon's highest support in three presidential races. McGovern's meager total (representing 3 million circulation) was the lowest recorded for a major candidate since the trade journal began its studies in 1936.

In 1960 Vice-President Nixon was supported by newspapers with 70.9 percent of the polled circulation in his unsuccessful race against John F. Kennedy, who had 15.8 percent. A dramatic reversal occurred in 1964. President Lyndon B. Johnson, who succeeded to the White House after Kennedy's assassination, faced a right-wing conservative Republican, Barry Goldwater. Johnson had the support of dailies representing 61.5 percent of the polled circulation; Goldwater, 21.5 percent. The trend swung back to the Republican side four years later, when Nixon faced Vice-President Hubert Humphrey, the Democratic nominee. Nixon had the support of newspapers representing 69.9 percent of polled circulation; Humphrey, 15 percent. Twelve papers supported George C. Wallace, the conservative third-party candidate.

REAGAN AND THE MEDIA

By 1986 it had become clear that President Reagan had bested the media in the duel for public perception of credibility. A longtime professional actor, Reagan was at his best striding across the White House lawn, smiling and waving his arm, as he left or returned from Camp David by helicopter, with the air of a "take charge" leader many hungered for. His scheduled news conferences, more infrequent than those of any president except Nixon, were judged ineffective; sharp questioning by correspondents left him uncertain, evasive, and prone to resort to anecdotal defenses of policies. Challenged by the reporters about the extent of unemployment and hunger, Reagan asserted that the media resorted to distortion by seeking out evidence, saying "Is it news that some fellow out in South Succotash has just been laid off?" Cartoonist Paul Conrad answered with a sign reading "Welcome to South Succotash. Population: 9,000,000 Unemployed." Others pointed out how Reagan had often used the example of one man in a store line using food stamps to buy ginger ale and cigarettes as justification for sharp slashes in federal aid to the poor. But the public generally accepted the administration's assertions of cheating in food stamps and soup lines.

Reagan's rigid anti-Communist stance, in which he portrayed the Soviet Union as the "source of all evil," enabled him to defend the need for escalating defense expenditures, placement of nuclear missiles in Europe, and 1983 military involvement in Lebanon and Grenada. Deaths of more than 240 U.S. Marines in Lebanon, and a Pentagon commission report criticizing both the president's policy and lack of precautions against enemy attacks, gave the administration pause. But the lightning invasion of Grenada to overthrow its Marxist government proved enormously popular among Americans, who focused primarily on the fact that a group of college students there had been snatched from presumed danger of becoming hostages (shades of Iran). Reagan answered media critics of his ban on news coverage of the first several days of that invasion by arguing that the public had no need of media coverage when it had the word of the armed forces and his own. This argument failed to win public support.

Secretary of State George Schultz defended the precedent-breaking exclusion of reporters by saying in World War II "reporters were involved all along. And on the whole, they were on our side. . . . It seems as though reporters are always against us. . . . They're always seeking to report something that's going to screw things up." Reagan agreed, saying, "Beginning with the Korean conflict and certainly in the Vietnam conflict, there was more criticizing of our own forces and what we were trying to do, to the point that it didn't seem there was much criticism of the enemy." Later Reagan quipped to Jimmy Doolittle, "How did you get away with your flight to Tokyo without taking the press along?"

Stung by these attacks upon the patriotism of newspeople, *Editor & Publisher* accused Reagan of seeking to undermine public confidence in a press that reported his administration's failures as well as successes. Others compared the charges that press criticism had led to American defeat in Vietnam to those made by Hitler that the German army had been betrayed in World War I.

THE GRENADA EPISODE. The Reagan administration's ability to deflect or "stonewall" media protests and inquiries was demonstrated during the Grenada episode. The American Newspaper Publishers Association's executive vice-president, Jerry W. Friedheim, himself a former assistant secretary of defense for public affairs, issued a public statement calling the news blackout of U.S. military operations in Grenada "unprecedented and intolerable," and requesting the President "to renounce the policy of secret wars hidden from the American people."

The presidents of ANPA and ASNE wrote the President on November 1, one week after the invasion began, asking for a White House conference with press executives. They received no reply. On December 1, they wrote again. Finally, on January 17 five leaders of ANPA, ASNE, and the Radio Television News Directors Association met with a group of White House officials. Their heels were well cooled, and action had passed them by.

In December the Pentagon had appointed a panel on media–military relations headed by retired Major General Winant Sidle, which heard the testimony of 18

On the island of Grenada, November 5, 1983, Cuban prisoners were evacuated to Cuba in groups of 50 under the guard of U.S. soldiers. Reagan banned all media coverage of the U.S. invasion of Grenada during the first few days. (Randy Taylor, Sygma)

media organizations. The following August Sidle's plan was approved by the Defense Department. Central to the plan was the creation of a rotating pool of experienced reporters whose members would be called upon at a moment's notice to cover military operations, with secrecy of the calls to be preserved. The Pentagon scheduled regular "dry run" tests to make certain of press readiness and security levels.

THE ATTACK ON LIBYA. In March 1986 the press access policy was given its first "live" usage when print and broadcast reporters were flown by helicopter to the decks of U.S. aircraft carriers sitting off the Gulf of Sidra while conducting actions against Libyan planes and naval craft. They missed, however, the nighttime bombing of Libya's capital.

There was extensive press criticism of the attacks on Libya, Reagan's insistence on military support of the "Contras" seeking overthrow of the Nicaraguan government, American longtime support of the corrupt Marcos dictatorship in the Philippines and the military dictatorship in Chile, and Reagan's failure to give support to the black majority in South Africa. When South Africa censored news coverage of turmoil there, there was no protest from the White House.

Whatever the protests, no matter how many White House miscues or failed policies, Reagan maintained a high level of public approval in the opinion polls. It was said he wore a "teflon coat."

Jack Nelson, Pulitzer Prize-winning Washington news chief for the conservative Lost Angeles *Times,* declared in a 1984 talk, "No recent president has so thoroughly controlled access to information that was once available to the public." Said Nelson:

> Mr. Reagan, with his amiable manner, comes across as a likeable guy and as an inspiration to many people. That's a major reason he has been able to deny public access to government information and at the same time remain popular. But behind that smile is a "we vs. them" attitude that has set the whole tone for his administration's relations with the press. It's not that he hates the press the way Mr. Nixon did, it's just that he's insensitive to the press' role in our society and sees the media generally as something to be manipulated, but not trusted.

IRAN-CONTRA SCANDAL. During six years in office President Reagan had outmaneuvered his press critics at nearly every turn. Then, in November 1986, the roof fell in. A series of adverse events, news disclosures, and personal misadventures left Reagan stripped of his teflon coat.

First, his seeming political invincibility was shattered when eight of nine senatorial candidates he had campaigned for across the country lost their races, giving the Democrats a solid majority in the Senate to match their grip on the House of Representatives.

But far more serious was the effect of a series of disclosures upon Reagan's credibility rating with the public. These began with the discovery that the *Wall Street Journal* had been the victim of a "disinformation" campaign designed by the White House to spread a false story that Libya was endangering U.S. military security, in order to justify bombing its capital. Next, a survivor of a plane shot down in Nicaragua, carrying arms for the rebel Contras, revealed a network of CIA military aid activity being carried on despite a Congressional ban.

Then a Lebanese magazine published a story telling how the Reagan administration had been secretly selling arms to Iran in exchange for hostages, in direct contradiction of an American policy that the administration had been promoting to its allies. The White House said its aim had only been to reestablish relationships with friendly Iranians. But as the story snowballed in the world press, and after ill-fated attempts to contain the story, Reagan found himself facing his 39th formal press conference on national television.

There, Reagan was subjected to what was undoubtedly the most pitiless cross-examination ever made of a President by the White House press. UPI's Helen Thomas led off by asking Reagan to "assess the credibility of your own administration in light of the prolonged deception of the Congress and the public in terms of your secret dealings with Iran, the disinformation (about Libya). . . ." Correspondents for news services, networks, and liberal and conservative dailies joined in blunt questions about duplicity and deception. Reagan refused to say any of the actions had been wrong. He denied—and admitted immediately afterward—the role Israel had played in facilitating arms deals with Iran. When six days later Attorney General Edwin Meese told an incredulous press conference that profits from the Iranian arms sales had been run through secret Swiss bank accounts so the money could be illegally diverted to the Contra campaign against Nicaragua, the disaster to the Reagan image was complete. The President denied any knowledge of the Contra aid diversion, but two months later public opinion polls showed 60 percent of respondents believing Reagan was lying (the word used in the query).

Two White House officials most involved were dismissed; the Congress established two select committees to investigate; and a special prosecutor with authority to examine both Iranian and Nicaraguan aspects was appointed. The Senate committee began its hearings and the prosecutor brought his first indictments in May 1987. The scandal, identified variously as "Iranamuck," "Gippergate," and "Contragate," generally dominated the political news.

The Media's

Legal Environment

How to Win a Pulitzer Prize

The Freedom of Information Act (FOIA) was 20 years old in 1986, a birthday marked by the winning of three 1986 Pulitzer Prizes by newspapers that used the provisions of the law to gather needed information.

Staff writers Craig Flournoy and George Rodrigue collected two dozen big packing boxes full of materials by using FOIA requests, as part of a 14-month job developing an eight-part series about public housing in America for the Dallas *Morning News.* The series, "Separate and Unequal," revealed a pattern of racial discrimination and segregation in public housing in the United States. It first won the Associated Press Managing Editors Association Public Service Award in 1985 and then the 1986 Pulitzer Prize for national reporting.

The Pittsburgh *Press* used FOIA to detail deficiencies in the operation of the federal Health Care Financing Administration for another Pulitzer Prize-winning series on organ transplants.

Federal bank records obtained through FOIA requests helped the San Jose *Mercury News* develop its Pulitzer Prize-winning series on the transfer of wealth out of the Philippines by former President Ferdinand Marcos. That story touched off such reaction in Manila that the movement to oust Marcos began.

Reporters encounter many difficulties in obtaining information through FOIA requests, but they can get help from the FOI Service Center in Washington, a project of the Reporters Committee on Freedom of the Press.

In this chapter we trace to the present day the historic press freedoms first discussed in Chapter 4, involving the right to print, the right to criticize, and the right to report.

Media leaders call the first of these freedoms "The First Amendment Battleground" in recognition of the writing of a ban on prior restraint into the First Amendment to the United States Constitution. In 1931 the Supreme Court handed down a bedrock doctrine banning prior restraint of printing by either Congress or the states in the case of *Near* v. *Minnesota.* The written decision, however, did not establish an absolute prohibition of prior restraint, as was demonstrated in the Pentagon Papers case of 1971 and later decisions.

In our discussion of the right of the media to criticize, we consider the areas of libel and slander, and particularly recent court decisions involving criticism of public figures. These decisions at first greatly expanded the area of safe criticism, then contracted it.

The "Freedom of Information Crusade" has been carried on during the past four decades and won passage by Congress of the Freedom of Information Act of 1966. FOI gained admittance to federal agency files and records for reporters and other citizens. ◆

LAWS AFFECTING THE MEDIA

In the relationships of the press to society, through governing bodies and the courts, eight types of laws affecting the media may be listed. They are, in summary form:

1. *Common law*—written and reinforced by court decisions through the centuries;
2. *Constitutional law*—both federal and state, including the crucial First Amendment to the United States Constitution;
3. *Statutory law*—that passed by legislative bodies;
4. *Criminal law*—which concerns the press largely in the areas of treason, criminal libel, publication of lottery information, and fraudulent advertising;
5. *Civil law*—dealing with such matters as libel, invasion of privacy, and unfair competition;
6. *Equity*—seeking relief from the courts, such as the government's suit in the Pentagon Papers case;
7. *Administrative law*—as enacted by such agencies as the Federal Communications Commission and the Federal Trade Commission;
8. *Moral law*—which has no distinct position in our modern legal system, but

which imposes a greater restriction on the press than any purely legal restraint. Conversely, it functions as a tremendous force that can overturn legal restraints and bring greater freedom for the press.

A discussion of moral law will introduce Chapter 24, in which the media's social responsibilities are discussed.

THE FIRST AMENDMENT BATTLEFRONT

Freedom to print without prior restraint has been a basic tenet of Anglo-American civilization since 1694. It was written into the First Amendment to the United States Constitution as a part of the Bill of Rights. The high watermark for this concept was reached in 1931 when the Supreme Court, by invalidating a state law, applied the press guarantees of the First Amendment to the states in the case of *Near* v. *Minnesota*. But as supportive of the freedom to print as that decision was, it did not establish an absolute prohibition of prior restraint. The Pentagon Papers case of 1971 marked a diminishment in support of the philosophy of the freedom to print and gave warning that the battlefront for even such an elementary freedom remained an active one.

Freedom to criticize is necessary to the realization of the proposition that the media are "the censors of their governors." A colonial jury's verdict in the John Peter Zenger trial of 1735 first challenged the theory of seditious libel, which had made it an automatic crime to criticize those in authority and thereby imperil their capacity to govern. But it was 1800 before Anglo-American law recognized the right to criticize public officials. The high watermark in the press-government duel was reached in the Watergate drama of 1974, but since then court decisions have whittled down this freedom.

The press has always had only a tenuous right to the freedom to report, first won when Parliament was opened to reporters in 1771 in England. What good is the freedom to print and to criticize, asked journalists, without access to news and information vital to the functioning of a democratic society? The frontier of freedom in this area was reached with passage by the U.S. Congress of the Freedom of Information Act in 1966 and its strengthening in 1974. But in the ebb and flow of the First Amendment battlefront, once again a reaction set in. The 1980s have thus been years of challenge and struggle for writers, editors, broadcasters, and photographers who want to bring their words and images to the public.

THE RIGHT TO PRINT

During the 1981 celebrations of the fiftieth anniversary of the Supreme Court decision in *Near* v. *Minnesota,* it was generally recognized that this was the bedrock case for all constitutional defenses of First Amendment rights. In giving his five-to-four majority decision, Chief Justice Charles Evans Hughes had quoted from Blackstone on prior restraint and postpublication punishment:

> The liberty of the press is indeed essential to the nature of a free state; but this consists in laying no *previous* restraints upon publications, and not in freedom from censure for

Pulitzer Prize winners George Rodrigue (left) and Craig Flournoy (right) of the Dallas Morning News show boxes containing one-third of the government documents they obtained under the FOI Act. Their stories revealed a pattern of racial discrimination and segregation in public housing in the United States. (See vignette opening this chapter.) (Reprinted by permission from Presstime, the journal of the American Newspaper Association.)

criminal matter when published. Every freeman has an undoubted right to lay what sentiments he pleases before the public; to forbid this is to destroy the freedom of the press; but if he publishes what is improper, mischievous, or illegal, he must take the consequences of his own temerity.

Hughes continued with a dictum, or observation, that weakened the case for absolute protection against prior restraint:

The objection has also been made that the principle as to immunity from previous restraint is stated too broadly, if every such restraint is deemed to be prohibited. That is undoubtedly true; the protection even as to previous restraint is not absolutely unlimited. But the limitation has been recognized only in exceptional cases.

The chief justice defined some such cases: military secrets, overthrow of the government, and obscenity. But he excluded publication of censure of public officers and charges of official misconduct.

It was under this latter exclusion that the Supreme Court ruled six to three in favor of the New York *Times* in the Pentagon Papers case in 1971 (see Chapter 22). The court's earlier five-to-four vote to continue a temporary restraining order stopping publication of the Pentagon Papers series strongly indicated that it would not support a plea for application of the principle of absolute protection against prior restraint, so the newspaper attorneys argued successfully that the articles did not affect national security. But the court's *per curiam* decision did include these quotations from its decisions in previous cases:

> Any system of prior restraints of expression comes to this court bearing a heavy presumption against its constitutional validity.
> The Government thus carries a heavy burden of showing justification for the enforcement of such a restraint.

The Progressive *Case*

When press and government clashed over prior restraint in 1979, the Justice Department relied upon the Atomic Energy Act to obtain a U.S. district court's preliminary injunction prohibiting *The Progressive* magazine from publishing an article that supposedly contained secret information vital to the construction of a hydrogen bomb. Publication would result in "direct, immediate and irreparable" injury to national security, the government argued, by allowing nations not having the bomb to more easily construct one. The government relied upon the Atomic Energy Act's secrecy provisions being considered one of Chief Justice Hughes' "exceptional cases."

But the matter did not reach the Supreme Court, or even an appeals court verdict. First, it was discovered that documents containing "restricted data" similar to that in the *Progressive* article had been mistakenly declassified and placed on open library shelves in Los Alamos. Then a computer programmer wrote an 18-page letter to a U.S. senator, using only library materials available to him, paralleling the *Progressive* article in content. He had sent the letter to several newspapers and magazines; one published it. The Justice Department immediately withdrew its suit, after six months of a previous restraint injunction, and *The Progressive* ran its article.

The Reporters Committee for Freedom of the Press stated: "But one thing remains clear; nothing was settled by *The Progressive* case, including the constitutionality of the Atomic Energy Act. The same type of complex and mostly secret court case could occur again the next time a publication has nuclear-related information that the government does not want published."

THE RIGHT TO CRITICIZE

Never had the press and a powerful political figure been so fiercely locked in struggle as in 1974, when the print and broadcast media persisted in pressing the Watergate inquiry until the courts and Congress forced President Nixon to make disclosures that brought about his resignation. The media were in danger, until the struggle had been won, for two reasons: the president had substantial support and the greater power of office, and many citizens thought it unwise to risk the political instability that might result from the forced resignation of a president. As we discussed in Chapter 22, the president's power evaporated, and the transition of office from Richard Nixon to Gerald Ford was a tranquil event.

Psychologically, the Watergate drama strengthened the historic press role of "censors of their governors." But perhaps in reaction to this demonstration of power on the part of the press, and more certainly as the result of the changing composition of the Supreme Court membership toward a more conservative stance, constitutional cases involving the right to criticize public officials began to go against the media. The media thereby found themselves more restricted in their ability to comment and more vulnerable to suits for libel and slander.

Libel and Slander

One constant challenge confronting the communications media is to avoid libeling or slandering individuals or easily identifiable groups. Laws designed to protect persons from unfair and damaging attacks create well-defined limits as to what may be broadcast or printed without risking legal action and possibly heavy financial losses.

Defamation is communication that exposes people to hatred, ridicule, or contempt; lowers them in the esteem of their fellows; causes them to be shunned; or injures them in their business or calling. Its categories are *libel,* mainly printed or written material; and *slander,* mainly spoken words. Because a person may be injured as greatly in a radio or television broadcast as in a printed publication, the courts have come to treat broadcast defamation as libel.

Some defamation is considered privileged, such as statements made on the official record during court trials and public meetings of government bodies. For example, council member Jones may call council member Smith "a liar and a thief" during an official session, and the allegation may be safely broadcast or published because it is privileged by law. However, if Jones should make such a statement about Smith in the corridor after the meeting adjourns, the newspaper or broadcast station that reports it would risk a libel or slander suit from Smith unless it could prove that the charge was true.

The principal defenses against libel actions involving the press are provable truth, the privilege of reporting fairly and truly an official proceeding, the right of fair comment, consent, and the U.S. Supreme Court ruling in *New York Times* v. *Sullivan* that state libel laws must yield to the First Amendment freedom of the press guarantees.

Historically, the libel and slander laws have protected individuals or small groups of easily identified persons, but not large, amorphous groups. There is pressure now to enlarge protection to cover broader groups, such as ethnic minorities, but the difficulty in writing such laws has discouraged their adoption.

Criticism of Public Figures

THE SULLIVAN RULING. A landmark case in broadening the media's right to comment was the Supreme Court ruling in *New York Times* v. *Sullivan* in 1964.

The Court held that a public official cannot recover damages for a defamatory falsehood relating to his or her official conduct without proving that the statement had been made with actual malice. This and related rulings have broadened the interpretation of "public official" to include relatively minor public employees and even "public figures" such as former officeholders and prominent personalities.

The Supreme Court in *Rosenbloom* v. *Metromedia* extended the Sullivan ruling in 1971 to include a private person involved in an event of public interest. However, in *Gertz* v. *Welch,* in 1974, the court seemed to reverse its position. In a five-to-four decision, the court held that a "private person," regardless of involvement in a public event, might recover such actual damages as could be proved for injury or harm resulting from publication of a defamatory falsehood, without proof of actual malice by the libeler, but with proof of negligence as determined by a state standard. Gertz, a Chicago attorney, won $100,000 actual damages and $300,000 punitive damages in a retrial ordered by the Supreme Court of his case against Robert Welch and a John Birch Society publication. A U.S. Court of Appeals upheld this verdict in 1982, leaving *Gertz* still the controlling case in libel suits involving public figures.

The Colorado Supreme Court became the first state high court to accept the *Gertz* ruling, in 1975. Using the "reckless disregard" standard, the judges reviewed seven articles published in the Colorado Springs *Sun* and awarded an antique dealer actual and punitive damages for allegations that he had purchased stolen merchandise.

In *Firestone* v. *Time Inc.,* the Supreme Court ruled in 1976 that the wife of Russell Firestone III, scion of a prominent industrial family, was not a "public figure," even though she was a well-known citizen of Palm Beach, Florida, society and held press conferences during her celebrated divorce trial. She was awarded $100,000 in a libel suit against *Time* magazine for incorrectly reporting that her husband had been granted a divorce from her on grounds of extreme cruelty and adultery.

The decision unnerved news media executives and lawyers, occurring as it did during a period when more than 500 libel suits were being filed each year and juries seemed willing to compensate plaintiffs for their injuries with large settlements. With expenses ranging up to $100,000 or more per case, even when won, fears mounted that the threat of such high costs would make the news media more timid in their pursuit of news. These fears were somewhat allayed by the decision by Mrs. Firestone in 1978 to drop the case rather than go through a second trial, ordered by the Supreme Court to determine *Time's* degree of negligence (in order for her to collect the $100,000). Media lawyers expressed hope that the proving of negligence would be a difficult matter in such cases.

Another blow fell in 1979, when the Supreme Court ruled that engaging in criminal activity did not automatically make one a public figure, even for purposes of comment on issues related to the conviction. Since journalists had long operated under a "calculated risk" theory that a criminal cannot be libeled, this was a decision narrowing further the definition of a public figure that had been expanded in *Sullivan.*

The *Wolston* v. *Reader's Digest Association, Inc.,* case arose when a book author mistakenly identified Ilya Wolston as a Soviet espionage agent, when in reality

Wolston had only been found guilty of criminal contempt for failure to appear before a grand jury in a case that had resulted his aunt and uncle pleading guilty to espionage. A U.S. district court ruled that the author made an honest error when Wolston sued for libel, asserting that, since Wolston was a public figure as a convicted criminal, he had to prove actual malice. Therefore, the court granted a defense motion for summary judgment in behalf of the book publisher.

When the case reached the Supreme Court, Justice William Rehnquist wrote the reversal decision. He further limited the *Gertz* definition of a public figure, saying it included only those who voluntarily participated in public controversies over which the public itself was divided. Professor Paul Jess, of the University of Kansas, analyzing *Wolston* and other cases of 1979, said that Justice Rehnquist's language seemed to have sounded the death knell for newsworthiness as a defense in libel actions.

Things were made even more difficult for media libel lawyers when Chief Justice Warren Burger commented in his decision of 1979, in the case of *Hutchinson* v. *Proxmire:* "We are constrained to express some doubt about the so-called 'rule' [of summary judgment on First Amendment grounds in libel cases]. The proof of 'actual malice' calls a defendant's state of mind into question . . . and does not readily lend itself to summary judgment." The District of Columbia Court of Appeals cited this Burger viewpoint in 1980 when it ordered columnist Ralph de Toledano to stand trial on libel charges brought against him by consumer activist Ralph Nader, rejecting de Toledano's argument that Nader was a public figure upon whom he had commented reasonably and that, therefore, there should be summary judgment. The Supreme Court refused to review the appeals court order, seemingly strengthening its opposition to the summary judgment pathway to libel defenses for the media. *Hutchinson* v. *Proxmire* also included a ruling that there was no immunity for those printing Senator Proxmire's press releases and newsletters. This, the court said, was an unwarranted extension of legislative immunity.

Another new rule for libel cases emerged from the decision in *Herbert* v. *Lando,* in 1979. This permits pretrial inquiry into the journalist's state of mind as a means of establishing the presence of actual malice in a libel action. Colonel Anthony Herbert, a Vietnam War veteran, sued CBS and producer Barry Lando of the "60 Minutes" program for falsely and maliciously depicting him as a liar (Herbert had agreed that he was a public figure). His attorneys asked for the right to explore the states of mind of CBS newspeople at the time they were making editorial decisions. A United States court of appeals held that requiring reporters to divulge their thoughts and to reveal the content of their discussions with colleagues would "strike to the heart of the vital human component of the editorial process." The Supreme Court, in a six-to-three decision, reversed the appeals court decision, saying such inquiries were valid and necessary if the plaintiff were to be able to prove actual malice. Disturbing as the prospect of inquiry into a journalist's state of mind might be, there was merit to the contention that it was necessary in cases involving the need for proof of actual malice.

RECENT PUBLIC FIGURE DECISIONS. During the years 1979 through 1985 there were no Supreme Court decisions in the area of criticism of public persons, leaving

Sullivan, as narrowed by *Gertz,* the controlling standard. In 1986 the Court gave further support to the *Sullivan* doctrine by ruling that a public-figure libel plaintiff must demonstrate "actual malice" by "clear and convincing evidence" to overcome a defendant's motion that a summary judgment dismissing the suit be granted by a trial judge. The Supreme Court's six-to-three decision in *Anderson* v. *Liberty Lobby* overturned a District of Columbia circuit court of appeals opinion written by Judge Antonin Scalia stating that columnist Jack Anderson and *The Investigator* magazine would have to defend themselves in court against the 1981 suit of the political action organization. The Supreme Court held that trial judges must apply the *Sullivan* "clear and convincing" evidentiary standard to determine whether a reasonable jury might find that the plaintiff had shown actual malice on the part of the defendant. Scalia, his future colleagues on the Supreme Court said, had failed to do so.

In another 1986 decision the Supreme Court widened the scope of the *Sullivan* doctrine by ruling that states may not place the burden on media libel defendants to prove truth in suits brought by private figures if they involve coverage of issues of public concern. Justice Sandra Day O'Connor, joining the Court's liberal wing to write the five-to-four opinion, acknowledged that at common law the defendant was required to prove that allegedly libelous statements were true. But, she declared, that to protect the constitutional interest in open debate on issues of public concern, private figures, as well as public figures and officials, must "bear the burden of showing falsity, as well as fault, before recovering damages." The case, *Hepps* v. *Philadelphia Newspapers Inc.,* arose from a series of articles in the Philadelphia *Inquirer* in 1975 and 1976 linking a beverage storeowner with members of organized crime. The *Inquirer* disputed the constitutionality of a Pennsylvania state law requiring libel defendants to show truth as a defense. The U.S. Supreme Court agreed, ruling the Pennsvania statute unconstitutional and overturning precedents in nine other states.

A third 1986 Supreme Court action bulwarked the "actual malice" standard when the Court let stand a U.S. court of appeals ruling affirming a summary judgment for the Columbia Broadcasting System dismissing a libel claim by Lt. Col. Anthony Herbert. This prevented Herbert from tasting the fruits of his earlier victory in winning the right to inquire into the states of mind of CBS writers in order to prove malice. The Court's action closing the Herbert case reaffirmed its similar action in 1984 letting stand a federal appeals court decision vacating a lower court libel verdict in *Bose* v. *Consumers Union* because it did not meet *Sullivan* standards.

The Multimillion Dollar Suits

A wave of libel suits against newspapers, broadcast networks and stations, and magazines swept through the courts beginning in the late 1970s. The Legal Defense Resource Center reported that juries awarded more than $1 million each to plaintiffs in 26 libel suits between 1976 and 1985. Verdicts from juries had gone against the media as much as 89 percent of the time during that period, although they had dropped to 60 percent during 1982–1984. Seventy percent of the verdicts were being reversed by appeals courts, on grounds the *Sullivan* standards had not been observed. This testified to the importance of the 1986 Supreme Court decisions affirming the use of summary judgments and defining appeals courts jurisdictions.

CBS, which spent 13 years defending itself and Mike Wallace in the Herbert libel case at a cost exceeding $4 million, spent even more defending itself against a suit for $120 million in damages brought by General William Westmoreland in the wake of the broadcast of another Wallace news documentary, "The Uncounted Enemy: A Vietnam Deception." After 18 weeks of trial, and a week before the case was to go to the jury, Westmoreland in early 1985 withdrew his suit. Testimony by fellow military officers had hurt his cause. Under an agreement between CBS and the general, both sides paid their own legal costs, and CBS made no apology or retraction.

Time magazine did not come off so fortunately defending itself against a $50 million libel suit brought by a discredited Israeli politician, Ariel Sharon, who accused the magazine of erroneously linking him to a massacre of 700 Arabs in a Lebanese refugee camp while he was Defense Minister of Israel. Sharon lost his suit because he could not prove *Time* had acted in malice and had known the story to be false or had serious doubts about its truth. But the jury issued a statement saying the magazine "acted negligently and carelessly in reporting and verifying" the information it published. A year later, in 1986, *Time* admitted before an Israeli court that its key charge against Sharon was erroneous, and agreed to pay some of Sharon's legal fees. Not only was *Time*'s reputation damaged, but Sharon was rehabilitated in Israeli politics.

The Washington *Post* eventually won its libel controversy. Mobil Oil president William Tavoulareas had gained a jury verdict of $2.05 million from the paper for stories charging him with improper business practices. The trial judge threw out

Retired General William C. Westmoreland is shown in this courtroom sketch as he testified in his $120-million libel suit against CBS. Westmoreland's attorney, Dan M. Burt, is at left and Judge Pierre Lavel at right. When photographers are barred from courtrooms, television producers use artists to depict the scene in major trials. This sketch is by NBC NewsCenter 4 artist Ida Libby Dengrove. (AP/Wide World)

the verdict, saying there was insufficient evidence of actual malice. The case, *Tavoulareas* v. *Washington Post,* then went to the District of Columbia circuit court of appeals, where judges Antonin Scalia and George MacKinnon reinstated the $2.05 million award. This decision was vacated, however, and the case was reheard by the entire D.C. court of appeals. In 1987 the court overturned the verdict, ruling seven-to-one that the *Post* story asserting that Tavoulareas had "set up" his son in business was "substantially true" and not libelous.

An early victim was the Alton, Illinois, *Telegraph,* caught in an editing error, and assessed $9.2 million in penalties, including $3.5 million punitive damages. The owners settled out of court for $1 million to save the paper. The *National Enquirer* paid Carol Burnett $200,000 in settlement of a $1.6 million verdict for reporting her drunk in a restaurant. Some other multimillion dollar claims, illustrating the trend: against *Philadelphia* magazine, $7 million; television showman Phil Donahue, $5.9 million; *Penthouse* magazine, $14 million; *USA Today,* $5 million; KSAT-TV, San Antonio, $1.6 million. The Supreme Court's 1986 decision calling on public-figure libel plaintiffs to provide clear and convincing evidence of actual malice if defendants ask for summary judgments was expected to ease such onslaughts.

THE RIGHT TO REPORT

While the narrowing of constitutional defenses in libel suits, particularly in reporting that involved public figures, became a problem for the media of the 1980s, erosion of the right to report was even more extensive.

Supreme Court decisions of the 1970s adversely affected the media in four areas: (1) requiring reporters to reveal their sources in certain situations or face fines and imprisonment; (2) allowing police raids of newsrooms; (3) allowing law enforcement agencies access to telephone records of news organizations; and (4) closing pretrial hearings and in some cases courtroom trials. These decisions, along with the erosion of the Freedom of Information Act that was gaining strength in the 1980s, affected not only the rights of newspeople, but of the public's right to know.

The Freedom of Information Crusade

Throughout American history, there has been conflict among the three branches of government—legislative, executive, and judicial. The acceptance of the principle of judicial review, making the Supreme Court the final authority on the constitutionality of legislative and executive actions, gave that branch relative freedom from conflict and attack. In the Watergate struggle, for example, President Nixon bowed to an eight-to-zero decision by the Court, which overruled his assertion of executive authority to suppress the Watergate tapes, and he relinquished the tapes. But the dueling between Congress and the White House over the principle of "executive privilege" continues unabated. The privilege of reporters to use public records and documents is involved in this infighting.

The Pentagon Papers case produced widespread realization that democratic principles are incompatible with the present sweep of executive privilege and its corollary, the executive practice of classification and withholding information from both the people and Congress. The knowledge that the government had classified the entire history of a foreign policy era, during which secret debate decided not only how but whether to conduct a war, resulted in the most concerted attack ever launched by the press and Congress on the classification system.

New Republic magazine reported that, since World War II, bureaucrats wielding classified labels had consigned 20 million documents to the government's "subterranean empire of buried information." Most of these documents had been classified under the authority of President Eisenhower's 1953 Executive Order 10501, which ruled that official secrecy would be limited to defense matters, under three categories: top secret, secret, and confidential. President Kennedy set up guidelines for declassification in 1961, but very little declassification actually took place.

THE FOI ACT. After 11 years of wrestling with the problem of the people's right to know the facts of government, Congress passed the Freedom of Information (FOI) Act in 1966. The law states basically that any person may go to court to gain access to public records, and the burden of proof that secrecy is necessary is upon the government.

The never-ending conflict between the news media, representing the public's right to know, and government officials who try to conceal information that might show them or their policies in a bad light is graphically depicted in this cartoon. (Reprinted with special permission of King Features Syndicate, Inc.)

In 1972 the House of Representatives and the Supreme Court began separate inquiries into the effectiveness of the FOI Act. Samuel J. Archibald, of the University of Missouri Freedom of Information Center, was commissioned to plot the trend of court interpretation of the act by studying significant cases. His analysis concluded that court judgments have leaned toward the people's right to know. The courts, however, generally have protected "investigatory files compiled for law enforcement purposes," and they have been wary of second-guessing executive decisions about matters that are kept secret "in the interest of national defense and foreign policy."

Declaring that his action was intended to challenge the government's security system, in 1972 syndicated columnist Jack Anderson released secret and sensitive documents that revealed that Dr. Henry Kissinger, the president's adviser on foreign policy, had directed administration spokespersons to support Pakistan against India in the war between those two countries. The fact that the anti-India policy had not been revealed even to Congress provoked further outcries against White House secrecy.

President Nixon established a new system for classification and declassification in 1972. Among other things, the system reduced the number of authorized "top secret" classifiers and made declassification, except for particularly sensitive information, automatic after six to ten years (amended to six years). Media response was mixed. Noting that the Pentagon Papers would have been ineligible for release under the time period, one newspaper editorialized, "If the Congress is to have a voice in war and nuclear testing, it must have quicker access."

AMENDMENTS. Congress moved to strengthen the Freedom of Information Act in 1974, by enacting its amendments into law over President Gerald Ford's veto. Ford argued that the amendments were "unconstitutional and unworkable" and a threat to legitimate military and intelligence secrets. The amendments, which went into effect in 1975, narrowed the scope of exemption that protected certain categories of government files from public disclosure, such as secrets that affect the national security. Congress also required agencies to answer information requests within ten days of receipt, broadened avenues of appeal and court authority to declassify disputed documents, and established penalty guidelines for wrongful withholding of documents.

Since passage of the law, agencies such as the FBI and CIA have provided copies of thousands of documents about individuals, companies, events such as the Kennedy assassinations, surveillance of known or presumed radical groups, and even, under court order, items such as the transcripts of background briefings and official conversations conducted by former Secretary of State Henry Kissinger. Private citizens were able to obtain copies of FBI files about themselves compiled through extraordinary surveillance during the Vietnam War and years of national unrest. Activist organizations likewise could clarify their status in government records. And reporters and writers could request and receive documents essential to their work. There were costs to pay for the searches, and delays in responses, as well as refusals based on security claims by the agency involved. But the system seemed to be working, until 1978.

By then the CIA was complaining that foreign agents were using the FOI Act to attempt to gain information, while the FBI maintained that organized crime was attempting to discover FBI information sources. The Federal Trade Commission and business-related cabinet departments said that the FOI procedure was being used, not by the general public, but by law firms and commercial competitors attempting to gain trade secrets and business advantages.

These arguments helped to build support in Congress for amendments to the FOI Act. The 1980 session passed a bill exempting most consumer information from being disclosed by the Federal Trade Commission. With the advent of President Ronald Reagan's administration in 1981, efforts to amend the act were intensified. Bills were introduced giving substantial or total exemptions from the act to the CIA and the FBI, two of the principal targets of the activists of the 1960s and 1970s. Also to be exempted was information from nuclear power plant archives and about offshore power plants. Fees for obtaining information were to be raised. But wrangling among members of Congress, and determined opposition by media groups, stalled the bills. In 1986, however, Congress finally enacted legislation giving federal law-enforcement agencies new authority to withhold documents they believe might compromise current investigations. Agencies also were granted authority to refuse either to confirm or deny that certain records exist at all. Under a new fee schedule, costs were lowered for news organizations and nonprofit groups seeking information, but increased for "commercial use," a category that makes up most of the requests to some agencies.

The Reagan administration's drive against freedom of information had included other successes: a Justice Department directive setting more restrictive guidelines for federal agencies in responding to FOI requests, the instituting of requirements for advance payments for information requests by several agencies, and an executive order making it easier for federal agencies to classify information and harder to get information unclassified. In two Supreme Court cases the Justice Department succeeded in blocking release of information sought by journalists under the FOI Act. The annual report of the federal Information Security Oversight Office stated that officials had wielded the secrecy stamp 22.3 million times during fiscal year 1985, a 14 percent jump over 1984. Only 8.1 million documents were declassified during the same period.

GOVERNMENT IN THE SUNSHINE. An encouraging sign in the battle for the right to know was the enactment by Congress of a Government in the Sunshine Law that took effect in 1977. This law requires more than 50 federal boards and agencies with two or more members to conduct most meetings in the open. The law allows closed meetings for certain specified reasons but requires that the reasons for any closed meetings be certified by the chief legal officer of the agency. In 1978 the House decided to open its debates to daily live broadcast coverage. The body voted, however, to control the broadcast feed itself rather than let a network pool produce it. Passage of "open-meetings" laws in individual states had begun during the 1950s, and by 1975 virtually all of the states had some form of open-meetings law as well as laws guaranteeing the opening of public records to reporters needing access to them.

A new era in news reporting of the U.S. Senate began when television cameras were permitted to cover sessions under tightly controlled conditions. Television technicians check the lighting in the Senate chamber. (UPI/Bettmann Newsphotos)

FURTHER LIMITATIONS. But despite such evidences of progress, Washington correspondents faced an increasingly hostile effort by the Reagan administration to limit media access to information and public access to a variety of information channels. In addition to its efforts to weaken the FOI Act, the Reagan administration barred the entry into the country of foreign speakers because of concern about what they might say opposing administration policies, inhibited the free flow of films about the danger of a nuclear holocaust in and out of the country, subjected almost 290,000 government officials to an unprecedented system of lifetime censorship of their writings, instituted polygraph tests for federal workers to help prevent so-called leaks of information, and flooded universities with threats relating to their right to publish and discuss unclassified information.

A climax came in 1986 when Patricia Lara, reporter for a leading Colombian newspaper, was arrested and deported when she arrived from South America to attend a ceremony at the Columbia University Graduate School of Journalism, her Alma Mater. Lara had written critically about Reagan administration policies, reported from Cuba, and written a book about her country's guerrilla movement. U.S. immigration officials rated her potentially dangerous or subversive; no amount of protest succeeded in restoring her visa.

Reporters' Confidentiality

In 1972 the Supreme Court, by a five-to-four vote, decided that news reporters have no special immunity under the First Amendment not to respond to grand jury subpoenas and provide information in criminal investigations, even at the risk of "drying up" their sources.

One broadcast and two newspaper reporters, in separate appeals, urged the court to make it clear that the First Amendment guarantee of a free flow of information gives reporters at least some degree of immunity to government subpoena powers. The appeals from contempt citations were made by Paul M. Branzburg, a Louisville *Courier-Journal* reporter who had investigated the use of illegal drugs; and by Earl Caldwell, New York *Times* reporter, and Paul Pappas, newsman employed by television station WTEV, New Bedford, Massachusetts, both of whom had investigated Black Panther Party activities.

Justice Byron R. White, writing the decision with the support of four Nixon administration appointees to the Court, stated: "The Constitution does not, as it never has, exempt the newsman from performing the citizen's normal duty of appearing and furnishing information relevant to the grand jury's task."

Justice Potter Stewart, in an opinion in which he was joined by Justices William J. Brennan and Thurgood Marshall, said that the decision "invites state and federal authorities to undermine the historic independence of the press by attempting to annex the journalistic profession as an investigative arm of government." He added: "The full flow of information to the public protected by the free press guarantee would be severely curtailed if no protection whatever were afforded to the process by which news is assembled and disseminated . . . for without freedom to acquire information the right to publish would be impermissibly compromised."

In his dissent, Justice William O. Douglas wrote: "If [a reporter] can be summoned to testify in secret before a grand jury, his source will dry up and the attempted exposure, the effort to enlighten the public, will be ended. If what the Court sanctions today becomes settled law, then the reporter's main function in American society will be to pass on to the public the press releases which the various departments of government issue."

The justices, however, did leave open some avenues for relief to the media:

1. They acknowledged, for the first time, that the process of newsgathering qualifies for some First Amendment protection. According to Justice White, the First Amendment might come into play to protect a reporter if he or she could show "a bad faith attempt by a prosecutor to harass a reporter and disrupt his relationship with his news sources" (a fact not in evidence in the three cases before the Court). Justice White declared that if a reporter does not believe a grand jury investigation is being conducted in good faith, the reporter could seek relief from the courts. That eventually might occur, he said, if the reporter is called upon to give information "bearing only a remote and tenuous relationship to the subject of the investigation" or if the reporter has "some other reason to believe that his testimony implicates confidential source relationships without a legitimate need for law enforcement."

2. The Court left the door open for Congress to enact legislation binding on *federal* courts and grand juries.

3. The Court declared that state legislatures could enact "shield" laws preventing reporters from being forced to reveal sources of information to *state* courts and grand juries.

4. The Court conceded itself "powerless" to bar state courts from construing state constitutions so as to recognize a reporter's privilege of some type.

"Shield" laws were enacted in a number of states. Many journalists, however, declined to support campaigns to persuade Congress and the states to pass protective legislation, on grounds that the First Amendment guarantee of press freedom would be endangered by such action.

In recent years numerous reporters and editors have been jailed on contempt of court charges for failing to reveal sources of information. One celebrated case was that of William Farr, a Los Angeles reporter who, during the mid-1970s, served 46 days in jail for protecting his sources for a story about the Charles Manson murder trial. Another case was that of Myron Farber, New Jersey correspondent for the New York *Times,* who spent 40 days in jail in 1978 and paid, along with the *Times,* $285,000 in fines. He had refused to relinquish to a judge documents subpoenaed by the defense in a murder case against a physician. When the doctor was acquitted, Farber was released from jail. The New Jersey legislature then weakened the New Jersey shield law to conform to the state supreme court's decision in the Farber case, only to see that court reverse itself in 1980 and uphold the shield principle. In 1982 the New Jersey governor pardoned Farber and the *Times* and ordered return of their fines.

In 1980 the voters of California approved, by a 73 percent majority, a state constitutional amendment that included the exact language of that state's reporter shield law. Thus a statutory protection became a constitutional one in California. Farr could breathe a sigh of relief, for his case had never been adjudicated.

Countless subpoenas also have been issued in both criminal and civil cases in which the protection of sources was not involved. In some cases newspeople have testified or given depositions; in others the media have provided clippings and tearsheets; and in still others the subpoena has been successfully refused, denied, or withdrawn.

Searches and Seizures

When police raided the offices of the student-run *Stanford Daily* in 1971 seeking photographs of a campus sit-in, the incident set off a series of events culminating in the signing of legislation by President Jimmy Carter in October 1980 that banned similar police raids on newsrooms. The legislative action was necessary because the Supreme Court's decision of 1978 in *Zurcher* v. *Stanford Daily* had declared that the First Amendment provides the press no special protection from police searches.

PRIVACY PROTECTION ACT. There had been two reactions to this Court decision. Police in various parts of the country carried out at least 27 similar raids in two years, armed only with search warrants, instead of subpoenas that required advance warning of their action. But the other reaction was a welcome rebellion in Congress against increasingly conservative decisions by the Supreme Court that negated basic individual rights as well as First Amendment rights. The result was the passage, virtually without opposition, of the Privacy Protection Act in 1980, sponsored by the Carter administration and leading members of Congress.

The bill requires federal, state, and local authorities either to request voluntary compliance or to use subpoenas—with advance notice and the opportunity for a court hearing—instead of search warrants when they seek reporters' notes, films, or tapes as evidence. It also covers authors, scholars, and others engaged in First Amendment activities. Searches are allowed only in very limited situations. The bill also calls for the attorney general's guidelines to limit the use of search warrants against nonsuspect third parties who are not covered by the First Amendment.

Presumably the Supreme Court would note this reaction by Congress and the president in its future deliberations involving First Amendment rights. As President Carter commented when signing the bill, "The Supreme Court's 1978 decision in *Zurcher* v. *Stanford Daily* raised the concern that law enforcement authorities could conduct unannounced searches of reporters' notes and files. Such a practice could have a chilling effect on the ability of reporters to develop sources and pursue stories. Ever since the court's decision, my administration has been working with Congress to prevent this result by enacting legislation."

SECRET SEIZURE OF TELEPHONE RECORDS. But in the case of *Reporters Committee for Freedom of the Press* v. *AT&T,* the Carter administration's Justice Department sided against the media in their effort to prohibit secret seizure of their telephone call records by law enforcement agencies. The case began with the disclosure in 1973 that various Nixon administration agencies had secretly subpoenaed both office and home telephone call records of columnist Jack Anderson and the bureau chiefs of the New York *Times,* St. Louis *Post-Dispatch,* and Knight-Ridder. The Reporters Committee for Freedom of the Press asked AT&T to agree not to permit such seizures without advance warning to the news persons involved so that they could seek relief within the courts. AT&T refused. The Reporters Committee went to court, seeking First Amendment rights. But it lost in the United States district court and court of appeals trials, at which the Justice Department argued that, "the First Amendment does not permit reporters to withhold information about their news sources . . . in the course of a legitimate criminal investigation." In 1979 the Supreme Court refused to hear the case, leaving unanswered the question of how reporters could protect themselves against highly dubious seizures and searches such as those made by the Nixon administration merely to find out who was leaking news—a noncriminal offense.

Reporters in the Courtroom

A Nebraska murder trial in 1976 brought about a press-bar confrontation when the trial judge entered an order restraining the news media from reporting the existence of any confession or admission made by the defendant until the trial jury had been impaneled. The order followed the guidelines developed after the Supreme Court had in 1966 overturned the murder conviction of Dr. Sam Sheppard in Ohio because he had been subjected to massive pretrial publicity. In the Supreme Court decision in *Nebraska Press Association* v. *Stuart,* Chief Justice Burger held that the press was entitled to report all evidence presented in an *open* preliminary hearing, including confessions and admissions. By that time the Nebraska trial had ended. It was noted that Burger's decision made it plain that the ruling did not prevent future "gag" orders, and that it did not cover the issue of First Amendment rights when pretrial hearings were closed.

Media people's fears were justified when in 1979 the Supreme Court ruled in *Gannett* v. *DePasquale* that members of the public have no constitutional rights under the Sixth and Fourteenth amendments to attend criminal trials. But apparently not all members of the Court realized the implications of the decision, which once again struck at a long-cherished individual right. Within a few months various justices were implying that the ruling had been misinterpreted by judges who were busy closing courtrooms to public and press. Within one year there were 160 successful closings of courts—126 pretrial proceedings and 34 trial proceedings.

The situation was clarified, to the satisfaction of First Amendment advocates, in 1980 when Chief Justice Burger read a seven-to-one decision in *Richmond Newspapers* v. *Commonwealth of Virginia* declaring that the public has a constitutional right to attend criminal trials even when defendants want to exclude them. The decision overturned a Virginia judge's closing of a murder trial in 1978. Burger cited First Amendment rights in his decision, but, as usual, warned that "the constitutional right to attend criminal trials is not absolute." The decision left pretrial hearings still subject to closing. A 1982 Supreme Court decision reaffirmed the *Richmond* ruling by declaring unconstitutional a Massachusetts law requiring courtrooms to be closed during testimony of young rape victims.

Justice John Paul Stevens called the *Richmond* decision a "watershed" case, saying: "Until today the court has accorded absolute protection to the dissemination of ideas, but never before has it squarely held that the acquisition of newsworthy matter is entitled to any constitutional protection whatsoever." And so, at least in one justice's mind, the right to report is a constitutional right.

The gap in the Supreme Court decisions about public attendance at criminal trials was closed in 1986 when the Court held seven-to-two in an opinion written by Justice Burger that the public has a First Amendment right to attend pretrial hearings in criminal cases over the objections of defendants. The case, *Press Enterprise Company* v. *Superior Court of California,* followed a 1984 case also brought by the Riverside paper which won the opening of the jury selection process to the public and press.

Cameras in the Courtroom

The U.S. Supreme Court ruled unanimously in 1981 in *Chandler* v. *Florida* that states have the right to allow television, radio, and photographic coverage of criminal trials, even if the defendant objects. Although the decision did not guarantee news media a right to insist on such coverage, it clarified the fact that any state is now free to allow cameras and microphones into courtrooms as long as the defendant's right to a fair trial is protected.

The decision bolstered the movement to permit still and television cameras in trial and appellate courts, which had spread to many states. Among them was Florida, where the courts had allowed their use in the courtroom during the conviction of two former police officers who said that television coverage of their burglary trials in Miami Beach deprived them of their constitutional rights to a fair and orderly proceeding. It was their appeal that produced the Supreme Court decision.

In 1965 the Supreme Court had overturned the swindling conviction of Billie Sol Estes in Texas after large, movie-type cameras and bright lights were used to televise his trial. But the Court indicated then that television coverage might be approved if unobtrusive equipment were used. In its 1981 decision the Court declared that the Estes ruling had not meant that TV and photographers must be banned forever under all circumstances. Regarding the Florida trials, the Court said, "The defendants have offered no evidence that any participant in this case was affected by the presence of cameras."

The decision left unchanged the ban against the use of cameras in *federal* courts. This restriction stemmed from a vote by the American Bar Association (ABA) in 1937, reinforced in 1979 when the ABA voted down a resolution to amend its long-standing Canon 35 (renumbered 3A7). But in 1982 the ABA house of delegates voted 162 to 112 to repeal its Canon 3A7. Judges voted in 1984, however, to continue prohibiting the use of TV and still cameras and radio equipment during federal trials.

THE MEDIA AND THE INDIVIDUAL

Free Press, Fair Trial

The reporting of arrests and trials, especially in crimes of a sensationalist nature, came under attack from the American Bar Association and certain civil rights groups during the 1960s. This development coincided with an increasing concern by the U.S. Supreme Court about the rights of defendants. Editors were accused by their critics of "trying the case in the newspapers" and printing or airing material prejudicial to the defendant.

In 1968 the ABA house of delegates adopted guidelines prepared by a special committee to restrict the reporting of crime news. The guidelines are known as the Reardon Report, named for the committee chairman, Associate Judge Paul C. Reardon of the Supreme Judicial Court of Massachusetts. Newspaper people protested that the attorneys had overstepped their role and were trying to sabotage freedom of the press. Eventually a press-bar committee, set up through the American Society of Newspaper Editors, resolved much of the conflict. Under court and ABA pressures, the newspapers grew more cautious with regard to what they printed about a crime and the suspects before the matter reached trial. Broadcast newspeople took similar precautions. In addition, the police became reluctant to disclose the facts of a crime to reporters—information ordinarily given freely in the past.

For many years courts have forbidden the reporting of trials by print photographers, television camera operators, and radio newspeople operating tape recorders. In order to improve public awareness of legal procedures, however, courts in 43 states by 1986 had begun permitting TV and still-photo coverage of trials.

In nontrial settings, numerous state legislatures have authorized television coverage, the House of Representatives and Senate permitted radio and television under controlled conditions, and network officials have urged the Supreme Court to follow suit. A coalition of 28 media organizations was formed in 1983 to seek such opening of all federal courts.

The Right of Privacy

Closely allied to libel and slander is the question of which is more important, the privacy of the individual or the privilege of the press. The right of privacy, perhaps the most cherished right of all, is guaranteed, but more and more it is coming into conflict in the courts with the First Amendment right to report news freely.

As previously discussed, public figures such as politicians, entertainers, and athletes give up their right to privacy in return for being public figures. But how much right to privacy does a person who is not a public figure have when that right conflicts with the rights of the press? Privacy rights have been obtained through a series of judicial rulings in this century.

An individual's privacy may be violated if that person is depicted in a "false light," an action that is similar to but separate from libel law, and if private facts about private persons are publicly disclosed. In a case pertaining to the latter, in 1975 the Supreme Court struck down a Georgia law that made it a misdemeanor to print or broadcast the name of a rape victim. Following a court hearing for six youths accused of raping a 17-year-old girl who subsequently died, presumably from rape-related trauma, Atlanta station WSB-TV used the girl's name in a newscast. Claiming serious disruption of the family's privacy, the girl's father filed suit. The Georgia courts upheld the suit as a matter of law, and the TV station appealed.

Although the Supreme Court ruled in favor of the Cox Broadcasting Corporation, it would not go so far as to make truth an absolute defense in invasion of privacy cases. The Court held that "once true information is disclosed in public court documents open to public inspection, the press cannot be sanctioned for publishing it." The Court then dampened the ruling somewhat by stating that it was confining its judgment to "the narrower interface between press and privacy" involved in printing the name of a rape victim rather than "the broader question whether truthful publications may ever be subjected to civil or criminal liability."

Despite the ruling, Georgia editors and broadcast news directors were quick to point out that they would continue to exercise great care in deciding whether it was necessary to report the names of rape victims.

Media lawyers hope that eventually the Court will permit the publication of any and all information about individuals unless clear and convincing proof can be shown that such information is false and that the communicator either knew it was false or acted in "reckless disregard" of the facts—the test laid out in the *New York Times* v. *Sullivan* case.

The Privacy Act of 1974 stipulated types of information about individuals that could not be disclosed by federal agencies and provided means whereby persons could determine the nature of information about themselves in official files. A Privacy Protection Study Commission, created by the act, undertook a two-year study of the application of the law and submitted a 654-page report to President Carter in 1977. The report listed five "competing social values" that must be taken into account in protecting personal privacy: the First Amendment, freedom of information, law enforcement interests, the cost of privacy protection, and federal-state relations.

The commission recommended that no action be taken that would affect the ability of the press to request or obtain information. The commission did suggest, however, that medical records be kept strictly confidential and that it be considered a crime to seek such information through misrepresentation or deception.

Further restrictions on the newsgathering function of the media were imposed when the federal Law Enforcement Assistance Administration (LEAA) decreed in 1975 that, effective December 31, 1977, if a state or community wanted federal money for collecting, storing, or disseminating criminal history records, policies would have to be enacted to limit the release of such information. That meant that the only information available to the public and the media would be police station "blotter" lists that are organized chronologically. The only way to obtain noncurrent records would be to have available the name of the person and the date of the arrest or court record.

The restrictions brought strong protests from media organizations and, in 1976, the LEAA decided to leave the matter up to individual states. Some states have adopted restrictive or modified policies; others have liberal dissemination plans, usually because an open record or "sunshine" law covers criminal history or arrest records; and some, with no plan, must follow the LEAA revised policies calling for open release of conviction data and restricted release of nonconviction information.

ACCESS TO THE MEDIA

The role of the mass media is enormous in influencing important public policy decisions, in maintaining or changing the status quo of our society, and in providing outlets for all types of views. So great is the impact of the media today that it has become common, though it is ungrammatical, to use the plural word "media" in the singular ("The media does this"). Gaining access to such a powerful force is the goal of innumerable business firms, ethnic organizations, labor leaders, consumers, government officials, and other special interest groups. All realize that much can be gained or lost through what is printed or broadcast.

Because of the theory that "the airwaves belong to the people," special interest groups have met with greater success in obtaining access to radio and over-the-air and cable television than to the print media.

Newspapers

In 1969 Jerome A. Barron, a law professor at George Washington University, proposed a new concept of the First Amendment in relation to newspapers. Pointing out that in the *New York Times* v. *Sullivan* case the Supreme Court had created a new relative freedom from libel for newspapers by the way it had interpreted the First Amendment, Barron said that similar techniques could be used to fashion a right of access to the press for the public:

> If this approach does not work, then a carefully worded right of access statute which would aim at achieving a meaningful expression of divergent opinions should be attempted. The point is that we must realize that private restraints on free expression have become so powerful that the belief that there is a free marketplace where ideas will naturally compete is as hopelessly outmoded as the theory of perfect competition has generally become in most other spheres of modern life.

In 1974 the Florida Supreme Court, in *Miami Herald Co.* v. *Pat L. Tornillo,* upheld a state law requiring that newspapers give "right of reply" space to political candidates criticized by newspapers. The U.S. Supreme Court, however, unanimously overturned the decision, its opinion reading in part as follows:

> The Florida statute fails to clear the barriers of the First Amendment because of its intrusion into the function of editors. A newspaper is more than a passive receptacle or conduit for news, comment, and advertising. The choice of material . . . the treatment of public issues and public officials—whether fair or unfair—constitutes the exercise of editorial control or judgment. It has yet to be demonstrated how government regulation of this process can be exercised consistent with First Amendment guarantees of a free press as they have evolved to this time.

Newspaper editors long have sought to obtain replies from possibly maligned individuals, companies, and institutions both before and after the printing of controversial stories. Letters to the editor columns traditionally have been open to all readers. A number of newspapers have solicited articles from the public to run in the columns opposite their main editorial pages.

Recognizing the pressures for greater access to their publications, however, many newspapers more recently have employed persons called *ombudsmen,* or have assigned certain staff members, to consider complaints; have endeavored to establish local and state press councils and given support to the now disbanded National News Council (discussed in Chapter 24); and have hired reporters and editors from minority groups. But the editors insist that the final decision as to what is printed must be theirs alone. Others call attention to the fact that today's technology permits persons with only limited capital to start their own newspapers.

About the only infringement upon publishers' prerogatives in recent years has been the federal requirement that in classified advertising male and female notices may no longer be kept separate.

Broadcasting

By contrast, broadcasters have had to contend with a multiplicity of efforts to gain access and influence what is aired: the Fairness Doctrine; threats by minority groups and others to take over their licenses; the necessity every few years—five years for television and seven years for radio—to prove that they have ascertained community interests and have been operating for the public good; bans on cigarette and smokeless tobacco advertising; "countercommercials," the airing of viewpoints replying to commercial spots; attacks on television documentaries; demands by citizen groups to provide special programming; network antitrust suits; efforts to reduce televised violence and children's advertising and to maintain good taste in programming; the control of prime-time program segments; access to cable channels; the staging of demonstrations and other "pseudo-events" to gain news attention ("Just do your thing; the press eats it up. Media is free. *Make news,*" proclaimed Yippie Abbie Hoffman). It is small wonder that the broadcaster is harried, but that is the price that must be paid for the prestige, pride in community involvement, and substantial profits that are attained in much of the broadcast world.

During the last two decades, minority groups have applied consistent pressure to station managements in efforts to achieve more programming of special interest to them, to have minorities presented favorably in existing programs, and to have greater ethnic representation on station staffs. These groups obtain agreements from individual stations and they also seek policy changes from the FCC and Congress, in part because of commission and federal court encouragement over the years and in part from an increasing awareness that broadcasters and the government often respond to pressure. Action before the FCC consists principally of participation in license renewal procedures, either as petitioners to deny or as parties to agreements that head off litigation. Many such groups form local coalitions in dealing with broadcasters.

Other special interest groups, such as Accuracy in Media (AIM), join in suits against both the networks and individual media in efforts to promote their causes if voluntary action to alter programming practices cannot be obtained. A discussion of the threats action groups make to the economic security of broadcasters is provided in Chapter 21.

Cable television and public broadcasting are the avenues most open to individuals and special interest groups. Almost 20 percent of the cable systems originate some local programming and many welcome community participation.

The Fairness Doctrine

For many of the nation's broadcasters, one specific legal requirement—the "Fairness Doctrine"—has had the effect of discouraging coverage of many important social issues. Since 1949, broadcasters have been obligated to offer reasonable opportunity for opposing sides to respond to the coverage of controversial public issues. This statutory requirement to be fair was based on two legal philosophies not relevant to print media: (1) the airwaves are public property; and (2) broadcasters are licensed to operate in the "public interest, convenience, and necessity." Public interest is served, Congress and the FCC have ruled, if the airwaves are made accessible to many differing viewpoints.

Most broadcasting leaders took issue with the Fairness Doctrine, charging that it abridged the principles of freedom of speech and press traditionally applied to electronic media by forcing the presentation of various sides of an issue, even when the views may be unfounded, untrue, or difficult to identify in a local community. Even more annoying to broadcasters was the *personal attack* clause of the Fairness Doctrine. This clause states that if an individual is attacked in an editorial or program, a script or tape of the attack must be sent to the individual, with an offer of a reasonable opportunity to reply. Furthermore, if the licensee endorsed or opposed legal candidates for office in an editorial statement, the same notice and offer of time must be made within 24 hours after the program is aired.

The industry considered the clause unconstitutional, a violation of freedom of the press. Its effect, it was argued, would be to curtail meaningful discussion of issues because of the expense involved in offering time for reply and because the licensee would avoid controversial issues if uncertain about the freedom to comment.

The Supreme Court did not agree with the broadcasters; in 1969 it held the personal attack rules constitutional, noting that "it is the right of the viewers and listeners, not the right of the broadcasters, which is paramount" in such instances. If broadcasters were not willing to present representative community views on controversial issues, Justice Byron White of the Court wrote, the granting or renewal of a license might be challenged. To make this threat of a license loss, he continued, "is consistent with the ends and purposes of those constitutional provisions forbidding the abridgement of freedom of speech and freedom of the press." In law circles, this became known as the *Red Lion* decision *(Red Lion Broadcasting Co.* v. *Federal Communications Commission).*

The FCC has been confronted with fairness questions covering a wide spectrum of material ranging from news and public affairs programs to commercials and political broadcasts. Its rulings have raised serious questions about the criteria for fairness. What is reasonable balance in the presentation of opposing views? How does a government agency determine whether a viewpoint is favorable, unfavorable, or neutral? In what amount of time, at what hour, and to what audience should an opposing viewpoint be presented? And the larger question: Should the government be involved in such matters at all? If so, how extensively?

Broadcasters, and many print journalists as well, have continued to oppose the doctrine as inhibiting the free flow of ideas, and measures have been introduced in Congress to eliminate the requirement. Many who once favored the doctrine have expressed the viewpoint that, now that, in their opinion, an abundance of electronic channels permits the airing of many viewpoints on controversial issues, the requirement should be eliminated. In June 1987 an effort by Congress to turn the policy into law was vetoed by President Reagan. Two months later, however, the FCC voted unanimously to abolish the doctrine. Unaffected were the equal time rule and other regulations such as license requirements calling for local programming. Broadcasting was on its way to achieving First Amendment parity with print.

COPYRIGHT LAW AND THE MEDIA

On January 1, 1978, a comprehensive copyright revision law, described by congressional leaders as "the greatest advance in copyright legislation in our nation's history," went into effect.

For more than two decades Congress had endeavored to revise the amended copyright law of 1909, which rapidly became outdated by advances in technology. The development of modern photocopying machines, cable television, and the computer had raised serious and complex problems primarily affecting authors, performers, book and magazine publishers and distributors, libraries, educational institutions, cable television broadcasters, and motion picture and other audio-visual program suppliers.

Copyright is *the exclusive right to reproduce, publish, and sell the matter and form of a literary, musical, or artistic work.* Designed to encourage the creation and dissemination of original works to the public, copyright was originally established by statute in England in 1556. Prior to that time, the only protection that existed was under common law. The United States had recognized common law copyright, which protected works before publication. The new law, however, established a single system of copyright protection for all copyrightable works, whether published or unpublished.

The law extends copyright protection from the former maximum of 56 years to the life of the author plus 50 years. For works made for hire and copyrighted by others, as well as anonymous material, the new term is 75 years from publication or 100 years from creation, whichever is shorter.

The measure provides for the payment, under a system of compulsory licensing, of certain royalties for the secondary transmission of copyrighted works on cable television systems. The fees are based on the amount of distant nonnetwork programming carried and on subscriber receipts. The assessments are paid to the Register of Copyrights for later distribution to the copyright owners by a copyright royalty tribunal.

The law permits archives and libraries, such as Vanderbilt University's TV news archives, to copy news programs for lending to researchers. The borrowers are restricted from using copies for profit or politics. An American TV and Radio Archives was established in the Library of Congress for collecting, cataloguing, and lending broadcast news and entertainment programs.

Noncommercial transmissions by public broadcasters of published musical and graphic works are subject to a compulsory license, thus eliminating the paperwork and legal costs of negotiation for the rights to such broadcast material. Public broadcasters are urged to negotiate their own royalty rates.

One section of the law recognizes the principle of "fair use" as a limitation on the exclusive rights of copyright owners. Within certain prescribed limits, copies may be made for purposes such as criticism, comment, news reporting, teaching (including multiple copies for classroom use), scholarship, or research. Libraries are permitted to make single copies of copyrighted works, also under stringent limitations. It quickly became apparent that the photocopying machines of the 1980s would disgorge increasing sheaves of materials for educational and research purposes.

The law retains the provisions added to the former law in 1972 that accord protection against the unauthorized duplication of sound recordings for commercial purposes. Compulsory licensing is provided for the recording of music.

The law removes the former exemption for performances of copyrighted music by jukeboxes. It substitutes a system of compulsory licensing based upon the payment by jukebox operators of an annual royalty fee to the Register of Copyrights for distribution to copyright owners. A 1984 U.S. Supreme Court decision, *Sony* v. *Universal,* exempted home use of video recorders from federal copyright laws.

Copyright secures only the property right in the manner and content of expression. Facts and ideas recited, or systems and processes described, are made freely available to the public. Although news itself is in the public domain and uncopyrightable, news accounts per se—that is, their particular literary arrangement—may be copyrighted, especially when they bear the mark of individual enterprise and literary style. "CBS Evening News With Dan Rather," for example, is copyrighted. Feature stories, editorials, columns, series of articles, cartoons, maps, photographs, and the like may be copyrighted. Newspapers usually copyright entire editions, by issue or weekly or monthly, in order to protect their advertising from piracy, although the copyright of an advertisement created solely by the advertiser may be retained by that person or company.

For infringement of copyright, courts may award statutory damages ranging from $250 to $10,000. In addition to or instead of a fine, conviction for criminal infringement carries a sentence of up to one year in prison.

Copies of the statute are available free of charge from the Copyright Office, Library of Congress, Washington, D.C. 20559.

The Media's Social
and Ethical Responsibilities

An Ethical Dilemma?

An emotionally troubled 18-year-old college student murdered his mother, father, and sister. Found mentally incompetent to stand trial, he underwent many years of intensive therapy and was found not guilty of murder on grounds that he was insane at the time.

The student obtained his college degree, married, and rose through journalistic ranks to become president of a large group of suburban weekly newspapers.

Twenty-one years after the slayings, however, a competing weekly paper disclosed his past. No other news medium picked up the story and many condemned the action.

This story illustrates a cardinal principle of journalism—*never* publish unsavory information about a long-ago happening without cause, such as a person's seeking public office. People, it is almost universally agreed, have a right to "live down" their past.

Probably no other editor would have run this particular story. But newspeople *are* confronted with ethical decisions almost daily: Does the public interest override individual privacy? Should a news source go unnamed? Should a "leak" possibly affecting national security be used? Should a rape victim's identity be disclosed?

General journalism codes call for truth, accuracy, impartiality, fair play. Most news media also have their own codes, generally enforced. Many decisions, however, test individual judgment and conscience.

Would *you* have run this story?

C an, or should, the mass media be held responsible for actions that many believe are harmful to society? Is such an accountability possible under the First Amendment? If so, to whom would the media be accountable? Is self-regulation the ultimate answer?

We open this chapter with a philosophical discussion of the moral law under which all our communications media, along with other institutions, must operate. We review the recommendations for responsibility of the Commission on Freedom of the Press.

We discuss complaints against media portrayal of violence, including terrorism; obscenity, including the contrasting reports of the Commission on Obscenity and Pornography in 1970 and the Commission on Pornography in 1986; and other matters concerning sex and good taste, including possibly objectionable lyrics in rock music recordings.

Public criticism of media ethics is reviewed as well as media codes and their enforcement. Efforts of the media to employ more minority personnel and women and advance them to management positions are explored. We conclude with a discussion of the roles played by numerous organizations in seeking to improve media performance. ◆

THE MORAL LAW

Of all the laws that the mass media and their supporting industries, advertising and public relations, must obey, the moral law is the strongest. Public opinion produced the First Amendment, and public opinion can take it away. As pointed out in Chapter 23, not only does moral law impose a greater restriction on the media than any purely legal restraint, it also functions as a force that can overturn legal restrictions and bring greater freedom for the press. A monumental example is the manner in which public opinion slowly overturned laws against the right to print and the right to criticize in the fifteenth through eighteenth centuries. A more familiar, specific example is the John Peter Zenger case in 1735, when an aroused public prevented the government from punishing an editor for criticizing it.

Moral law has grown principally out of religion and may be found embodied in the precepts of all major religions. In Christianity, for example, it is found in the Old and New Testaments, most notably in the Ten Commandments and the teachings of Jesus Christ; in the Muslim world, moral law is set forth in the Koran of the Islamic religion.

Circles of Control

Examine in Figure 24.1 the five concentric circles, each succeeding one placed within the other, much like the bull's-eye used in target practice. These may be termed the "circles of control affecting the mass media" (or, for that matter, most other human activities).

1. The innermost circle represents the professional standards and ethical practices of *individuals*—publishers, reporters, editors, station and network owners, news directors and film and videotape editors—the *gatekeepers* of what we read, see, and hear. In all that they do, these people must keep in mind the other four circles of control that surround them.

2. The second innermost circle represents the standards of practice and the codes of ethics established by the *individual media*. All the mass media—newspapers, magazines, broadcast stations, and so forth—operate under certain guidelines, whether these guidelines consist of written codes or simply unwritten assumptions, lore, and traditions. The persons who work for these media—those in the innermost circle—must subscribe to the standards and practices of organizations for which they work, or look elsewhere for their employment.

3. The third circle, moving outward, consists of *professional and industrywide* standards of conduct as embodied in the statements of sound practice affecting radio, television, film, newspapers, magazines, and books, and the codes of ethics of groups such as the American Society of Newspaper Editors, the Radio Television News Directors Association, and the Society of Professional Journalists, Sigma Delta Chi. Broadcast standards are enforced, only in part, however, by the Federal Communications Commission; print codes are entirely voluntary. Professionalism and peer pressure are the major forces leading to compliance by individual media and those working for them. There are other pressures, of course, economic considerations being among the strongest. Stories that an editor or news director regards as socially responsible and significant may strike some readers

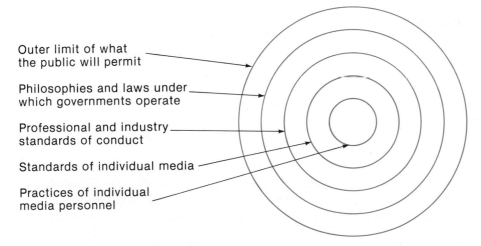

Outer limit of what the public will permit

Philosophies and laws under which governments operate

Professional and industry standards of conduct

Standards of individual media

Practices of individual media personnel

FIGURE 24.1
Circles of control of the mass media.

or listeners as obscene, or certain advertisers as harmful to their business. They may try to strike back economically by canceling their subscriptions, withdrawing their advertising, or, in the case of perceived lapses in good taste by broadcasters, filing a complaint with the FCC. Theoretically, such protests should not influence news decisions and most of the time, on better newspapers and broadcast stations, they do not directly. But the pressure exists.

4. The fourth circle represents the *basic press philosophies and the laws of individual governments.* In Chapter 4 we discussed the four theories of the press: authoritarianism, Soviet Communism, libertarianism, and social responsibility. Under the concept of social responsibility, so strongly insisted upon by today's press critics, it is the obligation of all owners and managers of the press to be socially responsible, to ensure that all public issues are presented fairly and fully so that the people may form their own opinions about the issues. Should the media fail to do so, its proponents insist, it may be necessary for some other agency of the public to enforce this concept. The threat of such action by the public—which would draw us dangerously back toward authoritarian control of the press—illustrates how important it is that the three innermost circles of control function as they should.

5. The fifth circle represents the *limits that people will tolerate regarding all types of human activity.* No individual or organization can pass beyond that outer limit without reprisal; history shows that even the most powerful governments eventually fall (as did that of ancient Rome) if they exceed the outer limit of what the people will permit. And those in the three inner circles also fall if they disregard that outer limit circumscribing their conduct.

These circles of social and legal control are not fixed, immutably, for all time. They shift from century to century, from generation to generation. For example, in the Western world the relative social permissiveness of the Chaucerian and Shakespearian eras may be contrasted to the puritanical restraints and Victorianism of the nineteenth century and they, in turn, may be contrasted with the permissiveness of the latter half of the twentieth century.

The outer limits vary, as do the inner circles. Governments rise and fall, greatly affecting human rights, including the freedom of the press. Governments in Portugal, Spain, and Greece provide examples. Codes of conduct stiffen, then relax, then stiffen again. The standards of the individual media respond to changing social mores as do the decisions of our media gatekeepers concerning what will be printed, filmed, or broadcast.

Commission on Freedom of the Press

In 1947 the report of the *Commission on Freedom of the Press,* whose chairman was the late Robert Maynard Hutchins, then chancellor of the University of Chicago, set forth twentieth-century America's requirements of the mass media. Although denounced by much of the media because no news person was a member of the commission, these requirements reflect the code of ethics enacted in the 1920s by the American Society of Newspaper Editors, and they have been incorporated in codes of ethics subsequently established by other media organizations. The press, the commission declared, should provide the following in a democratic society:

1. A truthful, comprehensive, and intelligent account of the day's events in a context which gives them meaning.
2. A forum for the exchange of comment and criticism.
3. The projection of a representative picture of the constituent groups in the society.
4. The presentation and clarification of the goals and values of the society.
5. Full access to the day's intelligence.

The communications media, of course, may choose not to attempt to fulfill these obligations: Indeed, the First Amendment permits irresponsibility as well as responsibility. But, as we have emphasized, they may do so only at their own peril —and ours.

VIOLENCE

Effects of Televised Violence

Because many families spend about half their waking hours at home watching television, a number of society's greatest concerns, such as the threat of nuclear annihilation, wars and other forms of violence, sexual excesses, crime, and drug and alcohol abuse, have reached a far sharper focus of debate than at any other time in U.S. history. No other communications medium is so powerful in mirroring human activity and in reinforcing or changing popular beliefs.

Violence is a major characteristic of humankind's history and literature, including even religious writings and children's fairy tales. In the United States, violence was an inevitable part of the expanding frontiers, with law and order coming slowly but leaving a heritage of violent behavior as a principal means of settling arguments. Hand-gun deaths in this country in 1979, for example, numbered 10,728, as compared with only 52 such deaths in Canada, 48 in Japan, and 8 in Britain. As Harry Henderson pointed out in an article in *The Press* in 1982, "This is a far more violent country than anyone wants to admit."

Because of its prime role in our lives, a dispute has raged for three decades over the effects of viewing acts of violence on television by the American public— particularly by children, other young people, and the emotionally disturbed. In response to public concern, the late Senator Estes Kefauver held hearings on the matter as far back as 1954, and testimony was heard again in the Senate in 1961.

As the rate of violent crime in America grew, a greater number of critics pointed to television as one of the possible causes. The assassinations of President John F. Kennedy, Senator Robert Kennedy, and the Rev. Martin Luther King, Jr., and the attempted assassination of former Governor George Wallace of Alabama, combined with civil disturbances, all focused attention on the violent behavior of Americans.

Hundreds of scholars have attempted to ascertain the root causes of violence.

A 1980 bibliography of television research on the subject lists about 300 titles published before 1970 and approximately 2500 titles published after that. Landmark reports of this research include the following:

1. The National Commission on the Causes and Prevention of Violence reported in 1969 that watching programs with violence made it more likely that a viewer would behave violently.

2. The Scientific Advisory Committee on Television and Social Behavior, appointed by U.S. Surgeon General Jesse L. Steinfeld, reported in 1972 that its massive study "does not warrant the conclusion that televised violence has a uniformly adverse effect nor the conclusion that it has an adverse effect on the majority of children." However, the report continued, "the evidence does indicate that televised violence may lead to increased aggressive behavior in certain subgroups of children, who might constitute a small portion or a substantial portion of the total population of young television viewers." The committee cited as significant other factors, such as parental attitudes and experience with violence and whether violence was punished in the programs.

3. The National Institute of Mental Health, of the U.S. Department of Health and Human Services, reported in 1982 that "the consensus among most of the research community is that violence on television does lead to aggressive behavior by children and teen-agers who watch the programs." Of the 2500 studies on which the report was based, "the great majority . . . demonstrate a positive relationship between televised violence and later aggressive behavior," and show that girls as well as boys are so influenced, the report declared. Moreover, "the viewer learns more than aggressive behavior from televised violence. The viewer learns to be a victim and to identify with victims. As a result, many heavy viewers may exhibit fear and apprehension, while other heavy viewers may be influenced toward aggressive behavior. Thus, the effects of televised violence may be even more extensive than suggested by earlier studies . . . and exhibited in more subtle forms of behavior than aggression."

After a 16-month study the American Academy of Pediatrics warned in 1985 that repeated exposure to TV violence can make children violent, and numb to the horror of real-life violence.

In that same year the American Psychological Association, citing the accumulated results of 1000 studies over 25 years, passed a resolution declaring: "Viewing televised violence may lead to increases in aggressive attitudes, values, and behavior, particularly in children." The psychologists likened the link between violent TV and violent children to that between cigarette smoking and lung cancer: One does not necessarily cause the other, but there is undeniable evidence that the two go together.

The issue was far from closed, however. ABC published a booklet titled, *A Research Perspective on Television and Violence,* asserting that "after more than 30 years of scientific investigation, the issue of television violence remains open

Controversy exists as to whether excessive gunplay and violence in popular television shows such as NBC's "Miami Vice" cause social harm by conditioning viewers to accept or to imitate violence. Detectives Tubbs (Philip Michael Thomas, left) and Crockett (Don Johnson) star in the fast-paced "Miami Vice." (AP/Wide World)

to debate." The CBS director of research told congressional investigators in 1983 that there is "still no convincing evidence," and challenged the methodologies endorsed by the institute report. NBC issued a report of a study of 2300 children and adolescents in Fort Worth and Minneapolis, which, it stated, found no evidence that watching television led to aggression.

The NBC researchers did find, however, that boys "in low socioeconomic circumstances," who are "socially insecure, have other emotional problems, and are not accepted by their parents," tend to become aggressive, although the researchers were not sure that these factors are indeed "causes of aggression." ABC researchers told a congressional body in 1983 that a survey of 400 studies found that only 1 percent of the researchers thought that television was *the* cause of aggressive behavior.

Public concern over televised violence had earlier intensified with news reports that a young woman was fatally set on fire with kerosene in a lonely Boston neighborhood soon after a similar scene had been depicted on television. Concern turned into outrage when three adolescents (two girls and a boy) raped a 9-year-old girl with a bottle in San Francisco only three days after, the attackers admitted to police, they had seen the made-for-television movie *Born Innocent.* (Observers were reminded of this incident in late 1984 when, after a woman played by Farrah Fawcett set her abusive husband on fire in the TV movie, *The Burning Bed,* a Milwaukee man was charged with torching his estranged wife while she lay in bed.) In the movie a 15-year-old girl was portrayed as being raped with the handle of a plumbing device in the shower room of a mental hospital by four other girls. On behalf of the real-life victim, suit was brought against NBC and the Chronicle Publishing Company, owner of the local television station. It alleged negligence and intentional wrongful conduct in presenting a program that eventually led to the physical and mental harm inflicted on the girl.

Charging that television had become "a school of violence and a college for crime," the California Medical Association filed a friend-of-the-court brief urging that NBC and the station be held accountable for the assault. The brief also pointed out that several months previously, "based on the overwhelming scientific and medical evidence," the American Medical Association had declared television violence to be "an environmental health risk."

After viewing the film and hearing arguments, Superior Court Judge John A. Ertola threw the case out of court. He ruled that the First Amendment gives broadcasters an absolute immunity from civil liability for personal injuries arising out of their programming.

An even more celebrated case occurred in Miami, Florida, where Ronald Zamora, 15 years old, in the state's first televised criminal trial, had been given a life term in prison for murdering his 83-year-old neighbor. A year later the youth and his parents sought $25 million from ABC, CBS, and NBC, claiming that TV programming "showed the impressionable teenager . . . how to kill." Zamora, the suit maintained, was a victim of "involuntary subliminal television intoxication" caused by viewing shows such as "Kojak" and "Police Woman."

District Judge William Hoeveler dismissed the suit on First Amendment grounds. He declared that otherwise he would have to "find in law a new duty, a new cause for action" and that it would be impossible to enforce any rule seeking to protect certain viewers. "Obviously there's a large segment of our population that wishes to see that violence," the judge said. "Presumably they have a right to watch it."

OTHER STUDIES. At about the same time the Chicago *Sun-Times* interviewed scores of psychologists and sociologists at universities and other research centers and reported general agreement that watching violence on television and movie screens indeed makes some children more violent. Even the minority of dissenters, the newspaper said, agreed that it is now the majority view that make-believe violence breeds real violence.

The newspaper reported the results of a study of 875 boys and girls in a semirural New York community over a 10-year period beginning in 1960, when they were third-graders. The study was made by Leonard D. Eron, editor of the *Journal of Abnormal Psychology* and chairman of the psychology department at the Chicago Circle campus of the University of Illinois.

Eron concluded that one of the best predictors of how aggressive a boy will be at age 19 is the violence of the television programs he prefers at age 8. "If you take those kids who were nonaggressive at age 8 but preferred and watched violent TV, at age 19 they were significantly more aggressive than children who were aggressive at age 8 but watched nonviolent TV," Eron stated, "which indicates it's the TV violence causing the aggression, rather than the other way around."

For girls, however, the study found that "viewing television violence may lead to lessened aggression," possibly because television may provide girls a vicarious outlet for aggression not socially acceptable in females or because women depicted on television are usually victims or passive observers of aggression.

Drs. Jerome L. Singer and Dorothy G. Singer, codirectors of the Yale University Family Television Research and Consultation Center, found in studying a group of 3-year olds from middle-class homes that most of them watch television four or five hours a day during winter, with an average of three hours a day for the total year. Some of the children in the sample watched as much as 50 hours a week. These psychologists reported evidence that viewing violent action stimulated aggressive behavior by the children.

Researchers at the Annenberg School of Communications at the University of Pennsylvania have found that persons who watch a great amount of television show greater fear and mistrust than those viewers who watch less. In answer to questions about their chances of encountering violence in real life, the former tend to express attitudes "more characteristic of the television world than of the real world." They tend to see themselves as potential victims, not aggressors. They believe there are more policemen than there really are and that "most people just look out for themselves, take advantage of others, and cannot be trusted."

In response to complaints, the networks insisted that program producers reduce the senseless mayhem on Saturday cartoon shows and also decrease depictions of violence on other programs, in accordance with the industry's broadcast standards. Several constructive juvenile programs were created. In 1975 the networks began devoting the first hour of prime time (8 to 9 P.M. on the East and West coasts, an hour earlier in the Central time zone) to programs considered suitable for family viewing. Warnings that parental viewing guidance should be exercised were flashed across the screen preceding some programs shown after that hour.

Nevertheless, the annual "violence profiles" for all network programming, produced by Annenberg's Dean George Gerbner, showed that, after a decline in 1977, the level of violence on all three television networks rose to near-record levels in the fall of 1978, with Saturday morning cartoons accounting for most of the increase. In 1986 Gerbner reported that TV's 8 to 9 P.M. time period—the "family hour"—included the most violent acts—168 per week—in his 19-year study. The National Institute of Mental Health's 1982 report had pointed out that the evening hours after 9 contain more violence than other hours, but that "over the last 10 years there has been more violence on children's weekend programs than on prime-time television." "Banging Daffy Duck on the head is fun! Hit him again!" This, the report said, is how the conditioning of children to violence is begun.

The institute report expressed the hope that schools will develop ways to teach children "how to watch and understand television. Much as they are taught to appreciate literature, to read newspapers carefully . . . they need to be prepared to understand TV as they view it in their homes. The field of critical TV viewing is essentially in its infancy, but it reflects the general trend toward setting the medium of TV in its place as part of the overall system of cognitive and emotional development."

Complaints against televised violence have been strongly registered with Congress, the FCC, stations, networks, and advertisers. Leaders of the protests include the Parent-Teachers Association, Action for Children's Television, American Medical Association, National Council of Churches, and other groups, including the so-called Moral Majority (which in 1986 became part of the more politically oriented Liberty Federation, formed by the Rev. Jerry Falwell). Many companies set their own standards for programs on which they would advertise. Concern was expressed that some of the violence was being replaced by the excessive use of sexual innuendoes and topics.

Violence in Newspapers

Because of the nature of the medium, the reporting of violent crimes in American newspapers has drawn less criticism than its display in television and films. However, through the years many readers have objected to sensationalistic treatment of murders, rapes, and other such crimes, often in the form of detailed front-page stories and photographs published under large headlines. Some people have felt that newspapers glorified violent activities, in effect making heroes of criminals. Objections have also been expressed against mayhem in the comic strips (although comic books were more severely criticized on this account) and against the reporting in some papers of almost every minor crime that occurs in the community. Newspaper accounts of violent actions, however, have a minimal impact compared with that which is televised and shown in movie houses.

The report of the Commission on Freedom of the Press, previously discussed in this chapter, decried sensationalism. The commission commented:

> To attract the maximum audience, the press emphasizes the exceptional rather than the representative, the sensational rather than the significant. Many activities of the utmost social consequence lie below the surface of what are conventionally regarded as reportable incidents: more power machinery; fewer men tending machines; more hours of leisure; more schooling per child; decrease of intolerance; successful negotiation of labor contracts; increase of participation in music through the schools; increase in the sale of books of biography and history.
>
> In most news media such matters are crowded out by stories of night-club murders, race riots, strike violence, and quarrels among public officials. The Commission does not object to the reporting of these incidents but to the preoccupation of the press with them. The press is preoccupied with them to such an extent that the citizen is not supplied with the information and discussion he needs to discharge his responsibilities to the community.

The press, however, has matured since those days; newspapers depending upon sensationalism for their circulation have, for the most part, been replaced by those such as the Washington *Post* and the Louisville *Courier-Journal,* which subordinate crime news of this sort to stories treating criminal activities in a sociological manner. One reason is that, since the advent of radio and television, single-copy street sales constitute only a minor part of most newspapers' circulation; most copies are delivered to homes. For such sales so-called screaming headlines and breathtaking accounts of crime are no longer necessary. Another reason is that most readers today, more educated than in the past, want their news in a different form. And the better newspapers are inquiring into the causes of conflict and violence, presenting in-depth background stories to throw more light on social problems.

Much of the nation's press, however, played up the 1977 arrest of David Berkowitz, suspected of killing six persons in New York City, in what critics called "a highly irresponsible manner" reminiscent of coverage of the noted Hall-Mills, Charles Lindbergh, and Sam Sheppard cases of earlier eras. Although some network and news magazine coverage was criticized, the charges, including those of exploitation and sensationalism, centered on the New York *Daily News* and on the New York *Post,* the latter owned by publisher Rupert Murdoch, noted for sensationalism.

The "Son of Sam" case, as it was termed, raised such thorny questions as: (1) the degree to which constitutional guarantees of press freedom imply unstated responsibilities; (2) the difference between reporting and exploiting the news; (3) the propriety of reporters' becoming part of the story they are covering; (4) the conflict between the public's right to know and the defendant's right to a fair trial; (5) the question of reporters' violating the law to obtain information; and (6) the ethics of the media's paying for information.

During the first part of the 1980s the New York *Post,* seeking to lure readers from its rivals, the *Daily News* and the New York *Times,* assumed an increasingly sensationalist tone. The typographic menu included such bannerline entrees as HEADLESS BODY IN TOPLESS BAR, UNCLE TORTURES TOTS WITH HOT FORK, and LEPER RAPES VIRGIN, GIVES BIRTH TO MONSTER BABY. Such stories were designed for the huge street sales necessary to keep the paper alive since major retail advertisers in 1986 were giving the tabloid only 7.2 percent of the total advertising in New York's major dailies, against 35.2 percent for the *Daily News* and 57.6 percent for the *Times.*

Terrorism and the Media

The substantial increase in terrorism throughout the world during the last decade or so poses other problems for the media. Public and media debate on this issue reached a crescendo with coverage of the hijacking of TWA Flight 847 in the Mideast during the summer of 1985. Charles Krauthammer, a *Time* magazine essayist, summed up the complaints as "insensitivity to the families; exploitation of the hostages; absurd, degrading deference to jailers; interference with diplomacy; appropriation of the role of negotiator. [ABC's] David Hartman to [Shiite terrorists' negotiator] Nabih Berri: 'Any final words to President Reagan this morning?') And finally, giving over the airwaves to people whose claim to airtime is based entirely on the fact that they are forcibly holding innocent Americans."

Former Secretary of State Henry Kissinger said the media should stop carrying news about such incidents, declaring that terrorists were cynically using the media to transmit their demands. Attorney General Edwin Meese III said the Department of Justice might ask newspapers and television to "withhold some interviews that might endanger (hostages in a terrorist situation) . . . or endanger the successful conclusion of the incident."

Columnist George Will complained about the "pornography of grief" in interviewing families of hostages and questioned whether media coverage jeopardized U.S. foreign policy. Noting the terrorists' demands that Israel release political prisoners, an action already planned, Jeanne Kirkpatrick, United Nations ambassador at the time, accused the press of creating tension that had not existed between the United States and Israel.

A House of Representatives foreign affairs subcommittee asked network executives how they might improve their coverage in the future, specifically in denying terrorists "the oxygen of publicity." This was the same phrase used by Britain's Prime Minister Margaret Thatcher when she called upon journalists to adopt a voluntary code of conduct. Democratic countries, she said, "must try to find ways to starve the terrorist and the hijacker of the oxygen of publicity on which they depend."

In response to the demand for partial or complete blackouts of hostage situations, media critic Ben Bagdikian, in an article in the September 1985 issue of *The Quill,* said: "Forcing news operations to react abnormally, to pretend that these are not frightening, dramatic events with political causes and consequences, not only misleads the American populace, but also can be an invitation for terrorists to escalate their violence until it becomes impossible to withhold or downplay news of their actions."

Contrasting the heavy media coverage of the TWA incident with the relative lack of publicity about seven Americans held captive in the Mideast for many months, syndicated columnist Carl Rowan wrote: "Media coverage of the TWA drama forced politicians to do some things they otherwise would not have done; lack of media pressure allows the politicians to go their old ways, doing nothing that would permit these seven remaining hostages to 'get in the way of national policy.'" The media, he argued, saved the lives of the TWA hostages.

During the networks' critiquing of their coverage, ABC announced that in the future its news division would supervise operations with no intrusion from its entertainment division (as in the case of "Good Morning, America"). Collective coverage was viewed by some media leaders as one means of avoiding the unseemly competition for interviews of captives by broadcast and print reporters alike.

Meese's proposal that the media and the government establish voluntary guidelines was rejected outright by editors of the New York *Times,* the Washington *Post,* the Los Angeles *Times,* and *USA Today.* "The United States government refused in the Beirut crisis to compromise its principles to terrorist demands," said *USA Today* editor John Quinn. "Certainly the U.S.A. principle of a free press deserves protection with equal vigor." Then New York *Times* executive editor A.M. Rosenthal called the Constitution "the best code ever drawn up, and I really don't see any need to tinker with it."

EARLIER TERRORIST ACTIVITIES. Even heavier television and print coverage had followed the Iranians' takeover of the U.S. Embassy in Tehran several years previously. The questions then asked: Did the media contribute unduly to the wave of anti-Iranian hysteria that swept the United States? Were they "used" by those holding the hostages, who were determined to focus American and worldwide attention on the crimes that they claimed had been perpetrated by the former Shah with the support of the United States government? One Department of State official called the whole affair a "tele-crisis." However, media spokespersons pointed out that the holding of hostages was news that had to be reported and that print and broadcast reporters provided almost the only informational link between Iran and the United States during that period.

Serious problems involving the media had arisen when Hanafi Muslims took control of the B'nai B'rith building in Washington, D.C., in 1977. News reports of a basket being lifted by rope to the fifth floor, where some people had evaded being taken hostage, were monitored by the Muslims and those hiding were discovered. Another report referred to Khaalis, the leader, as a Black Muslim. Khaalis, whose family had been murdered by Black Muslims, became enraged and threatened to kill the hostages in retaliation; he was pacified only when the reporter apologized. Another broadcaster reported that what appeared to be "boxes of ammunition" were being taken to the building in preparation for an assault. Fortunately, the terrorists did not hear this report, especially since the boxes contained food for the hostages.

Because publicity for a cause almost always is a major aim of terrorists, the media inevitably are drawn into such crises beyond their task of disseminating news. When a bomb goes off in a public place, at least one terrorist group invariably contacts a newspaper or broadcast station to claim responsibility. Sometimes, because lives are at stake, the media have no choice but to air grievances. Witness the front-page publication of reams of political material from the Symbionese Liberation Army after Patricia Hearst was kidnapped. Or consider the live broadcast in Indianapolis of the obscene verbal tirade by another kidnapper who had wired a shotgun to the head of his victim and demanded television time.

Calls for news blackouts also followed each of these incidents. "That's not serving the public's interest at all," CBS reporter Walter Cronkite replied. "All that it does is lead to rumor, speculation, to doubt that the press is telling the whole story under any circumstances." And Harold Kaufman, a professor of law

Coverage of bombings, hijackings, and kidnappings by terrorists involves difficult decisions by editors, who must try to cover the news without being used by the terrorists to circulate their propaganda.
(Pavolovsky/Sygma)

and psychiatry at Georgetown University, said he was persuaded that coverage of such events is helpful. "It allows whoever these people are to have some method of ventilating their anger and frustration, and making known their grievances," Kaufman said. "The more coverage is given, the more likely they are to see themselves as part of, rather than outside of, the system."

RESEARCH ABOUT TERRORISM. In 1986 about two dozen researchers in the United States and Canada were involved in a two-year study of the relationship between terrorism and the news media. The study was sponsored by the Mass Communications and Society Division of the Association for Education in Journalism and Mass Communication.

The project director, Professor Robert G. Picard of Louisiana State University, reported that his preliminary studies disclosed no credible evidence that media are an important factor in either inducing or diffusing terrorist acts. "As one reviews the literature," he wrote, "it becomes shockingly clear that not a single study based on accepted social science research methods has established a cause–effect relationship between media coverage and the spread of terrorism."

In 1977 the Task Force on Terrorism and Disorders had argued that, "The news media should devote more, rather than less, space and attention to the phenomena of extraordinary violence." If such coverage avoids glamorizing the perpetrators of violence, provides reliable information, and gives appropriate emphasis to the consequences of violence, it will increase public understanding, reduce public fear, and assist in reducing violence, the report indicated. Picard observed that this unproven theory, echoing Professor Kaufman's views, is unlikely to meet public favor.

As for the research project, Picard observed: "I suspect that we will find that media are a contributing factor in the spread of terrorism, just as easy international transportation, the easy availability of weapons and explosives, the intransigence of some governments' policies, the provision of funds to terrorists by a variety of supportive governments, and a host of other factors are to blame."

MEDIA SELF-REGULATION. Because the First Amendment precludes government censorship, media self-regulation appears to be the only feasible path to follow. After the TWA hostage crisis, media leaders were pleased that, by a stunning 66 percent to 28 percent margin in an ABC News–Washington *Post* poll, Americans expressed satisfaction with coverage of the 17-day ordeal. Nevertheless, the major media, which have always cooperated with legal authorities in voluntarily withholding salient information about crimes, checked aspects of their coverage against guidelines previously prepared. Americans have always demanded, and have a right to expect, thorough news coverage of all major happenings. In view of the competitive nature of the media, newspeople must continue to walk the tightrope between reporting and abetting terroristic activities.

OBSCENITY

Pornography in books, magazines, films, and cable television became big business during the 1960s and 1970s as sexual mores changed and a new permissiveness in regard to individual conduct permeated American society. At the same time serious works of art increasingly dealt with so-called adult themes and explicit sexual acts of every nature. The right to read and view what one desired conflicted with the opinions of those who felt that society had the innate right to proscribe such activities.

Obscenity, although a legal concept, is discussed in this chapter instead of Chapter 23 because of the difficulty in differentiating it from forms of pornography of broad social concern that are not considered obscene.

Obscenity usually is defined in terms of whether the materials are lewd, lascivious, prurient, licentious, or indecent. After more than three decades, however, the U.S. Supreme Court has been unable to draw firm legal lines as to what is obscene and what is not. Each of the nine justices has had his or her own definition ("I know it when I see it," declared Justice Potter Stewart), and until 1973 a majority could not agree on any one definition. Yet the Court maintained that certain materials are not protected by the First Amendment and that the government may suppress those materials. Recognizing the importance of safeguarding constitutional freedom, the Court in each decision has attempted to limit severely the kinds of materials that can be suppressed as obscene. The problem has remained, however, that fundamental First Amendment values have been encroached upon, and are in constant jeopardy, because all the Court definitions are, as three justices wrote in 1973, "so elusive that they fail to distinguish clearly between protected and unprotected speech."

For more than 70 years the so-called Hicklin rule, stemming from a landmark obscenity decision in England, was applied by courts in America. Under this rule published matter was regarded as obscene if isolated passages might be construed as depraving and corrupting even the most feebleminded reader. In a 1933 case involving the book *Ulysses* a U.S. judge said a better test would be the dominant effect of the entire book on the average reader, and the Supreme Court agreed.

In *Roth* v. *United States* (1957) the Supreme Court ruled that the standard for judging obscenity is "whether, to the average person, applying contemporary community standards, the dominant theme of the material, taken as a whole, appeals to the prurient interest." The Court ruled that obscenity is not within the area of constitutionally protected expression, declaring that, "All ideas having even the slightest redeeming social importance . . . have the full protection of the [constitutional] guaranties . . . but implicit in the history of the First Amendment is the rejection of obscenity as utterly without redeeming social importance."

To limit suppression of materials, the Court also declared: "Sex and obscenity are not synonymous . . . the portrayal of sex . . . is not itself sufficient reason to deny materials the constitutional protection of speech and press. Sex, a great and mysterious force in human life, has indisputably been a subject of absorbing interest to mankind through the ages; it is one of the vital problems of human interest and public concern."

In *Memoirs* v. *Massachusetts* (1966), involving the celebrated eighteenth-century novel *Fanny Hill,* the Court set forth a new definition of "obscene" wherein three elements must coalesce: "(1) that the dominant theme of the material taken as a whole appeals to a prurient interest in sex; (2) the material is patently offensive because it affronts contemporary standards relating to the description or representation of sexual matters; (3) the material is utterly without redeeming social value." The Court stressed that material must be "utterly"—unqualifiedly —worthless.

In *Miller* v. *California* (1973), however, the Court, in a five-to-four vote, revised its definition to "(1) whether the average person, applying contemporary community standards, would find that the work taken as a whole appeals to the prurient interest; (2) whether the work depicts or describes in a patently offensive way, sexual conduct specifically defined by the applicable state law; (3) whether the work taken as a whole lacks serious literary, artistic, political, or scientific value."

The *Miller* decision differed from the previous *Memoirs* test in three significant areas: First, community standards, as opposed to national standards, are to be used. The Court did not, however, specify what area it meant as "community." Second, the "utterly without redeeming social value" test became "lacks serious literary, artistic, political, or scientific value." This omits religious, entertainment, and educational genres and leaves more materials open to attack. Third, each state must specifically define the types of sexual conduct prohibited. Chief Justice Burger gave as an example: "(a) patently offensive representations or descriptions of masturbation, excretory functions, and lewd exhibition of the genitals; (b) patently offensive representations or descriptions of ultimate sexual acts, normal or perverted, actual or simulated."

In *Jenkins* v. *Georgia* (1974) the Court, ruling that the film *Carnal Knowledge* was not obscene, declared that "community standards" may be those of the state but do not necessarily have to be representative of any specific geographical boundary; they may be the jury's "understanding of the community from which they come as to contemporary community standards." On the other hand, the Court declared that juries do not have "unbridled discretion in determining what is 'patently offensive'" and may therefore be overruled on appeal (as here the decisions of the local and supreme courts of Georgia were reversed). The Court said that nudity alone is not obscene and prohibitions apply only to "public portrayal of hardcore sexual conduct for its own sake."

In 1987, in *Pope* v. *Illinois,* the Court largely reaffirmed the *Miller* ruling but voted, five-to-four, that judges and juries must assess the social value of the material from the standpoint of a "reasonable person," rather than apply community standards.

Pornography Commissions

As a result of the *Jenkins* ruling and another decision in 1974, the legislatures of almost every state set about revising their own obscenity laws. They did so in the light of the sexual revolution of the previous 20 years or so and the controversial report in 1970 of the Commission on Obscenity and Pornography, established by Congress. Concerning the effects of pornography, the commission declared:

> The conclusion is that, for America, the relationship between the availability of erotica and changes in sex-crime rates neither proves nor disproves the possibility that availability of erotica leads to crime, but the massive overall increases in sex crimes that have been alleged do not seem to have occurred. . . . In sum, empirical research designed

to clarify the question has found no evidence to date that exposure to explicit sexual materials is a factor in the causation of sex crime or sex delinquency.

In contrast to its recommendations affecting adults, the commission did recommend "legislative regulations upon the sale of sexual materials to young persons who do not have the consent of their parents." The commission was of the opinion, however, that only pictorial material should be legally withheld from children.

In 1986 a second such commission, appointed by former Attorney General William French Smith at the request of President Reagan, submitted an advisory report calling for a national assault on the pornography industry through a combination of more vigorous law enforcement and increased vigilance by citizens' groups.

In sharp contrast with the earlier report, the 11-member Commission on Pornography concluded that exposure to most pornography "bears some causal relationship to the level of sexual violence, sexual coercion or unwanted sexual aggression." Critics, including two commission members, contended that this conclusion was not based on firm scientific evidence, pointing out that social scientists are divided on whether most pornography is harmful.

In its 1960-page report the commission listed the titles of 2325 magazines, 725 books, and 1270 films found in "adults only" stores that it visited, and provided detailed, explicit descriptions of the activities depicted in some of those publications and films.

The commission urged concerned citizens to band together into "watch groups" to file complaints, put pressure on local prosecutors, monitor judges, and, if necessary, boycott merchants selling pornographic material. As reported in Chapter 8, a commission letter sent earlier to chain drug and convenience stores, suggesting that the owners might be cited in the report for distributing pornography, resulted in the removal of such magazines as *Playboy, Penthouse,* and *Forum* from hundreds of these establishments.

The commission rejected proposals to broaden the legal definition of obscenity, which embraces some but not all pornographic material. Instead, it said, current laws should be strengthened and enforced. In its report the commission used the word, "pornography," to mean material that is "sexually explicit and intended primarily for the purpose of sexual arousal."

Also rejected were proposals urging, on the basis of obscenity, prosecution concerning books that do not contain graphic pictures and drawings or focus on sexual abuse of children. Books consisting solely of printed text seem to be among the least harmful types of pornography, the panel said. The commission, however, recommended that booksellers be required to keep proof-of-age documents in child depictions. It also suggested the rewriting of an Indianapolis law, declared unconstitutional, that would have made publishers and booksellers liable for damages due to pornography, termed a form of discrimination on the basis of sex.

Although turning down proposals seeking regulation of movies with sexually explicit themes shown on cable television, the commission cited as harmful depictions of sex and violence on broadcast television, R-rated fare on cable TV, and X-rated movies distributed by satellite and home video. "Although the sexually violent material aired on network television is probably never legally obscene, the covering of breasts and genitals does not render the material any less harmful," the panel said.

The report recognized that cable operators, under the Cable Communications Act of 1984, are prohibited from airing obscene material and must, when asked, provide lock boxes to enable adults to prevent children from viewing certain channels. While critical of home video, the commission focused most of its attention on videos that may be legally obscene rather than on most of the adult videos found in neighborhood stores.

Numerous changes in federal and state laws were among the 92 recommendations, including curbs on the production, transmission, and possession of child pornography and sexually explicit material portraying violent abuse of women by men.

The report was widely praised as helpful in eliminating "the plague of pornographic pollution that has ravaged our society," as one group spokesperson put it. It was condemned by civil libertarian and other organizations and individuals as encouraging moral vigilantes—inviting inroads into First Amendment rights guaranteeing freedom of speech and the press. Attorney General Meese said it would not be used as a basis for censorship.

Several months later Meese established a Justice Department obscenity prosecution center to train prosecutors and advise local and state governments. He also created a task force of U.S. lawyers to help prosecute what Meese called "organized criminal enterprises" controlling pornography. Meese said laws would be sought to bar anyone under 21 years of age from performing in pornographic films, ban obscene cable TV programs, seize pornography sales proceeds, and end so-called "dial-a-porn" telephone services. The department planned to work with the National Center for Missing and Exploited Children to reduce exploitation through child pornography.

In 1987 a Media General-Associated Press poll found that most Americans believe pornography is not generally harmful to adults. According to the nationwide poll of 1402 adults, a majority oppose banning sexually explicit magazines in their communities. Most people, it was reported, seem to tolerate sexually related matter so long as it is kept under the counter or out of sight, and out of the hands of children.

Copies of the commission report may be obtained from the Government Printing Office, North Capitol and H Streets, N.W., Washington, D.C. 20401, or at its branches in various cities.

Other Obscenity Cases

Convictions for violating obscenity laws were relatively few during the years preceding the report. Between 1978 and 1986 only 100 people were indicted, and 71 convicted, of violating federal obscenity laws. Prosecutors took different approaches in seeking to obtain convictions.

It was on the grounds of the manner in which he advertised three publications —with "the leer of the sensualist"—that in 1966 the Supreme Court upheld the conviction of publisher Ralph Ginzburg for mailing obscenity. The publications were the magazine *Eros; Liaison,* a biweekly newsletter; and *The Housewife's*

Handbook of Selective Promiscuity. Ginzburg served eight months of a three-year sentence.

In 1976, rather than trying Al Goldstein and his copublisher of two magazines, *Smut* and *Screw,* in New York City, where they were published, the government brought suit in Wichita, Kansas, one of a number of cities to which the magazines were mailed and in which a more conservative jury presumably could be found. The two were convicted on 11 counts of using the mails to distribute obscene material, and on one count of conspiracy. The original conviction was thrown out because the prosecutor raised improper issues in his summation. The retrial was held in Kansas City, Kansas, where the jury was hung, nine to three, in favor of acquittal, and the case was later dismissed.

Actor Harry Reems earned $100 in Miami for one day's work in the movie *Deep Throat,* but suit was brought against him and his codefendants in Memphis, which he had never visited. His conviction on federal obscenity and conspiracy charges was overturned on the grounds that he had performed in the film before the *Miller* decision in 1973 and had been improperly tried by the standards of that case. The government decided not to retry him.

Larry Flynt published *Hustler* magazine in Columbus, Ohio, but was convicted by a Cincinnati, Ohio jury, on a misdemeanor charge of pandering and a felony charge of "engaging in organized crime." He was sentenced to 25 years in prison and fined $11,000 (and subsequently crippled by an assailant's gunfire during another obscenity trial in Lawrenceville, Georgia). Because *Hustler*'s content openly exceeded the limits set by competing sex-oriented magazines, many civil libertarians found it difficult to oppose the decision. A survey of the editors of men's and women's magazines disclosed, however, that more than three out of four considered the conviction a threat to their magazines' First Amendment rights.

Today "peepshow" movies, pornographic books, and magazines with explicit sexual content may still be found in most American cities. The courts, however, have upheld community zoning laws that provide either for dispersal of these establishments or their location in so-called erogenous zones, as may be found in large cities, and that also require that no such sexual materials may be viewed by passersby. As Charles Rembar wrote in an *Atlantic* magazine article, "Don't pluck my sleeve as I am passing by, stop poking your finger on my chest; freedom includes freedom from your assailing my senses . . . on theater marquees or posters, in storefront windows or newsstand displays." Protecting the privacy of consenting adults, seeking to prevent the exploitation of children in hardcore magazines and films, and restricting the dissemination of erotic material to children all seem to have the support of most Americans, including the staunchest First Amendment advocates.

SEX AND GOOD TASTE

Television

Not only violence, but also nudity, explicitly portrayed seductions, innuendoes, and obscene language—and more—have become common in the mass media and

American society during recent decades, pleasing some but offending others. The result is what sociologist and columnist Max Lerner has described as a sort of "Babylonian society," where almost anything goes.

Whereas magazines and books are directed to select audiences, mostly adult, and the audiences viewing motion pictures and plays in theaters may largely be controlled, free television enters practically every home and, of course, is viewed by young and old alike. The federal courts, however, have made distinctions that give cable wide latitude in program content. On grounds of vagueness or being too broad, the courts have struck down local ordinances for cable that sought to prosecute purveyors of what were regarded as obscenity, indecency, and profanity. There is a difference, say the courts, between cable, which subscribers buy and put into their own homes at their choice and cost, and broadcast television, which is so pervasive and unrestricted in its entry into the home that it must be held accountable to a higher standard of review. In 1987 the Supreme Court struck down a Utah law that restricted cable telecasts of nudity and sex acts that the state deemed "indecent" but that did not meet the Court's definition of obscenity.

The television industry developed its own Television Code of Good Practice and sought, with only mixed success, to follow its tenets. Adhering to the code, on a voluntary basis, was the primary responsibility of individual stations and networks. When parts of the code were held to violate antitrust laws in 1982, the National Association of Broadcasters suspended all its broadcasting code activities. Little change occurred, however, as the networks and stations continued their surveillance.

The department of broadcast standards of each network seeks to ensure that nothing is broadcast that exceeds generally accepted standards of public taste as represented by their huge national audiences. During a typical season, editors of each network make judgments on more than 2000 program outlines and scripts. They look at a variety of potential problems, including language, treatment of crime, use of narcotics, religious sensitivities, attitudes toward gambling and drunkenness, depiction of physical handicaps, the image of minorities, treatment of animals, and theatrical motion pictures and how they adapt to television. By far the most sensitive subjects are sex and violence.

Commercials also are closely examined. At ABC-TV, for example, editors review more than 50,000 submissions each year. In fact, of all new commercials received by ABC in 1984, more than one-third were rejected outright or returned for modification according to network commercial review standards. In 1985 NBC and CBS broadcast a public service TV announcement about preventing unintended pregnancies, but only after a reference to contraceptives was deleted. Network officals said that decisions about running commercials for contraceptives should be made by local stations, reflecting local community concerns.

In an effort to retain mass audiences while presumably downplaying violence, television producers during the late 1970s began to load situation comedies and dramas with scripts of an increasingly salacious nature, using themes such as pornography and sadomasochism, as well as suggestive dialogue. In so doing they seemed to be following the radically changed life styles of young people and many older persons as revealed by nationwide surveys of people's sexual habits such as those conducted by *Cosmopolitan* magazine. ABC's "Soap," "Three's Company," "Charlie's Angels," and several game shows led the way, followed in the 1980s by such shows as "Miami Vice" and "Hunter."

The Planned Parenthood Federation of America has long complained that network television programs promote sexual activity among teenagers without portraying the consequences. In 1986 the National Research Council voiced a similar concern. The council's report, based on a two-year study, stated that 1 million U.S. teenagers become pregnant each year and that the country's burden for taking care of these young mothers and children was about $16.6 billion in federal support in 1985. The council asked the networks to include mention of contraceptives in dramatic scenes in which sexual innuendos are made or when actors are seen in bed before or after sexual activity. Many persons, including some moral and religious groups, however, are strongly opposed to any mention of contraceptives.

Surveys have shown that sexual subject matter is acceptable to most viewers when it is presented with good taste and at times when children ordinarily are not watching. One survey found that people worry most about sexual themes that seem to impinge on the welfare of their children or their own concepts of normal family life. Some of the most strongly held opinions concerned child exploitation

Dancer Mikhail Baryshnikov, who defected from the Soviet Union, and his guest star Liza Minnelli, perform their version of the "Charleston" during a taping of his ABC-TV special. (AP/Wide World)

and homosexuality. Four out of five respondents, however, wanted to retain sex-related material on TV but at times when children were not watching, and with parents assuming responsibility. Few favored censorship, either by government or advertisers, although both were the objects of pressure from various organizations.

With only a few exceptions, such as an edited version of the movie *Midnight Cowboy,* commercial television has never shown X-rated movies. However, the popularity of hardcore films such as *Deep Throat* and softcore films such as the *Emmanuelle* series increased substantially with the advent of videocassettes, which could be shown in the privacy of one's home. In addition, some cable television stations showed so-called blue movies late at night, usually after midnight, and cable operations in a few metropolitan areas, notably New York City, provide facilities, as required by the FCC, for any person or group seeking access, and a few of the programs have bordered on public indecency. Even so, with its puritanical heritage, the United States has never witnessed such programming as is viewed in some other countries; for example, more than 150 private stations in Italy have presented hundreds of X-rated movies, striptease shows, nude exercise and sex-advice programs, and nude ballets.

Given the fact that television in the United States is constantly trying to please most of the people much of the time, without giving them more than they want, the medium has shown remarkable growth in intellectual freedom in recent years. Much of the maturation has gone virtually unnoticed because television has endeavored to keep pace with the reality of the nation's social growth. Twenty-five years ago subjects such as homosexuality, abortion, venereal disease, illegitimacy, incest, and adultery were unheard of in television drama. Today they are the focus of many intelligent and sensitive dramatic programs.

"Those of us in network television particularly do not wish to see a slowdown in the legitimate expansion of programming boundaries," said Herminio Traviesas, former vice-president in charge of broadcast standards for NBC-TV. "For while we do hear from our more conservative viewers, we also hear from the more liberal elements of our audience and, lest we forget, from the progressive people in the creative community. In a sense we are like Indians with our ears to the tube instead of to the ground. We are among the first to hear and witness new calls for greater freedom of expression. At the same time we are hearing complaints that television is going too far, too fast."

Radio

Profanity, obscenity, smut, and vulgarity are forbidden under the codes of conduct promulgated by the radio industry. Indeed, the Federal Communications Commission maintains a file of complaints against any such utterances and calls station managements to account at license renewal time if matters of sex and good taste have been violated.

When controversial "call-in" shows multiplied during the 1970s, a few stations encouraged late-night listeners openly to discuss their sex lives. This became known as "topless radio." Society's new permissive attitudes caused many listeners to accept such programs with equanimity; others were shocked. The industry in general and the FCC in particular, however, criticized instances of extreme verbal candor to such an extent that the practice has been abandoned except in such popular radio and cable television call-in shows as those of psychologist Dr. Ruth Westheimer, and in isolated instances of so-called "raunch radio," to be discussed shortly. One station, WGLD-FM, Oak Park, Illinois, was fined $2000 for broadcasting a call-in show on oral sex. The use of a device that delays the broadcast of telephoned observations for seven seconds, giving announcers time to delete offending remarks made by callers, has been a major help with call-in shows.

Station WBAI-FM, New York, was reprimanded by the FCC in 1978 for broadcasting George Carlin's "seven dirty words" comedy routine. The Supreme Court ruled that broadcasters do not have a constitutional right to air obscene words that apply to sex and excretion.

After receiving more than 20,000 protest letters, the FCC announced in 1987 that it would apply new rules to future decisions about "decency" on radio and television. The commission cited suggestive language used by so-called "shock radio" personality Howard Stern on WYSP-FM in Philadelphia, whose show was simulcast through WXRK-FM in New York and WBMW-FM in Fairfax, Virginia. Other targets included KCSB-FM, operated by students at the University of California at Santa Barbara, which aired sexually explicit rock songs; and WPFK-FM in Los Angeles, charged with broadcasting live talk show obscenities. Many station executives expressed apprehension at the increased involvement of the FCC in program content.

ROCK MUSIC. Rock music lyrics came under heavy attack in 1985 from the Parents' Music Resource Center and the Parent-Teachers Association. In a hearing before a Senate committee, the groups urged that a label of "R" (or even "X") be placed on records and tapes with lyrics that included explicit sexual language, profanity, or references to violence or the occult. The groups also wanted the lyrics of labeled music, as well as industry-wide guidelines, available to consumers before purchase. At issue were such albums as Bruce Springsteen's "Born in the U.S.A.," which includes the songs, "I'm on Fire" and "I'm Going Down."

In response, half of the 44 member companies of the Recording Industry Association of America, representing 80 percent of records released in the United States, agreed to urge the display of possibly objectionable lyrics on album covers or label the records, "Explicit Lyrics—Parental Advisory." For cassette tapes, which represent the majority of rock music sales, record companies may print, "See LP for Lyrics," on the tape box because there is often no space for lyrics on a cassette. No ratings would be made.

Some observers contended that the companies yielded partially to the pressure because of their vested interest in a pending House of Representatives bill (No. 2911) that would provide a 10 percent to 25 percent tax on taping devices and a penny-a-minute tax on blank tapes. The money would be allocated to the music publishers and record companies.

Accenting the parents' protests, a teenage fan of rock star Ozzy Osbourne shot himself to death with his father's gun in Los Angeles in 1986 after listening to a "death lullaby" of heavy-metal music. A lawsuit, later dismissed in court, contended that the lyrics of Osbourne's songs "Suicide Solution" and "Paranoid" helped push John McCollum, 19, over the brink to kill himself. He was still wearing stereo headphones when his body was found.

The Federal Communications Commission, although it has no jurisdiction over the recording industry, has warned broadcast stations that they would be held accountable for knowing the content of songs played on the air. Monitoring the records, however, has been no easy task.

Films

For many years criticism of commercial motion pictures focused on the artificial world they created. The vision of life presented in Hollywood films was far from everyday reality. It had excitement, glamour, romance, and comedy, but rarely paid attention to the perplexing problems of life. The filmmakers were selling noncontroversial entertainment featuring stars who had been made bigger than life by publicity. The major Hollywood studios, which dominated the market, had developed a successful formula and rarely deviated from it. Before television, they had no important rivals in presenting visual entertainment.

A factor that limited realism on the screen was the highly restrictive censorship code, conceived and enforced by the producers' association as a result of scandals that besmirched some silent film stars in the 1920s. Pressure from the Catholic Legion of Decency and other such groups strengthened enforcement of the code.

The taboos were so extreme that a husband and wife could not be shown together in the same bed. Mention of narcotics was forbidden. Criminals could not emerge as victors, although Hollywood made millions of dollars with gangster pictures full of violence by having the criminal lose at the last moment. A frequently heard claim that movies were intended for the mentality of a 12-year-old had much evidence to support it.

Shortly after World War II, the attitude in Hollywood began to change. The postwar world wanted more realism. Television's rapidly developing lure was keeping potential moviegoers at home. Filmmakers realized that they needed to alter their approach. More daring producers started making films that dealt with narcotics and contained suggestive sex scenes. They placed their products in theaters without the supposedly essential code seal of approval and drew large audiences.

Eventually enforcement of the code broke down completely. The growing permissiveness of American society emboldened the filmmakers; the increasingly frank films they released in turn contributed to the trend. Several U.S. Supreme Court decisions greatly broadening the interpretation of what was permissible under the obscenity laws speeded up the process. So did the success of films imported to this country, especially from Sweden. Although they were shown mostly in metropolitan "art" theaters, their impact on American filmmaking was intense.

The second half of the 1960s saw swift acceleration of boldness on the screen.

Nude scenes became commonplace. Sexual situations that had been only hinted at a few years earlier were shown explicitly. The imported Swedish film *I Am Curious (Yellow)* broke a barrier by showing actual scenes of sexual intercourse. Actors casually used language in films that was taboo in polite conversation a decade earlier. Films dealt openly with themes such as homosexuality. Greater liberality in these fields brought no reduction in the amount of violence shown, which was a major source of complaint by Europeans against American films. The complaints against motion pictures thus were reversed: Instead of being accused of sugar-coated blandness, they were charged with undue frankness. But with all its boldness, was American filmmaking being realistic? Many critics said no. They contended that, although sex and violence obviously existed, film producers were putting too much stress on them in order to cash in on shock value at the box office, and still were not coming to grips with the broader social problems of the country.

Anxious to preserve their profits from this new freedom and to prevent any government censorship moves, the Motion Picture Association of America adopted a new rating plan. Starting in 1968, each new Hollywood film was released bearing a code letter. This was to inform potential viewers what kind of picture to expect. The letter ratings are G—for general audiences, PG-13—special parental guidance urged for attendance of children under 13, PG—for adults and mature young people (parents should decide if their children should attend), R—restricted, those under 17 must be accompanied by a parent or adult guardian, and X—those under 17 not admitted.

Jack Valenti, president of the Motion Picture Association of America, has attempted to explain what determines each individual rating:

- G: *General audiences.* All ages admitted. This is a film which contains nothing in theme, language, nudity and sex, or violence that would be offensive to parents whose younger children view the film. . . . No words with sexual connotation are present in G-rated films. The violence is at minimum. Nudity and sex scenes are not present.
- PG-13: *Special parental guidance.* Parents are strongly cautioned to give special guidance for attendance of children under 13. Some material may be inappropriate for young children. (This rating category was added by the industry in 1984.)
- PG: *Parental guidance suggested.* Some material may not be suitable for pre-teenagers. . . . There may be profanity in these films but certain words with strong sexual meanings will vault a PG rating into the R category. There may be violence but it is not deemed excessive. Cumulative man-to-man violence or on-the-screen dismemberment may take a film into the R category. There is no explicit sex on the screen although there may be some indication of sensuality. Fleeting nudity may appear in PG-rated films, but anything beyond that point puts the film into R.
- R: *Restricted.* Under 17's require accompanying parent or guardian. . . . This is an adult film in some of its aspects and treatment of language, violence or nudity and sex. . . . The language may be rough, the violence may be hard,

and while explicit intercourse is not found in R-rated films, nudity and lovemaking may be depicted.

- X: *No one under 17 admitted. . . .* This is patently an adult film and no children are allowed to attend. It should be noted, however, that X does not necessarily mean obscene or pornographic. Serious films by lauded and skilled filmmakers may be rated X.

By using the code, the filmmakers placed the responsibility of censorship upon the audience, rather than upon themselves. They also discovered a profitable solution to competition from commercial television, which because of its home audience was more cautious in selection of material than theater operators were. As it turned out, relatively few G-rated and X-rated movies were produced. Audiences seemed to consider G-rated films "too tame." X-rated movies encountered two problems: the rating substantially reduced the number of moviegoers who could buy tickets and many newspapers refused to print advertisements for these films.

In 1984 the Motion Picture Association of America, in response to public

KILLINGS BY THE DOZEN

Gory violence, often committed in the causes of law and order and superpatriotism, was the dominant element in numerous hit motion pictures of the 1980s. Such behavior is a leading cause for films receiving R ratings.

Defenders of blood-and-death films contend that they merely reflect a tendency toward violence in the American character. Numerous sociologists and psychologists argue, however, that excessive violence in movies hardens audiences to the heedless taking of life and encourages viciousness.

A reviewer for the Los Angeles *Times* found that the movie *Cobra* starring Sylvester Stallone as a police lieutenant (1986) contained 67 violent deaths. The toll was 25 "good guys" and 42 "bad guys."

Good guy deaths included two women in cars by knifing, two men in a garage by axes; a hospital attendant, a nurse, and a bedridden patient by knives; a security guard in a garage smashed into a wall by a speeding car; a man in a supermarket and a security guard in a factory by guns; and 15 as victims of the Night Slasher.

Bad guys perished thus: two men in car on freeway by machine guns; four men by grenades; two killers outside Cobra's home by guns; one man in supermarket by Cobra's knife-gun combination; one run over by a truck; 27 on motorcycles by various guns; one set afire in factory by the flip of an electrical switch; one by fists; one drenched in gasoline and set afire by Cobra; one woman shot; one man beaten by Cobra, impaled on a gigantic hook, and incinerated.

complaints, toughened the ratings for language content. The single use of "one of the harsher, sexually derived words" now earns a movie a PG-13 label and repeated use of the worst four-letter epithets means an automatic R designation. In 1986 the association decreed that any movie that depicts any form of drug usage would be automatically rated PG-13, with the more restrictive X rating likely, depending upon the depiction of drugs in the film.

Undoubtedly the revolution in American films had made the films better related to the realities of life, more experimental and stimulating, and more influential in shaping the country's social patterns, especially among people under 30 years of age. (The rating system is also discussed in Chapter 14.)

MEDIA ETHICS

Criticism of the press has been commonplace in America since the publication of the first newspaper. However, ever since they gained widespread public attention as a powerful force not only reporting but also helping to shape the social and political upheavals of the 1960s and 1970s, the mass media have come under increasing attack for their perceived lapses in ethical and professional conduct. By almost any standard of measurement, the press today is more ethical and more responsible than in any previous period. Nevertheless, large money awards by unfriendly jurors in libel cases document some of the current public antipathy to the media. In this section we discuss some of the criticisms of media actions as well as the codes of ethics that have been established and the extent to which some of these codes apparently are enforced.

Criticism of Media Practices

Truth, honesty, and fairness are bedrock public expectations of all business and professional practitioners. But in poll after poll Americans rank the clergy, doctors, and police above mass communicators in terms of honesty and ethical standards. That was the finding, for example, of a poll reported by the American Society of Newspaper Editors in 1985. Television anchors achieved fourth place, the highest ranking for a communicator. Television reporters ranked sixth, newspaper editors seventh, and newspaper reporters eighth. Near the bottom of the list were advertising executives, just ahead of used car salespeople.

Among other perceived faults, the media are blamed for invading personal privacy, smearing reputations, practicing deception, unduly criticizing government and business leaders, emphasizing "bad news" over "good news" sensationalizing stories, reporting gossip and rumors, developing conflicts of interest, and failing to correct errors promptly and conspicuously or even admitting that mistakes had been made.

Extensive criticism followed the explosion of the Challenger shuttle in 1986. Some critics said safeguards were not taken in part because newspaper and television coverage had heavily and unfairly criticized delays in the launch. Leslie H. Gelb, a New York *Times* correspondent, wrote that, through its barrage of continuing TV and print reporting, the media, "almost without exception, quickly transformed tragedy into gruesome voyeurism and soap opera by its gross over-coverage." And when 300 reporters and camera operators converged on Concord, New Hampshire, to cover memorial services and to interview grieving family members and students of Christa McAuliff, the schoolteacher victim, George Wilson, publisher of the Concord *Monitor,* termed the spectacle "a very ugly scene . . . a classic horror show." These perceived lapses in media judgment and taste echoed those accompanying coverage of the terrorist hijacking of TWA Flight 847 only a half-year before, as discussed previously in this chapter.

The Miami *Herald* was accused of unethical conduct after it reported in May 1987 that Democratic presidential candidate Gary Hart had spent the night with a young woman, precipitating Hart's withdrawal from the race five days later. Hart angrily denied the report, denounced the *Herald* for spreading "false" information, and accused the media of harassing people in public life. Many criticized the paper for basing its account on a non-thorough stakeout of Hart's Washington, D.C., residence and for printing the story hurriedly against a deadline without giving Hart a full chance to explain himself. Others questioned the propriety of media inquiries into a candidate's sex life. A number of editors defended the *Herald*'s action as legitimate, coming as it did on the heels of widespread accounts of Hart's social activities including a report in *Newsweek* magazine that Hart "had been haunted by rumors of womanizing." Said Heath J. Meriwether, executive editor of the *Herald:* "We think the issues raised by our stories are germane to any consideration of a presidential candidate."

Condemned by mass communicators and the public alike are deceptive practices such as fabricating stories, quoting nonexistent sources, impersonating people when other means to obtain a story could be used, plagiarizing, unexpectedly confronting persons being interviewed on television with accusations, and preoccupation with dramatic TV or still pictures at the expense of accuracy and fairness.

Washington *Post* reporter Janet Cooke admitted that her sensational account of "Jimmy," an 8-year-old heroin addict, was a hoax, prompting her dismissal and the return of a Pulitzer Prize. Darrow "Duke" Tully resigned as publisher of the *Arizona Republic* and *Phoenix Gazette* after admitting that for more than 30 years he had lied about being a decorated Air Force pilot with extensive combat service in Korea and Vietnam. Writer Michael Daly admitted that he had used questionable journalistic techniques in "300 columns over two years." Revelations of fraud based upon the incognito operation of a Chicago bar, "The Mirage," by a team of Chicago *Sun-Times* reporters won some acclaim but not a Pulitzer Prize because of some judges' objections to the method employed. These are only a few of innumerable examples of deception troubling editors and the public alike.

Conflicts of interest, such as using unpublished information for financial gain and accepting gifts from news sources, represent another area of ethical concern. In 1985 R. Foster Winans was found guilty of "insider trading" under the Securities Act of 1934 when he "leaked" advance word of his *Wall Street Journal* columns to a stockbroker. A number of journalism organizations, although not condoning Winans's breach of journalistic ethics, argued unsuccessfully that extending "insider trading" prohibitions to journalists intruded into First Amendment rights of free speech.

In 1986 approximately 5000 media representatives accepted an expenses-paid trip to Disney World for an $8 million, 15th anniversary party outside Orlando, Florida. Some print and broadcast people paid their own way. The Society of Professional Journalists, Sigma Delta Chi, condemned the acceptance of gratuities as "a breach of ethical conduct that inescapably creates the appearance of journalists being bought in return for favorable publicity."

PHOTOGRAPHS. Although many newspaper editors defend their use, photographs of tragic events such as a drowning almost invariably evoke protests from readers on grounds of poor taste and invasion of privacy. Artificially contrived photographs also pose ethical problems as critics equate truthfulness in photojournalism with honesty in reporting.

MAGAZINES. Magazines, of course, also experience ethical problems, such as the acceptance by staff members of free tickets and trips, the occasional use of composite characters and fictional situations to make a point in articles, and editorial-advertising collaboration. Freelancers sometimes are paid by companies for stories submitted in their behalf.

TELEVISION AND RADIO. Television programs that feature heroes and villains drawn from the toy-store shelf or developed in conjunction with the marketing of goods unfairly exploit children, the American Academy of Pediatrics (AAP), a Congressional committee chairman, and a consumer group charged in 1986. "What the shows do is hook kids into these program-length commercials that in fact offer an engaging story but are designed to sell the product," Dr. William H. Dietz, chairman of the AAP's task force on children and television, said.

On different ethical grounds critics complain that radio stations, and to a lesser extent television stations, have reduced the amount of air time devoted to public affairs and news programming as a result of federal deregulation and the industry's changing economics. TV news coverage has been criticized for "its superficiality, its choppy brevity for fear of dial turners, its preoccupation with visual excitement (fires, hurricanes, riots)," as *Time* magazine's Thomas Griffith put it. Television production executive Norman Lear, at a Boston conference on TV and ethics, charged that, "The manufacturers of television entertainment, news and public affairs proceed with very little consideration for the ethics involved. . . . Commercial television's north star, from which nearly all bearings are set, is quite simply, 'How do I win Tuesday night at 8 o'clock?' "

The litany of complaints about media ethical violations seemingly is endless. When the subject arises, nearly everyone, it seems, is eager to attest to some media failing.

Codes of Ethics

Standards of professional conduct were strengthened after the harsh public distrust of all institutions—including the news media—that buffeted the nation during the Watergate era and that still widely persists.

Sensing the public mood, the Associated Press Managing Editors Association (APME), even before Watergate, began to examine influences on the probity of the press. The report of the APME professional standards committee in 1972 was the first salvo in what turned out to be a barrage of attention to the problem of media ethics.

The APME sent Carol Sutton of the Louisville *Courier-Journal* to report on the extent of gratuities received by the press during three fashion events in New York and Montreal. Two weeks later she returned with a new canvas suitcase filled with what her newspaper colleagues termed "loot" and "goodies"—assorted cosmetics, jewelry, tote bags, and other objects—along with a report of countless other gratuities offered at these events. She returned all the gifts she could and gave others to charity, in line with the Louisville newspapers' long-standing policy against the acceptance of gifts by staff members.

The Detroit *News* discovered that during one year alone at least $56,000 worth of free gifts and services were offered to its staff members. *New York* magazine reported on the receipt by media news staff members of free tickets to events at Madison Square Garden and the influence of public relations people with the New York *Times*.

The model for modern codes of ethics is the Canons of Journalism, established in 1923 by the American Society of Newspaper Editors. Accuracy, fair play, and responsibility are its hallmarks.

The Society of Professional Journalists, Sigma Delta Chi (SPJ, SDX) adopted the ASNE code as its own in 1926. Then, in 1973, SPJ, SDX broke new ground with the introduction of a new code of ethics. Two years later, APME and the National Conference of Editorial Writers adopted codes of their own. Other organizations either did likewise or closely examined standards they had previously established. In addition, more than 80 percent of the large newspapers spelled out rules of conduct for their staffs.

The foreword to the code of fair publishing practices adopted in 1955 by the Catholic Press Association points out that: "Like all promises, the code can be as effective as the will and determination of the members of the association make it. . . . But if it is not reaffirmed by practice and conduct it can become only an empty statement, a pledge ignored and a promise forgotten and broken. . . ." Moral law, it added, undergirds all such codes.

The code of the National Press Photographers Association affirms, in part, that: "It is the individual responsibility of every photojournalist at all times to strive for pictures that report truthfully, honestly, and objectively." The code ends with the statement: "No code of ethics can prejudge every situation; thus common sense and good judgment are required in applying ethical principles."

The code adopted in 1966 by the Radio Television News Directors Association is regarded as much more stringent than the former radio and television codes of the National Association of Broadcasters, which were criticized as containing "weak, ambiguous, evasive, and permissive language." The NAB codes, as previously stated, were abandoned after antitrust action in 1982, leaving the promulgation of standards largely in the hands of individual stations and the networks.

A study of journalists' opinions about gratuities, conducted by Keith P. Sanders and Won H. Chang of the University of Missouri School of Journalism, revealed "a strong regard for individual professionalism, a general distaste for freebies, a rejection of freebies as essential, and a general support for the SPJ, SDX code of ethics."

The respondents rated highest the statement: "A professional journalist, secure in himself and his understanding of his public trust, will report honestly not because of a code, but because of what he is and believes."

The APME's professional standards committee studied approximately 50 separate ethics codes adopted by individual newspapers. "None of the [survey] respondents expressed any negative thoughts about the wisdom of codes of ethics, either written or unwritten," the committee reported. "Most believe they are necessary to set a tone of behavior for all staffers while understanding that not every situation be specifically addressed in a code."

Journalists and journalism educators have mixed feelings about codes of ethics. Most media people seem to maintain that codes are useful as standards against which to measure their own value systems; others, steeped in the individualistic tradition, take a cavalier attitude toward codes, supporting conscience and principle but disdaining formalized strictures. An SPJ, SDX survey that included newspaper and broadcast news personnel disclosed in 1983 that a considerable tightening of ethical standards and practices had taken place during the preceding decade.

A study of the ethical views of more than 200 Chicago area journalists, conducted by Professor David Gordon of the University of Miami, revealed strong support for ethical behavior, with a slight plurality in favor of enforced codes. More than one-fifth of the respondents, however, said that ethical principles do not play a very large role in their professional lives. As might be expected, the journalists supported most strongly the statements that "freedom of the press is to be guarded as a vital right of mankind" and that "every journalist should be concerned with truthfulness, accuracy, and decency in his reporting."

Those who attack codes of ethics maintain, among other things, that the codes often contain internal contradictions, are poorly written, unwisely tend toward consensus thinking on the part of practitioners, and are largely products of management or organizations dominated by "management types," which, as Professor Richard A. Schwarzlose of Northwestern University states it, "tend to focus on things reporters cannot do (as a protection for corporate and product credibility), rather than on ways of uplifting the reporters' self-image."

It is evident that, because of substantial public concern, communication ethics will continue to be a hotly debated subject and schools of journalism and mass communications increasingly will seek better ways of sensitizing their students to the ethical decisions they must face as practitioners.

Enforcement of Ethical Codes

NEWSPAPERS. At least 48 newspaper journalists were fired and 30 suspended for ethical violations during 1983–1985, according to an informal survey by the ethics committee of the American Society of Newspaper Editors. Responses in the mail survey were received from 226 editors.

"Ethics violations ranged from sports copy editors who were making book on the newspaper's telephones to plagiarism to out-and-out fabrication of a story," the committee report stated. "The extent of unethical behavior is disturbing."

More than one of every three editors reported that at least one ethics violation had occurred at their papers during the three years. A total of 240 ethics violations were reported by the 122 correspondents who answered the question. Eleven papers reported six or more violations during the period.

The other findings were summarized as follows:

- About one of six editors said at least one newsroom employee had been dismissed because of ethics violations during the three years. Another 11 percent said at least one employee had been suspended for an ethics violation during the period.
- Slightly more than a third—37 percent—of the editors said they had a written code of ethics. More than half—54 percent—said they did not. Four percent said they were preparing one and 6 percent did not answer the question.
- An overwhelming majority of editors—87 percent—at papers with written codes of ethics said the code included exceptions. Among them: review tickets, tickets to sports events, and freelance work approved by a supervisor.
- Almost three of 10 editors at papers with written codes said the code included penalty provisions.
- Four percent of the editors said their papers require employees to sign a stock disclosure form.
- Half of the editors said their code applied only to the newsroom. (The survey did not, however, ask whether the business side had a separate code of ethics.)
- Five percent of the editors surveyed said they had a separate code of ethics for business reporters and editors.
- Plagiarism, using unpublished information for financial gain, and discounts for personal purchases made from companies the reporter or editor handled generally were viewed as the most serious ethical violations of those listed.
- Spouses owning stock in companies a reporter covers, and social relationships between newsroom personnel and newsmakers, were viewed as representing minor or no ethical problems.
- Social contacts between reporters, editors, and newsmakers, as well as reporters who rewrote competitors' stories without verifying any information, were the most frequently encountered situations of those listed.

MAGAZINES. A "rather dramatic shift of journalistic values" from those found in studies 10 years earlier was reported in 1985 by Professor Ralph Izard of Ohio University and Professor Vicki Hesterman of the University of Georgia. Their more recent surveys were answered by almost 2000 reporters, editors, and other members of the Associated Press Managing Editors Association, Radio Television News Directors Association, and the Society of Professional Journalists, Sigma Delta Chi.

Izard and Hesterman reported:

> While significant progress has been made in the last ten years toward developing more standard principles of news media performance, discrepancies still exist. Some journalists are allowed to receive free gifts; most are not. Some papers and stations will use the names and addresses of all crime victims; some will not. Some approve deception on occasion; some do not.
>
> In spite of these expected differences, a rather dramatic shift of journalistic values is indicated. . . . Journalists no longer believe that their search for information is unrestricted. They are much closer to those issues that are of importance to American citizens—such as individual privacy, public decency, basic honesty, and fair play.

Magazine journalists disagree significantly on how they would handle specific ethical dilemmas, Hesterman found in a survey of consumer magazine editors reported in 1986. Forty-nine of 100 editors responded to her questionnaire.

> Some take free trips, some take free tickets, some allow composite characters, some experience editorial–advertising collaboration. . . . Considering the fact that consumer magazines comprise a mere fraction of the magazine industry . . . arriving at any kind of a common code will probably not be a simple process.

PUBLIC RELATIONS. The Public Relations Society of America (PRSA) is the only professional communications organization that has created a grievance procedure taking action against members on ethical grounds. By 1986 approximately 165 complaints, mainly charging account piracy and job infringement, had been heard. Of these, the society warned two members, censured three, suspended two, and expelled two. PRSA's most notorious case occurred in 1986 when its national president, Anthony M. Franco, a Detroit counselor, was accused of improper insider trading by the Securities and Exchange Commission. Franco signed a consent decree and resigned his presidency and, later, his PRSA membership (see Chapter 18).

The International Association of Business Communicators, comprised mainly of publications editors and information specialists, has a generalized code of standards but no formalized grievance procedure. According to one member, the code "simply tells us to go out and do good." Norman G. Leaper, president, said the few letters of complaint received mainly concerned plagiarism.

News Councils

With the financial aid of the Don R. Mellett Fund of the Newspaper Guild, community news councils were established during the late 1960s in several states including California, Oregon, Illinois, and Colorado. The councils, composed of both public and media representatives, were intended to provide a forum for public criticism of the media and to enable editors and managers to respond. The idea, however, met with only limited success. Today, only the statewide Minnesota News Council and the Honolulu Media Council are in operation. In 1985 the Kentucky Press Association rejected a proposal to establish a news council.

Similar media and public lassitude marked the 10½-year operation of the National News Council. Creation of the council was recommended in 1973 by the

Twentieth Century Fund Task Force "to make press freedom more secure by providing an independent forum for debate about media responsibility and performance, so that such debate need not take place in government hearing rooms or on the political campaign trail."

With the support of eight foundations, the council began operation on August 1, 1973, as an objective, expert body, without sanctions, whose functions were (1) to examine complaints, (2) to speak out on press freedom issues, and (3) to analyze recurring problems of journalistic ethics. Similar news councils exist throughout the world. The oldest, the Swedish Press Council, was established in 1916 and the British Press Council, one of the best known, was formed in 1953.

The council, with headquarters in New York City, was gradually expanded in membership to include 18 widely known public and media leaders. They included such people as Richard S. Salant, former president of CBS News; Lucy Wilson Benton, former Under Secretary of State for Science and Technology and former president of the League of Women Voters; and Elie Abel, a professor of journalism at Stanford University, who represented the United States on UNESCO's International Commission for the Study of Communication Problems (see Chapter 25). Its paid staff, headed by William B. Arthur, former editor of *Look* magazine, grew to include four full- and part-time employees. Annual operating expenditures often exceeded $300,000.

The council examined and reported on complaints from individuals or organizations concerning the accuracy and fairness of news reporting by the national print and broadcast organizations, and by local news organizations if the matter in question were of national significance as news or for journalism. Complaints about editorial expression or personal opinion were not accepted unless the facts were in dispute. The council did not regulate or impose penalties; its only strength lay in the force of public opinion. In addition, the council issued "white papers" dealing with a wide variety of ethical problems confronting the media.

Media reaction was mixed, with only 40 or so news organizations helping to fund the council's operations. Proponents maintained that the council enhanced media credibility and effectively dealt with public complaints before they could translate themselves into a push for government controls detrimental to freedoms provided by the First Amendment. Opponents argued that the media already are criticized sufficiently by readers, viewers, and professional groups and that the council could be a forerunner of government control.

The council received varying levels of cooperation. In almost all instances, editors and news directors responded to requests for information adequately enough to enable the council, augmented by its own research, to act on complaints. A notable exception was the New York *Times,* but even so the council was able to reach decisions on 22 complaints against the newspaper, of which 7 were found warranted, in whole or in part, and 11 unwarranted; 4 were dismissed. On several occasions the council, with permission from a top editor, was able to discuss complaints with *Times* reporters.

Of the 249 complaints considered by the council, 35 percent were found fully or partially warranted and 49 percent unwarranted; 15 percent were dismissed; and 1 percent were withdrawn. Thirty-two percent of all complaints brought before the full council were against television networks, with 63 percent found unwarranted and 23 percent warranted. Complaints against newspapers totaled 29 percent of all handled, with 43 percent unwarranted and 49 percent warranted.

Reports of the complaints and the decisions reached were published in the *Columbia Journalism Review* and, later, *The Quill,* but were disseminated only sporadically or incompletely by the commercial media; as a result, even voracious consumers of news—print and broadcast—knew little or nothing about the council's work. "We were never able to build a public constituency," said President Salant. Lacking visibility and hobbled by lack of funds and "far too small a staff assigned to do too much," the news industry's watchdog ended its existence on March 31, 1984. Its files, records, and resources were turned over to the University of Minnesota's Walter Library for scholarly use.

EMPLOYMENT OF MINORITIES AND WOMEN

As is true with most American industries and professions, almost all of the print and broadcast media, filmmaking, advertising, and public relations companies in the United States are controlled by white males.

Leaders of many minority and women's groups contend that, as a consequence, the public gets a distorted or incomplete view of American life. After all, minority groups point out, the 1980 U.S. census showed that 12 percent of the population is black and 6 percent is Hispanic, but that these ratios are not reflected in the number of persons who make media decisions. Women professionals simply point to the relative scarcity of females in high-level positions.

At the heart of the issue, in the opinion of advocates of change, is power—the ability, through the employment of more women, blacks, and Hispanics in top-management positions, to help ensure a relatively even-handed and fair portrayal in the media of all social groups.

Women and minority group representatives have risen to prominence in the mass media in recent years. Among them is Connie Chung, an NBC-TV anchor. (AP/Wide World)

More than a dozen witnesses at a congressional hearing in 1983 complained that minorities are denied roles in many TV programs, are badly portrayed in others ("The Jeffersons" was cited as one example), and are systematically excluded from executive media positions. Nancy Hicks, former president of the Institute for Journalism Education, a minority training organization, summed up the viewpoint of many blacks: "The story so far has been, lamentably, [the portrayal of] minorities [as] less intelligent and more violent than whites, less hard-working and more inclined to take handouts than whites, less serious and a lot keener about drugs than whites, less able but on the whole better basketball players than whites." Since that time the success of the Bill Cosby Show, portraying Cosby as the physician-father of an upper-middle-class black family, has done much to dispel that view.

After the Kerner Commission expressed the opinion, following the shocking city riots of 1968, that inadequate coverage of the black community was partly to blame for the riots (see Chapter 22), both print and broadcast media set out to improve the situation.

Since then the number of minority journalists on newspapers has grown from about 400 to more than 3600 Asian Americans, blacks, Hispanics, and Native Americans, representing approximately 6.56 percent of a workforce of 54,700, according to a 1987 report of the American Society of Newspaper Editors (ASNE). Minority personnel occupied 13 percent of newsroom supervisory positions, an increase of 4 percent since 1985. The number of newspapers with no minority newsroom employees had dropped from 60 percent in 1984 to 56 percent in 1987.

During the eight previous years, recruitment efforts of the newspaper industry had concentrated mainly on a campaign by ASNE and the Association for Education in Journalism and Mass Communication (AEJMC) to achieve, by the year 2000, minority representation in newsrooms proportionate to that of the general population, a figure expected by that year to be 29 percent. Progress, however, was embarrassingly slow.

The campaign was broadened in 1985 when the newspaper industry as a whole began a concerted effort to recruit additional hundreds of minority personnel to work in all departments of newspapers. Twenty-nine organizations established an industry-wide Task Force on Minorities in the Newspaper Business. Aided in part by a five-year, $500,000 program begun by the American Newspaper Publishers Association Foundation, job fairs were held throughout the country, bringing together recruiters and minority prospects; newspapers planning minority programs were given detailed advice; high school recruiting was intensified; more scholarship and seminar programs were created; and a national newsletter was established. Publishers of several major dailies began demanding, not simply encouraging, the hiring of minority personnel.

The Society of Professional Journalists, Sigma Delta Chi, reported that during its two years' existence, 4629 calls were made on a toll-free number for minority persons interested in journalism careers. Callers received a brochure, and their names were forwarded to media organizations.

At the same time minority organizations accelerated their own efforts. They included the National Association of Black Journalists, Native American Press

Association, National Association of Hispanic Journalists, Asian-American Journalists Association, and the Institute for Journalism Education.

Both racial minorities and women have been aided by federal equal opportunity regulations regarding hiring, promotion, and pay. Class action suits have been partially responsible for improved conditions for women employees of some newspapers. As part of the settlement of a discrimination suit filed by the Wire Service Guild and seven female employees, the Associated Press agreed to pay $500,000 in legal fees and expenses and $1.5 million in back-pay to women and blacks employed between November 1972 and June 1983. In addition, the AP established a five-year affirmative action program for blacks and women. In 1987 a federal jury found that the New York *Daily News* had discriminated against four of its black employees between 1979 and 1982 by giving them fewer promotions, less desirable assignments, and lower salaries than were granted to white journalists with comparable experience and qualifications. The out-of-court settlement was reported to total about $3 million.

Of the more than 7500 film and television members of the Directors Guild of America, only about 160 are black. Of these, about 145 are directors and the others mainly assistant directors and production managers. Only a handful of black guild members make a living from their craft. Thomas Carter, who directed the "Miami Vice" pilot and won a 1985 Directors Guild award for a "Hill Street Blues" episode, said, "There really has been no entree for blacks into the business, except as performers. Part of the problem is that black people have not been around the film industry as a culture. They have not seen many role models behind the camera."

In 1985, women public relations specialists constituted 48.7 percent of the field, blacks 7.4 percent, and Hispanics 3.1 percent, according to the Bureau of Labor Statistics. Forty-eight percent of the members of the Public Relations Society of America in 1987 were women. The problems of minorities and women seem to be endemic to other mass media as well. An annual study conducted in 1985 by Professor Vernon A. Stone of the University of Missouri for the Radio Television News Directors Association revealed that women constituted almost a third of the broadcast news workforce at commercial radio and TV stations, while members of minority groups held about 1 of every 10 news jobs at the stations. Women were news directors at 21 percent of the radio stations but at only 10 percent of the TV stations, and minorities constituted only 3 percent of each. The FCC reported that in 1985 women constituted 29.7 percent, and minorities 10.2 percent, of broadcast executives.

Women held only 12.4 percent of the directing-editor jobs on U.S. dailies and Sunday newspapers listed in the 1986 *Editor & Publisher International Year Book,* Dorothy Jurney, a retired ASNE member, reported. This compares with 5 percent in 1977, when Jurney began her annual tabulation. However, it was far below the 32.4 percent of women executives in business and industry reported by the Bureau of Labor Statistics for 1984.

In fact, Jurney said, 37 more men were added in that year to the list of executives on newspapers exceeding 250,000 circulation, whereas the number of women dropped from 30 to 29, leaving them only 7.4 percent of the share of the field. Paraphrasing remarks about scientists made by Professor Stephen Jay Gould of Harvard University, Jurney said, "We desperately need more women as equal companions in this effort, not because the culture of feminism grants deeper vision but because we need as many good journalists with broad and deep vision as we can get."

Kay Mills, editorial writer for the Los Angeles *Times,* has cited one facet of the role of women in policy-forming positions. "I can point to many editorials that I know simply would not be in the *Times* if I were not there—either because the men are not in the network to hear of the issues emerging, or don't think they rank with cosmic world affairs when they do hear of them."

Because women constitute about 60 percent of total enrollments in journalism and mass communications schools, a percentage that increases each year, the influence of women in mass communications undoubtedly will increase. With minority students comprising only about 8 percent of school enrollments, the prospect for increased minority influence is not so bright.

ORGANIZATIONS SEEKING MEDIA IMPROVEMENT

Almost every mass communicator in the country either is a member of one or more journalism and mass communications associations or is represented by the organization for which he or she works. Generally, the managers fulfill institutional membership responsibilities and staff communicators belong to craft organizations. Thousands are active in local associations. The purposes of almost every organization are to interchange ideas for the advancement of professional ideals and to work collectively for the solution of common problems.

TRADE ASSOCIATIONS. One group is composed of the various trade associations. For newspapers there are the American Newspaper Publishers Association, representing the dailies; the National Newspaper Association, for weeklies and small dailies; the National Newspaper Publishers Association, serving the black press; and other groups, including the International Circulation Managers' Association, International Newspaper Marketing Association, International Newspaper Promotion Association, and Suburban Newspapers of America, Inc. There are also strong regional associations—Inland Daily Press Association, Southern Newspaper Publishers Association, New England Daily Newspaper Association, Western Newspaper Foundation, Northwest Daily Press Association—and state associations (usually emphasizing the concerns of weeklies). All issue publications of one sort or another, the most notable being ANPA's *presstime.*

The trade associations for other media include the National Association of Broadcasters, Magazine Publishers Association, Association of American Publishers, Motion Picture Association of America, Association of Business Publishers, American Association of Advertising Agencies, and American Advertising Federation.

Each trade association speaks for its industry in affairs of general interest to the members. The staffs represent the industries when necessary at congressional hearings and before other government organizations. The associations develop promotional materials for their media and operate central offices that act as clearinghouses for information about the industries. The daily newspapers organized a Bureau of Advertising that promotes their media; the Magazine Advertising Bureau, Radio Advertising Bureau, and Television Information Bureau do the same in their fields. The National Association of Broadcasters, Motion Picture Association of America, American Society of Magazine Editors, and American Association of Advertising Agencies have developed codes of conduct. Although they are primarily concerned with business matters, many of the associations sponsor discussions aimed at improving their media and encourage individual activities to raise the standards of members.

ORGANIZATIONS OF INDIVIDUALS. There are also groups of editors and writers. Most prominent is the American Society of Newspaper Editors (ASNE), limited primarily to editors, editorial page editors, and managing editors of dailies of 50,000 or more circulation. ASNE's convention proceedings are reproduced in book form in the *Problems of Journalism* series. The monthly ASNE *Bulletin* analyzes problems confronting editors and the press.

The National Conference of Editorial Writers meets annually in sessions providing small-group critiques of editorial pages. It publishes a quarterly, the *Masthead,* and has a code of principles "to stimulate the conscience and the quality of the American editorial page." The Associated Press Managing Editors Association (APME) continually studies the AP news report, each year publishes the *APME Red Book* reporting on committee findings and convention sessions, and has drawn up a code of ethics. The International Society of Weekly Newspaper Editors meets annually, publishes the quarterly *Grassroots Editor,* and presents a Golden Quill award for outstanding work in the weekly field.

The Radio Television News Directors Association has sought to elevate standards through adoption of a code of principles and has been instrumental in advancing the position of news and public affairs broadcasting in the industry. The International Association of Business Communicators serves writers, editors, audiovisual specialists, managers, and other business and organizational communicators. The Public Relations Society of America, the largest national group of public relations people, sets standards for its more than 13,000 members. All of these groups issue magazines.

The American Academy of Advertising brings together educators and practitioners in annual meetings and publishes the *Journal of Advertising.* The Business and Professional Advertising Association is also active in this field.

The Newspaper Guild has done much to improve the standards of the newspaper business through the raising of salaries and has attempted to carry out programs of self-improvement. Its publication is the *Guild Reporter.* Membership primarily consists of workers in larger daily newspapers and the news services. Its role as a trade union is discussed in greater detail in Chapter 6.

There are other groups: the Society of Professional Journalists, Sigma Delta Chi (previously discussed) and Women in Communications, Inc., both almost 80 years old and both operating chapters for working journalists as well for college students; Pi Delta Epsilon, honorary collegiate journalism fraternity; Kappa Tau

Alpha, journalism scholastic society; AAF/ADS, professional advertising society; Pi Alpha Mu, professional fraternity for men and women in the publishing, advertising, and journalistic management fields; Di Gamma Kappa and Alpha Epsilon Rho, professional broadcasting organizations; and the Public Relations Student Society of America. Most of them issue publications, *The Quill* of the Society of Professional Journalists being the best known.

CENTERS, INSTITUTES, AND ACTION GROUPS. Almost a dozen such organizations have been established in recent years. Some of these groups are providing legal and other aid for investigative journalists (Reporters Committee for Freedom of the Press, and Center for Investigative Reporting), encouraging print and broadcast media to improve their accuracy (Accuracy in Media, Inc.), advancing the cause of female journalists and teachers (Women's Institute for Freedom of the Press), helping high school students and teachers in press freedom causes (Student Press Law Center), and bolstering press freedom throughout the world (World Press Freedom Committee).

The American Press Institute has conducted seminars for newspaper people for many decades.

The Poynter Institute for Media Studies publishes books and provides fellowships for journalism students and professors. In cooperation with the American Society of Newspaper Editors, the institute each year offers seminars for news writing and editing instructors. Other seminars include those for teachers of newspaper graphics and video graphics and design. The institute was founded by the late Nelson Poynter, longtime publisher of the St. Petersburg *Times* and is directed by his hand-picked successor, Eugene Patterson.

The Gannett Center for Media Studies at Columbia University, established by the Gannett Foundation in 1985, publishes the *Gannett Center Journal,* and provides advanced study of mass communication and technological change for media professionals, journalism educators, and scholars from other fields through more than a dozen annual fellowships of three months to a year's duration. Gannett also makes monetary awards to schools of journalism and mass communications.

The Center for Communication, operating from both New York City and Washington, D.C., helps practitioners keep university students and professors up-to-date on communications development. Seminar videotapes are widely distributed. The center is supported by major newspaper and broadcast organizations.

In 1985 Harvard University opened a Center for Press, Politics, and Public Policy in its John F. Kennedy School of Government.

In the same year DePauw University established the Center for Contemporary Media, which, through workshops and seminars, seeks to foster an understanding of how the media collect, analyze, produce, and disseminate news and information. The multi-million-dollar gifts creating the center also provide an endowed scholarship program for outstanding high school seniors.

In 1986 the Freedom of Information Center at the University of Missouri, in operation since 1958, ended its publications program and, except for hundreds of thousands of clippings, transferred its voluminous holdings to the university's main library. The center's former *FOI Digest* became a section in the 3800-circulation *Investigative Reporters and Editors Journal,* published at the school.

The International Newspaper Advertising and Marketing Executives Foundation spends about $100,000 annually in strengthening the teaching of newspaper advertising in communications and business schools.

OTHER AID PROGRAMS. Since 1965, in a broad-based program designed to increase the number of competent journalists, the Ford Foundation has granted millions of dollars for postgraduate journalism education. The projects include an urban journalism program through the Northwestern University Medill School of Journalism, further development of the Graduate School of Journalism at Columbia University, a public affairs reporting program in cooperation with the American Political Science Association, a variety of study and seminar programs for journalists in the South in cooperation with the Southern Regional Education Board and the Southern Newspaper Publishers Association Foundation, and a program of study for journalists at the Yale University Law School.

Since 1973 the National Endowment for the Humanities has supported mid-career study for journalists at Stanford University and the University of Michigan.

For many years the William Randolph Hearst Foundation has conducted a nationwide student writing competition. Awards to students in accredited programs, with matching stipends to their schools, are given monthly through the academic year. In 1985–1986, the amount totaled $91,300. Additional stipends to participating schools during that period totaled $44,625. The foundation also underwrites minority workshops, scholarships, and research projects.

The Scripps-Howard Foundation provided more than $217,000 in scholarships during 1984–1985. Other grants for communications students were made that year to 89 colleges and universities.

The Dow-Jones Newspaper Fund, supported by Dow Jones and Company (publisher of the *Wall Street Journal, Barron's* financial weekly, the Dow Jones News Services, and Ottaway Newspapers, a wholly-owned subsidiary) has spent more than $5.5 million since 1958 in attracting talented young people to newsroom careers. The fund's program provides a clearinghouse for career information, summer study on college campuses for high school and junior college journalism teachers, summer intern programs with training courses and scholarships for undergraduate students and minority graduate students, recognition to high school teachers for outstanding performance, programs for minority high school students, and an editor-in-residence program to bring working newspeople to college campuses in cooperation with the American Society of Newspaper Editors.

Among numerous other assistance programs are the William Benton Fellowships in Broadcast Journalism at the University of Chicago and grants for research in broadcasting offered by the National Association of Broadcasters.

OTHER PUBLICATIONS. The Nieman Fellows, consisting of reporters and editors who have been given a year of study at Harvard University under the Nieman Foundation program, issue a quarterly, *Nieman Reports. The Columbia Journal-*

ism Review, published by the Columbia University Graduate School of Journalism, offers a quarterly analysis and criticism of media performance, as also is provided by the *Washington Journalism Review.*

Media practices are examined by a number of publications produced by critical reporters and editors, often with the support of journalism and mass communications educators. A few metropolitan radio and television stations have instituted programs designed to criticize press coverage. A number of university journalism schools publish periodicals containing media appraisal, among them being the *Montana Journalism Review,* of the University of Montana School of Journalism, and the *Iowa Journalist,* of the University of Iowa School of Journalism and Mass Communication. Other roles of journalism educators and the cooperation extended to them by the mass communications industries are discussed in Chapter 20. Articles in *TV Guide* assess industry practices. The Gannett Company issues *Gannetteer,* a monthly magazine. The Gannett Center for Media Studies began publication of its interest-winning *Gannett Center Journal* in 1987.

With this array of organizations and others providing such massive assistance both within and without the communications industry, the steady improvement in media performance that has characterized the last several decades seems certain to continue.

25

International Mass Communications

Internationalizing the News

A chemical leak in Bhopal, India, kills hundreds and sickens thousands. Journalists from major news organizations rush to the scene. But so does John D. Kimelman, a 27-year-old reporter for the Charleston (West Virginia) *Daily Mail.* The only other Union Carbide plant producing the deadly gas is situated less than 10 miles from that city.

It is not only to cover tragic events but also to investigate overseas problems such as immigration, trade, and international drug trafficking, as well as home-sponsored activities, that newspaper editors and broadcast news directors increasingly are dispatching staff members abroad. For example, the Quincy (Massachusetts) *Patriot Ledger* sent a reporter and photographer to Haiti—to chronicle missionary work of a local church group.

American interest in global happenings has become intense; one survey found that 40 percent of all national news exposure in 1985 was devoted to world news. On both large and some small media a cadre of reporters and camera operators is providing in-depth reports that tell not only what happened but also what an international event means to Main Street, U.S.A.

And they don't even have to leave home. A new Sigma Delta Chi Foundation book, *Main Street and the Third World,* compiled by John Maxwell Hamilton, details how a number of the print and broadcast media have learned that they can make foreign developments locally relevant. For instance, a news service report carried news of a new Malaysian consumer law requiring that food processing companies put dates on their products. Alerted by a reporter, a Keene, New Hampshire, industrial printing equipment firm began negotiations to sell one of its products in Malaysia.

Says ABC News anchor Peter Jennings in a foreword to the book: "There is no substitute for the powerful impression that the local news angle makes in revealing the impact of foreign relations."

*V*ery little happens anywhere in the world that does not have some effect upon citizens of other lands; this is true today as never before. As a consequence, international mass communications has assumed an importance in our lives little dreamed of only a few decades ago.

In this chapter we discuss the roles that the mass media and the major organizations concerned with mass communications internationally are playing in world society, and some of the vexing problems that have arisen.

Our survey covers the beginnings of international mass communications, foreign correspondents, national media systems, recent technological developments, the flow of news and cultural information, government and private sector organizations, advertising, public relations, research, education, Third World demands that a New World Order of Communications be effected, and qualifications for international mass communications careers. ◆

A BROADENING FIELD

For many years the term "Afghanistanism" was applied to editorial writing that avoided important local topics and instead focused on such seemingly inconsequential and faraway happenings as the overthrow of an Afghan leader, a poor rice crop in the Philippines, or tribal feuding in Somalia. But that ostrichlike posture no longer is tenable—if it ever was. The war between Iran and Iraq, the Soviet invasion of Afghanistan, and the turmoil in Lebanon, coupled with terrorism, inflation, and the spectre of world hunger, demonstrated anew to the American public what many observers have long realized—that there is scarcely a development anywhere that does not impinge upon our well being.

As a consequence, the maintenance of an open flow of communication has become a necessity, both for the United States and for all other countries. John E. Reinhardt, former director of the U.S. Information Agency, puts it this way:

> There are, of course, many elements that will determine our shared future on this planet. The one which is common to them all, however, is communications in its many forms —the sharing of ideas and emotions, the web of society. Only through an open communications system can we begin to hope for a stable world order. The alternative is national tribalism, economic protectionism, and social isolation—each of which feeds on ignorance of our common needs and of the prospects for meeting them.

Future communicators should be acquainted with the world's mass communications problems and be prepared to cope with them in their lives and careers. The days of Afghanistanism have ended.

HISTORICAL BACKGROUND

Origins

International mass communications may be identified as *any communication transmitted by the mass media across national boundary lines.* In the ancient world most communication was oral, augmented by signals, ceremonies, coins, and forms of architecture, and later by signs identifying places of business (the forerunner of our advertising today). The earliest writing was done on stones, on walls of caves, or on primitive materials such as bamboo strips. Conquerors, traders, and missionaries gradually spread their own language and writing to other parts of the world. Books were first produced laboriously by hand.

International communication was accelerated by Gutenberg's invention of movable type and the introduction of the printing press. News sheets, or *corantos,* relating the most wondrous of happenings, were carried from country to country by travelers. Important financial families such as the Fuggers and Rothschilds in Europe hired couriers to bring them news of political events and economic developments. Newspapers and magazines soon were printed and distributed by means of horseback and sailing ship, and later by means of steamship and train. When the telegraph, oceanic cable, radio, and improved newspaper presses appeared, international mass communication became an important element in modern world society.

The Global News Cartel

In 1835 Charles Havas, a Frenchman, began collecting European news for French newspapers. A few years later, Paul Julius Reuter, a German, began using homing pigeons to beat the Rothschilds' couriers. Telegraph lines linked continental countries but could not traverse the Skagerrak and the English Channel. Realizing that copper wire would revolutionize and standardize the newsgathering process, Reuter took his pigeons to London in 1851 and began gathering news for about a dozen newspapers in the British Isles. He then persuaded the British government to let him use government cables that were beginning to link the empire's outposts. Such an arrangement was mutually profitable: Reuter got his news, and his partner, the government, got favorable treatment in the news.

Finding that his service could not compete in world newsgathering with Reuter's use of the cables, Havas persuaded Reuter and Dr. Bernhard Wolff, who founded a German agency in 1849, that the world should be divided into three parts for the purposes of newsgathering. Havas covered the French empire, southwestern Europe, South America, and parts of Africa; Reuter covered the British empire, North America, Mediterranean countries, and most of Asia; Wolff covered the rest of Europe and Russia. Each agreed to exchange news with the others.

In the United States, the New York Associated Press had been organized in 1849 as forerunner of the modern AP. Since the British government wished to avoid offending its former colony, the cartel decided to admit the AP, and the agreement was formalized in 1887. Nevertheless, the AP was confined to the United States until early in the twentieth century, when it was permitted to gather news in Canada and Mexico and, near the end of World War I, in Central and South America. So it was that, from 1858 past World War I, news was never quite free of the taint of government propaganda. Kent Cooper, longtime general manager of the AP, expressed the opinion that the news cartel, by monopolizing the distribution of international news and by coloring that news in nationalistic hues to suit clients in each of the countries served, had been in part responsible for the war.

Dissatisfied with the cartel's method of newsgathering and reporting, major newspapers in the United States and other countries increased their number of foreign correspondents. Radiotelegraphy, a cheap alternative carrier, challenged the monopoly of the cables. The high-speed Hoe rotary press enabled newspaper circulations to rise, and many afternoon papers, with multiple split-second editions for street sales, developed. By 1909 the United States had three press agencies. The AP was reorganized in 1900; E. W. Scripps established the United Press Associations in 1907; and William Randolph Hearst's International News Service was formed two years later. The news cartel was finally broken by 1920, when through a friendship between a UP executive and the owners of *La Prensa* in Buenos Aires, the UP obtained contracts with a number of Latin American newspapers. At about the same time, several English provincial newspapers organized the British United Press and began exchanging news items with the UP.

Such major national news agencies as Stefani in Italy, Fabra in Spain, and the Press Association and Exchange Telegraph in England also had developed in the mid-nineteenth century. In the twentieth century the Associated Press of India, the Canadian Press, Japan's Domei, and Nazi Germany's DNB all appeared before the start of World War II. So did three other important government-controlled agencies: the USSR's TASS (1925), the New China News Agency, now called Xinhua, (1931), and Franco Spain's EFE (1938).

The Associated Press broke away completely from the cartel in 1934. The Havas agency ceased its operations in 1940, and British newspaper proprietors took over the Reuters agency in 1941. Stefani was succeeded a year later by the Agenzia Nazionale Stampa Associata, modeled after the AP and the new Reuters. An independent Agence France-Presse was organized in postwar France. Deutsche Press-Agentur succeeded DNB in the Federal Republic of Germany and Kyodo replaced Domei in Japan. EFE, TASS, and Xinhua survived as official news agencies, joined by Tanjug of Yugoslovia.

Today, four news agencies collect and distribute most of the world's news: AP, UPI, Reuters, and Agence France-Presse. Each has offices in all major news centers, employing hundreds of full-time and part-time correspondents, as described in Chapter 7. They are joined to a lesser extent in worldwide competition by TASS. All serve both print and broadcast media, as well as national and regional press agencies, in Arabic, English, French, German, Portuguese, Spanish, and other languages as necessary.

Most national and regional agencies exchange news with these services. The latter include specialized services offering coverage of the Third World. Among them are Inter Press Service, a Rome-based cooperative formed by journalists in 1964 to provide news services supporting political and social reform in Latin America but now also functioning in Africa, Asia, and Europe; its U.S. affiliate, Interlink, which also generates stories on its own; the Caribbean News Agency, founded in 1975 with United Nations aid and now serving 17 English-speaking countries; the Middle East News Agency; Pacific News Service; Asia-Pacific News Network; Gemini News Service; Pan African News Agency; and South-North News Service. The latter, based in Hanover, N.H., was founded in 1986 with $835,000 in grants, mostly from groups such as the Ford Foundation. Its editor-in-chief, Peter B. Martin, a former *Time* magazine staff member, said the agency's purpose is "to identify and train Third World reporters to write for First World publications." With about 175 correspondents, the agency sends six articles, generally features, to subscribers each week.

The Pool of News Agencies of Non-Aligned Countries was established in 1975 under the aegis of Tanjug, the Yugoslav news agency. Now the Tunisian news agency, Tunis Afrique Presse (TAP), using leased circuits, telex, and radioteletype channels, daily distributes approximately 40,000 words of news provided by the governments of about 50 countries. Influential in the Third World are the USSR's TASS, China's Xinhua, and the Press Trust of India, that country's cooperative news agency.

FOREIGN CORRESPONDENTS

Two London newspapers, the *Times* and *Morning Chronicle,* established foreign correspondence from the European continent in the 1820s and by 1850 had extended coverage to Asia and the United States. They thus pioneered the concept of individual newspaper enterprise to complement news agency services. William Howard Russell of the *Times* gained early fame by covering the Crimean War in 1854, and by reporting from Moscow, India, and the American Civil War.

James Gordon Bennett reported Queen Victoria's coronation for his New York *Herald* in 1838. Horace Greeley's New York *Tribune* boasted Charles A. Dana, Margaret Fuller, and Bayard Taylor as early European correspondents; Taylor was with Commodore Perry in Tokyo Bay in 1853. George W. Smalley opened the *Tribune*'s London bureau before 1870.

Major foreign news services, syndicated to other dailies, expanded rapidly in the 1920s, led by those of the New York *Times* and *Herald Tribune* and the Chicago *Daily News* and *Tribune.* Famous names were those of Walter Duranty, *Times* correspondent in the Soviet Union during the 1920s and 1930s; Paul Scott Mowrer and Edgar Ansel Mowrer of the Chicago *Daily News;* and Dorothy Thompson of the New York *Post* and *Herald Tribune.* The New York *Times* and Chicago *Tribune* services were joined in the 1960s by the syndicate sponsored by the Washington *Post* and Los Angeles *Times.* Other U.S. media organizations maintaining bureaus abroad, both then and in the 1970s and later, included the major broadcast networks, news and business magazines, and wire services; the *Wall Street Journal, Christian Science Monitor,* and Baltimore *Sun;* and the Hearst, Scripps-Howard, Block, and Knight-Ridder groups.

Peter Jennings was a foreign correspondent before becoming anchor of the ABC-TV World News Tonight. (Courtesy, Quill)

Despite increasing involvement by the United States in foreign affairs and the growing interdependency of the nations of the world, American mass media participation in reporting world news declined during the 1970s. Studies by Professor Ralph E. Kliesch of Ohio University for the Overseas Press Club revealed a 28 percent drop in the number of full-time persons employed abroad by the American media during the years 1969 to 1975. Of the total number of 676 employed, 429 were U.S. citizens, 8 percent of whom were women. The decline was attributed in large part to the major expense of maintaining a correspondent in another country, well in excess of $100,000 annually, causing many media instead to fly reporters and camera crews to obtain stories abroad.

During the 1980s, however, foreign coverage increased considerably. With such events as the Mid-East wars, the growth in terroristic activities, the African famine, fluctuations in the price of oil, and the increasing importation of electronic goods, automobiles, textiles, and other products to the United States at the expense of home industries, Americans became much more interested in foreign news and feature stories. Accelerating the trend was a signal effort by Western journalists to respond to Third World demands for portrayal of their complex economic, political, and cultural problems along with traditional stories on "coups and earthquakes." (Third World demands will be discussed later in this chapter.) In addition, advances in telecommunications made it possible to transmit copy and televised and still pictures much more rapidly than in the past.

A 1986 survey by the magazine *presstime* disclosed that 23 major U.S. daily newspapers had a total of 186 foreign correspondents, that all the papers had increased their contingents during the 1980s, and that there were more correspondents in Third World countries than ever before. In addition, middle-sized newspapers were expanding their network of "stringer" correspondents and sending reporters and photographers on more special projects abroad.

The Associated Press reported that it had about 400 full-time reporters, editors, and photographers working abroad, including 100 Americans. Most of its 45 percent growth in the number of Americans sent abroad since 1975 had been to posts in Third World countries. The news services also employed thousands of stringers native to their particular areas. Individual newspapers also reported increases in the number of foreign correspondents. The Los Angeles *Times,* for example, had one overseas correspondent in 1960; in 1986 it had 24 in 23 bureaus throughout the world.

The lives of American journalists, as well as those in other countries, were increasingly at risk. In a book titled, *The World's Most Dangerous Profession— Journalism,* Richard H. Leonard, vice president and associate editor of the Milwaukee *Journal* and former chairman of the International Press Institute, reported that in 1984 alone, 23 journalists were killed, 18 wounded, and 205 jailed or expelled. Freedom House, a New York-based human rights observation agency, reported that violence against journalists nearly doubled in 1985, while censorship and self-censorship continued to influence news reporting in three quarters of the world's nations. The tally: 30 journalists killed in 11 countries, 13 held hostage or disappeared, and 76 in 20 countries beaten, bombed, wounded, and otherwise harassed. Some broadcast and print journalists were withdrawn, or not sent, to the most hostile areas, but, overall, international correspondents and native journalists alike continued to pursue the news with scant abatement.

In 1986 the arrest in the Soviet Union of Nicholas Daniloff, correspondent for *U.S. News & World Report,* on seemingly trumped-up charges of spying produced an angry outcry in the United States. "The same thing can happen to you at any time," Daniloff warned his fellow correspondents in a Moscow news conference before his release and return to the United States.

NATIONAL MEDIA SYSTEMS

As may be expected, the mass media are most highly developed in the industrialized parts of the world, such as the United States, Japan, and the European countries. These countries have moved well beyond the simple oral forms that still characterize much of the public communication in the poorest nations, especially in Africa and Asia. Most societies, however, contain elements of both media and oral public communication. In national *media* systems, professional communicators provide information, interpretation, and entertainment to mass audiences via the media. In national *oral* systems information is conveyed by word of mouth directly to families and to worship and work groups by hierarchal leaders rather than by professional communicators.

In all countries the mass media help create and maintain a sense of nationhood, perform developmental tasks such as improving education and building political stability, distribute information for the formation of public opinion, provide a forum for public discussion, offer cultural information and entertainment, and, in nations where such activity is permitted, serve as a watchdog on government and prevent abuses of all kinds. Many of the poorer Third World nations, however, seek to use the media primarily for purposes of economic and social development and to maintain the governments in power.

Strengthening their communications facilities has been a primary aim of the more than 100 new nations—nearly all former colonies, almost all poor—that have been established during the last 35 years.

TELECOMMUNICATIONS

A Communications Explosion

So rapidly is world telecommunications expanding that, as pointed out in Chapter 1, its growth may best be described not as a revolution but as an explosion. Telecommunications, as defined by international convention, is *any transmission, emission, or reception of signs, signals, writing, images, and sounds or intelligence of any nature by wire, radio, optical, or other electromagnetic systems.* Thus it includes, among other means, the telegraph, telephone, telex, facsimile and data transfer between computers, and radio and television broadcasting.

Telecommunications takes place through the air, through land and oceanic cables, and, most dramatically, via satellite. It is used mostly for business and personal messages. Although almost 80 percent of the well over 400 million telephones have been installed in only ten countries, the telephone links all nations. It is estimated that more than 460 billion calls are made each year. The latest transatlantic cable can carry 4000 calls simultaneously, and the use of fiber optics and laser beams will increase that number tremendously. There are more than 10,000 satellite circuits transmitting far more messages than cable. Through the marriage of the computer and cable television, the telephone itself has become a mass medium.

Computers capable of performing one billion operations a second are linking all parts of the world with a flow of electronic data that can be stored, processed, analyzed, and retransmitted in oral and visual forms. Data processing, in a field known as informatics (after the French word, *informatique*), is rapidly transforming industrial, scientific, commercial, and government operations. It is estimated that about one-half of the workers in the United States are now engaged in some form of information processing.

Satellites

Futurist Arthur C. Clarke first put forward the idea of satellites more than 40 years ago. He pointed out that three satellites positioned over the Atlantic, Pacific, and Indian Oceans in geostationary orbit could cover with their beams almost all the inhabited areas of the earth. Today a host of communications satellites convey voice, radio, data, and television signals throughout the world.

Intelsat, started in 1965 and now operated by a consortium of more than 100 countries, serves nationally owned earth stations in most of these nations. (See Figure 25.1) The Communications Satellite Corporation, a private, profit-making company, was established in 1962 by Congress to own and operate the American segment of the system.

Intersputnik, the other global system, was created in 1971 by an agreement among the Soviet Union, Eastern countries, Cuba, and Mongolia. Available for use by all nations, it was developed from the Soviet Union's elliptical orbit system, consisting of satellites orbiting the earth every 12 hours, with a high arc over the northern hemisphere, and 40 earth stations. Simultaneous global diffusion of messages emanating from Intelsat and Intersputnik can be achieved by linking national and regional terrestrial networks.

Many countries have their own domestic and regional satellite systems, such as the United States' RCA and Comstar operations, and numerous others are planned. Additional satellite systems serve marine, aeronautical, weather, and military purposes. Because it costs no more to transmit a message 10,000 miles than it does to transmit one 300 miles, the satellite systems rapidly are replacing, as well as supplementing, terrestrial operations.

A number of satellites have been used for developmental purposes—to provide education, health care, social services, agricultural information, and cultural enrichment to less developed countries. In 1975–1976, the Indian Satellite Instructional Television Experiment (SITE), using a U.S. satellite, broadcast programs directly

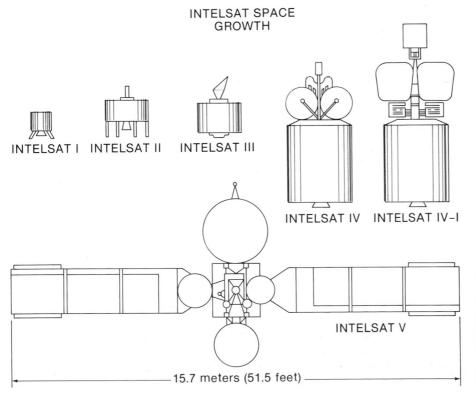

INTELSAT SPACE GROWTH

INTELSAT I INTELSAT II INTELSAT III

INTELSAT IV INTELSAT IV-I

INTELSAT V

15.7 meters (51.5 feet)

Figure 25.1
From the 1965 launching of INTELSAT I, better known as Early Bird, to today's INTELSAT V, five generations of COMSAT satellites have provided countries in most parts of the world with voice, computerized data, facsimile (electronic mail), and video transmission and reception. (Courtesy of COMSAT World Services Division.)

to villages across India. The Pacific Education and Communication Experiments by Satellite (PEACESAT), begun in the 1970s, links countries in and around the Pacific Ocean through more than 15 ground stations. The system enables members to engage in audio conferencing and classroom sessions and to exchange information on a variety of subjects.

Efforts are being made in a number of countries to establish direct satellite broadcasting systems (DBS). In its original, narrow sense, DBS is the transmission of messages from a high-power satellite directly to community receivers or to individual home sets without the need of local stations to receive and rebroadcast. These dish antennae can be as small as 64 centimeters and, when mass-produced, could cost as little as $200. Thus far technical and economic problems have delayed initiation of the system in most countries. A Japanese system failed, as did a planned North American operation.

Largely in anticipation of the advent of DBS, however, issues of equal access and *spillover* have been addressed in international forums. Because of the finite space available for satellites placed in geosynchronous orbit (GSO) 22,300 miles directly above the equator, less developed countries have been seeking access with those already positioned by industrialized nations. Since 1959 the International Telecommunication Union has accommodated demands, and, at World Administrative Radio Conferences (WARC) in 1977 and 1985, steps were taken to ensure future access by Third World countries.

The problem of spillover, which occurs when one country's signal creates what is known as a *footprint* in the territory of another nation, has created more spirited debate. The diffusion of standard satellite signals can largely be controlled from a few central locations, but DBS transmissions cannot be made to conform to nonoval-shaped national boundaries. The Soviet Union and the Eastern bloc, as well as many Third World and other countries, contend that a WARC provision absolutely forbids spillover and that prior consent must be obtained to prevent what they perceive to be politically destabilizing and culturally damaging programming from entering their territories. Most Western industrialized nations, desiring a free flow of information, favor little or no regulation.

Because a DBS signal can cover about 1 million square miles, an area about one-third that of the United States, the problem of spillover is especially acute in Europe, with its many countries. Resolution of the issue—if possible—will be extremely difficult.

Another complex problem yet to be resolved concerns the establishment of the legal and regulatory environment to enable newsgathering use of *remote-sensing* satellites. Images are obtained from sensors that record land-surface electromagnetic waves. The result is an image of terrain in varying colors or in black-and-white. Obtaining access to these images would enhance the ability of news organizations to report on military developments and political and economic issues around the world. National security interests, international obligations, and privacy concerns, however, are likely to conflict with media assertions of the right to use the data (for example, the First Amendment in the United States). Some such use for news purposes has been made, and U.S. media have contemplated launching their own satellite, but cost estimates ranging to $500 million appear prohibitive.

Television, Film, and Video

As the 1990s neared, satellite distribution systems, cable franchising, videocassette recorders, and the emergence of additional commercial television stations were transforming much of the world media scene, particularly in Europe.

EXPORT OF TELEFILMS. Hollywood films had long dominated the world market, but after 1962, when the 83 million television sets outside the United States for the first time surpassed the American total of 50 million, U.S. motion picture and TV production companies turned increasingly to the worldwide television market, which now encompasses well over 400 million receivers. They found ready acceptance because many countries had introduced TV and made heavy capital investments, but lacked the facilities and experience to produce much TV programming on their own. By 1986 approximately 160 major motion picture studios and both large and small independent producers and distributors were exporting programs to more than 100 nations, with revenues surpassing one-half billion dollars.

Videotaped game shows, as well as interview and variety programs, constitute only a small part of the exports. Because, except for Japan, U.S. videotape cannot be used in other countries without costly conversion, the programs are usually shot on 16-mm or 35-mm film for worldwide distribution, as well as on videotape for domestic TV consumption.

Approximately 85 percent of the total telefilm sales to other countries are programs produced by the nine members of the Motion Picture Export Association: MCA, Metro-Goldwyn-Mayer, Allied Artists, Avco Embassy, United Artists, Columbia, Paramount, Twentieth Century-Fox, and Warner Bros. Six countries—Canada (15 percent), Great Britain and Italy (13 percent each), Australia (12 percent), and Germany and Japan (11 percent each)—account for three-fourths of the total dollar income from foreign distribution. Brazil, Mexico, France, and Venezuela comprise other large markets. Many films are distributed to smaller countries under a less costly "bicycling" arrangement whereby the film print is shipped successively to other nations.

As a result of soaring production costs and increased import restrictions in many parts of the world, among other reasons, the cofinancing/coproduction of telefilms has become widespread. By placing quotas on imported products, countries seek to protect and develop their own film and television industries. France, Great Britain, and Germany, for example, limit the showing of foreign-made programs to, respectively, 12, 14, and 22 percent of broadcast time. In Canada and Australia the limit is 40 percent. In some countries even stricter regulations are placed on cable TV. Coproductions overcome these restrictions in the countries involved. Because U.S. outlets represent 50 percent of the worldwide market, at least one version of all American-European programs must be in English. The dubbing of voices, shooting of scenes twice, and other techniques increase costs but they are readily recouped by profitable U.S. syndication markets.

"Actually, we are evolving into a worldwide market rather than separate countries," Professors Jean-Luc Renaud and Barry B. Litman of Michigan State University, on whose research the foregoing is based, have stated, "International program distributors are beginning to wonder if the proliferation of satellite-fed programming services across Europe, in particular, requires a shift away from selling program rights to individual countries. Putting programming up on a satellite in Europe creates footprints by language. This problem may be alleviated by having coproduction partners in as many countries as possible.''

CULTURAL DIFFUSION. Great Britain, France, and West Germany also export much programming. In Mexico, where the "novella," patterned after the American soap opera, is highly popular, many programs are sold to other Latin American countries. Brazil also produces novellas. Nations in the Middle East obtain most of their programs from Egypt. Programs produced in communist countries are broadcast mainly in other such nations.

A cultural imbalance, however, is evident. According to a survey by Tapio Varis, a Finnish researcher, less than 2 percent of commercial and noncommercial program viewed in the United States and China is received from foreign sources; in the Soviet Union, 5 percent; in France, 9 percent; and in Japan, 10 percent. By contrast, countries such as Chile, Mexico, Uruguay, Saudi Arabia, Italy, Australia, and Zambia import more than 50 percent of the programs viewed by their citizens —Saudi Arabia, in fact, imports 100 percent.

Charges of cultural imperialism by the Western media have been advanced vigorously by many less developed countries during the last two decades. Critics charge that the United States, in particular, is unduly imposing on other countries its set of beliefs, values, knowledge, and behavioral norms as well as its overall life style. TV programs such as "Dallas," "Hill Street Blues," and "Miami Vice" have been cited as most harmful. In response, media spokespersons have pointed out that these countries are not forced to buy these products, although they recognize the scarcity of production facilities and expertise that would enable the nations to fill their TV and cinema screens. In some countries the problem is slowly being rectified.

Although American movies are viewed almost everywhere, the United States is far from being the leader in theatrical film production. Of the estimated 3000 feature-length films produced worldwide each year, India makes the most, followed in order by Japan, the United States, France, Italy, and the Soviet Union. About one-half of the world's full-length entertainment films are made in 11 Asian countries and about one-third in Europe and the Soviet Union. Language and cultural differences, as well as the expense of dubbing voices or placing limited translations at the bottom of film frames, are major problems.

COMMERCIAL TELEVISION. France, West Germany, and several other countries followed the lead of Great Britain and Italy in granting the establishment of commercial television stations in Europe in the mid-1980s. Traditionally a government monopoly, television had been opened to commercials in Great Britain in 1954 with creation of an Independent Broadcasting Authority, whose 15 regional stations successfully compete with the government-controlled British Broadcasting Company. A policy change in Italy in 1976 led to the creation of four private commercial networks and an astonishing number of more than 775 privately owned stations. They compete with three state-owned networks and more than 2200 state-owned stations.

The government-operated television network in India began accepting sponsored shows in 1985, enlivening programming. Approximately 60 million Indians —about 7 percent of the population—watched more than 5 million TV sets. By 1991 the numbers were expected to increase to 300 million viewers and 50 million sets.

The French government awarded one license to British publisher Robert Maxwell. His satellite channel, supported entirely by advertising, is broadcast in English but dubbed versions are provided to France and Germany. Those initially receiving the channel included Holland, Belgium, and Switzerland by cable and southern England by antenna.

The other license went to a French–Italian consortium, with Silvio Berlusconi, the principal developer of Italian privately owned TV, a 40 percent owner. A third new commercial TV station broadcasts music. Luxembourg, which had anticipated receiving a license, planned a new, direct broadcast satellite, to compete with a French satellite station in beaming television programs to European receivers.

West Germany had only one fully commercial TV station, but more than 1 million German households were connected to cable systems to allow viewers access to the 18 European commercial broadcast services available via satellite. Cable TV, however, had its greatest development in Belgium, the Netherlands, and Switzerland. Although these nations accounted for only 8 percent of European homes, they had two-thirds of all households equipped for cable TV. Sky Channel, owned by Rupert Murdoch, the Australian, British, and American media developer, reached 5 million subscribers, but Maxwell's satellite was strongly competing.

In 1985 America's Turner Broadcasting System began beaming its 24-hour Cable News Network to Great Britain and western Europe. Its strongest competitor was Britain's Visnews. Turner also exchanges news with Intervision, the Eastern bloc's consortium of TV systems and has cooperated in the production of a six-hour documentary, "Portrait of the Soviet Union."

France was unchallenged as Europe's telecommunications leader. The country already had established a leading position in several fields of advanced telecommunications, including digital switching equipment, electronic telephone directories, and videotex services under a system known as Minitel. In 1987 well over 2.5 million terminals were in use. With a $6 billion, government-sponsored plan the nation was being linked with videophones and fiber optic cables capable of handling vast quantities of information and images. It was anticipated that, by the end of 1988, 3.1 million homes would be connected. The government installed the videophones and charged homeowners only for calls. The table-top *videophone* incorporates a telephone, television screen, and movable video camera. Customers are automatically billed for all uses, including videotex services and videocassette programs ordered from a library of more than 2000 titles.

Less spectacular advances were being made in many other parts of the industrialized world and in some Third World countries as well. Among other achievements, Japan, with more than 10,000 TV stations and 60 million TV sets, introduced pay-TV services. In the People's Republic of China, the country's first communications satellite was sending programs to approximately 40 million TV sets. Beijing residents were reported to be viewing television an average of 90 minutes a day. Three-fourths of the programming consisted of sports and other entertainment.

VIDEOCASSETTES. Viewing of videocassette programs was a worldwide phenomenon. One estimate placed the number of recorders at about 100 million worldwide. The Japanese were building most of the sets and Americans were producing most of the movies and other entertainment and informational programs. In view of the cost of the recorders, as low as $190, and the heavy demand for both original and pirated programs, prerecorded tapes could be found everywhere, including the Soviet Union, which encountered difficulty in keeping Western products out of the country.

Radio

Anywhere in the world a person with a shortwave or mediumwave radio may tune in voices in a multiplicity of languages, as well as music and Morse code signals, projected by powerful transmitters in many countries. Where boundaries are not far distant, regular mediumwave broadcasts from other countries may be heard.

International radio broadcasting is that which is intended, either exclusively or in part, for audiences outside the frontiers of the country from which the broadcast originates. Potential audiences are vast. With the development of portable transistor radios, many of which are capable of receiving the programs of international broadcasters, it is estimated that more than one billion sets are in use. The British Broadcasting Corporation (BBC) estimates that about 75 million adults listen to its programs at least once a week. The United States' Voice of America reaches a comparable audience, well over one-half of which is in the Soviet Union.

In 1922 Germany began daily propaganda news broadcasts to other countries in Morse code. During the mid-1920s, the Soviet Union became the first country to produce foreign language broadcasts in several languages, and Great Britain and other countries soon followed. During the early 1930s, several commercial stations in Europe, such as Radio Paris and Radio Luxembourg, began broadcasting on longwave or mediumwave in several languages.

In the United States companies such as General Electric, NBC, and CBS built and operated shortwave transmitters, mostly relaying domestic programs but also transmitting some in foreign languages. Pearl Harbor convinced the U.S. government that it could not rely solely on commercial broadcasters for an international service, so the Voice of America was created in 1942 as a part of the Department of State. By 1946 it was broadcasting in 24 languages. During the Cold War the American effort was increased with the establishment in Munich, Germany, of Radio Free Europe and Radio Liberation (now Radio Liberty), both financed by the Central Intelligence Agency. Radio Free Europe broadcasts in Bulgarian,

Czech and Slovak, Hungarian, Polish, and Romanian. Radio Liberty sends its broadcasts to the USSR in Russian and 15 other languages. The stations are now financed by the U.S. government and managed by the Board for International Broadcasting. They are not, however, part of the Voice of America.

Today the countries engaged in the most international broadcasting, ranked in order of number of programming hours each week, are the Soviet Union (broadcasting in 82 languages), United States (42 languages), People's Republic of China, Federal Republic of Germany, United Kingdom, North Korea, Egypt, and Albania. In addition, many privately owned stations seek international audiences for religious, commercial, and clandestine purposes, the latter often seeking to provoke revolutions. Most of the stations intend their broadcasts for particular portions of the world.

Why do so many countries broadcast internationally? The answer takes many forms: promoting national interest, enhancing national prestige, keeping in touch with nationals abroad, promoting understanding among nations, disseminating news with accuracy and objectivity, spreading a particular creed or doctrine, attempting to influence the internal affairs of another country, fostering the national culture including the teaching of the national language, and reserving a place in the broadcasting spectrum against a future need.

Allocations on the overly crowded spectrum are made by the International Telecommunication Union. The claims of the many new developing countries for increased allocations are now being considered in the aftermath of the World Administrative Radio Conference which convened in Geneva in 1979 and Copenhagen in 1985. With an estimated 4600 shortwave stations in the world, audibility is a genuine problem, so some leading broadcasters send taped material to relay stations that boost their output, or they transmit programs to them directly by shortwave or by satellite. Holding and increasing their audiences is a constant problem; therefore, in recent years many stations, including Radio Moscow, have improved the quality and style of their programming. Jamming of broadcasts from other countries is frequently attempted; the Soviet Union greatly increased its jamming of American broadcasts in the 1980s, before relenting in 1987.

World competition for listeners is expected to become more intense when direct radio reception from satellites becomes more widespread. The number of receivers in use, particularly in the Third World, is expected to increase, and tuning has been made easier on sets with digital frequency displays.

THE PRINT MEDIA

Illiteracy is widespread throughout the world—it is estimated that only about one of every four persons 15 years of age or older can read and write at a minimal level. Although there are more than 3500 identified languages, perhaps no more than 500 languages and dialects exist in written form. UNESCO estimates that more than two-thirds of printed materials are produced in English, Russian, Spanish, German, and French. In view of these facts, it is clearly evident that mass communication takes place far more widely by electronic means than by newspapers, magazines, and books. Nevertheless, the print media remain the primary base for enhancing and preserving world civilization.

Newspapers

There are approximately 10,000 daily newspapers in the world and far more weeklies and semiweeklies. One estimate sets worldwide distribution of dailies in excess of 420 million copies. Europe, North America, and Japan account for four-fifths of these sales. Sweden and Japan have the highest circulations of dailies, nearly 600 for every 1000 inhabitants. Some large cities in the developing countries have high-quality newspapers, but beyond those urban areas the quality of content and appearance falls off sharply, largely because of illiteracy, the multiplicity of vernacular languages, low per capita income, and lack of distribution facilities.

As in the United States, the growth of chains and conglomerates characterizes much of the world's press. Except where resisted by unions, such as in England and Paris, modern printing techniques increasingly are being employed by newspapers in many countries. In England major battle lines were drawn between management and labor unions in 1986 as two major publishers, Rupert Murdoch and Robert Maxwell, introduced the new technology.

Newspapers in many less-developed countries are printed with nearly worn-out equipment on antiquated flat-bed presses. Most of the world's daily newspapers are privately owned, but direct and indirect government controls are evident in many countries.

Because of its mass nature, much of the world's press is sensationalist and somewhat superficial in its treatment of the news. With the exception of a few countries including the United States, where the *Wall Street Journal* now enjoys the greatest daily circulation of any newspaper, dailies with the largest circulations almost always are those that emphasize entertainment value. Most countries, however, with the exception of a few in Africa and Asia, do have at least one high-quality daily newspaper that deals primarily with social and political ideas and issues and reflects the best practices of journalism. John C. Merrill and Harold A. Fisher, in their 1980 book, *The World's Great Dailies,* provide profiles of 50 newspapers that they consider, by reputation and the consensus of serious observers, to be the world's finest. To a considerable degree, the editors of these dailies read each other's newspapers and, with the serious magazines of their countries, help maintain a dialogue among themselves and their readers about important national and world issues.

An around-the-world traveler examining copies of these dailies might pick up *The Times* in Great Britain, *Le Monde* in France, *Corriere della Sera* in Italy, *Al Ahram* in Egypt, *Pravda* in the Soviet Union, *The Statesman* in India, *The Age* in Australia, *The Straits Times* in Singapore, *Renmin Ribao* in the People's Republic of China, *Asahi Shimbun* in Japan, *Estado de S. Paulo* in Brazil, and the Los Angeles *Times* in the United States. The tourist might not be able to read all these papers, but, since English-language newspapers are published almost everywhere, the tourist could keep up with news developments of major importance reasonably well.

Thanks to satellite transmissions of completed newspapers to distant printing plants, a choice of major publications is available simultaneously on several continents. The oldest is the *International Herald Tribune,* established in Paris in 1887 and now printed in London, Zurich, Hong Kong, Singapore, Marseille, The Hague, and Miami, the latter for distribution in Latin America and North America. The paper is owned jointly by the New York *Times,* Washington *Post,* and Whitney Communications Company. Others include the *Wall Street Journal,* in Asian and European editions; *USA Today,* in more than 40 countries; the international weekly edition of the *Christian Science Monitor,* in Europe and Australia; Miami *Herald,* distributed throughout Latin America; and *The Stars and Stripes,* serving U.S. armed forces overseas. Other newspapers distributed internationally include the *Financial Times* of London, *Die Zeit* of Hamburg, Toronto *Globe and Mail,* and several Chinese and Japanese dailies.

World Paper, a monthly founded in 1978 in Boston to give an international perspective to the news, is distributed in 23 countries. In 1987 the 16-page publication began appearing as an insert in *China and the World,* a magazine published by the New China News Agency.

Magazines

Because so many magazines throughout the world begin and cease publication frequently, and their reported category range is so variable, estimates as to the total number vary widely, from only about 125,000 to more than 400,000. UNESCO has estimated that about 100,000 scientific and technical periodicals alone are published.

U.S. magazines in strong demand through both subscription and newsstand sales abroad include *Reader's Digest, Time, Newsweek, Business Week, Fortune, National Geographic, Playboy,* and *Penthouse.* According to *Folio* magazine, the leading American magazines purchased at the U.S. cover price from foreign newsstands in 1985 were *Penthouse,* with sales exceeding $10 million, and *Playboy,* with $5.5 million in sales. Others, in order of newsstand sales volume, were *National Enquirer, National Geographic, Muscle & Fitness, Life, Gallery, Vogue, Business Week/World Wide,* and *Byte.*

Reader's Digest distributes about 11.5 million copies abroad—40 national editions in more than a dozen languages, and books in 26 languages as well. *Time* sells about 1.5 million copies abroad, including 400,000 in Europe, where 37 editions with regional advertising are published. *Newsweek*'s foreign circulation approaches 2 million.

In 1986 the United Daily News group of 12 newspapers and magazines began translating weekly editions of America's *U.S. News & World Report.* More than 45,000 copies are distributed to 18 countries and areas on four continents. Bilingual versions of five regular features of the magazine are especially useful for

The Paris-based International Herald Tribune, *long a fixture on European news racks, now is distributed via satellite to English-speaking readers in the Orient and Latin America.* (Courtesy, International Herald Tribune)

International Herald Tribune

The Global Newspaper
Edited in Paris
Printed Simultaneously in
Paris, London, Zurich,
Hong Kong, Singapore,
The Hague and Marseille

Published With The New York Times and The Washington Post

No. 31,911   ZURICH, WEDNESDAY, SEPTEMBER 25, 1985   ESTABLISHED 1887

French Spy Agency Questions 3 Officers in Greenpeace Leaks

By Joseph Fitchett
International Herald Tribune

Paul Quilès

Third World's Nations Facing Tougher Crisis

By Carl Gewirtz
International Herald Tribune

World Debt

A New Phase

First of two articles

Dollar Stable After Freefall

PARIS — The dollar stabilized Tuesday in nervous foreign-exchange markets after a plunge Monday that marked the currency's biggest one-day drop since fixed exchange rates were scrapped in February 1973.

10 Are Injured in Bombing in Central Vienna
Ten persons were injured by flying glass and debris when a bomb exploded Tuesday at the Hungarian Central Exchange and Credit Bank on Kaernter Strasse, Vienna's main shopping street. The blast toppled mannequins in a nearby fashion shop. Police said no motive had been determined.

SEEKING RELATIVES — Placido Domingo, the opera star, standed with rescuers as work faster in seeking survivors of the Mexican earthquake. The death toll exceeded 4,000 on Tuesday as officials debated whether to continue search efforts. Page 6.

Soviet Plan Reportedly Calls for 40% Arms Cut

By Walter Pincus
Washington Post Service

WASHINGTON — Soviet officials have indicated that Foreign Minister Eduard A. Shevardnadze will propose this week to the Reagan administration that both superpowers reduce strategic nuclear missiles and warheads by 40 percent, according to a congressional source.

Edward A. Shevardnadze

China to Allow Inspection of Nuclear Plants

Compiled by Our Staff From Dispatches

VIENNA — In a surprise move, China said Tuesday that it would follow the lead of the world's other nations with nuclear weapons and allow outside inspection of some nonmilitary nuclear facilities.

Zhou Ping, chief delegate to the annual congress of the International

China completes a historic shift of Politburo leaders. Page 5.

Shiites May Demand Less For Freeing U.S. Captives

By David B. Ottaway
Washington Post Service

WASHINGTON — Shiite Moslems may release the six Americans they are holding in Lebanon if Kuwait agrees to free two Lebanese Shiites imprisoned among 17 convicted as terrorists, according to a well-placed Arab diplomatic source and relatives of the hostages.

Legislators Question Reagan's Claim of Soviet Arms Superiority

By George C. Wilson
Washington Post Service

WASHINGTON — President Ronald Reagan's declaration last week that the Soviet Union is ahead of the United States "in literally every kind of weapon" has prompted charges of verbal overkill and raised questions in Congress about what the nation's $1 trillion spent on defense in the past four years has bought the taxpayers.

INSIDE

🔲 An informer said the Mafia helped select two presidents of the Teamsters union.   Page 3

🔲 New York has moved feelings about having the United Nations as a tenant.   Page 3

🔲 U.S. ships will be issued to a private group of North America.   Page 5

🔲 Libia completed the shift of Politburo leaders.   Page 5

Most analysts believe the United States has never

BUSINESS/FINANCE

🔲 U.S. retail prices rose only 2 percent in August for the fourth straight month. Page 15

SPECIAL REPORT

🔲 China and Britain call forward in talks on transition rule in Hong Kong.   Page 9

Six years later than originally planned, the Picasso Museum in Paris is opening.   Page 24

The worldwide popularity of Reader's Digest *is evident by its numerous foreign editions. (© 1986 The Reader's Digest Association, Inc.)*

language students. The editions include a four-page supplement about Chinese people and events, also translated into Chinese.

Other top news magazines include *L'Express* of France, *Der Spiegel* of West Germany, and *Asiaweek,* circulating throughout the Orient. News magazines with strong economic emphases include *The Economist* of London, one of the world's great quality periodicals, and the *Far Eastern Economic Review* of Asia. One of the best picture magazines is *Paris-Match* of France.

Books

A post–World War II revolution in book production and distribution techniques, with emphasis on the paperback, has characterized the world book publishing industry. Between 1955 and 1976, world book production more than doubled in number of titles published annually, and tripled in number of copies printed. It is estimated that more than 590,000 titles and about eight billion copies per year are now marketed. Books were the first mass medium exported in large numbers when European publishers opened up markets and, later, subsidiaries in former colonies. The more limited book publishing in the Third World is overwhelmingly of an educational nature.

In many countries publishing is primarily a private enterprise, although governments of almost all nations have their own printing departments and some subsidize private operations. In communist nations publishing is part of the planned public economy.

U.S. publishing firms export more than $590 million in books each year. About

85 percent of these are sent to other industrialized nations and the Philippines. Canada, the United Kingdom, and Australia represent the largest markets. The leading countries from which books are imported into the United States are the United Kingdom, Canada, and Japan. Even so, American foreign book sales, comprising less than 10 percent of the total, are far below those of the British, who sell almost a third of their books in other countries.

Educational books, particularly those of a high-level scientific and professional nature, represent about one-fourth of U.S. total export revenues. For example, almost one-half of the encyclopedia revenues of American publishers are accounted for through international sales. Mass-market paperback publishers, however, sell about 10 percent of their millions of copies in other countries.

In 1987 Random House purchased a leading British book publishing group, Chatto, Virago, Rodley Head & Jonathan Cape, Ltd. It was the first purchase of a major European trade-book publisher by an American company, representing a reversal of a trend of foreign companies acquiring American book publishing houses. Previously, Doubleday, Dell and Henry Holt had been sold to West Germany publishers; New American Library and E. P. Dutton to a British company; and Grove Press to Ann Getty and Lord George Weidenfeld. In addition, Harper & Row was acquired by Rupert Murdoch, a naturalized American who invited the British book company of which he is a director and holder of a 42 percent interest, William Collins & Sons, to obtain an equity interest and become directly involved in management.

Some other American firms have copublishing arrangements with their own subsidiaries and independent houses abroad. Because of the limited market for English-language editions, translated versions are authorized for publication in many countries. These licensing arrangements often are promoted by the U.S. Information Agency, seeking, in part, to counter extensive Soviet Union publication of both English-language and translated works. Mainly because they represent poor markets, most Third World countries are not part of these licensing plans. In recent years some countries, such as India, have strengthened their own publishing efforts. A number of U.S. firms employ foreign printing houses to produce four-color work and also manufacture entire books. China looms as a sizable market; that country increased its publications imports from $10 million in 1977 to more than $60 million in 1985.

Tariffs on the importation of books increase prices and reduce sales in some countries. In 1986 Canada reimposed a 10 percent tariff on U.S. trade books, both hardcover and paperback, and on certain classifications of magazines. The government action was prompted by imposition of a 35 percent U.S. tariff on Canadian cedar shakes and shingles, followed by a tariff of almost 41 percent on Canadian steel. One analyst estimated that the Canadian action would cost U.S. book publishers $13.3 million of their annual income of about $240 million from sales in Canada.

Piracy is another major concern worldwide. It has been estimated that foreign publishing firms that reproduce books and audiovisual materials without authorization reap profits of $2 billion each year, 70 percent of which represents revenues that should accrue to American publishers and authors. New technologies have accelerated the rate of piracy. The United States is a member of the Universal

Copyright Convention, established in 1952, but is not (along with the Soviet Union and China) a member of the century-old Berne Convention. That convention prohibits formalities, such as registration, as a condition for copyright protection, and this restriction has been considered incompatible with American copyright law. Nevertheless, a renewed campaign against piracy is under way. A major victory occurred in 1986 when South Korea agreed to take steps to protect U.S. copyrights.

ORGANIZATIONS

The United Nations

International communication has been a major concern of the United Nations since its founding in 1946. In that year the UN issued a Declaration on Freedom of Information, which stated that "all states should proclaim policies under which the free flow of information within countries and across frontiers will be protected. The right to seek and transmit information should be insured in order to enable the public to ascertain facts and appraise events." Because of conflicting legal and ideological positions, a convention as to how this principle would be invoked has never been worked out.

In 1948 the UN General Assembly issued a Universal Declaration of Human Rights, which, although not legally binding, carries great moral and psychological weight with UN members. Article 19 of the document proclaims that: "Everyone has the right to freedom of opinion and expression; this right includes freedom to hold opinions . . . and to seek, receive, and impart information and ideas through any media and regardless of frontiers." Article 2 extends the document's affirmation of basic human rights to every individual "without distinction of any kind" including the "limitation of sovereignty." Resolution 110 (II), passed in 1947, condemns all forms of conflict-inciting propaganda, and Article 4 of the International Convention on Elimination of Racial Discrimination, passed in 1963, condemns all forms of racist propaganda. The issue of human rights was reaffirmed with the International Covenant on Civil and Political Rights in 1966 and by the Helsinki agreements in 1975.

With the launching of the first space satellites, the UN became involved in questions relating to outer space, and in 1959 the Committee on the Peaceful Uses of Outer Space was established. A declaration in 1963 was followed by passage of the Outer Space Treaty in 1967, as previously discussed in this chapter. It declared that outer space was to remain the "province of all mankind" to which all nations shall have equal access, that its uses should be nonmilitary but contributing to international peace and security. Two years later, with 102 nations in favor and the United States opposed, the UN called upon its committee to "elaborate principles governing the use by States of artificial earth satellites for direct television broadcasting with a view toward concluding an international agreement or agreements."

UNESCO. The involvement of the United Nations Educational, Scientific, and Cultural Organization (UNESCO) with mass communications was mandated in

Article 1 of its constitution, which states that the organization shall "collaborate in the work of advancing the mutual knowledge and understanding of peoples, through all means of mass communication, and to that end recommend such international agreements as may be necessary to promote the free flow of ideas by word or image." UNESCO is composed of official delegations of all member nations, which convene biennially. Between these general conferences, UNESCO's work is carried out by its Secretariat, based in Paris. Its activities include research, field projects, meetings of experts, regional conferences, and seminars. Among its actions was a declaration in 1972 calling for the principle of prior consent to be applied to broadcasts from satellites. In recent years UNESCO has become the primary forum for Third World communication complaints, which will be reviewed later in this chapter.

INTERNATIONAL TELECOMMUNICATION UNION. This UN agency traces its history back to an 1865 European conference establishing rules for transmission of telegraph messages across national boundaries. The telegraphic union thus formed was followed in 1906 by the establishment of a radio-telegraphic union. The two merged in 1932 to form the International Telecommunication Union (ITU), which became a UN agency in 1947. Its primary function is engineering —to govern frequency allocation and coordinate procedures for the world's electromagnetic spectrum. In recent years the ITU has become highly politicized as new nations have sought space on the crowded spectrum and older countries have sought largely to preserve the "first-come, first-served" principle that has given them priority. Primary World Administrative Radio Conferences, conducted every 20 years, are supplemented by special conferences dealing with satellites and other matters.

National Government Organizations

The governments of virtually every country have one or more departments involved in international communications. Almost all oversee broadcast operations, and many exercise direct and indirect control over the print media including fields such as news and editorial content, the acquisition of newsprint and equipment, the collection and dissemination of news by foreign correspondents in their countries, the news agencies that receive and transmit information, and their international information and propaganda activities.

The United States Information Agency administers a wide variety of information, educational, and cultural exchange programs around the world. The agency reports to the president and receives policy guidance from the secretary of state.

USIA employs approximately 8600 persons, of whom about 4200 are non-Americans serving abroad. About one-half of the USIA's 3400 employees in the United States are engaged in the broadcasting operations of the Voice of America. Many of the others provide supporting services for 600 Foreign Service information and cultural affairs officers working overseas alongside colleagues from the Department of State and other U.S. agencies at more than 200 embassies, consulates, and other missions in 125 countries. Among other activities, USIA operates regional libraries, plans exhibits and tours of performing groups, produces radio and television programs and research reports, and provides opportunities for foreign residents to learn English.

In 1983 USIA established a one-way video, two-way audio WORLDNET television service providing viewers in 75 countries with regular access to prominent American newsmakers as well as videoconferences on public diplomacy themes. By 1986 more than 170 "interactive" conferences had been conducted. USIA Director Charles Z. Wick asked Congress early in 1987 to approve a charter stating professional guidelines for handling WORLDNET news. The charter, patterned after one approved by Congress in 1976 for the Voice of America, is designed to guarantee integrity and credibility in USIA's television news.

In 1985 USIA began operation of Radio Marti, a medium-wave station in Florida, transmitting, according to its congressional mandate, "news, commentary, and other information about events in Cuba and elsewhere to promote the cause of freedom in Cuba," along with music. The station maintains a bureau in Miami, coverage in Washington, D.C., and a worldwide network of more than 60 part-time correspondents.

The Office of International Communication Policy of the Department of State performs various functions such as preparing the U.S. position for World Administrative Radio Conferences. As do the Soviet Union's KGB and the intelligence agencies of other countries, the Central Intelligence Agency engages in numerous clandestine communications activities abroad on behalf of American interests.

Nongovernment Organizations

Hundreds of private mass communications organizations operate throughout the world. A few of them will be noted here.

FÉDÉRATION INTERNATIONALE DES ÉDITEURS DE JOURNAUX. The International Federation of Newspaper Publishers (FIEJ), founded in 1948, links more than 25 national publishers' organizations on five continents in the free world to promote their interests in such fields as management, marketing, news-editorial, and freedom of information.

INTERNATIONAL PRESS INSTITUTE. Founded in 1950, the IPI is an association of about 2000 editors, publishers, broadcast executives, and associates in 63 nations dedicated primarily to promoting press freedom, fostering research, and training Third World journalists. The IPI continuously protests the imprisonment and murder of outspoken journalists.

INTER AMERICAN PRESS ASSOCIATION. The IAPA, organized in 1942, among other activities monitors press situations in all Western hemisphere countries, protests restrictive measures, sends special missions to problem countries, and promotes the exchange of journalists for educational purposes.

INTER-AMERICAN ASSOCIATION OF BROADCASTERS. The IAAB provides representation and technical and educational help for broadcast stations and associations in South and North America.

INTERNATIONAL FEDERATION OF JOURNALISTS. Through 28 national unions in 24 countries, the federation seeks to raise professional standards, defend press freedom, and help news media in developing nations.

INTERNATIONAL ORGANIZATION OF JOURNALISTS. This Marxist organization, headquartered in Czechoslovakia and linked to groups in 109 countries, promotes various journalistic activities.

WORLD PRESS FREEDOM COMMITTEE. Activated in the United States in 1976, the WPFC links 32 national and international media organizations in monitoring perceived challenges to world press freedom and in providing training programs, equipment, and consultants for Third World countries.

THE THIRD WORLD COMMUNICATIONS CONTROVERSY

Not only is the majority of the world's news transmitted by Western news agencies, but the Western powers are also the most advanced in the use of telecommunications channels, including satellites. The nonaligned and some other nations view this dominance of communications channels as a vestige of colonialism that must be shaken off if they are to develop culturally, politically, and economically. They believe that their goal of a New World Economic Order cannot be realized without a corresponding New World Communications Order. Their principal demands, as detailed in a document written by Mustapha Masmoudi, a Tunisian government official, have included the following:

- Establishing independence and equity in access to global communication resources in order that their own views, values, and developmental efforts might be reported more fully.
- Substantial help from the West to speed their own communication development.
- Western support of the Pool of News Agencies of Non-Aligned Countries, mentioned previously in this chapter.
- Legitimizing the right of governments to limit access to news sources and the right to censor or restrict the flow of information across national borders.
- The adoption by UNESCO of resolutions proclaiming the right of governments to become involved in the licensing of journalists in order to "protect" them, and in the adoption of an international code of ethics and an international right of reply.
- Establishment of a supranational tribunal by UNESCO to monitor media behavior throughout the world.

The Third World complaints gained the full attention of the Western nations in 1976, when the Soviet Union's draft copy of a declaration proposed for adoption by UNESCO stipulated the "use" of the mass news media for certain purposes and made independent journalists subject to control by governments. Alarmed, Western governments and the independent news media mounted a strong defense that won a two-year delay, based mainly on promises of increased aid to Third World news media. A 16-person International Commission for the Study of Communication Problems was created under the chairmanship of Sean MacBride of Ireland, recipient of both the Lenin and Nobel Peace Prizes.

By making further pledges to help Third World countries develop their news agencies and media, and by skillful maneuvering, Western leaders again warded off the state control threat at the 1978 UNESCO conference. A declaration was adopted that dropped the phrase, "free and balanced flow of information," the antithesis of a free flow, and called for "a new equilibrium and greater repricocity" —a balancing of news reports between the developed and developing countries and among the developing nations. The declaration also noted "the aspirations of the developing countries for the establishment of a new, more just, and more effective world information and communication order."

Through the World Press Freedom Committee, American news organizations already had raised more than $500,000 toward an initial goal of $1 million and were engaged in spending almost $300,000, mainly for training programs on three continents, soliciting donations of used equipment, and sending consultants abroad from a pool of 900 volunteer consultants. Plans were made to seek funding for substantial technology transfer through the United Nations Development Program, the International Telecommunication Union, and the World Bank.

THE MACBRIDE REPORT. When the MacBride Commission released its final report in 1980, the World Press Freedom Committee noted the following *positive* aspects of the report, from its traditional democratic–capitalist point of view:

- Censorship in all forms is condemned.
- The right of access applies to private as well as public sources of information.
- Journalists should have no special protection; they will be protected when the rights of all citizens are guaranteed.
- Licensing of journalists is rejected because it would require stipulation by some authority as to who is eligible and on what basis.
- Employment of journalists by intelligence agencies of any country is condemned.

Negative aspects from the Western point of view:

- A proposed International Center for Study and Planning of Information and Communications, to be established within UNESCO, conceivably could become a training ground for those challenging the Western concept of privately owned news businesses operating with traditional Western news values.

- News media (including the international news agencies and other transnational communication enterprises) would be pressured, or required, to promote government-set social, cultural, economic, and political goals.
- Private ownership of news media and communication facilities is questioned.

Because of the moderate tone of the MacBride Commission's report, UNESCO Director-General Amadou Mahtar M'Bow of Senegal—who has favored Third World aims while trying to avoid a blowup with the West—declined to present the report for formal adoption at UNESCO's twenty-first conference in Belgrade, Yugoslavia, in 1980. Instead M'Bow asked the delegates simply to consider it.

After several weeks of wrangling, delegates adopted a resolution calling for the free flow of information; expressing the need to safeguard freedom of opinion, expression, and information; supporting the widest and most democratic access possible to the functioning of the mass media; and repudiating censorship and licensing.

No concrete steps were taken toward the establishment of a New World Communications Order; however, the delegates agreed to underwrite a three-year study of what would be included in such a document. In addition, they authorized funding for a series of ten regional conferences on topics (mainly objectionable to the West) such as the protection of journalists, a definition of journalistic standards, international right of reply and rectification, responsibility in communications, and the advertising content and management of the media.

THE IPDC PROGRAM. A decision also was made to establish the International Program for the Development of Communications (IPDC), stemming from a U.S. proposal at the 1978 conference. Goals are: (1) to gather information about the communications needs of developing countries and (2) to mobilize financial and technical support to help meet those needs. The United States contributed $700,-000 toward a $10 million budget. While operations were to be partially supported by UNESCO, funding for specific projects would be developed through voluntary contributions.

The 35-member council of IPDC met in Acapulco, Mexico, in 1982 and reviewed proposals for 24 regional, 27 national, and 3 worldwide projects. Africa was accorded top priority as the most needy area, and, among 14 regional projects awarded $741,000 as first-year funding, the Pan African News Agency was allocated $100,000. An additional $2 million for the African project was sought from the Gulf States Program for United Nations Organizations.

Among numerous projects supplementary to the IPDC program, the U.S. Telecommunications Training Institution was created in 1982 to provide tuition-free training for Third World personnel. Participating companies included AT&T, COMSAT, and Hughes Aircraft Corporation. Additional technology transfer programs were announced by the World Press Freedom Committee.

With the IPDC program in place, representatives of Western governments and news organizations sought unsuccessfully at UNESCO's 1983 general conference to have the organization abandon elements of the proposed new information order aimed at establishing norms of international communications conduct. Some of these goals were indeed "watered down" by the conferees, who also approved studies of the watchdog role of the press in exposing government corruption and wrongdoing and of the effects of media censorship. In addition, a Soviet-sponsored resolution was defeated that would have empowered UNESCO to issue a blacklist of news organizations allegedly in violation of press guidelines drawn up in 1978.

This only-partial response to Western demands for UNESCO reforms, coupled with a decision to increase the 1984–1985 budget to $374.4 million despite U.S. insistence that the budget not be enlarged, precipitated a long-considered announcement by the United States that it would withdraw from the organization at the end of 1984.

A Department of State spokesman, Alan Romberg, said the United States contends that UNESCO had "politicized virtually every subject it deals with, exhibited hostility toward the basic institutions of a free press, and demonstrated unrestrained budgetary expansion." Gregory Newell, assistant secretary of state for international organizations, said the decision to withdraw would be reconsidered if significant and permanent changes were made in UNESCO's fundamental policies—a prospect that seemed unlikely.

UNESCO ACTIVITIES REDUCED. The UNESCO budget was reduced 25 percent by U.S. withdrawal from membership in 1985, and another 4.6 percent with Great Britain's withdrawal a year later. Both countries announced that the money saved would go directly to developing countries, to promote UNESCO-type objectives. UNESCO subsequently fired more than one-fourth of its more than 2000 staff members and canceled or phased out a number of its programs.

No "reforms" of the type urged by the United States and Great Britain had been made when UNESCO held its general meeting in Sofia, Bulgaria, in 1985. The body did reject a Soviet proposal spelling out the "responsibilities" of journalists as well as efforts to water down a planned UNESCO study of censorship, supported by Western powers. Renewed efforts were made, however, to sanction government intrusions on journalistic independence and to establish guideposts in international documents designed to outlaw certain kinds of news.

Requested by UNESCO to comment on its proposed 1988–1989 budget and programs, the International Federation of Newspaper Publishers (FIEJ) called on the agency to abandon its theoretical studies and research programs and stick to concrete projects for helping the media, particularly in developing countries. FIEJ recommended that UNESCO "concentrate its energies on monitoring new communication technologies closely, for example teletext and data banks, and investigate the possibilities of, and problems created by, satellites operational across national borders." The resolution added that, "In our view, the examination should be pursued from the point of view of a better and freer flow of information and not in support of restrictive attitudes on the part of national governments as applies today."

UNITED NATIONS. Thwarted thus far in their UNESCO efforts, proponents of the New World Information Order shifted their campaign to the United Nations. In 1986 the 60-nation UN Committee on Information approved a resolution precisely refusing to accept the consensus language accepted at UNESCO conferences that described the concept as an evolving and continuous process rather than something to be mandated and imposed. The UN General Assembly, in approving the resolution, called for establishment of the "new order," praised UNESCO efforts toward "clarification, elaboration, and application" of the plan, emphasized a role for public information in promoting universal disarmament, supported efforts to implement a 1978 mass media declaration, and requested UNESCO studies on the socioeconomic and cultural impact of new communication technology. No Western nation voted for the resolution. The campaign continued at a roundtable sponsored by the UN and UNESCO in Denmark.

Dana Bullen, executive director of the World Press Freedom Committee, expressed the Western view and that of Third World moderate nations in the June 1986 issue of *presstime* magazine. He suggested that, "in place of rhetoric about duties and restrictions," an approach should be put forward at UN and other meetings that:

- Rejects rather than ignores widespread censorship in the world.
- Promotes the free flow of news as mandated by Article 19 of the 1948 Universal Declaration of Human Rights instead of bending and limiting it.
- Opposes shutting down newspapers or turning off radio stations for reporting what angers somebody in power.
- Allocates resources at least evenly between independent and government media, rather than exclusively for the latter.
- Opposes channeling of all incoming news to a country through a government-run "national news agency," blocking direct access by news media.
- Finds a way to stop the killing, kidnapping, and jailing of journalists.

DECLARATION OF TAILLOIRES. The proposed agenda reflects a policy statement known as the Declaration of Tailloires, adopted by leaders of independent news-gathering organizations from 20 countries at a meeting in Tailloires, France, in 1981. As one outcome of the meeting, foreign correspondent George Krimsky prepared a comprehensive list of the approximately 300 programs in more than 60 countries that aid Third World journalists. In 1985 American publishers opened the Center for Foreign Journalists in Reston, Virginia, with Krimsky as director. The center maintains the list and provides workshops for foreign journalists.

The Tailloires declaration was reinforced in 1987 when 150 journalists from 15 countries adopted a plan of action to combat censorship. This so-called Declaration of London set forth nine "basic principles that should apply in maintaining a universal, free, and uncensored flow of information" throughout the world.

LICENSING OF JOURNALISTS. In November 1985 the Inter-American Court of Human Rights, an autonomous judicial arm of the 32-member Organization of American States, ruled seven-to-zero that a law requiring the licensing of journalists violated the right to free expression. Stephen Schmidt, an American reporter, had been found guilty in 1983 of practicing journalism in Costa Rica without a required license and had received a three-month suspended sentence from that nation's Supreme Court. The human rights court held that "the compulsory licensing of journalists is incompatible with Article 13 of the American Convention on Human Rights insofar as it denies some persons access to the full use of the news media as a means of expressing themselves or imparting information." Eleven Latin American nations and Spain are among countries that require such licensing. Free-press advocates expressed hope that the ruling would begin a reversal of the licensing trend.

THE PERSUASIVE ARTS

Advertising

World trade expands constantly, and with the growth of multinational companies has come the growth of multinational advertising agencies to serve multinational clients. As trade barriers have fallen, manufacturing distribution and advertising agency practices have become international activities in which the old concept of home as distinct from overseas markets is increasingly irrelevant. Coca-Cola, Toyota automobiles, Gillette products, and Tide—these and hundreds of other products are sold throughout the world; Gillette, for example, spends more than $100 million in advertising each year in 170 countries.

The earlier American dominance of world advertising has been diminished by increasingly more sophisticated practice in many other countries. Edward Ney of Young & Rubicam International states: "Today great advertising can and does happen everywhere in the world. The U.S. no longer has a monopoly, no longer has to dispatch its advertising missionaries abroad and spread the faith because they've got religion over there; and, like the traditional converts, these once benighted natives are frequently more dedicated practitioners than those born to the faith."

During the last two decades, huge multinational advertising conglomerates took shape as a number of major American advertising agencies joined forces with companies in Europe and elsewhere. In 1889 the J. Walter Thompson Co. opened its first overseas office in London. The international merger movement, however, got under way during the 1950s when McCann-Erickson began building its Interpublic Group of Companies' empire. In 1969 the Chicago-based Leo Burnett Company startled the advertising world with the acquisition of the major agency parts of the London Press Exchange, then the second largest London-based agency.

The movement assumed mega-agency proportions in 1986. Three of the top global agencies—BBDO International, the Doyle Dane Bernbach Group, and Needham Harper Worldwide—formed a holding company, Omnicom Group, to handle about $6 billion a year in billings. In that same year England's Saatchi & Saatchi Company acquired America's third largest agency, Ted Bates Worldwide, and became the world's largest agency with annual billings of $7.5 billion. Several

Japanese agencies, headed by Dentsu, also grew extensively. Despite the agency-engulfing mergers, many observers believe that medium-sized agencies will still be a strong force in most countries (see Chapter 17).

Multinational business firms operate subsidiaries in a number of countries, which often have vastly differing political, cultural, economic, and legal environments. Some companies centralize their marketing and advertising operations, while others assign much decision making to their foreign managers. The environmental variables are so numerous and often so subtle—in areas such as eating patterns and customs, social class structure, income levels, and legal restraint—that creative sales and promotion strategy, to a considerable extent, must be custom-tailored for each country. With regard to the European market, Professor S. Watson Dunn of the University of Illinois at Champaign-Urbana has concluded that, "the best approach is to preserve some covert multinationalism in the campaign but to add a deft touch that is distinctively French or British or Italian."

As in the United States and Canada, the consumer movement has gained momentum in recent years in most industrialized nations. Legislation to regulate and control advertising has been proposed or passed in Australia, Canada, Finland, Germany, Japan, Norway, the United Kingdom, the United States, and other countries. Cigarette and children's advertising, along with that considered dishonest, have been primary concerns. Statutes vary from country to country. Some countries, such as the United Kingdom and Ireland, rely on self-discipline by business itself. Most companies subscribe to the International Chamber of Commerce code of advertising practice. The International Advertising Association, composed of about 2500 individual members and more than 300 international companies and other groups, states that, in order to gain acceptance for self-regulation, its members should eliminate abuses in the marketplace and act as the champion of the public's interests in quality and performance of goods and services.

American companies with foreign branches often publish advertisements in the languages of their host countries. (Courtesy of the Coca-Cola Company)

No Western advertising agencies are permitted to operate in the Soviet bloc countries. In the Third World nations advertising is less developed but international agencies operate extensively. Some Third World countries seek to establish guidelines regarding advertising content and the values and attitudes it fosters, which are often perceived as contrary to national cultural values. Some of these nations also tax advertising, or plan to do so, in order to provide funding for national media development.

Public Relations

International public relations is the planned and organized effort of a company, institution, or government to establish mutually beneficial relations with the publics of other nations. It is an integral part of the foreign manufacturing, marketing, and investment operations of virtually all major corporations of the world.

Scores of U.S. public relations firms work with these companies, although mainly with those based in this country. The giant in the field is Hill & Knowlton. Other top U.S. agencies involved include Burson-Marsteller; Ruder, Finn & Rotman; Daniel J. Edelman; Doremus Public Relations; Ketchum Public Relations; Manning, Selvage & Lee; and Fleishman-Hillard.

American managers of U.S. corporations provide the continuing, overall strategy, but—because every country's customs and values are different, and substantial variations often exist even within companies—its application must be carried out primarily by public relations employees and outside consultants native to each country.

Companies everywhere are confronted with essentially the same public relations problems as those in the United States, including relationships with local and national governments, consumer groups, the financial community, and employees. For a company operating outside the borders of its own country, these problems often are aggravated by, among other things, the differences in language, longer chains of command, evident and subtle differences in customs, and the varying levels of media and public relations development.

A number of American public relations firms help foreign industries attain their sales and investment goals in this country. These firms seek to (1) hold off protectionist moves threatening a company's operations, (2) defeat legislation affecting the sale of a client's products, (3) support the expansion of the client's markets, and (4) keep the foreign company informed about important developments that may affect its interests in this country.

United States counseling firms also are retained by foreign governments, at large fees. Among other things, they seek to (1) advance their client's political objectives, (2) advise regarding probable reactions to projected actions, (3) advance commercial interests such as tourism, (4) help the client communicate in English, and (5) modify laws and regulations inhibiting the country's activities in the United States. For example, Hill & Knowlton has represented Indonesia and Morocco; Burson-Marsteller, Argentina, Costa Rica, Hungary, and the Soviet Union (the latter mainly in trade fairs); and Ruder & Finn, El Salvador, Israel, and Japan.

Hundreds of noncorporate groups depend upon international support for their undertakings. Vigorous public relations programs are maintained by such organizations as the International Red Cross, World Council of Churches, International Council of B'nai B'rith, and the International Chamber of Commerce, along with numerous foundations, educational enterprises, labor unions, and government-support agencies. For effective operation, their images must be kept as spotless as possible; like corporations, they must constantly monitor their environments, maintain proper relationships with the governments and publics of the countries in which they operate, and be prepared to handle crises.

With the development of satellite systems, many companies and governments conduct conferences in various parts of the world via satellite broadcasting. *Teleconferencing* has become an important international public relations and marketing tool.

Public relations associations have been organized in about 50 countries. In Great Britain more than 2500 practitioners belong to the British Institute of Public Relations. Because the German language has no close equivalent, practitioners in Germany have formed an association known as the Deutsche Public Relations Gesellschaft. In Japan, where more than 1000 consultants practice, the Public Relations Society of Japan has been formed. Regional associations include the European Center of Public Relations, the Pan Pacific Public Relations Federation, and the Inter-American Federation of Public Relations.

As noted in Chapter 18, the International Public Relations Association has members in more than 60 countries. Its objectives are to provide a means whereby members may exchange information and ideas, improve skills and ethical standards, and work toward a better understanding among the peoples of the world. Also, as previously noted, the International Association of Business Communicators rapidly is extending its membership to other countries.

RESEARCH

Cooperative research among nations is a strong component of mass communications research throughout the world. This is *true* international communications research, as exemplified by the study of the flow of news among nations and the determination of the international uses and effects of the transmission of information and cultural programs via satellite. Much more international communications research, however, is comparative in nature; for example, researchers may analyze media systems within individual countries and regions and then compare their findings with analyses of systems in other countries and regions that have been made by themselves or by researchers interested in only one country. In another category researchers endeavor, for example, to determine the effects, within a particular country, of communication received from outside its borders; or they may analyze the nature and operations of the communicators who send messages to other countries.

International communications scholars employ all the methodologies for gaining scientific information used by researchers in other fields. Their research may be *quantitative* in nature, employing such methodologies as content analysis, surveys, polling, and experimental techniques, or they may be *qualitative* studies, such as those of a descriptive, historical, and legal nature. These researchers are joined in international communications studies by scholars in other fields such as sociology, anthropology, economics, geography, and linguistics.

In the United States some international communications research began in the 1920s, when concern developed over matters such as World War I propaganda, the intermedia competition between newspapers and radio, and the impact of the rapidly growing mass media upon society. The real boom began during the period in which the United Nations was founded: after World War II, when the United States sought, in the words of one observer "to develop an art and science of international and crosscultural communication and opinion, in the hope of reducing international confusion and irritation." International communications research slowly developed from its parent disciplines into a field of its own which, although still in its infancy, is exercised predominantly through the universities, independent research centers often supported by foundations, government agencies, and business corporations intent on developing foreign markets.

In recent years much study has focused on the dissemination of innovation—how new technological and cultural inventions and ideas have been accepted in various countries—and in rural, family planning, and development communications in Third World countries. Research under way at centers throughout the world seeks answers to all sorts of communications problems plaguing the developing world. Among these centers are the East-West Communication Institute at Honolulu, the Asian Mass Communication Research and Information Centre at Singapore, and the Centre for Mass Communication Research in Leicester, England. Other regions in the Third World are seeking to develop their own research centers. For more than three decades UNESCO has developed research worldwide. During the 1950s the organization was mainly preoccupied with compiling information about the mass media and news agencies, but since the early 1960s it has turned much of its attention to development communication and, at present, to planning related to the entire communications technological explosion.

Increasingly influential was the International Association for Mass Communication Research (IAMCR), which by 1987 counted about 1000 members in 62 countries. Founded by a group of western European university research scholars, IAMCR was financially nurtured by UNESCO in the 1950s and led by the editor of *Journalism Quarterly,* Raymond B. Nixon. The group took over sponsorship of the Dutch research quarterly, *Gazette,* and began biennial general assemblies featuring discussion sessions and presentation of research papers. By 1987 substantial blocs of members from eastern Europe and the United States had joined with the western European founders of IAMCR, along with members from India, Asia, Latin America, and Africa. The 1986 assembly in New Delhi drew 360 participants from 42 countries. IAMCR headquarters, directed by James D. Holloran, were at the University of Leicester Centre for Mass Communication Research.

EDUCATION

Closely related to research has been the widespread development of training and professional education centers throughout the world. Much of this development took place during the 1950s and 1960s, when, under the Fulbright (later Fulbright-Hays) and Smith-Mundt programs, American mass communications educators went abroad at the rate of more than one dozen per year to help establish schools of journalism and strengthen others that had already begun. They took with them the concept that a liberal education, as provided by a university or other institution, in combination with professional instruction, would best serve a country's long-term communications needs.

Because the inculcation of professional standards and principles in a country's journalists is perhaps the greatest guarantee of a free press, the established centers of journalism education, both national and regional, are now playing an increasingly important role in the full development of the media in Third World countries and elsewhere. Of note are the professional education programs in the universities of Mexico, Peru, Brazil, and Argentina, as well as at the University of the West Indies; at Cairo University; in Kenya, Nigeria, and Ghana; in India, Taiwan, Hong King, the Philippines, Malaysia, and Thailand; and in Spain and Portugal.

During a typical academic year mass communications educators from American universities study or lecture in countries such as Egypt, Indonesia, Mexico, Britain, Japan, Jamaica, India, Brazil, Portugal, Colombia, Liberia, Nigeria, Australia, and Singapore. At the same time Fulbright lecturers and researchers come to the United States from Peru, Bulgaria, Japan, the Federal Republic of Germany, France, Norway, Argentina, Britain, South Korea, and elsewhere. For example, approximately 400 international graduate students from 73 countries studied mass communications in 58 schools and departments of journalism in the United States during the 1978–1979 academic year. To varying degrees, the exchange of educators and students is taking place among numerous other countries.

Seminars, institutes, and other educational programs throughout the world are supported each year by organizations such as the International Press Institute, World Press Freedom Committee, Inter American Press Association, Ford Foundation, Thomson Foundation, Friedrich Naumann Stiftung (Foundation), Konrad Adenauer Stiftung, UN Fund for Population Activities, UNESCO, and the International Development Research Centre. The news services and print and broadcast media and organizations sponsor training programs annually.

Under the operating philosophy that Third World journalists may best be educated and trained in their own environs, governmental and private sector efforts are now being concentrated on the development of regional centers of professional and technical education, a movement coinciding with the growth of regional news agencies. Classes taught by native instructors who have studied in other countries and who write and use textbooks indigenous to each region's language and culture are in great demand.

Meanwhile, international communications instruction in American universities is advancing slowly, impeded by increased student enrollments that are straining resources needed for all areas of instruction. Instruction is further constrained by accrediting requirements that state that communications instruction must occupy no more than approximately 25 percent of a student's total course of study.

WHAT *IS* THE THIRD WORLD?

To talk about *the* Third World is as descriptive as saying that Korean *kimchee* and Central American refried beans are, after all, both food. Not surprisingly, countries so labeled don't like the term "Third World," which implies that they hold a lower status than other nations. "First World," after all, is usually taken to mean the democratic industrialized nations, whereas the Eastern Bloc countries are sometimes placed in the "Second World," a phrase that is also loaded with value judgments.

The phrase "Third World" is originally French and not pejorative. French intellectual Alfred Sauvy seems to have used *le tiers monde* first, in *L'Observateur* in 1952, to describe nations shaking off colonial rule in the same way that commoners—the Third Estate—sought equality with the nobility and the clergy during the French Revolution. In the words of French Revolutionary Emmanuel-Joseph Sieyes, "What is the Third Estate? Everything. What is it asking? To become something."

So what is the Third World? It is India with 750 million people and Fiji with 700,000. It is Communist China and conservative Singapore. It is Burkina Faso and Bangladesh, with annual per capita incomes of less than $200, and it is newly industrialized countries (so-called MICs or middle-income countries) like Brazil and Seychelles, with per capita incomes of $2000. It is oil-rich Saudi-Arabia, Venezuela, and Nigeria; and oil-poor Tanzania and South Korea. It is anti-American Cuba and pro-American Philippines, and it is countries that fight each other, Iran and Iraq. It's also Turkey and Tunisia, Chile and Costa Rica, Sudan and Senegal, Thailand and Taiwan, and Yugoslovia.

And it is in flux. White-ruled Rhodesia, some thought, was not in the Third World; its black-ruled successor, Zimbabwe, is.

Qu'est-ce que le tiers monde? Too complex for neat definitions. Too big to be ignored. (Reprinted from *The Quill,* September 1986, by permission of *The Quill* and the author, John Maxwell Hamilton, compiler of a Sigma Delta Chi Foundation book, *Main Street America and the Third World,* detailing how the media increasingly are localizing foreign news.)

JOB OPPORTUNITIES IN INTERNATIONAL COMMUNICATIONS

Students interested in international communications work will most likely find their first opportunities when, as beginning reporters and editors, they cover assignments involving international matters and, as gatekeepers, edit international news stories. As magazine and freelance writers, they may be assigned to stories with an international flavor. Those assuming advertising and public relations duties with business corporations will need to work their way into the international departments of those companies. The tourism and development divisions of state government may afford an entry point. U.S. Foreign Service examinations are the beginning requirement for those seeking federal government positions leading to international communications work. Military service often provides yet another opportunity.

For those who seek foreign assignments with newspapers, magazines, broadcast networks, and news services, the road to those assignments most likely will be long, with service first in the United States to acquire experience and establish a personnel record recommending the applicant for overseas service. The same is true for advertising and public relations people who wish to work abroad. Equally long will be the road for those desiring university teaching and research professorships or work with independent research organizations that will lead to travel and study in other countries. Foreign service work with innumerable federal agencies, such as USIA, also often requires a substantial period of government or mass media service in this country before foreign assignments are received. In terms of adventure and salary, however, the rewards for those who "do their homework," preparing themselves adequately through experience and individual study, are ample.

Most USIA foreign service information officers begin their careers via the Career Candidate Program. Applicants take a written examination offered each December at many locations in this country and abroad. The examination tests general knowledge, English expression, and aptitude for information, cultural, economic, political, administrative, and consular work. To qualify for the USIA, candidates must receive passing grades in all areas and show particular strength in their knowledge of American culture, history, government, and society and current affairs. Other evaluations follow this examination. After orientation and training in Washington, D.C., including geographic area studies and language instruction as appropriate, a career candidate is assigned to a USIA post overseas for approximately one year. This training assignment is followed by a tour of duty in positions such as assistant cultural affairs officer, assistant information officer, program assistant, and occasionally public affairs officer at a branch of a USIA post in a large country such as India or Brazil. Permanent tenure may then be awarded in the form of a presidential commission. A foreign service information officer usually spends about two-thirds of his or her career overseas. Inquiries about USIA positions should be made to the agency at 1776 Pennsylvania Avenue, N.W., Washington, D.C. 20547.

An assignment as a foreign correspondent for a newspaper, news magazine, network, or news service has been the dream of many young journalists. As previously noted, however, such assignments are limited. Because it costs so much to maintain a correspondent overseas, assignments often go to unmarried persons who require less financial outlay. Sometimes they are employed by a media news bureau abroad. One encouraging trend among major American newspapers is to send staff members on specific overseas assignments, lasting perhaps several months, which is less costly than assigning living quarters abroad. This gives more persons an opportunity to do reporting overseas.

Because an extensive knowledge of national history, customs, laws, and language is highly desirable, advertising and public relations personnel often are natives of the countries or regions in which they work. For example, Richard C. Christian, former president of Burson-Marsteller, has observed that a new breed of marketing executive has emerged in Europe who is "multinational in attitude and multilingual and young."

Students interested in international communications careers of any type are advised to direct their programs of study toward obtaining substantive knowledge in international aspects of the social sciences, humanities, business, law, or other areas closely related to their individual talents and preferences. The choices are so numerous that career objectives should be narrowed quickly. For orientation, course work in international communications is highly desirable. Graduate study undoubtedly would be an asset.

The same necessity for early career decisions also applies to languages. Students should learn to speak and read one foreign language as well as they can. They may depend upon later intensive study or living experience in another country for the language mastery that will be necessary.

Bibliography

This is a selected, annotated bibliography of books dealing with mass communications and journalism. It is organized to correspond with the six principal parts and 25 chapters of this book.

It is the authors' aim to introduce readers to some of the basic books that, if they have the time and interest to explore them, will take them beyond the necessarily limited syntheses of an introductory survey of mass communications. A student reader who has the interest and opportunity to elect further studies in the field will encounter many of these books again in advanced courses; if the student goes no further, this bibliography will provide a personal reading list for more detailed examination of various facets of the field. It is in no sense an all-inclusive bibliography; for that purpose the reader is referred to Eleanor Blum and Frances Wilhoit, *Mass Media Bibliography: Reference, Research, and Reading* (Urbana: University of Illinois Press, 1988). Its 1200 annotated entries cover general communications, newspapers, broadcasting, film, magazines, advertising, and public relations. For more depth, particularly in historical areas and biographies, see the 3147 entries in Warren C. Price's *The Literature of Journalism: An Annotated Bibliography* (Minneapolis: University of Minnesota Press, 1959) and the 2172 entries in a 10-year supplement to it compiled by Price and Calder M. Pickett, *An Annotated Journalism Bibliography* (1970).

Communication Booknotes, edited since 1969 by Christopher H. Sterling and published monthly by him at the Department of Communication and Theatre, George Washington University, offers extensive listings and annotations of books in all communication and media areas. Some currently published bibliographies include Joseph P. McKerns, *News Media and Public Policy: An Annotated Bibliography* (New York: Garland, 1985); Robert Armour, *Film: A Reference Guide* (Westport, Conn.: Greenwood Press, 1980); George Rehrauer, *The Macmillan Film Bibliography* (New York: Macmillan, 1982); Bruce A. Austin, *The Film*

Audience; An International Bibliography of Research (Metuchen, N.J.: Scarecrow Press, 1983); Fred K. Paine and Nancy E. Paine, *Magazines: A Bibliography of Their Analysis with Annotations* (Metuchen, N.J.: Scarecrow Press, 1987); Arthur F. Wertheim, *American Popular Culture: A Historical Bibliography* (New York: ABC-Clio Information Services, 1984); Benjamin F. Shearer and Marilyn Buxford, *Communications and Society: A Bibliography on Communications Technologies and Their Social Impact* (Beverly Hills, Calif.: Sage, 1983); Albert N. Greco, editor, *The Graphic Arts Bibliography* (New York: New York University, 1984); and Roland E. Wolseley, *The Journalist's Bookshelf* (Indianapolis: R.J. Berg, 1984). See also the bibliographies in research journals listed below.

A remarkably useful encyclopedia, by Robert V. Hudson, appeared in 1987, titled *Mass Media: A Chronological Encyclopedia of Television, Radio, Motion Pictures, Magazines, Newspapers, and Books in the United States* (New York: Garland, 1987). Its detailed entries are given by years, organized in 16 sections from 1638 to 1985. A 75–page index is vital.

The Encyclopedia of American Journalism (New York: Facts on File, 1983), edited by Donald Paneth, contains more than 1000 entries covering print and electronic media, documentaries and newsreels, and also bibliographies. Three other valuable reference-research guides are *The Aspen Handbook on the Media,* edited by William L. Rivers, Wallace Thompson, and Michael J. Nyhan (New York: Praeger, 1977); *The Mass Media: Aspen Guide to Communication Industry Trends,* edited by Christopher H. Sterling and Timothy R. Haight (New York: Praeger, 1978); and its update, *Electronic Media: A Guide to Trends in Broadcasting and Newer Technologies, 1920–1983,* edited by Christopher H. Sterling (New York: Praeger, 1984). A general source book is the annual Directory issue of *Journalism Educator,* published by the Association for Education in Journalism and Mass Communication (AEJMC) for the Association of Schools of Journalism and Mass Communication. *Journalism Abstracts* (published by AEJMC) is an annual annotated listing of Ph.D. and M.A. theses; *Communication Abstracts* (Beverly Hills, Calif.: Sage) reports on research in the field.

This bibliography also lists the principal journals and trade publications with which students of mass communications should be familiar, and in a few instances makes references to articles in them. In cases where books have gone through revised editions, the date given is for the most recent revision. In subsequent listings of a book, place and date of publication are not repeated.

PERIODICALS, ANNUAL PUBLICATIONS, AND DIRECTORIES

General Research Journals

Journalism Quarterly Published by the Association for Education in Journalism and Mass Communication, devoted to research articles in journalism and mass communications. Contains extensive book reviews and bibliographies of articles in American and foreign journals.

Public Opinion Quarterly Emphasizes political and psychological phases of communication. Book reviews and summaries of public opinion polls. Published by the American Association for Public Opinion Research.

Journal of Communication Research quarterly focusing on methodology; material in speech and interpersonal communication areas; book reviews. Published by the International Communication Association.

Communication Research International quarterly focusing on research methodology. Published by Sage Publications.

Human Communication Research Quarterly concerned with the empirical study of diverse communication subfields. Published by the International Communication Association.

Public Opinion Bimonthly journal; articles, reports on public opinion polls. Published by the American Enterprise Institute.

AV Communication Review Reports on research activities and findings in the communication area. Published quarterly by the Association for Educational Communications and Technology.

Quarterly Journal of Speech Research articles, book reviews. Published by the Speech Communication Association.

Communication Monographs Published serially by the Speech Communication Association for research findings falling between article and book lengths.

Critical Studies in Mass Communication Quarterly focusing on critical scholarship in the field. Published by the Speech Communication Association.

Telematics and Informatics International research quarterly in applied telecommunications and information sciences. Published by Pergamon Press.

Journalism Monographs Published serially by the Association for Education in Journalism and Mass Communication, beginning in 1966, for research findings falling between article and book lengths; approximately quarterly.

Gannett Center Journal Published by the Gannett Center for Media Studies, Columbia University, New York. Scholarly discussion of media issues.

Mass Comm Review Quarterly publication of the Mass Communications and Society Division of the Association for Education in Journalism and Mass Communication; articles.

Journalism History Research quarterly; articles, notes, book reviews for mass communications history. Published by the California State University Northridge Foundation with the support of the Association of Schools of Journalism and Mass Communication.

American Journalism Quarterly journal of the American Journalism Historians Association; articles, reviews.

Journal of Popular Culture Quarterly publication with wide interests in field; articles, book reviews. Published by Bowling Green State University in cooperation with the Popular Culture Association.

American Quarterly Journal of the American Studies Association; articles, reviews.

Journal of Mass Media Ethics Semi-annual; articles, essays. Published at the University of Utah.

Southwestern Mass Communication Journal Semi-annual; articles. Published at

Trinity University by the Southwest Education Council for Journalism and Mass Communication.

General Professional Journals

Professional journals with general interest articles on press problems: *Nieman Reports* (Nieman Foundation); *Columbia Journalism Review* (Columbia University Graduate School of Journalism); *Quill* (Society of Professional Journalists, Sigma Delta Chi); PRO/COM (Women in Communications, Inc.); *Journalism Educator* (Association of Schools of Journalism and Mass Communication); *Communication: Journalism Education Today* (Journalism Education Association); *Community College Journalist* (Community College Journalism Association); *Washington Journalism Review* (College of Journalism, University of Maryland); *News Media and the Law* (Reporters Committee for Freedom of the Press); *Communications and the Law* (Meckler Communications); *feed/back* (San Francisco State University Department of Journalism); *Media History Digest (Editor & Publisher); Media Report to Women* (Women's Institute for Freedom of the Press); *nfpw* (National Federation of Press Women).

International Journals

Sources for those interested in international communications and media include the following publications:

RESEARCH JOURNALS AND PUBLICATIONS. *Gazette* (Department of Mass Communications, University of Amsterdam); *The Nordicom Review of Nordic Mass Communication Research* (Department of Political Science, University of Göteberg); *Canadian Journal of Communications* (Ottawa); *Communication Research Trends* (Centre for the Study of Communication and Culture, London); *European Research* (European Society for Opinion and Market Research); *European Journal of Communication* (Sage Publications); *The Media Reporter* (quarterly, London); *Media Bulletin* (European Institute for the Media, University of Manchester); *Chronicle of International Communication* (International Communication Projects, Inc.); *Intermedia* (International Institute of Communications); *Media Asia* (Asian Mass Communication Research and Information Centre, Singapore); *The Communicator* (Indian Institute of Mass Communication); *Europa Yearbook; Media International; Television International; Space Communication and Broadcasting.*

PROFESSIONAL PUBLICATIONS. *World Press Review* (general monthly); *IPI Report* (International Press Institute); *FIEJ Bulletin* (International Federation of Newspaper Publishers); *IFJ Information* (International Federation of Journalists); *Democratic Journalist* (International Organization of Journalists); *IAPA News* (Inter American Press Association); *International Communication Bulletin* (AEJMC); *WACC Journal* (World Association for Christian Communication); *East–West Perspectives* (East–West Center, Hawaii); *AMCB Bulletin* (Asian Mass

Communication Centre, Singapore); *Indian Press* (New Delhi); *Asian Messenger* (Chinese University of Hong Kong).

BROADCASTING. *EBU Review* (European Broadcasting Union); *Telecommunication Journal* (International Telecommunication Union); *OIRT Information* (International Radio and Television Organization); *Combroad* (Commonwealth Broadcasting Conference); *ABU Newsletter* (Asian Broadcasting Union).

DIRECTORIES. George Kurian, editor, *World Press Encyclopedia* (New York: Facts on File, 1982); *World Communications* (UNESCO, 1975); *Ulrich's International Periodicals Directory* (New York: R. R. Bowker); *Editor & Publisher International Year Book* (daily newspapers), and the British-published *Benn's Press Directory* and *Willing's Press Guide; Television Factbook* (*TV Digest,* U.S.A) and *World Radio–TV Handbook* (Denmark); *Japanese Press* (Japan Newspaper Publishers and Editors Association).

Newspapers

RESEARCH JOURNALS. *Newspaper Research Journal* (Newspaper Division, Association for Education in Journalism and Mass Communication); *News Research Report* series (News Research Center, American Newspaper Publishers Association).

PROFESSIONAL JOURNALS. *presstime* (American Newspaper Publishers Association); *ASNE Bulletin* (American Society of Newspaper Editors); *Masthead* (National Conference of Editorial Writers); *APME News* (Associated Press Managing Editors Association).

TRADE JOURNALS. *Editor & Publisher,* whose focus is on the daily newspaper and general industry problems, but which reports on advertising, marketing, and public relations areas; *Publishers' Auxiliary* (National Newspaper Association), primarily covering weeklies and small dailies; *Guild Reporter* (Newspaper Guild); *Circulation Management; Inland Printer,* for the printing industry.

ANNUAL PUBLICATIONS. *APME Red Book,* containing the record of the annual meeting and the reports of the continuing studies committee of the Associated Press Managing Editors Association; *Problems of Journalism,* covering the annual meeting of the American Society of Newspaper Editors.

DIRECTORIES. *Editor & Publisher International Year Book,* source for statistics and information about dailies; N. W. Ayer and Son, *HMS/Ayer Directory of Publications,* covering all newspapers and magazines; *National Directory of Weekly Newspapers* (National Newspaper Association).

Television, Radio, Cable, and Video

RESEARCH JOURNALS. *Journal of Broadcasting & Electronic Media* (Broadcast Education Association); *Television Quarterly* (National Academy of Television Arts and Sciences); *Public Telecommunications Review* (National Association of Educational Broadcasters); *Historical Journal of Film, Radio, and Television.*

PROFESSIONAL PUBLICATIONS. *RTNDA Communicator* (Radio Television News Directors Association); *Access* (National Citizens Committee on Broadcasting); *Channels of Communications; Television; World Broadcast News; Telecommunications; COMSAT Magazine; Satellite Communications; Electronic Media; Perspective on Cable Television* (National Cable Television Association); *Cable Marketing; Cable Communications* (Canada); *TV Communications* (cable); *Videocassette and CATV Newsletter; Feedback* (Broadcast Education Association).

TRADE PUBLICATIONS. *Broadcasting,* the voice of that industry; *TV Guide; Television/Radio Age; The Dial,* for public television; *Variety,* voice of the entertainment world; *Billboard,* music and record industry; *Cable/Vision; Satellite Orbit; Media Mix, Video, Video Review, Videography, Video Trade News, Video International.*

DIRECTORIES. *Broadcasting/Cablecasting Yearbook,* source for statistics about radio and television, station listings; *Television/Cablecasting Factbook; Broadcasting Cable Sourcebook; The Video Handbook; The Video Register.*

Film, Photographic and Graphic Communications

RESEARCH JOURNALS. *American Film* (American Film Institute, Kennedy Center for the Performing Arts); *Cinema Journal* (Society for Cinema Studies); *Film Comment* (Film Society of Lincoln Center); *Film & History* (Historians Film Committee); *Journal of Popular Film* (Bowling Green University); *Literature/ Film Quarterly* (Salisbury State University); *Journal of Typographic Research* (Cleveland Museum of Modern Art); *Printing History; Publishing History.*

PROFESSIONAL PUBLICATIONS. *Film Critic* (American Federation of Film Societies); *Film Quarterly* (University of California Press); *American Cinematographer; News Photographer* (National Press Photographers Association); *Infinity* (American Society of Magazine Photographers); *Aperture* (fine photography); *Portfolio* (graphic arts); *Print* (fine graphic arts); *Communication Arts* (graphic); *Typeworld.*

TRADE PUBLICATIONS. *Variety,* motion pictures; *Modern Photography; Popular Photography; Photo Marketing; Graphic Arts Monthly.*

DIRECTORIES. *International Film Guide* (London), to international film, TV film, and documentary markets; *Kemps International Film & Television Year Book*

(London); *500 Best American Films to Buy, Rent or Videotape,* selected by the National Board of Review of Motion Pictures (New York: Simon and Schuster, 1986); Anthony Slide, editor, *International Film, Radio and Television Journals* (Westport, Conn.: Greenwood Press, 1985), descriptions and evaluations of more than 200 periodicals.

Magazines and Book Publishing

PROFESSIONAL AND TRADE JOURNALS. *Folio,* for the magazine area; *Publishers Weekly,* for the book publishing industry, whose focus is primarily on general trade and children's books; *BP Report,* for the book trade; *The Retail Bookseller; Bookbinding and Book Production; Author and Journalist, Writer,* and *Writer's Digest,* for freelance magazine writers.

DIRECTORIES. *Literary Market Place* (R. R. Bowker) for book publishing; *HMS/Ayer Directory of Publications* (N. W. Ayer and Son), for magazine statistics and information; *Writer's Market* and *Writer's Year Book,* guides for magazine article writers; *House Magazine Directory* (Gebbie Press); *Magazine Industry Marketplace* (R. R. Bowker).

Advertising and Public Relations

RESEARCH JOURNALS. *Journal of Marketing* (American Marketing Association), articles and book reviews; *Journal of Marketing Research* and *Journal of Advertising Research* (Advertising Research Foundation); *Journal of Advertising* (American Academy of Advertising); *Public Relations Review* (Foundation for Public Relations Research and Education), annual bibliography.

PROFESSIONAL JOURNALS. *Public Relations Journal* (Public Relations Society of America); *PR News,* newsletter; *Communication World* (International Association of Business Communicators); *IABC News,* newsletter.

TRADE JOURNALS. *Advertising Age* and *Adweek,* major organs of the advertising industry; *Advertising Agency; Advertising Requirements; Sponsor,* for buyers of broadcast advertising; *Industrial Marketing; Sales Management; Direct Marketing; Marketing & Media Decision.*

DIRECTORIES. Standard Rate and Data Service, *Consumer Markets; Editor & Publisher Market Guide; Broadcasting Marketbook.*

PART ONE: THE ROLE OF MASS COMMUNICATIONS

Chapter 1: The Communication Explosion

Four books introducing the student to the communication explosion of the 1970s and 1980s are Lynne Schaefer Gross, *Telecommunications: An Introduction to Radio, Television, and the Developing Media* (Dubuque, Ia.: Brown, 1986), reporting on the history and current status of cable, pay TV, low-power TV, direct broadcast satellite, videotex, teletext, compact discs, videocassettes, and videodiscs; Wilson P. Dizard, Jr., *The Coming Information Age* (New York: Longman, 1985), an overview of technology, economics, and politics; George E. Whitehouse, *Understanding the New Technologies of the Mass Media* (Englewood Cliffs, N.J.: Prentice-Hall, 1986); and the prophetic Anthony Smith, *Goodbye Gutenberg–The Newspaper Revolution of the 1980s* (New York: Oxford University Press, 1980).

Emerging systems are reviewed by Paul Hurly, Matthias Laucht, and Denis Hlynka in *The Videotex and Teletext Handbook* (New York: Harper & Row, 1985); by David Weaver in *Videotex Journalism: Teletext, Viewdata and the News* (Hillsdale, N.J.: Lawrence Erlbaum Associates, 1982); in *The Videocassette Recorder: An American Love Affair* (Washington, D.C.: Television Digest, 1985), compiled from 1983–1985 files; by Stuart Crump, Jr. in *Cellular Telephones: A Layman's Guide* (Blue Ridge Summit, Pa.: Tab Books, 1985); and in the National Association of Broadcasters' readable summary, *New Technologies Affecting Radio and Television Broadcasting* (Washington, D.C.: NAB Books, 1982).

A good introduction to cable is Thomas F. Baldwin and D. Stevens McVoy, *Cable Communication* (Englewood Cliffs, N.J.: Prentice-Hall, 1983), which surveys cable technology, services, public policy, organization, and operations. Christian Williams analyzes Atlanta's cable and television king in *Lead, Follow or Get Out of the Way: The Story of Ted Turner* (New York: Times Books, 1982).

Two analyses of the problems raised are Leonard Lewin, editor, *Telecommunication: An Interdisciplinary Text* (Dedham, Mass.: Artech House, 1984), and Jeremy Tunstall, *Communication Deregulation: The Unleashing of America's Communications Industry* (New York: Basil Blackwell, 1986).

Chapter 2: The Media and Society

See bibliographical references for Chapter 24.

Chapter 3: Mass Communication: Process and Effects

An excellent introduction to the study of the communication process and to research in mass communication is found in Wilbur Schramm and William E. Porter's *Men, Women, Messages and Media* (New York: Harper & Row, 1982), a readable survey of communication theory, mass communication audiences, effects, and social controls. John C. Merrill and Ralph L. Lowenstein have contributed their prize-winning *Media, Messages, and Men: New Perspectives in Communication* (New York: Longman, 1979), analyzing the changing role of the mass media, the communicators and their audiences, and media concepts and ethics.

Two new introductory studies are Leo W. Jeffres, *Mass Media: Processes and Effects* (Prospect Heights, Ill.: Waveland Press, 1986), an extensive research-based overview, and Ray E. Hiebert and Carol Reuss, editors, *Impact of Mass Media* (New York: Longman, 1985).

Communication effects are analyzed in W. Phillips Davison, James Boylan, and Frederick T. C. Yu, *Mass Media Systems and Effects* (New York: Praeger, 1976);

The Process and Effects of Mass Communication, edited by Wilbur Schramm and Donald F. Roberts (Urbana: University of Illinois Press, 1971); and Joseph T. Klapper, *The Effects of Mass Communication* (New York: Free Press, 1960). A review of 25 years of literature on television audience effects is provided in George Comstock, Steven Chaffee, Nathan Katzman, Maxwell McCombs, and Donald Roberts, *Television and Human Behavior* (New York: Columbia University Press, 1978). Communicator studies are reviewed in James S. Ettema and D. Charles Whitney, editors, *Individuals in Mass Media Organizations: Creativity and Constraint* (Beverly Hills, Calif.: Sage, 1982).

Several books of readings deal with the role of mass communications in society. Listed in order according to the increasing complexity of their materials, they are *Interpretations of Journalism,* edited by Frank Luther Mott and Ralph D. Casey (New York: Crofts, 1937), a historical collection of utterances about the press over 300 years; *Enduring Issues in Mass Communication,* edited by Everette Dennis, Arnold Ismach, and Donald Gillmor (St. Paul: West Publishing, 1978), a study of media impact, roles, and reforms; *Communications in Modern Society,* edited by Wilbur Schramm (Urbana: University of Illinois Press, 1948), 15 essays on communications problems and research trends; *Mass Communications,* edited by Wilbur Schramm (Urbana: University of Illinois Press, 1960), selected readings on mass communications "through the windows of the social sciences"; and *Reader in Public Opinion and Communication,* edited by Bernard Berelson and Morris Janowitz (New York: Free Press, 1966), dealing with public opinion theory, media content, audiences, and effects.

A cross section of current research is found in the *Mass Communication Review Yearbook,* Beverly Hills, Calif.: Sage Publications (Vols. 1–2, edited by G. Cleveland Wilhoit and Harold de Bock, 1980, 1981; Vols. 3–4, edited by Ellen Wartella and D. Charles Whitney with Sven Windahl, 1982, 1983; and Vol. 5, edited by Michael Gurevitch and Mark R. Levy, 1985). Sage also publishes *Communication Yearbook,* a review appearing since 1977 and sponsored by the International Communication Association.

The complex and specialized area of communications theory may be approached through a readable survey of contemporary theory by Melvin L. DeFleur and Sandra Ball-Rokeach, *Theories of Mass Communication* (New York: Longman, 1982); Alexis S. Tan, *Mass Communication Theories and Research* (New York: Macmillan, 1986); Dennis K. Davis and Stanley J. Baran, *Mass Communication in Everyday Life: A Perspective on Theory and Effects* (Belmont, Calif.: Wadsworth, 1980); Everette E. Dennis, *The Media Society, Evidence About Mass Communication in America* (Dubuque, Ia.: Brown, 1978); and Dennis McQuail, *Mass Communication Theory: An Introduction* (Beverly Hills, Calif.: Sage, 1983). An overview is provided in Ernest G. Bormann, *Communication Theory* (New York: Holt, Rinehart and Winston, 1980). Provocative discussions are found in Marshall McLuhan's *Understanding Media: The Extensions of Man* (New York: McGraw-Hill, 1964); his earlier *The Gutenberg Galaxy: The Making of Typographic Man* (Toronto: University of Toronto Press, 1962); and *The Medium Is the Massage* (New York: Bantam Books, 1967).

A 1000-page reference volume for the serious scholar of communication theory is *Handbook of Communication* (Chicago: Rand McNally, 1973), edited by Ithiel de Sola Pool and Wilbur Schramm. Among collections of scholarly articles on mass communications research are three of the annual reviews published by Sage Publications: *Current Perspectives in Mass Communication Research,* edited by F. Gerald Kline and Phillip J. Tichenor (1972); *New Models for Mass Communication Research,* edited by Peter Clarke (1973); and *The Uses of Mass Communications: Current Perspectives on Gratification Research,* edited by Jay G. Blumler and Elihu Katz (1974). The latter was updated by Karl Erik Rosengren, Lawrence A. Wenner, and Philip Palmgreen, editors, *Media Gratifications Research: Current Perspectives* (Beverly Hills, Calif.: Sage, 1985).

Included among books in the theory area are William Stephenson, *The Play Theory of Mass Communication* (Chicago: University of Chicago Press, 1967); Alex S. Edelstein, *The Uses of Communication in Decision Making* (New York: Praeger, 1974) and *Comparative Communication Research* (Beverly Hills, Calif.: Sage, 1982); and the classic *The Measurement of Meaning* by Charles E. Osgood, George Suci, and Percy Tannenbaum (Urbana: University of Illinois Press, 1957).

Among the leading books on public opinion are Bernard C. Hennessy, *Public Opinion* (Belmont, Calif.: Wadsworth, 1985), a text in its fifth edition; Alan D. Monroe, *Public Opinion in America* (New York: Harper & Row, 1975), emphasizing the political process; and Dan Nimmo, *Political Communication and Public Opinion in America* (Santa Monica, Calif.: Goodyear Publishing, 1978). The place of the media in controversial policy decisions is analyzed in Phillip J. Tichenor, George A. Donohue, and Clarice N. Olien, *Community Conflict and the Press* (Beverly Hills, Calif.: Sage, 1980), and by Kathleen Hall Jamieson and Karlyn Kohrs Campbell, *The Interplay of Influence: Mass Media & Their Publics in News, Advertising, Politics* (Belmont, Calif.: Wadsworth, 1982).

The role of the mass media, particularly television, in politics has been studied by Austin Ranney in *Channels of Power: The Impact of Television on American Politics* (New York: Basic Books, 1983); by Gladys Lang and Kurt Lang in *Politics and Television Re-Viewed* (Beverly Hills, Calif.: Sage, 1984), an update of a 1968 study; by Elisabeth Noelle-Neumann in *The Spiral of Silence* (Chicago: University of Chicago Press, 1983), an analysis of the public opinion formation process; by Garth S. Jowett and Victoria O'Donnell in *Propaganda and Persuasion* (Beverly Hills, Calif.: Sage, 1986); and by Kathleen Hall Jamieson in *Packaging the Presidency: A History and Criticism of Presidential Campaign Advertising* (New York: Oxford University Press, 1984), covering 1952 to 1980. The uses of polls in politics is the subject of *Polling and the Democratic Consensus,* edited by L. John Martin for the *Annals* of the American Academy of Political and Social Science, Vol. 477 (Beverly Hills, Calif.: Sage, 1985).

The impact of public opinion and the mass media upon politics is analyzed by Walter Lippmann in his classic *Public Opinion* (New York: Harcourt, Brace, 1922); by Douglass Cater in *The Fourth Branch of Government* (Boston: Houghton Mifflin, 1959), a study of the key role of the Washington press corps; by Bernard C. Cohen in *The Press and Foreign Policy* (Princeton, N.J.: Princeton University Press, 1963), a study of Washington diplomatic reporting; by James Reston in another study of press influence on foreign policy, *The Artillery of the Press* (New York: Harper & Row, 1967); by Elmer Cornwell, Jr., in *Presidential Leadership of Public Opinion* (Bloomington: Indiana University Press, 1965); and by William L.

Rivers in *The Opinionmakers* (Boston: Beacon, 1965), a study of leading Washington journalists, and *The Adversaries* (Boston: Beacon, 1970), a study of press manipulation by public officials.

A research-oriented contribution to the subject was made in the 1975 Sage Publications review of communication research edited by Steven H. Chaffee, *Political Communication: Issues and Strategies for Research.* Others are Bernard Rubin, *Media, Politics, and Democracy* (New York: Oxford, 1977); Donald L. Shaw and Maxwell E. McCombs, editors, *The Emergence of American Political Issues* (St. Paul: West, 1977), studies of the agenda-setting function; Sidney Kraus and Dennis Davis, *The Effects of Mass Communication on Political Behavior* (State College: Penn State Press, 1976); L. John Martin, editor, *Role of the Mass Media in American Politics,* a special issue of the *Annals* of the American Academy of Political and Social Science (September, 1976); and Thomas E. Patterson and Robert D. McClure, *The Unseeing Eye* (New York: Putnam, 1976), television's role in elections.

PART TWO: THE PRINT MEDIA

While it is primarily a history of the print media, the most widely ranging of the journalism histories is Michael and Edwin Emery, *The Press and America: An Interpretive History of the Mass Media* (Englewood Cliffs, N.J.: Prentice-Hall, 1988). It correlates the narrative of journalism history with social, political, and economic trends and is especially comprehensive in its treatment of twentieth-century media—newspapers, magazines, radio and television, press associations, motion pictures, books, advertising, public relations—and the relationship of the mass media to government and society.

Frank Luther Mott's *American Journalism: A History, 1690–1960* (New York: Macmillan, 1962) is designed for both classroom and reference shelf, contains much rich detail in its comprehensive treatment of newspapers, but puts little emphasis on other media. Alfred McClung Lee's *The Daily Newspaper in America* (New York: Macmillan, 1937) offers a sociological approach and much valuable data in its topical treatment of subjects such as newsprint, printing presses, labor, ownership and management, news, advertising, and circulation. Willard G. Bleyer's *Main Currents in the History of American Journalism* (Boston: Houghton Mifflin, 1927) remains an excellent account of American journalism until the early twentieth century, with emphasis on leading editors.

Kenneth Stewart and John Tebbel, in *Makers of Modern Journalism* (New York: Prentice-Hall, 1952), sketch early American journalism history and concentrate on twentieth-century journalism personalities. Tebbel, in his *Compact History of the American Newspaper* (New York: Hawthorn, 1969) and his *The Media in America* (New York: Crowell, 1975), does the reverse, sketching twentieth-century journalism in only the broadest terms. Sidney Kobre adds details in his sociologically based *Development of American Journalism* (Dubuque, Ia.: Brown, 1969). Robert A. Rutland wrote a brief popularized account in *The Newsmongers* (New York: Dial, 1973), as did George N. Gordon in *The Communications Revolution* (New York: Hastings House, 1977).

Reproductions of full front pages of newspapers on an extensive, planned scale are found in Edwin Emery's *The Story of America as Reported by Its Newspapers 1690–1965* (New York: Simon and Schuster, 1965), and in *America's Front Page News 1690–1970,* edited by Michael C. Emery, R. Smith Schuneman, and Edwin Emery (New York: Doubleday, 1970). A collection of the best magazine articles about leading American newspaper editors and publishers of all periods is found in *Highlights in the History of the American Press,* edited by Edwin H. Ford and Edwin Emery (Minneapolis: University of Minnesota Press, 1954).

Two portraits of American newspeople in the 1970s and 1980s are found in John W.C. Johnstone, Edward J. Slawski, and William W. Bowman, *The News People: A Sociological Portrait of American Journalists and Their Work* (Urbana, Ill.: University of Illinois Press, 1976), based on 1300 interviews in 1971; and in David H. Weaver and G. Cleveland Wilhoit, *The American Journalist: A Portrait of U.S. News People and Their Work* (Bloomington, Ind.: Indiana University Press, 1986), a similar survey updating to 1982. Two biographical works about journalists are Joseph P. McKerns, *The Biographical Dictionary of American Journalism* (Westport, Conn.: Greenwood Press, 1988), detailing some 500 newspeople in a variety of positions; and *American Newspaper Journalists,* edited by Perry J. Ashley in five volumes of the *Dictionary of Literary Biography* (Chicago: Gale Research, 1983 ff.).

J. William Snorgrass and Gloria T. Woody compiled *Blacks and Media: A Selected, Annotated Bibliography 1962–1982* (Tallahassee, Fla.: Florida A&M University Press, 1985). James P. Danky was editor and Maureen E. Hady compiler of two major listings: *Native American Periodicals and Newspapers, 1829–1982: Bibliography, Publishing Record and Holdings* (Westport, Conn.: Greenwood Press, 1984), and *Women's Periodicals and Newspapers from the 18th Century to 1981* (Boston: G.K. Hall, 1982).

The role of women in American journalism history is explored by Marion Marzolf in *Up From the Footnote: A History of Women Journalists* (New York: Hastings House, 1977), a good synthesis. A research guide is Maurine Beasley and Sheila Silver Gibbons, *Women in Media: A Documentary Source Book* (Washington, D.C.: Women's Institute for Freedom of the Press, 1977). Eighteen women's careers are told in *Great Women of the Press* by Madelon Golden Schilpp and Sharon M. Murphy (Carbondale: Southern Illinois University Press, 1983). Barbara Belford deals with 24 in her biographical anthology, *Brilliant Bylines* (New York: Columbia University Press, 1986).

The best historical accounts of specific print media areas are found in the following:

NEWS SERVICES. Victor Rosewater, *History of Cooperative News-Gathering in the United States* (New York: Appleton, 1930) and a four-volume series by Robert W. Desmond: *The Information Process: World News Reporting to the 20th Century* (Iowa City: University of Iowa Press, 1978), *Windows on the World 1900–1920* (1981), *Crisis and Conflict: World News Reporting Between Two Wars 1920–1940* (1982), and *Tides of War: World News Reporting 1940–1945* (1984).

MAGAZINES. Frank Luther Mott's monumental *A History of American Magazines,* in five volumes (Vol. 1, New York: Appleton, 1930; Vols. 2–5, Cambridge,

Mass.: Harvard University Press, 1938–1968); James Playsted Wood, *Magazines in the United States* (New York: Ronald, 1956); Theodore Peterson, *Magazines in the Twentieth Century* (Urbana: University of Illinois Press, 1964); and John Tebbel, *The American Magazine: A Compact History* (New York: Hawthorn, 1969).

BOOK PUBLISHING. John Tebbel, *A History of Book Publishing in the United States,* 4 vols. (New York: Bowker, 1972–1981); Hellmut Lehmann-Haupt and others, *The Book in America: History of the Making and Selling of Books in the United States* (New York: Bowker, 1951); Frank A. Mumby, *Publishing and Bookselling: A History from the Earliest Times to the Present* (London: Jonathan Cape, 1956); and Douglas C. McMurtie, *The Book: The Story of Printing and Bookmaking* (New York: Oxford University Press, 1943).

GRAPHICS. Isaiah Thomas, *The History of Printing in America* (Albany, N.Y.: Joel Munsell, 1810 and 1874), is the earliest journalism history account; Daniel B. Updyke's two-volume *Printing Types: Their History, Forms and Use* (Cambridge, Mass.: Harvard University Press, 1937) is the standard work; S. H. Steinberg, *Five Hundred Years of Printing* (Baltimore: Penguin, 1974), is a briefer survey.

Additional references, by chapter topic, follow.

Chapter 4: Historic Press Freedoms

Companion books trace the story of American press freedom: Leonard W. Levy, *Freedom of the Press from Zenger to Jefferson,* and Harold L. Nelson, *Freedom of the Press from Hamilton to the Warren Court* (Indianapolis: Bobbs-Merrill, 1966). They are excellent surveys.

Elizabeth Eisenstein focuses on cultural and intellectual movements accompanying *The Printing Revolution in Early Modern Europe* (Cambridge: Cambridge University Press, 1984). Lucy M. Salmon's *The Newspaper and Authority* (New York: Oxford University Press, 1923), is an extensive historical survey of restrictions placed on newspapers. Important periods of the history of press freedom struggles are covered in Fred S. Siebert, *Freedom of the Press in England, 1472–1776* (Urbana: University of Illinois Press, 1952); Leonard W. Levy, *Emergence of a Free Press* (New York: Oxford University Press, 1985), a revision of *Legacy of Suppression: Freedom of Speech and Press in Early American History* (Cambridge, Mass.: Harvard University Press, 1960); Clyde A. Duniway, *The Development of Freedom of the Press in Massachusetts* (New York: Longmans, Green, 1906); John C. Miller, *Crisis in Freedom: The Alien and Sedition Acts* (Boston: Little, Brown, 1951); Frank Luther Mott, *Jefferson and the Press* (Baton Rouge: Louisiana State University Press, 1943); and Zechariah Chafee, Jr., *Free Speech in the United States* (Cambridge, Mass.: Harvard University Press, 1941), a study emphasizing the effects of modern wartime conditions. James E. Pollard, *The Presidents and the Press* (New York: Macmillan, 1947), covers presidential press relations from Washington to Truman, and is supplemented by Pollard's *The Presidents and the Press: Truman to Johnson* (Washington: Public Affairs Press,

1964). John Tebbel and Sarah Miles Watts covered from Washington to Reagan in *The Press and the Presidency* (New York: Oxford University Press, 1985).

Excellent discussions by newspaper editors of problems in protecting freedom of information and access to news are found in James Russell Wiggins, *Freedom or Secrecy* (New York: Oxford University Press, 1964), and Herbert Brucker, *Freedom of Information* (New York: Macmillan, 1949). More detailed studies are Harold L. Cross, *The People's Right to Know* (New York: Columbia University Press, 1953), and Zechariah Chafee, Jr.'s, two-volume *Government and Mass Communications* (Chicago: University of Chicago Press, 1947).

Philosophical problems of press freedom are analyzed by the Commission on Freedom of the Press in *A Free and Responsible Press,* by William E. Hocking in *Freedom of the Press: A Framework of Principle* (Chicago: University of Chicago Press, 1947), and by Fred S. Siebert, Theodore Peterson, and Wilbur Schramm in *Four Theories of the Press* (Urbana: University of Illinois Press, 1956). Among discussions of press freedom by journalists are Walter Lippmann, *Liberty and the News* (New York: Harcourt, Brace, 1920); Elmer Davis, *But We Were Born Free* (New York: Bobbs-Merrill, 1954); Alan Barth, *The Loyalty of Free Men* (New York: Viking, 1951), and *The Rights of Free Men* (New York: Random House, 1984).

Chapter 5: Growth of Newspapers

The best historical discussion of the news function is Frank Luther Mott's *The News in America* (Cambridge, Mass.: Harvard University Press, 1952), a survey of the concepts, forms, and problems of news. Jim A. Hart traces the history of the editorial, from 1500 to 1800, in *Views on the News* (Carbondale: Southern Illinois University Press, 1971), and Allan Nevins continues in the introductions for sections in his collection of editorials, *American Press Opinion: Washington to Coolidge* (New York: Heath, 1928). Michael Schudson, *Discovering the News* (New York: Basic Books, 1978), and Dan Schiller, *Objectivity and the News* (Philadelphia: University of Pennsylvania Press, 1981), deal with the rise of objectivity and Thomas C. Leonard, *The Power of the Press* (New York: Oxford University Press, 1986), with the birth of political reporting.

Arthur M. Schlesinger, *Prelude to Independence: The Newspaper War on Britain, 1764–1776* (New York: Knopf, 1958), analyzes one period of major press influence. Nevins' *American Press Opinion* has an excellent section on the partisan journalism of the 1790s. C. C. Regier, *The Era of the Muckrakers* (Chapel Hill: University of North Carolina Press, 1932), examines magazines during the Progressive era; Louis Filler, *Crusaders for American Liberalism* (New York: Harcourt, Brace, 1939), also discusses newspaper people. So does Jonathan Daniels in *They Will Be Heard: America's Crusading Newspaper Editors* (New York: McGraw-Hill, 1965), a 200-year survey. Writings of the muckrakers are edited by Arthur and Lila Weinberg in *The Muckrakers* (New York: Simon and Schuster, 1961).

The best anthologies are *Voices of the Past,* edited by Calder M. Pickett (Columbus, Ohio: Grid, 1977); *A Treasury of Great Reporting,* edited by Louis L. Snyder and Richard B. Morris (New York: Simon and Schuster, 1962); Bryce W. Rucker's *Twentieth Century Reporting at Its Best* (Ames: Iowa State University Press, 1964), John Hohenberg's *The Pulitzer Prize Story* (New York: Columbia University Press, 1959), and *The Best of Pulitzer Prize News Writing,* edited by William David Sloan, Valarie McCrary, and Johanna Cleary (Columbus, Ohio: Publishing Horizons, Inc., 1986), an anthology of 71 articles.

Top-flight biographies of key figures in the development of the news function include Esmond Wright, *Franklin of Philadelphia* (Cambridge, Mass.: Harvard University Press, 1986), and Ronald W. Clark, *Benjamin Franklin* (New York: Random House, 1983); Oliver Carlson, *The Man Who Made News: James Gordon Bennett* (New York: Duell, Sloan and Pearce, 1942); Francis Brown, *Raymond of the Times* (New York: Norton, 1951); Fayette Copeland, *Kendall of the Picayune* (Norman: University of Oklahoma Press, 1943); Candace Stone, *Dana and the Sun* (New York: Dodd, Mead, 1938); Raymond B. Nixon, *Henry W. Grady: Spokesman of the New South* (New York: Knopf, 1943); W. A. Swanberg, *Pulitzer* (New York: Scribner's, 1967); Julian Rammelkamp, *Pulitzer's Post-Dispatch 1878–1883* (Princeton, N.J.: Princeton University Press, 1966); George Juergens, *Joseph Pulitzer and the New York World 1883–1887* (Princeton, N.J.: Princeton University Press, 1966); Oliver Knight, *I Protest: Selected Disquisitions of E. W. Scripps* (Madison: University of Wisconsin Press, 1966), both a biography and a collection of Scripps' writings; W. A. Swanberg, *Citizen Hearst* (New York: Scribner's, 1961); John Tebbel, *The Life and Good Times of William Randolph Hearst* (New York: Dutton, 1952); Gerald W. Johnson, *An Honorable Titan: A Biographical Study of Adolph S. Ochs* (New York: Harper, 1946); Merlo J. Pusey, *Eugene Meyer* (New York: Knopf, 1974); James H. Markham, *Bovard of the Post-Dispatch* (Baton Rouge: Louisiana State University Press, 1954); Homer W. King, *Pulitzer's Prize Editor: A Biography of John A. Cockerill* (Durham, N.C.: Duke University Press, 1965); Mary E. Tomkins, *Ida M. Tarbell* (New York: Twayne, 1974); Marion K. Sanders, *Dorothy Thompson* (Boston: Houghton Mifflin, 1973); and Robert V. Hudson, *The Writing Game: A Biography of Will Irwin* (Ames: Iowa State University Press, 1982).

Leading biographies of opinion makers include John C. Miller, *Sam Adams: Pioneer in Propaganda* (Boston: Little, Brown, 1936); Mary A. Best, *Thomas Paine* (New York: Harcourt, Brace, 1927); Glyndon G. Van Deusen, *Horace Greeley: Nineteenth Century Crusader* (Philadelphia: University of Pennsylvania Press, 1953); Paula Blanchard, *Margaret Fuller* (New York: Delacorte, 1978); George S. Merriam, *The Life and Times of Samuel Bowles* (New York: Century, 1885); Joseph F. Wall, *Henry Watterson* (New York: Oxford University Press, 1956); Joseph L. Morrison, *Josephus Daniels Says* (Chapel Hill: University of North Carolina Press, 1963); and Ronald Steel, *Walter Lippmann and the American Century* (Boston: Little, Brown, 1980). William Cullen Bryant and Edwin Lawrence Godkin are most easily read about in Allan Nevins, *The Evening Post: A Century of Journalism* (New York: Boni and Liveright, 1922).

The McCormick and Patterson families and their Chicago *Tribune* and New York *Daily News* are analyzed by John Tebbel in *An American Dynasty* (New

York: Doubleday, 1947). Lindsay Chaney and Michael Cieply begin in 1951 with their *The Hearsts: Family and Empire—The Later Years* (New York: Simon and Schuster, 1981). Ten publishers are examined in Piers Brendon, *The Life and Death of the Press Barons* (New York: Atheneum, 1983). David Halberstam traced the influence of the Washington *Post* and Los Angeles *Times* publishers and the heads of *Time* and CBS in *The Powers That Be* (New York: Knopf, 1979).

The best autobiographies are Benjamin Franklin, *Autobiography* (New York: Putnam, 1909); *The Autobiography of William Allen White* (New York: Macmillan, 1946); *The Autobiography of Lincoln Steffens* (New York: Harcourt, Brace, 1931); Horace Greeley, *Recollections of a Busy Life* (New York: Ford, 1868); Fremont Older, *My Own Story* (New York: Macmillan, 1926), the memoirs of a crusading San Francisco editor; Josephus Daniels, *Tar Heel Editor* (Chapel Hill: University of North Carolina Press, 1939), volume one of a five-volume series; and E. W. Howe, *Plain People* (New York: Dodd, Mead, 1929), the story of a Kansas editor and his readers; also told in Calder M. Pickett, *Ed Howe: Country Town Philosopher* (Lawrence: University Press of Kansas, 1969).

Excellent reminiscences of journalists include Melville E. Stone, *Fifty Years a Journalist* (New York: Doubleday, Page, 1981); Will Irwin, *The Making of a Reporter* (New York: Putnam, 1942); Webb Miller, *I Found No Peace* (New York: Simon and Schuster, 1936); Harrison E. Salisbury, *A Journey for Our Times* (New York: Harper & Row, 1983); William L. Shirer, *The Nightmare Years: 1930–1940* (Boston: Little, Brown, 1984); and Vincent Sheean, *Personal History* (Boston: Houghton Mifflin, 1969 reissue). The best of a great writer's news work is found in William White's *By-Line Ernest Hemingway* (New York: Scribner's, 1967), and in the biography by Carlos Baker, *Ernest Hemingway* (New York: Scribner's, 1969). Lee G. Miller, *The Story of Ernie Pyle* (New York: Viking, 1950) is very readable as is *Ernie's War,* the best of Pyle's dispatches edited by David Nichols (New York: Random House, 1986).

Ishbel Ross, *Ladies of the Press* (New York: Harper, 1936), and John Jakes, *Great Women Reporters* (New York: Putnam, 1969), tell the story of dozens of women journalists. Helen Thomas in *Dateline: White House* (New York: Macmillan, 1975) tells the story of one and Sarah McClendon another in *My Eight Presidents* (New York: Wyden Books, 1978).

Among important histories of individual newspapers are William E. Ames, *A History of the National Intelligencer* (Chapel Hill: University of North Carolina Press, 1972); Frank M. O'Brien's *The Story of the Sun* (New York: Appleton, 1928), covering the New York *Sun* from 1833 to 1928; Gerald W. Johnson and others, *The Sun-papers of Baltimore, 1837–1937* (New York: Knopf, 1937); Meyer Berger, *The Story of the New York Times* (New York: Simon and Schuster, 1951); and a later study, Gay Talese, *The Kingdom and the Power* (New York: New American Library, 1969); Richard Kluger, *The Paper: The Life and Death of the New York Herald Tribune* (New York: Knopf, 1986); Chalmers M. Roberts, *The Washington Post–The First Hundred Years* (Boston: Houghton Mifflin, 1977), heavy on recent years; Erwin D. Canham, *Commitment to Freedom: The Story of the Christian Science Monitor* (Boston: Houghton Mifflin, 1958); Will C. Conrad,

Kathleen F. Wilson, and Dale Wilson, *The Milwaukee Journal: The First Eighty Years* (Madison: University of Wisconsin Press, 1964); Lloyd Wendt, *Chicago Tribune* (Chicago: Rand McNally, 1979); Robert Gottlieb and Irene Wolt, *Thinking Big: The Story of the Los Angeles Times* (New York: Putnam, 1977), and Jack R. Hart, *The Information Empire: The Rise of the Los Angeles Times and the Times Mirror Corporation* (Washington: University Press of America, 1981); Jerry Martin Rosenberg, *Inside the Wall Street Journal* (New York: Macmillan, 1982); and Lloyd Wendt, *The Wall Street Journal* (Chicago: Rand McNally, 1982).

Two basic historical studies of the black press are Frederick G. Detweiler, *The Negro Press in the United States* (Chicago: University of Chicago Press, 1922), and Vishnu V. Oak, *The Negro Press* (Yellow Springs, Ohio: Antioch Press, 1948). A comprehensive survey is *The Black Press, U.S.A.,* by Roland E. Wolseley (Ames: Iowa State University Press, 1971). *Perspective of the Black Press, 1974* (Kennebunkport, Maine: Mercer House, 1974) is an extensive anthology edited by Henry G. La Brie III, whose *A Survey of Black Newspapers in America* appeared from the same press in 1979. Henry Lewis Suggs edited *The Black Press in the South 1865–1979* (Westport, Conn.: Greenwood Press, 1983). James and Sharon Murphy did a comprehensive synthesis in *Let My People Know: American Indian Journalism 1828–1978* (Norman: University of Oklahoma Press, 1981).

Among books on the alternative and protest press are a good survey across 200 years by Lauren Kessler, *Against the Grain: The Dissident Press in America* (Beverly Hills, Calif.: Sage, 1984), dealing with feminists, immigrants, blacks, utopians, radicals, and pacifists; Everette E. Dennis and William L. Rivers, *Other Voices: The New Journalism in America* (San Francisco: Canfield, 1974); an anthology edited by Tom Wolfe, *The New Journalism* (New York: Harper & Row, 1973); David Armstrong, *A Trumpet to Arms, The Alternative Press in America* (Los Angeles: Torcher, 1981); and Nancy L. Roberts, *Dorothy Day and the Catholic Worker* (Albany: State University of New York Press, 1984).

Magazine editors and writers are the subjects of books by Oswald Garrison Villard, *Fighting Years* (New York: Harcourt, Brace, 1939), the memoirs of the editor of the *Nation;* Peter Lyon, *Success Story: The Life and Times of S. S. McClure* (New York: Scribner's, 1963); S. S. McClure, *My Autobiography* (New York: Stokes, 1914); Kathleen Brady, *Ida Tarbell: Portrait of a Muckraker* (New York: Seaview Putnam, 1984); John Tebbel, *George Horace Lorimer and the Saturday Evening Post* (New York: Doubleday, 1949); George Britt, *Forty Years—Forty Millions: The Career of Frank A. Munsey* (New York: Farrar and Rinehart, 1935); James Thurber, *The Years with Ross* (Boston: Little, Brown, 1957), the story of editor Harold Ross and the *New Yorker;* Raymond Sokolov, *Wayward Reporter: The Life of A. J. Liebling* (New York: Harper & Row, 1980), longtime *New Yorker* writer; Brendan Gill, *Here at the New Yorker* (New York: Random House, 1975); Norman Cousins, *Present Tense* (New York: McGraw-Hill, 1967), by the *Saturday Review's* editor; W. A. Swanberg, *Luce and His Empire* (New York: Scribner's, 1972); and Robert T. Elson, *Time Inc.* (New York: Atheneum, 1968) and *The World of Time Inc.* (New York: Atheneum, 1973 and 1986), a three-volume history covering 1923–1941, 1941–1960, and 1960–1980.

The story of a famous book editor is told by A. Scott Berg in *Max Perkins, Editor of Genius* (New York: E. P. Dutton, 1978).

Two individual histories of news services are Oliver Gramling, *AP: The Story of News* (New York: Farrar and Rinehart, 1940), and Joe Alex Morris, *Deadline Every Minute: The Story of the United Press* (New York: Doubleday, 1957).

Chapter 6: Newspapers Today

TEXTBOOKS ON REPORTING AND NEWSWRITING. Curtis D. MacDougall, *Interpretative Reporting* (New York: Macmillan, 1982), a 50-year veteran carried on after MacDougall's 1985 death by coauthor Robert D. Reid in a 1987 ninth edition; Warren K. Agee, Phillip H. Ault, and Edwin Emery, *Reporting and Writing the News* (New York: Harper & Row, 1983); George A. Hough, 3rd, *Newswriting* (Boston: Houghton Mifflin, 1988); Everette E. Dennis and Arnold H. Ismach, *Reporting Processes and Practices* (Belmont, Calif.: Wadsworth, 1981); Brian Brooks, George Kennedy, Daryl Moen, and Don Ranly, *News Reporting and Writing* (New York: St. Martin's Press, 1985); Mitchell and Blair Charnley, *Reporting* (New York: Holt, Rinehart and Winston, 1979); Melvin Mencher, *News Reporting and Writing* (Dubuque, Iowa: Brown, 1987); William L. Rivers, *News in Print* (New York: Harper & Row, 1984); John Chancellor and Walter R. Mears, *The News Business* (New York: Harper & Row, 1983); William Metz, *Newswriting* (Englewood Cliffs, N.J.: Prentice-Hall, 1985); Hiley Ward, *Professional Newswriting* (New York: Harcourt Brace Jovanovich, 1986); M.L. Stein, *Getting and Writing the News* (New York: Longman, 1985); Mitchell Stephens and Gerald Lanson, *Writing & Reporting the News* (New York: Holt, Rinehart and Winston, 1986); Douglas A. Anderson and Bruce D. Itule, *Contemporary News Reporting* (New York: Random House, 1984); Fred Fedler, *Reporting for the Print Media,* (New York: Harcourt Brace Jovanovich, 1984); Ralph S. Izard, Hugh Culbertson, and Donald A. Lambert, *Fundamentals of News Reporting* (Dubuque, Iowa: Kendall/Hunt, 1983); Julian Harriss, Kelly Leiter, and Stanley Johnson, *The Complete Reporter* (New York: Macmillan, 1985); Judith L. Burken, *Introduction to Reporting* (Dubuque, Iowa: Brown, 1979); Daniel R. Williamson, *Newsgathering* (New York: Hastings House, 1979); Ken Metzler, *Newsgathering* (Englewood Cliffs, N.J.: Prentice-Hall, 1986); and John Hohenberg, *Concise Newswriting* (New York: Hastings House, 1987).

Valuable adjuncts to the reporting texts are E. L. Callihan, *Grammar for Journalists* (Radnor, Pa.: Chilton, 1979); William Zinsser, *On Writing Well* (New York: Harper & Row, 1980); R. Thomas Berner, *Language Skills for Journalists* (Boston: Houghton Mifflin, 1984); Terry Murphy, *Classroom to Newsroom* (New York: Harper & Row, 1983); and Lauren Kessler and Duncan McDonald, *When Words Collide* (Belmont, Calif.: Wadsworth, 1984). Wayne Overbeck and Thomas M. Pasqua did an overview for college paper staffs in *Excellence in College Journalism* (Belmont, Calif.: Wadsworth, 1983).

Information gathering, ranging from library resources to data bases, is the subject of two books: Jean Ward and Kathleen A. Hansen, *Search Strategies in*

Mass Communication (New York: Longman, 1986), and Lauren Kessler and Duncan McDonald, *Uncovering the News* (Belmont, Calif.: Wadsworth, 1987).

Offering instruction in writing for all media are James G. Stovall, *Writing for the Mass Media* (Englewood Cliffs, N.J.: Prentice-Hall, 1985); Earl R. Hutchison, *Writing for Mass Communication* (New York: Longman, 1986); and Doug Newsom and James A. Wollert, *Media Writing: News for the Mass Media* (Belmont, Calif.: Wadsworth, 1985).

SPECIAL FIELDS OF REPORTING. Clark Mollenhoff, *Investigative Reporting* (New York: Macmillan, 1980); Paul Williams, *Investigative Reporting* (Englewood Cliffs, N.J.: Prentice-Hall, 1978); Philip Meyer, *Precision Journalism* (Bloomington: Indiana University Press, 1979), a reporter's introduction to social science methods; Henry H. Schulte, *Reporting Public Affairs* (New York: Macmillan, 1981); George S. Hage, Everette E. Dennis, Arnold H. Ismach, and Stephen Hartgen, *New Strategies for Public Affairs Reporting: Investigation, Interpretation, Research* (Englewood Cliffs, N.J.: Prentice-Hall, 1983); Ronald P. Lovell, *Reporting Public Affairs* (Belmont, Calif.: Wadsworth, 1982); Gerry Keir, Maxwell E. McCombs and Donald L. Shaw, *Advanced Reporting: Beyond News Events* (New York: Longman, 1986); Investigative Reporters and Editors, *The Reporter's Handbook* (New York: St. Martin's Press, 1983); Shirley Biagi, *Interviews that Work* (Englewood Cliffs, N.J.: Prentice-Hall, 1985); Sharon M. Friedman, editor, *Scientists and Journalists: Reporting Science News* (New York: The Free Press, 1985); Warren Burkett, *News Reporting: Science, Medicine and High Technology* (Ames: Iowa State University Press, 1986); Douglas A. Anderson, *Contemporary Sports Reporting* (Chicago: Nelson-Hall, 1985); Bruce Garrison and Mark Sabljak, *Sports Reporting* (Ames: Iowa State University Press, 1985); Claron Burnett, Richard Powers and John Ross, *Agricultural News Writing* (Dubuque, Iowa: Kendall/Hunt, 1973); Todd Hunt, *Reviewing for the Mass Media* (Radnor, Pa.: Chilton, 1972); and John W. English, *Criticizing the Critics* (New York: Hastings House, 1979).

EDITORIAL PAGE AND OPINION WRITING. Harry W. Stonecipher, *Editorial and Persuasive Writing* (New York: Hastings House, 1979); Kenneth Rystrom, *The Why, Who and How of the Editorial Page* (New York: Random House, 1983); A. Gayle Waldrop, *Editor and Editorial Writer* (Dubuque, Iowa: Brown, 1967); Curtis D. MacDougall, *Principles of Editorial Writing* (Brown, 1973); John L. Hulteng, *The Opinion Function* (New York: Harper & Row, 1973).

NEWS EDITING AND COPYREADING. Bruce Westley, *News Editing* (Boston: Houghton Mifflin, 1980); Martin L. Gibson, *Editing in the Electronic Era* (Ames: Iowa State University Press, 1984); Roy H. Copperud and Roy Paul Nelson, *Editing the News* (Dubuque, Iowa: Brown, 1983); William L. Rivers, *News Editing in the '80s* (Belmont, Calif.: Wadsworth, 1983); Gene Gilmore, *Modern Newspaper Editing* (New York: Boyd & Fraser, 1983); Floyd K. Baskette and Jack Z. Sissors, *The Art of Editing* (New York: Macmillan, 1982); and Robert E. Garst and Theodore M. Bernstein, *Headlines and Deadlines* (New York: Columbia University Press, 1982), a New York *Times* classic.

COMMUNITY JOURNALISM. John Cameron Sim, *The Grass Roots Press: America's Community Newspapers* (Ames: Iowa State University Press, 1969); Morris Janowitz, *The Community Press in an Urban Setting* (New York: The Free Press, 1967); and Bruce M. Kennedy, *Community Journalism: How to Run a Country Weekly* (Ames: Iowa State University Press, 1974).

MANAGEMENT. Herbert Lee Williams, *Newspaper Organization and Management* (Ames: Iowa State University Press, 1979); D. Earl Newsom, editor, *The Newspaper* (Englewood Cliffs, N.J.: Prentice-Hall, 1981), 28 articles focusing on small dailies and weeklies; Ardyth B. Sohn, Christine L. Ogan and John E. Polich, *Newspaper Leadership* (Englewood Cliffs, N.J.: Prentice-Hall, 1986), describing the "total" approach; and W. Parkman Rankin, *The Practice of Newspaper Management* (New York: Praeger, 1986), based on studies of four major newspapers and the programs of the Newspaper Advertising Bureau and ANPA.

Chapter 7: News Services and Syndicates

The best picture of the major Western news services is in Jonathan Fenby, *The International News Services* (New York: Schocken Books, 1986), which covers the histories and roles of AP, UPI, Reuters, and Agence France-Presse. There is no one book solely devoted to the U.S. news services. Frank Luther Mott paints a picture of the Associated Press operation in a chapter of *The News in America.* Emery and Emery trace their history in *The Press and America* and Phillip H. Ault tells youthful readers how big stories are covered in *News Around the Clock* (New York: Dodd, Mead, 1960).

Oliver Gramling, *AP: The Story of News,* and Joe Alex Morris, *Deadline Every Minute: The Story of the United Press,* capture a good deal of the reportorial excitement of the news services. Hugh Baillie, *High Tension* (New York: Harper & Row, 1959), is the readable autobiography of a former president of UP. *Kent Cooper and the Associated Press* (New York: Random House, 1959) is the second personal account by the most famous general manager of the AP; the first, *Barriers Down* (New York: Farrar and Rinehart, 1942), is Cooper's story of his efforts to break up international news monopolies. Melville E. Stone, *Fifty Years a Journalist,* is the autobiography of the first AP general manager.

A UNESCO publication, *News Agencies: Their Structure and Operation* (New York: Columbia University Press, 1953), gives summary accounts of the AP, UP, and INS and analyzes other world news agencies. John C. Merrill, Carter R. Bryan, and Marvin Alisky, *The Foreign Press* (Baton Rouge: Louisiana State University Press, 1970), includes world news agencies in its overall picture. UNESCO's *World Communications: A 200-Country Survey of Press, Radio, Television, Films* (New York: UNESCO, 1975) is a reference work for international communications. (For further references, see bibliography for Chapter 25.)

The annual July *Syndicate Directory* issued by *Editor & Publisher* updates Elmo Scott Watson, *A History of Newspaper Syndicates, 1865–1935* (Chicago: Publishers' Auxiliary, 1936).

Chapter 8: Magazines

A factual supplement to the magazine field texts is Leonard Mogel's *The Magazine: Everything You Need to Know to Make It in the Magazine Business* (Englewood Cliffs, N.J.: Prentice-Hall, 1979). William H. Taft's *American Magazines for the 1980s* (New York: Hastings House, 1982) is a state-of-the-art summary. So is *The Handbook of Magazine Publishing,* compiled by the editors of *Folio* magazine in 1983.

An overview of the field is provided by Roland E. Wolseley's *Understanding Magazines* (Ames: Iowa State University Press, 1969), which treats editorial and business operations of consumer, business, and specialized publications. Wolseley's *The Changing Magazine* (New York: Hastings House, 1973) traces trends in readership and management. *Magazine Profiles* (Evanston, Ill.: Medill School of Journalism, 1974) presents studies by 12 graduate students of nearly 50 current magazines. John Tebbel's *The American Magazine: A Compact History* (New York: Hawthorn, 1969) emphasizes an industry-wide survey. James L. C. Ford, *Magazines for Millions* (Carbondale, Ill.: Southern Illinois University Press, 1970), tells the story of specialized publications in fields such as business, religion, labor, and homemaking.

Views of specialized magazine work can be obtained from Jan V. White, *Designing for Magazines* (New York: Bowker, 1982); Ruori McLean, *Magazine Design* (London: Oxford University Press, 1969); Rowena Ferguson, *Editing the Small Magazine* (New York: Columbia University Press, 1976); Don Gussow, *The New Business Journalism* (San Diego: Harcourt Brace Jovanovich, 1984); and Julien Elfenbein, *Business Journalism* (New York: Harper & Row, 1960), a classic.

Textbooks on editing and writing include Betsy P. Graham, *Writing Magazine Articles With Style* (New York: Holt, Rinehart and Winston, 1980); William L. Rivers and Alison R. Work, *Freelancer and Staff Writer* (Belmont, Calif.: Wadsworth, 1986); J. W. Click and Russell N. Baird, *Magazine Editing and Production* (Dubuque, Iowa: Brown, 1986); Roy Paul Nelson, *Articles and Features* (Boston: Houghton Mifflin, 1978); William L. Rivers, *Magazine Editing in the '80s* (Belmont, Calif.: Wadsworth, 1983); J. T. W. Hubbard, *Magazine Editing* (Englewood Cliffs, N.J.: Prentice-Hall/Spectrum, 1982), a how-to-do-it manual; and Myrick Land, *Writing for Magazines* (Englewood Cliffs, N.J.: Prentice-Hall, 1987).

Chapter 9: Book Publishing

Charles G. Madison's *Book Publishing in America* (New York: McGraw-Hill, 1967) is the definitive survey of the book publishing industry by a former editor and publisher. There are many useful insights into the art of publishing and the history of the major companies. A well-rounded picture of the trade or general side of the book publishing industry is given by a score of specialists in *What Happens in Book Publishing,* edited by Chandler B. Grannis (New York: Columbia University Press, 1967).

Some of the economic factors behind publishing house mergers and sales are presented in Benjamin M. Compaine, *The Book Industry in Transition: An Eco-*

nomic Analysis of Book Distribution and Marketing (White Plains, N.Y.: Knowledge Industry Publications, 1978).

Sir Stanley Unwin, *The Truth About Publishing* (New York: Bowker, 1960), is highly readable. John P. Dessauer, *Book Publishing: What It Is, What It Does* (New York: Bowker, 1981), gives an excellent overview. William Jovanovich, *Now, Barabbas* (New York: Harper & Row, 1964) presents thoughtful essays on his field by a publishing executive.

Elizabeth A. Geiser has edited papers from the University of Denver Publishing Institute in *The Business of Book Publishing: Papers by Practitioners* (Boulder, Colo.: Westview Press, 1985). Roger Smith, editor, *The American Reading Public: A Symposium* (New York: Bowker, 1964), is a particularly succinct and useful collection of authoritative essays by a number of publishing executives.

John Tebbel has completed his four-volume *A History of Book Publishing in the United States* (New York: Bowker). The first three volumes appeared in 1972, 1975, and 1978. They cover the years 1630 to 1865, 1865 to 1919, and 1920 to 1940. The last appeared in 1981. A single volume summary, *Between Covers,* was issued in 1986.

The most complete history of paperbacks is Kenneth C. Davis, *Two-Bit Culture: The Paperbacking of America* (Boston: Houghton Mifflin, 1984). Thomas L. Bonn wrote *Under Cover: An Illustrated History of American Mass Market Paperbacks* (New York: Penguin, 1982). Roy Walters presents a collection of his trade journal columns for the 1970s and early 1980s in *Paperback Talk* (Chicago: Academy Chicago, 1985).

PART THREE: THE ELECTRONIC AND FILM MEDIA

Chapter 10: Growth of Radio, Television, and Film

An eight-year editing project by Lawrence H. Lichty and Malachi C. Topping resulted in more than 700 pages of *American Broadcasting: A Sourcebook on the History of Radio and Television* (New York: Hastings House, 1975). Two one-volume distillations are Christopher H. Sterling and John M. Kittross, *Stay Tuned: A Concise History of American Broadcasting* (Belmont, Calif.: Wadsworth, 1978), and F. Leslie Smith, *Perspectives on Radio and Television* (New York: Harper & Row, 1984).

Other historical accounts include Erik Barnouw's three-volume history of American broadcasting, *A Tower in Babel, The Golden Web,* and *The Image Empire* (New York: Oxford University Press, 1966, 1968, 1970); Sydney W. Head and Christopher Sterling, *Broadcasting in America* (Boston: Houghton Mifflin, 1987); Hugh G.J. Aitken, *The Continuous Wave: Technology and American Radio 1900–1932* (Princeton, N.J.: Princeton University Press, 1985); Gleason L. Archer's classics, *History of Radio to 1926* (New York: American Historical Society, 1938) and *Big Business and Radio* (1939); and Llewellyn White's *The American Radio* (Chicago: University of Chicago Press, 1947).

Broadcasting magazine issued a volume compiled from its files on its fiftieth anniversary in 1981, *The First 50 Years of Broadcasting,* an informal history.

Biographies include Kenneth Bilby, *The General: David Sarnoff and the Rise of the Communications Industry* (New York: Harper & Row, 1987); Ann M. Sperber, *Murrow: His Life and Times* (New York: Freundlich, 1986); Alexander Kendrick, *Prime Time: The Life of Edward R. Murrow* (Boston: Little, Brown, 1969); Roger Burlingame, *Don't Let Them Scare You: The Life and Times of Elmer Davis* (Philadelphia: Lippincott, 1961); Irving E. Fang, *Those Radio Commentators!* (Ames: Iowa State University Press, 1977); and Barbara Matusow, *The Evening Stars* (Boston: Houghton Mifflin, 1983), portraits of news anchors.

Autobiographies are William S. Paley, *As It Happened: A Memoir* (Garden City, N.Y.: Doubleday, 1979); Lowell Thomas, *Good Evening Everybody* (New York: Morrow, 1976); Dan Rather, *The Camera Never Blinks* (New York: Morrow, 1977); *Father of Radio: The Autobiography of Lee De Forest* (Chicago: Wilcox & Follett, 1950); and H. V. Kaltenborn, *Fifty Fabulous Years, 1900–1950: A Personal Review* (New York: Putnam's, 1950). Two collections of writings are *In Search of Light: The Broadcasts of Edward R. Murrow 1938–1961* (New York: Knopf, 1967) and *Looking Ahead: The Papers of David Sarnoff* (New York: McGraw-Hill, 1968).

Historical accounts of networks are found in Sterling Quinlan, *Inside ABC: American Broadcasting Company's Rise to Power* (New York: Hastings House, 1979), and for CBS in David Halberstam's *The Powers That Be* (New York: Knopf, 1979).

Relationships with government are analyzed in Walter B. Emery, *Broadcasting and Government* (East Lansing: Michigan State University Press, 1971); and in John R. Bittner, *Broadcast Law and Regulation* (Englewood Cliffs, N.J.: Prentice-Hall, 1982). For sources, see Frank J. Kahn, *Documents of American Broadcasting* (Englewood Cliffs, N.J.: Prentice-Hall, 1984). Donald G. Godfrey compiled *A Directory of Broadcast Archives* (Washington: Broadcast Education Association, 1983).

Leading historical surveys of motion pictures are Paul Rotha and Richard Griffith, *The Film Till Now* (London: Spring Books, 1967), a world cinema survey; and Richard Griffith and Arthur Mayer, *The Movies* (New York: Simon and Schuster, 1970), American film history. Alan Casty offered an account of world filmmaking in *Development of the Film: An Interpretive History* (New York: Harcourt Brace Jovanovich, 1973). Two other top accounts are Gerald Mast, *A Short History of the Movies* (New York: Bobbs-Merrill, 1981), and Arthur Knight, *The Liveliest Art* (New York: Macmillan, 1978).

The history of documentary films is told by Paul Rotha, Sinclair Road, and Richard Griffith in *Documentary Film* (London: Faber and Faber, 1966), and by A. William Bluem in *Documentary in American Television* (New York: Hastings House, 1965). Charles Montgomery Hammond, Jr., updated Bluem in *The Image Decade: Television Documentary 1965–1975* (New York: Hastings House, 1981). Newsreels are covered in Raymond Fielding's *The American Newsreel, 1911–1967* (Norman: University of Oklahoma Press, 1972).

Chapter 11: Radio

Introductory books for radio include Robert L. Hilliard, *Radio Broadcasting* (New York: Longman, 1985), and Peter Fornatele and Joshua Mills, *Radio in the*

Television Age (Woodstock, N.Y.: Overlook Press, 1980). A specialized history is J. Fred MacDonald, *Don't Touch That Dial! Radio Programming in American Life 1920–1960* (Chicago: Nelson Hall, 1979). Two books about radio's comedy programs are Jim Harmon, *The Great Radio Comedians* (New York: Doubleday, 1970), and Arthur Wertheim, *Radio Comedy* (New York: Oxford University Press, 1979).

Books dealing with radio news include John and Denise Bittner, *Radio Journalism* (Englewood Cliffs, N.J.: Prentice-Hall, 1977), including documentaries; F. Gifford, *Tape: A Radio News Handbook* (New York: Hastings House, 1977); G. Paul Smeyak, *Broadcast News Writing* (Columbus, Ohio: Grid, 1977); and Mitchell Stephens, *Broadcast News* (New York: Holt, Rinehart and Winston, 1980).

Lewis B. O'Donnell, Carl Hausman and Philip Benoit collaborated on *Modern Radio Production* (Belmont, Calif.: Wadsworth, 1986) and *Announcing: Broadcast Communicating Today* (Wadsworth, 1987). In radio management and production, two key books are Edd Routt, *The Business of Radio Broadcasting* (Blue Ridge Summit, Pa.: TAB Books, 1972), one of a series issued by that publisher, and Robert Oringel's *Audio Control Handbook* (New York: Hastings House, 1972), a guide to radio sound. Jonne Murphy offers *Handbook of Radio Advertising* (Radnor, Pa.: Chilton, 1980). An excellent book about announcing is Stuart W. Hyde, *Television and Radio Announcing* (Boston: Houghton Mifflin, 1983).

See the listings for Chapter 13 for books dealing with both radio and television.

Chapter 12: Recording

Celebrating the centennial of the phonograph with its third edition was Roland Gelatt's *The Fabulous Phonograph: 1877–1977* (New York: Macmillan, 1977). A popular history is C. A. Schicke, *Revolution in Sound: A Biography of the Recording Industry* (Boston: Little, Brown, 1974). Another is R. Serge Denisoff, *Solid Gold: The Popular Record Industry* (New Brunswick, N.J.: Transaction Books, 1975). Paul E. Farnsworth wrote *The Social Psychology of Music* (Ames: Iowa State University Press, 1969).

Chapter 13: Television

Introductory books for television include John R. Bittner, *Broadcasting and Telecommunication: Introduction* (Englewood Cliffs, N.J.: Prentice-Hall, 1985); Marvin Smith, *Radio, TV, and Cable* (New York: Holt, Rinehart and Winston, 1985); Giraud Chester, Garnet R. Garrison, and Edgar Willis, *Television and Radio* (Englewood Cliffs, N.J.: Prentice-Hall, 1978); and Horace Newcomb, *TV: The Most Popular Art* (Garden City, N.Y.: Doubleday Anchor, 1974), an analysis of popular TV programming.

Books that deal with television news are Irving E. Fang, *Television News, Radio News* (Minneapolis, Minn.: Rada Press, 1985); Richard Yoakam and Charles F. Cremer, *ENG: Television News and the New Technology* (New York: Random House, 1985); David K. Cohler, *Broadcast Journalism: A Guide for the Presentation of Radio and Television News* (Englewood Cliffs, N.J.: Prentice-Hall, 1985);

Carolyn D. Lewis, *Reporting for Television* (New York: Columbia University Press, 1984); Ted White, Adrian J. Meppen, and Stephen B. Young, *Broadcast News Writing, Reporting and Production* (New York: Macmillan, 1984); Edward Bliss, Jr., and John M. Patterson, *Writing News for Broadcast* (New York: Columbia University Press, 1978); Vernon Stone and Bruce Hinson, *Television Newsfilm Techniques* (New York: Hastings House, 1974); and Edd Routt, *Dimensions of Broadcast Editorializing* (Blue Ridge Summit, Pa.: TAB Books, 1974).

Books treating various types of writing are Martin Maloney and Paul Max Rubenstein, *Writing for the Media* (Englewood Cliffs, N.J.: Prentice-Hall, 1980); Daniel E. Garvey and William L. Rivers, *Broadcast Writing* (New York: Longman, 1982); Peter B. Orlik, *Broadcast Copywriting* (Boston: Allyn & Bacon, 1982); Robert L. Hilliard, *Writing for Television and Radio* (New York: Longman, 1984); and Milan D. Meeske and R. C. Norris, *Copywriting for the Electronic Media* (Belmont, Calif.: Wadsworth, 1987).

MANAGEMENT AND PRODUCTION. Norman Marcus, *Broadcast and Cable Management* (Englewood Cliffs, N.J.: Prentice-Hall, 1986); Charles Warner, *Broadcast and Cable Selling* (Belmont, Calif.: Wadsworth, 1986); Thomas D. Burrows and Donald N. Wood, *Television Production: Disciplines and Techniques* (Dubuque, Iowa: Brown, 1986); Stanley R. Alten, *Audio in Media* (Belmont, Calif.: Wadsworth, 1986); Alan A. Armer, *Directing Television and Film* (Belmont, Calif.: Wadsworth, 1986); Susan Tyler Eastman, Sydney Head, and Lewis Klein, *Broadcast Programming* (Belmont, Calif.: Wadsworth, 1980); Richard Breyer and Peter Moller, *Making Television Programs* (New York: Longman, 1984); Herbert Zettl, *Television Production Handbook* (Belmont, Calif.: Wadsworth, 1984), a classic text; Alan Wurtzel, *Television Production* (New York: McGraw-Hill, 1979); Gerald Millerson, *The Technique of Television Production* and *Effective TV Production* (New York: Hastings House, 1972, 1976); Michael Murray, *The Videotape Book: A Basic Guide* (New York: Taplinger, 1975); Arthur Englander and Paul Petzold, *Filming for Television* (New York: Hastings House, 1976); and Richard L. Williams, *Television Production: A Vocational Approach* (Salt Lake City: Vision, 1982). Stuart W. Hyde, *Television and Radio Announcing* (Boston: Houghton Mifflin, 1983), is excellent in its field.

The advertising area is described in Elizabeth J. Heighton and Don R. Cunningham, *Advertising in the Broadcast Media* (Belmont, Calif.: Wadsworth, 1984); Charles A. Wainright, *Television Commercials* (New York: Hastings House, 1970); and Sherilyn K. Zeigler and Herbert H. Howard, *Broadcast Advertising: A Comprehensive Working Textbook* (Columbus, Ohio: Grid, 1978).

Methods of displaying textual information on a video display screen are described in *Videotext,* edited by Efrem Sigel (White Plains, N.Y.: Knowledge Industry Publications, 1980).

Chapter 14: The Film

Gerald Mast's *A Short History of the Movies* (New York: Bobbs-Merrill, 1981), offers detailed, highly readable descriptions and analyses, primarily of American and European films. A competitor is David A. Cook, *A History of Narrative Film*

(New York: W. W. Norton, 1981). To the major film histories, Rotha and Griffith's *The Film Till Now* and Griffith and Mayer's *The Movies,* may be added Arthur Knight, *The Liveliest Art* (New York: Hastings House, 1978), particularly good for the years 1895 to 1930; D. J. Wenden, *The Birth of the Movies* (New York: Dutton, 1975), covering 1895 to 1927; William K. Everson, *American Silent Film* (New York: Oxford University Press, 1978), copiously illustrated; Harry Geduld, *The Birth of the Talkies: From Edison to Jolson* (Bloomington, Ind.: Indiana University Press, 1975); David Bordwell, Janet Staiger, and Kristin Thompson, *The Classical Hollywood Cinema: Film Style and Mode of Production* (New York: Columbia University Press, 1985), a first-rate new version of film history, 1895 to 1960; John Fell, editor, *Film Before Griffith* (Berkeley, Calif.: University of California Press, 1984), 29 essays; Alan Casty, *Development of the Film: An Interpretive History* (New York: Harcourt Brace Jovanovich, 1973); James Monaco, *How to Read a Film* (New York: Oxford University Press, 1977); Jack C. Ellis, *A History of Film* (Englewood Cliffs, N.J.: Prentice-Hall, 1985); John L. Fell, *A History of Films* (New York: Holt, Rinehart and Winston, 1979), designed for the survey course; and James Monaco, *American Film Now* (New York: Oxford University Press, 1979), films of the 1970s.

The best social history is Garth Jowett, *Film: The Democratic Art* (Boston: Little, Brown, 1976), updating Lewis Jacobs' *The Rise of the American Film* (1939). Another is Robert Sklar, *Movie-Made America* (New York: Random House, 1975). Gerald Mast edited an anthology tracing the cultural importance of movies, *The Movies in Our Midst* (Chicago: University of Chicago Press, 1981).

The standard work on the history, principles, and technique of the documentary motion picture is Paul Rotha, Sinclair Road, and Richard Griffith, *The Documentary Film* (London: Faber and Faber, 1966). Others are Lewis Jacobs, *The Documentary Tradition* (New York: W. W. Norton, 1979); Alan Rosenthal, *The New Documentary in Action: A Casebook in Film Making* (Berkeley: University of California Press, 1971); Richard M. Barsam, *Nonfiction Film: A Critical History* (New York: Dutton, 1973); Richard D. MacCann, *The People's Films* (New York: Hastings House, 1973), a history of United States government documentaries; and Erik Barnouw, *Documentary: A History of the Non-Fiction Film* (London: Oxford University Press, 1974), a well-integrated analysis.

Among introductory texts are Thomas and Vivian Sobcheck, *An Introduction to Film* (Boston: Little, Brown, 1980), and Bernard F. Dick, *Anatomy of Film* (New York: St. Martin's Press, 1978). John L. Fell's *Film: An Introduction* (New York: Praeger, 1975) is designed for survey courses as is Roy P. Madsen's *The Impact of Film* (New York: Macmillan, 1973). Suitable for text use is Thomas W. Bohn and Richard L. Stromgren, *Light and Shadows: A History of Motion Pictures* (Port Washington, N.Y.: Alfred Publishing, 1975).

Film genres—westerns, musicals, detectives, horror, and so on—are described by Stuart M. Kaminsky and Jeffrey H. Mahon in *American Film Genres* (Chicago: Nelson-Hall, 1985). Brian G. Rose edited *TV Genres: A Handbook and Reference Guide* (Westport, Conn.: Greenwood Press, 1985).

Among recent film biographies are Richard Schickel, *D.W. Griffith: An American Life* (New York: Simon and Schuster, 1984); David Robinson, *Chaplin: His Life and Art* (New York: McGraw-Hill, 1985); Charles Higham, *Orson Welles* (New York: St. Martin's Press, 1985); and Leonard Mosley, *Disney's World* (New York: Stein and Day, 1985).

A pathbreaking reworking of contemporary film theory is offered by Edward Branigan in *Point of View in the Cinema: A Theory of Narration and Subjectivity in Classical Film* (Berlin: Mouton Books, 1984). Also in the field of theory and criticism are Gerald Mast and Marshall Cohen, editors, *Film Theory and Criticism* (New York: Oxford University Press, 1985); J. Dudley Andrew, *The Major Film Theories* (New York: Oxford University Press, 1976); Garth Jowett and James M. Linton, *Movies as Mass Communication* (Beverly Hills, Calif.: Sage, 1980); and Pauline Kael, *Reeling* (Boston: Little, Brown, 1976), *When the Lights Go Down* and *Taking It All In* (New York: Holt, Rinehart and Winston, 1980, 1984), and *State of the Art* (New York: Dutton, 1985), by the noted film critic.

Lewis Jacobs, *The Emergence of Film Art* (New York: Hopkinson and Blake, 1969), offers carefully selected essays to illustrate the evolution of the motion picture as an art from 1900 to the present. Roger Manvell, in *New Cinema in Europe* (New York: Dutton, 1966), gives brief descriptions of movements, filmmakers, and films in postwar feature filmmaking in Europe. Gregory Battcock's *The New American Cinema* (New York: Dutton, 1967) is a stimulating collection of essays covering theory and practice of experimental filmmakers.

Film direction is examined by Eric Sherman in *Directing the Film* (Boston: Little, Brown, 1976), and by Louis Giannetti in *Masters of the American Cinema* (Englewood Cliffs, N.J.: Prentice-Hall, 1981). Personalities from the silent film era are interviewed in Kevin Brownlow, *The Parade's Gone By* (New York: Knopf, 1968). Also of note is Andrew Sarris, *The American Cinema: Directors and Directions 1929–1968* (New York: Dutton, 1968).

Chapter 15: Video

Book references are scant for this newest entry in the communications explosion. See the bibliography for Chapter 1, particularly Gross, *Telecommunications,* and *Television Digest*'s anthology, *The Videocassette Recorder: An American Love Affair.* Other references include Eli M. Noam, editor, *Video Media Competition* (New York: Columbia University Press, 1985), covering research and statistics, including VCRs; Fiona Richardson, editor, *Video in the UK and US* (London: Financial Times Business Information, 1984), an historical and current overview of the videocassette, videodisc, and marketing; Mark Nadel and Eli M. Noam, editors, *The Supply and Demand for Video Programming: An Anthology* (New York: Columbia University Graduate School of Business, 1983); and *The Video Register* (White Plains, N.Y.: Knowledge Industry Publications), an annual directory of users and suppliers.

In the "how-to-do-it" category, but also explaining the medium are Peter Utz, *Today's Video: Equipment, Setup, and Production 1987* (Englewood Cliffs, N.J.: Prentice-Hall, 1987); Pamela Levine, et al., *Complete Guide to Home Video Production* (New York: Holt, Rinehart and Winston, 1984); Ingrid Wiegand, *Professional Video Production* (White Plains, N.Y.: Knowledge Industry Publications, 1985);

Frank Leslie Moore, *The Video Moviemaker's Handbook* (New York: New American Library, 1984); and Welby A. Smith, *Video Fundamentals: A Practical Handbook for the Entry-Level Video User* (Englewood Cliffs, N.J.: Prentice-Hall, 1983).

Shemus Culhene offers an anecdotal discussion and explanation of animation on film in *Talking Animals and Other People* (New York: St. Martin's Press, 1986).

Chapter 16: Photographic and Graphics Communication

PHOTOGRAPHIC HISTORY AND DEVELOPMENT. Beaumont Newhall, *The History of Photography from 1839 to the Present* (New York: Museum of Modern Art, 1982); Helmut and Alison Gernsheim, *History of Photography* (London: Oxford University Press, 1970); Peter Pollack, *Picture History of Photography* (New York: Abrams, 1969); Nathan Lyons, *Photographers on Photography* (Englewood Cliffs, N.J.: Prentice-Hall, 1966); R. Smith Schuneman, *Photographic Communication: Principles, Problems and Challenges of Photojournalism* (New York: Hastings House, 1972); A. William Bluem, *Documentary in American Television* (New York: Hastings House, 1965); and Paul Rotha, Sinclair Road, and Richard Griffith, *Documentary Film* (London: Faber and Faber, 1966).

PHOTOGRAPHIC TECHNIQUES. Harold Evans, *Pictures on a Page* (Belmont, Calif.: Wadsworth, 1979), by the former editor of the *Sunday Times,* London; Kenneth Kobre, *Photojournalism: The Professionals' Approach* (Somerville, Mass.: Curtin and London, 1980); Phil Davis, *Photography* (Dubuque, Iowa: Brown, 1986); Robert B. Rhode and Floyd H. McCall, *Introduction to Photography* (New York: Macmillan, 1981); David H. Curl, *Photo-Communication* (New York: Macmillan, 1979); Philip C. Geraci, *Photojournalism* (Dubuque, Iowa: Kendall/ Hunt, 1984); Frank P. Hoy, *Photojournalism: The Visual Approach* (Englewood Cliffs, N.J.: Prentice-Hall, 1986); Marvin J. Rosen, *Introduction to Photography* (Boston: Houghton Mifflin, 1982); and Robert L. Kerns, *Photojournalism: Photography with a Purpose* (Englewood Cliffs, N.J.: Prentice-Hall, 1980), with a focus on public relations.

BIOGRAPHICAL. James Horan, *Mathew Brady: Historian with a Camera* (New York: Crown, 1955), and *Timothy O'Sullivan: America's Forgotten Photographer* (New York: Crown, 1966); Judith Gutman, *Lewis W. Hine and the American Social Conscience* (New York: Walker, 1967); Richard Griffith, *The World of Robert Flaherty* (New York: Duell, Sloan and Pearce, 1953); Karin Becker Ohrn, *Dorothea Lange and the Documentary Tradition* (Baton Rouge: Louisiana State Press, 1980); Margaret Bourke-White, *Portrait of Myself* (New York: Simon and Schuster, 1963); Vickie Goldberg, *Margaret Bourke-White* (New York: Harper & Row, 1986); Ansel Adams, *An Autobiography* (Boston: Little, Brown, 1985); Richard Whelan, *Robert Capa* (New York: Knopf, 1986); David Douglas Duncan, *Yankee Nomad* (New York: Holt, Rinehart and Winston, 1966); Carl Mydans, *More Than Meets the Eye* (New York: Harper & Row, 1959); Gordon Parks, *A Choice of Weapons* (New York: Harper & Row, 1966); Edward Steichen, *A Life in*

Photography (Garden City, N.Y.: Doubleday, 1963); Cornell Capa, *Robert Capa* (New York: Grossman, 1974); Dora Jane Hamblin, *That Was the Life* (New York: W. W. Norton, 1977).

PICTURE BOOKS. Alfred Eisenstaedt, *Witness to Our Times* (New York: Viking, 1966); David Douglas Duncan, *War Without Heroes* (New York: Harper & Row, 1970); William S. Johnson, editor, *W. Eugene Smith: Master of the Photographic Essay* (Millerton, N.Y.: Aperture, 1982); Carl Mydans, *Photojournalist* (New York: Abrams, 1985); Robert Capa, *Photographs* (New York: Knopf, 1986); *Life, the First Fifty Years* (Boston: Little, Brown, 1986); John Phillips, *It Happened in Our LIFETIME* (Boston: Little, Brown, 1985); John Szarkowski, *The Photographer's Eye* (New York: Museum of Modern Art, 1966); Leonard Freed, *Black in White America* (New York: Grossman, n.d.); Cornell Capa, editor, *The Concerned Photographer* (New York: Grossman, 1969), 200 photos of protest by six leading photographers; Charles Harbutt and Lee Jones, *America in Crisis* (New York: Holt, Rinehart and Winston, 1969); Associated Press, *The Instant It Happened* (New York: Associated Press, 1974), great news photos from the Civil War to Watergate. The University of Missouri Press began issuing an annual, *The Best of Photojournalism,* in 1975.

GRAPHICS AND PRODUCTION. Edmund C. Arnold, *Designing the Total Newspaper* (New York: Harper & Row, 1981), and *Ink on Paper 2* (New York: Harper & Row, 1972); Arthur T. Turnbull and Russell N. Baird, *The Graphics of Communication: Typography, Layout and Design* (New York: Holt, Rinehart and Winston, 1980); Anthony Smith, *Goodbye Gutenberg—The Newspaper Revolution of the 1980s* (London: Oxford University Press, 1980); Mario R. Garcia, *Contemporary Newspaper Design* (Englewood Cliffs, N.J.: Prentice-Hall, 1987); Roy Paul Nelson, *Publication Design* (Dubuque, Iowa: Brown, 1987); Sean Morrison, *A Guide to Type Design* (Englewood Cliffs, N.J.: Prentice-Hall, 1986); Daryl R. Moen, *Newspaper Layout and Design* (Ames: Iowa State University Press, 1984); Wendell C. Crow, *Communication Graphics* (Englewood Cliffs, N.J.: Prentice-Hall, 1986); Roy Paul Nelson, *Design of Advertising* (Dubuque, Iowa: Brown, 1985); Ralph Ayers, *Graphics for Television* (Englewood Cliffs, N.J.: Prentice-Hall, 1984); and Society of Newspaper Design, *Seventh Edition: The Best of Newspaper Design 1985–1986* (Washington, D.C.: The Newspaper Center, 1987).

PART FOUR: THE PERSUASIVE PROFESSIONS

Chapter 17: Advertising

Three recent books, complementing each other in presenting the history of American advertising, are noteworthy additions to media literature. Daniel Pope's *The Making of Modern Advertising* (New York: Basic Books, 1983), is a thoughtful, analytic account of advertising's growth to 1920, using theoretical perspectives grounded in economics. The major contribution is Roland Marchand's *Advertising the American Dream* (Berkeley: University of California Press, 1985), which uses a cultural approach to the formative period of advertising, 1920 to 1940, describing it as both promoting technological modernity and offering relief from self-image anxiety. Stephen Fox, in *The Mirror Makers: A History of American Advertising and Its Creators* (New York: William Morrow, 1984), carries the story through the 1970s, concentrating on the impact of creative people.

Among other histories, the standard account is Frank Presbrey, *The History and Development of Advertising* (New York: Doubleday, Doran, 1930). James Playsted Wood, *The Story of Advertising* (New York: Ronald, 1958), is very readable. E. S. Turner, *The Shocking History of Advertising* (New York: Dutton, 1953), is constructively critical. Michael Schudson, *Advertising: The Uneasy Profession* (New York: Basic Books, 1984), is a critical historical analysis.

The role of advertising in society is discussed in John W. Wright, editor, *The Commercial Connection: Advertising and the American Mass Media* (New York: Dell/Delta, 1979); in Kim B. Rotzoll, James E. Haefner, and Charles H. Sandage, editors, *Advertising in Contemporary Society* (Columbus, Ohio: Grid, 1976); and in John S. Wright and John Mertes, *Advertising's Role in Society* (St. Paul, Minn.: West, 1976).

Research areas are outlined in Alan D. Fletcher and Thomas A. Bowers, *Fundamentals of Advertising Research* (Columbus, Ohio: Grid, 1983), and in James Leigh and Claude R. Martin, Jr., editors, *Current Issues and Research in Advertising* (Ann Arbor: University of Michigan, 1978), a brief reader. Two books on marketing strategy are Leo Bogart, *Strategy in Advertising: Matching Media and Messages to Markets and Motivation* (Chicago: Crain, 1984), and David J. Luck and O.C. Farrell, *Marketing Strategy and Plans* (Englewood Cliffs, N.J.: Prentice-Hall, 1985), using numerous case histories.

Among the general text and reference books on advertising are Charles H. Sandage, Vernon Fryburger, and Kim Rotzoll, *Advertising Theory and Practice* (Homewood, Ill.: Irwin, 1983); Jack Engel, *Advertising: The Process and Practice* (New York: McGraw-Hill, 1980); S. Watson Dunn and Arnold Barban, *Advertising: Its Role in Modern Marketing* (New York: Dryden, 1986); John S. Wright, Daniel S. Warner, and Willis L. Winter, Jr., *Advertising* (New York: McGraw-Hill, 1981); Philip Ward Burton and William Ryan, *Advertising Fundamentals* (Columbus, Ohio: Grid, 1980); Thomas Russell, W. Ronald Lane, and Glenn Verrill, *Kleppner's Advertising Procedure* (Englewood Cliffs, N.J.: Prentice-Hall, 1988), published since 1925; and Maurice Mandell, *Advertising* (Prentice-Hall, 1984).

Media is the topic of discussion in Donald Jugenheimer and Peter Turk, *Advertising Media* (Columbus, Ohio: Grid, 1980); in Arnold M. Barban, Donald W. Jugenheimer, and Lee F. Young, *Advertising Media Sourcebook and Workbook* (Columbus, Ohio: Grid, 1975); in Jack Z. Sissors and Jim Sutmanek, *Advertising Media Planning* (Chicago: Crain, 1982); and in Anthony F. McGann and J. Thomas Russell, *Advertising Media: A Managerial Approach* (Homewood, Ill.: Irwin, 1988). Prentice-Hall offered two 1986 books about cable: David S. Barr, *Advertising on Cable,* and Kensinger Jones, Thomas F. Baldwin, and Martin P. Block, *Cable Advertising.*

Management is covered in David A. Aaker and John G. Myers, *Advertising Management* (Englewood Cliffs, N.J.: Prentice-Hall, 1982), and in John D. Leckenby and Nugent Wedding, *Advertising Management* (Columbus, Ohio: Grid, 1982).

Copywriting techniques are described by David L. Malickson and John W. Nason in *Advertising—How to Write the Kind That Works* (New York: Scribner's, 1977) and by Philip Ward Burton in *Advertising Copywriting* (Columbus, Ohio: Grid, 1979). Copy, design, and production are covered by A. Jerome Jewler in *Creative Strategy in Advertising* (Belmont, Calif.: Wadsworth, 1985), while Sandra E. Moriarty emphasizes theory in *Creative Advertising: Theory and Practice* (Englewood Cliffs, N.J.: Prentice-Hall, 1986). Two classic writers on copy were Aesop Glim (George Laflin Miller) in *Copy—The Core of Advertising* (New York: Dover, 1963) and *How Advertising Is Written—and Why* (1961); and Clyde Bedell, *How to Write Advertising That Sells* (New York: McGraw-Hill, 1952).

GRAPHICS AND DESIGN. Arthur T. Turnbull and Russell N. Baird, *The Graphics of Communication: Typography, Layout, Design* (New York: Holt, Rinehart and Winston, 1980); Roy Paul Nelson, *The Design of Advertising* (Dubuque, Iowa: Brown, 1985); and Edmund C. Arnold, *Ink on Paper 2* (New York: Harper & Row, 1972).

ADVERTISING AGENCIES. Herbert S. Gardner, Jr., *The Advertising Agency Business* (Chicago: Crain, 1983), is a practical guide. Martin Mayer, *Madison Avenue, U.S.A.* (New York: Harper, 1958), provides a good picture of advertising agencies; Ralph M. Hower, *The History of an Advertising Agency: N. W. Ayer & Son at Work, 1869–1939* (Cambridge, Mass.: Harvard University Press, 1939) is a documented history of one agency. David Ogilvy tells a fascinating story about work in an agency in *Confessions of an Advertising Man* (New York: Atheneum, 1963; Dell paperback, 1964). The story of the pioneering Albert Lasker is told by John Gunther in *Taken at the Flood* (New York: Harper & Row, 1960).

Chapter 18: Public Relations

Books to read in exploring the public relations field reflected changes in 1986. New to the field was *Public Relations: Strategies and Tactics* by Dennis L. Wilcox, Phillip H. Ault, and Warren K. Agee (New York: Harper & Row, 1986), combining breadth and depth with coverage of "hot" topics and extended case studies. A third author was added for the sixth edition of *Effective Public Relations* by Scott Cutlip, Allen H. Center, and Glen M. Broom (Englewood Cliffs, N.J.: Prentice-Hall, 1985); H. Frazier Moore and Frank B. Kalupa brought out the ninth edition of *Public Relations: Principles, Cases and Problems* (Homewood, Ill.: Irwin, 1985), a text begun by Bertrand R. Canfield. It was the second edition for Doug Newsom and Alan Scott, *This Is PR: The Realities of Public Relations* (Belmont, Calif.: Wadsworth, 1985).

Other general books include those by Bill Cantor, *Inside Public Relations* (New York: Longman, 1984), edited by Chester Burger; Fraser P. Seitel, *The Practice of Public Relations* (New York: Charles E. Merrill, 1980); James E. Grunig and Todd Hunt, *Managing Public Relations* (New York: Holt, Rinehart and Winston,

1983); John E. Marston, *Modern Public Relations* (New York: McGraw-Hill, 1979); Raymond Simon, *Public Relations: Principles and Practices* (New York: John Wiley, 1984); and Allen H. Center and Frank E. Walsh, *Public Relations Practices: Managerial Case Studies* (Englewood Cliffs, N.J.: Prentice-Hall, 1985).

Groups of public relations professionals contributed chapters for *Public Relations Handbook,* edited by Philip Lesly (Englewood Cliffs, N.J.: Prentice-Hall, 1978), and *Handbook of Public Relations,* edited by Howard Stephenson (New York: McGraw-Hill, 1971). A leading counselor, John W. Hill, tells his story in *The Making of a Public Relations Man* (New York: McKay, 1963). New York's practitioners are described by Irwin Ross in *The Image Merchants* (Garden City, N.Y.: Doubleday, 1959). Edward L. Bernays, in *Public Relations* (Norman: University of Oklahoma Press, 1979), presents a case history type of discussion by a longtime practitioner. His memoirs are in *Biography of an Idea* (New York: Simon and Schuster, 1965). Ray E. Hiebert contributed the biography of another pioneer in his *Courtier to the Crowd: The Life Story of Ivy Lee* (Ames: Iowa State University Press, 1966). Alan R. Raucher traced early PR history in *Public Relations and Business 1900–1929* (Baltimore: The Johns Hopkins Press, 1968).

Writing techniques are analyzed in Lawrence W. Nolte and Dennis L. Wilcox, *Effective Publicity: How to Reach the Public* (New York: John Wiley, 1984); Doug Newsom and Bob Carrell, *Public Relations Writing: Form & Style* (Belmont, Calif.: Wadsworth, 1986); Frank E. Walsh, *Public Relations Writer in a Computer Age* (Englewood Cliffs, N.J.: Prentice-Hall, 1986); and David L. Lendt, editor, *The Publicity Process* (Ames: Iowa State University Press, 1975).

Bibliographies are Scott M. Cutlip, *A Public Relations Bibliography* (Madison: University of Wisconsin Press, 1965), and its extension, Robert L. Bishop, *Public Relations: A Comprehensive Bibliography* (Ann Arbor: University of Michigan Press, 1974).

PART FIVE: RESEARCH AND EDUCATION

Chapter 19: Mass Communications Research

A major effort to describe mass communications research was made in *Research Methods in Mass Communication,* edited by Guido H. Stempel III and Bruce H. Westley (Englewood Cliffs, N.J.: Prentice-Hall, 1981). It examines both social science and documentary research fields. Two research area studies are John D. Stevens and Hazel Dicken Garcia, *Communication History* (Beverly Hills, Calif.: Sage, 1980), and Klaus Krippendorff, *Content Analysis* (Beverly Hills, Calif.: Sage, 1980). An historical account is Shearon A. Lowery and Melvin L. DeFleur, *Milestones in Communication Research* (New York: Longman, 1983). The first communication research reference guide is *Communication Research: Strategies and Sources* (Belmont, Calif.: Wadsworth, 1986), by Rebecca B. Rubin, Alan M. Rubin, and Linda Piele.

Books that introduce the reader to research methods are Roger D. Wimmer and Joseph R. Dominick, *Mass Media Research* (Belmont, Calif.: Wadsworth, 1987); Frederick Williams, *The New Communications* (Belmont, Calif.: Wadsworth,

1983), and *Technology and Communication Behavior* (Wadsworth, 1987); Mary S. Mander, editor, *Communication in Transition* (New York: Praeger, 1983); Paul M. Hirsch, Peter V. Miller, and F. Gerald Kline, *Strategies for Communication Research* (Beverly Hills, Calif.: Sage, 1977); Maxwell E. McCombs and Lee Becker, *Using Mass Communication Theory* (Englewood Cliffs, N.J.: Prentice-Hall, 1979); Werner Severin and James Tankard, Jr., *Communication Theories: Origins, Methods, Uses* (New York: Hastings House, 1979), media-oriented; Albert H. Cantril, editor, *Polling on the Issues* (Cabin John, Md.: Seven Locks Press, 1980), with 21 contributors; Frederick Williams, *Reasoning with Statistics: Simplified Examples in Communication and Education Research* (New York: Holt, Rinehart and Winston, 1978); Pamela Alreck and Robert Settle, *The Survey Research Handbook* (Homewood, Ill.: Irwin, 1985); Floyd J. Fowler, Jr., *Survey Research Methods* (Beverly Hills, Calif.: Sage, 1984), a succinct textbook; and Hugh M. Beville, Jr., *Audience Ratings: Radio, Television, Cable* (Hillsdale, N.J.: Erlbaum Associates, 1985), a history of ratings.

Advertising research methods are outlined in Daniel Starch, *Measuring Advertising Readership and Results* (New York: McGraw-Hill, 1966); in Charles Ramond, *Advertising Research* (New York: Association of National Advertisers, 1976), summarizing knowledge; and in Alan D. Fletcher and Thomas J. Bowers, *Fundamentals of Advertising Research* (Columbus, Ohio: Grid, 1979).

Many of the references listed for Part One of this bibliography also are pertinent to this chapter, especially those dealing with effects, the communication process, and public opinion.

Chapter 20: Education for Mass Communications

The early growth of journalism education is reviewed in Albert A. Sutton, *Education for Journalism in the United States from Its Beginning to 1940* (Evanston, Ill.: Northwestern University Press, 1945). *The Training of Journalists* (Paris: UNESCO, 1958) is a worldwide survey on the training of personnel for the mass media, updated by *Mass Communication: Teaching and Studies at Universities,* edited by May Katzen (Paris: UNESCO, 1975). A history of journalism educator organizations in the United States is found in a 1987 *Journalism Monographs* issue, *AEJMC: 75 Years in the Making,* by Edwin Emery and Joseph P. McKerns.

William R. Lindley's monograph, *Journalism and Higher Education* (Stillwater, Okla.: Journalistic Services, 1976), traces the development of four major American journalism schools.

Books about career opportunities include Gregory Jackson, *Getting Into Broadcast Journalism* (New York: Hawthorn, 1974); John Tebbel, *Opportunities in Publishing Careers* (Louisville: Vocational Guidance Manuals, 1975), book publishing; Elmo I. Ellis, *Opportunities in Broadcasting* (Skokie, Ill.: National Textbook Co., 1981); and Roland E. Wolseley, *Careers in Religious Communications* (Scottdale, Pa.: Herald Press, 1977). Available in paperback are Arville Schaleben's *Your Future in Journalism* and Edward L. Bernays' *Your Future in Public Relations* and *Your Future in Advertising* (New York: Popular Library, updated regularly).

The Career Directory Series has compiled books for the fields of advertising, magazine publishing, book publishing, and public relations, available from Career Publishing Corp., 505 Fifth Ave., Suite 1003, New York City, N.Y. 10017.

Career information is available from the office of the Executive Secretary, Association for Education in Journalism and Mass Communication, College of Journalism, University of South Carolina, Columbia, S.C. 29208. *Education for a Journalism Career* is available from the Accrediting Council on Education in Journalism and Mass Communications, School of Journalism, University of Kansas, Lawrence, Kansas 66045.

Other pamphlets available include the following:

ADVERTISING. *A Career in Newspaper Advertising* (Newspaper Advertising Bureau, P.O. Box 147, Danville, Ill. 61832); *Advertising: A Guide to Careers in Advertising* (American Association of Advertising Agencies, 666 Third Ave., New York, N.Y. 10017); *Business-to-Business Communications* (Business/Professional Advertising Association, 205 E. 42nd St., New York, N.Y. 10017); *Jobs in Advertising* (Bureau of Education and Research, American Advertising Federation, 400 K St., N.W., Washington, D.C. 20005); and *Where Shall I Go to College to Study Advertising?* (Advertising Education Publications, 3429 55th St., Lubbock, Tex. 79413).

BOOK PUBLISHING. *Getting Into Book Publishing* (R.R. Bowker Company, 205 E. 42nd St., New York, N.Y. 10017).

BROADCASTING. *Careers in Broadcast News* (Radio Television News Directors Association, 1735 DeSales St., N.W., Washington, D.C. 20036); *Careers in Cable* and *Directory of Cable Education and Training Programs* (National Cable Television Association, 1724 Massachusetts Ave., N.W., Washington, D.C. 20036); *Careers in Radio* and *Careers in Television* (National Association of Broadcasters, 1771 N St., N.W., Washington, D.C. 20036); and *Women on the Job: Careers in the Electronic Media* (American Women in Radio and Television, 1321 Connecticut Ave., N.W., Washington, D.C. 20036).

MAGAZINES. *Magazines in the U.S.A.* (Magazine Publishers Association, 575 Lexington Ave., New York, N.Y. 10022); and *Careers in the Business Press* (Business Press Educational Foundation, 205 E. 42nd St., 19th Floor, New York, N.Y. 10017).

NEWSPAPERS. *Journalism Career and Scholarship Guide* (Dow Jones Newspaper Fund, P.O. Box 300, Princeton, N.J. 08540); *Journalism, Your Newspaper Career and How to Prepare for It* (National Newspaper Foundation, 1627 K St., N.W., Suite 400, Washington, D.C. 20006); *Newspaper Jobs You Never Thought of . . . Or Did You?, Newspapers . . . Your Future?,* and *Your Future in Newspapers* (American Newspaper Publishers Association Foundation, The Newspaper Center, Box 17407, Dulles International Airport, Washington, D.C. 20041); and *Suburban Newspaper Careers* (Suburban Newspapers of America, 111 E. Wacker Dr., Chicago, Ill. 60601).

PHOTOJOURNALISM. *Careers in News Photography* (National Press Photographers Association, P.O. Box 1146, Durham, N.C. 27702).

PUBLIC RELATIONS. *Careers in Public Relations, Your Personal Guidebook PRSA,* and *Occupational Guide to Public Relations* (Public Relations Society of America, 845 Third Ave., New York, N.Y. 10022).

GENERAL. *Careers in Communications* (Women in Communications, P.O. Box 9561, Austin, Tex. 78766); *Careers in Journalism* (Quill & Scroll, University of Iowa, Iowa City, Iowa 52242); and *Getting Started in Writing* (Writer's Digest, Dept. JSG, 9933 Alliance Rd., Cincinnati, Ohio 45242).

MINORITIES. *Journalism Career Guide for Minorities* (Dow Jones Newspaper Fund, P.O. Box 300, Princeton, N.J. 08540); *Career Guide for Minority Journalism Students* (Dr. Clint C. Wilson, II, School of Journalism, University of Southern California, Los Angeles 90089, or Dr. Marilyn Kern-Foxworth, College of Communications, University of Tennessee, Knoxville 37916); and *Who's What and Where,* a directory of America's black journalists (Who's What and Where, P.O. Box 921, Detroit, Mich. 48231).

Catalogues describing the curricular offerings of individual schools and departments of journalism and mass communications are available upon request to the school or department concerned or to the registrar of the institution.

PART SIX: CRITICISMS AND CHALLENGES

An excellent basis for any discussion of the duties and the performance record of the mass media is the summary report of the Commission on Freedom of the Press, *A Free and Responsible Press* (Chicago: University of Chicago Press, 1947). The commission printed four studies already cited, Chafee's *Government and Mass Communications,* Hocking's *Freedom of the Press,* White's *The American Radio,* and Ruth Inglis' *Freedom of the Movies,* as well as *Peoples Speaking to Peoples,* by Llewellyn White and Robert D. Leigh (Chicago: University of Chicago Press, 1946), an analysis of international news channels.

An in-depth study of four major media institutions and their principal operating heads is found in David Halberstam, *The Powers That Be* (New York: Viking, 1978). The four institutions are CBS, Time Inc., the Washington *Post,* and the Los Angeles *Times,* with the New York *Times* hovering in the background. The reportorial process is examined in Gaye Tuchman, *Making News* (New York: Free Press, 1978), and the editing process in Herbert Gans, *Deciding What's News: A Study of CBS Evening News, NBC Nightly News, Newsweek & Time* (New York: Pantheon, 1979). Tom Wicker is reflective in *On Press* (New York: Viking, 1978).

Criticisms of the mass media are summarized in John L. Hulteng's *The Messenger's Motives* (Englewood Cliffs, N.J.: Prentice-Hall, 1984), by analyzing cases involving ethical problems. In a similar vein is *Groping for Ethics in Journalism* by H. Eugene Goodwin (Ames: Iowa State University Press, 1983). Criticism of press managers is the theme of Ben H. Bagdikian in *The Effete Conspiracy and Other Crimes by the Press* (New York: Harper & Row, 1972). Hillier Krieghbaum examines this topic in *Pressures on the Press* (New York: Crowell, 1972). Daniel J. Czitrom traced developing years of the telegraph, movies, and radio, then discussed media theory to 1960 in *Media and the American Mind: From Morse to McLuhan* (Chapel Hill: University of North Carolina Press, 1982), Everette Dennis and John C. Merrill took opposing sides in *Basic Issues in Mass Communication: A Debate* (New York: Macmillan, 1984). Probing the media scene are J. Herbert Altschull, *Agents of Power* (New York: Longman, 1983); John L. Hulteng, *The News Media: What Makes Them Tick?* (Englewood Cliffs, N.J.: Prentice-Hall, 1979); David Shaw, *Journalism Today* (New York: Harper's College Press, 1977); and John Hohenberg, *The News Media* (New York: Holt, Rinehart and Winston, 1978). Bryce W. Rucker presents a comprehensive survey of media dilemmas while updating Morris Ernst's 1946 study by the same title, *The First Freedom* (Carbondale: Southern Illinois University Press, 1968). Ben H. Bagdikian's *The Information Machines* (New York: Harper & Row, 1971) projects the impact of technological change on the media and offers a wealth of research data based on findings of RAND Corporation research teams.

Two books edited by Warren K. Agee provide extensive criticisms of the media: *The Press and the Public Interest* (Washington: Public Affairs Press, 1968) contains the annual William Allen White Lectures delivered by 18 of America's leading reporters, editors, and publishers; in *Mass Media in a Free society* (Lawrence: Regents' Press of Kansas, 1969) six media spokesmen discuss challenges and problems confronting newspapers, television, motion pictures, and magazines. Other criticisms of press performance are found in *The Press in Perspective,* edited by Ralph D. Casey (Baton Rouge: Louisiana State University Press, 1963), a series of 17 lectures by leading journalists at the University of Minnesota over 16 years.

Selected readings on both media issues and the mass communications industries and professions are presented in *Maincurrents in Mass Communications,* edited by Warren K. Agee, Phillip H. Ault, and Edwin Emery (New York: Harper & Row, 1986). A comprehensive collection of articles focusing on major media issues and criticisms is found in Michael C. Emery and Ted Curtis Smythe, *Readings in Mass Communication: Concepts and Issues in the Mass Media* (Dubuque, Iowa: Brown, 1986). Other books of readings include Alan Wells, *Mass Media and Society* (Palo Alto, Calif.: Mayfield, 1979); Donald F. Ungurait, Thomas W. Bohn, and Ray Hiebert, *Media Now* (New York: Longman, 1985): Robert Atwan, Barry Orton, and William Vesterman, *American Mass Media: Industries and Issues* (New York: Random House, 1985); and Glen O. Robinson, *Communication for Tomorrow: Policy Perspectives for the 1980s* (New York: Praeger, 1978), an Aspen-sponsored publication.

Among general introductory surveys are Samuel L. Becker, *Discovering Mass Communication* (Glenview, Ill.: Scott, Foresman, 1986); Jay Black and Frederick C. Whitney, *Introduction to Mass Communication* (Dubuque, Iowa: Brown, 1983); Joseph R. Dominick, *The Dynamics of Mass Communication* (Reading, Mass.: Addison-Wesley, 1987); Edward J. Whetmore, *Mediamerica* (Belmont, Calif.: Wadsworth, 1987); Melvin L. DeFleur and Everette E. Dennis, *Understanding Mass Communication* (Boston: Houghton Mifflin, 1985); John R. Bittner, *Mass Communication: An Introduction* (Englewood Cliffs, N.J.: Prentice-Hall, 1986);

Don R. Pember, *Mass Media in America* (Palo Alto, Calif.: Science Research Associates, 1983); Ray Hiebert, Donald F. Ungurait, and Thomas W. Bohn, *Mass Media IV* (New York: Longman, 1985), research-oriented; Peter M. Sandman, David M. Rubin, and David B. Sachsman, *Media: An Introductory Analysis of American Mass Communications* (Englewood Cliffs, N.J.: Prentice-Hall, 1982); Joseph Turow, *Media Industries: The Production of News and Entertainment* (New York: Longman, 1984); Charles R. Wright, *Mass Communication: A Sociological Perspective* (New York: Random House, 1985); and Robert D. Murphy, *Mass Communication and Human Interaction* (Boston: Houghton Mifflin, 1977).

PRINT MEDIA. Two studies of the status of the daily press are found in Ernest C. Hynds, *American Newspapers in the 1980s* (New York: Hastings House, 1980), and John L. Hulteng and Roy Paul Nelson, *The Fourth Estate* (New York: Harper & Row, 1983). A. Kent MacDougall collected *Wall Street Journal* articles in *The Press: A Critical Look from the Inside* (New York: Dow Jones, 1972). Selections from the *Nieman Reports* make a comprehensive survey of news problems and trends in Louis Lyons, *Reporting the News* (Cambridge, Mass.: Harvard University Press, 1965). Hillier Krieghbaum discusses one problem in *Science and the Mass Media* (New York: New York University Press, 1967). Curtis D. MacDougall, *The Press and Its Problems* (Dubuque, Iowa: Brown, 1964), is a revision of his *Newsroom Problems and Policies.* Lucy M. Salmon's *The Newspaper and the Historian* (New York: Oxford University Press, 1923) is a classic historical study.

Among professionals' criticisms, Herbert Brucker's *Freedom of Information* is an enlightened defense and analysis of the newspaper press. By contrast, Carl E. Lindstrom uses for the title of his book *The Fading American Newspaper* (Garden City, N.Y.: Doubleday, 1960). A. J. Liebling brought together his satirical articles on press shortcomings, written for the *New Yorker,* in *The Press* (New York: Ballantine, 1964), and in *The Wayward Pressman* (New York: Doubleday, 1948), devoted mostly to New York papers. Silas Bent, *Ballyhoo* (New York: Liveright, 1927) is strongly critical of the newspaper press of its day, as are Upton Sinclair's *The Brass Check* (Pasadena, Calif.: Published by the author, 1920), and George Seldes' *Freedom of the Press* (Indianapolis: Bobbs-Merrill, 1935). Oswald Garrison Villard, *The Disappearing Daily* (New York: Knopf, 1944), and Morris L. Ernst, *The First Freedom* (New York: Macmillan, 1946), exhibit a critical concern over newspaper ownership concentration trends but are not statistically accurate.

BROADCASTING AND CABLE. A comprehensive collection of readings is in Ted C. Smythe and George A. Mastroianni, *Issues in Broadcasting: Radio, Television, and Cable* (Palo Alto, Calif.: Mayfield, 1975). The best of *TV Guide's* articles of the 1970s are collected in Barry Cole's *Television Today* (New York: Oxford University Press, 1981). Leo Bogart objectively analyzes scores of research studies, seeking to determine the social impact of television, in *The Age of Television* (New York: Frederick Ungar, 1972). The Television Information Office in 1985 issued *A Broadcasting Primer: With Notes on the New Technologies,* including data from 1946 to 1985.

Among effective criticisms are two edited guides to popular culture, *Watching*

Television by Todd Gitlin and its companion *Reading the News* by Robert Manoff and Michael Schudson (New York: Pantheon, 1986); David Marc, *Demographic Vistas: Television in American Culture* (Philadelphia: University of Pennsylvania Press, 1984); Todd Gitlin, *Inside Prime Time* (New York: Pantheon, 1985); Robert T. Bower, *The Changing Television Audience in America* (New York: Columbia University Press, 1985), research-oriented; Philip Drummond and Richard Paterson, editors, *Television in Transition* (London: British Film Institute, 1986), papers from the 1984 International Television Studies Conference; George Comstock, *Television in America* (Beverly Hills, Calif.: Sage, 1980); Frank Coppa, editor, *Screen & Society: The Impact of Television* (Chicago: Nelson Hall, 1979); Horace Newcomb, editor, *Television: The Critical View* (New York: Oxford University Press, 1982): Muriel Cantor, *Prime Time Television: Content and Control* (Beverly Hills, Calif.: Sage, 1980); Ron Powers, *The Newscasters* (New York: St. Martin's, 1977); Edwin Diamond, *The Tin Kazoo: Television, Politics, and the News* (Cambridge, Mass.: MIT Press, 1975); and Edward Jay Epstein, *News from Nowhere: Television and the News* (New York: Random House, 1973), an evaluation of 1968 to 1969 network news. Critical appraisals by the Alfred I. DuPont–Columbia University Awards committee were begun with *Survey of Broadcast Journalism 1968–1969,* edited by Marvin Barrett (New York: Grosset & Dunlap, 1969). Seventh of the series was *The Eye of the Storm* (New York: Harper & Row, 1980).

Two collections of scholarly original essays appearing in 1981 were *The Entertainment Functions of Television,* edited by Percy H. Tannenbaum, and *Television and Social Behavior,* edited by Stephen Withey and Ronald P. Abeles (Hillsdale, N.J.: Lawrence Erlbaum Associates). Coming from the Aspen Institute Program on Communications and Society are *Understanding Television: Essays on Television as a Social and Cultural Force,* edited by Richard Adler (New York: Praeger, 1980); *The Future of Public Broadcasting,* edited by Douglass Cater (New York: Praeger, 1976); *Television as a Social Force* and *Television as a Cultural Force,* edited by Douglass Cater and Richard Adler (New York: Praeger, 1975, 1976); *Cable and Continuing Education,* edited by Richard Adler and Walter S. Baer (New York: Praeger, 1973); Richard M. Polsky, *Getting to Sesame Street: Origins of the Children's Television Workshop* (New York: Praeger, 1974); and *The Electronic Box Office: Humanities and Arts on the Cable,* edited by Richard Adler and Walter S. Baer (New York: Praeger, 1974).

Additional references, by chapter topic, follow.

Chapter 21: Who Owns the Media?

Ben Bagdikian's answer to this question is an exposé of corporate influence on publishing, in *The Media Monopoly* (Boston: Beacon Press, 1983). Loren Ghiglione presents ten case studies in *The Buying and Selling of American Newspapers* (Indianapolis, Ind.: R.J. Berg, 1984).

The Mass Media: Aspen Institute Guide to Communication Industry Trends, by Christopher H. Sterling and Timothy R. Haight, is a primary source. For data and trends analysis, see Benjamin N. Compaine, editor, *Who Owns the Media? Concen-*

tration of Ownership in the Mass Communications Industry (White Plains, N.Y.: Knowledge Industry Publications, 1979), and Compaine's *The Newspaper Industry in the 1980s* (White Plains, N.Y.: Knowledge Industry, 1980).

Jon G. Udell, *The Economics of the American Newspaper* (New York: Hastings House, 1978), was sponsored by the American Newspaper Publishers Association and contains articles contributed by newspaper business people. James N. Rosse, Bruce M. Owen, and David L. Grey wrote a brief data-filled study of one problem for an FCC hearing, published as *Economic Issues in the Joint Ownership of Newspaper and Television Media* (Stanford, Calif.: Stanford University Research Center in Economic Growth, 1970).

Bryce Rucker, *The First Freedom* (Carbondale: Southern Illinois University Press, 1968), has a wealth of statistics and analysis. Trends in concentration of newspaper ownership historically are reported in Chapter 20 of Emery and Emery, *The Press and America,* and by Raymond B. Nixon in *Gazette* (1968, No. 3).

Chapter 22: Credibility: Media and Government

Four major research studies of press credibility and public support for the media were published in 1985 and 1986. The most elaborate, *The People & the Press,* was carried out by the Gallup Organization for the Times Mirror newspaper group (Los Angeles: Times Mirror, 1986). Two other national studies were done by MORI Research, Minneapolis: *Newspaper Credibility: Building Reader Trust* (Reston, Va.: American Society of Newspaper Editors, 1986), and *Journalists and Readers: Bridging the Credibility Gap* (Reston, Va.: Associated Press Managing Editors Association, 1985). A 50-year review of the literature, *The Media and the People,* summarizes the studies described above (New York: Gannett Center for Media Studies, Columbia University, 1986).

David H. Weaver and G. Cleveland Wilhoit update earlier communicator studies in *The American Journalist: A Portrait of U.S. News People and Their Work* (Bloomington, Ind.: Indiana University Press, 1986). Ben Wattenberg attacks conventional wisdoms of the press in *The Good News Is the Bad News Is Wrong* (New York: Simon and Schuster, 1984). Also pertinent are Rodney A. Smolla, *Suing the Press* (New York: Oxford University Press, 1986); Norman E. Isaacs, *Untended Gates: The Mismanaged Press* (New York: Columbia University Press, 1986); and J. Edward Gerald, *News of Crime* (Westport, Conn.: Greenwood Press, 1983).

The Continuing Study of Newspaper Reading, sponsored by the American Newspaper Publishers Association and the Advertising Research Foundation from 1939 to 1952 and covering readership studies of 142 newspapers, offers evidence of readership trends. The results were analyzed by Charles E. Swanson in "What They Read in 130 Daily Newspapers," *Journalism Quarterly* (Fall 1955). Gary A. Steiner, *The People Look at Television* (New York: Knopf, 1963), is a voluminous study of viewing habits and attitudes of the American people by sex, education, income, religion, and so on.

A 1000-page study of the Watergate years of 1972 to 1974, objectively presented with detailed documentary support and many cross-references integrating various facets of the episode, forms the basis for analysis of that gigantic crisis of media and presidential credibility. The volume is *Watergate: Chronology of a Crisis* (Washington: Congressional Quarterly, 1975), edited by Mercer Cross and Elder Witt with a staff of 30 from that research organization and contributors. Gladys Engel Lang and Kurt Lang approached Watergate from a social science perspective in *The Battle for Public Opinion: The President, the Press, and the Polls During Watergate* (New York: Columbia University Press, 1983).

Among the most useful books about Watergate are Carl Bernstein and Bob Woodward, *All the President's Men* (New York: Simon and Schuster, 1974); Jimmy Breslin, *How the Good Guys Finally Won* (New York: Viking, 1975); William E. Porter, *Assault on the Media* (Ann Arbor: University of Michigan Press, 1976); and the fifth Dupont–Columbia University survey of broadcast journalism, *Moments of Truth?* (New York: Crowell, 1975). Backgrounds for the government and political leaders involved in a decade of credibility crisis are provided in Dan Rather and Gary Paul Gates, *The Palace Guard* (New York: Harper & Row, 1974), and David Halberstam, *The Best and the Brightest* (New York: Random House, 1972). Harrison Salisbury gives an insider's view of the New York *Times* during the Pentagon Papers and Watergate crises in *Without Fear or Favor* (New York: Times Books, 1980). The Kennedy years are analyzed by Montague Kern, Patricia W. Levering, and Ralph B. Levering in *The Kennedy Crises: The Press, the Presidency, and Foreign Policy* (Chapel Hill, N.C.: University of North Carolina Press, 1983).

Television news crises are covered admirably in William Small, *To Kill a Messenger* (New York: Hastings House, 1970), covering the 1960s with its crises of war, violence, rioting, and political polarization. Small was then CBS Washington bureau chief. One of television's problems was the subject of Newton Minow, John Bartlow Martin, and Lee M. Mitchell in *Presidential Television* (New York: Basic Books, 1973). A first-hand criticism of network policy affecting CBS News appears in Fred W. Friendly, *Due to Circumstances Beyond Our Control . . .* (New York: Random House, 1967). The 1969 speeches of Vice-President Spiro T. Agnew attacking the fairness of television commentators and other media news are collected in Spiro T. Agnew, *Frankly Speaking* (Washington: Public Affairs Press, 1970). Even stronger attacks were made by Edith Efron in *The News Twisters* and *How CBS Tried to Kill a Book* (Los Angeles: Nash, 1971, 1972).

Two recent studies of political reporting are Michael B. Grossman and Martha J. Kumar, *Portraying the President* (Baltimore, Md.: Johns Hopkins University Press, 1981), and Stephen Hess, *The Washington Reporters* (Washington: Brookings Institution, 1981). A more general study is William L. Rivers, *The Other Government: Power and the Washington Media* (New York: Universe, 1982). James Deakin, White House correspondent from 1955 to 1980 for the St. Louis *Post-Dispatch,* wrote *Straight Stuff: The Reporters, the White House and the Truth* (New York: William Morrow, 1984). Sam Donaldson of ABC contributed *Hold On, Mr. President!* (New York: Random House, 1987).

One of the best reports on the 1972 campaign press corps was Timothy Crouse, *The Boys on the Bus* (New York: Random House, 1973). Another aspect of political reporting is surveyed in 50 selections edited by Robert Blanchard for *Congress and the News Media* (New York: Hastings House, 1974). Two interesting studies of press performance during political campaigns are Nathan B. Blumberg's *One Party Press?* (Lincoln: University of Nebraska Press, 1954), a report on how 35 metropolitan dailies covered 1952 presidential campaign news, and Arthur E. Rowse's *Slanted News: A Case Study of the Nixon and Stevenson Fund Stories* (Boston: Beacon Press, 1957).

For details on studies of violence in riots, see Robert K. Baker and Sandra J. Ball, *Violence and the Media* (Washington: Government Printing Office, 1969), a staff report to the National Commission on the Causes and Prevention of Violence giving a historical treatment and a review of research. Two major citations in commission reports are *Report of the National Advisory Commission on Civil Disorders* (Kerner Report, 1968), Chapter 15, "The News Media and the Disorders," and *Rights in Conflict,* the Walker Report to the National Commission on the Causes and Prevention of Violence, 1968, pages 287–327, "The Police and the Press."

The *Aspen Notebook on Government and the Media,* edited by William L. Rivers and Michael J. Nyhan (New York: Praeger, 1973), offers a spirited debate of government-media relations and regulatory issues.

Chapter 23: The Media's Legal Environment

Two extensive casebooks on press law are Donald M. Gillmor and Jerome A. Barron, *Mass Communication Law: Cases and Comment* (St. Paul: West, 1984), and Marc A. Franklin, *Cases and Materials on Mass Media Law* (Mineola, N.Y.: Foundation Press, 1986). Two major case-oriented accounts are Harold L. Nelson and Dwight L. Teeter, Jr., *Law of Mass Communications* (Mineola, N.Y.: Foundation Press, 1986), and William E. Francois, *Mass Media Law and Regulation* (New York: John Wiley, 1986). Steering a middle course between casebook and narrative are Ralph Holsinger, *Media Law* (New York: Random House, 1986); Don R. Pember, *Mass Media Law* (Dubuque, Iowa: Brown, 1987); and Wayne Overbeck and Rick D. Pullen, *Major Principles of Media Law* (New York: Holt, Rinehart and Winston, 1985). Accompanying Franklin's casebook is yet another major work, *The First Amendment and the Fourth Estate: The Law of Mass Media* by T. Barton Carter, Marc A. Franklin, and Jay B. Wright (Minneola, N.Y.: Foundation Press, 1985). The same trio and publishing house produced *The First Amendment and the Fifth Estate: Regulation of Electronic Mass Media* in 1986.

The area of broadcast law is also the focus of John R. Bittner, *Broadcast Law and Regulation* (Englewood Cliffs, N.J.: Prentice-Hall, 1982), and of Douglas H. Ginsburg, *Regulation of Broadcasting: Law and Policy Towards Radio, Television, and Cable Communications* (St. Paul: West, 1979).

Specialized books are Maurice R. Cullen, Jr., *Mass Media and the First Amendment: An Introduction to the Issues, Problems, and Practices* (Dubuque, Iowa: Brown, 1981), and John D. Stevens, *Shaping the First Amendment: The Development of Free Expression* (Beverly Hills, Calif.: Sage, 1982), a brief, model-based discussion.

Supreme Court trends are traced in William A. Hachten's *The Supreme Court on Freedom of the Press* (Ames: Iowa State University Press, 1968) and later in Kenneth S. Devol's *Mass Media and the Supreme Court* (New York: Hastings House, 1982). J. Edward Gerald's *The Press and the Constitution* (Minneapolis: University of Minnesota Press, 1948) analyzes constitutional law cases involving press freedom from 1931 to 1947. David L. Grey reports on court coverage in *The Supreme Court and the News Media* (Evanston, Ill.: Northwestern University Press, 1968). Donald M. Gillmor analyzes a major conflict in *Free Press and Fair Trial* (Washington: Public Affairs Press, 1966).

Chapter 24: The Media's Social and Ethical Responsibilities

William L. Rivers, Wilbur Schramm, and Clifford G. Christians, *Responsibility in Mass Communication* (New York: Harper & Row, 1980), is the best treatment of communications ethics. It discusses the role of the mass communicator in developing the political, social, and economic fabrics of a democratic society, and the development of modern mass communications. In a similar vein are John L. Hulteng, *The Messenger's Motives: Ethical Theory in the Mass Media* (Englewood Cliffs, N.J.: Prentice-Hall, 1984); Edmund B. Lambeth, *Committed Journalism: An Ethic for the Profession* (Bloomington, Ind.: Indiana University Press, 1986), a framework of principles for ethical journalism; and Clifford G. Christians, Kim B. Rotzoll, and Mark Fackler, *Media Ethics: Cases and Moral Reasoning* (New York: Longman, 1987), a leading textbook.

The American Society of Newspaper Editors sponsored Philip Meyer's *Editors, Publishers and Newspaper Ethics* (Reston, Va.: ASNE, 1983), and *Drawing the Line: How 31 Editors Solved Their Toughest Ethical Dilemmas,* edited by Frank McCulloch (Reston, Va.: ASNE, 1984). Meyer later published *Ethical Journalism* (New York: Longman, 1986), based on his surveys. On the critical side are Tom Goldstein, *The News at Any Cost: How Journalists Compromise Their Ethics to Shape the News* (New York: Simon and Schuster, 1985), and Patrick Brogan's *Spiked: The Short Life and Death of the National Press Council* (New York: Priority Press, 1985), a 20th Century Fund study of a largely ignored effort. Other books include Lee Thayer, editor, *Ethics, Morality and the Media* (New York: Hastings House, 1980); John C. Merrill, *The Imperative of Freedom* (New York: Hastings House, 1974); Lee Brown, *The Reluctant Reformation* (New York: David McKay, 1974); and Bruce Swain, *Reporters' Ethics* (Ames: Iowa State University Press, 1978).

VIOLENCE AND SENSATIONALISM. William D. Rowland, Jr. reviews 50 years of futile efforts to force the American media to reduce violence in *The Politics of TV Violence* (Beverly Hills, Calif.: Sage, 1983). Linda S. Lichter and S. Robert Lichter argue that television sensationalizes and distorts in *Prime Time Crime: Criminals and Law Enforcers in TV Entertainment* (Washington: The Media Institute, 1983). Sex and violence in television programming are explored in Geoffrey Cowan, *See No Evil* (New York: Simon and Schuster, 1979). Muriel Cantor, in *Prime Time Television: Content and Control* (Beverly Hills, Calif.: Sage, 1980), concludes that varied forces, pressures, and prejudices determine the final form of a television show.

Terrorism and hostage-taking are the subjects of two books: Dan Nimmo and James E. Combs, *Nightly Horrors: Crisis Coverage in Television Network News* (Knoxville, Tenn.: University of Tennessee Press, 1985), and Sarah Midgley and Virginia Rice, editors, *Terrorism and the Media in the 1980s* (Washington: The Media Institute, 1984), proceedings of a 1983 conference of news directors, politicians, and former hostages.

There are two collections of articles on these issues. One, with reasoned but conservative views, is edited by Victor B. Cline, *Where Do You Draw the Line? An Exploration into Media Violence, Pornography, and Censorship* (Provo, Utah: Brigham Young University Press, 1974). The other is the research-based *Violence and the Mass Media* (New York: Harper & Row, 1968), edited by Otto N. Larsen. Of historical importance are Helen M. Hughes, *News and the Human Interest Story* (Chicago: University of Chicago Press, 1940), a sociological study; and Simon M. Bessie, *Jazz Journalism: The Story of the Tabloid Newspapers* (New York: Dutton, 1938).

Research findings have been reported by George Gerbner, et al., annually, and summarized in *Violence Profile No. 8: Trends in Network Television Drama and Viewer Conceptions of Social Reality, 1967–1976* (Philadelphia: Annenberg School of Communication, University of Pennsylvania, 1977). The Government Printing Office issued a 1982 two-volume summary and research report, *Television and Behavior: Ten Years of Scientific Progress and Implications for the Eighties.*

CHILDREN AND TELEVISION. Widely acclaimed was *The Early Window: Effects of Television on Children and Youth,* by Robert Liebert, Joyce N. Sprafkin, and Emily Davidson (New York: Pergamon Press, 1982). Included in the extensive literature are Mariann Pezzella Winick and Charles Winick, *The Television Experience: What Children See* (Beverly Hills, Calif.: Sage, 1979); Ellen Wartella, editor, *Children Communicating* (Beverly Hills, Calif.: Sage, 1979); Scott Ward, Daniel Wackman, and Ellen Wartella, *How Children Learn to Buy* (Beverly Hills, Calif.: Sage, 1977); and Jerome Johnson and James Ettema, *Positive Images: Breaking Stereotypes with Children's Television* (Beverly Hills, Calif.: Sage, 1982).

CENSORSHIP. Ruth Inglis, *Freedom of the Movies* (Chicago: University of Chicago Press, 1947), argued the case for self-regulation for the Commission on Freedom of the Press. In discussions of censorship trends, the film area is covered by Ira H. Carmen, *Movies, Censorship and the Law* (Ann Arbor: University of Michigan Press, 1966), and by Richard S. Randall, *Censorship of the Movies* (Madison: University of Wisconsin Press, 1968); and books by Richard McKeon, Robert K. Merton, and Walter Gellhorn, *The Freedom to Read: Perspective and Program* (New York: Bowker, 1957). Movie and television censorship is decried in Murray Schumach's *The Face on the Cutting Room Floor* (New York: Morrow, 1964).

PORNOGRAPHY. The two-volume (1960-page) *Final Report of the Attorney General's Commission on Pornography* (Washington, D.C.: Government Printing Office, 1986) explores the subject and makes recommendations for law enforcement and citizen action.

MINORITIES AND MEDIA. A major discussion of the evolving relationship between the American mass media and non-European minorities is contributed by Clint C. Wilson II and Félix Gutiérrez in *Minorities and Media* (Beverly Hills, Calif.: Sage, 1985). They discuss media reporting about blacks, Asians, Latinos, and Native Americans, and the rise of a segmented media. Problems of employment of minorities by the mass media are analyzed. Ana Veciana-Suarez, a Miami *Herald* journalist, has produced a narrative guide and directory, *Hispanic Media, USA* (Washington, D.C.: Media Institute, 1987), based on research and interviews.

MEDIA ORGANIZATIONS. There are three histories of media organizations: Edwin Emery's *History of the American Newspaper Publishers Association* (Minneapolis: University of Minnesota Press, 1950), Alice Fox Pitts' *Read All About It!—50 Years of ASNE* (Reston, Va.: American Society of Newspaper Editors, 1974); and W. F. Cento, editor, *Fifty and Feisty: APME, 1933 to 1983* (St. Paul, Minn.: North Central Publishing, 1983).

Chapter 25: International Mass Communications

Of merit as texts for international communications classes are two 1983 Longman entries. Twenty scholars wrote chapters about six major aspects of mass media, from Western, communist, and Third World viewpoints, in *Comparative Mass Media Systems,* edited by L. John Martin and Anju Grover Chaudhary. John C. Merrill and six coauthors surveyed the world's mass media in *Global Journalism.* Another general text is Heinz-Dietrich Fischer and John C. Merrill, editors, *International and Intercultural Communication* (New York: Hastings House, 1976), with 45 articles by scholars in many countries. George Kurian's two-volume *World Press Encyclopedia* (New York: Facts on File, 1982) and a UNESCO publication, *World Communications: A 200-Country Survey of Press, Radio, Television, Films* (New York: Unipub, 1975), are basic reference works for international media study. Another international survey is John C. Merrill, Carter R. Bryan, and Marvin Alisky, *The Foreign Press* (Baton Rouge: Louisiana State University Press, 1970).

More detailed studies of the world's leading newspapers were made for John C. Merrill's *The Elite Press* (New York: Pitman, 1969) and its 1980 update by Merrill and Harold A. Fisher, *The World's Great Dailies: Profiles of 50 Newspapers* (New York: Hastings House, 1980). Anthony Smith's brief *The Newspaper: An International History* (London: Thames and Hudson, 1979) offers a worldwide account and 111 illustrations.

Some regional accounts include Kenneth E. Olson, *The History Makers* (Baton Rouge: Louisiana State University Press, 1966), a survey of European press history; James W. Markham, *Voices of the Red Giants* (Ames: Iowa State University Press, 1970), a study of the Soviet and Chinese mass media systems; Mark W. Hopkins, *Mass Media in the Soviet Union* (New York: Pegasus, 1970); John A. Lent, editor, *The Asian Newspapers' Reluctant Revolution* (Ames: Iowa State University Press, 1971); William A. Hachten, *Muffled Drums: The News Media in Africa* (Ames: Iowa State University Press, 1971); G. A. Cranfield, *The Press and*

Society: From Caxton to Northcliffe (London: Longman, 1978), a British overview; Francis Williams, *Dangerous Estate: The Anatomy of Newspapers* (New York: Macmillan, 1958), a social study of the British press since 1702; Anthony Smith, compiler, *The British Press Since the War* (Totowa, N. J.: Rowman and Littlefield, 1974); and Wilfred H. Kesterton, *A History of Journalism in Canada* (Toronto: McClelland and Stewart, 1967).

Three books by Burton Paulu, all published by the University of Minnesota Press in Minneapolis, offer detailed studies of European broadcasting: *Radio and Television Broadcasting on the European Continent* (1967), *Radio and Television Broadcasting in Eastern Europe* (1974), and *Television and Radio in the United Kingdom* (1981). Asa Briggs has produced four volumes of his *History of Broadcasting in the United Kingdom* (New York: Oxford University Press, 1961–1979).

A worldwide broadcasting survey was published by Sydney W. Head in *World Broadcasting Systems: A Comparative Analysis* (Belmont, Calif.: Wadsworth, 1985). Other broadcast books: Walter B. Emery, *National and International Systems of Broadcasting* (East Lansing: Michigan State University Press, 1969); John A. Lent, editor, *Broadcasting in Asia and the Pacific* (Philadelphia: Temple University Press, 1978), with many chapters by nationals of the countries described; and Elihu Katz and George Wedell, *Broadcasting in the Third World: Promise and Performance* (Cambridge, Mass.: Harvard University Press, 1978).

Among studies of international news flow and press associations, the scholarly synthesis is Robert W. Desmond's *The Information Process: World News Reporting to the Twentieth Century* (Iowa City: University of Iowa Press, 1978). *Windows on the World 1900–1920* (1981), *Crisis and Conflict: World News Reporting Between Two Wars 1920–1940* (1982), and *Tides of War: World News Reporting 1940–1945* (1984), continued a project interrupted by death. The best history and current description of the four Western transnationals (AP, UPI, Reuters, AFP) is Jonathan Fenby, *The International News Services* (New York: Schocken Books, 1986). Robert L. Stevenson and Donald L. Shaw analyze news reports of the four Western news agencies and the mass media of 17 countries in *Foreign News and the New World Information Order* (Ames: Iowa State University Press, 1984). Oliver Boyd-Barrett, *The International News Agencies* (Beverly Hills, Calif.: Sage, 1980), examines the five transnational news agencies and two Third World ones. John Hohenberg covered foreign correspondents in his *Foreign Correspondence— The Great Reporters and Their Times* (New York: Columbia University Press, 1964). UNESCO surveyed press associations in *News Agencies: Their Structure and Operation* (New York: Columbia University Press, 1953). Two news service histories are Graham Storey, *Reuters* (New York: Crown, 1951), and Theodore E. Kruglak, *The Two Faces of Tass* (Minneapolis: University of Minnesota Press, 1962) (see bibliography for Part Two, Chapter 7, for other news service citations). Francis Williams briefly analyzed news transmission in *Transmitting World News: A Study of Telecommunications and the Press* (New York: Arno, 1972).

The dominant name in international communications research and writing has been that of Wilbur Schramm, beginning with his *Mass Media and National Development* (Stanford, Calif.: Stanford University Press, 1964). Two conferences at the East–West Communication Institute in Hawaii produced two books: Daniel

Lerner and Wilbur Schramm, editors, *Communication and Change in the Developing Countries* (Honolulu: East-West Center, 1967) and Schramm and Lerner, editors, *Communication and Change: The Last Ten Years—and the Next* (Honolulu: University of Hawaii Press, 1976).

Hamid Mowlana provides a research-oriented overview in *Global Information and World Communication: New Frontiers in International Relations* (New York: Longman, 1986). Other research studies: Lucian W. Pye, *Communications and Political Development* (Princeton, N.J.: Princeton University Press, 1963); E. Lloyd Sommerlad, *The Press in Developing Countries* (Sydney, Australia: Sydney University Press, 1966); Colin Cherry, *World Communications: Threat or Promise? A Socio-Technical Approach* (New York: Wiley, 1971); George Gerbner, editor, *Mass Media Policies in Changing Cultures* (New York: Wiley, 1977); Alan Wells, *Mass Communication: A World View* (Palo Alto, Calif.: National Press, 1974); Wilbur Schramm, *Big Media, Little Media: Tools and Technologies for Instruction* (Beverly Hills, Calif.: Sage, 1977); Peter Habermann and Guy de Fontgalland, editors, *Development Communication—Rhetoric and Reality* (Singapore: Asian Mass Communication Research and Information Centre, 1978); and Syed A. Rahim, et al., *Planning Methods, Models, and Organization: A Review Study for Communication Policy Making and Planning* (Honolulu: East-West Communication Institute, 1978).

A research study of "what might have been" by Margaret A. Blanchard, *Exporting the First Amendment: The Press-Government Crusade of 1945–1953* (New York: Longman, 1986), documents the exporting of the U.S. value system of free press through joint efforts of the press and the Truman administration. But this forerunner to fulfillment of Third World news aspirations was abandoned in 1953.

Basic documents of UNESCO's International Commission for the Study of Communication Problems (the MacBride Commission) include "The New World Information Order," a document presented by Mustapha Masmoudi of Tunisia as a spokesman for the Third World, in July 1978; the Commission's "Interim Report on Communications Problems in Modern Society," published by UNESCO in September 1978; and the Commission's "Final Report" submitted in December 1979 and published as *Many Voices, One World* (Unipub, 1980).

The Third World campaign for a New World Information Order is analyzed in a superbly written 133-page book by William A. Hachten, *The World News Prism: Changing Media, Clashing Ideologies* (Ames: Iowa State University Press, 1981); in a balanced compilation of major scholarly articles edited by Jim Richstad and Michael H. Anderson, *Crisis in International News: Policies and Prospects* (New York: Columbia University Press, 1981), and by Rosemary Righter in *Whose News? Politics, the Press, and the Third World* (London: Times Books, 1978). Various viewpoints on free flow versus balanced flow are found in Philip C. Horton, editor, *The Third World and Press Freedom* (New York: Praeger, 1978). The International Press Institute in London published *UNESCO and the Third World Media: An Appraisal* in 1978. Sage Publications produced *International News: Freedom Under Attack,* edited by Dante B. Fascell, and containing four essays (Beverly Hills: Sage, 1979). The essays, also published separately by Sage, were *International Broadcasting: A New Dimension of Western Diplomacy,* by David M. Abshire; *Mass News Media and the Third World Challenge,* by Leonard R. Sussman; *International News and the American Media,* by Barry Rubin; and *Access Denied: The Politics of Press Censorship,* by Sean Kelly. Television's impact is analyzed in Chin-Chuan Lee's *Media Imperialism Reconsidered* (Sage, 1980). Donald Shanor and Donald H. Johnston edited the proceedings of a 1982 conference in Columbia Journalism Monograph No. 4, *Third World News in American Media* (New York: Columbia University, 1983). Michael H. Anderson used case studies from China, Singapore, Malaysia, and Indonesia in *Madison Avenue in Asia: Politics and Transnational Advertising* (Rutherford, N.J.: Fairleigh Dickinson University Press, 1984). Thomas L. McPhail forecasts the future of international broadcasting and communication in *Electronic Colonialism* (Sage, 1987).

Criticisms of the American mass media abroad, giving substance to Third World arguments, were voiced by Herbert I. Schiller in *Mass Communications and American Empire* (Boston: Beacon Press, 1969) and in *Communication and Cultural Domination* (White Plains, N.Y.: International Arts and Sciences Press, 1976). William H. Read's *America's Mass Media Merchants* (Baltimore, Md.: Johns Hopkins University Press, 1977), focuses on press agencies, news magazines, the *Reader's Digest,* television, and the movies. Thomas H. Guback described *The International Film Industry: Western Europe and America Since 1945* (Bloomington: Indiana University Press, 1969). And Jeremy Tunstall wrote *The Media Are American: Anglo-American Media in the World* (New York: Columbia University Press, 1977).

Appendix: The Language

of Mass Communications

Many words and phrases have special meanings in mass communications. This guide will help students understand more fully a number of the expressions, words, and concepts used in this textbook.

Account executive The key person providing liaison between an advertising agency, or a public relations firm, and a client.

Accreditation Certification by a government or nongovernmental agency of the competence of an individual, institution, or other enterprise offering its services to the public.

Actuality A brief on-the-scene report, live or on tape, inserted into a radio news program.

Advertising Any paid form of nonpersonal presentation and promotion of ideas, goods, or services by an identified sponsor.

Advocacy advertising Advertising in which companies take sides on important issues. (See *Commercial speech.*)

Affective aspect of mass communication The ability of the media to change attitudes of readers, listeners, or viewers.

Agenda-setting The ability of the media to influence the salience of events in the public mind, shaping public awareness and action.

AIM Accuracy in Media, Inc. An organization founded in the 1960s to investigate and report publicly on what it considers to be serious errors in news reporting.

Alternative press A designation used to group various publications outside the norm. Feminist, radical, black, Latino, underground are examples.

A.M. newspaper One distributed primarily in the early morning hours.

AM radio Amplitude modulation transmission sent high into the air.

Analog   Mechanical method of using changes in electrical voltage to create sound and pictures.

Anchor   Person on a television news program who reads news items and introduces stories taped in the field.

Audiocassette   Magnetic tape on which sound may be recorded.

Authoritarian theory   The assumption that a small ruling class should determine what others read, hear, and know.

Behavioral aspect of mass communication   The success of the media in moving people to action, as in voting decisions.

Bit   The smallest unit of computer data. Shortened form of "binary digit."

Blockbuster   Trade jargon characterizing a major, expensive movie and also a broadcast commercial of 90 to 120 seconds in duration.

Byte   Computer term representing eight bits, enough to identify one character.

Cable television   The method of delivering television pictures to a receiving set by wire rather than over the air.

Cathode ray tube (CRT)   A vacuum tube that generates and guides electrons to produce such images as characters or graphic displays on a fluorescent video display screen.

Cellular telephone   Mobile telephone, such as one in an automobile, whose call is transferred from one low-powered transmitter to another as the instrument is moved into a new geographic zone.

Channel   One of the mass media.

Channel noise   Anything that interferes with the fidelity of the physical transmission of a message, such as static on the radio.

Channel research   Studies of various media, called channels of communication by researchers, to determine their characteristics and most effective uses.

Character-generated text   Delivery of information on a television screen in simple text block form.

Chip   A tiny disc, generally of silicon, on which electronic circuits are etched.

Cinéma vérité   Film format that uses a camera to record reality in an unbiased and unmanipulated manner. Also known as spontaneous, or direct, cinema. (See *Documentary.*)

Cognitive aspect of mass communication   The effectiveness of media in shaping thought.

Commercial speech   The First Amendment right of a company to express its views through advertising and other means. Subject to legal regulation. (See *Advocacy advertising.*)

Communication   The act of transmitting information, ideas, and attitudes from one person to another.

Compact disc   Small recording whose content encoded in digital form can be heard when "read" by a laser beam, as contrasted to a grooved recording played with a needle.

Comparative advertising   Advertising that refers specifically to a competitor's product or service.

Computer   A machine that accepts and processes information and provides the results in desired form. The digital computer is the most widely used type.

Computer animation   Creation and movement of objects in motion pictures, television, and video production. Also called *electronic animation.*

Conglomerate   A corporation owning companies in several different fields of endeavor.

Connotative   The emotional or evaluative meaning of a word or other symbol.

Content analysis   Methodical study of print or broadcast messages to determine the subject matter of items, writer's style, editor's intent, and so forth.

Controlled circulation newspaper   A publication distributed free to every home in its area. Sometimes called a *shopper.*

Coproduction   A filmed or videotaped presentation produced through financial and other arrangements between companies in one or more countries.

Corporate public relations   The efforts of an incorporated company to establish mutually beneficial relationships with its various publics.

Counselor   In public relations, a person or firm that provides advice, and often services, for a fee.

Countercommercial   Broadcast advertising that replies to claims made by other commercials.

Cross-media ownership   A corporation's owning properties in more than one media field, such as television stations and newspapers.

Crossover   In popular music, the switching by a performer from one type of music to another, as from country to rock.

C-SPAN   The Cable Satellite Public Affairs Network.

Cultural dissemination   The transmission of messages and values among different racial, ethnic, and other groups or across national boundaries. At times called *cultural imperialism* or *cultural invasion.*

Daguerreotype   Photographic image produced on pewter plate in the nineteenth century. Named after its inventor, Louis Daguerre.

Database   System incorporating information of a like kind. Most commonly used in reference to computer storage.

Decisive moment   The instant out of many available when a photograph will capture the essence of an action.

Decoder   The person who receives a message (symbols) sent through a communication channel from an encoder (communicator).

Defamation   Communication that exposes people to hatred, ridicule, or contempt, thereby lowering them in others' esteem or injuring them in their business or calling.

Denotative   The common, or dictionary, meaning of a word or other symbol.

Desktop publishing   Writing, editing, setting textual material, preparing artwork, and laying out a letter-size page that can be sent to a printer for multiple reproduction. The operator uses a personal computer, software, hard-disc drive, and laser printer, all of which generally are situated together on a desk or table.

Developmental journalism   Use of the media as committed agents of a government for development of its country.

Digital   Electronic method of translating signals into binary and decimal notations.

Direct broadcast satellite (DBS)   In its original, narrow sense, transmission of televised material by a high-power satellite directly to extremely small reception dishes.

Diskette   A thin magnetic disc that stores computer data or programs. Also known as a *floppy disc.*

Dissonance   The discomfort experienced by the recipient of a message because of its variance with that person's experience or attitudes.

Documentary   Photo or film depicting real life. (See *Cinéma vérité.*)

Electronic animation   See *Computer animation.*

Electronic camera   Filmless camera with digitalized circuits and motors capable of producing still or motion pictures that may be viewed on a television monitor or printout.

Electronic carbon   Copy of a news story transmitted from one computer to another for publication or reference, for example, from a member newspaper to an Associated Press office.

Electronic darkroom   Term used to describe the computerized processing of photographs, which then may be printed or sent to computer storage. Contrasts with a darkroom in which pictures are processed by chemical means.

Electronic mail   Messages exchanged among operators of computer terminals through a network linked by telephone circuits.

Electronic publishing   Delivery of a newspaper's content on the television screen rather than on newsprint.

El-hi text   Textbook produced for use in elementary or secondary schools.

Encoder   The communicator, who prepares a message (symbols) to be sent through a communication channel to a recipient (the decoder).

External publication   Magazine, newspaper, and so forth, produced mainly for the publics served by a company or institution.

Fairness doctrine   A 1949 Federal Communications Commission requirement that broadcasters are obligated to provide reasonable opportunity for opposing sides to respond to coverage of controversial public issues.

FCC   The Federal Communications Commission, established by Congress in 1934 to regulate broadcasting and other use of the air waves.

Fiber optics   Transmission of signals through highly transparent strands of extremely thin glass, instead of by wire.

Feedback   The responses of the receiver that shape and alter subsequent messages.

Field study   A research study in which independent and dependent variables are related and hypotheses tested in an effort to establish causal relationships.

Flack   Derogatory designation of a public relations person, most often by news personnel.

Flexible film   A transparent photographic film on a flexible support developed by the Eastman Kodak Company.

Flexography   A method of newspaper printing employing a new inking system that largely eliminates the ruboff of ink onto the reader's hands.

Floppy disc   See *Diskette.*

FM radio   Frequency modulation transmission along the line of sight to the horizon.

FOI   Freedom of information. Specifically, the FOI Act of 1966, which gave the media and members of the public access to many federal government agency files.

Frame of reference   A person's knowledge, based upon his or her own life experience. (See *Stored experience.*)

Free press, fair trial   A balancing concept developed out of concerns for the right of an accused to a fair trial and the right of the press to access to information about a criminal proceeding.

Freebie   A gratuity offered to a newsperson in hope of obtaining publicity or better treatment in the media than otherwise might be accorded.

Freelance writer   A person who earns all or a portion of income by writing articles for publication.

Gatekeeping   Selection or rejection of a news item or other materials by a media editor or manager.

"Gold" record   An album that has sold 500,000 copies and a single record that has sold 1 million. Records that attain double these sales are called *platinum*.

Graphics   The use of lines and figures to display data, as opposed to the use of printed characters.

Halftone   An engraving produced by photographing a picture through a screen onto a metal plate so that small dots of varying size will display lights and shadows when printed. The smaller and more distant the dots, the whiter the image.

"Hammocking" a show   Placing a new network program between two proven shows in prime-time schedule.

Hardcore pornography   Materials designed to arouse a person sexually and graphically depicting *actual* intercourse. Differentiated from softcore pornography, in which sexual intercourse is *simulated*.

Hardware   A computer and its auxiliary equipment, as distinguished from software. (See *Software.*)

Holography   The projection of a three-dimensional image of an object by laser beams.

Hype   Promotional efforts for personalities, entertainment events, and other activities. Used as both noun and verb. (See also *Press agentry.*)

Iconoscope   Electronic television tube invented by Dr. Vladimir Zworykin in 1925. A "breakthrough" development.

Image processing   Enlarging, enhancing, or otherwise transforming a representation on a computer screen.

Industrial advertising   That employed by producers of industrial goods to sell their products to other industries.

Infomercial   A commercial on cable television, running several minutes, in which the emphasis is on information instead of hard selling.

Information overload   The mass of information in general circulation from which individuals must select material that helps and pleases them.

Institutional public relations   The efforts of a nonprofit organization, such as a charitable group, to establish mutually beneficial relationships with its various publics.

Intercultural communication   Transmission of values across national borders, often through films and television programs.

Intern   A student employed temporarily by a media organization to obtain work experience.

Internal publication   Magazine, newspaper, and so on, produced mainly for employees of a company or institution.

International communication   Transmission of information, ideas, and attitudes across national borders.

Interpersonal communication   Transmission of information, ideas, and attitudes by directing a message to one or more of an individual's senses of sight, sound, touch, taste, or smell.

Interpretive reporting   A reporting style, beginning in the 1930s, growing out of the need to provide background in coverage of breaking news of government, science, labor, agriculture, education, and other complex fields.

Intrapersonal communication   The communication transaction that takes place within an individual—"talking to oneself."

Investigative reporting   Searching below the surface of ordinary news in an effort to discover information of social value that otherwise might not be revealed.

Jamming   Deliberately interfering with the reception of radio communication.

Jazz journalism   The sensationalized U.S. press of the 1920s' "jazz age," usually tabloid in format.

Journalism   The occupation in which news is reported and interpretation and opinions based on the news are given.

Kerner report   A study by the National Advisory Commission on Civil Disorders, with Illinois Governor Otto Kerner as chairman, into media responsibility for ghetto riots in 1967.

Kid vid   Slang description of videotapes designed for viewing by children.

Kinetoscope   A four-foot box in which a motion picture could be shown. Its invention by Thomas A. Edison and his assistants in 1889 laid the foundation for the motion picture industry.

Laser   Intense beam of light energy created when solid, liquid, gas, or plasma molecules are excited by electricity, heat, or other means. From the descriptive phrase *(l)*ight *(a)*mplification by *(s)*timulated *(e)*mission of *(r)*adiation.

Laser disc recording   See *Compact disc.*

Libel   Mainly printed or written defamatory material. (See *Defamation.*)

Libertarian theory   Free access by all segments of society to a free marketplace of ideas.

Lithography   See *Offset printing.*

Low-power television (LPTV)   Transmission by a television station whose authorized power is sufficient only to reach homes in a 15-mile or so radius.

Marriage mail   Several advertising circulars combined into a package for distribution by third-class mail in competition with newspaper advertising.

Mass communication   The process of transmitting information, ideas, and attitudes to relatively large, heterogeneous, and anonymous audiences through media developed for that purpose.

Mass communications   The multitude of messages that are transmitted, most often through the mass media, to large, heterogeneous, and anonymous audiences. Frequently used as a synonym for *mass media.*

Mass-market paperback   Paperbound book sold mainly through newsstands and chain retail stores.

Media system   Patterned methods of distributing information within a nation in oral and mediated form.

Media voices   Those of all separate ownerships of media seen, heard, and read in a community.

Mega-agency   Global advertising agency, incorporating a holding company and subsidiaries.

Microfilm   A film often in the form of a strip 16-mm or 35-mm wide bearing a photographic record on a reduced scale of printed or other graphic matter that can be enlarged for viewing.

Modem   An instrument that enables computer signals to be transmitted over telephone circuits.

Muckraking   A term used by Theodore Roosevelt to describe crusading magazines of the early 1900s and adopted by them as a badge of honor.

Multinational   In the communication field, the designation for a company or organization, such as a major news agency, cable or wireless operator, and television or film distributor, that operates as a single entity in more than one country. Distinct from a transnational company. (See *Transnational.*)

Multiple-system operator (MSO)   A company that operates more than one cable television system.

Narrowcasting   Designing a radio station's programming to serve the interests of a limited, closely defined audience.

Neorealism film   Movie produced with natural lighting in nonstudio locations, employing only a few professional performers, and aimed at depicting actual life situations.

New Journalism   A designation originally applied to the newspapers of the 1880s that won mass readership by being low priced, entertaining, objective in basic hard news, and advocates of social and economic reform. Used in the 1960s to identify an impressionist, activist writing style.

New Wave   Experimental film genre popular from about 1958 to 1964 in many countries, notably France. Films were produced generally without chronological continuity, carefully plotted story lines, or "stagey" performances.

News pool   An organization of agencies of various countries formed to exchange news and other information. Also, a group of reporters chosen voluntarily to gather and exchange news for a number of news organizations.

Newspaper group   Two or more dailies in different markets under common ownership. Also described (not to the groups' liking) as a *chain.*

Newspaper Guild, The   The labor union representing newspaper editorial employees and some other staff members.

Newspaper Preservation Act   Created an exemption to the antitrust law permitting a failing newspaper to combine business and mechanical operations with those of a successful paper in the same city. Editorial departments must remain separate.

Nonverbal communication   Communication without the use of words, through facial expression, eye movement, posture, and so forth. Also known as *silent language.*

O and Os   Television stations owned and operated by networks.

Obscenity   Depiction of materials of a lewd, lascivious, prurient, licentious, or indecent nature. Subject to a broad range of interpretation.

Offset printing   A method of printing, based on lithography, used by a large majority of newspapers.

Ombudsman   A person employed by a news organization with independent authority to respond to reader complaints and to call attention to discrepancies in the handling of news.

One-to-a-market rule   A Federal Communications Commission regulation prohibiting a company from owning more than one type of medium in a city. For example, a newspaper owner cannot purchase a television station in the same city.

Op-ed page   Short for *opposite editorial page,* on which columns and other opinion material are published.

Optical character recognition (OCR)   A machine that feeds typewritten material into a computer or a phototypesetting machine.

Outdoor   A branch of advertising using billboards and signs.

Over the transom   Unsolicited manuscripts received by book and magazine publishers.

Pagination   The process of making up an entire newspaper page on a videoscreen, ready for transmission to a printing plate.

Pay cable   Supplementary programming services distributed by a cable television system, for which the recipient pays additional fees beyond the basic cable charge.

Payola   Under-the-counter payment of cash or other favors to radio station personnel who play certain records frequently.

Penny press   The designation of a new style of newspaper reporting, appearing in the 1830s and 1840s, that was low priced, popularly written, and edited to include human interest stories and important news appealing to a broad base of readers.

Pentagon Papers   A 47-volume study of the origins of the Vietnam War ordered by Secretary of Defense Robert McNamara. Publication of a summary by the New York *Times* brought an unsuccessful effort to impose prior restraint.

People meter   Hand-held instrument used by rating services to measure the size and demographic elements of television audiences.

Photographic communication   Transmission of ideas, information, and attitudes through use of one or more photographs for all types of purposes, including news and advertising.

Photojournalism   A combination of words and photograph(s) designed to communicate information or attitudes. A branch of photographic communication.

Piracy   Unauthorized acquisition and use of property. Commonly used in reference to the foreign appropriation of copyrighted books and other materials for financial gain.

Pixel   Definable location on a video screen used to form images. For graphic displays, screens with more pixels generally provide sharper images.

P.M. newspaper   One distributed primarily in late afternoon.

Positioning   Differentiating a product or service, mainly through marketing and advertising, from those of its competitors.

Press agentry   Promotion of an idea, product, service, or individual(s) through shrewd and often extravagant notices to the media, staged events, and other such devices. (See also *Hype.*)

Press association   An agency that gathers and transmits news, such as the Associated Press.

Prime time   In broadcasting the three peak evening viewing hours when the networks present their most important programs.

Printout   Computer-generated hard copy, as distinguished from data in nonpermanent form on a video screen.

Prior restraint   Action by government to prevent publication, as by licensing or censorship.

Professional association   An organization formed to advance the interests of people who perform public services in a particular field of learning, such as law and medicine, for which special educational preparation and other requisites are essential.

Public-access channel   A cable television channel on which are shown programs prepared by members of the public.

Public figure   Person defined by Supreme Court decisions whose ability to recover damages for defamatory falsehood is limited because of such status.

Public opinion   The prevailing frame of mind publicly expressed by a significant number of people on an issue of public concern.

Public relations   The planned and organized effort of a company or institution to establish mutually beneficial relationships with its publics.

Publicity   Nonpaid promotion of goods, services, and people, generally in the media.

Publics   The various groups of people who are affected by—or who may affect—the operations of a particular company or institution.

Rating   Percentage of all households having television sets that viewed a particular program. (See *Share.*)

Redundancy   Repetition of a message to help ensure that it is received.

Regress   To restudy a message for clarification of meaning.

Right of reply   Ability of a government to require dissemination in other countries of materials designed to counterbalance or correct allegedly false information. One goal of the New World Information Order.

Satellite   A device in orbit 22,300 miles above the Equator. Electronic signals from earth are bounced off transponder pads on its surface, back to receiving dishes on earth.

Satellite master antenna system (SMATV)   A receiving dish on private property that receives programs by satellite and distributes them to adjacent dwelling units.

Satellite newsgathering (SNG)   Use of satellite transmission units by reporters in the field to send stories quickly to their home studios.

Semantic noise   Interference with the reception of a message that occurs when the message is misunderstood even though it is received exactly as transmitted. (See *Connotative* and *Denotative.*)

Sensationalism   Overemphasized treatment of reports of a sexual, criminal, or scandalous nature in the mass media.

7-7-7 rule   A Federal Communications Commission regulation that formerly permitted a single company to own only seven AM radio stations, seven FM radio stations, and seven television stations. (See *12-12-12 rule.*)

Share   The percentage of households with television sets having their sets turned on to a given station at a given time. (See *Rating.*)

Shield law   State legislation preventing reporters from being forced to reveal sources of information to state courts and grand juries.

Shopper   See *Controlled circulation newspaper.*

Slander   Mainly spoken defamatory words. (See *Defamation.*)

Softcore pornography   Materials designed to arouse a person sexually but depicting only simulated (not actual) sexual activity of a graphic nature.

Software   A set of instructions written in computer language that makes a computer do as it is told.

Sound   In radio, the choice of music and vocal technique that make a station's programming easily recognizable.

Specialty advertising   Useful articles of merchandise imprinted with an advertiser's message and distributed without obligation to the recipient.

Spectrum   Electromagnetic energy in the form of wavelengths or frequencies laid out in numerical order and including light and radio waves.

Spinoff   A new television show created around a popular character or characters taken from another situation series.

Sponsored film   Motion picture, paid for by a company or organization, that delivers information or a message, usually without charge.

Standard Advertising Unit   Uniform system adopted by many newspapers in 1984 providing conformity in mechanical requirements and billing procedures for advertisers.

Stereotype   The image of another person or entity that people have in their minds, reflecting attitudes and general extent of knowledge about that person or entity. Also and originally (as a verb), to convert a flat newspaper page form into a semicyclindrical metal plate to fit a rotary press.

Stored experience   Knowledge based upon what one has observed, encountered, or undergone. (See *Frame of reference.*)

Subscription television   Programs delivered over the air in scrambled form, then unscrambled for a fee at the receiving set.

Survey research   Through a scientific sample gathering demographic information or sociological facts, as well as opinions and attitudes.

Symbol   The component of a message, usually a word, picture, or sign, transmitted by a communicator.

Syndicate   An organization that sells comic strips and other features to newspapers.

Syndicated television show   A program leased by its producer for rerun showing after it has appeared on a network.

Tabloid   A newspaper with about half the dimensions of a standard-sized newspaper.

Target marketing   Aiming a marketing campaign at a special demographic or psychographic group.

Technology transfer   Transmission of the products of technology and knowledge of their operation from one individual, company, or country to another.

Teleconferencing   Linking groups of people by telephone and/or television, often via satellite, generally for business purposes. When television is used, often called *videoconferencing.*

Telefilm   A dramatic or informative presentation shot on 16-mm or 35-mm film for television transmittal within the majority of countries that cannot use American videotaped programs without costly conversion.

Teletext   System of delivering news and other information to a television screen in which the viewer can select certain portions of the material to watch.

"Tell" story   A brief news item read by an anchorperson on television without accompanying videotape or film action.

Third World   The less technologically advanced nations of Asia, Africa, and Latin America. The First World consists of the so-called Western powers and the Second World of the communist bloc of nations.

Tiering   System under which a cable television subscriber pays for a basic package of channels, then pays extra fees for additional channel reception as desired.

"Till forbid" (tf)   Arrangement under which a feature provided by a syndicate is published in a newspaper indefinitely, until the editor sends in a cancellation notice.

Time-shifting   Practice of recording a television program on a videocassette recorder for viewing at a later time.

Trade advertising   That employed by producers and distributors of branded and non-branded consumer goods in order to sell these products to wholesalers and retailers.

Trade association   An organization formed to advance the interests of a number of people engaged in a particular enterprise for profit.

Trade book   A fiction or nonfiction book marketed to the general public, mainly through bookstores and libraries.

Traffic   Programs and commercials scheduled by a broadcast station.

Transnational   In the communication field the designation for a corporation that owns or controls one or more affiliated companies in foreign countries. Distinct from a multinational firm, which operates as a single entity in more than one country. (See *Multinational.*)

12-12-12 rule   A Federal Communications Commission ruling that permits a single company to own only 12 AM radio stations, 12 FM radio stations, and 12 TV stations, provided that collectively the TV stations serve no more than 25 percent of the nation's television households. (UHF stations are counted as serving only one-half of the TV homes within their markets.) A company may own 14 stations in each of the AM, FM, and TV categories if two each are subsidiaries controlled by minorities.

UHF television   Ultra high frequency transmission of signals.

Underground press   Publications appearing in the 1960s that mirrored the discontent of many, particularly youths, with status quo social and political conventions and restrictions.

VHF television   Very high frequency transmission of signals.

Video   General term applied to movies and other material prerecorded on videotape, as well as programs recorded from television, that are shown on a television screen by a videocassette recorder. Originally, a synonym for *television. Music video* is a brief taped performance by a popular group whose music is accompanied by a visual representation of its message.

Videocassette   Magnetic tape on which pictures and sound may be recorded.

Videocassette recorder   Instrument attached to a television set that can play prerecorded videotapes on the screen, as well as record and replay television programs.

Videodisc   Disc resembling a phonograph record on which visual and sound material is recorded for later showing on a television screen.

Video display terminal (VDT   A cathode ray machine with keyboard and display screen on which (in journalism) news stories are written and dispatched into a computer, and on which they can be called up from the computer for editing.

Videoconferencing.   See *Teleconferencing.*

Videophone   A telephone equipped with a television screen and a movable video camera to transmit sound and images from one point to another.

Videotex   Two-way interactive television service in which the viewer can respond to material shown on the screen and conduct business and other transactions.

Violence profile   Annual record, by George Gerbner and associates, of incidences of violence on network television programs.

Walker report   A study by the National Commission on the Causes and Prevention of Violence, with attorney Daniel Walker as chairman, which placed primary blame on police for violence and rioting at the 1968 Democratic national convention in Chicago.

Watergate   A term used to describe a series of illegal actions taken by Nixon administration officials, including a 1972 break-in at Democratic party offices in the Watergate Tower apartment building in Washington, D.C.

Wet plate   A glass plate coated with a light-sensitive solution that must be kept wet until exposed in the camera and processed in a darkroom. Used before the invention of flexible film.

Word processing system   A software system that processes text on a video screen, performing such functions as paragraphing, paging, left and right justification of margins, rearrangement of lines, and printing the text.

Index